Second Thoughts
Critical Thinking for a Diverse Society

SECOND EDITION

Wanda Teays

Mount St. Mary's College

Boston   Burr Ridge, IL   Dubuque, IA   Madison, WI   New York
San Francisco   St. Louis   Bangkok   Bogotá   Caracas   Kuala Lumpur
Lisbon   London   Madrid   Mexico City   Milan   Montreal   New Delhi
Santiago   Seoul   Singapore   Sydney   Taipei   Toronto

McGraw-Hill Higher Education

A Division of The McGraw-Hill Companies

SECOND THOUGHTS: CRITICAL THINKING FOR A DIVERSE SOCIETY

Published by McGraw-Hill, a business unit of The McGraw-Hill Companies. Inc., 1221 Avenue of the Americas, New York, NY, 10020. Copyright © 2003, 1996, by The McGraw-Hill Companies, Inc. All rights reserved. No part of this publication may be reproduced or distributed in any form or by any means, or stored in a database or retrieval system, without the prior written consent of The McGraw-Hill Companies, Inc., including, but not limited to, in any network or other electronic storage or transmission, or broadcast for distance learning. Some ancillaries, including electronic and print components, may not be available to customers outside the United States.

This book is printed on acid-free paper.

2 3 4 5 6 7 8 9 0 DOC/DOC 0 9 8 7 6 5 4 3

ISBN 0-7674-2562-6

Publisher: *Kenneth King*
Sponsoring editor: *Jon-David Hague*
Marketing manager: *Greg Brueck*
Senior project manager: *Jean Hamilton*
Lead production supervisor: *Lori Koetters*
Coordinator of freelance design: *Mary E. Kazak*
Supplement associate: *Kate Boylan*
Cover design: *Cassandra Chu*
Interior design: *Jamie O'Neal*
Typeface: *10/12 Sabon*
Compositor: *G&S Typesetters, Inc.*
Printer: *R.R. Donnelley and Sons Company*

Library of Congress Cataloging-in-Publication Data

Teays, Wanda.
    Second thoughts : critical thinking for a diverse society / Wanda Teays.—2nd ed.
        p. cm.
    Includes index.
    ISBN 0-7674-2562-6 (softcover : alk. paper)
    1. Reasoning. 2. Critical thinking. 3. Multiculturalism. I. Title.
BC177.T4   2003
160—dc21   2002071810

www.mhhe.com

To Anita

I have the dew,
A sunray falls from me,
I was born from the mountain.
I leave a path of wildflowers.
A raindrop falls from me.
I'm walking home.
I'm walking back to belonging.
I'm walking home to happiness.
I'm walking back to long life.
—Leslie Marmon Silko

Preface

Then I was standing on the highest mountain of them all,
And round beneath me was the whole hoop of the world.
And while I stood there I saw more than I can tell
And I understood more than I saw.

—BLACK ELK

Standing on the hills above Los Angeles, I see people united by a common desire to improve our lives and communities. I see people struggling to solve global violence and societal problems like poverty, homelessness, and racism. One of the tasks of a critical thinking course is to enable students to approach such issues, assess evidence, examine assumptions, sort out moral, legal, and social considerations, and arrive at decisions. To do this well, we need a receptive and reflective disposition, guided by a desire for truth and fairness.

What I do in *Second Thoughts* is integrate diverse perspectives in critical reasoning and help students acquire the tools to put their thinking skills to use. There are many opportunities in the text for students to integrate what they learn and apply it to cases, exercises, and readings. Students then become adept at transferring their knowledge to real-life examples. It is important to expose students to ideas and varying points of view—and to provide them with techniques for organizing their own thoughts and assessing those of others. Social and moral problems need to be examined in a thoughtful way. Students want to see the relevance and significance of what we learn to the lives we lead. As instructors, we can relate what we teach to the world we live in and reshape curricula and pedagogy to recognize and meet a wider audience.

The book is set out in three units. The first unit focuses on skill building through argumentation, language, analysis, fallacies, and an introduction to inductive and deductive reasoning. The second unit consists of carefully constructed applications chapters. These range over social issues, the Internet, the news media, advertising, film and television, problem solving, questioning techniques and writing skills. The third unit focuses on fundamentals of logic—rules of replacement, inductive reasoning, syllogisms, and rules of inference. Together these three units offer a solid foundation for developing critical thinking techniques and skills.

Goal of this Text

I wanted a textbook that offered a range of perspectives, accessible language, interesting examples, and varying levels of complexity. Given the diversity of our society, it is important to broaden the playing field. This ensures many voices, not just one, in this textbook. Students then have many opportunities to examine how perspective influences the ways problems are defined and solved. My goal was a text that would be engaging and challenging, while providing tools that students could use in their college courses and in their own lives.

Key Features

1. *Restructuring of the Text into Three Units.* (1) Acquiring Critical Thinking Skills (fundamentals); (2) Going Out in The World (applications); and (3) The Logic Connection (inductive and deductive reasoning). This format makes it easy for instructors to use a modular approach or select chapters to emphasize specific areas and applications of critical thinking.
2. *Three New Chapters. The Social Dimension* (Chapter 7) applies critical thinking skills to social, ethical, and legal issues. *Voices of the Community: the News Media* (Chapter 9) focuses on the role of the news media in a democracy and offers tools and guidelines for evaluating news coverage. *Web Sight: Critical Thinking and the Internet* (Chapter 11) centers on Internet analysis, search tools, analyzing web pages, web hoaxes and deceptive practices, checklists, and tools for evaluating web sites.
3. *Updated Chapters.* Applications and exercises have been added to provide another level of complexity and allow instructors more flexibility. Timely examples and case studies show relevance of concepts and skills to real life situations. New and updated readings for class discussion or writing exercises provide thought-provoking material for putting students' critical reasoning to use. This allows instructors to meet students at their level and help them develop as critical thinkers.
4. *Discussion and Exercises Incorporating Levels of Difficulty and a Range of Skills.* This includes exercises drawing from current events, and popular culture; case studies for class discussion, group projects, and individual exercises; statistical tables for analysis; examples of both strong and weak reasoning; and exercises that stimulate class discussion while building skills.

Examples and exercises vary in difficulty in terms of analytical skills. Instructors can then structure their classes to meet the various levels and needs of their students without being hampered by a book that is either too easy or too hard.

5. *Focus on Diverse Perspectives for a Broader Outlook.* This includes a variety of readings and case studies from different points of view; both global and national examples; a chapter on the oppressive and liberating aspects of language; techniques and exercises on prejudicial ways of thinking and acting; illustrations ranging across the humanities and the sciences; topical issues centered on class, race, religion, gender, and disability; and group exercises to build mental dexterity.

6. *Exercises and Readings on Current Events.* Topics include freedom of the press, DNA dragnets, Timothy McVeigh's execution, terrorism, censorship, gun control, performance enhancing drugs, racist language, violence in the media, filtering software vs. open access to the Internet, anthrax vaccines, hate speech, cloning, biotechnology, and many more. Examples provide timely, interesting applications for developing critical thinking skills.

7. *Expanded Selection of Readings and Articles for Analysis and Discussion.* These include Nobel prize-winners Elie Wiesel and the Dalai Lama, internationally-renowned writers and thinkers (including Mario Vargas Llosa, Susan Brison, Jane Caputi), legal scholars, journalists, writers on popular culture and current events, advertisements, and news items.

8. *Appendices for Easy Access of Supplemental Material:* Truth tables and Venn diagrams (Appendix A); logic puzzles (Appendix B); student essays and supplemental readings (Appendix C). Available on Instructor's CD-ROM.

9. *A Glossary of Key Terms.*

Organization

Second Thoughts consists of three parts that can be used singularly or in combination. Part One (Chapters 1 to 6) covers the nuts-and-bolts of critical thinking. This includes the obstacles to clear thinking, frames of reference, speculation, description versus inference, basics of argument, assumptions, weighing evidence, credibility, concerns with language, fallacies, analysis, and an overview of inductive and deductive reasoning.

Part Two (Chapters 7 to 12) covers specific applications of critical thinking skills, so students can put their tools to use. Chapter 7 (the social dimension) presents cases and examples on current events, moral, legal, and social problems. Chapters 8, 9, and 10 provide applications to advertising, the news media, and film/TV, respectively. Chapter 11 looks at critical thinking and the Internet. With Chapter 12 we turn to specialized tools of problem solving, question techniques, and writing.

Part Three (Chapters 13 to 16) provides the fundamental tools of logic. Chapter 13 focuses on key inductive arguments—cause and effect reasoning, use of analogy, and statistical reasoning. Chapter 14 examines propositions, the rules of replacement, and the square of opposition. Chapter 15 presents syllogistic reasoning (Appendix A has Venn diagrams). Chapter 16 looks at the rules of inference. Those preparing for standardized tests like the LSAT will find chapters in Part Three and the logic puzzles (Appendix B, on Instructor's CD-ROM) especially helpful.

When I went to the dance, I went only to see
and to learn what the people believed;
but now I was going to stay and use the power
that had been given me.

—BLACK ELK

Acknowledgments

Thanks to all my students. You are my collaborators! There is a great satisfaction in seeing students develop the skill and confidence to take risks with their own thinking and writing—and to demonstrate how imaginative and insightful they can be. Such moments remind me why I love to teach. It is my hope that knowledge and compassion can shape the course of events; and so I teach and write. Looking at all the gifts in my students and their deep sense of fairness there is reason to be optimistic.

I am grateful to all those who graciously allowed me to use their work. This allowed me to bring in a richness of ideas, of voices, of diverse perspectives on issues and events. I am also grateful for the support of friends and colleagues. Ruth Rhoten, Jane Caputi, and Mary Anne Warren have touched me with their courage and insight. Patricia Davidson, Ann Garry, Judy Miles, Jody Baral, Vicky Loschuk, Judith Meyer, and my fellow philosophers at Mount St. Mary's College provide ongoing moral support. Thanks especially to dear Silvio, Willow, and Anthea. How lucky I am to have so many wonderful people in my life. Something tangible happens when others believe in us.

I appreciate the thoughtful criticism and insights of the reviewers. Their constructive criticism and those of colleagues Paul Green and Darin Dockstader helped shape this new edition. I want also to thank my editor, Jon-David Hague and all those at McGraw-Hill, especially Jean Hamilton, Gretlyn Cline, and Kaila Wyllys who helped in production.

All these people, all this kindness—it makes all the difference in the world. Woodrow C. Teays, my father, died from exposure to nuclear testing while a navigator in the Air Force. He infused my life with a sense of purpose and helped me realize there is no time to waste. His compassionate spirit lives on in my brother Steve and in my sister Anita. My mother, Rose Teays, had to find the inner strength to overcome poverty and an oppressive childhood. That she did is testimony to the human spirit.

I am carrying the torch that was never passed to her.

Wanda Teays

Contents

PART THREE
The Logic Connection   497

Acquiring Critical Thinking Skills

CHAPTER ONE

Out of the Fog: The Pathway to Critical Thinking

Nothing was clear to lonesome Quoyle. His thoughts churned like the amorphous thing that ancient sailors, drifting into arctic half-light, called the Sea Lung; a heaving sludge of ice under fog where air blurred into water, where liquid was solid, where solids dissolved, where the sky froze and light and dark muddled.

—E. ANNIE PROULX, *The Shipping News*

The ability to think critically and articulate ideas is powerful and compelling. It helps give meaning to our lives and it gives us a tool to change the world. Critical thinking helps us handle both the positive and the negative. Knowing how to think clearly means we can separate well-reasoned from weak arguments, sift out unwarranted assumptions, and spot opinions that are camouflaged as evidence. With analytical skills at our disposal, we'll be able to present solid arguments and, consequently, make our own best case. There is no doubt about the value of a well-trained mind!

Think about what happens when analytical skills are missing or in disrepair: you can't think straight, you miss the obvious—much less the subtle or hidden, and you are vulnerable to the most flimsy argument imaginable. Plus, faulty reasoning has the potential for harm. Many people who have power abuse it and many more make decisions resting on the slimmest thread of good sense. It is stunning how often racist, sexist, and other oppressive attitudes and kinds of behavior are subtly or overtly expressed.

People with analytical skills can detect weak or potentially harmful reasoning and are able to dismantle it. Because we tend to expect fairness and justice in dealing with others, acts or statements that are unjust or insensitive may take us by surprise. Sometimes we speak out, sometimes we don't. Sometimes we know how to speak out, sometimes we don't. For instance, we may hear a racist joke and not know how to respond. Critical thinking gives us the skills to address that sense of powerlessness. It also makes us realize that we have moral obligations and that those who do nothing still bear responsibility for what happens in the world.

With critical thinking skills we can assess the reasoning of others, look at issues more carefully, and reflect on our own attitudes. It is not easy to examine our own assumptions or to see how values color our perceptions and shape our understanding of the world. It is not easy to look at the ways a person's own perspective and vested interests shape the ways questions are asked and answered. But it is liberating to be able to approach problems in a systematic way, to put forth our own ideas in a defensible manner, and to confront shoddy thinking. We are then able to sort through evidence, weigh it, and arrive at conclusions about what we should or should not do.

Critical reflection on long-held beliefs might turn over some stones and force us to look at the creatures that crawl out—such as our own stubbornness, rigidity, and prejudice. The more facile we feel, the better we can "think on our feet," address injustice, recognize prejudice and bias, unravel convoluted arguments (i.e., claims together with the evidence meant to support them), and defend our own beliefs. There is a great sense of power in this.

We grow as individuals when we are able to subject our own systems of thought to scrutiny. We grow as thinkers when we acquire the tools to reflect, examine issues, solve problems, evaluate positions, defend our own ideas, and assess decision making. Something happens when people can recognize repressive systems of thought. Our lives change when we can think clearly and defend our own ideas and insights.

When people learn to think for themselves, it is much harder to keep repressive systems and oppressive governments in place. When people learn to speak and write effectively, they can make their voices heard. Being able to examine hate speech and offer liberating alternatives, for example, is empowering. Look at the ways in which large numbers of seemingly powerless people have brought about societal transformations by rallying together in unions, peaceful protests, prayer meetings, boycotts, civil rights marches, e-mail campaigns, and so on.

An educated citizenry is at the heart of the true democracy. People who can think critically cannot be manipulated into believing lies are truth. Our system of governance rests on voters not only being informed, but also caring enough to act on their convictions. The entire jury system depends on people who are able to tell the difference between opinions and facts, between weak and well-supported reasoning. "Misinformation campaigns" work only when we fall for them, when we accept unsupported claims and tolerate sloppy thinking.

To determine the truth or falsity of claims, we must subject them to careful scrutiny. Failure to do so is a victory for ignorance or mean-spiritedness. This is true with any claims made by a credible source: Assertions may or may not be true, but they may raise concerns that warrant consideration. Some claims, such as those about sexual harassment or ethnic slurs, rest on the word of one person against another. The absence of witnesses or direct support poses problems for evaluating evidence. But the difficulty of ascertaining truth or assessing collaborating details does not negate the value of the quest. The messiness of the journey should not stop us from seeking the truth.

We should aspire to base our knowledge on solid ground. Even so, we may discover that there is no one "truth" to be found, such as when we are choosing between two worthwhile options. There may be equally strong arguments for both options, but we still have to make a decision. Neither option may be a disaster for us, but one may ultimately be the better choice.

Whatever the focus of our thinking, it is important to ensure that the groundwork is in place for us to examine, analyze, criticize, defend, decide, study, and reflect. All of these things require clear thinking, so we should eliminate possible obstacles that may trip us up and cause our reasoning to veer off in the wrong direction.

Moral Framework

Critical thinking is rooted in a system of values and beliefs, a moral framework that presupposes basic human rights. For example, the fact that Nazis took bids from companies so they could build cost-efficient crematoria to commit genocide does not demonstrate critical thinking skills. The fact that serial killers carefully plan their next murder testifies only to their being organized and having a twisted sort of predictability. Corporate officials' valuing profitability over workers' lives may show minimal reasoning skills but lacks moral depth. There is much more to clear thinking than short-range business acumen or mere shrewdness.

Moral awareness is fundamental to critical thinking. In that sense, Paolo Freire's term "critical consciousness" can help us understand that we are not talking about a mechanistic enterprise here, but something value based. We need to see how we are unique in terms of our own experience and ways of living in the world; but also that we are not separate. We are part of a community—a neighborhood, a society, a world of others both like and unlike ourselves. This fact of our uniqueness and yet our connectedness shapes everything we do. Through our actions we demonstrate the degree to which we have highly developed ways of thinking. And through art, literature, music, speeches, movies, TV, journalism, Internet sites, and other forms of expression we can make our voices heard.

CNN reporter Christiane Amanpour once said, "There are some situations one simply cannot be neutral about, because when you are neutral you are an accomplice. Objectivity doesn't mean treating all sides equally. It means giving each side a hearing" (as noted by Eric Schmitt, "Five Years Later, The Gulf War Story Is Still Being Told," *The New York Times*, 12 May 1996). One of our tasks as critical thinkers is to learn how to give each side a hearing, so we can fairly assess the evidence in light of all the relevant considerations weighing upon the issue at hand.

Obstacles to Clear Thinking

All sorts of things can trip us up; for instance when we rush into decisions without thinking about the consequences. At times we are impulsive, at times obedient or submissive, letting others think for us. Do you listen to yourself and sometimes hear the voice of your mother, father, or friend like a tape playing inside your brain? Do you detect in yourself patterns of behavior that are unhealthy or destructive? Each one of us has a few failings, cultural baggage, and blind spots. These need to be overcome if we want to attain clarity and quickness of mind. Let us examine some of the more obvious obstacles to clear thinking.

Survival Issues

We tend to assume others' basic needs are being met, so they have the ability to focus, learn, and reason. But this may not be the case. Some people struggle with physical or emotional survival issues, such as an abusive environment, alcoholism, eating disorders, and a stress-inducing lifestyle. Take responsibility to reach out to such individuals. If you are dealing with survival issues like these, get help.

Prejudice, Bias, and Oppression

Prejudice comes in many forms. It may be racial or ethnic prejudice, gender bias, ageism or speciesism, or hatred of fascists, right-wingers, leftists, conservatives, or liberals. Bias functions as a kind of blinder or filter that must be set aside if we want to think clearly, formulate strong arguments or assess those of others, and act out of a sense of justice.

Prejudice and bias have to do with attitudes and states of mind—oppression involves action. All three are associated with a set of values and beliefs that we need to examine. This is true even if our bias seems justified. Some deplorable or even horrific acts and policies stemmed from what seemed to be justifiable, such as slavery, whites-only laws, lynching, Japanese internment camps in World War II, antigay ordinances, and the forced relocation of Native Americans. Cases such as the police abuse of Abner Louima, the torture–murder of gay college student Matthew Shepherd, and the post 9–11 violence against people who looked Middle Eastern illustrates how prejudice can lead to devastating consequences. Of course, racism and prejudice can become manifest in a number of ways.

Writing about the subtle ways in which racism can be manifested within "good" Christians, Pat and Art McFarlane observe the following:

> Racism often masquerades as "concern." . . . For example, an individual may express a concern about using someone from another race or ethnic group in the local church or business setting. Since "good" Christians know they should not be openly racist, they may raise a "concern" that will effectively bar that person from a church position or promotion in the organization.
>
> Racism usually includes an element of disrespect. Since another is deemed less valuable, the thoughts and feelings of that individual cannot matter much. It is only another short step to a disrespect of that individual's rights to equal education, employment and housing opportunities. (See Pat and Art McFarlane, "Beyond Scratching The Surface: Moving Toward a Multicultural Society," *Goshen University News Bulletin,* June 1998)

It is a short distance from racist or biased ways of thinking to actions and policies, underlining how vital it is to watch for this obstacle to clear thinking.

Unreflective Acceptance of Cultural and Societal Attitudes

Cultural traditions and societal attitudes help shape our lives. Those associated with holidays like Thanksgiving, Easter, Passover, Christmas, and Ramadan can be sources of strength and comfort. However, even traditions may have negative aspects, such as the materialistic dimensions of Christmas, weddings, and birthday celebrations. Cultural attitudes can act as blinders in viewing others and in evaluating evidence and testimony.

We see this, for example, when juries exhibit culturally biased attitudes toward people of different cultures, races, genders, economic classes, and employment status. Consequently, a young Latino or African-American male might be more likely viewed as a gang member than a teenager who is white or Asian, a crime victim who is a prostitute tends to have less credibility than other female victims, and so-called white-collar crime is rarely taken as seriously as other types of crime.

Societal assumptions can also inhibit clear thought. For example, some people believe children cannot tell the difference between fantasy and reality. If we assume this is true, it may be hard to evaluate children's claims of molestation or abuse. We think children are vulnerable to manipulation. We assume that children often exaggerate or lie and, therefore, children's claims about violence, incest, or inappropriate behavior can be ignored. However, we risk dismissing a child who needs help.

We operate with a set of attitudes about children, adults, people with disabilities, the elderly, religious groups, and members of racial and ethnic groups. We may also have outmoded views about those from other societies (we are "civilized" they are "primitive"). We make assumptions about people on the basis of weight (fat = self-indulgent, loser; thin = healthy, disciplined), looks (pretty = nice, interesting; plain = mousy, boring), economic class (wealthy = sharp, deserving, lucky; poor = inept, undeserving, unlucky), age (old = dowdy, helpless; young = attractive, energetic), sexual orientation (gay or lesbian = queer, deviant, unnatural; heterosexual = natural, emotionally stable) and so on.

To unthinkingly adopt a societal or cultural attitude creates an obstacle that critical thinkers will eventually have to remove from the path. This means we must examine our assumptions to see which ones are justifiable and which are not.

Falling Prey to Stereotypes

Think of all the stereotypes that bog down our thinking: Catholics want big families, Jews are money-grubbing, Hindus oppress women, men shouldn't cry, women are emotionally unstable, white men can't jump, black women are oversexed, white women are frigid, Latinas are submissive, Asian women are both sexy and submissive, boys can't concentrate, girls are not athletic, elderly people are easily confused, young people aren't politically savvy, rich people know how to manipulate the system, poor people are lazy, and so on. All such assumptions impede clear thinking and put barriers up in our relationships with others. For example, Roscoe Pond discusses coping with racist stereotypes in the film business. He says,

> When I first started out in the [film] business I was stereotyped as just an American Indian. Now with experience behind me I have come to explore other areas of choice in

ethnic roles. I recently have gone on auditions for Hispanic, Korean, and Japanese parts. My agent even went as far as categorizing me as a dark Italian. After years of relying on my long flowing black hair for just Indian roles, I cut it all off to get rid of a stereotype and to explore more range as an actor. (See "Hollywood Struggle, Indian Style," *Oklahoma Indian Times,* Jan./Feb. 2001)

Unfortunately, we are regularly confronted with stereotypes. Todd Jones notes: "Two stereotypes that can be found everywhere in American culture are the "dumb jock," brawny and stupid, and the weak, bespectacled "science nerd." Throughout popular culture, thinking people tend to be stereotyped as 98-pound weaklings, whereas strong or powerful people are characterized as dullards (see Todd Jones, "The Dumb Jock and the Science Nerd," *The Humanist,* Sep.–Oct. 1996).

Such stereotyping of all makes and models of people has serious pitfalls and we need to be on the lookout for them. We need also to reflect upon the reason people resort to stereotypes. In discussing stereotypes in her book *Black Looks,* bell hooks says: "They are a fantasy, a projection onto the Other that makes them less threatening. Stereotypes abound when there is distance." It's time to cut the distance.

Blind Obedience and Unquestioning Deference to Authority

Every day we see ads using movie stars, athletes, or other celebrities to sell a product. It's easy to draw unwarranted connections between such "authority" figures and the products they are selling. Similarly, blindly following a politician or religious leader can be as bad as—or worse than—the unquestioning acceptance of a movie star's endorsement.

Look, for example, at the case of cult leader Jim Jones, who moved his followers from San Francisco to Guyana. There he led 900 of them to commit mass suicide by drinking cyanide-laced fruit punch. In this case, trusting obedience was the beginning of the end. On a much larger scale is the example of Pol Pot, Cambodian dictator. He came into power in 1975 and led the Khmer Rouge secret police on a reign of terror, torture, and mass genocide (over 1 million Cambodian men, women, and children were massacred). He did not accomplish this by himself, but with the help of loyal followers. Such violence cannot likely be accomplished without the participation of others.

On the other hand, there are authority figures whose testimony has merit. Authority figures may be credible sources whose advice is worth heeding. But we need to assess that credibility first. We can make use of the advice of an authority, but we should never be manipulated by it.

Biased Language

German philosopher Martin Heidegger claimed that every seeking gets guided beforehand by what is sought. The very way in which an inquiry is structured, the very terms that are used, and the criteria for arriving at a resolution, affect the results of the inquiry. In this sense, language literally shapes our thoughts.

Language has power. The words we use affect the thoughts we have and our ideas for defining, as well as solving, problems. Just think about the power one word or phrase can have compared to another one. Calling someone a welfare "recipient" versus a welfare "bum" colors the way the person is perceived. Calling someone a "substance abuser" versus a "crackhead" can affect our perceptions of drug treatment programs. Calling someone a "surrogate mother" versus a "gestational carrier" or a "uterine hostess" can affect decision-making around reproductive technology. Calling someone an "abortion provider" versus a "baby killer" affects how we think about Internet sites containing "Wanted" posters with names and addresses of doctors who help terminate pregnancies. Describing shredded documents as "disposed of" versus "destroyed" affects the way we view participants in the Enron scandal. (See "Enron Documents 'Disposed Of,'" *news.bbc.co.uk*, 10 Jan. 2002). Referrring to yourself, as did Tony Soprano, local mafia head in the TV show *The Sopranos*, as being in the "waste management" business, makes murder sound socially useful.

Such biased and loaded language must always be routed out. Look for it and assess its impact. Try to achieve a balanced assessment. We need not be colorless to be unbiased, but we must be on the watch for the ways language is used to deceive, to mislead, or to otherwise block us from seeing an issue and evaluating the evidence.

Habit and Conformity

As the writer Samuel Beckett said, "Habit is the great deadener." We must take care that unwholesome habits do not intrude upon our actions and decision making. Not only might they blind us from seeing a good opportunity for ourselves or even getting out of stagnation and decay, but they could even result in harming others. To the extent that we are victims of habitual ways of doing things and falling into routines, we dull our skills at observation and description. There is a reason people describe habits as "traps," for habits act as blinders or restrictions on perceiving the world and evaluating what is seen.

Many people vote along party lines (such as Democrat, Republican, Tory, NDP, Green Party, and so on) without even considering the candidate or the issues. Voting out of habit is not only a failure of critical thinking but has a wider social impact. If you voted for the party without looking at the candidate, you could miss crucial short-term problems and potential consequences for the political party. For example, when, in June 2001, Senator Jim Jeffords in Vermont bolted from the Republican Party to become an Independent, power in the Senate transferred from Republican to Democrat. His decision had repercussions for both parties. It is not obvious that Republicans in Vermont supported Jeffords' decision, but it certainly brought issues up regarding the direction of the party. Furthermore, Ralph Nader's candidacy for U.S. president in 2000 not only impacted the Green Party, but also the two major parties.

Coach Phil Jackson of the Lakers basketball team is celebrated for his ability to stay cool even in the most heated moment. He once spoke of the importance of not being trapped by habitual modes of thinking and said,

The truth is that you can only settle down your mind by providing a large pasture for it to run around in. Among other things, meditation has taught me that I am bigger than my mind. I certainly believe in boundaries, but I want my boundaries to be spacious enough to allow for extreme flexibility. So when I'm coaching, I try not to let myself get too rigid. My own personal tendency is to be fairly tight, precise and dogmatic, but a dictatorial coach can frighten his team. My daily meditation practice frees me from habitual behavior, allows me to be a little loose, to be open to having fun, and to react more to the breath of the moment. (See Charley Rosen, "No More Bull," *Cigar Afficionado,* Sep.–Oct. 1998)

Once we free ourselves from habitual behavior and provide a "large pasture" for our minds to move in we will be in a much stronger position to think clearly and be able to reflect on both the bigger picture and the particular aspects of any given issue. This obstacle, as Phil Jackson implies, is more important than we may realize in terms of moving beyond rigidity of thought.

Limited Access to Information or Evidence

We are not always able see the big picture. Sometimes we lack information or we are given only one perspective so we don't quite see what's going on. This may be due to someone else controlling access to information, as in the case of a teacher, supervisor, doctor, family member, or friend. Or it may be that the information provided has been censored or edited, as with news coverage. This can happen in high profile cases, like the FBI discovery of boxes of evidence long after the trial of Timothy McVeigh, convicted of killing 168 people in the Oklahoma City bombing. This discovery temporarily delayed his execution and raised many questions about the FBI's handling of evidence.

In October 2001, the five major U.S. television networks reached an unprecedented agreement to limit broadcasts of statements by Osama bin Laden and his associates after U.S. national security advisor Condoleeza Rice called the heads of the networks (see "U.S. Limits bin Laden Coverage," BBC News, *news.bbc.co.uk,* 11 Oct. 2001). In addition, the news coverage of the war in Afghanistan (the "war on terrorism") was hampered by severe restrictions placed on journalists by the Pentagon. The Pentagon had a policy of forbidding news reporters from covering raids or other military encounters firsthand—a policy that limited access to information. (See "Lingering Limits on War Coverage Frustrates Washington Press Corps," *The Reporters Committee for Freedom of the Press, www.rcfp.org,* 24 Oct. 2001)

Whenever there is limited or controlled access, critical thinking is handicapped. When this happens, we need to seek other sources of information (say, international news sources in the case of news, or other friends and family members in the case of our personal lives). Become adept at piecing together puzzles and drawing inferences from nuggets of details. The Freedom of Information Act, for instance, allows us to approach the FBI for information about ourselves or about others. The information obtained from the FBI on public figures, however, will not be given to us without editing. Sometimes documents are withheld for "security reasons." Those that are sent may be heavily censored, with words and whole passages deleted or blacked out. Using such information means working around those censored sections and trying to piece the available information together in a useful and defensible way.

Sometimes, however, not even edited information can be obtained. For example, after being a hostage in Lebanon for seven years, Terry Anderson wanted to know what the U.S. government did to try to bring about his release. He filed Freedom of Information Act requests with the FBI and the Drug Enforcement Administration, but was met with this response: Because of privacy considerations, they couldn't release their files unless Anderson first obtained permission from his captors (see Richard A. Ryan, "Access to Public Information Still a Fight," *The Detroit News*, 4 July 1996). Later this decision was rescinded and Anderson got files from the FBI; however they had a number of sections blacked out—supposedly for security reasons.

Self-Esteem Problems

Debra Moon, president of the Hopi Pu'tavi Project, Inc., at Second Mesa, Arizona, observes that self-esteem problems can get in the way of good reasoning. She's right. For those who have a healthy sense of their own self-worth and the confidence to function more or less effectively in the world, it may be difficult to understand what happens when that balance is thrown off. When people either suffer low self-esteem or have inflated views of themselves, their perception of the world, their own affairs and those of others can be somewhat distorted.

For example, people who have bloated egos often assume that their concerns should always take priority over the rights and concerns of others. And those who have a diminished sense of self may not be able to think clearly or make good, or fair, decisions—and antisocial behavior (e.g., sadistic or masochistic) may follow. An example of this is when victims of domestic violence or incest stay bonded to their abuser(s), often suffering "learned helplessness" and unable to protect themselves and their loved ones from the situation escalating further.

Some think that these extremes operate on societal levels as well—for instance, when those from "developed" countries like the United States and Canada fail to fully understand or respond to problems facing Third World countries. Similarly, there may be imbalances within a "developed" country; for example, when the wealthy fail to appreciate the hardships of those who are economically impoverished. Greed and excess can sometimes blind us to the consequences of our collective actions and policies. Fortunately, we have the tools to address these imbalances. But we need to be aware of this potential obstacle.

Weaseling

Everyone makes mistakes. Some poeple are gracious, while some are uncomfortable, uneasy, or embarrassed. Others become nasty and brutish with anyone who tries to confront them. Nonetheless, being honest about our mistakes is crucial for clear thinking. We can't adequately examine our own or others' reasoning if we mislead, deny, pass the buck, or otherwise act like a weasel.

It may require humility, integrity, and a sense of humor to acknowledge our own gaffes, but operating otherwise is not to anyone's benefit. Even the most respected sources trip up occasionally. Just look at the following editorial or journalistic errors (as noted in "And Now, a Few Words We Wish Had Never Been Written," *The New York Times*, 20 Jan. 2002). It can only be hoped that no one assumed the newspaper's advice was correct (see error 3) on when it's safe to eat oysters:

ERROR 1:

A report in the "Sunday" pages included erroneous data from the *Farmer's Almanac* about occurrences of full moons. The last month with no full moon was February 1980, not February 1866. The next month without a full moon will be February 1999, not some month 2.5 million years from now. (25 Feb. 1996)

ERROR 2:

An article about [California's then] Governor Pete Wilson's role in eliminating affirmative-action programs at University of California campuses rendered a word incorrectly in a quotation from Sherry Bebith Jeffe, a former legislative aide. Ms. Jeffe said of Mr. Wilson: "He's been biding his time on this, knowing all along what he was going to do when the time was ripe. It's ripe. He's picked." She did not say, "He's pickled." (24 July 1995)

ERROR 3:

An article about the collapse of Long Island oyster harvest misstated the traditional rule about oyster eating. In any month without an "r" in its name, oysters are to be avoided, not eaten. (20 Dec. 1998)

One-Sided Thinking

This obstacle to critical thinking comes about when information or evidence is offered from only one point of view when looking at the problem from another perspective could result in a completely different picture. Often a limited perspective results in too narrow a focus and, with that, exclusion of vital information. At times a narrow frame of reference functions like blinders, blocking us from a clearer understanding of what's going on. Each person who tells a story looks at the topic through a particular filter. That filter is made up of values, beliefs, assumptions, experiences, knowledge or ignorance, and, at times, even desire (see Figure 1-1).

We cannot remove ourselves from our own set of interests, at least not entirely. No one sees out of eyes cut off from emotions, experiences, ways of thinking and feeling about the world. But we can become more aware. And we gain from getting a sense of how our own world view gets shaped by our own particular (and often personal) vantage point.

FIGURE 1.1
As Calvin found out, seeing things from multiple perspectives changes everything.

We see this when a story from the perspectives of different characters—as William Faulkner did in *The Sound and the Fury* and as Toni Morrison did in *Beloved.* We can also see how perspectives differ when we shift from one group to another. Think of the TV show *Law and Order,* which shifts from the police to the prosecutors or *Third Watch,* which shifts frames of reference each week from firefighters to the police and to paramedics. In our own lives, we can notice how a particular frame of reference affects how stories are told, how problems are formulated and solved, and how arguments are structured. Once we notice this crucial dimension, we can give a more accurate analysis.

Take nothing for granted. Be careful not to assume the *deadly triad* of the *status quo + habit + stereotypical thinking.* This triad is formed by the mindset of the dominant culture, the habitual ways of approaching things, and belief systems that lock attitudes and stereotypical ways of thinking into place. Think of this deadly triad as conceptual snow goggles. We stare through them, seeing the world through tiny slits. Sure we focus on this or that particular item, but we're unable to get beyond a narrow range of vision. To get the entire vista in perspective, we need to yank the goggles off. Similarly, we have to get rid of habitual ways of thinking and seeing so that we can get a wider perspective.

So it is with these obstacles to critical thinking: we see some things quite clearly, but we miss an awful lot. We are doomed to a restricted view of the world unless we free ourselves of our mental blinders. It is important to avoid preconceptions and cultural baggage that would prevent us from in-depth thinking. Here, too, we must remove our conceptual goggles.

Exercise

Read the following excerpt and then answer the questions below.

In a 1995 survey, nearly 200 aspiring American Olympians were asked if they would take a banned substance that would guarantee victory in every competition for five years and would then cause death; more than half answered yes. A recent seminar on teenage steroid use, held in New York City, revealed these desperate efforts to boost athletic performance: A female basketball player asked a doctor to break her arms and reset them in a way that might make them longer; pediatricians were being pressured by parents to give their children human growth hormones to make them taller and perhaps more athletic; doctors were being asked by the parents of football players to provide steroids so their sons might gain college scholarships.

A molecular scientist, speaking on condition of anonymity, said in an interview that a foreign exchange student staying with the scientist's family was approached at a swimming pool by a stranger and was told "You are absolutely beautiful; I'll give you $35,000 for one of your eggs." The student accepted the offer. It is not inconceivable that some parent looking to create an elite athlete would offer far more money for such an arrangement with, say, Marion Jones, the world's fastest woman. (See Jere Longman, "Pushing the Limits," *The New York Times,* 11 May 2001)

Answer the following:
1. State the major obstacles to clear thinking you see in the quest for a more perfect body (e.g., by using performance-enhancing drugs or nutritional supplements) in both amateur and professional athletes.
2. Assuming we don't want young athletes to find doctors who will break their arms so they might have an athletic advantage and black markets in genetically engineered human eggs, what sorts of steps could be taken to address this situation?
3. Was the beautiful foreign exchange student thinking clearly when she agreed to sell her genetic material for $35,000?

Now we have looked at some of the obstacles to clear thinking, let's get an overview of the territory ahead. There are a number of skills and dispositions we can acquire to be good at reasoning, as we will see in the discussion that follows.

CASE STUDY

The Barstow Beauty Queen

In May 2001, just weeks after being named "Miss Barstow" in the small California town's beauty contest, Emily Arnold, a high school senior, was celebrating winning the crown, her 18th birthday, her pending graduation, and her acceptance to the University of Arizona, she did a prank never imagining what was about to happen.

Read the excerpt below about what transpired and decide what YOU think should have been done to address the misdeed:

At a rival classmate's house, she impulsively grabbed a piece of chalk and scrawled the words "NOT NICE" and "MEAN" on a car windshield. The schoolmate's father [Stan Clair], a California Highway Patrol (CHP) sergeant, caught her in the act, called for backup—three squad cars showed up—and had her and six friends arrested. The father wants the district attorney to file charges of vandalism.

Tonight, Emily Arnold—cheerleader, honor student and class treasurer, so long the beneficiary of small-town life, now the victim of it—will give back her crown. The sudden controversy has left Barstow divided "There are some people who felt that she should be asked to leave [the position], and others who felt that she should not," said Kris Watson, director of the Miss Barstow contest for the last 12 years. (See Scott Gold, "The Short, Sad Reign of Miss Barstow," *Los Angeles Times,* 28 June 2001)

1. Do you agree with Mr. Clair's response to the incident? Set out three pros and cons of his action in light of his own daughter's behavior:

But [the CHP officer] Stan Clair, a member of the school board, insisted on pressing charges of vandalism, a crime that can bring a $1,000 fine and a year in jail. Some criticize him for that, pointing out his own daughter had been accused of shooting a neighbor's house and car with a paint-ball gun only hours before the notorious chalk incident. That situation, they say, was resolved without need for law enforcement. (From "The Short, Sad Reign of Miss Barstow")

2. What three or four thoughts would you share with Kris Watson, director of the Miss Barstow contest?
3. As you might expect, the public responded. Label or categorize each of the three responses, noting which one you think made the strongest points:

Response 1. Wally Roberts:

Any reasonable father in such circumstances would have made the errant teens clean up the mess and apologize . . . in the circumstances, he grossly overreacted and used his authority as a CHP [California Highway patrol] officer to do so.

Response 2. Mark Herder:

I want to commend Sgt. Clair and the CHP for their courageous takedown of Miss Barstow. Few people know or even care about the growing epidemic of teenage beauty queens run amok. Just yesterday I caught one scribbling "wash me" with her finger on the dusty windshield of my car. Sgt. Clair, where were you and your three squad cars of brave highway patrolmen when I needed you?"

Response 3. Mark Espenschied:

Shame on Clair, shame on the Kiwanis Club and shame on half the citizens of Barstow. . . . In a perfect world, Clair would be reprimanded by the CHP and kicked off the school board. By all means, get out of town, Emily Arnold. Go to where you can continue to excel.

▦ Overview of Critical Thinking

You just get home and turn on the TV. On comes an ad, "More people prefer Sammy's to Pizza House pizza." Ready to place your order for a BBQ chicken pizza, you glance at the TV screen. "In a study of 300 people, 156 people preferred Sammy's."

The ad agency for Sammy's underestimates you, however, as your brain cells are on standby for action! Fortunately, you are able to figure out that of the 300 people studied, 156 preferred Sammy's and 144 preferred Pizza House pizza. This is a difference of only 8 people, or 2.6 percent. Allowing a margin of error of 2 or 3 percent, the study actually revealed very little, other than that the contest was virtually a draw.

When studying critical thinking you acquire skills and tools to construct or take apart arguments, examine data, weigh evidence, read more carefully, subject your own reasoning to assessment, reflect on your beliefs, and articulate your own ideas clearly and defensibly. The result is that you think with more care and precision. You start to feel like a mental acrobat, no more the fool.

Arguments: The Common Ground of Logic and Critical Thinking

Propositions are the building blocks of arguments. A proposition is an assertion that is either true or false. Declarations and rhetorical questions may operate as propositions, in order to clarify what's being asserted. Propositions can function together as a body of evidence offered in support of a particular claim. This forms an argument.

Argumentation is central to both critical thinking and logic. An argument has two major parts: the conclusion and the evidence. This means arguments consist of a set of propositions, at least one of which (called a premise) is offered as evidence for accepting another proposition (called the conclusion). Our main concern is to look at the relationship between them to see if the conclusion is really supported by the premises. Dismantling and assessing arguments is the bread and butter of critical thinking.

Arguments bombard us from every side. We meet them everywhere—in advertisements, newspapers, TV, radio, political campaigns, family conflicts, personal choices we anguish over, and in decisions about what to buy, where to live, and how we relate with each other. Some arguments are of little importance. Some have changed the world. In a strong argument, the premises—the evidence cited—provide sufficient support for the conclusion. This standard means that the conclusion should follow from the evidence, so if all the evidence is true, we'd expect the conclusion to also be true. Here's a strong argument: "All race car drivers take risks. Some race car drivers are killed in accidents at professional auto races. Therefore, some risk takers are killed in accidents at professional auto races." If the two premises were true, the conclusion follows and would also be true.

However, many arguments fall short of this goal. For instance, the premises may offer some support, but the support may not be as convincing as we'd like. There may be missing pieces, so the overall picture is twisted and the argument deficient. Or the argument may be poorly worded or badly constructed. There are a lot of ways an argument can have problems. On the other hand, the evidence could present an airtight case. Our task is to figure this out.

Comparison of Logic and Critical Thinking

Being a good critical thinker and being a good logician are similar, but different. The key similarity is that both emphasize analysis and careful reasoning. The key difference is that logic is more narrowly focused, whereas critical thinking has a broader scope. By a comparison of the two areas, we can get a sense of how the two fields intersect and yet have distinct concerns.

Logic focuses almost entirely upon argumentation, with the task of the logician to determine the strength of the evidence. They want to see if the evidence is sufficient for the conclusion that is being drawn. The logician makes *three key distinctions:* What kind of argument is this? How convincing is it? Does it rest on evidence we know (or can determine) to be true? Each question lays the foundation for all further steps the logician will take, as we'll see below:

Three Key Questions in Logic
What kind of argument is it?

Logicians divide arguments into two categories: deductive and inductive. With *deductive* arguments, it is claimed or implied that the premises *completely* support the conclusion. With *inductive* arguments, there are missing pieces of evidence or the evidence is not sufficient for the conclusion to follow with certainty. This results in a degree of probability, likelihood, and uncertainty in even the best inductive arguments. The difference between these two categories of reasoning is analogous to operating with a full deck of cards versus a deck in which there are missing cards.

How convincing is the argument on its face value?

With deductive arguments logicians seek to determine if the conclusion will *certainly* be true if we assume the premises are all true. With inductive arguments we are assessing how *probable* is the conclusion if we assume the premises are all true. The focus here is basically structural. If we examine the argument on its face value—where, if we give the speaker the benefit of the doubt and assume the evidence cited is in fact true—we want to see if the conclusion would have to be true as well. In the case of deductive arguments, logicians call these logically *valid* arguments.

Does the argument pass the truth test?

Here we look at the question: Are the premises true—is the evidence cited really the case? Resting an argument on truth is always better than relying on what is uncertain, doubtful, or false. Of course we may not know if a piece of evidence is true or false (think of historical claims about a lost tribe from centuries ago or hypotheses about alien autopsies). So long as there's doubt, we don't know if the argument will pass the truth test. When there's a false premise, the argument cannot be considered sound, even if the argument is well structured.

These three distinctions structure all of logic, with logicians centering their work on the first two questions. One of the main tasks of the logician is to decide if the evidence really offers the quality of support being claimed (or implied) by the person who is setting out a position. This corresponds to the standard of proof in criminal trials ("beyond a reasonable doubt").

Classically, logicians studied only arguments in which the conclusion was thought to follow directly from the evidence. That is, traditional logic focused on the relationship between the evidence and the conclusion, where the evidence was claimed to be sufficient to establish the truth of the conclusion. The main objective of logicians of the past was certainty (they did not want there to be any doubt in their reasoning) and the model was mathematics. Now, however, that is not necessarily true. Think how often people cite statistical studies, try to explain what causes an event to happen, and use comparisons to convince others that they are right.

Many arguments rest on probability or rely upon unproven assumptions. Think, also, about the standard of proof in civil trials, which rests on a "preponderance of the evidence" (that is, just a majority of the evidence pointing to one conclusion). Logic gives us the tools to examine arguments that claim to contain an element of certainty and those that rest on probability or likelihood in terms of the relationship between the evidence and what is concluded. That is one reason the tools of logic are valuable in critical thinking.

Critical Thinking: A Broader Scope

Critical thinking encompasses much more than argumentation and, so, is a broader discipline than logic. This is shown by the range of concerns. To be good thinkers, we need to be observant. If we are oblivious to what's going on around us, we may miss a vital detail. We need to watch carefully, get a sense of the big picture, take note of the unusual or questionable, and have our antennae out. We want little, if anything, to escape our attention.

Look, for instance, at the way the Unabomber case was solved. Crucial to the FBI's arrest of Ted Kaczynski was the attentive eye of Kaczynski's brother Dave and sister-in-law Linda Patrik. The FBI spent years trying to catch the Unabomber, who was responsible for several deaths and injuries from his (usually letter) bombs. One day while she was reading the Unabomber's manifesto published in *The Washington Post,* Kaczynski's sister-in-law (a philosophy professor!) had an "ah-ha" moment. She noticed a similarity in the style of writing and shared her suspicion with her husband (Kaczynski's brother), who then notified the FBI. Her analysis of the writing sample was the key to solving the case.

We need to be attentive to the specific elements of a situation, while not losing sight of the framework. And we must never take anything for granted—look at the familiar as if we were seeing it for the first time. There could be serious consequences if we are oblivious, "asleep at the switch," make mistakes, or overlook something that we should have caught. Here's an example: In 1999 the CIA provided incorrect targeting data that led U.S. warplanes to bomb the Chinese Embassy in Yugoslavia during a NATO air war. Evidently, "The CIA had not noticed the embassy's new address in the Belgrade [Yugoslavia] telephone directory" (See Bob Drogin, "School for New Brand of Spooks," *Los Angeles Times,* 21 July 2000). Duh! You can imagine why the CIA wants to make sure that doesn't happen again.

Examining the Evidence

One aspect of critical thinking not normally found in logic centers on how evidence is gathered and examined. This involves surveying the situation, clarifying goals, looking at the process by which evidence was obtained, keeping an eye out for any missing evidence, and weighing the evidence. Weighing evidence involves recognizing evidence from background information, deciding on a set of criteria, and sorting and weighing evidence.

For example, if the criteria for getting a scholarship centered on academic excellence and leadership capabilities, then such matters as financial need would not be a factor. If the sole requirements for an ideal mate are that the person be attractive, muscular, and rich, then traits like integrity, generosity of spirit, or sense of humor would be of little relevance. If your criteria for a good movie include lots of special effects, then you probably wouldn't like the old classics but would be drawn to movies like *The Matrix, The Time Machine,* or *Lord of the Rings.*

Sorting for Relevance

Being able to pinpoint relevant evidence is crucial, as a great deal may rest on this decision. The more relevant the evidence is, the greater its role or impact. We are often faced with a glut of information (think of trying to get information from a study of websites). Or perhaps the information is a bit off-topic or is out of date. Or perhaps someone is intentionally deceptive. Think, for instance, about advertising and how little relevant information is actually given about the product. Ads often omit information that a careful consumer requires to make a good decision. The goal of advertising is to persuade. In that sense, ads often fail to provide detailed information about the product.

Consider two advertisements, one for yogurt and one for cigarettes. The ad for Yoplait berry banana and kiwi daiquiri yogurt has a photo of three young, pretty, women who are laughing and appear to be having fun. In the top left corner is written "It's Like . . . Girls' Night Out" and at the bottom right in large letters is "Good!" Nothing in the ad addresses the virtues of Yoplait yogurt—the "girls" are not even eating yogurt. In the second example, a Marlboro cigarette ad, we are presented with a photo of a building (night club?) in midnight blue. In the center of the ad is written, "There are no strangers here. Only friends we haven't met."

These last words are positioned so we might connect the idea of meeting these new "friends" with smoking Marlboros.

In both cases, the evidence for concluding that we should get this yogurt or that cigarette centers on an imagined experience. With this is the implicit promise of a feeling of satisfaction that using the product is supposed to bring. However, this overlooks more relevant factors for making a good decision—such as the nutritional value of the yogurt or the health concerns of smoking. As we will see, though, that's when critical thinking tools can come to the rescue.

Analysis

The heart of critical thinking is analysis, because it is there that all of the other elements we've mentioned come together. When we analyze, we need to be observant to detail and able to clarify problems, tasks, and goals; we need to separate fact from opinion; we need to recognize speculation as opposed to giving evidence for a position; we need to be able to evaluate testimony and assess credibility; we need to be attentive to moral reasoning; and we need to be able to dismantle arguments and evaluate them.

Speculation is a form of guesswork. People speculate all the time, for example, when they offer their theory as to why their dog bit your ankle or why one idea may give better results than another. We normally use the term "speculation" to apply to hypotheses that have little, if any, evidence to back them up. There may be a kernel of evidence, but not enough to draw a solid conclusion. In such cases, speculation can run rampant. On the other hand, some speculation seems like it's within the realm of possibility, even if we can't be sure about it.

Take, for instance, the speculation of Dr. Susan Solomon who wrote a history of the Scott expedition in Antartica in 1912. The expedition resulted in the death of explorer Robert F. Scott and four men. Having weather reports of the region and diaries as the main evidence to study, Solomon had to deal with missing data. Trying to fill in the holes about why they died only 11 miles from a depot of food and heating oil, she ended up offering a bit of speculation about their last days, saying, "The full answer is a human question beyond the powers of science to answer."

> She speculated that Scott, who was now suffering from frostbite, could not go farther and that Wilson and Bowers decided not to leave him. Since they were still able to leave the tent, she surmises, they may have told Scott that there was a blizzard so he would not know they had chosen to follow their leader into death. (As quoted by Kenneth Chang, "How Bad Luck Tipped the Scales to Disaster," *The New York Times*, 28 Aug. 2001).

Dr. Solomon may be entirely correct in her speculation. On the other hand, it may be that Wilson and Bowers told Scott the truth and wanted to abandon the frostbitten chap and save their own hides, but Scott implored them to die with dignity, all together. However, this could be entirely wrong. Perhaps they all just gave up, that the long perilous journey wore them out and they lost the will to live.

Or the real reason they died together in the tent may come to light when another investigator finds a shred of missing data and throws off all the speculation thus far.

Speculation is a fact of life. When we don't have all the pieces, but do want to offer an explanation or a theory—we often speculate. But remember: speculation is guesswork. It may be informed guesswork, but it is still guesswork. We should keep that in mind as we offer our own tentative explanations—or examine those of others.

The Role of Ideas in Analysis

Without the ability to analyze effectively, we would flounder. And in situations that require us to dismantle reasoning or solve a problem facing us, our analytical skills are crucial. Another aspect of analysis is the ability to work on the level of ideas. This is one of the creative dimensions of analysis. Through ideas and insights, we are able to move forward, solve problems, break deadlocks, and bust through mental paralysis.

There are two key aspects to the role of ideas in critical thinking: one is having ideas (the very fact of synthesizing what we know, contemplating goals, imagining scenarios, formulating hypotheses, and bursts of creativity and insight) and another is being able to use and examine ideas (applying our insights, seeing how ideas can take shape, evaluating the value of an idea, being detached enough to scrutinize our own, as well as others' ideas). This means we need to look at our own ideas and at the ideas of others and determine if they have merit. We weigh in what we know about the issue to be addressed, along with the various parameters that may act as constraints, such as time, money, and available resources.

Sometimes our ideas are triggered by the things right around us, those aspects of our lives with which we are most familiar. Take the case of Philip McCrory, a hairdresser, who was watching footage of an otter's fur soaking up oil from the *Exxon Valdez* spill when he had an idea. If otters' fur can soak up oil, why couldn't human hair? He ran an experiment: He filled a child's swim pool with water, dumped a quart of motor oil in it and then tossed in 4 pounds of hair stuffed in a pair of tights. It soaked up the oil in two minutes.

Sharing his idea with others, he was put into contact with Maurice Hale at NASA's Marshall Space Flight Center. After a diesel oil spill at the center, McCrory took his idea to the next step: He made a filter of 16 pounds of hair and dumped it in and, again, the water was cleaned up enough to empty down a sewer (17 parts per million of oil). Hale then computed how this could have been applied to the *Exxon Valdez* spill: 1.4 million pounds of hair in mesh pillows would have soaked up the 11 million gallons spilled in about a week. Evidently Exxon spent $2 billion for an extended attempt to clean up the oil, but was only approximately 12 percent successful. As Hale's experiment showed, maybe Exxon would have done a lot better using hair collected from beauty salons. (See "Oil Spills? Ask a Hairdresser," *The New York Times,* 9 June 1998)

Exercises

1. In the dialogue below, Adam and Sandra are discussing a courtroom drama that occurred when convicted murderer Richard Allen Davis was sentenced. Read the discussion and answer the questions that follow.

   NEWS REPORTER: When Richard Allen Davis was sentenced to be executed for the murder of Polly Klaas, he accused Marc Klaas, Polly's father, of having molested her. Davis said that the main reason he did not attempt any lewd acts before he killed Polly, was because the little girl said, "Just don't do me like my Dad. I have to pay my dues, so should you." When he made this accusation, Polly's grandmother burst into tears and covered her face. Marc Klaas jumped to his feet and yelled, "Burn in Hell Davis," and gestured obscenely at Davis. Still screaming at Davis, Marc Klaas was dragged out of the courtroom.

   ADAM: Given Klaas' reaction was so immediate and so strong, it seems obvious that there must be some truth to what Davis said. It doesn't make sense Polly would have accused her father this way if it wasn't really true. Plus, Marc Klaas wouldn't have gone berserk with anger if it were a lie. I think Marc Klaas must have molested his own daughter at some point before Davis murdered her.

   SANDRA: You've got to be kidding! That's not what this tells us at all. What happened in the courtroom shows us how much Marc Klaas loved Polly. Plus, he felt protective of his mother who, as Polly's grandmother, was grief stricken by Polly being murdered. Klaas yelled at Davis because he was so upset to see his mother crying.

   Answer the following:
   a. State Adam's conclusion and set out all the evidence supporting it.
   b. State Sandra's conclusion and set out all the evidence supporting it.
   c. What alternative conclusion might be drawn from what happened in the courtroom?

2. In an article on tobacco advertising, Diane Marleau, gave the following argument. Read it and then answer the questions below:

   We will not permit the marketing and sale of a product that kills so many Canadians to go unregulated. Tobacco products are like no other. They are highly addictive, they are hazardous, and they are lethal in their consequences. . . . What we're going to try to get is a total ban on [cigarette] advertising." (See Times Wire Services, "Canada to Seek Total Ban on Tobacco Ads," *Los Angeles Times,* 12 Dec. 1995)

   Answer the following:
   a. What is Marleau's goal?
   b. What evidence does she give for her position?
   c. What might Ms. Marleau be assuming in taking this position?

3. In their book, *Prime Time: Network Television Programming*, Richard Blum and Richard Lindheim said program executives are concerned with the following elements in making TV episodes:
   - Giving the audience a reason to watch.
   - Having a strong and suitable conflict in the episode.
   - Providing worthy adversaries for the lead characters.
   - Sustaining faithfulness to the overall series concept.
   - Offering viewers the right amount of predictability.

   Answer the following:
   a. What does this list tell us about how program executives approach TV?
   b. What sorts of assumptions do they make about the audience?
   c. Can you think of any successful TV shows that violate these guidelines? If so, what does that tell you about viewers?

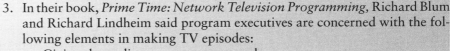 Profile of a Clear Thinker: Skills and Dispositions

Critical reasoning gives us the tools to look at problems, sort through possible solutions, make decisions, be a more reflective person, and examine the various issues we face. Here are some of the tools critical thinkers learn how to use:

Surveillance Tools: Perceive problems (define problems, clarify relevant concerns, sort out relevant from irrelevant information), recognize unsupported opinions vs. facts and supported claims, spot prejudicial or biased modes of thinking, recognize the different uses of language (e.g., racist diatribes, hate speech, motivational speech, liberatory voice), watch for what is not said, omitted, downplayed, or discarded

Analytical Tools: Weigh evidence, construct or dismantle arguments, analyze the various aspects of reasoning, acquire a facility for both inductive and deductive reasoning, and determine the strength of the reasoning holding an argument together

Assessment Tools: Assess a situation in light of any relevant policies and priorities, examine assumptions and underlying values and beliefs, and assess moral and legal reasoning

Synthesis Tools: Articulate goals and decisions using a defensible set of criteria; resolve personal conflicts and professional dilemmas; recognize the role of ideas and creativity in problem solving; evaluate decisions, plans, and policies; summarize arguments and synthesize information; and examine our own thinking processes and decision-making strategies

Critical thinking calls us to look more carefully at how we approach a situation and our own ways of thinking. This means that good critical thinkers have some or all of the following dispositions and attitudes: they are receptive, flexible, open-minded, careful listeners, attentive to detail, observant, questioning, willing to persevere. Personal traits include being unbiased, nonjudgmental, willing to take risks, and able to look at problems from different vantage points. Critical thinking helps us become more systematic and more effective at problem solving.

Good critical thinkers are able to see the big picture, sort and weigh evidence, examine assumptions, and are attentive to diverse perspectives. This includes being willing to chuck what doesn't work and start all over, while being careful not to reject ideas that challenge long-held beliefs. Be willing to rethink basic assumptions and admit when mistakes are made. Operate with a sense of fairness and try to be curious and open-minded in approaching situations.

Group Exercise

A jewelry firm called American Design sells a "Fat-Be-Gone" ring. The online ad was said to claim that, "when worn on the little finger, the ring slims the thighs. The ring finger is for the stomach, thumb for the face and so on—all with 'no drugs, no starving, no sweating.'" Lynn McAfee, director of the Council on Size and Weight Discrimination observes, "I don't think it's unreasonable that we want to have a miracle." She evidently has a Fat-Be-Gone ring, saying, "In the back of my mind, I say, 'Well, maybe it will work.'" (see Greg Winter, "Fraudulent Marketers Capitalize on Demand for Sweat-Free Diets," *The New York Times*, 29 Oct. 2000)

Answer the following:
a. Is there any harm (and maybe even good) in wearing a Fat-Be-Gone ring?
b. What concerns should be raised about allowing a company to market a Fat-Be-Gone ring?
c. What elements of being a good critical thinker will help you in deciding whether or not there is any merit to such a diet cure as this?

Exercises

1. In his article, "Coyote Goes Hollywood," Rennard Strickland relays the following story. Read it and then answer the questions that follow.

    There is a story told about the shooting in Monument Valley of one of the epic Westerns directed by the renowned John Ford. The cameras stop. The Navajo actors dismount and take off their Sioux war bonnets. One of the film crew says to the Indian, 'That was wonderful, you did it just right.' An Indian actor replies,

'Yeah, we did it just like we saw it in the movies.'" (See *Native Peoples* magazine, Fall 1997).

Answer the following

a. Discuss whether Strickland is right to say, "Without question, the American view of the 'Indian' is 'just like we saw it in the movies.'"

b. Set out the issues and concerns about this from the perspective of a Native American.

2. Discussing the treatment of Latinos in film, Aaron Leff says:

Hollywood and other outlets of mainstream media, with few exceptions, have formulated the Chicano experience into nihilistic, 40-ounce–drinking, blunt-smoking gang members. This formula makes it seem inherent that Chicano youth has some gene correlating to "thug life," and thus putting a price on Chicanismo. (See "Shout from the Abyss," in *Grandemesa*)

Answer the following:

a. Can you cite any examples to back up Leff's observations?

b. Can you cite any examples that would disprove or offer contrary evidence to Leff's observations?

3. Read about the case of Rebecca Corneau and then set out three or four questions you would want answered before deciding if the judge's decision was well founded:

On August 31, 2000, a Massachusetts Juvenile Court judge, Kenneth Nasif, ruled that Rebecca Corneau, 9 months pregnant, should be hospitalized against her will until the birth of her child. Corneau is the member of a small Christian cult in which two children died. One died by starvation and her infant son, Jeremiah, died during a home birth. The cult shuns modern medicine—leading to concerns about potential harm to Corneau's unborn child. In his ruling, the judge was reported to have said that he could hear the unborn child's voice. "And it said, 'I want to live. I do not want to die. I do not want to die like my brother Jeremiah did.'" After the baby was born, she was taken into custody by the Department of Social Services. The case is without precedent (see Elizabeth Mehren, "Pregnant Sect Member's Case Is a Rights Quandary," *Los Angeles Times*, 9 Sep. 2000).

CASE STUDY

Egyptian Feminist Charged with Blasphemy

People often hold strong views about the ways in which people should practice their faith. Sometimes these views come into conflict, as in the case of an Egyptian woman named Nawal El Saadawi. In June 2001 there was an international protest against threatened sanctions of the respected writer and feminist scholar who was charged with blasphemy and separation from

Islam. Her critics are taking her to court to try to make force her to be divorced from her husband. Arguing on the basis of a concept, *hisba*, which allows individuals to police their neighbors for religious piety, a critic of Dr. El Sadaawi has placed charges against her.

This case made the front page of American newspapers and brought an outcry from human rights advocates. In a nutshell, here's the case:

CAIRO—Since Nawal Saadawi, Egypt's most outspoken feminist, first started writing about women's issues more than 30 years ago, she has been thrown in jail, stripped of her job, even forced to flee the country for a time because of her controversial views. Now her critics are trying to take away her husband.

Relying on an obscure and rarely applied Islamic principle called *hisba*, a lawyer here has filed suit against the fiery author seeking to have her forcibly divorced from her husband of 37 years on the basis of statements she made that the attorney says are insulting to Islam. The lawsuit is only the second time in modern Egyptian history that *hisba* has been sought and, as in the first case, this one targets an academic whose ideas infuriate fundamentalists.

Saadawi's supporters say a judge's decision last week to consider the suit is another sign of a pervasive spirit of repression in Egypt. Just last month, a court sentenced a prominent Egyptian American professor, Saad Eddin Ibrahim, to seven years in prison in part because it said his efforts to promote civil rights made Egypt look bad. "Even a madman would not have thought to do this if he did not have support," said Dr. Sherif Hetata, Saadawi's husband. "It is linked to the general atmosphere in the country, the growth of fundamentalist culture."

The lawyer behind the suit, Nabih Wahsh, says he is not a fundamentalist but an average Muslim who "loves and respects Dr. Saadawi" but feels that he must stop her because she has

crossed a red line." (See Michael Slackman, "Egypt May Force Feminist to Divorce," *Los Angeles Times,* 27 June 2001)

In light of the case of Dr. El Saadawi noted above, human rights advocates worldwide launched a letter-writing campaign in an attempt to influence the Egyptian ambassador and assert political pressure to back off prosecuting Dr. El Saadawi. One of the many groups speaking out in her support was Sociologists for Women in Society. Read the letter below from Myra Marx Ferree, the president of the Sociologists for Women in Society.

Answer the following:
1. How does Dr. Ferree set out her defense of Dr. El Saadawi?
2. What methods does she use to persuade the Egyptian ambassador to help block the charges against Dr. El Saadawi?
3. How does Dr. Ferree bring in different perspectives in order to make her case?

Ahmed Maher El Sayed
Ambassador to the United States
2301 Massachusetts Avenue NW
Washington DC 20004

Your Excellency:

On behalf of Sociologists for Women in Society (SWS), I am writing to urge that you and other authorities in Egypt take steps to block the charges of blasphemy and separation from Islam that are being brought against Nawal El Saadawi. Dr. El Saadawi's work and writings have focused on women and gender, and raised important questions about the status of women in all countries, not only in Egypt.

Hers has been an important voice for equality and decency, and attempts to silence her reflect poorly on the overall state of human rights in Egypt. Efforts to separate her from her husband of many years and to make her fear for her safety are attacks on the free circulation of ideas that is at the heart of all scholarship.

Sociologists for Women in Society is the oldest and largest national membership organization of sociologists concerned with women's rights and gender equity anywhere in the world. We are deeply concerned that Dr. El Saadawi's situation was produced by an effort to end any and all attempts to explain and defend women's rights. As fellow researchers in this area, we deplore all attempts to limit scholarship on gender. The effort to intimidate and silence Dr. El Saadawi appears to violate international human rights standards, including Article 19 of the Universal Declaration of Human Rights:

Everyone has the right to freedom of opinion and expression; this right includes freedom to hold opinions without interference and to seek, receive and impart information and ideas through any media and regardless of frontiers.

We are gravely concerned about the conditions under which discussion of women's issues occurs in Egypt. We urge an immediate end to actions Against Dr. El Saadawi. Taking such actions against her can only undermine the image of Egypt's regard for human rights and of Islam's respect for women among scholars anywhere in the world.

Sincerely,

Myra Marx Ferree

President,
Sociologists for Women in Society

cc: Maher Abdel Wahab, General Prosecutor
    Ahmed Maher El Sayed, Ambassador to
    the US
    Victoria Baxter, AAAS

Reprinted with permission of Myra Marx Ferree.

Case Update.   The Cairo court threw out the petition to forcibly divorce Dr. El Saadawi from her Muslim husband on the grounds that she had abandoned her Islamic faith. The court ruled that no individual could petition a court to forcibly divorce another person. The court held that such cases have to be raised by a state prosecutor.

▓ Frame of Reference

If you were to tell the story of your life, certain things would jump out at you as most significant. But if your mother or father told *your* life story, you can bet that the story would differ considerably from your version of your life. And if your best friend told the story of your life, you can bet that this story would be quite different from both your story and your parent's story. As we might gather from the case about Dr. El Sadaawi, assessing her work from the frame of reference of her critic, Nabih Wahsh, will lead to different results than approaching it from the perspective of such feminist scholars as Jane Caputi and Myra Marx Ferree.

None of us are completely dispassionate observers. Each of us has a particular vantage point from which events are seen and understood. This is what is known as our *frame of reference*. This framework is shaped by our prior knowledge, assumptions, values, or language, among others. Assumptions and values may also influence our perceptions.

For example, a psychologist once suggested that a victim of robbery who is traumatized can often help the police by trying to see the robbery from the perspective of the robber (and not that of the victim). Patients with cancer often find it helpful to join a cancer support group to be able to talk to others facing the same sort of medical hurdles—for they share a common reference point and often a similar frame of reference on their disease.

Shifting perspectives helps us see the subject in an entirely different way.

Look at the HEMA map (Figure 1-2) of the world from the "upside-down" perspective. If you lived in Australia, for example, you wouldn't necessarily think of yourself as "down under." Rather, you might justifiably argue that you're on the top of the world and those people in the United States and Canada, for example, are all from down under.

FIGURE 1.2
It's amazing how our view of the world is affected by where we stand.

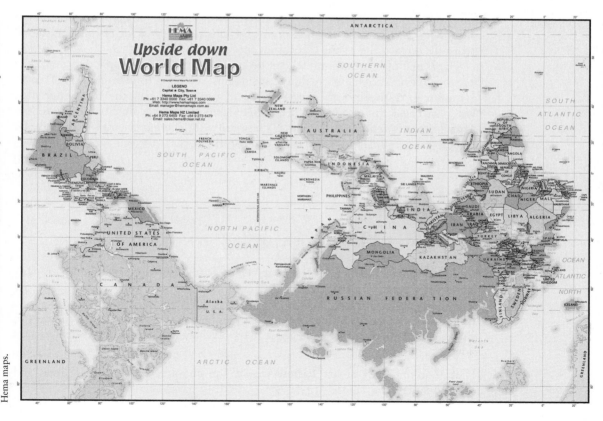

The familiar tale is no longer quite so familiar, causing us to rethink our assumptions and habits of thought. For example, in the movie *Babe,* the story is told from the frame of reference of a young pig, named Babe. As a result, such events as the killing of the Christmas goose (fellow resident at the farm) takes on a different meaning than if the story was told from the perspective of the farmer or his wife.

Filmmakers shift perspectives all the time, inasmuch as they often remake earlier films (e.g., *Planet of the Apes, Sleepless in Seattle,* and adding the "prequel" to the *Star Wars* saga). Filmmakers rework European films for an American audience (e.g., *Vanilla Sky, City of Angels, Three Men and a Baby,* and *La Femme Nikita*). They use novels as their base (e.g., *Harry Potter and the Sorcerer's Stone, All the Pretty Horses, Joy Luck Club, The Fugitive*). They also use video games as the inspiration for a movie (e.g., *Resident Evil, Lara Croft: Tomb Raider, Streetfighter, Mortal Kombat,* and *Super Mario Bros.*) and even TV shows (e.g., *The X-Files*).

Even the use of evidence is influenced by the researcher's perspective or a frame of reference weighted down by personal or cultural baggage. Some researchers refuse to abandon theories long after others fail to find confirmation. Of course, evidence that could contradict a researcher's hypothesis may be overlooked or misinterpreted. Scientist Stephen Jay Gould describes how an eminent scientist in the mid-1800s consistently mismeasured and miscalculated skull sizes in trying to prove the superiority of the Caucasian race.

The frame of reference model can be very helpful. When people disagree, they may be talking about slightly different subjects, referring to different sets of information (e.g., authority versus peer opinion), and interpreting the facts differently. When we speak out of our own personal life experience, we must be careful to recognize what is unique and what is common with the experiences of others. Be careful not presume any more than you can support.

Group Exercise

Anthropologist and teacher Dr. Mary Anne Saul cites observations (set out below) that students made after reading excerpts from two different works on the !Kung people of southern Africa. List 1 shows the ideas derived from one source. List 2 shows the ideas derived from the other source. List 3 shows the ideas both works agreed on. Read over the three lists and then answer the questions Dr. Saul raises:

1. Looking only at list 1, how would you characterize the !Kung men and women?
2. Looking only at list 2, how would you characterize the !Kung men and women?

3. Using only list 3, how would you characterize the !Kung society?
4. What things do we still need to find out to determine which gender is dominant in the !Kung society?
5. Who's right? Set out your criteria for deciding which of the two sources should be considered most credible or dependable.

Anthropological Study of the !Kung

List 1. From *The !Kung of Nyae Nyae* by Lorna Marshall:
- In some ways women lean on the men, look to them for protection, and depend on them in !Kung society.
- !Kung women are less outgoing than the men.
- Some !Kung women say the men know more than they do.
- Returning hunters are greeted with excitement; returning gatherers are not.
- Gathering is drudgery.
- Adjectives the author uses to describe !Kung women: quiet, modest, gentle, compliant.
- Possible hypothesis to explain this data: In !Kung society, men are dominant

List 2. From "!Kung Women: Contrasts in Sexual Egalitarianism in Foraging and Sedentary Contexts" in *Toward an Anthropology of Women* by Patricia Draper:
- A relaxed and egalitarian relationship exists between !Kung men and women in their traditional society.
- Small groups of !Kung women forage 8 to 10 miles from home with no thought that they need protection.
- Gathering requires great skill and includes collecting information about game.
- Women derive self-esteem from their work.
- Returning gatherers are greeted excitedly by the children.
- Women retain control over the food they gather.
- Adjectives the author uses to describe !Kung women: vivacious, self-confident, independent, self-contained.
- Possible hypothesis to explain this data: In !Kung society, women are not dominated by men.

List 3. Ideas and Information both authors agree upon:
- Women gather most vegetable food.
- 60 to 80 percent of !Kung diet is vegetable food.
- Men hunt large game.
- Meat is considered the most desirable food by both men and women.
- There is no system of offices or rules giving !Kung men power over women.
- We speak and we write out of a particular perspective, drawing from a set of values and rooted in a specific race, gender, nationality, class, and age.

Societal Impact of Frame of Reference

Recorded history tends to be imprinted by the most powerful members of society. The definitions, the very terms of the inquiry, are usually given at the outset according to the interests of the dominant class. Generally these interests work to preserve the status quo. For example, at the end of World War II the federal government set out an ad campaign to persuade women to leave their jobs and become housewives, so the returning soldiers could resume their (rightful!) position in the workplace.

Even when the dimensions of power do not come into the frame of reference, a set of values is often at work. Our view of the world is not value-free. Rather, we are influenced by different contexts, such as temporal and conceptual frameworks. That is, we approach the world within a certain temporal context (like the 1980s, 1990s, 2000s), a certain sociocultural context (like the Tex-Mex, Boston Irish, Confederate Southerners, the Amish), a certain linguistic framework (like urban slang, formal English, computer speak, rap, military lingo), a certain religious framework (like atheistic, agnostic, Jewish, Christian, Muslim, Hindu, Buddhist), and a certain conceptual framework (like Marxist, Jungian, Freudian, Sartrean).

The frame of reference influences the ways issues are presented and potentially "stacks the deck" for one interpretation versus another. Look, for example, at the use of American Indian mascots for high schools. As of April 2001, at least 135 high schools in the State of New York still had Indian mascots or team names. For example, even though the high school in Massena, N.Y., has Mohawk (Indian) children attending the school, the team is called the "Red Raiders" and the Onteora Central School District in the Catskills, N.Y., reinstated the buckskin-dressed mascot used since the 1950s and their high school prom is called the Tomahawk Dance.

In contrast, the Los Angeles school board banned American Indian logos, as did over 20 school districts in the state of Wisconsin. From the perspective of those who favor "time-honored tradition," giving up the Indian names and mascots for the teams is met with resistance, if not outrage. As the New York school commissioner, Richard P. Mills, put it, "There are cherished traditions surrounding many of the mascots." On the other hand, Bear Clan representative Brian Patterson said, "Often, Indian people are stereotyped. The mascots are derogatory and slanderous and misrepresent what Indian life is really about" (see James C. McKinley Jr., "Schools Urged to Stop Using Indian Names," *The New York Times,* 6 April 2001).

There is a moral for us in this; namely always be aware of the frame of reference used. We should look at its impact, consider who, or what, is most affected, and try to determine what would change if there was a shift in perspective.

Diverse Perspectives in Critical Thinking

When we assess arguments involving public policy and institutional decision making, it helps to be aware of whose interests prevail, whose history has priority, whose frame of reference determines the norm, and who sets the criteria by which important decisions are to be made. These are all aspects of the *perspective* taken on ideas or events and the framework of assessing them.

People know when they are being valued, or devalued. People know the parameters of race, class, gender, sexual orientation, age, and ethnicity—although self-imposed denial keeps a certain amount of illusion intact. Nevertheless, people who have experienced even subtle demonstrations of prejudice have a sense of injustice, however difficult it is to face. It may be hard not to laugh at jokes you are the butt of. It may be hard not to buy into a mentality that is ultimately degrading and destructive. We are all affected by justice and by injustice. We ignore this at our peril.

One source of strength is the knowledge that we affect each other's lives. We have an impact on the course of events, and on the public consciousness. That impact may be slow in coming and not easily pinpointed, but it is undeniable over time. One of our failings is not having celebrated that enough. We are just starting to examine the significance of that legacy at institutional levels. We don't use our power as judiciously as we might. This can change.

To look at ethical and political decision making as clearly separate from culture, class, gender, and ethnicity is to, effectively, assume a mistaken sense of neutrality. This universalizes values without any real justification for doing so. For example, we think of Martin Luther King, Jr., the Dalai Lama, Mahatma Gandhi, and Cesar Chavez as heroes. But if we fail to examine their concern for human cruelty, injustice, and systemic racism, we turn them into caricatures, instead of sources of spiritual strength, leadership, and guidance.

Advantages of Diverse Perspectives

Critical thinking gives us such techniques as analysis, observation, and reflection. These are powerful tools. Our knowledge grows when we recognize diverse perspectives, when we go beyond the routine (and narrow) interpretations of events, when we look at the broader picture. We can then see how stereotypical modes of thought have shaped our values, laws, and policies. We can also see ways to use positive and life-affirming visions to guide us and acquire techniques to address oppressive practices.

Take racism, for instance. People complain that racism goes both ways. Some say the oppressed are unjust to members of the dominant class if given the chance, that women can be as sexist as men, that nothing much changes when the tables are turned. It is certainly true that human cruelty takes all forms. The oppressed can be as vicious as the oppressor. We are capable of behaving horribly. But that's no reason not to reflect on the human condition, not to study the interplay of culture and morality, not to raise questions about how we treat one another.

The fact that members of disadvantaged groups seem ungrateful or angry should prod us to action. We need to understand what dynamics come into play when we relate to each other. Being raised on gospel or Kentucky hill music, rap or rock and roll plays a role in our identity. So do family barbecues, corn on the cob, and traditions around religious holidays. The task for us is to see what those influences have been and determine their effects. We can bring in different perspectives and get a wider view of events and issues. By looking at the relationship between power and policies, we can understand our society and better understand the way we think and act. This can be summarized as follows:

Frame of Reference

- Point of view presented
- Strengths/weaknesses/omissions
- Alternate points of view that could be taken
- New concerns and questions raised
- Results of a shift in frame of reference

Power Dimensions

- Ways power is manifested here
- Authority or power figures
- Possible shifts in the balance of power
- Likely changes (e.g., language, style, issues, values, criteria) if the power balance shifted

Values and Beliefs

- Set of values that predominate
- Alternative systems of belief that could be used
- Major assumptions of the author (warranted or unwarranted)
- Ways assumptions and language reflect values and beliefs

Race and Ethnicity

- Race/ethnicity of the key players
- How race affects the way the problem or issue is perceived
- How race affects the solution offered
- Other racial perspectives that might be raised
- Results of a shift of perspective

Class

- Economic class perspective that is dominant and how manifested
- Results from a shift of perspective (to a higher or lower class)
- Values that link to class
- Assumptions that reflect a class bias

Gender

- Gender of author and intended audience (and how expressed)
- What is left out with a focus on only one gender
- Likely result from a shift of gender focus (e.g., material emphasized, language, key arguments)

Language

- Biased or prejudicial use of language
- Ways use of language evokes images or expresses a set of values
- Likely result if different language is used (less technical, more casual or formal, more neutral, more subjective or objective)

There are various aspects and perspectives that factor into the way people reason, the policies they recommend, and the way in which events and issues are interpreted. It is, therefore, helpful to keep this in mind when we undertake an analysis. For that, we need to incorporate the various perspectives. Here is a useful guideline of how to do this:

Steps to Incorporating Diverse Perspectives

1. Try to determine the points of view being presented. *Ask yourself:* From whose point of view is this article written, this story told, this song sung, this versions of events made public? Clarify whose perspective is dominant.
2. Try to determine what would change with a shift of perspective. *Ask yourself:* What would be added or omitted if this were presented through a different set of eyes or in a different voice? Acquire the facility of shifting points of view to get a more well-rounded understanding.
3. Try to determine where the power rests, what forces are setting the agenda. *Ask yourself:* Who stands to gain or lose? Who are the players? Who is most powerful and most vulnerable? See how power or control is revealed in the way problems are addressed. Make note of what would likely change if the power shifted.
4. Try to determine the set of priorities and underlying values. *Ask yourself:* What set of values and beliefs are being subscribed to, and where might conflicts arise? Consider how a different set of values might shift the priorities, problems, and solutions.
5. Try to determine the extent to which you see diversity. *Ask yourself:* Is there enough diversity in terms of critical factors, like race, ethnicity, class, gender, and underrepresented groups? Look to see how this relates to, or challenges, the status quo. Make note of who determines the criteria used.
6. Try to determine the extent to which economic factors, like class, shape the discourse. *Ask yourself:* Does the perspective of a particular class dominate or shape the presentation, or issue at hand? Examine what would happen if you shifted to a higher or lower socioeconomic level. Look for any assumptions reflecting a class bias.
7. Try to determine the extent to which gender and sexual orientation slants the inquiry. *Ask yourself:* Do gender and sexual preferences affect the content and values being expressed? Watch for the expression of attitudes and assumptions (e.g., about what is "deviant" or "natural"). Look at the impact of the gender/sexual orientation of both the author and the intended audience.

8. Try to determine the ways in which language is used to create an effect. *Ask yourself:* How does the use of words, quotes, humor, clichés, and other sorts of expression reveal a set of values or way of seeing the world? Note the use of images, analogies, poetic or inspiring language. Be conscious of what a change in the writing would bring.

9. Try to determine how the intended audience shapes the dialogue or affects the presentation. *Ask yourself:* Who is this aimed at? Why this, rather than some other, audience? See if you discern ways in which one set of interests is catered to over other, competing, interests.

10. Try to determine how factors such as age, religion, nationality, ability versus disability shape the inquiry. *Ask yourself:* What assumptions and values are at work in terms of how old or young are the participants (or audience)? What is the role of geography, culture, nationality, and religious faith? Do factors like physical limitations, health status, or formative life experiences change the problems that are perceived and assessed?

Exercises

1. Think about the sorts of moral and social problems around us. Then:
   a. List the five greatest moral or social problems you see us facing as a society.
   b. What major obstacles need to be addressed before we can solve those problems?

2. After the school killings and violence at Columbine and then later school shootings, people sought to understand how violence could erupt on a school campus. One concern was that some of the student–murderers were bullied at school, and this may have been a factor in the shootings. Others ask if the media has made violence an acceptable way to vent rage. Still others see the root problem of school shootings is the ready access to guns.

   Answer the following:
   a. Set out your three best ideas on how to address campus killings.
   b. For each suggestion, note your frame of reference (e.g., from that of a victim, a murderous or angry student, a teacher, a parent of a child who was shot, a parent of the killer).

3. Virtually every urban area faces problems with poverty and homelessness.
   a. List five ways to address the effects of poverty and homelessness on children.
   b. Which two would you say are your best ideas?
   c. Taking your two best ideas, sketch a way they might be put into motion.
   d. Write two paragraphs in favor of one of your ideas for addressing homelessness and poverty on the local level.

4. What do you think of coach Phil Jackson's method of motivating the Lakers basketball team? Read the excerpt below and then share your response:

> He has been known to regale players with tales of the sacred white buffalo of the plains, coach them in meditation techniques and burn sage to reverse a losing streak. Relating to players through books would later become one of the hallmarks of his unique approach to coaching. He has assigned *To Kill a Mockingbird* to Horace Grant and Nietzsche to Shaq. During the Bulls' first championship run, he intercut sequences of the team with scenes from *The Wizard of Oz*. Like the Wizard, Jackson was making his subjects realize the heart, courage and brains latent within them. (See José Klein, 'Phil Jackson, The Zen-iest Coach in Basketball Has a Cruel Streak. He's Weird and It Works,'" *www.salon.com*)

Group Exercises

Discuss how you think the point of view dominant in U.S. society shapes the way Americans have viewed Mexico. How do you think stereotypes about Mexico and Mexicans have shaped the policies around the drug war and around immigration? What sorts of stereotypes are prevalent? Note any cultural attitudes or fears (e.g., of the rich about the poor, or fears about the "criminal element" and gangs). Note any racism that may be a factor in how Mexico and Mexicans are viewed. Discuss how the following excerpt illustrates the power of a person's frame of reference:

> For two decades, the distorting prisms of the wars on migrants and drugs and communism have made American panjandrums paint Mexico as a pretty scary place, but one that could be tamed by projecting American political and economic power. . . . And when the war on cocaine replaced the war on Communists, Washington's drug czar, retired Gen. Barry McCaffrey, praised his Mexican counterpart in the war on drugs as a man of "absolute unquestioned integrity." Days later, the very same man, Gen. Jesus Gutierrez Rebollo, was arrested; he was later convicted for working for the drug lords.
>
> What made the high and mighty misread Mexico? More than wishful thinking, it was mirror-imaging: projecting American thought process and value systems on everyone else. Adm. David E. Jeremiah, a former vice chairman of the Joint Chiefs of Staff, has critiqued it as "this 'everybody thinks like us' mindset," a classic American cultural assumption that underlies cockeyed intelligence and myopic policy." (See Tim Weiner, "America's Dream: A Mexico Like Itself," *The New York Times*, 18 Feb. 2001).

Exercises

Part One

1. Discuss the frame of reference (perspective) of the author and any biases evident in the following:

   Those bums that come up to your car and beg sure drive me nuts! They ruin a downtown area by accosting people on the street trying to get money. Anyone with the least bit of self-respect wouldn't live like that. They ought to get off their butts and work like decent American citizens! I'm sick and tired of people who want to suck the blood of the country by living on welfare or being some homeless slob on the street. We ought to just gather them up and ship them out of town. They don't deserve to live in a nice place like this. And we sure don't deserve to have them ruining our city.

2. Discuss the frame of reference of the author and any biases evident in the following:

   Men who smoke are disgusting. Soon as I see a guy pull out a cigarette, I feel nauseated. Don't they realize they are rotting themselves from the inside out? Don't they see that they are aging their skin and ruining their lungs? Can't they tell that they stink? Have they no respect for others? It simply mystifies me why any woman on earth would date a smoker, much less marry one.

3. The state of Florida has gotten rid of computers and typewriters in its prison law libraries. As a result, Florida prisoners who wish to appeal their cases will have to draw up their legal appeal by longhand. Read about the case and answer the questions that follow:

   The Corrections Department removed computers and typewriters in May 2001, arguing that they had to do so to save money. Florida has 71,000 inmates, the 5th largest prison system in the U.S. Florida has executed 51 prisoners since 1979 (behind only Texas and Virginia) and has 371 people on death row. Prisoners' Rights groups argue that removing the computers and typewriters limits what prisoners can do. Kara Gotsch of the ACLU says, "When it's handwritten, it's not as effective for them." Rebecca Trammell of the American Association of Law Libraries, says most state prisons provide typewriters to prisoners. Allen Overstreet of the Florida Corrections Department said only around 5% of prisoners use the law libraries and it would save $50,000 a year (on repairs and upkeep) to get rid of the typewriters. (See Jackie Halifax, "Florida Prisoners Lose Access to Typewriters," *Los Angeles Daily [Law] Journal,* 25 June 2001).

   Answer the following:
   a. Set out the concerns from perspective of prisoners in Florida.
   b. Set out the concerns from the perspective of prisoners in states that currently have computers and typewriters available for inmate use.
   c. Set out the concerns from the perspective of Florida officials, pressured by taxpayers, to cut costs.

4. Discuss the excerpt below, noting the issues and concerns the author raises:

   It is hard to say which crash in recent years has generated the greatest amount of fallacious fear mongering. Most likely that honor belongs to TWA Flight 800. To this day speculation continues about a terrorist attack. The New York Times tossed out heavy hints that the plane had been bombed. One story noted that, "TWA's connection to one of the world's most turbulent regions, the Mideast, has been long and prominent." Another spoke of "the lax scrutiny of air cargo loaded on passenger planes." And a column by Clyde Haberman opened with: "This may seem to be jumping the gun, since so much is still not known about what brought down TWA Flight 800. But it is probably time for Americans to accept terrorism as a fact of life requiring certain impositions, like personal searches in public places, to preserve communal safety." (See Barry Glassner, "Fear of Flying," *Wall Street Journal,* 2 Nov. 1999)

5. Your college newspaper, *The Oracle,* wants to run a story on faculty members dating students. How would the issue be seen if you were (pick two and set down each perspective): a 30-year-old single professor, a happily married student, a 19-year-old student who is single and lonely, a 22-year-old student, an administrator, and a parent of an 18-year-old student attending the college.

6. Study the way people are *described* in your local newspaper. Try to determine if there is any prejudice, bias, or value judgment in the language of description. Include a representative excerpt from the articles attached to your paper (cut out and number each article).

7. Share your thoughts on the decision of the University of North Colorado who named their intramural basketball team the "Fightin' Whites" (the team is multiracial), as reported by CNN:

   The students named their intramural basketball team, made up of American Indians, Hispanics, and whites, "The Fightin' Whites." They printed up jerseys saying, "Every thang's going to be all white," with a caricature of a middle-aged white man. "The Fightin' Whites," however, have taken on a life of their own. More than 1,600 e-mails have flooded into the university. . . . Some say it's about time that a white person is made a mascot for a sport team. Others complain the idea is perpetuating yet another racial stereotype. . . .

   The American Indian Movement has weighed in supporting the name. The team chose the name after it couldn't persuade nearby Eaton High School to abandon its nickname, the Fightin' Reds, and the American Indian caricature on the team logo. The students say the logo is offensive. The school superintendent denies the logo is derogatory and called the group's criticism insulting. (See " 'Fightin' Whites Whip Up Controversy," *CNN.com,* 16 Mar. 2002)

Part Two

Directions: In the excerpt below, Rena Diamond discusses the ways reviews of ethnic restaurants often fall prey to stereotypical thinking and the trivialization of groups and cultures. Read the following and set out the key claims and the strengths of her reasoning:

An investigation of restaurant reviews reveals a great deal about how cultural difference is absorbed, ingested and digested, while a perfect example of how contemporary cultural imperialism facilitates the perpetual marginalization of immigrant groups in America . . . In restaurant reviews, as in colonialism, the non-dominant culture is exoticized, fetishized, and consumed. The rituals of the "other" are appropriated for "our" use. . . .

In order to get a good review, ethnic establishments must momentarily satisfy the critic/consumer's desire for authenticity and difference by magically bringing the eater into a foreign world. For example, Connie's, a West Indian restaurant, is praised for being an "island . . . much more than a restaurant . . . if you prefer, a trip." . . . One Greek restaurant is as "close as you're going to get without a passport." . . . "The ambiance of Morocco comes brilliantly alive" . . . One Swiss restaurant miraculously "exudes the charm of the mother land": there are "pretty young waitresses dressed like Heidi!" . . . to make the transformation complete. Cafe Central is a "Mexican restaurant so authentic, you can easily forget that you are north of the border." . . .

In these reviews, critics describe fictitious lands that are static, immune to political strife, poverty, and any oppression due in part to intervention from the so-called first-world. . . . For example, "With raised dining areas, bamboo or burnished wooden columns and lots of thatch, plants, and native artifacts," one place "achieve(s) Vietnamese village visions." . . . A similarly simplistic representation was found in a review of an "authentic" soul food establishment: "How authentic? By the time you leave the place, you'll be doing the James Brown leap and the O'Jay's kick." . . .

There is no acknowledgment of the fundamental contradiction: how can someone who is not even a member of the group in question deem its product "authentic"? (See Rena Diamond, "Become Spoiled Moroccan Royalty for an Evening: The Allure of Ethnic Eateries," *Bad Subjects*, Issue #19, Mar. 1995)

Writing Exercise

Sketch out how you would rewrite a TV show so that it presents (pick one):

1. Using positive role models, taking into consideration race, gender, class, and age. Exactly what needs to change—and how would you change it?

2. A radical shift in terms of sexual orientation, religion of the lead characters, ethnicity, physical attributes. If, for example, the lead character is gay instead of straight, a Buddhist instead of a Christian, a Chicano instead of white, and so forth—what would the show be like?

CHAPTER TWO

Sharpening Our Tools:
The Basics of Argument

It takes a lot of time to be a genius,
You have to sit around so much
Doing nothing,
Really doing nothing.
—GERTRUDE STEIN

You just finished your shift and stopped at the cafeteria. The five people at your table are discussing a talk show about whether a young man on a hunger strike should be force-fed if he's near death and slips into unconsciousness. You start to follow their conversation to see what you can learn about how people defend what they think. Everyone at the table wants to be heard. See what you think of their reasoning.

Opinion versus Reasoned Argument

ALISHA: Anyone stupid enough to go on a hunger strike deserves to die! Forget them!

JESS: What's wrong with you, Alisha? Either you die for a noble cause or your life has no meaning!

ANDY: I don't know why you two are fighting. Didn't you study history? Mahatma Gandhi went on hunger strikes for what he believed in, so hunger strikes must be a good thing. We should follow the steps of good leaders.

FRANCESCA: Mahatma Gandhi went on hunger strikes when he was competent to decide what was worth dying for. There's some question here whether we should consider anyone on a hunger strike competent to make an informed decision. When in doubt, choose what's best for the patient's health. Therefore, we should intervene when lives are at stake, whether it's for a hunger strike or anything else.

ERIN: Really, Francesca, why should we listen to your position? You're no expert on hunger strikes. In fact, you barely made it through high school and had to go to a community college for your degree!

As you might have inferred, not all of the reasoning in the above discussion rests on a solid foundation. Let's look at this more closely and see just what's going on.

Dismissing with a Wave of the Hand: First, Alisha dismisses people who go on hunger strikes ("stupid"). But she doesn't offer any reasons for her judgment. Such name-calling doesn't count as reasoned argument. We need evidence!

Presenting False Either/Or Choices: Jess gives his argument; but his "either/or" argument ignores the fact that there are more than two options. Since there are alternatives to dying for a noble cause and living a meaningless life, Jess's reasoning is flawed.

Appealing to Famous Figures as Evidence: Andy turns to history, but fails to explain why, if Gandhi did it, then it must be right. Andy needs to go beyond simply citing Gandhi as a role model. A few words of explanation would make all the difference.

Reasoned Argument: Francesca gives us evidence for her conclusion. She sets out several reasons for intervening to save a person who is on a hunger strike. Those reasons can be assessed to see how convincing they are, but at least her argument gives us something to work with.

Personal Attack: Erin thought she could take down Francesca's argument by a personal attack. However, whether Francesca went to public school or read books she dug out of the garbage is irrelevant to the issue being argued. The question is, "Does Francesca offer good reasons for her conclusion?"

We encounter arguments virtually every day. We need to be able to examine the structure of an argument, set out the evidence, and evaluate it. Without the fundamental concepts and basic techniques of critical thinking, we will just be moving about in an intellectual fog, guided only by gut instinct and a prayer. Once we understand the nuts and bolts of argumentation we can incorporate them into our own thought processes.

Argumentation

Arguments consist of *propositions*. These are assertions that are either true or false. As we know from Chapter 1, an argument presents us with a proposition (called a *conclusion*) drawn on the basis of a body of evidence (called *premises*). An argument consists of *only one* conclusion and <u>at least one</u> premise. If the same set of evidence is used to support two propositions, we have to erect two separate arguments and analyze each one.

First, we should set out the argument, so the conclusion is identified and the body of evidence grouped together as the set of premises. We are then in a position to evaluate the argument and see if the reasoning is strong. In order to determine whether the premises support the conclusion, we need to develop our skills at dismantling and evaluating arguments. We'll need these skills whether we are analyzing the reasoning of others or erecting our own arguments. If we are setting out our own argument, we should make sure we have sufficient evidence to make a strong case. Let's see how to accomplish this goal.

Exercise

Read Kate Crisp's letter to the editor of *Shambhala Sun* magazine and then answer the questions that follow. Note that Ken Wilber writes in the area of spirituality and consciousness studies and has published over a dozen books.

For the past two years I have been dissing Ken Wilber all over town. I just hate the guy. Years ago I was at an art event and a gangly man flailing his arms about knocked me down and didn't apologize. I asked my cohorts who he was and got the reply: "Oh, that's Ken Wilber." After that rude encounter I saw Mr. Ken all around town. I always gave him a surly look and he always ignored me. He would always somehow end up in a line near me, at the post office, at Kinko's, wherever, and he would always be giving a grand, boring discourse to someone. He frequently was with a girl who gazed at him with reverential rapture. Nausea was my m.o. when I saw this "great mind of the western hemisphere."

But the thing that really bugged me about Ken Wilber was the photos. When I saw that photo of him on the cover of the September *Shambhala Sun*, I just knew I had his number. . . . on top of all his faults, he was VAIN! I mean really, Ken Wilber does NOT look like that picture at all. Well, maybe a little bit, but obviously the picture was 20 years old or majorly retouched. He looks ancient in real life and his head is about 40 times bigger than that photo reveals.

Well, wouldn't you know it, last week I strolled in Business Express and standing right in front of me was the REAL Ken Wilber, the one on the *Sun* cover. Not MY Ken Wilber, not the person I had been seeing and loathing for years, but someone else. This WAS the person on the magazine cover. I felt totally deflated. Here I had spent all this mental energy hating Ken Wilber and it wasn't even HIM!

Now who the hell was this fake Ken? At least ten people have told me that fake Ken IS Ken. "Look, there is Ken Wilber!" someone always said, much to my annoyance. One of my friends even went up to fake Ken and had a conversation with him and excitedly reported to me "Ken's" words of wisdom.

I am sorry to say that real Ken Wilber just does NOT work as an object of my aggression. True, he does look kind of "LA" in his brand new white Range Rover. And true, he does wear little tank tops and swoopy down jeans that show off his buffy physique. True, he kind of waltzes through space as if to say, "Hey there everybody, I'm smart AND I'm sexy!" but real Ken just doesn't cut it for me. There just isn't enough material for me to work with. The show is over. And the worst part is NOW I've lost another object for all my pent-up aggression. (Letter to the editor, *Shambhala Sun*, Mar. 1997)

Reprinted with the permission of the Shambala Sun.

Answer the following:

1. What is Crisp's main argument about the fake Ken Wilber? Set out her evidence for concluding that she "hates" (is bugged by) the man she thinks is Ken Wilber.

2. What does she conclude, after she realizes this was NOT the real Ken Wilber?

3. State the strongest claims supporting her statement, "And the worst part is NOW I've lost another object for all my pent-up aggression."

FIGURE 2-1
A few minutes after detonation of the atomic blast in Operation Cue. How would you describe this? What can we infer from this photo?

Source: (Office of Civil and Defense Mobilization, 5 May 1955 (from the National Archives, Ref. 304-OC-703) . Reprinted with the permission of the National Ar-

FIGURE 2-2
What do you observe? What
do you infer?

FIGURE 2-3
What do you observe? What
do you infer?

Exercises

Part One

Look at the photographs of the toddler and man (Figures 2-2 and 2-3).

Answer the following for each photograph:
1. Describe what you see in the photo. (Draw up a list of descriptions for each photo.)
2. What do you think the photo is about? Draw some inferences on the basis of what you see. What is going on here?
3. Look over both your description list and list of inferences and answer this:
   a. What is different about the two lists?
   b. What sorts of assumptions came into play when you made your inferences?

Part Two

1. Describe the three flags (see Figure 2-4). What can you infer from these photos?
2. Given the association of the Confederate flag with racism and injustice, did the state of Georgia go far enough in changing the state flag? List four pros and four cons.

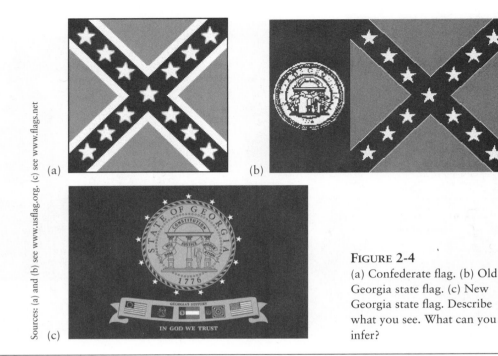

Sources: (a) and (b) see www.usflag.org. (c) see www.flags.net

(a)

(b)

(c)

FIGURE 2-4
(a) Confederate flag. (b) Old Georgia state flag. (c) New Georgia state flag. Describe what you see. What can you infer?

▦ Description versus Inference

When we describe, we try to objectively state a set of facts. An *inference* is a conclusion drawn on the basis of some evidence or observations. An inference is an answer to the question, "What's it about? What story does this tell?" Let's look at this summary of a pregame collapse of Marcus Camby, a New York Knicks player, when he was on the U Mass Boston team in 1996. We will set out the statements of fact and separate any inferences (conclusions) drawn (inferences will be put in bold type):

Marcus Camby, star center for the UMass [Boston] basketball team collapsed minutes before a game against St. Bonaventure and was hospitalized in Olean, NY, where he was listed in stable condition last night. He was taken to the hospital by ambulance and was accompanied by UMass Coach John Calipari. Brian Nash, an assistant coach for St. Bonaventure, said he was on the phone in the corridor leading to the locker room when he saw Camby leave the gym floor after the warm-ups.

"**He seemed to be in some discomfort** and was holding his head," Nash said. Then Nash saw him collapse "right in front of me. He took a step through the door and dropped." Ed Baron, brother of St. Bonaventure Coach Jim Baron, said of Camby, "His eyes were open. **He looked more scared than anything.**"

Before the game, fans were chanting, "Where is Marcus," before stopping at the request of a security guard. Few realized the severity of Camby's condition until he was taken away by ambulance. Moments before the game, UMass players gathered for a quick prayer for Camby. Tears rolled down their faces. "Just about everybody was crying, junior guard Carmelo Travieso said. "You don't want anything to happen to anybody, but **when someone goes to the hospital, you know it's pretty serious.**" (See "Camby Remains Stable after Pre-Game Collapse," *Associated Press,* 14 Jan. 1996 emphasis added)

Exercises

1. Draw two inferences that seem well supported by the descriptions of Camby's collapse and the reaction of those around him.

2. In an article on tennis star Andre Agassi, the reporter drew an inference that Agassi's rude behavior was due to impending fatherhood. Assess her reasoning and offer some alternative conclusions:

   Now we know why Andre Agassi hasn't been himself lately. He yelled at a spectator in his fourth-round match at the French Open and lost it in the next. . . . A couple of weeks later, Agassi melted down against Patrick Rafter in the semifinals at Wimbledon. He hit a ball in the general direction of a lineswoman who angered him. . . . He had a perfectly plausible reason for his nerves, edgiress, his irritation at almost any question not about tennis. Impending fatherhood." (Lisa Dillman, "Great Expectations," *Los Angeles Times,* 13 July 2001).

Descriptions

Descriptions, like a set of facts, are statements about what is or is not the case. Generally, each item in a description is either true or false, which could be verified by an examination. For example, we might describe a friend by giving her height, weight, eye color, hair color, style, and so forth. Occasionally an inference sneaks in as a description, for example, when someone says, "He's tall, thin, and a real hunk!" One woman's "hunk" is another woman's wallpaper, so such value-laden judgments would have to be pulled out and placed in the inference category, because they can be very problematic.

For instance, if you were trying to find someone in a crowd who your brother described as a "striking brunette," and there are dozens of brunettes around you, you'd have to know what he thinks is "striking." That's not always easy and, so we have to watch what counts as the description. Descriptions act as evidence, or support, for inferences we then draw using the descriptions or other pieces of evidence as a foundation. An inference may or may not be well supported by the evidence given.

Al's Demand Letter to Milly

You <u>will</u> see to it:

(1) That my clothes and linen are kept in order,
(2) That I am served three regular meals a day *in my room,*
(3) That my bedroom and study are always kept in good order and that *my desk is not touched by anyone other than me.*

You <u>will</u> renounce all personal relations with me, except when they are required to keep up social appearances. In particular you will not request:

(1) That I sit with you at home,
(2) That I go out with you or travel with you.

You <u>will</u> promise explicitly to observe the following points in any contact with me:

(1) You will expect no affection from me and you will not reproach me for this.
(2) You must answer me at once when I speak to you,
(3) You must leave my bedroom or study at once without protesting when I ask you to go.

You <u>will</u> promise not to denigrate me in the eyes of the children, either by word or deed.

Source: "His Head in the Ether, He Was Among a 'Sorry Herd of Humans,'" *The New York Times,* 10 Nov. 1996)

Let's look at another example, one involving struggles in the marriage of Al and Milly. Here are some demands the husband, Al, made in a letter to his wife, Milly:

What do you think about this man? What sort of marriage do these two people have? These two questions are issues of drawing inferences. What evidence supports your conclusion about what kind of man makes these sorts of demands and what sort of marriage this is? This is an issue of evidence. Perhaps the fact that this letter was written in 1914 might affect how you see the man and the marriage. This is an issue of context. Perhaps the fact that Al was famous may cause you to think twice about your conclusions. Or the fact that he was a scientist, versus, say an artist, surgeon, gardener, or truck mechanic may color your interpretation.

At times, our inferences are influenced, if not shaped, by personal traits that we find attractive or can relate to in terms of our own interests and lifestyle. Many more factors into our assessments of people than we often realize. For example, would your inference be different if you knew that "Al" is Albert Einstein, more famous for his work in physics and mathematics than his marital finesse. "Milly" is Mileva Maric, whom Einstein met when they were both students (she was the only female at the university studying physics).

Exercise

In the box below are a list of dates and titles of press releases from the U.S. Department of Justice, Bureau of Statistics website. Go through the list and select any five titles and write down what you think the statistical data indicate. You are drawing inferences on the basis of these data. Note when you might conclude quite different (even conflicting) pictures of the society from the same press release.

U.S. Department of Justice
Bureau of Justice Statistics Press Releases

8/12/01:   Nation's State prison population falls in second half of 2000. First such decline since 1972.

7/1/01:   Firearms purchase applications declined during 2000. About 2 percent of the requests were rejected.

3/18/01:   Differences in rates of violent crime experienced by whites and blacks narrow. American Indians are the most victimized by violence.

3/11/01:   Half of all contacts with law enforcement officers are in traffic stops.

1/26/01:   Nearly 3 percent of college women experienced a completed or attempted rape during the college year, according to a new Justice Department report.

11/29/00:   Two of three felony defendants represented by publicly-financed counsel.

8/30/00:   Almost 1.5 million minor children have a mother or father in prison.

7/23/00:   U.S. Correctional Population reaches 6.3 million men and women—represents 3.1 percent of the adult U.S. population.

5/17/00:   Intimate partner violence against women declined from 1993 through 1998. One-third of all murdered females were killed by partner.

2/27/00:   The number of people under 18 sent to adult State prisons more than doubled between 1985 and 1997.

1/9/00:   People 65 years old and older less likely to be victims of violent crime than younger U.S. residents.

7/11/99:   More than a quarter million prison and jail inmates are identified as mentally ill.

2/14/99:   American Indians are victims of violent crime at double the rate of the general population.

Source: www.ojp.usdoj.gov/bjs/press.htm.

Drawing Inferences

People regularly conclude one thing or another on the basis of what they see or hear. One of the ways this process is referred to is that they are drawing inferences. An inference is the same as a conclusion. Sometimes the inferences we draw are well founded. Sometimes they are not.

Think of one of those stories about someone who shoots a family member in the middle of the night: a woman is awakened by a noise and, because it is two or three in the morning when everyone should be tucked in bed, she infers that the noise is due to some vicious criminal out to rob or kill the family. She grabs the shotgun out of the closet and, when the door opens to their bedroom, lets the suspect have it. Only after it's too late does she realize that she's just killed Uncle Roy, who dropped by to give them a surprise present.

Whether it's in the dark of night or the cool light of day, drawing inferences is a part of our lives. We need to think about evidence to avoid a hasty conclusion. Consider this example: In July 2001, Kevin Pullum, convicted of attempted murder, managed to stroll out of the Los Angeles Twin Towers jail wearing a badge with a photo of Eddie Murphy from *Dr. Doolittle 2*. Although the escapee is black, he bears little resemblance to Eddie Murphy. Apparently no one checked Pullum's fake badge as he passed by the security booth. As Bill Cunningham of the Cook County Sheriff's Department in Chicago put it: "He's walking around with a picture of Eddie Murphy on an ID and no one noticed? That's bad. One small mistake can compromise security for the entire jail" (see Beth Shuster and Kenneth Reichs, "Jail Escapee Is a No-Show at Surrender," *Los Angeles Times*, 17 July 2001).

Not all inferences create the set of problems like the case above. Sherry Turkle, Sociologist of Science at MIT, did a study of children and toys. She observes,

> I have found that children describe these new toys [Furbies—bear-like electronic toys] as "sort of alive" because of the quality of their emotional attachments. . . . I predict that our children will have expectations of emotional attachment to computers, not in the way that we have expectation of emotional attachments to our cars and stereos, but in the way we have expectations of emotional attachments to people. (See "Toys to Change our Minds," in Sian Griffiths, *Predictions*).

What Turkle did is this: based on her research, she described the ways in which children related to computer-based toys like Furbies. She then drew inferences about what the study told us about children and what we need to keep in mind when thinking about the future. For Turkle the future with toys is this: "To relate to the doll, you have to relate to its state of mind" (see "Toys to Change our Minds").

As Dr. Turkle's research illustrates, we draw inferences as part of our work as students and faculty. But we also draw inferences in relationships (think what Milly must have inferred about her husband, Al, from his letter). We also draw inferences whenever we are bombarded with information and especially so when we come across issues that potentially impact our lives.

inference is a conclusion...

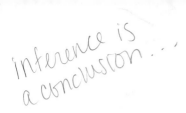

Group Exercise

What can you conclude from the excerpt below about human cloning experiments going on in secret labs in the United States? State all the claims being asserted and what can be inferred from the following:

> For Brigitte Boisselier, cloning a human being isn't just good science—it's a religious imperative. As a trained chemist and a bishop of a sect that believes scientists from another planet created all life on Earth, Boisselier and other followers of the "Raelian" religion say cloning is key to humanity's future. Despite warnings from scientists who say such practices are fraught with potential health risks, some Raelians have built a secret U.S. laboratory and vowed to create the first human clone this year. . . .
>
> Food and Drug Administration agents visited the lab recently and ordered any human cloning experiments to cease. Says one official: "There's a timeout in force." For months, Boisselier has told reporters that she has three scientists and a physician trying to resurrect an 11-month-old infant—the deceased son of a former state legislator, whom the Raelians refuse to identify—through genetic regeneration.
>
> Rael, who says he was contacted by a UFO in 1973, has tens of thousands of followers, largely in France, Canada, and East Asia. . . . Dozens of young Raelian women, including Boisselier's daughter, have volunteered to donate eggs and act as surrogate mothers for a cloned embryo. (See Nell Boyce and David E. Kaplan, "The God Game No More: The Feds Crack Down on a Human Cloning Lab," *U.S. News and World Report,* 9 July 2001)

Exercises

Part One

1. Given the information below, what can you infer about actor Angelina Jolie and observer Noah Taylor?

   [Angelina Jolie speaking] . . . on that famous amulet around her neck containing a drop of husband Billy Bob Thornton's blood: "I'm obsessed with Billy. I always want more. I can't have enough of him. So I wanted his blood to make me feel closer to him."

   "She speaks her mind," observes Noah Taylor, who spent months working with Jolie on the film in London and Iceland. "She'll actually answer your questions honestly. I wish there was more of that in Hollywood." (See Benjamin Svetkey, "Wonder Woman," *Entertainment Weekly,* 15 June 2001)

2. What can you infer from the comments of Jesse Ventura, Governor of Minnesota, stated below:

I didn't need this job. I ran for governor to find out if the American dream still exists in anyone's heart other than mine. I'm living proof that the myths aren't true. The candidate with the most money isn't always the one who wins. You don't have to be a career politician to serve in public office. You don't have to be well connected. You don't even have to be a Democrat or a Republican. You can stand on your own two feet and speak your mind, because if people like where you're coming from, they will vote you in. The will of the people is still the most powerful force in our government.

Politics is not my life. I have a career in radio and another career in film. I have a wife who is the sweetest person in the world and two kids who are growing up into terrific, well-rounded people. I don't want to spend the rest of my life in politics. When I'm finished with my term as governor, I'm going back to the life that's waiting for me in the private sector. (See *Ain't Got Time to Bleed*, 1 Jan. 1999, as noted by *www.issues2000.org*).

3. What can you infer about this reporter's view of Toronto, Canada, from this excerpt from his newspaper column:

The streets [of Toronto, Canada] are garbagey now with pickups less frequent. . . . The schools hold bake sales to buy books and pencils. There's been no major office construction and virtually no new rental accommodation downtown since 1995. The number of two-parent families with kids using homeless shelters grew by 545 per cent between 1988 and 1999. . . . We are in the decline and fall phase. . . . Decline and falls are part of the lives of cities, countries and individuals. Then they rise again, sometimes. As a Jewish character defiantly told Tony Soprano when Tony and his pals were about to cut the man's fingers off: "My people fought the Romans. Tell me, where are the Romans now?" And Tony answered, "You're lookin' at 'em." (See Rick Salutin, "John, Paul, and the Fall of Toronto," *The Globe and Mail* (Toronto), 6 July 2001)

4. Note what you can infer about Sarah from the following conversation that takes place in the movie, *The Hustler:*

SARAH: How did you know my name is Sarah?
FAST EDDIE: You told me last night.
SARAH: I always lie when I drink.
FAST EDDIE: Okay, so what is your name today?
SARAH: Sarah.

5. State what you can infer about the impact cell phones have had on our society from the following:

Perhaps the most famous breach of cell phone–church etiquette happened at the Vatican in May when 155 Roman Catholic cardinals bowed in prayer during a rare meeting called by Pope John Paul II. A cell phone went off and kept ringing until one very embarrassed cardinal—his face undoubtedly matching his scarlet cap—reached into his black cassock and silenced the phone.

[And another example:] At a picturesque church near Victorville in June, the bride and groom stood before the Catholic priest when his cell phone went off. "At first, I thought maybe it was some kind of joke," said Mary Lou Fulton of Long Beach, whose cousin was getting married. The phone rang three more times during the ceremony. "I felt so bad," she said. "It was quite a culture clash—the ancient rites of marriage and someone fumbling with a cell phone." (See William Lobdel, "Cell Phone Etiquette Sins Hit a New Low," *Los Angeles Times,* 2 July 2001)

6. Is it safe to conclude that watching the World Cup (soccer match) is the reason for falling rates of domestic violence? Look at the argument below and assess the strength of the reasoning.

World cup soccer is keeping Israeli men glued to their TV sets, and calls to domestic violence hotlines have dropped by half since the start of the competition. "Soccer lets men act out their aggressions and it's keeping them busy," Ronit Lev-Ari, director of the country's (Israel's) largest counseling service for battered women, said Thursday.

"If the World Cup didn't already exist, women would have had to organize it," said Mrs. Lev-Ari. She said the four violence hotlines of Naamat, the women's organization of Israel's trade union federation, usually receive about 30 calls for help a day from battered women. Since the World Cup started in mid-June, the number of calls has dropped to about 15. (Associated Press, "Calls to Domestic Violence Hotline Drop Sharply During Cup," 30 June 1994)

7. Share your thoughts about (a) younger vs. older viewers and (b) TV decision making from the following excerpt about modeling TV news after computers:

Increasingly, we're going to see TV work like computer screens," said industry analyst Larry Gerbrandt of Carmel-based Paul Kagan Associates. "The problem with television is that it's linear, it can only do one thing at a time," he said. "This is a way of multi-tasking, and it's clear from the way people use computers and Web sites that they can do more than one thing at a time." . . . As part of its makeover, ESPNEWS will roughly double the information grid at the bottom of the screen, said spokesman Mike Soltys. . . .

Can there be an overload? TV viewer Bruce Beasley, 44, of Corona, who works in the real estate industry, thinks so. "It's distracting," he said of the information already on news channels like CNN and MSNBC. His 18-year-old son, Matthew, a Web page designer, disagrees. "When I turn on ESPNEWS or CNN, I want news. I'd like it (an expanded display), especially if I'm trying to get a particular score or news story and don't wait to wait before they rotate again. As a teen-ager, I'm very impatient."

He's part of the younger, computer-savvy demographic which CNN Headline News . . . expects will most easily adapt to the new format. "Focus testing comes back off the charts," said Turner chief executive officer Jamie Kellner. "If you get really a lot of older people, you'll start getting confusion. But with the core (audience) that you want for this, which is 18–49, 25–54, there's a very, very solid response." (See "TV News Bows to the Computer Age," Associated Press, 18 July 2001)

8. The results of a poll released on March 12, 2002, suggest that photocopier rage is an issue for millions of Canadians (see Ian Johnson, "Millions Prone

to Photocopier Rage," *The Globe and Mail*, 12 Mar. 2002). Discuss what is revealed by the poll:

- The national poll found that 12 percent of Canadians who have used a photocopier at work have become so frustrated that they have actually kicked or hit it.
- Another three in 10 say that they have "seriously wanted to kick or hit" their photocopier, but ultimately restrained themselves.
- "The results suggest that more than five million Canadian office workers have fought back the urge to kick or hit their office photocopier, while more than two million have actually struck their machine," said Mr. Desmarais of Hewlitt Packard (Canada).
- People with university educations are the group most likely to physically attack a photocopier? 13 percent have, and 34 percent admitted a serious desire to do so.
- Those with higher-income jobs are also at higher risk, with 14 percent dishing out a swift boot at some point and 35 percent having given it serious thought.

Part Two

Examine the FBI table of bias-crime statistics from 1995, noting the range of incidents depending upon the traits of the victim (see the FBI website, *www.fbi.gov*). Note that an "incident" refers to the event and "offenses" refers to actions committed on the victim(s). Draw four inferences on the basis of any or all of these statistics.

U.S. Department of Justice
Federal Bureau of Investigation
Criminal Justice Information Services
Uniform Crime Reports

Incidents, Offenses, Victims, and Known Offenders by Bias Motivation, 2000[1]

BIAS MOTIVATION	INCIDENTS	OFFENSES	VICTIMS[2]	KNOWN OFFENDERS[3]
Total	8,063	9,430	9,924	7,530
Single-Bias Incidents	8,055	9,413	9,906	7,520
Race:	4,337	5,171	5,397	4,452
Anti-White	875	1,050	1,080	1,169
Anti-Black	2,884	3,409	3,535	2,799
Anti-American Indian/ Alaskan Native	57	62	64	58
Anti-Asian/Pacific Islander	281	317	339	273
Anti-Multiracial Group	240	333	379	153

Bias Motivation	Incidents	Offenses	Victims[2]	Known Offenders[3]
Religion:	**1,472**	**1,556**	**1,699**	**577**
Anti-Jewish	1,109	1,161	1,269	405
Anti-Catholic	56	61	63	33
Anti-Protestant	59	62	62	23
Anti-Islamic	28	33	36	20
Anti-Other Religious Group	172	187	210	77
Anti-Multireligious Group	44	46	52	18
Anti-Atheism/Agnosticism/etc.	4	6	7	1
Sexual Orientation:	**1,299**	**1,486**	**1,558**	**1,443**
Anti-Male Homosexual	896	1,023	1,060	1,088
Anti-Female Homosexual	179	211	228	169
Anti-Homosexual	182	210	226	153
Anti-Heterosexual	22	22	24	18
Anti-Bisexual	20	20	20	15
Ethnicity/National Origin:	**911**	**1,164**	**1,216**	**1,012**
Anti-Hispanic	557	735	763	694
Anti-Other Ethnicity/National Origin	354	429	453	318
Disability:	**36**	**36**	**36**	**36**
Anti-Physical	20	20	20	22
Anti-Mental	16	16	16	14
Multiple-Bias Incidents[4]	**8**	**17**	**18**	**10**

[1] Because hate crime submissions have been updated, data in this table may differ from those published in *Crime in the United States, 2000.*

[2] The term *victim* may refer to a person, business, institution, or society as a whole.

[3] The term *known offender* does not imply that the identity of the suspect is known, but only that the race of the suspect is identified which distinguishes him/her from an unknown offender.

[4] A *multiple-bias incident* is a hate crime in which two or more offense types were committed as a result of two or more bias motivations.

Facts, Opinions, and Ideas

When we think of facts, we think of things rooted in reality, or truth. This covers actual occurrences and actions performed, as well as pieces of information corresponding to an objective reality. Facts are actually the case, known by observation or authentic testimony, as opposed to what is inferred, conjectured or invented. Statements of fact include all that we can say is "true." As Philip K. Dick says,

"Reality is that which, when you stop believing in it, doesn't' go away." The *Oxford English Dictionary* offers examples of facts:

- "The very great advantage of being a fact and not a fiction."
- "Imagination is often at war with reason and fact."
- "She was detected . . . in the very fact of laughing . . . at the description"

Generally we think of facts as empirically verifiable. That is, facts can be proved by means of our five senses—sight, smell, touch, taste, and hearing. These are all facts: "Carrots are vegetables," "Bread is a starchy food," "Water freezes at 32° Fahrenheit." Mathematical definitions, axioms, and proven theorems are usually considered facts as well, even though the ordinary person may not be able to establish their truth. In that sense, they operate as facts, because they are thought to be true by definition or derivation (e.g., derived from theorems and postulates in geometry or calculus).

Factual judgments are often treated as facts, as we see with "Smog is bad for your lungs." These are generally inferences drawn from earlier observations, for instance, about the sorts of ingredients of smog and the studies that show the effects of those ingredients on the respiratory system. Some argue that factual judgments are not really facts and, thus, should be assessed carefully, because they can mislead us. The rule of thumb here is: A factual judgment is not normally as strong as a fact, because it is at least one step away. This step means that the inference drawn on the basis of the fact cannot be assumed to be true, but must be scrutinized.

Opinions are statements of belief. Some opinions rely upon facts or are in response to them, but are insufficiently supported and, so, opinions are disputable. This is seen with: "The best music is rhythm and blues" and "Practicing verb drills is a drag." Opinions are generally based on perception—and because opinions are relative to the speaker's own experience or state of mind, people can say, "Well, that's just a matter of opinion." Opinions tend to function like beliefs, varying from one speaker to the next. However, in a legal context, they may be expressed as a formal statement, a ruling, or considered advice. Court opinions, for example, function as an explanation for a decision that becomes law. The *Oxford English Dictionary* offers these examples of opinions:

- "Opinion in good men is but knowledge in the making."
- "Let them stand, or fall in the public opinion."
- "It is not to control opinions, but actions, that Government is instituted."

Fact, analysis, and opinion are often linked, though opinions may or may not have a factual basis. It is a fact that we utter words. What they signify requires analysis and whether the speaker thinks they make sense or not is a matter of opinion. When people set out the reasons for an opinion, we now have an argument.

Red Flags

An *unsupported opinion* should raise a red flag. Just saying what you think does not make it true. State your reasons. Without support, your opinion is flapping in the wind. Only when we know the foundation they rest on can we decide whether or not they have merit. People often state opinions alongside a set of facts—the two are often intertwined. They are not the same, however, and shouldn't be used interchangeably. Even so, there is not always a clear line between facts and opinions. For instance, "Ice cream is sweet" or, worse, "This pie is *too* sweet." Verifying the two claims involves an empirical taste-test. But taste may vary from one person to the next and may be influenced by differing diets, medication, or other conditions.

Given this, there may be gray zones requiring something like the "reasonable person" standard in law. To determine the factual nature of a claim and distinguish it from mere opinion, look for universal agreement as to the truth of the claim (e.g., drawing across competent members of different groups, classes, cultures, genders). If the response to the claim varies according to class, ethnicity, or gender, and so on, it may not be considered a fact.

Exercises

Part One

1. Discuss whether the "facts" in the *Ayds* diet candy ad from 1951 are sufficient to conclude "It Works," as did actress Paulette Goddard. Note also what questions you'd want answered (what other facts you want to know) before you'd recommend trying the candy:

   Ayds is a specially made candy containing health-giving vitamins and minerals. It acts by reducing your desire for those extra fattening calories . . . works almost like magic. Easily and naturally you should begin to look slimmer, more beautiful day by day.

2. Go to an Internet site with archives of ads, such as *www.adflip.com*. Select three to four ads, each from a different decade (e.g., the 60s, 70s, 80s, 90s). State what sorts of facts or factual claims are presented, and what sorts of opinions are expressed. Attach the ads and set out the facts and opinions you see on each.

Part Two

Read over the information about Firestone tires connected with deaths involving Ford Explorers. State the key <u>facts</u> and your <u>opinion</u> of the situation.

1. After being blamed as the cause of numerous accidents and as many as 88 deaths involving Ford Explorers, Firestone has begun a recall of several of their tires in the South and southwestern states.

2. Other regions of the country are expected to become part of the recall in the future.

3. Included in the recall are the Firestone Wilderness and ATX lines, both tires are used as the original equipment fitment for the Ford Explorer.

4. Thus far only tires in the size of P235/75R15 with a serial number beginning with the letters "VD" are subjected to the recall.

5. Firestone has in the past recalled the same tires on vehicles in South America and the Middle East.

6. Consumers who own Ford Explorers or other SUVs equipped with these tires would be advised to visit their local Firestone dealer or other tire retailer in order to have their tires inspected.

7. Ford CEO Jacques Nasser stated that the defects claimed to have caused 88 deaths in the United States are "a tire issue, not a vehicle issue." He also said the Ford was "sorry that these tires are on our vehicles."

8. Firestone is allowing drivers to be reimbursed for the purchase of non–Firestone brand tires up to $100 per tire.

9. Several newspaper articles (in Sep. 2000) claimed that Ford officials as early as 1989 knew that the Explorer, which replaced the Bronco II, was susceptible to rolling over.

10. This air pressure change while increasing handling and lessening the likelihood of rollover can cause an overheating of the tires and hinder the dissipation of that heat which could lead to tire failure. (See Garth R. Smith, "Firestone Tires and the Ford Explorer," *www.suite101.com,* 19 Sep. 2000)

Ideas

Ideas take the form of solutions, intentions, plans of action, even theories. The ancient roots of the word go back to a general or ideal form, pattern, or standard by which things are measured. More commonly now, we use it to refer to insights, purposes, or recommendations. Some ideas are creative leaps, springing from visions or mental images, connected by often the finest of threads. In contrast, some ideas are mental constructs we generate from our observations or factual data.

Some ideas directly link to specific issues or problems; others have no clear relationship to reality. Ideas may strike like lightning, unexpected and piercing, and may appear in dreams, or daydreams, with no clear stimulus. The *Oxford English Dictionary* offers these examples of ideas:

- "That's not the Big Idea, I know; it's the idiotic one, but the market for idiocy is unlimited."
- "Gosh, he's always reading now. It's not my idea of having a good time in vacation."
- "You're an idea man, and that's what they pay off on in Hollywood."

Ideas sometimes come through a side door, when our attention is focused elsewhere—or not at all. You know this if you ever sat down to write a paper and stared fruitlessly at the blank sheet for hours. You give up and are in the middle of doing dishes or talking on the phone, when an idea springs forth from the top of your head. That's the creative dimension of ideas that cannot be forced or programmed. Anyone can have an opinion, but not everyone can have an idea—much less a good idea.

A set of facts may give rise to an unlimited number of ideas. For example, here is a set of facts: My refrigerator has in it mustard, mayonnaise, chocolate sauce, Maraschino cherries, and (in the freezer) vanilla ice cream; the humidity today is 84 percent and it is 100°F outside, I am hungry for a snack, and I am bored. Here are some ideas: We can make an ice cream sundae with the ice cream, fudge sauce, and cherries; We can make a revolting mixture of ice cream and mustard; We could smear ice cream all over our bodies and take photos for *Playmate* magazine.

Do you see how a fact differs from an idea or an opinion? An opinion is usually a personal response (e.g., "Your dog is a monster," "Oranges taste nicer than grapefruits," or "Birds are disgusting animals because they poop so much"). Customarily, opinions are stated without citing evidence and allow for a contrasting interpretation ("I'm of another opinion"). An idea is not simply a statement of affairs, like "This dog is attacking people," "Oranges grow on trees," or "Birds are not capable of living at the bottom of the ocean." Ideas are often in response to a set of facts (e.g., "You should take your dog to obedience school," "We ought to make marmalade from all those oranges," or "Birds should be trained to wear diapers or use a tiny toilet"). In many cases an idea could be expressed in the form "We should . . ." or "We ought to . . ." or "We might try . . ." or "This may be the cause of . . ." or "This may solve the problem."

German philosopher Ludwig Wittgenstein said that ideas "sometimes fall from the tree before they are ripe." We've probably all experienced a few of these—ideas that are not fully formed, with potential maybe, but need to be reshaped. Not all ideas are good or even workable ideas. However, just generating a set of ideas can lay the foundation for a major breakthrough. That's one reason problem-solving sessions often start with brainstorming ideas—generating ideas freely, quickly, and without editing or criticism.

Exercises

Part One

Directions: In the sentences below, mark which ones are F (facts), I (ideas), or O (opinions) and then note the basis for your decision.

1. Leftover pizza makes for a tasty breakfast.
2. New York City is known as the "Big Apple."
3. Women with firm muscles are beautiful.

4. In order to increase tourism, the Yellowknife Chamber of Commerce should put ads in *People* magazine.

5. A well-balanced diet is generally good for your health.

6. Perhaps if you try a gas additive, you could improve the mileage of your SUV.

7. Yellow is a color that makes people feel happy.

8. Women love it when men wear cologne.

9. If you want an emotionally stable bird, you shouldn't cut its wings.

10. You ought to sing while driving to combat boredom.

11. Lemons are members of the citrus family.

12. If you aren't a U.S. citizen, you cannot be a member of Congress.

13. Only snooty people prefer the sound of a violin over an electric guitar.

14. Mariah Carey is a better singer than Madonna, but not as interesting a performer.

15. Smoking statistically increases the chance of lung cancer and emphysema.

16. To increase revenue, Mexican restaurants should set up a tamale home-delivery service.

17. Watching movies without a big box of popcorn is a drag.

18. *American Beauty* won for Best Picture in the 2001 Academy Awards.

19. Haley Joel Osment was robbed of the Oscar for Best Actor for his great job in *Sixth Sense*—he was sensational!

20. To train for the Boston marathon, you ought to increase your intake of carbohydrates and work on endurance.

Part Two

For each set of <u>facts</u> from Jeffrey Abramson's book *We, The Jury*, state your inference and any opinions or ideas you have in response:

1. In 1990 there were 9826 jury trials in U.S. district courts, out of a total of 20,433 trials. Of the jury trials, 5061 were criminal and 4765 were civil.

2. Of all convictions, 86.5% were through guilty pleas or pleas of no contest—only 13.5% convictions were in cases where the defendant proceeded with a not guilty plea.

3. Eighty percent of defendants going to trial in federal courts in 1990 were found guilty.

4. In 1990, juries convicted 84% of the defendants coming before them, whereas the conviction rate in trials before judges was 62.7%.

Part Three

CASE STUDY

Bigger Breasts through Vacuum Cups

Just when you thought the breast-enlargement business had gone about as far as it could, a new product called Brava hit the market in the summer of 2001. The target is an estimated 16 million women who want to have larger breasts; and the company hopes for a windfall. Brava is a vacuum-based system in which large plastic domes, acting as suctions over the breasts, presumably increase the fluid level in the breasts. With the increased fluid, the breast will be fuller up to one cup size. Unfortunately, to get this result women have to wear the suction domes at least 10-hours a day for 10 weeks.

The device is recommended for women between 18 and 40 years old who hope to plump up the breast or help a sagging (but not too sagging!) breast. It is not for those who are pregnant, breast-feeding, have breast cancer, or have scarring in the breast from past surgeries. Within four months, 1000 women have been fitted with the Brava breast vacuum. The average cost is around $2500 each. Dr. Roger Khouri, inventor of Brava, insists the product is safe. The FDA (Food and Drug Administration) elected not to regulate it, considering it a very low risk. However, the FDA did not assess its effectiveness. The manufacturer claims the process is not painful, but can cause an uncomfortable pulling sensation. Also, it requires a lifestyle adjustment (such as sitting up straight) so the vacuum seal is not broken.

Apparently breast cancer surgeon, Dr. Susan Love, does not think it will do any short-term harm. However, Dr. Susan Downey of the University of Southern California doubts if the changes would be permanent. Nevertheless, the company is optimistic about the potential market. Individual women using Brava have to make major adjustments. For example,

[Customer Linda Langer] is curbing her social life because she has to be home by 8 p.m. to have sufficient time to strap the device on, hook it up and keep it running while she tries to sleep. With an alarm system that lately has been going off about three times a night—whenever her movements break the domes' vacuum seal, she's suffering from lack of sleep. She's also been forced to change many habits. Because she does a lot of writing at the computer, she had to learn to sit "very erect. You can't slump because you'll lose the seal." (For a fuller discussion, see Jane E. Allen, "Breast Enhancement in the Privacy of Your Own Home," *Los Angeles Times,* 2 July 2001)

Exercises

1. Given what you learned about Brava in reading the description and excerpt above, answer the questions below:
   a. What facts are claimed about Brava?
   b. What opinions are expressed about the device?
   c. In terms of your own ideas and insights, what are some reasons women may want to purchase a Brava breast-enhancement device?
   d. What are some reasons women may be leery about using this product?

2. Share your ideas and insights on ONE of the following:
   a. What would you say to a woman contemplating getting a Brava breast vacuum cup?
   b. What would you say to Dr. Khouri sharing your ideas on his invention of the Brava breast vacuum cup?

3. What would you say in response to Steve Lopez, journalist, who writes:

   I don't expect to ever understand the opposite sex in my lifetime. But one woman, whose identity must be withheld, would toss my shorts into the street in about two seconds if I suggested she place her privates into suction domes for roughly 10 hours a day through mid-September. First of all, she doesn't like to vacuum anything. Second, she would say something about women trying to make themselves look like beer commercial bimbos for "idiot men."

   "Have they thought about strapping that thing to their heads?" she'd ask. Dr. Khouri, creator of Brava, actually liked the idea. "Smart women tell me that's the most important sex organ," he said. "We could call it Brainva." It's a good thing the anonymous woman didn't see the ad that ran near the Brava story. It was from a surgeon looking for "Buttock Enhancement" patients. Wasn't it just yesterday that women were trying to lose weight back there? And how about the noble work of the surgeon? Children are dying in mosquito-infested villages without doctors, and this guy's doing butt surgery on Jennifer Lopez wannabes." (*Los Angeles Times*, 4 July 2001)

Good Arguments, Bad Arguments

Arguments are all around us; the question is what to make of them. The first step in tackling an argument is to locate the conclusion. If we don't know where the argument is headed, we're lost in a fog. Once the conclusion is clear, we can see how the argument is structured. This entails setting out the evidence—the premises—and examining the role of any assumptions that may be a factor. If there are any unwarranted assumptions, we'd need to make note of that and decide if there are any glaring omissions. In this way, we can dismantle the argument before us.

In order to examine and evaluate the arguments, keep in mind:

- The evidence should provide a clear link to the conclusion.
- The case needs to be as strong as possible.
- If it seems like a strong case, see how the evidence supports the conclusion.
- Determine the weakest link, in case you need to bolster it.
- If the argument is not convincing, find the weaknesses in the reasoning.

Let's look at the reasoning in the cartoon "Failed Laundry Detergents" by Roz Chast. Here we find three arguments, one for each type of detergent: Reason, the first failed laundry detergent, offers dirty laundry this argument, "You are not really wanted; therefore, you should leave." The second failed detergent, Snub, offers the consumer this reasoning, "These soap flakes will totally ignore dirt. Most dirt that is totally ignored goes away. Therefore, hopefully this dirt will go away." The last failed detergent is Empty Threat. Here the detergent argues, "Unless this dirt dissolves this instant, there will be hell to pay." Presumably, the argument continues with, "There is no hell to pay. Therefore, the dirt dissolved this instant."   **FIGURE 2-5**

However, in the nightmare world of filthy laundry the argument could have proceeded: "The dirt did not dissolve this instant. Therefore, there will be hell to pay." As you can see, all three arguments are weak; thus clarifying for us why these are all *failed* laundry detergents.

Not all arguments have the problems of failed laundry detergent. Some arguments *are* convincing. If the support is strong and clearly supports the conclusion if we assume it were true, we'd say we have a good argument. Let's look at an example of an argument that is well constructed.

In "Paying a Price for Drinking Men under the Table," Nancy Wartik discusses the results of heavy alcohol consumption in women (see *The New York Times,* 24 June 2001). Here are some of her observations and key pieces of evidence:

Observation 1: In recent years, studies have found many ways in which the drinking life takes a greater toll on women than men.

Observation 2: Dr. Mary Dufour, deputy director of the National Institute of Alcoholism and Alcohol Abuse, said, "Every organ and cause of death that we look at suggests women are more susceptible and die at greater rates than men do."

Observation 3: Women appear to suffer many alcohol-related problems and illness at an earlier stage than men. Their risk of sustaining some kinds of liver, cardiac or neurological damage is greater, and their depression rates are higher.

Observation 4: Four million American women already suffer from alcohol use disorders, with 14 percent of both male and female eighth graders admitting in a survey to having taken five drinks in a row in the two weeks before the survey done by the University of Michigan in 2000.

Observation 5: Researchers discovered that drinking raised women's blood alcohol levels higher than men's; on average, one drink for a woman is worth nearly two for a man, partly because women are smaller and have less water in their bodies to dilute the alcohol.

Observation 6: It is already clear from an abundance of studies that alcoholic women are much more likely than men to contract liver disease and to die from it at an earlier stage in their drinking lives.

Observation 7: The risk of cirrhosis, the chief cause of death in alcoholics, starts to increase for men at 2.5 to 4 drinks a day, but for a woman, the risk starts to increase at less than two.

Observation 8: Alcoholic women are more prone to hepatitis and less likely to recover from liver disease even if they stop drinking.

Observation 9: A federal study in 2001 found that alcoholics' brains tend to atrophy and the rate was almost twice as great for women as for men, after fewer years of chronic drinking.

Observation 10: Women in the alcoholic category were generally more than twice as likely to report being hindered in daily life as men in the alcoholic category, and far more likely to report being depressed.

Conclusion: We need to get across that even for women without alcohol problems, it's not cool to try and drink your male counterparts under the table.

Group Exercise

Examine Wartik's argument above and then answer the following:

1. What is the strongest evidence she cites?
2. How effective is her comparison of men and women?
3. Note what facts and statistics she cites and whether they are crucial to her argument.

Exercises

1. State two possible premises for the conclusion: "People who vote keep democracy alive."
2. State two possible premises for the conclusion: "It is inappropriate for a talk show host to ask teenagers about their sex lives."
3. State two possible premises for the conclusion: "Taking photos of movie stars in public places without their permission is not a violation of their privacy."
4. List three inferences you could draw from the report that the United Nations plans to use comic books to educate people about land mines in the following:

   Last week, the United Nations secretary general helped launch a comic book starring the Man of Steel [Superman] and Wonder Woman. The publication is designed to inform Central American children of the dangers posed by undetonated mines left from the wars that plagued the region in the 1980s. (See *U.S. News and World Report*, 22 June 1998).

5. Here are the premises (facts). Draw two possible conclusions:

   P1: About one out of every five children in this country lives in poverty.
   P2: About one out of every two black children lives in poverty.
   P3: About two out of every five Hispanic children live in poverty.

6. What are three different conclusions that could be drawn from this claim: "The average 5-foot-8-inch Miss America contestant weighed 132 pounds in 1954 and 117 pounds in 1980"?

7. What is the author arguing in the following assessment of the 2002 Olympics? State his conclusion and how he supports it:

   It was Oscar Wilde who said, "Moderation is a fatal thing. Nothing succeeds like excess." Salt Lake proved Wilde's point. Fire and ice, reds and blues, deserts and mountains, hot and cold were used over and over and over again to link venue to venue, ceremony to stage, opening to closing, athlete to spectator, performer to audience, look to print, print to broadcast, medal to torch, start to finish.

Like an ice crystal, the repetition bred enchantment, not contempt. It lent form and vitality, not predictability and dullness. Banners along the cold streets transitioned from icy blues to warm reds, drawing people from the cold outdoors to the heat of the athletic competition inside. At the top of ski runs, warming huts were wrapped in red, while the alpine runs were trimmed in blues. As the alpine racers crossed the finish lines, they passed into "finish corrals" dressed in reds and lined with screaming, adoring fans. (See Matthew Porter, "Olympic Winter Games of 2002, " *Communication Arts*, March/April 2002)

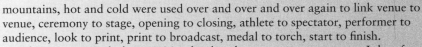 Premise-Indicators and Conclusion-Indicators

It is not always clear what is the conclusion and what are the premises. For example, what if someone said to you, "Asbestos is dangerous. It poisons the atmosphere. It is a known carcinogen." Is the conclusion obvious, or has it even been stated? If you clutch your head in confusion, you can understand the value of signposts in locating the terms of the argument.

Indicator words such as "because" and "therefore" functioning as signposts, eliminate the need for guessing as to the premises and the conclusion. These words and phrases tell us that a premise or conclusion immediately follows. If you can replace the term with "therefore" without changing the argument, the term is a conclusion-indicator, if you can replace it with "because" it's a premise-indicator. Fortunately, arguments often have premise-indicators or conclusion-indicators and, so, the job of setting out the argument is much easier. Some common indicators are as follows:

Premise-Indicators	Conclusion-Indicators
Because . . .	Therefore . . .
Since*	Consequently . . .
In light of . . .	Hence . . .
Whereas . . .	It follows that . . .
Given that . . .	Subsequently . . .
For the reason that . . .	Thus . . .
For . . .	In conclusion . . .
	Accordingly . . .
	As a result . . .
	So . . .

* *Be careful:* Sometimes "since" is a temporal indicator, as in "Since I dyed my hair purple, men have found me attractive." If "since" can be replaced by "from the moment," then it is a temporal indicator, NOT a premise-indicator. If "since" can be replaced by "because"—e.g., "Since I love ice cream, I'll get a sundae"—then it functions as a premise-indicator.

premise → have more than 1
↓
conclusion   because + therefor

Transition Words

Words like, "however," "although," whenever," "if," and "then" have various functions. When you see a "however" or an "although" treat them as conjunctions (. . . and . . .). They do not function as premise- or conclusion-indicators, unless clearly shown as such in the context (say a list of premises or conclusions being itemized or numbered). And when you see an "either . . . or," treat it like a disjunction (. . . or . . .). Be careful: these words could appear anywhere—in a premise OR in a conclusion. There are a number of transition words and, so, it helps to have a general sense of the range. Here are some of the more common transition words:

Transition Words

Amplification:	Moreover, furthermore, in addition, provided that, similarly, also, likewise, first, second, third
Introduction:	In order to, primarily, the first reason, initially, in the first place, to begin, in general
Clarification:	That is, to restate, in other words, in simpler terms, briefly, to repeat, to put it in another light, to put it differently, as seen by
Emphasis:	In fact, notably, nonetheless, nevertheless, in effect, above all, indeed, and rightly so, as such
Illustration:	To illustrate, for example, for instance, specifically, namely, a case in point
Contrast:	However, alternatively, on the other hand, notwithstanding, in opposition to, and yet, conversely, at the same time, in spite of, despite

Exercises

Part One

1. Circle all the premise-indicators below:

However	Since	Because	Although
Therefore	Whereas	If	Subsequently
Despite	Unless	Given that	Hence
Moreover	Conversely	Accordingly	For the reason that

2. Circle all the conclusion-indicators below:

Conversely	Yet	Whereas	Consequently
As a result	Since	Because	In light of the fact that
Thus	In fact	Given that	In conclusion
Indeed	To restate	Hence	Accordingly

3. Circle all the transitional words below:

However	Given that	Therefore	Although
In fact	Since	Accordingly	For the reason that
Above all	Specifically	Hence	Furthermore
Thus	Because	Despite	Initially

4. Clarify the difference between premise-indicators, conclusion-indicators, and transitional words.

Part Two

Directions: Circle the conclusion and underline the premises in the following:

1. Since cheese is so tasty, we ought to put it on top of our fried eggs. This is especially true given that Gabe likes cheese. ↑ conclusion

2. All your friends think you look better as a blonde. Green hair is unnatural. People with strangely colored hair attract trouble. Therefore, you should get rid of that ghastly green hair!

3. In spite of his lucrative film career, Russell Crowe seems to enjoy his band, 30 Odd Foot of Grunts. Consequently, directors who are impatient with Crowe's wanting to take time out for music should think twice before casting him in a movie.

4. You should restrict your yodeling to when you're in the shower. This is the case since, if you make a bunch of noise in the shower, it doesn't usually offend people. Plus, I know how much you like to yodel.

5. Men should love well-educated women. These women are smart. They are interesting. Moreover, they can't be taken for granted and we know men love women who can't be taken for granted.

6. Guys who've seen the world can explain words like *joie de vivre*. They have a kind of self-confidence impossible to get from staying in one place. They may get a bit restless, but worldly men are never boring. So if you want a great companion, go for a worldly man any day over a couch potato.

7. Escargot is another word for "snail." That's why I don't eat them, because I see snails every day in my front yard and they disgust me.

8. Alligators live in the swamp. Therefore, you ought to carry a weapon when you go wading, in light of the fact that alligators are vicious and they have been known to attack people.

9. Darin loves the movie *Babe*. He's probably watched it dozens of times. He doesn't mind the funny way the animals' mouths moved when they "talk." In fact, he thinks that's cool! He especially likes the way the little runt of a pig ends up transforming everyone in his world.

10. Politicians are a strange lot, or so my mother said. She thought they were all corrupt also. According to her only crooks became politicians. Given all this, she never voted, not even once.

11. Sniffing wallpaper paste is something you should avoid. It is causally linked to respiratory disease. It ages your skin dreadfully. Those who sniff paste have bad breath. Plus, it looks repulsive to see people sticking their noses next to wallpaper paste.

12. Tiger Woods is a lot like Keanu Reeves: he is tall, famous, and loves movies. Tiger Woods is a good golfer; therefore Keanu Reeves will be a good golfer too.

13. Stephen Jay Gould must have been a child genius, since he's such an intelligent man and has made his mark in biology.

14. Since Maria Martinez can't decide whether to run for office or not, people are going to have to send her a message. This is especially the case since she'd be a lot better at it than that politician, Ray Dubey, who's been in politics so long he looks like Count Dracula.

15. Tiny Tom prefers not to run for mayor. He is happy in his singing career and he could not bear the political headaches of politics. Moreover, Tom hasn't been approached by either party!

16. Arnold Schwarzenegger is thinking of running for governor of California. He is a popular actor, who was really great in the two *Terminator* movies. Because he has lots of political support, it would, therefore, be a good thing to have Schwarzenegger in the race.

17. Not all students eligible to vote have registered. They insist that politicians do not care about their concerns. Their numbers are very great. They are, consequently, a silent potential voice in the direction of this country.

18. You ought to get a parrot. They are intelligent, but not obnoxious. They don't require a nightly walk. There's no litter box to clean out. You can even teach them to talk if you are clever—not like cats or dogs, whose language skills are pathetic. Also they are loyal—remember how the parrot in the movie *Paulie* kept trying to find his owner, Marie? That movie brought tears to my eyes, it was that good!

19. "You chose the bread for the irresistible cinnamon swirls. Deciding what goes on top is easy. Margarines, spreads, and all things artificial need not apply. Don't you deserve the simple goodness of Land O Lakes butter? Butter is better." (Ad for Land O Lakes butter)

20. Cinderella had two mean stepsisters who made her life miserable. Her father was negligent, leaving her alone a great deal. Consequently, it is no wonder Cinderella married a man she just met—particularly if you also consider how cruel her stepmother was.

21. Cinderella may have been an abused child, but she was no wimp. She managed to get a dress to go to the ball. She showed courage in going out so late at night. She knew the importance of getting home before the curfew. This goes to show that Cinderella deserves more recognition than just being the pretty girl who woos a prince.

22. Sleeping Beauty now has trouble with insomnia. This is due to her childhood being cut short by that witch's cursing her. After a hundred-year long sleep it's hard to want to lie down and even take a nap! She must be terrified she won't wake up again.

23. Even though Ursula was an octopus, she developed her feminine charms. She wore bright red lipstick to flaunt her sexuality and had no qualms about wearing a low-cut dress. Subsequently, Ursula could be viewed as a kind of sea-goddess, not a witch. This is especially the case if we consider how generously she gave Ariel advice about men.

24. Rumplestiltskin is a bit of a toad. As a result, it's no wonder he's never appeared in any Disney cartoons. Just think about it: He was willing to take a baby from an exploited young woman. He could care less about the devastating effect it'd have on her life. Granted, she made the deal with him in exchange for spinning gold. But her stupidity and greed should not hide the fact that that nasty little Rumplestiltskin deserved a fast trip to the underworld!

25. "The dementors affect you worse than the others because there are horrors in your past that others don't have." (Said to Harry Potter by Professor Lupin)

Part Three

1. Set out the arguments by listing the premises and then stating the conclusion:
   a. People who only watch TV news must have a very different view of the world from those who read a newspaper. For one thing, they hear about all the murders, drive-by shootings, gang activity, and neglected children as soon as the news starts. Also, they must think the police put car chases as a top priority, since newscasts are often interrupted so viewers can watch police chasing someone on the freeway and city streets. And, finally, they must think people talk very little, since TV interviews rarely exceed 15 seconds.
   b. Televised executions are suggested from time to time. This is because some people think seeing murderers die will be a powerful deterrent to potential criminals. Furthermore, people like the idea of "an eye for an eye." Watching public executions could also give satisfaction to the victims' families.
   c. Children who watch TV before breakfast are less likely to eat a nutritious meal than children who run and play. The reason for this is that watching TV inputs the brain with far more signals than the young brain can handle before they are fully awake. Also, children watching morning TV want to eat and watch at the same time. When that happens, kids just don't pay attention to their meals.
   d. Bruce doesn't seem to get tired of Pokemon. He has Pokemon T-shirts, a Pokemon lunch pail, and he even has a key ring with Pokemon hang-

ing on it. As a result, Bruce will probably be crazy about that Pokemon body suit you got him for his snorkeling lessons!

e. Given that you keep flipping the channels, I am turning off the television.

f. Ryan loves to hear stories about Egypt and was fascinated by the video on the pyramids. He spent all of his $20 gift money on a plastic statue of the Sphinx when he went to Universal City Walk. Other kids went for toys, but Ryan bought that Sphinx and guarded it like it was the treasure of King Tut. Consequently, that mummy costume you got him for Halloween will be a major hit for sure!

g. Some time travel would be a good thing. You could get a sense of the future and have fewer risks. You could go back and study your past and get another chance to see what mistakes you made. You could make a few key changes in your past. Plus you could rewrite history.

2. Read the following discussion of the use of jingles in commercials and then set out the argument in as much detail as you can:

Audiences today are too intelligent and sophisticated for jingles. People easily identify jingles as advertising and tune them out. Music in ads these days should not dare sing the praises of the product, or even mention it.

Jingles aimed to elicit brand-name recall, but ads now work by "borrowing interest"—transferring value from the music to the product. Commercials not only borrow interest from music, they borrow our interests, milking our memories and desires, and selling them back to us. (Adapted from Carrie Mclaren's "Why Jingles Died and Licensed Pop Rules," *Village Voice Worldwide, www.villagevoice.com*)

3. State the argument below about virtual reality, noting the conclusion and the supporting evidence:

Our relationship to physical space and our known reality don't need to correspond with any familiar perspective. Not only can virtual worlds be realistic or imaginative, and defy the laws of physics, they can also transcend human physical and perceptual limitations. We are free to experience new worlds in completely new ways. Virtual worlds enable us to see the invisible, to shrink into microscopic worlds—we can go right down into the smallest molecule of the DNA helix—or, on a galactic scale, to travel through the solar system. (See Steve Holtzman, *The Aesthetics of Cyberspace: Digital Mosaics*)

4. Set out the conclusion and key claims made by Steve Peralta in the following excerpt:

The relationship between the United States and Mexico is a tenuous one, to say the least. But let it be known that there is hope for the Latino culture. Let it be known that the sacrifices that our ancestors have made will not be ignored. The contemporary Latino has "wised up" and the face of Latino America is finally changing.

The young and enterprising Latino no longer seeks out the acceptance that seemed to be so important before. The young Latino is blazing a new frontier that will eventually change the American mindscape. The young Latino refuses to accept that there are no opportunities for an inner city scholar with a north side

Denver accent. He has struggled as hard as the white suburban kid to get into the freshman class at Harvard and will not make any more cultural sacrifices.

The contemporary Latino has finally realized that culture and *ganas* can work together to mold a truly unique individual. The contemporary Latino makes no investment in statistical odds or figures because he realizes that figures lie and liars figure. . . . The Latino culture has reached a crossroads and in order to choose the right path we must be on the *same path*. When the Latino culture is unified, America can be unified. ("The Changing Face of Latino America," *www.grandemesa.com*)

5. Set out the argument and discuss the reasoning of this ad for Neff appliances. Discuss any assumptions about the consumer's values or lifestyle:

Who says money can't buy you happiness? With Neff appliances—ovens, hobs, microwaves, washing machines, dryers—for your kitchen and laundry areas, you can be sure that they will not only look wonderfully stylish, but will work like a dream, ensuring that your home life run as smoothly as possible. Neff allows you to get on with the more important things in life, whether it be cooking a cordon bleu meal for friends, going to the theatre or just simply putting your feet up. (Neff ad)

6. Set out the premises and conclusion in the argument below:

Although good intentions are meant by the protesters in controlling cutting, thin cutting is needed to promote a healthy growing environment. The crowded tree-to-tree situation within the Tillamook State Forest is a disaster in waiting, akin to the past Tillamook Burn fires. These trees, when planted, were placed 6 to 8 feet apart, but are now 50 to 70 feet high with crowns touching. If thin cutting is not allowed, the past 50 years could be for naught with all lost to another disastrous fire. The students who planted these trees did so with the understanding that they would be managed as a renewable resource, to be used for typical timber uses, from which we all profit. (Jerry Harding, Letter to the Editor, *Portland Oregonian,* 13 Oct. 2001)

7. Set out the premises and conclusion in the argument below:

Though not much good can come of a burned custard, Stephanie Tatin proved more than 100 years ago that not all culinary accidents need be irreversible disasters. Having forgotten the crust in an already-baking apple tart, she hastily placed a round of pastry on top of the pan in the oven. Once the crust was golden, she flipped the pan over, serving her upside-down tart as the now famous *Tarte Tatin.* (Shelton Wiseman, *Bon Appetit* magazine)

8. Set out the premises, the conclusion, and any assumptions in Jacqueline Bobo's argument below:

Black people watch a lot of television and spend a lot of money going to see commercial films. And these may not be films that they find particularly useful, or that they even enjoy. Consequently, I believe that if more works produced by black film and video makers were available, the Black audience would cultivate the habit of watching, and watching critically. It is, of course, difficult to assess any group's reactions to specific cultural works. Media audiences in general, not just Black audiences, have proven to be unruly and unpredictable." (See Jacqueline Bobo, "The Politics of Interpretation," in *Black Popular Culture*)

Part Four

Directions: State the conclusion and the premises in the following (longer) arguments:

1. "If you believe, as I do, that one important measure of our humanity is our regard for other living beings, then the grisly practices of industrial ranching are immoral. I'm speaking of what is hidden from sight: such horrors as the butchering of live steers, the periodic starving of chickens to stimulate greater egg production and the rigid confinement of animals in cages where they can hardly move for the entirety of their lives." (See John Balzar, "Cruel Slaughter of Food Hits a Nerve," *Los Angeles Times,* 13 July 2001)

2. "Marijuana is not just the recreational drug of students on their lunch hour, although it is that, but of people in almost every other phase and stage of Canadian society. The marijuana culture is embraced by lawyers, teachers, aboriginals, government officials, and probably butchers and bakers and candlestick makers. For an astonishing number of Canadians, marijuana is no big deal. The suspicion is that a good many parliamentarians understand that and may share the attitude. . . . The Dutch simply stopped enforcing the law on marijuana long ago, and Dutch society seems to be the better for it. . . . The nonmedical use of drugs has been studied to death. . . . What more needs to be known? . . . Of course, it is not knowledge that is lacking but fortitude. There may be thousands of Canadians convicted every year and crushed with a criminal conviction, but, what the hell, they probably don't vote anyway." (See John Gray, "Free us From this Reefer Madness," *The Globe and Mail (Toronto),* 13 July 2001)

3. "Because U.S. reconnaissance satellites had not yet been able to survey all of the vast Soviet landmass, the Air Force's assistant chief of staff, intelligence, disagreed with the estimate of 10–25 ICBMs." (See Philip J. Klass, "CIA Papers Reveal Spy Satellites' Role," *Aviation Week & Space Technology*)

4. "Your teenagers may have something to teach you about the American work ethic. In fact, they might be working *too* hard. . . . A Junior Achievement poll reports that 86.2% of teens planned to hold down a job this summer—virtually unchanged from the 87% who planned to work last year. . . . [N]early three out of five 16-year-olds work for an employer at some time during the school year. (Editorial, "How They Spend Their Summer Vacation," *The Wall Street Journal,* 14 July 2001)

5. Dutiful moral consciousness is most graphically depicted [in *The Simpsons* TV show] in the character of second-grader Lisa Simpson. Lisa has

an acute sense of moral duty . . . Lisa's morality arises out of precocious personal reflection on the great themes of moral life: truthfulness, helping others in need, a commitment to human equality, and justice. Lisa shows us how difficult it sometimes is to live up to such principles in the face of thoughtless conventional compromises with the status quo. (James Lawler, "The Moral World of the Simpson Family: A Kantian Perspective," in William Irwin, Mark T. Conard, and Aeon J. Skoble, eds., *The Simpsons and Philosophy: The D'oh! of Homer*)

6. "Government can fairly be said to have adopted a pro-crime policy for decades in America. It subsidized the mechanization of agriculture that pushed masses or rural poor into the cities, simultaneously encouraging the flight of the urban industry and employment. Similarly, it subsidizes the transfer of capital and jobs overseas, and routinely adopts monetary and fiscal policies, in the name of fighting inflation, that create widespread unemployment and its resulting community and family fragmentation." (Eliott Curie, *Confronting Crime: An American Challenge*)

7. Very little reason exists to believe that the present capital punishment system deters the conduct of others any more effectively than life imprisonment. Potential killers who rationally weigh the odds of being killed themselves must conclude that the danger is nonexistent in most parts of the country and that in the South the danger is slight, particularly if the proposed victim is black. Moreover, the paradigm of this kind of murderer, the contact killer, is almost by definition a person who takes his chances like the soldier of fortune he is. (Jack Greenberg, *Against the American System of Capital Punishment*)

8. Thompson points out that there is a great range of activities in which it is justifiably assumed that parents have a legitimate right to determine their children's participation. There is no general reason to suppose that childbirth is different; there are no compelling grounds (such as the expectation of great harm) to justify overriding the parent's prerogative. Hence insofar as the fetus needs an advocate, there is no reason to regard the physician rather than the pregnant woman as the appropriate advocate. (Christine Overall, *Ethics and Human Reproduction*)

9. [W]hile electronic toys have succeeded in seducing children, much of the technology added to toys threatens to change the way children play in fundamental ways. Often, electronic toys are less creative, do not involve much imagination and encourage more passive reactions than older toys, experts say. . . . "There is a passivity that comes from having toys that entertain you." (Julian E. Barnes, "Where Did you go, Raggedy Ann? Toys in the Age of Electronics," *The New York Times*, 10 Feb. 2001)

10. According to the most recent Nielsen ratings, the average Black household watches eleven hours of television every day—about two-thirds of their waking hours. In addition, they spend at nearly five times their proportion

of their population at movie theaters. Distinctions no longer exist between movies and news, television and real life. (Jacqui Jones, "The Accusatory Space," in *Black Popular Culture*, Gina Dent, ed.)

Analyzing Arguments

People usually offer more than one premise to support the conclusion. There has to be at least one premise to have an argument. If you have no evidence to cite, there's no argument. And you may make a statement such as "Elvis impersonators need to get a life," but that does not constitute an argument. To have an argument you need both the claim "Elvis impersonators need to get a life" and evidence offered in support of the claim ("Elvis impersonators live in the shadow of Elvis," "People who live in anyone else's shadow need to get a life," etc.).

Only the combination of evidence and the conclusion said to follow from the evidence can form an argument. We can then see how strong the argument actually is. It helps to be organized. Here's the strategy to take:

- Find the conclusion. This gives us a sense of where we're headed. If you don't know the conclusion, you cannot analyze an argument.
- List the premises (the pieces of support for the conclusion) one by one.
- Examine the evidence (premises) to see if it is sufficient to support the conclusion. Look for any holes; such as missing premises, unwarranted assumptions, biased language, or fallacious reasoning.
- Listing the premises one by one above the conclusion makes the argument easier to read.

You then have the premises and conclusion clearly set out, so you can examine the relationship between them; and you are less likely to overlook a piece of evidence.

Group Exercise

In July 2001 the Wisconsin Supreme Court upheld a probation order barring a man, 34-year-old David Oakley, from having more children unless he shows that he can support all his offspring. He had been convicted of failure to pay child support and owes $25,000 in support. Oakley has nine children by four women. If he violates the order, Oakley will face eight years in prison. The Court noted the problem of collecting child support: one family in three with a child support order received no money at all and parents who did not pay deprived children of about $11 billion a year (see Tamar Lewin, "Father Owing Child Support Loses a Right to Procreate," *The New York Times,* 12 July 2001, and see the court opinion at the Wisconsin Bar website, *www.wisbar.org/Wis3/98-1099.htm.*) Groups should examine the arguments (pro and con) below and then answer the questions that follow:

Arguments FOR the Decision:

1. A spokeswoman for the Association for Children for Enforcement of Support said the decision is a useful tool for ensuring that children are taken care of.

2. The Court majority saw the restriction as "narrowly tailored to serve the state's compelling interest of having parents support their children." The restriction would expire in five years, when probation ends and, in the Court's view, the alternative of incarcerating Oakley would further victimize his children, ages 4 to 16.

Arguments AGAINST the Decision:

1. Dissenting Justice Ann Walsh Bradley wrote:

   Today's decision makes this court the only court in the country to declare constitutional a condition that limits a probationer's right to procreate based on his financial ability to support his children. Ultimately, the majority's decision may affect the rights of every citizen of this state, man or woman, rich or poor. (See Tamar Lewin, "Father Owing Child Support Loses a Right to Procreate," *The New York Times,* 12 July 2001)

2. Julie Sternberg of the American Civil Liberties Union argued:

   [U]ntil now I don't know of any appeals court that has upheld that kind of condition. It's a very dangerous precedent. The U.S. Supreme Court has said that the right to decide to have a child is one of the most basic human rights. And in this case there were all kinds of less restrictive alternatives, like attaching his wages, to make sure child support would be paid. (See Tamar Lewin, "Father Owing Child Support Loses a Right to Procreate," *The New York Times,* 12 July 2001)

   Answer the following:
   Group 1: Speak in favor of the Wisconsin Supreme Court's ruling.
   Group 2: Speak against the ruling.
   Group 3: Discuss whether the various mothers of the children are contributing to the problem.
   Group 4: Give your response to journalist Tom Richards, who said:

   Now, I don't know any more of this case than I read in the paper, but Oakley sounds like a creep, one of those jerks who thinks that making babies somehow proves his masculinity. Any animal can do that. I am not and would not defend him. But what is wrong with those women? Didn't their mamas warn them about men like this? OK, so a woman might marry him the first time. Even the second time, well, a lot of people have bad first marriages. But a third time? Wouldn't you say this was a bad gamble? And any woman who would be his fourth wife and have children with him is just plain stupid. And there are women who had children with him without being married to him. Incredible. (See "Congress Is Too Obsessed to Screw Up," *Wisconsin Post Crescent*, 16 Jan. 1999)

Exercises

Part One

1. Circle the arguments below (Be sure there's a conclusion and at least one premise):
   a. It would be immoral and selfish not to use animals in experimentation, given the harm that could come to future generations if such animal experimentation was halted.
   b. What is politically good cannot be bad, unless the rules of the society make no sense.
   c. I like Otis Redding's music best of all. It has a good beat, I can sing along, and I just love soul. Otis has soul.
   d. In Iowa, the striped skunk is one of the animals most likely to be flattened on the highway, even though it is easy to spot a skunk.
   e. Ubu got closed in a drawer for 5 hours. The kitten, however, was not the slightest perturbed. He hopped out of the drawer and, the next day, jumped in an open file cabinet! Consequently, cats don't seem to learn from their mistakes.
   f. What George needs to do is believe in himself. People who believe in themselves are winners and everyone loves a winner.
   g. Rebecca feels bad for her lungs that she started smoking again, but thinks it'll help keep her weight under control.
   h. Lashanda says everyone she works with cleaning fish down at the pier whines and complains. She says not a day goes by without someone blowing up over the smell. She says it does get a bit smelly by the end of the day. She says it's peaceful, though, looking out at the ocean during her lunch break.
   i. Jamal insists that the problem with Rosa's laptop computer was a virus that corrupted her email program. Rosa is convinced, however, that the real problem isn't a virus; it's a problem with autoformatting. Sure Jamal is a trained techie, but it's Rosa who fixed the hardware problem in the lab. Therefore, it must be the autoformat function that's messing up Rosa's laptop.
   j. Although *Men in Black* is hilarious, Kwame says he'd rather rent the video *Seven Samurai*.

2. How do you tell a relevant premise from one that is irrelevant? Give an example of (a) a relevant premise and then (b) an irrelevant premise for the conclusion, "Therefore, children under 10 years old should not be allowed to see *Silence of the Lambs*."

3. State the premises and conclusion in each of the following arguments:
   a. The Chinese have not got the sense of individual independence because the whole conception of life is based upon mutual help within the home . . . it is considered good luck to have children who can take care of one. One lives for nothing else in China. (See Lin Yutang, "Growing Old Gracefully," in *Vice and Virtue in Everyday Life*, 4th ed., Christina and Fred Sommers, eds.)
   b. There is good reason for deceiving one another—it works. It works not only for the liar but also for the listener. Many of us are unprepared to speak the truth or to hear the truth, particularly about those things we care about, such as ourselves, friends or family, or even our ideals. (See Alexander E. Hooke, *Virtuous Persons, Vicious Deeds*)

4. State the premises and conclusion in the argument below:

   Since drug testing is a means for obtaining information, the information sought must be relevant to the contract if the drug testing is not to violate privacy. (See Joseph R. Desjardins and Ronald Duska, "Drug Testing in Employment")

5. In your own words, explain what the author is arguing below:

   TV's true violence consists not so much in the spectacle's techniques or content, but rather in the very density and speed of TV overall, the very multiplicity and pace of stimuli; for it is by overloading, overdriving both itself and us that TV disables us, making it hard to think about or even feel what TV shows us—making it hard, perhaps, to think or feel at all. (See Mark Crispin Miller, "Deride and Conquer," from Todd Gitlin, ed., *Watching Television*)

6. What could you conclude about music videos or our society from the following (explain your answer)?

   Music videos have no heroes, because they do not feature individuals in the sense that plot-driven entertainment does. Music video offers unadulterated celebrity. The living human beings do not play characters, but bold and connotative icons. Frequently, those icons evoke sex roles (not sexuality).

   In her hit video "Like a Virgin," Madonna alternately takes on the aspect of a whore—in black bad-girl clothes—and a virgin, in white ballroom and wedding-type dresses. In other videos, movie-Mafioso types abound; performers strut in white ties and black shirts, projecting macho images of power and money. A bold image is crucial to video and, now, recording-artist celebrity.

   Bryan Adams, whose hit video "Cuts Like a Knife," was widely criticized for its sadomasochistic elements, was pleased that the video removed a hint of weakness from his pop-rock image. "The most important thing [the video did] for me was establish my look," he said. (See Pat Aufderheide, "The Look of the Sound," in Todd Gitlin, ed., *Watching Television*).

7. What might you conclude from the following (explain your answer)?

In her research on human development, cognitive psychologist Carol Gilligan found an essential difference between the sexes: while men tended to make judgments according to abstract moral principles, women were much more likely to decide on the basis of how their actions would affect other people. On daytime soaps, the split dissolves: both men and women are judged by the values of the women's world. Men discuss romance, family, and personal problems with the same intensity as women.

   Only on soaps do men value the verbal intimacy that Lillian Rubin, in *Intimate Strangers,* found lacking in most traditional marriages. In the soap's world, everyone is preoccupied with personal life, and the community is the family writ large. It is a community no one is supposed to leave. Many covet wealth, but happiness is defined by the bonds that bind. (See Ruth Rosen, "Search for Yesterday," in Todd Gitlin, ed., *Watching Television*).

8. Discuss what is being said about our society and what else you could conclude by the following excerpt from a movie review:

Money, money, money. The creepiest aspect of *A Perfect Murder* is that there really is no contest between love and money. The movie is right in tune with the icy Darwinian mood fostered by the booming late-90's economy. In a climate like this, the hottest sex in the world doesn't stand a chance against the possibility of raking in a quick half-million." (See Stephen Holden, "Perfect Plan: Kill My Wife, Please," *The New York Times,* 5 June 1998)

Part Two

Read the excerpt below on the link between video games and TV viewing and violence and then answer the questions that follow.

In the [video] games, you do not bleed or feel pain when hit. And when you kill your opponent, nothing comes out of the wound and there is no suffering. You do not get any sensation of how dangerous real fighting is, or what suffering you cause your opponent. You can do cruel things with a light heart. This feeling is truly dangerous.

   We have raised a generation that thinks nothing of killing. Now we are seeing the shocking results. I refer to the murder of an elementary school student in Kobe's Suma Ward in May [1997] and the dismemberment of the corpse.

   What can be done to stop the computer-nurtured generation from turning to crime? At least as far as virtual reality is concerned, the only antidote is actuality. After every hour spent in front of the TV or game terminal, young people should be made to spend another reading a novel or on outside sports. They need to be continually returned to the real world. In this respect, the family environment is particularly important. I would like to see every family set and rigidly keep to a fixed number of hours per day for the children to spend watching TV and playing computer games, even when they do so with classmates who come round to the house. Our most essential task now is to reflect on where we have gone wrong. By doing so, perhaps we will be able to come up with a new set of lofty ideals to pursue as the twenty-first century dawns." (See Masuzoe Yoichi, "Violence in Virtual Reality," in *Japan Echo,* Vol. 24, No. 4, Oct. 1997)

Answer the following:
1. What is Maszoe Yoichi's concern and main recommendations?
2. What are her key claims she gives as support?
3. Is there anything Yoichi should add to make the argument a stronger one?
4. Do you find Yoichi's argument persuasive? Explain why/why not.

Part Three

1. On December 1, 1997 basketball player Latrell Sprewell attacked his coach and tried to choke him. He returned later and punched the coach. This resulted in a suspension from the league for one year and the termination of his contract with the Golden State Warriors. Latrell is a black man and his coach is white. On March 5, 1998, an independent arbitrator reduced the sentence and ordered the team to reinstate Sprewell (see *www.pbs.org/ newshour/bb/sports/jan-june98*). Discuss the quality of the reasoning of the two journalists in the interchange with PBS national correspondent.

   IRA BERKOW, *New York Times:* I thought it was a terrible decision [to reduce the sentence and reinstate Sprewell]. I thought that a business organization has the right to fire someone who punches the employer, or boss, or in this case the coach. And the—and as far as the league imposing a one-year suspension on the player, I thought that was fair as well. He's able to come back next season; he's a young man; he's one of the best players in the league; and numerous teams have expressed interest in him. They expressed interest in him shortly after the incident, and so there's really no question that he's going to be able to reap a nice benefit from it for playing basketball.

   PHIL PONCE: Mike Bruton, is that a fair comparison, comparing one's action towards one's boss in the work place to what goes on in the NBA?

   MIKE BRUTON, *Philadelphia Inquirer:* No, I don't think the comparison is fair. I think that the professional sports culture is different from your garden-variety corporate situation. That's not to condone what Sprewell did. It definitely was wrong. But I think one must understand that in game or even practice type situations sometimes emotions are elevated. The type of behavior and decorum that is observed in corporate situations are not always observed in those situations. I believe that is was fair for the Golden State Warriors to fire Latrell Sprewell, but I don't believe it was fair for David Stern to come and give him a one-year suspension simply because he knew that there was at least five or six owners who would have signed Sprewell. That goes to punishing Sprewell for deficits that the owners may have. (*www.pbs.org/newshour/bb/sports/jan-june98*)

2. Analyze one of (a), (b), (c), or (d). Go into detail, discussing the quality of the reasoning:
   a. Performance-enhancing drugs should be legalized, because it would give whites a chance at beating black sprinters.
   b. Performance-enhancing drugs should be legalized, because it would allow athletes to reach their potential.

   c. Performance-enhancing drugs should be legalized, because it would put an end to cheating.
   d. Performance enhancing drugs should be banned because they cost too much.

3. Discuss the quality of the reasoning in one of these two ads and set out your reasons why the ad has been so successful in selling the product:
   a. (Coke ad): "Coke is Life"
   b. (Marlboro cigarette ad): "Come to Where the Flavor Is"

4. On March 19, 2001, the Pizza Wars ended. It started with Pizza Hut declaring "war" on poor-quality pizza and daring anyone to come up with a better pizza. Papa John's ad, "Better Ingredients. Better Pizza" hit Pizza Hut like a torpedo. Pizza Hut sued Papa John's, arguing this constituted false advertising (see Donald M. Gindy's "True Lies," *Daily Journal*, 26 June 2001). Papa John's claimed that its "vine ripened tomatoes" were superior to the "remanufactured tomato sauce" used by Pizza Hut. Plus its fresh dough and filtered water created a better-tasting pizza. (See entire article at end of this chapter).
   a. Discuss whether you have enough information to conclude whether Papa John's ad was false advertising.
   b. If not, what would you want to know, what questions you would want answered, before you could decide who won the war, Pizza Hut or Papa John's?

Part Four
Constructing Arguments

1. The State Department needs your help handling a public relations nightmare around the use of depleted uranium in NATO weapons. Read the paragraph below and then (a) set out the issues and concerns and then (b) construct an argument explaining what the State Department can do:

   Many Europeans suspect that depleted uranium contained in NATO weaponry has caused or contributed to numerous cases of leukemia suffered by alliance troops deployed in the Balkans. The leukemia deaths of several European soldiers who served in Kosovo or Bosnia-Herzegovina prompted the U.S. Army report. . . .
   On Thursday, two German arms makers reported having tested weapons containing depleted uranium during the 1970's, intensifying public concerns that some Germans may have been exposed to the low-level radiation released by such weapons. (See Carol J. Williams, "U.S. Warned Germany of Uranium Leaks," *Los Angeles Times*, 20 Jan. 2001)

2. North-South Airlines needs you to help them keep a problem for frequent fliers from erupting into a public relations disaster with both flight crews and customers. What will you advise them, given the information below?

   On June 12, 2001, it was reported that frequent fliers—and especially flight crews—face radiation risks. The problem is the ionizing radiation emitted by the sun. When the sun is at the peak of its "storm" season, the solar wind is supplemented by bursts of protons called solar flares. These flares can expose people flying at high altitude to ionizing radiation. Occasionally airlines reroute polar flights to avoid solar storms. Though there is no evidence this exposure is dangerous, experts agree that a pregnant woman could be exposed to enough radiation on a single flight to exceed government health guidelines. Crew members who fly polar flights for years can accumulate doses that are large relative to those received by nuclear power plant workers and other "radiation workers."

Dr. Robert J. Barish, medical radiation specialist, says, "People may be hurt." Airlines don't have radiation monitors on board so that they could change altitude or reroute to avoid the solar storms. Overall, flight crews have higher rates of a variety of diseases, but it's not clear if it's connected to the radiation risk or the disruption of their biorhythms. European authorities have gone so far as to classify flight crews as radiation workers. In the U.S. the FAA does the same, but it does not require employers to track exposure. A United Nations committee estimated that aircrew members (approximately 250,000 compared to nearly four million people worldwide who are occupationally exposed to radiation) received about 24% of all the occupationally related exposure to radiation. (For a fuller discussion see Matthew L. Wald, "The Frequent Flier and Radiation Risk," *The New York Times,* 12 June 2001)

3. How would you respond to Donna Langston's argument that class is the key influence on what we are and become:

Class is more than just the amount of money you have; it's also the presence of economic security. For the working class and poor, working and eating are matters of survival, not taste. However, while one's class status can be defined in important ways in terms of monetary income, class is also a whole lot more—specifically, class is also culture. As a result of the class you are born into and raised in, class is your understanding of the world and where you fit in; it's composed of ideas, behavior, attitudes, values, and language; class is how you think, feel, act, look, dress, talk, move, walk; class is what stores you shop at, restaurants you eat in; class is the schools you attend, the education you attain, class is the very jobs you will work at throughout your adult life. (See "Tired of Playing Monopoly?" in Timko and Hoff, eds., *Philosophies for Living*)

4. Examine the arguments in the following article by Donald M. Gindy. Please note that legal citations have been removed to make it easier to focus on the discussion.

True Lies
Duel Between Pizza Hut and Papa John's Comes to an End

Donald M. Gindy
Daily Journal —June 26, 2001

With a resounding thud, the pizza wars ended March 19, when the U.S. Supreme Court refused to review the decision of the 5th U.S. Circuit Court of Appeals in *Pizza Hut Inc. v. Papa John's International Inc.* (2001). The nature of the lawsuit was a claim of false advertising under the Lanham Act allegedly committed by Papa John's when it claimed "**Better Ingredients. Better Pizza.**"

Pizza Hut threw down the gauntlet as its president, from the deck of a World War II aircraft carrier, declared "war" on poor-quality pizza. Pizza Hut "dared" anyone to come up with a better pizza. At about the same time, Papa John's was launching a new advertising campaign proclaiming that it sold a better pizza because it used better ingredients. The matter went to trial in Dallas, resulting in a verdict in favor of Pizza Hut. Under the Lanham Act, "a plaintiff must demonstrate that the commercial advertisement or promotion is either literally false, or that it is likely to mislead and confuse consumers." Pizza Hut relied on a theory that Papa John's ads were deceptive and were intended to mislead purchasers of pizza.

On appeal, the 5th Circuit threw out the verdict. Their decision points out that a prima facie case of false advertising requires that the following occur:

- There is a false or misleading statement of fact about a product.
- Such a statement either deceives or had the capacity to deceive a substantial segment of potential consumers.
- The deception is material, in that it is likely to influence the consumer's purchasing decision.
- The product is in interstate commerce.
- The plaintiff has been or likely will be injured as a result of the statement at issue.

But was Papa John's ad mere "puffery"? That is to say, was the claim an expression of opinion or a type of boasting on which no reasonable person would rely? The court concluded that "Better ingredients. Better Pizza," standing alone, would not mislead consumers. But Papa John's lost its bragging rights when it coupled the slogan with misleading statements of specific differences in the ingredients used.

Pizza Hut asserted that its competitor had placed before the public "a measurable claim,

capable of being proved false or of being reasonably interpreted as a statement of objective fact." Papa John's claimed that its "vine ripened tomatoes" were superior to the "remanufactured tomato sauce" used by Pizza Hut and that its fresh dough and filtered water created a better-tasting pizza. By pointing to specific differences between itself and Pizza Hut and by failing to present at trial any scientific support or the results of independent surveys to substantiate its claims (such as taste tests), Papa John's had, in fact, left the arena of opinion and entered the realm of quantifiable fact. As a result, it subjected itself to a claim that it misled consumers.

However, the burden of proving false advertising falls on the shoulders of the plaintiff. It is essential to a cause of action for false advertising based on misleading ads that the plaintiff prove not how consumers would react but how they actually do react. "The success of a plaintiff's implied falsity claim usually turns on the persuasiveness of consumer survey." The test thus becomes, assuming that the ads were misleading, whether they actually influence a reasonable consumer in his or her purchasing decision. Since the court found that Pizza Hut had neglected to present such evidence, it had failed to satisfy the element of the cause of action relating to the "materiality" of Papa John's ads. In the absence of such a survey, Pizza Hut's entire action had to fail.

An actionable claim of false advertising also may proceed where a plaintiff is able to prove "literal falsity" of the claim. In *S.C. Johnson v. The Clorox Co.*, which was rendered Feb. 23, Johnson, the manufacturer of Ziploc Slideloc bags, brought an action under the Lanham Act against Clorox, the manufacturer of GLAD-LOCK resealable storage bags. The suit challenged the truthfulness of a television commercial and a print advertisement.

On television, Clorox presented ads of side-by-side comparisons of its bag and Johnson's. The bags were filled with water and turned upside down while an animated goldfish in a state of distress in the Ziploc bag complained of water dripping from his bag. The Slideloc bag leaks rapidly while the GLAD-LOCK bag does not leak at all. An expert hired by Johnson conducted "torture testing" on the Slideloc bags and proved that a significant number did not leak at all and that others leaked at a substantially slower rate than depicted in the advertisement. The vice in this presentation, according to the trial court, was "no depiction in the visual images to indicate anything else than the fact that the type of fairly rapid and substantial leakage shown in the commercials is simply characteristic of that kind of bag."

The court concluded that the presentation was literally false. S. C. Johnson was, therefore, entitled to permanent injunctive relief until Clorox is able to portray in a "truthful and fair way" the differences between its product and the Slideloc product.

These cases amply demonstrate the two methods of proving false advertising claims. Literal falsity is proved by demonstrating that the tests employed "are not sufficiently reliable to permit one to conclude with reasonable certainty that they established the claim made." *Procter & Gamble Co. v. Cheeseborough-Pond's Inc.* However, there is no need to demonstrate how the particular advertisement had "impact on the buying public." *PPX Enterprises Inc. v. Audiofidelity Enterprises Inc.*

However, implied falsity requires extrinsic evidence in the form of consumer surveys that clearly reflect that consumers are misled or confused. "The question in such cases is—what does the person to whom the advertisement is addressed find to be the message?" *Johnson & Johnson v. Smithkline Beecham Corp.* It is not for a judge to decide intuitively that the consumer has been misled. Rather, it must be established that a "statistically significant" and "not insubstantial number of consumers" holds the false belief allegedly communicated in the ad. In the absence of such a showing, the claim for false advertising will fail.

Accordingly, one may conclude that an action based on implied falsity is an expensive endeavor, fraught with statistical problems, conflicting expert testimony and a less-than-certain result whereas seeking relief for literal falsity presents the court with a bright line. The advertising as presented is either true or it is not. In such circumstances, plaintiffs may proceed with more assurance of the outcome of the litigation.

However, the common characteristic in most of these cases is a giant company challenging another of equal strength. Counsel for the proponent of the comparison advertising should encourage their clients to proceed with caution in these head-to-head encounters. Don't expect your opponent to sit back and accept an advertisement that disparages its product. Be circumspect, for the outcome can be costly and embarrassing.

Donald M. Gindy practices intellectual-property law in Century City.

Source: © 2000 Daily Journal Corporation. All rights reserved. Permission granted by the Daily Journal.

CHAPTER THREE

Out of the Silence:
The Power of Language

Looking at a pot, for example, or thinking of a pot, . . . it was in vain that Watt said, Pot, pot. Well, perhaps not quite in vain, but very nearly. For it was not a pot, the more he looked, the more he reflected, the more he felt sure of that, that it was not a pot at all. It resembled a pot, it was almost a pot, but it was not a pot of which one could say, Pot, pot, and be comforted. It was in vain that it answered, with unexceptionable adequacy, all the purposes, and performed all the offices, of a pot, it was not a pot. And it was just this hair-breadth departure from the nature of a true pot that so excruciated Watt.

—SAMUEL BECKET, from *Watt*

Many of us empathize with Watt, the Beckett character who struggles to find words to apply to his situation. Watt wrestles with words, frustrated that they seem to work for others, but not for him. His losing battle with the word "pot" in the quote above is but one example of the struggle between words and silence played out every day in Watt's world. And, in the case of the pot, "the true name had ceased, suddenly, or gradually, to be the true name for Watt. For the pot remained a pot, Watt felt sure of that, for everyone but Watt. For Watt alone it was not a pot, any more."

On the other hand, some people believe they have the upper hand on language, that there is no real battle between words and silence. They are in control. They believe words have no power to penetrate our outer exterior, that we have skulls like helmets and bodies like armor, so words can just bounce off and land in the dust. But this, we all know at heart, is just a ruse, a game of deception—or self-deception—about the power of language. Language can have incredible power, both positively and negatively.

Whoever said, "Sticks and stones may break my bones, but words can never hurt me" was mistaken. Words can hurt. Words can be used to threaten and co-erce, to galvanize whole populations, to drill images of self-hate into young minds, and to convey stereotypes. Language can be an instrument of oppression. Given the power language has, it is vital that we always be aware of its potential to shape—even manipulate—our thoughts.

But language can also be an instrument of liberation. Just as words can harm us, words can be used to unite us as a people, to move us to a higher moral plane, to calm, to communicate, and to achieve spiritual strength. Language can help us see the beauty of the earth and the potential for greatness in ourselves and in others. As bell hooks says, "We are rooted in language, wedded, have our being in words. Language is also a place of struggle. The oppressed struggle in language to recover ourselves—to rewrite, to reconcile, to renew. Our words are not without meaning. They are an action—a resistance."

In this chapter, we will examine the uses of language that are most significant for critical thinking. The key uses of language that have the greatest persuasive power are these:

Key Uses of Language

1.   Words as weapons.
2.   Symmetrical versus asymmetrical descriptions.
3.   Culturally defined uses of language.
4.   Euphemisms, hedging, and loaded language.
5.   Ambiguity (linguistic fallacies).
6.   Concepts and definitions.
7.   Jargon, buzzwords, and technical terms.
8.   Metaphors and images.
9.   Exclusive language.
10.   The liberatory voice.

Words as Weapons

Words can be used in uplifting ways, but also in degrading, even violent ways. Words can act like weapons. We see this when people succumb to name-calling. The effect of name-calling is to create a negative impression, biasing or slanting an argument in such a way that we may unfairly prejudge the case. When this occurs, we've fallen into a kind of fallacious reasoning known as question-begging epi-thets (see Chapter 4 on fallacies).

For example, in *Mein Kampf,* a book on the Nazi ideology, Adolf Hitler wrote:

Nothing gave me more cause for reflection than the gradually increased insight into the activities of Jews in certain fields. Was there any form of filth or profligacy, above all in cultural life, in which at least one Jew did not participate? When carefully cut-ting open such a growth, one could find a little Jew, blinded by the sudden light, like a maggot in a rotting corpse.

The Jews' activity in the press, in art, literature, and the theater, as I learned to know it, did not add to their credit in my eyes. All unctuous assertions were of little or no avail. It was enough to look at the bill-boards, to read the names of those who produced these awful works for theaters and movies if one wanted to become hardened for a long time. This was pestilence, spiritual pestilence with which people were infected, worse than the Black Death of former times! And in what quantities this poison was produced and distributed! Of course, the lower the spiritual, and the moral standard of such an art manufacturer, the greater his fertility, till such a fellow, like a centrifugal machine, splashes his dirt on the faces of others. Besides, one must remember their countless number; one must remember that for one Goethe, Nature plays a dirty trick upon mankind in producing ten thousand such scribblers who, as germ carriers of the worst sort, poison the minds of the world.

Given the effect Hitler's speeches had on inciting an entire populace, we ought never underestimate the power of language to move people to action—positively or negatively. Whether or not we should allow such hate speech to be publicly expressed is a moral problem people have wrestled with.

Hate speech can also occur in the context of sexual violence and racism. Law professor Catharine MacKinnon has written about racial and sexual harassment, including a book on pornography. She argues that,

> Sexual words and pictures, delivered in context, work the way pornography works: they do not merely describe sexuality or represent it. In a sense, they have sex. . . . When male workers say, "Hey pussycat, come here and give me a whiff," it is a sexual invasion, an act of sexual aggression, a violation of sexual boundaries, a sex act in itself. (See *Only Words*)

In other words, MacKinnon would include such verbal taunts and sexual images as a kind of weapon. This weapon, in her view, is principally used against women, children, men of color, and gay men—all of whom have been victimized by sexual words functioning as a kind of hate speech. This empowerment of the perpetrator and traumatization of the victim happens, because of the experience words embody and convey (e.g., a rapist calling a woman a "bitch" imbues the word with the associated action). MacKinnon observes that in Argentina under the junta, "when people were rounded up and tortured and disappeared because they were Jewish, 'Jew' used as a taunt and term of torture had such a meaning." (See Chapter 11 for a discussion of hate speech on the Internet.)

 CASE STUDY

The John Rocker Case

In December of 1999, *Sports Illustrated* published an interview with Atlanta Braves pitcher John Rocker. In it he referred to a black team- mate as a "fat monkey," and let loose a series of comments that shook sports. *Sports Illustrated* reported some of Rocker's opinions, such as:

- On ever playing for a New York team: "I would retire first. It's the most hectic, nerve-racking city. Imagine having to take the [Number] 7 train to the ballpark, looking like you're [riding through] Beirut next to some kid with purple hair next to some queer with AIDS right next to some dude who just got out of jail for the fourth time right next to some 20-year-old mom with four kids. It's depressing."

- On New York City itself: "The biggest thing I don't like about New York are the foreigners. I'm not a very big fan of foreigners. You can walk an entire block in Times Square and not hear anybody speaking English. Asians and Koreans and Vietnamese and Indians and Russians and Spanish people and everything up there. How the hell did they get in this country?" (See Jeff Pearlman, "At Full Blast," *Sports Illustrated,* Dec. 1999.)

Exercises

1. Give your assessment of Rocker's comments and how seriously they ought to be taken.

2. Discuss what allowances, if any, should be made for reporter Pearlman's comment, "Rocker is rarely tongue-tied when it comes to bashing those of a race or sexual orientation different from his. 'I'm not a racist or prejudiced person,' he says with apparent conviction. 'But certain people bother me.'"

3. In response to Rocker's comments, Baseball Commissioner Bud Selig said,

   Major league baseball takes seriously its role as an American institution and the important social responsibility that goes with it. We will not dodge our responsibility. Mr. Rocker should understand that his remarks offended practically every element of society and brought dishonor to himself, the Atlanta Braves and major league baseball. The terrible example set by Mr. Rocker is not what our great game is about and, in fact, is a profound breach of the social compact we hold in such high regard. (*Associated Press* statement, *atlanta.about.com/blrockernews,* 1 Feb. 2000)

   Answer the following:
   a. If you assume baseball players and teams DO have a social responsibility, what sort of official response would you find appropriate?
   b. Indicate what should have been the official response to Rocker's comments.

4. Set out your views on whether or not the punishment given Rocker is just. Read the following and then state whether you think this was appropriate:

   John Rocker was suspended until May 1 by baseball commissioner Bud Selig on Monday for racial and ethnic remarks that "offended practically every element of society." The Atlanta Braves reliever also was fined $20,000 and ordered to undergo sensitivity training for disparaging foreigners, homosexuals and minorities in a magazine interview. The players' union said it intends to fight the ruling." (Associated Press, *atlanta.about.com/blrockernews.htm,* 1 Feb. 2000)

To John Rocker's credit, he issued an apology that addressed the "foul language" ("I've been a poor example"), the racist comments ("I'm not a racist, although I can understand how someone who did not know me could think that"), and his unprofessional behavior ("my comments concerning my team were totally unprofessional and out of line"). Rocker admitted that his words demand action: "An apology is no more than just words unless it is followed by actions. I hope in this coming year I may somehow redeem myself."

Addressing Name-Calling ✗

One solution to the problem of name-calling is that the group in question (whether it is gays, blacks, Asians, Latinos, etc.) could be allowed to determine what is an acceptable referent. We need a preferential option for the linguistically oppressed, whereby those most vulnerable to a descriptive word or phrase become the ones to decide if it warrants use. For example, there has been some conflict over the use of the words Native American and Indian. It may be advisable for those in the dominant culture to allow those who fit these labels to decide if either or both are acceptable terms. Name-calling can occur in virtually any setting and, so, don't think it is reserved only for street use.

For example, *The New York Times* reported that the prosecutor, Stephen G. Murphy, built much of his case in the Bensonhurst murder case around a personal attack. He focused on one of the witnesses, Gina Feliciano, calling her a "crackhead" and a "contemptible liar." Sometimes such name-calling works to convince a listener, sometimes it backfires—but it is always a poor replacement for making your case with solid evidence.

Labeling ✗ → Not necessarily demeaning

If we think of name-calling as inherently negative in terms of its impact (regardless of whether or not it was intended as such), then it functions a bit differently from labeling. Not all labeling of people is experienced as demeaning by the one so named. Sometimes labels (such as 'married' vs. 'single,' 'gay' vs. 'straight,' 'vegetarian' vs. 'meat-eater,' 'lacto-vegetarian' vs. 'non-dairy ' are used to categorize people to a potentially positive effect.

Sometimes the labels themselves are open to a range of interpretations. For instance, there are those who call themselves 'vegetarian' who eat poultry and fish. Look at the way Richard Ford struggles with the label 'foodie' that was attached to him:

Alas, I am not a *foodie* (as I once told a cookbook writer when she asked me at a cocktail party in Tennessee if I was, in fact, a *foodie*) the word still frightens me. For one thing, I don't eat red meat (game yes, fish yes). I don't eat fried food, I don't eat potatoes, white rice, most bread, cream sources. I eat butter only reluctantly (and if I don't know it's there). I generally steer a course away from dairy, most desserts, all pastries, cheese, high-sodium this, high-cholesterol that. And anything I do eat I never eat a lot of . . . I realize that at the end of my life I will not so much die as simply one day disappear due to the accumulated removal of all those things that I fear will kill me, but that are also necessary to keep me, if not alive and healthy, at least visible" (See Richard Ford, "Satisfaction," *Gourmet,* Mar 01).

Exercises

Part One

1. On one half of a piece of paper, write the word "single man" and the other half "single woman."
   a. List all the words and phrases used to name or describe single men. Allow three minutes for this exercise.
   b. List all the words and phrases used to name or describe single women. Allow three minutes for this exercise.
   c. Look at your two lists, noting values and beliefs that the lists reflect. What do your lists indicate about societal values?
   d. How do your two lists compare to the ways in which single men and women are referred to in popular music or popular culture?

Part Two

In the excerpts below, make note of the ways in which racism or prejudice gets expressed, how stereotypes are used, how hatred and fear factor into the author's reasoning.

1. From "Dilemma of a Norwegian Immigrant," in *Annals of America,* 1862, author unknown:

   You are not safe from [Indians] anywhere, for they are as cunning as they are bold. The other evening we received the frightening message that they have been seen in our neighborhood; so, we hitched our horses and made ready to leave our house and all our property and escape from the savages under the cover of darkness. But it was a false alarm, God be praised, and for this time we could rest undisturbed. How terrible it is thus, every moment, to expect that you will be attacked, robbed, and perhaps murdered! We do not go to bed any night without fear, and my rifle is always loaded. . . .

   It is true that some cavalry have been dispatched against these hordes, but they will not avail much, for the Indians are said to be more than 10,000 strong. Besides, they are so cunning that it is not easy to get the better of them. Sometimes they disguise themselves in ordinary farmers' clothes and stalk their victims noiselessly. . . .

2. From Stephen A. Douglas, The Lincoln-Douglas Debates: First Debate, 21 August 1858:

I ask you, are you in favor of conferring upon the Negro the rights and privileges of citizenship? Do you desire to strike out of our state constitution that clause which keeps slaves and free Negroes out of the state and allows the free Negroes to flow in and cover your prairies with black settlements? Do you desire to turn this beautiful state into a free Negro colony in order that, when Missouri abolishes slavery, she can send 100,000 emancipated slaves in Illinois to become citizens and voters, on an equality with yourselves? . . .

For one, I am opposed to Negro citizenship in any and every form. I believe this government was made on the white basis. I believe it was made by white men, for the benefit of white men, and their posterity forever, and I am in favor of confining citizenship to white men, men of European birth and descent, instead of conferring it upon Negroes, Indians, and other inferior races. . .

Now I do not believe that the Almighty ever intended the Negro to be the equal of the white man. If he did, he has been a long time demonstrating the fact. . . He belongs to an inferior race and must always occupy an inferior position.

3. From the Mississippi Penal Code, 1865:

Section 1. Be it enacted by the legislature of the state of Mississippi, that no freedman, free Negro, or mulatto not in the military service of the United States government, and not licensed so to do by the board of police of his or her county, shall keep or carry firearms of any kind, or any ammunition, dirk [dagger], or Bowie knife; and, on conviction thereof in the county court, shall be punished by fine, not exceeding $10, and pay the costs of such proceedings, and all such arms or ammunition shall be forfeited to the informer; and it shall be the duty of every civil and military officer to arrest any freedman, free Negro, or mulatto found with any such arms or ammunition, and cause him or her to be committed for trial in default of bail.

4. From *The Turner Diaries* by William L. Pierce:

I'll never forget that terrible day: November 9, 1989. They knocked on my door at five in the morning. I was completely unsuspecting as I got up to see who it was. I opened the door, and four Negroes came pushing into the apartment before I could stop them. One was carrying a baseball bat, and two had long kitchen knives thrust into their belts. The one with the bat shoved me back into a corner and stood guard over me with his bat raised in a threatening position while the other three began ransacking my apartment.

My first thought was that they were robbers. Robberies of this sort had become all too common since the Cohen Act, with groups of Blacks forcing their way into White homes to rob and rape, knowing that even if their victims had guns they probably would not dare use them. Then the one who was guarding me flashed some kind of card and informed me that he and his accomplices were "special deputies" for the Northern Virginia Human Relations Council. They were searching for firearms, he said. . . .

Right after the Cohen Act was passed, all of us in the Organization had cached our guns and ammunition where they weren't likely to be found. Those in my unit had carefully greased our weapons, sealed them in an oil drum, and spent all of one tedious weekend burying the drum in an eight-foot-deep pit 200 miles away in the woods of western Pennsylvania.

Descriptions and Societal Attitudes

Descriptions often reveal societal attitudes. How we refer to people can have enormous significance. In the history of the world, we see example after example of ethnic groups being referred to in degrading ways, as we saw earlier. The effect of such language is to make the targeted group into aliens, not even human, or only barely so. What this does is create an *asymmetry* in that the sorts of ways of talking about or describing the targeted group (or individual) is distinctly different from the ways we talk about and describe the dominant group (or favored individual). This sort of "special treatment" makes the targeted group or individual appear deviant, rather than included in the norm.

Newspapers often describe women in ways not usually accorded to men. For example, we often find women's make-up (or lack of it) and hair described in amazing detail. For example, in an article on Caroline Thompson, director of the movie *Black Beauty,* the *Los Angeles Times* reported,

> "Girlish" isn't an adjective that would sit well with Thompson, who's direct and unaffected, doesn't wear makeup and walks with a purposeful stride. But her pale skin and inverted bowl of dark hair evoke the moppet she must have been as a kid, and the lightness in her handshake suggests a construction of bone china. A man's plaid buttoned shirt and dark pants don't conceal the length and delicacy of her frame—nor the muscles of hips and thighs built up from years of guiding a half-ton or more of horse. (See Lawrence Christon, "MOVIES Taking the Reins for the First Time Screenwriter Caroline Thompson parlayed her track record in Hollywood and her love of horses to become the director of *Black Beauty,*" *Los Angeles Times,* 24 July 1994)

To get a sense of the asymmetry, picture an article on Carl Thompson in which it is reported that: "'Boyish' isn't a term Thompson likes to describe himself. He is straightforward and unassuming, doesn't shave on a daily basis and walks with a sense of his own importance. His red hair and freckles suggest what a rascal he must have been as a kid, but his powerful grip when he shakes hands lets us know that his bones are made of steel. His construction jacket can't hide his massive frame—nor the bulging biceps built up from years of shoveling hay at his dad's farm." As we'll see, men are starting to be victims of such descriptions, though not to the degree seen with descriptions of women.

Watch for differences in descriptions of physical attributes and ask yourself if there's any asymmetry in what you see. For example, on June 24, 2001, *The New York Times* published an article about actress Angelina Jolie focusing solely on descriptions by film critics of her lips (see Tom Kuntz, "Lip Crit: It Smacks of Angelina"). The range of descriptions was as follows: "Jolie has had so much collagen pumped into her lips that they threaten to become duck-like," she "has lips that look as if she ran into a wall," "famously bee-stung lips," "lips that look more tarantula than bee-stung," her lips, "those plumy pods of puffed perfection," "huge, pillowy lips," "gargantuan, and as uneven as lunar terrain," and so on. In order to test the asymmetry, replace the subject, Angelina Jolie, with a male actor (say her father, John Voigt, or a younger actor, say Tom Cruise). You decide how likely it is for an entire article to focus on either of these men's lips.

On the other hand, men are not immune from being examined for their physical traits. Look at the way in which a trait traditionally thought unattractive in men— baldness—has been turned on its head in the following excerpt in *The Australian*:

> Shane Warne looks pretty ugly these days. . . . Warnie began his transformation by shaving off his blond mop before the third Test against India. It seemed to be a response to the good advice of close-cropped Andre Agassi, who said Pat Rafter's long hair had trapped heat against his skull and worn him out in the Australian Open tennis final. Combined with his jowls, Warnie's naked skull made him look like somebody you would bargain hard to avoid having to share a cell with. However, by the end of the one-day series, Warnie was sporting a thick, neat, red beard to set off his stubbly head. Sensational. . . .
>
> He is, in fact, the dead opposite of the blond beach boy persona. He is volatile and impetuous. Shrewd and intelligent. He is not rabid about physical fitness training but doesn't hesitate to put in extra months of hard work when an English county makes the price right. He is acquisitive. . . . Blond beach boys seek to be loved. Burly, bald, redbeards don't really give a bugger.
>
> Blond beach boys, especially counterfeit ones, can't take a knockback from a pretty girl in an English pub. It's not the way the plot is supposed to run. They go bonkers. By contrast, experience has told red-bearded baldies with a spare tyre or two that life holds no less than a fair share of knockbacks for them. (See Frank Devine, "The Bald Truth Is, Everyone Loves An Ugly Bloke," *The Australian*, 9 Apr. 2001)

Symmetrical versus Asymmetrical Descriptions

As we saw above, the language of description may vary according to who or what is being described. The same trait, say height or weight, may be discussed in quite different terms according to the subject. A woman may be described as "plump" where an overweight man is called "beefy" or "stocky." For example, Mel Gibson's character in *What Women Want* is described by as a being like "a stocky athlete with Gene Kelly in his heart" (see *www.salon.com*). Men can be "tall," but never "willowy" or "petite." Women can be "large," but would not likely be called "bullish" or a "steam roller."

Look, for instance, at this description of a hockey star: "Eric Lindros . . . certainly isn't playing hockey, and hasn't since game 7 of last year's NHL Eastern Conference Final. That's when the normally bullish Lindros was himself bulled over by a steamroller named Scott Stevens" (see Rob Sinclair, "Lindros in Limbo, "Hockey Night in Canada," *CBC Sports*, 31 Mar. 2001).

Men can be the recipients of negative descriptions, too, though men rarely warrant as much detail. This asymmetry in description is common, although articles on the tenor Luciano Pavarotti occasionally contain remarks about his weight (e.g., "There is a *Tosca* at the Met this evening, but really only one story: Luciano Pavarotti. "The Fat Man," as he is known reverently among some of his fans (and enemies), is, as it happens, in glorious voice." (*www.nypress.com,* 27 Oct. 1999) And sports-related descriptions of male athletes are far more likely to get into physical descriptions than in other types of news coverage. This suggests that men are not beyond public scrutiny of their appearance.

We also see asymmetry in news coverage of how people dress. It is much more common to see details about items of clothing worn by women than by men. This is the case even when the focus of the discussion has little if anything to do with appearance. For example, in a news report on the trial of Marjorie Knoller, whose dog viciously attacked and killed a San Francisco woman, we find a description of Knoller's attire: "Knoller, 46, wearing a periwinkle blazer and with her hair pulled back in a ponytail, spoke clearly and strongly, but broke down in tears several times." (See Anna Gorman, "Dog Could Not Be Stopped, Owner Says," *Los Angeles Times,* 12 Mar. 2002)

Some words and descriptions are only applied to females and quite different ones describe the same or similar actions by males. Look at the asymmetry: Men talk, shoot the bull, or chew the fat; women chat, gossip, or nag; men laugh or chuckle, but never giggle or titter (only females do these). Married men may be "henpecked" but there's no similar word for married women. The closest would be that men "bully" or "browbeat" another person, male or female. A woman who has a number of sexual partners could be called "promiscuous," but it would be unlikely for this to be applied to a man.

Issues with asymmetrical uses of language can tap into some strong feelings, as the next example shows. Looking at the drug, Viagra, a treatment for male impotence, the *Augusta Chronicle* noted that at least some insurance plans cover Viagra, while most refuse to cover female contraception, stirring controversy by their editorial comment:

> This is a paradox that seems impossible to justify. After all, impotence is not a life-threatening condition, but some unwanted pregnancies, certain uterine cancers and ovarian cancer certainly are. At the same time, though, no insurance company or employer should have to subsidize *promiscuity* by paying for elective birth control. (*Augusta Chronicle,* 14 May 1998)

Reader Julie Kendall's letter to the editor blasted the use of the word "promiscuity" here. In Kendall's estimation, the editorial showed asymmetry in their use of language. She wrote,

> I was appalled by that statement! It reinforces the outdated and backward notion that only women can be promiscuous. Is there any chance that formerly impotent men who are helped by Viagra can now be promiscuous themselves? Or can only women be promiscuous, while at the same time men are, well, just being men and are applauded for being so virile? Is this kind of reasoning still prominent in our male-oriented society? (Letter to the *Augusta Chronicle,* 18 May 1998)

Connotations of Words and Descriptions

Think of all the words used as synonyms of the term "male," with a wide range of connotations: man, gentleman, guy, dude, fellow, boy, hunk, jock, stud, beefcake, dreamboat, lone wolf, sport, shark, and so on (add to the list). Think of all the words used as synonyms of the term "female," with a wide range of connotations: woman, gal, girl, chick, bunny, broad, lady, fox, vixen, bombshell, bimbo, tomato, cupcake, cheesecake, honey, hen, babe, kitten, doll, witch, hag, crone, and so on (add to the list). What do you think these terms tell us about our culture and our values?

Study descriptions, watching for such concerns as symmetry. Not only do we see differences in the ways males and females are described, but we also see differences according to other factors, such as age, class, celebrity or renown, and race. If you examine your own descriptions of people, do you see differences according to gender, age, race, class, or any other factor?

Group Exercise

In July 2001, a proposal surfaced that could change the way in which fetuses are viewed for health care purposes. The proposed plan is to consider the fetus an "unborn child" and, thus, allow the fetus access to federal health-care dollars. Read the following strongly worded editorial and then answer the questions below:

> A back door effort to undermine abortion rights has emerged in a proposal circulated by the Federal Department of Health and Human Services to expand the availability of prenatal care. While the goal is unassailable, the method surely is not.
>
> The goal is to provide insurance coverage for pregnant women in families that earn too much to qualify for Medicaid, thus enabling them to get prenatal care. But the plan under consideration by Tommy Thompson, the secretary of health and human services, looks to be designed primarily to advance the right-to-life movement's long-standing goal of establishing a legal precedent for recognizing the fetus as a person.
>
> Under the proposal, which is described in a draft letter to state health officials, states would be allowed to define an "unborn child" as eligible for medical coverage under the federal Children's Health Insurance Program, known as CHIP. The qualifying beneficiary, in other words, would be the fetus, not the pregnant woman, but counting the fetus as a child would allow prenatal services to be delivered to the mother on its behalf. Like the benign-sounding Unborn Victims of Violence Act, which the House passed in 1999 and again this April, the plan is a backdoor assault on *Roe v. Wade.* (See "Counting the Fetus as an Unborn Child," *The New York Times,* 7 July 2001)

Groups discuss the following:

1. Discuss how the *New York Times* editorial sets out its opposition to considering the fetus an "unborn child."

2. List all the words or terms used in the passage that suggest the author's own set of values.

3. Do you think using the term "unborn child" rather than "fetus" necessarily creates a bias (and thus favors the right-to-life movement's goals)? (Note the connotations of the term "unborn child" compared to those associated with the word "fetus.")

Role of Context in Asymmetry

Often societal expectations determine our use of language, and the power dynamics of the relationship factor in. Even in our relationships, issues around asymmetry pop up. We see asymmetry when words that function similarly mean one thing in one context and something else in a different context.

For example, Martin Luther King, Jr., relayed a story about his father being stopped by a police officer, who called him "boy." It seems highly unlikely that he would have used this term if Mr. King, Sr., had been a white man. What is defined as acceptable uses of language varies according to the context (such as living rooms, parks, offices, restaurants, classrooms, workplaces).

For example, students and patients generally get referred to on a first name basis, while doctors and teachers are usually referred to more formally. Even such business practices as having waiters and waitresses (or "servers," to adopt a more gender-neutral term) introduce themselves on a first name basis puts them in a seemingly subservient position, with the customer (who does not have to tell his or her first name) in the dominant, more powerful, role.

Exercises

1. Make a list of ways you could describe yourself (try for a balances of positive, negative, and neutral descriptions). Then write two to three paragraphs discussing how description affects the way we think about people.

2. Discuss American attitudes toward drinking by examining the words used to describe alcohol consumption, like tipsy, sloshed, plastered, pie-eyed, soused, potted, three sheets to the wind, smashed, or tanked up.

3. Discuss the use of language in the following excerpt:

   Different as she and her husband may be—the poor little black boy from Leeds, Alabama, who was deserted by his father, to be raised by his mother and grandmother, and the prosperous white girl from a big, happy, traditional Catholic family in Bucks County, Pennsylvania—they share one common fundamental. Just as everybody put him down for being fat, everybody kidded her for being a hopelessly skinny twig with big, funny feet. But then he grew up to be Charles Barkley, and she grew up to be a beautiful, willowy woman who dared marry a famous black man named Charles Barkley. (See Frank Deford, "Barkley's Last Shot," *Vanity Fair*, Feb. 1995.)

4. Discuss the following description of actor Chris Tucker, including any assumptions about gender stereotypes and societal attitudes:

   Tucker took character roles in two movies: Quentin Tarantino's *Jackie Brown* and *The Fifth Element*, in which he played a transvestite radio deejay. It wasn't too big a stretch . . . his voice is already up in that range where the genders meet, he can be campy and over-the-top, and he has beautifully fine bones that can swing either way. But believe, me, Chris Tucker is all man. Chicks dig him, of course, and he has a girlfriend and a son, but he generally keeps his private life to himself. (See Rick Cohen, "Chris Tucker in Phat City," *GQ*, Aug. 2001)

Culturally Defined Uses Of Language

Our society and culture shape our use of language, by setting out a system of norms as to who can say what to whom, who can speak and in what order, who gets the first and last word, in public gatherings or in family dynamics. Some words are about as neutral as a number (think of "the" or "and" or "or") but nouns, pronouns, and verbs are flavored with cultural meaning and significance.

Think of phrases like "Children should be seen and not heard" and "Speak when you're spoken to." The understanding is that it is, in certain contexts, deemed inappropriate for children to speak. Adults are similarly linguistically restricted in some contexts—for example, in meetings with your supervisor at work, when stopped by the police for a traffic violation, and in church.

Political Expectations and Restrictions

In Canada, where many people speak both French and English, language often reflects political allegiances and even tensions between French Canadians and English Canadians. As James Crawford notes in *Language Loyalties,* "As a practical medium and a 'marker' of ethnicity, language becomes a predictable source of tension." Discussing the low status of French in Canada, he says, "Language discrimination by design and by neglect, created a mutual estrangement over time and loosened the bonds of the Canadian federation."

In the United States, many people are bilingual, but the expectation is that everyone ought to speak English. This links to frustrations connected with the changing ethnic composition of society. Illustrating such frustrations, Mitsuye Yamada discusses an incident in her childhood:

> In first grade I was forced to sit crouched in the kneehole of the teacher's desk for hours in punishment for speaking to my brother in Japanese (only a year apart, we started first grade together). Did I know that this was being done "for my own good" so that I would learn English more quickly? Among other things, I learned that speaking Japanese in public leads to humiliation. The lines were clearly drawn. English is like Sunday clothes and is the superior language. By extension I learned that the whites who speak it must be the superior race, and I must learn to speak as the whites do. (See "The Cult of the 'Perfect' Language; Censorship by Class, Gender, and Race," in *Sowing Ti Leaves*)

Political Ramifications

In some contexts, culturally defined uses of language have political ramifications. The words leaders use can have considerable impact. A recent misunderstanding illustrates this.

After the Middle East peace accord, Yasser Arafat, seemingly inadvertently, set off a controversy: He called for a Muslim *jihad* over Jerusalem. The term *jihad* has several possible meanings, one being a "holy war" and another having a religious reference about working for peace. The *Los Angeles Times* reported, "Arafat said he was the victim of a linguistic mix-up" after a radio station played a tape of him saying, "*Jihad* will continue . . . our main battle is Jerusalem." He meant working for peace, not a holy war and, thus, was forced to explain his intention by using this word (see "Arafat Clarifies *Jihad* Call; Peres Accepts Explanation," *Los Angeles Times*, 19 May 1994).

After the terrorist attacks in New York and Washington, D.C., there were many references to a call for a *jihad*. And, as with the earlier case with Arafat, this evoked uncertainty regarding what exactly was being said, however, in this later case, interpreting bin Laden's use of the term *jihad* to mean a "holy war." This is much closer to what Benjamin R. Barber described as, "The mood is that of *Jihad*: war not as an instrument of policy but as an emblem of identity, an expression of community, an end in itself" (see Benjamin R. Barber, "Jihad vs. Mcworld," *www.theatlantic.com*). In this case, with this one word, a great deal follows from its interpretation. A failure to fully understand what is meant when it is being used could be disastrous on a number of levels. Language is that powerful.

As a society, we have had to adapt to the range of ethnicities and languages in our midst. This means institutional policies have had to be reshaped to reflect the fact that we are not a unilingual society. Take, for example, the Queensland, Australia, governmental guide for health professionals. Under the section on language, we find:

> Serbian and Croatian are usually understood by most people although there are dialectic differences. In Australia, younger migrants may have good English but may not be used to the Australian accent. Especially at stressful times such as illness, an interpreter may be required. When translation is required, it is important to discuss the ethnicity of the interpreter as well as the language desired by the client, due to the political tension. (*www.health.qld.gov.au*)

Wider Ramifications

Language is a carrier of values. Words can convey or connote a set of beliefs. Language also can express prejudice and racist attitudes. Our thoughts and perceptions take place in a certain time and space. Consequently, ideas and concepts are not isolated from the world.

Rather, we learn and understand language at the same time that we live in the world and come to a sense of how people should interact with each other. Ask yourself whether or not describing an athlete as having a "Mexican *bandido* moustache" has the potential to contribute to racist stereotyping.

Exercises

Part One

1. Do you think Mitsuye Yamada is right to think that non-English speakers are pressured to speak English? Go into detail in your answer, bringing in any examples you can find or think of that will boost your position.

2. Give an argument for or against instituting an "English only" law for public institutions and workplaces.

3. Do a study of what happened when the province of Quebec instituted a requirement that French be the dominant language (e.g., stores with English signs had to either replace them with signs in French or at least have bilingual signs, with the French letters larger than the English translation).

4. Pick any *one* popular song. Study the lyrics, looking at the way words are used in terms of emotional impact.

5. Select two or three phrases from the list below and discuss the way the phrase reveals values or cultural attitudes:

drug-infested neighborhood	gang attire
solid American citizen	homemaker
sexual predator	hacker
workaholic	soccer mom
running off at the mouth	airhead (or bimbo)
groupie	womanizer
a man's man	yuppie
sponging off the system	Generation X
confirmed bachelor	wimp
old maid	head honcho
cyberspace	underclass
chill	chatfly
nerd	stool pigeon
party pooper	feminazi
jock	drama queen
lone wolf	hatchet man

6. Think of all the words or phrases that are connected to financial/economic status (like rich, loaded, fat cat, bourgeois, poor, welfare bum, broke, etc.). After drawing up your list, try to determine what these words indicate about our societal values.

7. Do an Internet study of the ways in which the word *jihad* has been used and understood (or misunderstood). After you gather some sense of the range of interpretations, share your reflections on what this shows us about language as a bearer of values.

Part Two

Directions: Answer any two of the following questions (1–5):

1. Do a study of descriptions around any *one* topic that has social significance, such as weight, age, looks, hair, economic class, professional status.

2. Do a study of magazine or newspaper articles that focus on celebrities (movie stars, singers, famous figures, or political leaders) and list all the words to describe them, keeping tabs on males versus females. Note any differences and see if there are changes when other factors come in, such as race, class, age, nationality, and popularity.

3. Do a study of the sports pages of the newspaper. Examine the different ways male and female athletes are described. Find as many examples as you can (try a week's worth of articles). Then draw some inferences from your study as to what this tells us about our society's values and beliefs.

4. Do a study of the ways in which religion is discussed in magazines or newspapers and see if you detect any bias or weighted descriptions.

5. Do a study of the way people use language to describe *one* of these groups: the disabled, children, teenagers, the elderly, gays or lesbians, single versus married people, working class versus upper class, any one ethnic or racial group, any one religious group, urban versus rural residents.

Euphemisms

When people want to avoid the repercussions of using a particular term, they may turn to a euphemism. A euphemism acts as a substitute for the targeted word, in order to achieve a particular end. The goal may be to defuse a situation that is controversial or it could be to slant it with a set of political or other values more favorable to the speaker. Whatever the motivation, the result is a slippery word that is used to refocus the audience's attention.

In an article on euphemisms in news reporting, Robert Kuttner observes that we need to be attentive to the lessons of Orwell's *1984*. He warns against such euphemisms as Stalin's term "liquidation" to describe the execution of political enemies. And he argues that replacing the term "school voucher" by "tuition support" masked a game of political manipulation. He asserts, "This is Orwellian because with public education there is no need for tuition support; public schools are free" (see Robert Kuttner, "Shame on Journalists for Forgetting Orwell," *Boston Globe*, 1 July 2000).

Similarly, there have been recent debates about the use of the terms "internment camps" and "relocation camps" instead of "concentration camps" to describe the forced imprisonment of Japanese-American citizens during World War II. In such cases, euphemisms may be perceived by oppressed groups to be harmful or hurtful. (See Chapter 4 for a discussion of the way a euphemism can create a question-begging epithet, which can cause us to draw an incorrect conclusion.)

Let's look at some more examples. In an article on mythological language, Steve Hoenisch gave two examples:

First: "security officials. This euphemism, found on the April 11, 1997, front page of *The New York Times*, should be recast as secret police when appropriate, as it would have been in the case of the *Times*'s article, which was referring to Vevak, the Iranian secret police."

Second: "some cutback on duplicate staffing appeared in a story on rising wages and stable prices on the front page of *The New York Times*, April 11, 1997. Writers should use 'layoffs' or 'firings' if that's what they mean to say." (See Steve Hoenisch, "The Mythological Language of American Newspapers," *www.criticism.com,* emphasis mine)

Some of the wildest euphemisms relate to moral issues. For example, a couple using a surrogate mother who wanted her to abort one of the twin fetuses, referred to the abortion as "selective reduction" and the law around surrogacy in the state of Florida calls the gestational surrogate (who does not provide the egg, only the womb) a "gestational carrier," as if she were a piece of luggage, instead of a human being.

Hedging

As we saw above, use of a euphemism is one form of loaded language. Another is hedging. In addition to watching adjectives and other terms of description, watch for the use of hedging or qualifying terms, as well as language that is loaded in terms of the values it adheres to and prescribes.

Hedging has the effect of undercutting the claim or raising doubts about it. Hedging can take two forms: (1) it can indicate a shift from one position to a much weaker one; or (2) it can undercut a claim or suggest a negative connotation of a phrase or claim being made.

Hedging is more often found in oral communication than written expression. This may explain why we get rejection *letters* rather than phone calls telling us another applicant got the job. It also explains why it's easier to write a "Dear John" letter than to place a "Dear John" phone call or have direct, face-to-face meetings.

On the political plane, the results of hedging can be dramatic. For example, on 4 Aug. 2001, the British Broadcasting Corporation (BBC) announced to its journalists that the word "assassination" could no longer be used to describe the actions of Israelis murdering guerilla opponents. Robert Fisk reports that:

> In a major surrender to Israeli diplomatic pressure, BBC officials in London have banned their staff in Britain and the Middle East from referring to Israel's policy of murdering its guerrilla opponents as "assassination." BBC reporters have been told that in future they are to use Israel's own euphemism for the murders, calling them "targeted killings."
>
> BBC journalists were astonished that the assignments editor, Malcolm Downing, should have sent out the memorandum to staff, stating that the word "assassinations" "should only be used for high-profile political assassinations." There were, Mr. Downing said, "lots of other words for death." (See Robert Fisk, "BBC Staff Are Told Not to Call Israeli Killings 'Assassination,'" *news.independent.co.uk,* 4 Aug. 2001)

Exercises

1. State the issues and concerns in the BBC by trying to control the use of language in reporting on Israelis (e.g., assignments editor, Malcoln Downing sent a memo to reporters on when to use the term "assassinations").

2. Share your thoughts on Fisk's comment that, "Mr. Downing's memorandum suggests that the murder of a leading Israeli—the late Prime Minister Yitzhak Rabin, killed by an Israeli extremist—is worthy of the word 'assassination' while the killing of Palestinians is not."

3. Investigate euphemisms: Find two euphemisms and discuss how they function and what would likely change in the context if we shifted to a less slanted or deceptive use of language.

4. Discuss the social and political impact of the euphemism used in the quote below:

> A storm of criticism forced the White House last week to play down talk of a new amnesty for illegal Mexican immigrants. But a conditional amnesty, cloaked in a euphemism, remains on a complex list of immigration issues being negotiated by the two countries.
>
> Some form of amnesty—which both nations now call "regularization"—has been on the agenda of unprecedented U.S.–Mexico talks for the last three months. Negotiators are trying to complete a framework by the time President Bush and his Mexican counterpart, Vicente Fox, meet in Washington in September. . . . the "regularization" of a yet-to-be-determined portion of the estimated 3-million-plus illegal Mexican immigrants already in the United States. Mexican authorities are willing to let these immigrants qualify only for practical benefits such as Social Security numbers and driver's licenses, rather than the eventual promise of full U.S. citizenship. (See Patrick J. McDonnell, "Amnesty by Any Name Is Hot Topic," *Los Angeles Times,* 22 July 2001)

▨ Loaded Language

As indicated by the discussion of euphemisms and name-calling, we have to be on the lookout for a fallacy called question-begging epithets. This occurs when language is biased so that it stacks the deck in either a positive or negative direction and we are drawn to an incorrect conclusion. This results from the slanted language causing us to unfairly prejudge the case. (See Chapter 4 on fallacies.)

Such loaded language must be guarded against in our own writing and speaking. And when spotted in the ways in which others express themselves, we need to watch for language stacking the deck, creating poorly reasoned arguments. This does not mean, however, that the use of language has to be dull and dry. Quite the contrary.

Loaded versus Colorful Language

Loaded language is to be distinguished from colorful, or figurative, language. With the latter, striking images (from ugly to funny to beautiful) are evoked because of the vivid use of language, but it does not function as a means of persuasion for a particular conclusion.

For example, "He's as subtle as a hog in heat," or "My hair feels greasier than an oil well!" may be considered colorful uses of language. We might even consider use of irony as a form of colorful, or figurative, language. For example, when Steve Forbes dropped out of the 2000 U.S. presidential campaign, he quipped: "we were nosed out by a landslide" (*Boston Globe,* as noted by *www.Issues.2000*).

In contrast, referring to Jews as "vermin" (as did the Nazis) is using a loaded phrase. It was used to help lay the foundation for the "final solution" (also loaded) to the "Jewish problem" (also loaded) that Jews must be eliminated and, therefore, mass-genocide must be instituted. It isn't a question of "vermin" being a *colorful* use of language, but that such words were used as part of a context, that is, to persuade. The loaded language used by the Nazis was a powerful tool of anti-Semitism. Those who heard (and were encouraged to use) such words and phrases were meant to draw both general and specific conclusions about Jews as a whole and what ought to be done with them (terminate them). The point is, loaded language acts to *bias* the reader or listener.

People frequently use loaded terms when they write or speak. Think of someone being described as a "thug": Would you think well of them? Both words—vermin and thug—are so loaded, that it is hard to look at the evidence in a fair manner.

Connotations of Loaded Language

Words are not usually neutral. Words are not like numbers or a symbolic language. You get a very different effect—and reaction—depending on whether you call a police officer, an officer or a cop or pig; as you will whether you call a female a woman, lady, gal or broad or a male a man, guy or dude. Each word carries its own set of connotations, so watch for both the overt and covert meanings of words.

Author Karl E. Meyer, tells the story of an old-time Chicago columnist, Sydney Harris. Harris used to tease his readers with a word game: "My religion is a denomination, yours is a sect and theirs is a cult." In citing this, Meyer is trying to nudge the reader to look at the ways in which language is used and how that use may vary to suit the political or ethical persuasion of the speaker.

CASE STUDY

Farrakhan's Mission: Fighting the Drug War—His Way

How Loaded Language Shapes Interpretation
The use of language can affect our understanding of an article, by looking at the following excerpt from an article on Louis Farrakhan.

He is soft-spoken, patient and polite—the very antithesis, or so it seems, of the <u>fire-breathing</u> apostle of black racism that many Americans believe him to be. But Minister Louis Farrakhan, leader of the little-understood Black Muslim sect known as the Nation of Islam, has much on his mind these days and for better or worse he is making himself heard. . . .

To listen to Farrakhan is to <u>walk on the wilder shores of racial paranoia</u>. He believes,

<u>apparently</u> sincerely, that George Bush wants to have him killed, and that the late Elijah Muhammad, former leader of the Nation of Islam, spoke to him in a vision aboard a gigantic UFO. . . .

<u>Incendiary Ideology</u>: Farrakhan's tendency toward <u>apocalyptic ranting</u> makes it all too easy for white Americans to ignore the power of his message to the economically distressed, <u>drug-ravaged</u> neighborhoods of the inner city . . . he has recently tempered the more incendiary elements of his ideology. (See Lynda Wright and Daniel Glick, *Newsweek,* 19 Mar. 1990, emphasis mine)

In this quote, we see the second kind of hedging. Many of the emphasized phrases undercut Farrakhan, raising suspicions about his credibility. For example, look at the use of "his way," "or so it seems," "for better or worse," and "apparently sincerely." All suggest something is off: "his way" as opposed to everyone else's; "or so it seems" implies some questions about the truth of the claim; "for better or worse" connotes a negative, a doubt; and "apparently sincerely" raises concerns about whether this sincerity is an illusion.

Look also at the terms "fire-breathing," "black racism," "wilder shores of racial paranoia," "incendiary," "sect," "ideology." Each term has impact. We can see this by looking at the sorts of images conjured up by the word or phrase:

- "Fire-breathing" What sorts of things are fire-breathing? Dragons, principally, maybe some monsters, but nothing human.
- "Black racism" draws up fears of revolt, of blacks waging war on whites.

- "Wilder shores of racial paranoia" has three words that are forceful; "wilder," "racial" and "paranoia." All tap into societal fears about race war, about citizens out of control, about deranged individuals.
- "Incendiary": This connotes something that creates a fire, linking back to the "fire-breathing" image in the article's opening sentence. It's also an image of destruction, because of some dangerous, little known "sect."
- "Sect" is also loaded. "Religious group" would have been more neutral. "Sects" are groups of people who are disenfranchised from ordinary society or subscribe to strange beliefs.
- "Ideology" suggests a theoretical/social set of beliefs that is on the fringe, unacceptable by ordinary criteria. We hear it used like this: Marxist ideology, Communist ideology. You never hear the phrase "Democratic ideology," though that would not be an inappropriate use. We do not hear ideology used in the positive, basically, because it isn't normally thought of as such.

We tend to expect a degree of objectivity in what we read and hear, unless it we understand it to be a persuasive piece. The expectation is that there is an attempt at fairness. If there is controversy, as in the case of Louis Farrakhan, we may expect to be given a balanced report, but that is not always the case.

The use of language is often tinged with the values of the author. That is not necessarily a bad thing, but it is something we must stay attentive about. This is why critical thinking should come into play whenever you read. You must always be on the lookout for loaded terms.

Exercises

Bertrand Russell once set out a conjugation of words to see how synonyms of a word can carry a range of connotations. He offered this one: "I am firm. You are stubborn. He is a pig-headed fool." Here are a few others: "I am svelte. You are thin. She is skinny as a green bean." "I am pleasingly plump. You are overweight. He is a blimp." "I am reserved. You have a chip on your shoulder. She is a stuck-up princess."

1. Come up with four conjugations of your own.
2. Write two to three paragraphs discussing the range of the three terms and the impact of the different connotations.

Ambiguity (Linguistic Fallacies)

When it comes to the use of language, clarity is important. Problems can occur when words, grammar, or sentence structure is used in ways that create an ambiguity. Sometimes the problems are like seeing in a fog; whereby the confusing use of language allows a variety of interpretations. Of course, some people use slippery language intentionally, manipulatively—twisting their words to suit their purposes. In this case, we've got "weasel words."

Sometimes it's just that the use of language is ambiguous—at times because the issue is not clearly defined or the writer/speaker is hedging on where to stand. In this situation, the various interpretations will eventually call for clarification. David Harel points out that we utilize an enormous amount of knowledge in clarifying and understanding ordinary language, besides just the words and grammar. He illustrates this with the way the following sentences differ in the relationships between their various parts (see David Harel, *computers Ltd.*):

The thieves stole the jewels, and some of them were later sold.
The thieves stole the jewels, and some of them were later caught.
The thieves stole the jewels, and some of them were later found.

We see ambiguity in the discussion over stem cell research, which would involve the use of cells from human embryos. Some favor such use, for example, for medical advances; others think it is immoral. When the eyes turned to President Bush to see where he stood and examined his record, they ran into a brick wall. As Robert Pear observes,

> Administration officials on both sides of the debate, trying to frame the issue for a decision by President Bush, have been reviewing his campaign statements, which generally expressed disapproval of research that used embryonic stem cells. But officials said they had found ambiguities in his statements that might allow some research to go forward. (See Robert Pear, "Bush Administration Is Split over Stem Cell Research," *The New York Times,* 13 June 2001)

President Bush did not exactly clear out the ambiguity when he later said, "I oppose federal funding for stem cell research that involves destroying living human embryos. I support innovative medical research on life-threatening and debilitating disease, including promising research on stem cells from adult tissue." There comes a time, however, when ambiguity has to yield to a clear-cut position (either directly or indirectly, either by word or deed).

When ambiguities lead to an incorrect conclusion, we are looking at fallacious reasoning. In this case, we end up in a dead end because of the confusing language. The three key linguistic fallacies are: equivocation (where there's a shift of meaning in a word or phrase leading to an incorrect conclusion), accent (where the emphasis of a word or phrase leads us to an incorrect conclusion), and amphiboly (where the sentence structure or use of grammar creates an ambiguity, leading to an incorrect conclusion). Here are a few examples:

Equivocation: That was such a bad movie it deserves jail time! (This plays on different senses of the word "bad."). This is also seen in the ad for Philip Morris cigarettes, Basic Lights: "THE BEST THINGS IN LIFE ARE BASIC."

Accent: **One Month Rent Free** when you sign a lease for three years. (The visual emphasis about the "free" rent is misleading, given the terms that follow.)

Amphiboly: I saw the Lone Ranger with his horse, so I gave him a carrot. (The ambiguous sentence structure makes it unclear whether it is the Lone Ranger or the horse getting the carrot.)

Being able to spot ambiguity and any resulting fallacies is important. We are much less likely to be manipulated by slippery uses of language if we know fallacies and are able to tackle any other sorts of ambiguity we run into.

Concepts and Definitions

It can be crucial to see how concepts and definitions function in the way language is used. We need to ask what the term is meant to include and how it is to be applied. Philosopher Ludwig Wittgenstein once advised, "Don't look at the meaning—look at the use!" There may be any number of possible definitions for a word; but the context of its use, how the person is using it in the sentence, may more clearly reveal the intended meaning.

Watch for hidden assumptions or exclusions in the way language is used in speaking, writing, policy guidelines, and laws. For example, if policies speak of employees as male, then it's hard to know what to do with pregnant women (e.g., with regard to maternity leave, fetal protection issues, time off for birth). Should pregnancy be put in the same category as illness? Historically, women who took a leave to have a child lost both her seniority and accumulated benefits—and sometimes her job. This was due to overtly discriminatory laws and to societal attitudes that were encapsulated in the language of employer–employee relationships.

Similarly, in female-dominated fields like nursing, males have had an uphill battle addressing both gynocentric (female-centered) language and stereotypes. Patrick Thornton, a nurse midwife talks about his work: "I think a lot of people expected that because I was a man, they were going to be treated like a doctor treats them. When they found out that wasn't true, then that seemed to help" (see Christopher Snowbeck, "Male Nurse Midwife Adopts a Supportive Attitude," *Post Gazette* [Pittsburgh], 27 Mar. 2001). The term "midwife" alone creates problems for Thornton—even though it means "with woman" and does not mean that the midwife is a female.

Components of a Definition

There are two parts to any definition: first, the word or phrase to define or clarify. This is called the *definiendum*. Then you have the explanation—words meaning the same as the word or phrase in question. This is called the *definiens*. *Synonyms* are words that are similar in meaning (e.g., warm and toasty), whereas *antonyms* are words that are opposite in meaning (e.g., hot and cold).

Syntax and Semantics

It is important to use words clearly and, to avoid ambiguity, specify what definition you are using. Questions about *syntax* have to do with punctuation, grammar, word order, and sentence structure. Questions of *semantics* have to do with the meanings of words, what they signify. This includes both denotation and connotation: the *denotation* of a word is the literal meaning, whereas the *connotation* is what the word suggests, implies, or conjures up in our minds.

Syntactical errors may seem less worrisome than semantic problems. However, grammatical or structural errors can create havoc. We simply may completely miss the point if the syntax is a mess. An example of a syntax error is "Rosa had been lifting weights for five years when she dropped a barbell on her foot." Watch also your use of semantics, because the use of a word or phrase that means something other than you thought may lead the reader to the wrong conclusion. In either case, be on the watch.

Definition versus Use

Realize that the strict definition of a concept may differ from the way the concept is used. We use terms and concepts in a social context; one in which values and cultural beliefs may color the use of a word. Realize also that our understanding of a concept can have significant consequences.

For example, if the word "person" were generally understood to include fetuses and embryos in applying the Constitution, laws around abortion and fetal experimentation would have to be reinterpreted. Historically the concept "person" referred to postnatal humans, but recently there has been a shift toward greater protection for fetuses. You see this, for example, in euphemistic references to the fetus as an "unborn child" or a "preborn person." The concept of "fetal rights" has much more meaning and significance than it had 50, or even 20, years ago.

Role of Values in Understanding a Concept

Let us take an example to see how attitudes and values get captured in how concepts are used. In law there is a thing called the "reasonable person" standard. It used to be called the "reasonable man" standard and it is used to judge certain actions. In order to assess whether what someone did was outrageous and unacceptable or "reasonable" and within the scope of the law, we were to ask ourselves, "What would a reasonable man do in this set of circumstances?"

Role of Social Norms in Understanding Concepts

Societal norms shape the scope of our concepts and definitions. If the norm is white people's experiences, anyone who is not white will be judged falling outside the norm. If the norm is the middle class, anyone who is not middle class will fall outside the norm. If the norm is men, women fall outside the norm. If the norm is able-bodied people, what we include in the design and construction of schools and other institutions has consequences for people who are disabled (such as the location of light switches, the size of hallways, the presence or absence of elevators, the height of toilets, the use of Braille in elevators). As a result, how we define the norm has considerable social, and linguistic, consequences.

Interpretations

We must watch how the terms are used and examine the possible interpretations of concepts. Think of it this way: What if our understanding of what it means to be a "person" was any human over 7 feet tall who was an excellent athlete? A disproportionately large proportion of those fitting these criteria would be males and especially African-American males. Entire ethnic groups would be excluded altogether.

Exercises

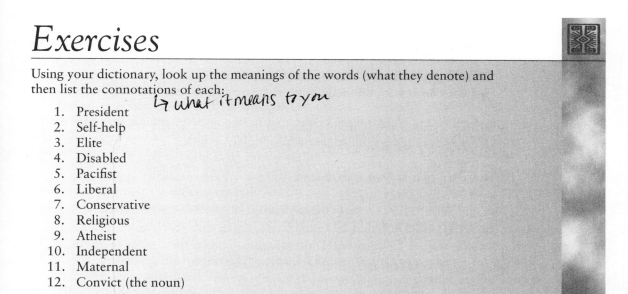

Using your dictionary, look up the meanings of the words (what they denote) and then list the connotations of each: ↳ *what it means to you*

1. President
2. Self-help
3. Elite
4. Disabled
5. Pacifist
6. Liberal
7. Conservative
8. Religious
9. Atheist
10. Independent
11. Maternal
12. Convict (the noun)

Jargon, Buzzwords, and Technical Terms

It is wise to watch out for jargon and buzzwords. First, we need to decide what exactly is being meant. Try to articulate your understanding of the word or phrase. "I understand this term to mean . . ." is one way to clarify your sense of a concept. Spell out how you think the term is being used.

Readers should not have to feel like they're cracking a secret code to understand how an author is using a term. Look, for example, at the Los Angeles Unified School District's use of the term "morphosyntactic skills" in their published glossary of acronyms and terminology. The glossary doesn't define the term; it only translates it to the Spanish "conocimientos morfosintacticos." Most just scratch their heads in befuddlement over what in the world this phrase means (for a fuller discussion, see Duke Helfand, "*Edspeak* is in a Class by Itself," *Los Angeles Times*, 16 Aug. 2001).

Basically, your goal is to be clear enough so your audience can understand what's being said. If not, we may end up like Dr. Hibbert talking to Homer (from the TV show *The Simpsons,* as noted on *www.imdb.com*):

DR. HIBBERT: Homer, I'm afraid you'll have to undergo a coronary bypass operation.
HOMER: Say it in English, Doc.
DR. HIBBERT: You're going to need open-heart surgery.
HOMER: Spare me your medical mumbo-jumbo.
DR. HIBBERT: We're going to cut you open and tinker with your ticker.
HOMER: Could you dumb it down a shade?

Some writers seem to use jargon to impress others or themselves, or to make the audience feel incompetent and unfit to challenge the work. If we don't know what is meant by a term, it is difficult to go very far. If the term is not in the dictionary (keep one nearby!), analyze the author's intent and examine the context surrounding the use of the term. Look at the way it is used, as Wittgenstein suggested.

Legal terms often are used quite specifically, so never assume they have an ordinary usage. Since a lot may follow from the interpretation of a legal concept, it is vital that the concept be examined. To see how a legal term can be transformed by court decisions, look at the concept of "medical treatment."

CASE STUDY

Evolution of Terms:
The Elizabeth Bouvia Case

Ordinarily when we think of medical treatment, we think of prescription drugs, special diets, and therapeutic treatments. In the case of Elizabeth Bouvia, this changed. Bouvia was a 28-year-old woman with cerebral palsy who checked herself into a hospital, wanting to starve herself to death. As she put it, "I'm trapped in a useless body." Doctors refused to go along with this wish, and ended up putting a feeding tube down her, against her will. She sued.

In a landmark decision, the California Court of Appeals ruled that "medical treatment" included nutrition and hydration through a feeding tube. Since a competent adult has the right to refuse treatment, Bouvia had the right to refuse having the feeding tube, even if it resulted in her death. In 1993, this concept was stretched further, when an ill prisoner sued for the right to refuse food and water under the umbrella of the right to refuse medical treatment. He won and, in so doing, the legal concept of medical treatment took yet another step beyond the Bouvia decision. By 2001 the issue was whether a severely incapacitated person who was "minimally conscious" could, at his wife's request, have his feeding tube removed and die. The California Supreme Court denied the request, but the issue continues and the language of the debate continues to evolve.

Since legal decisions have potentially significant consequences for future cases, a great deal may follow from the understanding of the legal term in question.

Directions: List 2–3 words or phrases you can think of that have shifted meaning.

Exercise

State all you can infer about the Kellogg Company from the following item taken from their website, under their Legal Information link:

Any communication or material you transmit to the Site by electronic mail or otherwise, including any data, questions, comments, suggestions, or the like is, and will be treated as, non-confidential and non-proprietary. Anything you transmit or post may be used by Kellogg's or its affiliates for any purpose, including, but not limited to, reproduction, disclosure, transmission, publication, broadcast and posting. Furthermore, Kellogg's is free to use any ideas, concepts, know-how, or techniques contained in any communication you send to the Site for any purpose whatsoever including, but not limited to, developing, manufacturing and marketing products using such information. (*www.thekelloggcompany.co.uk*)

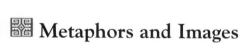 Metaphors and Images

Descriptions may take colorful, dramatic turns. When we study language, we see the power of metaphors, images, and value-laden terms. Of course, it's possible to go over the top with metaphors. This is noted in the "Metaphor Alert" in the *Wall Street Journal Online:*

In a Saturday *New York Times* article (link requires registration) on the Civil Rights Commission Democrats' report, reporter Katharine Seelye writes: "At an occasionally icy four-hour hearing, the eight-member commission waded through nearly 200 pages of text and ironed out its language before voting, 6 to 2, to accept the report." (*Wall Street Journal,* 11 June 2001)

People often turn to metaphor when words fail them. That is, when we are unable to find words to apply to our situation or to describe an experience, metaphors and images become the linguistic paintbrush to convey our thoughts and feelings. Think of the struggle to find words to apply to the terrorist attack on the World Trade Center and the Pentagon. Michiko Kakutani put it this way:

Language failed this week.
"Beyond comprehension," "beyond our worst imaginings," "beyond belief"—those were the phrases heard again and again in the last two days. As people struggled to describe the events of Tuesday morning, they reached for metaphors and analogies that might capture the horror of what they had seen. One witness on NBC local news described the World Trade Center collapse as "one more circle of Dante's hell." Brian Williams on MSNBC compared it to Mount St. Helen's [volcanic explosion]. Tom Brokaw on NBC compared it to "nuclear winter." Diane Sawyer on ABC compared it to standing on "the edge of a crater of a volcano."
Chris Matthews said it was "bigger than the Hindenberg, bigger than the Titanic."
. . . words felt devalued and inadequate to capture the disasters at the World Trade

Center, the Pentagon and near Pittsburgh. (See "Struggling to Find Words for a Horror beyond Words," *The New York Times*, 13 Sep. 2001)

Metaphors and images can shape an interpretation. They can be ruinous, but they also can be highly effective. This may be due to the visual nature of most metaphors and the fact that we are suckers for stories and images. Used well, metaphors can leave an impression that goes far beyond mere linear argumentation. Think of all the memorable speeches throughout history; many used powerful metaphors and images.

Vivid, even jolting, metaphors can have a powerful effect on the audience. Take the words of Malcolm X who said, "You don't stick a knife in a man's back nine inches and then pull it out six inches and say you're making progress. No matter how much respect, no matter how much recognition, whites show towards me, as far as I'm concerned, as long as it is not shown to every one of our people in this country, it doesn't exist for me" (as quoted by Cornel West, *Race Matters*). You don't have to know much about Malcolm X to be struck by his use of language; the imagery evokes both fear and horror.

Metaphors should generally be used sparingly for maximum impact. Like all advice, however, there are always exceptions and each writer or speaker has to decide how to parcel out the use of metaphors, analogies, or other potentially powerful uses of language.

Exercises

Part One

Directions: Pick two current events; such as a current issue from national news, a local story, a news item about a famous person, or an event in sports.

1. Using an analogy to a fairy tale, children's story, film character or cartoon character, write a brief description of the event. Your goal is to *be as colorful as you can.*

2. Now write your reflections on your use of language to create an effect, why you picked the metaphor/analogy you did, and how it could shape the way we see the event being described.

Part Two

1. Investigate the reappropriation of loaded terms, where a term that has been seen as highly charged is claimed by the targeted group and transformed:
   a. Find as many examples as you can of ethnic or cultural groups that take a term (e.g., crone, nigger, queer, chick, hag) that has been perceived as offensive and, turning the tables, apply it to themselves. For example, this was done in the movie *Menace II Society* with the term "nigger."

b. Why do you think they are reappropriating these words? Is it an expression of power, as Mary Daly, suggests when she applauds women for using terms like "witch," hag," and "crone?"

c. In the movie *Hardball*, African-American boys who are members of a Little League–type baseball team, regularly call each other "bitch" as a term of address (not anger). What does this use signify, in your estimation?

2. Do a study of the way the news media used the term "terrorist" or "terrorism" in the first two months after the attacks on the World Trade Center and the Pentagon in September 2001.

3. Do a study of the use of language in two or three song lyrics, noting the different uses of language that you see. Be sure to point out uses of language that you find particularly striking, appealing, or effective.

4. Do a study of the nightly news, answering *one* of the following questions:
a. How are people referred to or described in the various news segments (leading stories, sports, human interest stories, etc.)?
b. How do the descriptions of current events show a bias or reveal a cultural attitude?

Exclusive Language

Assume you moved to a town where people called Native-American men "chiefs" and the women "squaws," Asians "gooks," Latinos "bean-eaters," Middle Easterners "sand niggers," and Italians "wops." Would you start using any of those terms just because it was the tradition in that area? Would you call a gay man a "fag" and a lesbian a "dyke" just because those around you do? It's not always easy to opt out of the norm, even when the norm is morally flawed.

The use of demeaning or vitriolic language tends to ignite and sustain prejudice. All too easily this leads to disrespectful behavior and even hate crimes. It may make us all uncomfortable to think these are intertwined, but justice demands that we look at such links anyway. For the most part, racist and sexist language is hurtful and offensive. This may occur when we categorize individuals or groups. Think of terms like "primitive peoples" or "natives." Far better to use the term "indigenous." Think also of references to "developing nations"—instead try "Third World countries."

Look, for instance, at a *Newsweek* article about people taking classes in arts and crafts to be exposed to different cultures. The article mentions "another culture—*overseas or in a remote locale in the United States.*" The author describes arts and crafts lessons of "foreign" cultures in "remote" locales in Utah, Tennessee, and Texas alongside those in Guatemala, Nepal, Italy, and Madagascar (see Debra Klein, "Walking with the Buffaloes: To Really Dig Into Foreign Cultures, Learn Their Crafts," *Newsweek* 9 July 2001, emphasis mine).

This suggests that those in "remote" areas of the United States are as foreign as those in Madagascar, whose arts and crafts we can dabble in like anthropologists on vacation. In seeing the other as truly "other," as "foreign," we risk class and cultural bias. Plus, we risk alienating the very people we may want to connect with. We should be sensitive to the potential harm of our use of language. Sensitivity and empathy go a long way in building communication.

Recognizing the Connection between Language and Thought

Racism and sexism are never right. Language is part of the way prejudice gets perpetuated. By changing the language, we can help change the attitudes behind racism and sexism. Racist or sexist language reflects racist or sexist values. As a student in Chicago said, "You don't start out racist. We're all racist now" (*New York Times,* 29 May 1994). Although the remark was in response to a particular issue at the school, it has a broader significance.

We need to look carefully at the extent to which racist attitudes enter our language and our thought. Mari J. Matsuda looks at the issue of protecting racist speech under the First Amendment. Recognizing the harms that have been wrought because of hate speech, Matsuda proposes a narrow interpretation of the First Amendment. Because hate speech presents "an idea so historically untenable, so dangerous, and so tied to perpetuation of violence and degradation of the very classes of human beings who are least equipped to respond," she thinks it should be outside the domain of protected discourse. Matsuda argues that hate speech could be restricted and the society not end up in a problematic moral dilemma around censorship if three characteristics are used to identify hate speech. These are:

Matsuda's Three Characteristics of Hate Speech

1. The message is that one group is racially inferior.
2. The message is directed against a historically oppressed group
3. The message is persecutory, hateful, and degrading.

Exercises

1. Using Matsuda's three characteristics, find four to five examples of hate speech on at least two to three different websites on the Internet.

2. Is it right to try to censor hate speech in a Democracy? State your position and support.

3. What do you think should be a company or college policy around the use of hate speech in email or within publications, such as college newspapers or office newsletters? Set out your recommendations.

4. Do a study of contemporary music for examples of hate speech. Give an argument for or against censoring music lyrics.

5. If Matsuda's definition is expanded to include sexism, works of music, literature, film, and published articles would be included. Give your argument for or against expanding the criteria above to include sexism as well as racism.

6. What do you think should be done about hate speech on the Internet? You can easily find examples by going to websites for neo-Nazis, skinheads, Aryan Brotherhood, Ku Klux Klan, among others, as well as statements by individuals and organizations expressing their concerns. Set out your views in three to four paragraphs.

Group Exercise

Read over the excerpt below from Judy Shepherd, the mother of Matthew Shepherd (murdered in 1999) and share your thoughts on the ways in which speaking out, as she does here, can effect social change:

Statement from Judy Shepard
Mother of Matthew Shepard

March 23, 1999

While it is true, perpetrating violence on another individual is against the law regardless of the motivation, violence motivated by hate has deep ramifications and is often times meant to intimidate entire groups of people. Hate crimes laws first send a message that these crimes will not be tolerated in our society, a message that sadly needs to be heard by some people. Equally as important, these laws would provide law enforcement with tools they might need in pursuing these cases and making sure that justice is served.

There is ample evidence that hate crimes laws are needed. . . . It is my firm belief that this legislation is necessary in all 50 states and at the federal level. . . . There is no guarantee that these laws will stop hate crimes from happening. But they can reduce them. They can help change the climate in this country, where some people feel as though it is Ok to target specific groups of people and get away with it. If just one is stopped. If just one potential perpetrator gets the message of this legislation and there is one less victim, then it will be worthwhile.

On behalf of my family, I call on the Congress of the United States to pass the Hate Crimes Prevention Act without delay. Also, a state and federal partnership combating hate crimes can save lives. I urge the 21 state legislatures which have hate crimes laws that exclude sexual orientation to include it. I also urge the 8 state legislatures that have no hate crimes laws, including my home state of Wyoming, to enact them. And, I urge Gov. George W. Bush of Texas to reconsider his opposition to hate crimes laws that include sexual orientation. There is no excuse for inaction.

Source: www.matthewsplace.com.

Addressing Racist Language

We need examine the ways racism is expressed. We are not always in a position to confront the racist. It may be unwise or even dangerous to do so. But we are not powerless, either. By recognizing and understanding the mechanisms of hate and hate speech, we can be party to social change.

Writing about the Vietnam War, Ron Ridenhour discusses the role of racist language in creating a mindset that permits someone to kill "enemies." One way in which this was done was to refer to the Viet Cong (North Vietnamese) as "gooks." Ridenhour writes about the horrific consequences, namely:

> I first came face to face with my own intimate knowledge of gooks in Vietnam. First time I heard the word was on the way to Vietnam. "When you get to Vietnam," one of my first drill sergeants said, "you'll have one job. Killing gooks." Seemed straightforward enough.
>
> By the time I got to Vietnam, just before Christmas 1967, everydamnbody was talking about killing gooks. Gooks this, gooks that. The gooks, the gooks, the gooks. At first there was some confusion. How did you tell gooks from the good Vietnamese, for instance? After a while it became clear. You didn't have to. All gooks were VC [Viet Cong] when they were dead. (See Ron Ridenhour, "Jesus Was a Gook," Part I, *lists.village.virginia.edu/sixties/HTML_docs*)

Justice does not come about by a few people in powerful places making decisions to be blindly followed by the masses. Justice comes about when everyday people bring it into each aspect of their lives. And that means that change is possible. We can help others acquire the tools to recognize racist language and thought. We can also eradicate it out of our own speech and ways of thinking.

The issue doesn't appear to be going away: Even the Sydney Olympics in 2000 was shadowed by protests over racism. For example, one reporter inferred, "The push to demonize Aboriginal welfare recipients as ungrateful 'bludgers' and asylum seekers fleeing persecution as 'illegals' and 'queue jumpers' reflects a growing desperation on the part of the Australian ruling class" (see Simon Butler, "Why We'll Be Protesting at the Olympics," *Green Left Weekly,* 23 Aug. 2000).

Nonsexist Language

Source: *Reprinted with the permission of Virginia L. Warren and The American Philosophical Association.*

Incorporating Virginia L. Warren's Guidelines

Instead of:	Use:
Man	Person, individual, people
Mankind	Humanity, humankind
Person/he	People/they, person/he or she (*Person/they is becoming more acceptable*)
Person/he	Person/he, person/she (alternating) (*Avoid using "she" or "he" with stereotypical roles or behavior*)
One/his	We/our or one/one's
Actress, stewardess, waitress	Think of the job, not the person; actor, flight attendant, server
Policeman, policewoman	Police officer
Fireman	Firefighter
Stuntman, camera man	Stunt person, photographer
Bachelorette, bachelor girl	Bachelor, single woman

Use Plural Nouns:

The politician uses his knowledge	Politicians use their knowledge

Try New Constructions

If the writer plans ahead, he will save a lot of effort	The writer <u>who</u> plans ahead will save a lot of effort (*Use "who"*)
The manager must submit his budget by March 1st	The manager must submit <u>a</u> budget by March 1st (*Use articles like "the" and "a"*)
The manager . . . he	The manager . . . this person (*Use nouns instead of the pronoun "he"*)
The manager must submit his budget	The budget must be submitted by the manager (*Use passive voice for verbs, but use sparingly*)

Sexist versus Nonsexist Language

Most people think of language as both neutral and unchanging. It is neither. Language has power, positive and negative. Language helps shape our perceptions and behavior. Language also changes over time, as society changes.

We can be active agents of change so that degrading or stereotypical constructions fade away from ordinary use. One of the most significant ways this can be done is through our own use of language. Philosopher Virginia L. Warren wrote a valuable guide to nonsexist language for the American Philosophical Association. These guidelines are set out above.

Linguistic Lethargy

Some people do not want to change their way of speaking or writing. Some cite tradition as their reason for sticking with the "good ole way" of saying person/he. Some claim it is awkward or inconvenient to say "he or she" instead of "he." These arguments from tradition and from convenience are both pathetic. Doing what is just should always take precedence over doing what is convenient.

Some works are blatantly racist. Sometimes the author does not intend to write a racist diatribe, but shows a deep-seated prejudice that is unconscious. On the other hand, sometimes the writer is not only aware of such attitudes but seeks to perpetuate them. As critical thinkers, our task is to discern the ways in which attitudes and lethargy are expressed.

Exercises

1. Select two ethnic groups from the following: Asians, African Americans, Pacific Islanders, Latinos, Native Americans, Middle Easterners, Jews, Muslims, Anglos.
    a. Write down all the different stereotypes, myths, and descriptive terms you can think of for each of your three groups.
    b. Looking over your list, circle all the negative stereotypes, myths, and descriptions. Compare with the number of positives or neutrals.
    c. How do these stereotypes affect how we see members of the groups that are referred to stereotypically?

2. Study advertising as a kind of consumer propaganda.
    a. How is language used in ads to shape our thoughts and values?
    b. How are men and women described in ads?
    c. How are items made more appealing by the words used (e.g., in cigarette ads the word "taste" is often used, though we don't normally eat cigarettes)?

3. Do a study of stereotypes (focus on *one* area—race, ethnicity/nationality, gender, religion, age, weight) in sports. You can find articles in newspapers and on the Internet to gather examples and issues.

4. Find some examples to either <u>support</u> or <u>disprove</u> the claim made by Reggie Rivers at a Harvard University panel about gay experiences in athletics:

    Reggie Rivers, an African-American former NFL player who is heterosexual, equated the current climate of socially acceptable discrimination against homosexuals with the overt discrimination against blacks in the 1950s. "It seems that we are free to say anything about gay people without a societal reprimand," said Rivers, who now hosts a radio talk show and pens a column for the Denver Post. (See Daniel E. Fernandez, "Speakers Discuss Gay Experience in Athletics," *The Harvard Crimson,* 20 Feb. 2001)

Writing Exercises

1. Research the ways in which racism and racist language was used by any *one* of these groups: the Ku Klux Klan, the Nazis, neo-Nazis, white supremacists, or the Aryan Nation.
2. Research the ways in which racism and racist language was used by the American media and/or the U.S. government in the treatment of one group (Germans, Soviets, Asians, etc.) in (select one): World War II, Cold War, Korean War, Vietnam War, Grenada invasion, war in El Salvador, the Panama invasion, Gulf War.
3. Study the use of language by the media within the first month after the terrorist attacks on September 11, 2001, in New York and Washington, D.C., focusing on how issues of religion, race and/or racism were dealt with.

Addressing Prejudicial Language

We must look out for prejudicial language and name it when we see it. And we do not have to perpetuate it as an acceptable means of discourse. To say "man" and assume it includes women is to try to twist your brain around a linguistic pretzel. Clearly the issue is not simply one of convention or convenience. The underlying assumptions hiding behind sexist language need to be rooted out. Similarly, racist or other forms of biased language should be unacceptable, however easy it may be to use. We can start by making sure that we don't personally succumb to prejudicial language and take steps to address it when we see it in others.

Breaking the Chain

Language perpetuates a set of beliefs. If we find those beliefs oppressive or unjust, we must, therefore, be very careful to keep them from being sanctified through the ordinary day-to-day language we use.

In a satire on sexist language, Douglas Hofstadter illustrates how convoluted is the thought behind those who use exclusive language. In using an analogy to race, Hofstadter shows how ludicrous are the claims of inclusivity when such slanted language is being used. As he puts it,

> the libbers propose that we substitute "person" everywhere where "white" now occurs. Sensitive speakers of our secretary tongue of course find this preposterous. There is great beauty to a phrase such as "All whites are created equal." Our forebosses who framed the Declaration of Independence well understood the poetry of our language. Think how ugly it would be to say "All persons are created equal," or "All whites and blacks are created equal." Besides, as any school whitey can tell you, such phrases are

redundant. In most contexts, it is self-evident when "white" is being used in an inclusive sense, in which case it subsumes members of the darker race just as much as fairskins. (Douglas F. Hofstadter, from "A Person Paper on Purity in Language," in *Metamagical Themas: Questing for the Essence of Mind and Pattern*)

Exercises

1. Take a stand on one of the following and set down your position:
   a. Since we are not certain of the gender of God, we should not refer to God as *He. Note:* If you write in favor of the claim, discuss offering alternate ways of referring to God.
   b. Since roads and buildings are named after men, mountains and rivers should be named after women.
   c. Religious hymns, the Bible, and patriotic music like the national anthem should be rewritten to eliminate any exclusive language like *mankind* and *brotherhood of man."*

2. Discuss the use of language in this excerpt from an antiabortion article targeting then-President Clinton:

   Two years ago, our President [referring to Clinton] said to you and me to the effect: "If you will make me your President again, I promise I will suck the brains out of your babies heads!" We elected him and he kept his promise! All the severe problems which the administration of our beloved country is now experiencing are not so much because of the sexual abuse of young women, perjury, obstruction of justice, or tampering with witnesses, but the real reason for evil that prevails in the United States, is because our President kills Jesus Christ's babies. (*www.lambsofchrist.com*)

3. Read the following excerpt discussing Thoraya Obaid, head of the United Nations Population Fund and a participant in a UN special session on how best to combat AIDS. Then answer the questions that follow.

   Arab nations have resisted explicit wording on gay sex as well as on women's rights and adolescent sexuality. But then, so have representatives of the Vatican and some members of the Bush administration, to the consternation of American anti-AIDS campaigners. That confrontation, Ms. Obaid said . . . should serve as warning about the need for participants to be sensitive to cultural differences.
        From her vantage point, she added, the battle over semantics still often masks a more basic global split. The frank and explicit language about sex that is often demanded by Westerners when United Nations documents are written makes compromise—and progress on vital issues—difficult, she said. "The North needs to change the way it addresses the South," she said. "Because if you attend the debates, it always appears as if the South is wrong and they have to change—that they have nothing good in their culture or their society and we are teaching them what needs to be done. (See Barbara Crossette, "A Muslim Woman with a New View of Culture," *The New York Times,* 20 June 2001)

Answer the following:
a. What issues and concerns does Obaid raise in the excerpt above?
b. What sorts of obstacles might interfere with attempts to address AIDS, given the participants are from such different cultures?

CASE STUDY

The Deaf Culture

Rachel Stone, superintendent for the California School for the Deaf was fired in June 2001. State officials refused to discuss the basis of their decision, but parents suspect it was because Stone is a visionary. They said she empowered deaf students by making American Sign Language their primary form of communication. In short, she is "deaf and proud—a combination that doesn't sit well with the school's old guard," says journalist Scott Gold.

Basically, it appears that she challenged the stereotype that deaf people should model themselves after the dominant, hearing culture, even if no one can hear the words they are trying to say. She also takes issue with past attempts to determine the course of deaf education and the low expectations placed on deaf children. Stone says,

There are different cultures. We are all human beings, and in the past we were told that we were not. We were told that we could not be successful. That's all I'm trying to change. For years, deaf education has been run by people who think they know what's best for deaf people, and they have failed and failed and failed. I want to put a stop to that. (See Scott Gold,

"Controversial Head of School for Deaf Removed," *Los Angeles Times*, 21 June 2001)

Stone is trying to empower deaf children to use sign language, their "native" language instead of having teachers reciting their lecture out loud with a student in the class translating it. She hired faculty fluent in sign language and encouraged them not to speak (voices off). Parents reported that the children swelled with pride, having their own language, their own means of communication without an intermediary. Gold quotes Stone, who says, "This is my language. Why doesn't deaf education recognize that?"

Stone's detractors say American Sign Language is not English and students should be allowed to try to speak it. Hearing teachers felt marginalized, some were said to feel harassed, and some resigned. State officials made Stone clarify that she was not banning speaking, only encouraging signing. Faculty seemed divided in their support versus opposition of Stone's methods. One observer felt that her philosophy caught people off guard and moved too fast. Nevertheless, her vision may have been far-fetched, but was possible.

Exercises

1. Why do you think people appeared to be threatened by her demand that sign language rule in the deaf classroom?

2. Was Stone out of line to deemphasize, if not discourage, learning to speak out loud?

3. If you were a parent or family member who was part of the hearing culture, what concerns might you have about the children being taught "voices off"?

4. If you were asked to defend Stone, what would you say?

The Liberatory Voice

Language can degrade, as we have seen. But language can also exalt, as we saw with the case of the deaf children who were proud to have "their own language." Language can be an incredibly powerful tool. As William Raspberry says, "And, yes, words matter. They may reflect reality, but they also have the power to change reality—the power to uplift and to abase."

Out of Silence into Speech

We've all had to deal with psychic numbing, in our own way. We've all known what it is to live with the awareness that humans now have the capacity to vaporize us all, to commit mass genocide, to explode the vast nuclear arsenal.

Many of us have fathers and mothers who, naïve and trusting of their government stood before nuclear weapons testing or lived downwind from it. Many of us have uncles or aunts who worked in uranium mines or factories in which they were exposed to deadly toxins, radiation, or biological weapons. Many of us have brothers or sisters who took part in the Vietnam War, the Gulf War, or the war in Kosovo and now are living with the consequences of Agent Orange, nerve gas, mustard gas, biochemical agents, or uranium-tipped weapons. Many of us have neighbors who worked in agricultural fields touching pesticide-covered crops or in buildings breathing asbestos. We grieve the cancers they now have. We are numbed by that. Some of us, most of us, are numbed into silence.

Some, however, come out of their silence into speech. Think of those who have stood up against injustice and raised their voices in opposition. Think of those who have galvanized an entire community to confront oppression and work for social change. Think of those who have written down their thoughts and ideas, even in the most repressive environments, like prisons, internment camps, boarding schools, plantations, abusive households, and violent relationships. Such acts are inspiring and even transforming. That is why the liberatory voice must be recognized. And celebrated.

Look at this piece of the "I Have a Dream" speech by Martin Luther King, Jr., which has been called the most famous public address of the 20th century. It was given on August 28, 1963. Even in this brief excerpt, you can get a sense of King's power with words. And, if you go to the Internet, you can hear the speech itself (see, e.g., *douglass.speech.nwu.edu* for the speech and notes).

You will then see how those words came to life when he spoke and how he was able to call upon the best in us to work for civil rights. We get an idea, by just this segment:

> I have a dream that one day this nation will rise up and live out the true meaning of its creed: "We hold these truths to be self-evident: that all men are created equal."
>
> I have a dream that one day on the red hills of Georgia the sons of former slaves and the sons of former slave owners will be able to sit down together at a table of brotherhood.
>
> I have a dream that one day even the state of Mississippi, a desert state, sweltering with the heat of injustice and oppression, will be transformed into an oasis of freedom and justice. (Martin Luther King, Jr., "I Have a Dream")

Group Exercise

Discuss the way in which the Crow Indian chief, Curley, voiced his rejection of the government's offer to buy his land. Note how this conveys Curley's belief about the relationship between the land and the people:

> The soil you see is not ordinary soil—it is the dust of the blood, the flesh, and the bones of our ancestors. We fought and bled and died to keep other Indians from taking it, and we fought and bled and died helping the Whites.
>
> You will have to dig down through the surface before you can find nature's earth, as the upper portion is Crow.
>
> The land as it is, is my blood and my dead; it is consecrated; and I do not want to give up any portion of it. (As noted in Vine Deloria, Jr., *God is Red*)

Language and Transformation

As Isabel Allende says, "Writing is an act of hope." Some confront their terrors of what they see—whether it be about the dangers of warfare or technology, the dangers of humans interacting with one another, even in their own homes—and they speak and write. For them, and for all of us, language is a source of strength, a source of inspiration, a vehicle for liberation. It is the liberatory aspect of language that moves us to organize, to effect political change, to address the ills of society, to take one small step to make our voices heard, to inject reason in the face of madness, goodness in the face of evil.

Look at some of the ways language has been used to transform society. For example, Abraham Lincoln changed this country with "The Gettysburg Address." Thich Nhat Hanh has changed people's lives and helped them find spiritual wisdom. Cesar Chavez united the farm workers, a disenfranchised group, and helped them organize to effect political and social change. The Proclamation of the Delano Grape Workers called for an international boycott in 1969. Prominent African-American leader, John S. Rock, issued in 1862 his "Negro Hopes for Emancipation," a call to end slavery. Elizabeth Cady Stanton was a major figure in women gaining the right to vote in this country. And both the Dalai Lama and Eli Wiesel won the Nobel Prize for Peace.

CASE STUDY

The Dalai Lama's Nobel Peace Prize Acceptance Speech

The Dalai Lama, Buddhist monk and spiritual leader of Tibet, is one of the most influential religious figures in the world today. He was forced to flee Tibet as a young man, because of the violent overthrow of Tibet by the Chinese army. The Dalai Lama is now a world citizen, traveling from country to country, raising awareness about the power of nonviolence, the importance of happiness (which, for him, involves justice and social awareness), and working to bring Tibet back into the hands of the Tibetans. His unpretentious manner, humility, and integrity strike both Buddhists and non-Buddhists alike.

Read his acceptance speech for the Nobel Peace Prize of 1989 and make note of what is distinctive about his writing, including any transformative aspects that you see. It may help to read this twice—once silently and once aloud—in order to bring out the different elements—and power—of his writing style.

Nobel Prize Acceptance Speech
His Holiness the Dalai Lama
University Aula, Oslo, 10 December 1989

Your Majesty, Members of the Nobel Committee, Brothers and Sisters.

I am very happy to be here with you today to receive the Nobel Prize for Peace. I feel honored, humbled and deeply moved that you should give this important prize to a simple monk from Tibet. I am no one special. But I believe the prize is a recognition of the true value of altruism, love, compassion and non-violence which I try to practice, in accordance with the teachings of the Buddha and the great sages of India and Tibet.

I accept the prize with profound gratitude on behalf of the oppressed everywhere and for all those who struggle for freedom and work for world peace. I accept it as a tribute to the man who founded the modern tradition of non-violent action for change Mahatma Gandhi, whose life taught and inspired me. And, of course, I accept it on behalf of the six million Tibetan people, my brave countrymen and women inside Tibet, who have suffered and continue to suffer so much. They confront a calculated and systematic strategy aimed at the destruction of their national and cultural identities. The prize reaffirms our conviction that with truth, courage and determination as our weapons, Tibet will be liberated.

No matter what part of the world we come from, we are all basically the same human beings. We all seek happiness and try to avoid suffering. We have the same basic human needs and concerns. All of us human beings want freedom and the right to determine our own destiny as individuals and as peoples. That is human nature. The great changes that are taking place everywhere in the world, from Eastern Europe to Africa are a clear indication of this.

In China the popular movement for democracy was crushed by brutal force in June this year. But I do not believe the demonstrations were in vain, because the spirit of freedom was rekindled among the Chinese people and China cannot escape the impact of this spirit of freedom sweeping many parts of the world. The brave students and their supporters showed the Chinese leadership and the world the human face of that great nation.

Last week a number of Tibetans were once again sentenced to prison terms of up to nineteen years at a mass show trial, possibly intended to frighten the population before today's event. Their only 'crime' was the expression of the widespread desire of Tibetans for the restoration of their beloved country's independence.

The suffering of our people during the past forty years of occupation is well documented. Ours has been a long struggle. We know our cause is just because violence can only breed more violence and suffering. Our struggle must remain non-violent and free of hatred. We are trying to end the suffering of our people, not to inflict suffering upon others.

It is with this in mind that I proposed negotiations between Tibet and China on numerous occasions. In 1987, I made specific proposals in a Five-Point plan for the restoration of peace and human rights in Tibet. This included the conversion of the entire Tibetan plateau into a Zone of Ahimsa, a sanctuary of peace and non-violence where human beings and nature can live in peace and harmony.

Last year, I elaborated on that plan in Strasbourg, at the European Parliament. I believe the ideas I expressed on those occasions are both realistic and reasonable, although they have been criticized by some of my people as being too conciliatory. Unfortunately, China's leaders have not responded positively to the suggestions we

have made, which included important concessions. If this continues, we will be compelled to reconsider our position.

Any relationship between Tibet and China will have to be based on the principle of equality, respect, trust and mutual benefit. It will also have to be based on the principle which the wise rulers of Tibet and of China laid down in a treaty as early as 823 A.D., carved on the pillar which still stands today in front of the Jokhang, Tibet's holiest shrine, in Lhasa, that "Tibetans will live happily in the great land of Tibet, and the Chinese will live happily in the great land of China."

As a Buddhist monk, my concern extends to all members of the human family and, indeed, to all sentient beings who suffer. I believe all suffering is caused by ignorance. People inflict pain on others in the selfish pursuit of their happiness or satisfaction. Yet true happiness comes from a sense of brotherhood and sisterhood. We need to cultivate a universal responsibility for one another and the planet we share. Although I have found my own Buddhist religion helpful in generating love and compassion, even for those we consider our enemies, I am convinced that everyone can develop a good heart and a sense of universal responsibility with or without religion.

With the ever-growing impact of science on our lives, religion and spirituality have a greater role to play reminding us of our humanity. There is no contradiction between the two. Each gives us valuable insights into the other. Both science and the teachings of the Buddha tell us of the fundamental unity of all things. This understanding is crucial if we are to take positive and decisive action on the pressing global concern with the environment.

I believe all religions pursue the same goals, that of cultivating human goodness and bringing happiness to all human beings. Though the means might appear different, the ends are the same.

As we enter the final decade of this century, I am optimistic that the ancient values that have sustained mankind are today reaffirming themselves to prepare us for a kinder, happier twenty-first century.

I pray for all of us, oppressor and friend, that together we succeed in building a better world through human understanding and love, and that in doing so we may reduce the pain and suffering of all sentient beings.

Thank you.

His Holiness, the Dalai Lama

Source: *www.tibet.com/DL/nobelaccept.html.*

Exercises

Here are excerpts from works that have inspired political and religious action. Select one of the passages and read it carefully to see its power and ability to transform lives. Write a brief analysis of the use of language, focusing on one of these issues: (1) how the language is inspiring; (2) how the language could or should be changed to reflect other values or concerns, (3) what the writer seems to assume.

1. **First Passage—Abraham Lincoln's "The Gettysburg Address"**

   Four score and seven years ago our fathers brought forth on this continent a new nation, conceived in liberty and dedicated to the proposition that all men are created equal.

   Now we are engaged in a great civil war, testing whether that nation or any nation so conceived and so dedicated can long endure. We are met on a great battlefield of that war. We have come to dedicate a portion of that field as a final resting place for those who here gave their lives that that nation might live. It is altogether fitting and proper that we should do this.

   But, in a larger sense, we cannot dedicate—we cannot consecrate—we cannot hallow—this ground. The brave men, living and dead, who struggled here have consecrated it far above our poor power to add or detract. The world will little note nor long remember what we say here, but it can never forget what they did here. It is for us, the living, rather, to be dedicated here to the unfinished work which they who fought here have thus far so nobly advanced.

   It is rather for us to be here dedicated to the great task remaining before us— that from these honored dead we take increased devotion to that cause for which they gave the last full measure of devotion; that we here highly resolve that these dead shall not have died in vain; that this nation, under God, shall have a new birth of freedom; and that government of the people, by the people, for the people shall not perish from the earth.

2. **Second Passage—Thich Nhat Hanh from *The Sun My Heart***

   Peace can exist only in the present moment. It is ridiculous to say, "Wait until I finish this, then I will be free to live in peace." What is "this?" A diploma, a job, a house, the payment of a debt? If you think that way, peace will never come. There is always another "this" that will follow the present one. If you are not living in peace at this moment, you will never be able to. If you truly want to be at peace, you must be at peace right now. Otherwise, there is only "the hope of peace some day." . . .

The peace we seek cannot be our personal possession. We need to find an inner peace which makes it possible for us to become one with those who suffer, and to do something to help our brothers and sisters, which is to say, ourselves. I know many young people who are aware of the real situation of the world and who are filled with compassion. They refuse to hide themselves in artificial peace, and they engage in the world in order to change the society.

They know what they want; yet after a period of involvement they become discouraged. Why? It is because they lack deep, inner peace, the kind of peace they can take with them into their life of action. Our strength is in our peace, the peace within us. This peace makes us indestructible. We must have peace while taking care of those we love and those we want to protect.

3. Third Passage—Proclamation of the Delano Grape Workers

We have been farm workers for hundreds of years and pioneers for seven. Mexicans, Filipinos, Africans, and others, our ancestors were among those who founded this land and tamed its natural wilderness. But we are still pilgrims on this land, and we are pioneers who blaze a trail out of the wilderness of hunger and deprivation that we have suffered even as our ancestors did.

We are conscious today of the significance of our present quest. If this road we chart leads to the rights and reforms we demand, if it leads to just wages, humane working conditions, protection from the misuse of pesticides, and to the fundamental right of collective bargaining, if it changes the social order that relegates us to the bottom reaches of society, then in our wake will follow thousands of American farm workers. . . .

Our example will make them free. But if our road does not bring us to victory and social change, it will not be because our direction is mistaken or our resolve too weak, but only because our bodies are mortal and our journey hard. For we are in the midst of a great social movement, and we will not stop struggling 'til we die, or win! . . .

Grapes must remain an unenjoyed luxury for all as long as the barest human needs and basic human rights are still luxuries for farm workers. The grapes grow sweet and heavy on the vines, but they will have to wait while we reach out first for our freedom. The time is ripe for our liberation.

4. Fourth Passage—John S. Rock from "Negro Hopes for Emancipation," 1862 speech before the Massachusetts Anti-Slavery Society

The situation of the black man in this country is far from being an enviable one. Today, our heads are in the lion's mouth, and we must get them out the best way we can. To contend against the government is as difficult as it is to sit in Rome and fight with the pope. It is probable that, if we had the malice of the Anglo-Saxon, we would watch our chances and seize the first opportunity to take our revenge. If we attempted this, the odds would be against us, and the first thing we should know would be—nothing! The most of us are capable of perceiving that the man who spits against the wind spits in his own face!

This nation is mad. In its devoted attachment to the Negro, it has run crazy after him; and now, having caught him, hangs on with a deadly grasp, and says to him, with more earnestness and pathos than Ruth expressed to Naomi, "Where thou goest, I will go; where thou lodgest, I will lodge; thy people shall be my people, and thy God, my God." . . .

This rebellion for slavery means something! Out of it emancipation must spring. I do not agree with those men who see no hope in this war. There is nothing in it but hope. Our cause is onward. As it is with the sun, the clouds often obstruct his vision, but in the end, we find there has been no standing still. It is true the government is but little more antislavery now than it was at the commencement of the war; but while fighting for its own existence, it has been obliged to take slavery by the throat and, sooner or later, must choke her to death.

5. **Fifth Passage—Elizabeth Cady Stanton, "A Slave's Appeal," speech to the New York State Legislature, 1860.**

Now, gentlemen, do you talk to woman of a rude jest or jostle at the polls where noble, virtuous men stand ready to protect her person and her rights, when alone in the darkness and solitude and gloom of night she has trembled on her own threshold awaiting the return of a husband from his midnight revels? . . .

The fairy tale of Beauty and the Beast is far too often realized in life. Gentlemen, such scenes as woman has witnessed at her own fireside where no eye save Omnipotence could pity, no strong arm could help, can never be realized at the polls, never equaled elsewhere this side the bottomless pit. No, woman has not hitherto lived in the clouds surrounded by an atmosphere of purity and peace; but she has been the companion of man in health, in sickness, and in death, in his highest and in his lowest moments. She has worshipped him as a saint and an orator, and pitied him as madman or a fool.

In paradise man and woman were placed together, and so they must ever be. They must sink or rise together. If man is low and wretched and vile, woman cannot escape the contagion, and any atmosphere that is unfit for woman to breathe is not fit for man. Verily, the sins of the fathers shall be visited upon the children to the third or fourth generation.

You, by your unwise legislation, have crippled and dwarfed womanhood by closing to her all honorable and lucrative means of employment, have driven her into the garrets and dens of our cities where she now revenges herself on your innocent sons, sapping the very foundations of national virtue and strength. Alas! For the young men just coming on the stage of action who soon shall fill your vacant places, our future senators, our presidents, the expounders of our constitutional law! Terrible are the penalties we are now suffering for the ages of injustice done to women.

6. **Sixth Passage—Elie Wiesel, Winner of the Nobel Prize for Peace, 1986, in a speech at the White House**

The Perils of Indifference:
Lessons Learned from a Violent Century
Elie Wiesel
White House Symposium, April 12, 1999

Fifty-four years ago to the day, a young Jewish boy from a small town in the Carpathian Mountains woke up, not far from [18th C German romantic poet] Goethe's beloved Weimar, in a place of eternal infamy called Buchenwald. He was finally free, but there was no joy in his heart. He thought there never would be again.

Liberated a day earlier by American soldiers, he remembers their rage at what they saw. And even if he lives to be a very old man, he will always be grateful to them for that rage, and also for their compassion. Though he did not understand their language, their eyes told him what he needed to know—that they, too, would remember, and bear witness.

And now, I stand before you, Mr. President, the Commander-in-Chief of the army that freed me and tens of thousands of others, and I am filled with a profound and abiding gratitude to the American people. Gratitude is a word that I cherish. Gratitude is what defines the humanity of the human being.

Indifference is . . . a strange and unnatural state in which the lines blur between light and darkness, dusk and dawn, crime and punishment, cruelty and compassion, good and evil.

We are on the threshold of a new century, a new millennium. What will the legacy of this vanishing century be? How will it be remembered in the new millennium? Surely it will be judged, and judged severely, in both moral and metaphysical terms. These failures have cast a dark shadow over humanity: two World Wars, countless civil wars, the senseless chain of assassinations—Gandhi, the Kennedys, Martin Luther King, Sadat, Rabin; bloodbaths in Cambodia and Nigeria, India and Pakistan, Ireland and Rwanda, Eritrea and Ethiopia, Sarajevo and Kosovo; the inhumanity in the gulag, and the tragedy of Hiroshima. And, on a different level, of course, Auschwitz and Treblinka.

So much violence, so much indifference.

What is indifference? Etymologically, the word means "no difference." A strange and unnatural state in which the lines blur between light and darkness, dusk and dawn, crime and punishment, cruelty and compassion, good and evil.

What are its courses and inescapable consequences? Is it a philosophy? Is there a philosophy of indifference conceivable? Can one possibly view indifference as a virtue? Is it necessary at times to practice it simply to keep one's sanity, live normally, enjoy a fine meal and a glass of wine, as the world around us experiences harrowing upheavals?

Of course, indifference can be tempting—more than that, seductive. It is so much easier to look away from victims. It is so much easier to avoid such rude interruptions to our work, our dreams, our hopes. It is, after all, awkward, trouble some, to be involved in another person's pain and despair. Yet, for the person who is indifferent, his or her neighbors are of no consequence. And, therefore, their lives are meaningless. Their hidden or even visible anguish is of no interest. Indifference reduces the other to an abstraction.

Over there, behind the black gates of Auschwitz, the most tragic of all prisoners were the "Muselmanner," as they were called. Wrapped in their torn blankets, they would sit or lie on the ground, staring vacantly into space, unaware of who or where they were, strangers to their surroundings. They no longer felt pain, hunger, thirst. They feared nothing. They felt nothing. They were dead and did not know it.

Rooted in our tradition, some of us felt that to be abandoned by humanity then was not the ultimate. We felt that to be abandoned by God was worse than to be punished by Him. Better an unjust God than an indifferent one. For us to be ignored by God was a harsher punishment than to be a victim of His anger. Man can live far from God—not outside God. God is wherever we are. Even in suffering? Even in suffering.

In a way, to be indifferent to that suffering is what makes the human being inhuman. Indifference, after all, is more dangerous than anger and hatred. Anger can at times be creative. One writes a great poem, a great symphony, have done something special for the sake of humanity because one is angry at the injustice that one witnesses. But indifference is never creative. Even hatred at times may elicit a response. You fight it. You denounce it. You disarm it. Indifference elicits no response. Indifference is not a response.

Indifference is not a beginning, it is an end. And, therefore, indifference is always the friend of the enemy, for it benefits the aggressor—never his victim, whose pain is magnified when he or she feels forgotten. The political prisoner in his cell, the hungry children, the homeless refugees—not to respond to their plight, not to relieve their solitude by offering them a spark of hope is to exile them from human memory. And in denying their humanity we betray our own.

Indifference, then, is not only a sin, it is a punishment. And this is one of the most important lessons of this outgoing century's wide-ranging experiments in good and evil.

In the place that I come from, society was composed of three simple categories: the killers, the victims, and the bystanders. During the darkest of times, inside the ghettoes and death camps . . . we felt abandoned, forgotten. All of us did.

And our only miserable consolation was that we believed that Auschwitz and Treblinka were closely guarded secrets; that the leaders of the free world did not know what was going on behind those black gates and barbed wire; that they had no knowledge of the war against the Jews that Hitler's armies and their accomplices waged as part of the war against the Allies.

If they knew, we thought, surely those leaders would have moved heaven and earth to intervene. They would have spoken out with great outrage and conviction. They would have bombed the railways leading to Birkenau, just the railways, just once.

And now we knew, we learned, we discovered that the Pentagon knew, the State Department knew. And the illustrious occupant of the White House then, who was a great leader and I say it with some anguish and pain, because, today is exactly 54 years marking his death—Franklin Delano Roosevelt died on April the 12th, 1945, so he is very much present to me and to us.

No doubt, he was a great leader. He mobilized the American people and the world, going into battle, bringing hundreds and thousands of valiant and brave soldiers in America to fight fascism, to fight dictatorship, to fight Hitler. And so many of the young people fell in battle. And, nevertheless, his image in Jewish history—I must say it—his image in Jewish history is flawed.

The depressing tale of the *St. Louis* is a case in point. Sixty years ago, its human cargo maybe 1,000 Jews—was turned back to Nazi Germany. And that happened after the Kristallnacht, after the first state-sponsored pogrom, with hundreds of Jewish shops destroyed, synagogues burned, thousands of people put in concentration camps. And that ship, which was already on the shores of the United States, was sent back.

I don't understand. Roosevelt was a good man, with a heart. He understood those who needed help. Why didn't he allow these refugees to disembark? A thousand people—in America, a great country, the greatest democracy, the most generous of all new nations in modern history. What happened? I don't understand. Why the indifference, on the highest level, to the suffering of the victims?

But then, there were human beings who were sensitive to our tragedy. Those non-Jews, those Christians, that we called the "Righteous Gentiles," whose selfless acts of heroism saved the honor of their faith. Why were they so few? Why was there a greater effort to save 55 murderers after the war than to save their victims during the war?

Why did some of America's largest corporations continue to do business with Hitler's Germany until 1942? It has been suggested, and it was documented, that the Wehrmacht could not have conducted its invasion of France without oil obtained from American sources. How is one to explain their indifference?

And yet, my friends, good things have also happened in this traumatic century: the defeat of Nazism, the collapse of communism, the rebirth of Israel on its ancestral soil, the demise of apartheid, Israel's peace treaty with Egypt, the peace accord in Ireland. And let us remember the meeting, filled with drama and emotion, between Rabin and Arafat that you, Mr. President, convened in this very place. I was here and I will never forget it. And then, of course, the joint decision of the United States and NATO to intervene in Kosovo and save those victims, those refugees, those who were uprooted by a man whom I believe that because of his crimes, should be charged with crimes against humanity. But this time, the world was not silent. This time, we do respond. This time, we intervene.

Does it mean that we have learned from the past? Does it mean that society has changed? Has the human being become less indifferent and more human? Have we really learned from our experiences? Are we less insensitive to the plight of victims of ethnic cleansing and other forms of injustices in places near and far? Is today's justified intervention in Kosovo . . . a lasting warning that never again will the deportation, the terrorization of children and their parents be allowed anywhere in the world? Will it discourage other dictators in other lands to do the same?

What about the children? Oh, we see them on television, we read about them in the papers, and we do so with a broken heart. Their fate is always the most tragic, inevitably. When adults wage war, children perish. We see their faces, their eyes. Do we hear their pleas? Do we feel their pain, their agony? Every minute one of them dies of disease, violence, famine. Some of them—so many of them—would be saved. . . .

I'd like to tell you a story. The story is [about] how to fight indifference; really [the best way] is to assume it and to take it as something that belongs to me, and for me to deal with it.

The story is that, once upon a time, there was an emperor, and the emperor heard that in his empire there was a man, a wise man with occult powers. He had all the powers in the world. He knew when the wind was blowing what messages it would carry from one country to another. He read the clouds and he realized that the clouds had a design. He knew the meaning of that design.

He heard the birds. He understood the language of the birds; the chirping of the birds carried messages. And then he heard there was a man who also knew how to read another person's mind. I want to see him, said the emperor. They found him. They brought him to the emperor. Is it true that you know how to read the clouds? Yes, Majesty. Is it true you know the language of the birds? Yes, Majesty. What about the wind? Yes, I know. Okay, says the emperor. I have in my hands behind my back a bird. Tell me, is it alive or not?

And the wise man was so afraid that whatever he would say would be a tragedy, that if he were to say that the bird is alive, the emperor, in spite, would kill it. So he looked at the emperor for a long time, smiled, and said, Majesty, the answer is in your hands.

It is always in our hands.

And so, once again, I think of the young Jewish boy from the Carpathian Mountains. He has accompanied the old man I have become throughout these years of quest and struggle. And together we walk towards the new millennium, carried by profound fear and extraordinary hope.

I conclude on that.

Reprinted with the permission of Elie Wiesel.

CHAPTER FOUR

Fallacies, Fallacies: Steering Clear of Argumentative Quicksand

So that was Mrs. Lundegaard in there? I guess that was your accomplice in the wood chipper. And those three people in Brainerd. And for what? For a little bit of money. There's more to life than money, you know. Don't you know that? And here ya are, and it's a beautiful day. Well. I just don't unnerstand it.

—Marge,
From *Fargo*

There are many errors in reasoning that we come across. One special kind, called a *fallacy,* is especially important for us to study. Fallacies are not only pervasive; they often convince people to positions that are not supported by the evidence. In other words, a fallacy is a deceptive or misleading argument that may persuade us, but is nevertheless unsound. Upon careful scrutiny, we can see that fallacies should not be given credence. Sometimes we catch ourselves slipping into a fallacy—hopefully before it's too late.

Let's see how this happens. In a summer 2001 letter to the editor of *Tricycle: The Buddhist Review,* Melissa Chianta writes: "When I broke up with my first boyfriend in college, I told a friend, 'He bastardizes Eastern religions to suit his own emotional limitations.' . . . I realized that ten years later I have done the same thing!"

This awareness of one's own bad reasoning could be seen as the flipside of the "ah-ha" effect when we finally get it (= mental breakthrough). Catching ourselves in a fallacy is the "uh-oh" effect (= mental sinkhole). With the tools of this chapter, hopefully you'll be able to catch yourself before plunging into a sinkhole of bad reasoning!

Every fallacy contains a fundamental flaw in reasoning. The flaws can take any number of forms and may involve structural or linguistic errors, mistaken assumptions, or premises that are irrelevant to the conclusion stated. Fallacies could employ appeals to flawed statistical studies, the irrelevant testimony of a famous person, threats, patriotism, personal attacks, and so on. We will look at the major forms of fallacies in this chapter, so we can avoid making such errors in our own thinking and be able to defend ourselves against falling for such arguments made by others.

Have you ever seen an ad that rests on a play of words? Have you ever felt manipulated, but couldn't pinpoint why? You may have been a victim of fallacious reasoning. Fallacies tend to fall into particular forms or patterns and it is this form or pattern that gives the fallacy its name. Whatever form they take and no matter how persuasive they are, fallacies are always incorrect. They are always unsound arguments, either because the truth of the premises simply fails to guarantee the truth of the conclusion or because the premises are not true.

Watch the reasoning in this conversation:

HEATHER: Euthanasia is killing and, since it is wrong to kill, euthanasia must be wrong.

LEO: You're just a woman, what could you possibly know about euthanasia? Stick to the kitchen!

HEATHER: Why should I listen to you—you are a member of the National Rifle Association, you'd certainly be biased!

LEO: Get off it! Hey, did you hear about Ruben? He bought a sports car! Man, either you drive the best or you are a dud.

HEATHER: That's the truth! And if you don't drive a great car then you cannot meet interesting people. And then you will not have any kind of social life. Pretty soon, you'll be sitting home staring at the ceiling, your entire life rotting away in front of your eyes!

LEO: Sure thing, Heather. Hey, there's my bus. Catch you later!

Fallacy Busters.   First Leo dismisses Heather's argument without considering her reasons. The fact Heather's a woman (irrelevant in this case) was enough to dismiss her. Her reply is just as bad, because she points to his membership in a group to discredit him. Leo, then, switches the topic to their friend's new car, adding the "either/or" comment. Since there are more options than the two stated, he commits another fallacy. Then, Heather replies with another fallacy called a slippery slope, where she argues that not owning a car will doom you to a dreary life.

There are four major kinds of fallacies: fallacies of relevance, fallacies of presumption, fallacies of ambiguity, and formal fallacies. We'll start with an overview and then look at each fallacy.

Fallacies of Relevance.   In these fallacies the premises simply fail to support the conclusion; they are beside the point. *For example:* "Mickey Mouse loves Camembert cheese; therefore you should buy some today!"

Fallacies of Presumption.   In these fallacies the argument depends upon an unwarranted assumption causing the fallacy. *For example:* "Either you know Harry

Overview of the Fallacies

Fallacies of relevance are invalid and unsound because the premises are simply irrelevant to the conclusion being drawn.

Fallacies of presumption are invalid and unsound because of unfounded or unsupportable assumptions underlying them.

Fallacies of ambiguity are invalid and unsound because of unclear and confusing use of words, grammar, or sentence structure leading to an incorrect conclusion being drawn.

Formal fallacies are invalid and unsound because the very form or structure of the argument leads to an incorrect conclusion being drawn.

Fallacies of Relevance

- Ad hominem
- Ad hominem circumstantial
- Tu quo
- Ad populum
- Ad verecundiam
- Ad baculum
- Ad misericordiam
- Ad ignorantiam

Fallacies of Presumption

- Accident
- Hasty generalization
- Biased statistics
- Bifurcation
- Complex question
- Post hoc
- Red herring
- Slippery slope
- Straw man
- Begging the question

Linguistic Fallacies
(Fallacies of Ambiguity)

- Equivocation
- Accent
- Amphiboly
- Composition
- Division

Formal Fallacies (See Chapter 16)

- Fallacy of affirming the consequent
- Fallacy of denying the antecedent

Potter or you are a cultural toad. With 110 million Harry Potter books in print worldwide, published in 47 languages, there's no excuse for being a cultural toad. Therefore, you better get reading one of the Harry Potter books."

Fallacies of Ambiguity (also Known as Linguistic Fallacies). These fallacies center on the use of language in terms of emphasis, interpretation, sentence structure, or the relationship between the parts and the whole. This ambiguity results in an incorrect conclusion being drawn, causing the fallacy. *For example:* "Popeye is a fun guy and so is Olive Oyl. They should get married—together they'd be a dynamite couple!"

Formal Fallacies. These fallacies occur because of a structural error. As a result, the very form of the reasoning is incorrect. The truth of the premises will never guarantee the truth of the conclusion in a formal fallacy. *For example:* "If Wimpy eats one more hamburger, he will have to take a nap. Wimpy had to nap. Consequently, Wimpy must have eaten one more hamburger."

▦ Introduction to the Fallacies of Relevance

Fallacies of relevance rest on evidence that's beside the point and, thus, irrelevant. There is always a glaring gap between the premises and the conclusion drawn in a fallacy of relevance. For instance, you might be persuaded to hand over your shoes if George G. Geezil threatens you, but that doesn't make the threat a <u>good reason</u> for surrendering your shoes to Geezil.

The key is what counts as a good reason, not what counts as <u>persuasive</u>. A good reason is something that offers solid evidence for holding a position.

Examples of Fallacy Busters

We should see a direct connection between that evidence and the conclusion. If not, something is wrong. Let's look at some cases.

First Case:

RAY: Carl Johnson would make a great mayor: He's been active in government for 15 years. He has helped people get back on their feet. Plus, he has been instrumental in transforming the downtown so that it's not a haven for drugs.

LUCILLE: Don't you know he is gay? Would you vote for a gay man for mayor? Surely you are kidding!

Fallacy Busters.   You probably saw this one. Reasons are offered for voting for Johnson for mayor, but they are not dealt with. Instead, Johnson is discredited because of a personal characteristic. Lucille needs to explain why sexual orientation is a relevant consideration for mayor. The candidate is dismissed without getting a fair hearing.

Second Case:

ANNIE: Mommy, why do I have to go to bed? It is only seven o'clock and I am not at all sleepy. Can't I read for a while?

MOMMY: I'll tell you why you have to go to bed. If you do not go to bed right now I'll paddle your behind with a wooden spoon. Get moving!

Fallacy Busters.   Mommy threatens Annie—she did not give her a good reason, such as the need for sleep. The mother's reasoning is not acceptable from the standpoint of good thinking. She should try to persuade with evidence, not threats.

Third Case:

Even though Mr. Weiss is dishonest, he should be store manager, because he has six children, his wife left him and his last employer is suing him. Give that man a break!

Fallacy Busters.   Why does Mr. Weiss deserve a good job? Presumably, he is dishonest and his last employer is suing him (Because of that dishonesty? We don't know). We might feel pity for Mr. Weiss and perhaps even ought to refer him to counseling or social services. But that is a separate matter from hiring him. What if the job demands high-level skills that he lacks? What if the job involves handling important documents? Sympathy should not cloud our reasoning. That does not mean there is nothing to be done. In fact, seeing people suffer should prod us to act on their behalf. This need not entail giving the person a particular job.

Fourth Case:

DR. BERKOWITZ: Students, be honest throughout your entire academic career since it will make you an honorable person.

YU ZHAN: How can you say that, Dr. Berkowitz, when you plagiarized your master's thesis? Why should I pay attention to the advice of a cheater?

Fallacy Busters.   Here Dr. Berkowitz offered a reason for being honest, but he is dismissed for not "practicing what he preaches." We might justifiably expect someone to act on the standards by which they judge others. The unwillingness to do so points to a moral weakness, but does not mean that their <u>reasoning</u> is flawed. Whether or not the speaker lives in accordance with those reasons (the premises) is a separate issue from the argument at hand.

Key Fallacies of Relevance

By becoming familiar with the fallacies, we'll be able to spot incorrect reasoning in ourselves and in others and, hopefully, stop ourselves from falling into any fallacious thinking.

1. Argumentum Ad Hominem

This fallacy occurs when, instead of dealing with the issue at hand, there is a personal attack or an attempt to discredit someone. The personal attack aims at the individual, zeroing in on a characteristic—like age, weight, height, gender, race, class, nationality, sexual orientation—that is difficult, if not impossible, to change. Nevertheless, that very characteristic is treated as sufficient to negate the person's testimony or position.

Examples of Ad Hominem:
   a. PETE: *The death penalty is savage and has no place in a civilized society.*
      LUIS: *How would you know? You only went to high school.*
   b. KIM: *El Burrito is the best Mexican restaurant in Norwalk. They use the freshest ingredients and make their own tortillas. Everything I've eaten there is delicious.*

> ARTHUR: *Okay, but since you're Japanese you are hardly an expert on Mexican food! Why take your advice?*
>
> c. *Jackson's maid said she had reason to think he was not acting properly with the young boys who visited him, but, hey, she's only a maid. We'd be ill advised to listen to what she has to say.*

2. Argumentum Ad Hominem Circumstantial

This fallacy occurs when, instead of dealing with the reasons for accepting a particular conclusion, there is an attempt to discredit a speaker because of a religious, political, or social affiliation (such as a member of a group, club, or organization).

> *Examples of Ad Hominem Circumstantial:*
> a. PETE: *Physician-assisted suicide and has no place in a civilized society.*
>   MAX: *Oh yeah, how would you have anything to say on this, when you a member of the Hemlock Society and they are known for favoring a right to kill yourself?*
> b. *Of course he opposes rent control. He is a member of Condo Owners of America, isn't he?*
> c. *Rosalind suggested Mother Theresa as an example of a heroic woman in the 20th century, since Mother Theresa has done so much for the poor people in India. But Rosalind is a Catholic; she would clearly be biased.*

This fallacy differs from ad hominem since the person is discredited by virtue of their membership in a particular group or organization, not because of some uniquely <u>personal</u> trait. People generally choose to join a group, but have little if any choice over such personal traits as race, gender, class, or age.

3. Tu Quo (or Tu Quoque—"You're Another One")

This fallacy occurs when there's an attempt to discredit someone because their actions are not in keeping with their words or they don't "practice what they preach." Even if the one setting out an argument appears to be a hypocrite—his or her own actions are contrary to what is being argued—it doesn't mean the argument is flawed. We are all fallible. Some of us fail to take our own good advice. Study the evidence when assessing reasoning. For instance, the fact that a woman with emphysema smokes until her last gasp doesn't negate the validity of the argument that smoking can kill you.

> *Examples of Tu Quo:*
> a. BOB: *Hey LaShanta, you really should stop eating so much chocolate— it causes dreadful skin problems, it is linked to breast cancer and is physiologically addictive.*
>   LASHANTA: *What nerve! You've been eating chocolate since you were four—who are you to tell me to stop?*

   b. MARIA: *Will you please slow down, Richard? You're driving 20 miles over the speed limit, which is dangerous in the rain. I'm scared!*
      RICHARD: *I don't have to listen to you. You got a speeding ticket last month. Point your finger at me and it points right back at you!*
   c. *How can he tell me to exercise, when all he does is sit behind a desk?*

4. Argumentum Ad Populum (Appeal to the Masses)

This fallacy occurs when there is an attempt to persuade on the basis of popular appeal, mass sentiment, or patriotism, rather than giving good reasons to accept the conclusion. "Snob appeal" would be included here.

   Examples of Ad Populum:
   a. *Thousands of college students protested the bombing of Afghanistan—perhaps you ought to rethink your support of the administration on this.*
   b. *Be Cool! Smoke cigars! All the cool people do!*
   c. *What's wrong with you? Forget getting a Nissan. Support your country and buy an American car.*

Note how we are asked to get behind our country, be a member of the crowd, or join the bandwagon. The pressure here is to fall in line, not dissent. It is important, though, to seek good reasons for a call to conformity, rather than merely acquiescing. Blind obedience is not a sign of higher intelligence.

5. Argumentum Ad Vericundiam (Appeal to Authority)

This fallacy occurs when, instead of drawing upon solid evidence, a famous person or celebrity is cited in order to get a conclusion accepted. What makes it a fallacy is that the authority cited is not a credible expert in the area. Thus, it is expected that we'll be persuaded by the endorsement, rather than good reasons for the conclusion.

   Examples of Ad Verecundiam:
   a. *Einstein loved to play the violin so should you!*
   b. *Michael Jordan thinks Nike makes the best shoes. Buy some today.*
   c. *John Lennon opposed the Vietnam War. Therefore, it must have been a big mistake.*

The center of the fallacy is that the "expert" cited, however talented otherwise, is not a credible source for the topic under discussion. We may agree with the celebrity's product choice or their endorsement. But agreement is not enough—we need good reasons for the argument to be strong.

Note: Expert testimony does have its place, however. But the person cited must be an expert in the field under dispute. In some cases we should use more than one source or "expert" whenever there is some difference of opinion about the fundamental facts or topic. For instance, there is disagreement on the cause and transmission of AIDS, the medical benefits of marijuana, or concerns about strategies for computer privacy.

6. *Argumentum Ad Baculum (Appeal to Force or Coercion)*

This fallacy occurs when there is the use of force, the threat of force, or coercion in order to get a conclusion accepted. This includes verbal or sexual harassment, blackmail, extortion, and threat of violence used to "persuade" someone to a position. A variation is bribery, where the coercion comes in the form of a promise, offer, money, or position that motivates with a combination of desire (to have something) and fear (that the opportunity will pass if we turn down the bribe).

> *Examples of Ad Baculum:*
> a. PETE: *I believe the death penalty to be savage and it has no place in a civilized society.*
>   CHUCK: *Well if you don't vote in favor of it in the coming election, I will tell your parents you keep whiskey in your locker.*
> b. MR. SWARTHMORE: *Barbara, I would like you to come discuss your job promotion with me tonight. Meet me at my hotel and wear some sexy lingerie! Give a little and you'll get something back.*
> c. NURSE KRATCHIT: *Good to see you back on the ward, Dr. Hernandez. I hear you've called the press about the screw up last week in the emergency room. Please keep a lid on this. You know I could tell the media about that nasty medical malpractice case you had last year?*

In these cases, there is a threat of physical force (the most blatant), an implied threat (coercion), fear of loss (bribery, extortion) or harassment (sexual, verbal).

7. *Argumentum Ad Misericordiam (Appeal to Pity)*

This fallacy occurs when there is an irrelevant appeal to pity or a set of sorrowful circumstances in order to get a conclusion accepted. A sympathetic response may be called for when knowing of someone's personal difficulties. But that does not, in itself, substitute for good reasons that directly support a conclusion.

> *Examples of Ad Misericordiam:*
> a. *He should be a senator, given his history—his wife ran off with Judge Thornton, his grandmother died of sausage poisoning, and his children are all in gangs.*
> b. *Dr. Gonzales, I deserve an A in Logic. My boyfriend married my cousin, Alice, and the transmission went out on my car. My life is a mess! I deserve an A for my pain.*
> c. *Please officer, don't cite me for drunk driving. I know it's my second time in two years, but my parents will put me in a rehab program and my social life will be ruined.*

The sad tales may be relevant to a call for help or advice, but are not relevant reasons to be senator, to get an A in a class, to get a job, or to avoid a DUI charge. In some cases, as in affirmative action or preferential treatment programs, it may be legitimate to take into consideration factors beyond bare qualifications (like SAT scores or grades). It may be justified to factor for such hardships as poverty or discrimination. Legitimate attempts to provide a balance could be seen in terms of justice, not pity.

Generosity born of pity may be the correct moral response in a particular situation. Yet we must weigh it carefully, so that we not fall into a fallacy of ad misericordiam.

8. *Argumentum Ad Ignorantiam (Appeal to Ignorance)*

This fallacy occurs when it is argued that something is the case (either true or false) simply because you cannot prove otherwise. This is the "if you can't prove me wrong, then I must be right!" defense.

Examples of Ad Ignorantiam:
   a. *This house is haunted. You cannot prove it's not haunted, so it must be the case!*
   b. *My physics professor is an alcoholic—unless you have evidence that I'm wrong, I must be right!*
   c. *Belief in reincarnation is unwarranted, since no one can definitively demonstrate that the soul can enter another body and come back on earth.*

What is happening in all of these examples is that the person argues on the basis of a lack of proof to the contrary. However, a failure to disprove something does not mean the opposite is true. The fact that you cannot prove your brother is not dreaming of Sedna, the sea goddess, does not prove that he *is* dreaming about her. And when it comes to legal matters, a *presumption* of innocence is quite different than *proof* of innocence.

Exercises

Part One

Directions: Discuss the reasoning below.

Who Uses Creatine?
Some estimate that 75% of the Denver Broncos and 60% of all major league baseball players use Creatine: including Brady Anderson and Mark McGwire (and you keep hearing that the *ball* is juiced). Bodybuilders around the world are making use of the most effective sports supplement with no proven negative side effects (provided you do not abuse it). (See *www.powersupplements.com/creatine.htm*)

Part Two

Directions: Name the fallacy of relevance in the examples below. If you forget the name, describe what is happening in the argument: look for the pattern and the name may become apparent.

1. I heard that Nicholas Cage ate a live cockroach in *The Vampire's Kiss,* so it must be okay.

2. Smith's ketchup is all-American! Buy some!

3. Keith said it's smart to drive at a safe speed and be polite to other drivers. However, I see no reason to follow his advice, since he drives like a race car driver and has no qualms about cutting off other drivers. Who is he to talk?

4. Hundreds of people saw lights flashing on a wall and they declared it a miracle and a sign of the Virgin Mary. Scientists cannot explain the strange phenomenon. No one has been able to prove that it's not a sign of the Blessed Virgin, so it must be!

5. CARRIE: Angelica said that people should not use ivory, because so many elephants are killed and that's wrong.
   LEN: Don't you realize she's a member of Latinas United and couldn't possibly know anything about African elephants!

6. Most women think men who recite poetry are romantic. Therefore, if Angelo wants to impress his girlfriend, Mandy, he'd better start reciting poetry.

7. Movie star Jackie Chan says martial arts keep him in shape. Maybe your parents should sign up for lessons—they are getting a tad flabby!

8. Richard Alton Harris was beaten as a fetus and is a victim of fetal alcohol syndrome. Therefore, he should not have been convicted for the murder of those two teenagers.

9. Any law-abiding citizen stands behind the country in a time of war. Therefore, it was immoral of your Uncle Ted to register as a conscientious objector during the Gulf War. He should be ashamed of himself!

10. Hey Dr. Garry, I deserve an A on this exam. If you do not give me one, I will follow you home and feed moldy food to your guinea pigs. I'll give your shoes to your dog, Blue, so he can chew them to shreds. Tell me, will you give me the A or not?

11. I hear you have been raising questions about the government's response to the terrorist attacks. That's really disgusting. Don't you know the president's popular support was over 80 percent in the week after the attacks? You should take a cold, hard look at your lack of patriotism, because right now you appear to be spineless. I highly suggest you get behind the war effort.

12. George Washington said cutting down trees was good for building up your biceps. So why don't we all go cut down some trees this weekend?

13. Since no one has proven exorcism is not effective, we should call in a priest to examine Carrie. She needs help!

14 Dr. Johnson, I hope you can arrange to get an organ donor for my infant son. If you drag your heels, I'll make sure your wife knows about your affair with that cute nurse in ObGyn last year!

15. Charley Spengler, shortstop for the Redding Ravens, says chewing snuff is bad for your health and rots your teeth. Like we should pay attention to what he has to say? He has been chewing snuff since he made it to the minor league.

16. URSULA: Jack, you should vote for Proposition 112—there are so many reasons it will help the homeless.

    JACK: Really? How would you know? You're from Sweden.

17. Angelina Jolie wears a vial of Billy Bob's blood around her neck. Why don't all women show their love for their husbands in this manner? Get with it!

18. The pharmaceutical sales rep said we should not drink Screech, that alcoholic home brew the McGregors made. She said it is a disgusting habit and Screech is a probable cause of liver cancer. But her advice is questionable, given the alcohol I smelled on her breath.

19. You should be pretty skeptical about anything Oliver says about reproductive rights. He's active in the Defenders of the Unborn and you know what an extreme group they are!

20. MARIO: Angela, honey, what's this frozen chicken breast doing on the table instead of dinner?

    ANGELA: Mario, you big lug, if you don't get helping with dinner I'll toss the entire contents of the fridge out on the front lawn! I've had it! So, I suggest you change your ways, starting today.

21. How can you doubt the importance of drinking Paw Paw Spritzer, when you have the testimony of the famous singing group, the Rubber Bands, to vouch for it being good?

22. Don't believe everything Mario says about Angela. He's Italian—you know how those Latin men tend to exaggerate. They can't be trusted to tell the truth.

23. Bill Clinton deserves a break. He had a really hard time after they tried to impeach him, plus everyone got mad at him over those pardons right before the end of his presidency. I bet his wife wasn't too happy with him, especially given his previous problems with the Monica Lewinsky scandal. Then he was in Europe during the terrorist attacks, so had a hard time getting a plane home. He's had his share of problems.

24. Senator Feinstein supports the Identity Theft Protection Act intended to set down restrictions so access to personal information is made more difficult.

But Senator Feinstein cannot prove for certain that this act is really going to change anything, so it must not be any good. She sure blew it supporting that act!

25. Did you hear that two-thirds of American children and teens have read at least one Harry Potter book? I can't understand why your cousin, Bosco, isn't crazy about Harry Potter too. He should get with it.

26. It isn't wise of you to trust just any stockbroker, given the potential for bias. I know for a fact that your stockbroker, Alan Greenspine, is a Democrat. It'll be a cold day in Hades when a Democrat can figure out the stock market. You ought to change your stockbroker today. Give me a call and I'll get you the phone number of mine—she's a Republican and that gal knows her money.

27. Tennis great Andre Agassi deserved to win at Wimbledon. I hear he and Stefie Graff just had a baby and he was distracted by the coming event. Plus, he hardly slept and was probably too exhausted to be at his best. There should be a rematch!

28. Hey Ralph, you should fix my car. If you don't, I will tell your wife about those photos you took of your neighbor, Alicia, when she was sunbathing in her backyard.

29. The universe must be infinite, since no one has proven it is finite.

30. I'm not sure President Bush is seeing very clearly when it comes to the energy crisis. First off, he's worked for the oil industry. Second, he's from Texas, and they've got cheap gas there in that state. Don't count on him to help those of us paying over $2.00 a gallon for gas.

Part Three: Quick Quiz on Fallacies of Relevance

1. What fallacy occurs when, instead of giving reasons for accepting a conclusion, someone is asked to give sexual favors in exchange for a job or salary raise?

2. What fallacy occurs when an advertiser uses snob appeal, such as suggesting that eating their mustard will make us feel like we own a Rolls Royce?

3. What fallacy occurs when someone makes an irrelevant appeal to a recent disaster as a reason for getting a job, raise, or better grade?

4. What fallacy occurs when someone argues that something must be true because you can't prove it is false (or vice versa)?

5. What fallacy occurs when someone argues that a position should not be accepted, even if good reasons are offered, simply because the speaker does not follow his or her own advice and the speaker's actions suggest hypocrisy?

6. What fallacy occurs when someone is discredited solely on the grounds of a characteristic like race, age, or gender?

7. What fallacy occurs when someone tries to bribe another person?

8. What fallacy occurs when someone argues for a position solely on the basis of patriotism?

9. What fallacy occurs when someone is being discredited because of a political, religious or social affiliation?

10. What fallacy occurs when an argument rests on the irrelevant testimony of a famous person, like a movie star or athlete?

Fallacies of Presumption

We have all fallen victim to unwarranted assumptions. People make unwarranted assumptions all the time. Some of the major ways this occurs have been categorized and named, as we will see. What makes fallacies of presumption unsound arguments is that they all contain an unstated assumption that, being erroneous, causes the argument to sink. For example, what if your friend assumed that having her lucky stone in her pocket was the cause of her passing her physics final? It may have made her feel more confident than if she'd left her stone at home, but her success is more likely due to her having studied for the last two weeks before the exam.

Fallacy Busters.   See if you can spot any shady reasoning in this conversation:

KEN: Hey! What's happening? Are you coming to the rally with me? Either you're with us or you're against us!

BERNIE: I'm with you, Ken; you know that! Have you always been a dupe?

KEN: Watch it there pal. Things have been going good for me lately. How about you? Wait, what is that I see? What's that hundred-dollar bill sticking out of your pocket?

BERNIE: Oh, Ken, you have an interesting T-shirt on. I like the idea of Tweetie Bird chasing Godzilla! What a hoot! Where do you find such things?

Did you notice all the unwarranted assumptions? In the first case, Ken sets up a false "either/or" choice. In the second case, Bernie asks Ken a loaded question, where he cannot answer either *yes* or *no* without implicating himself. In the third case, when Ken asks about the $100 dollar bill, Bernie switches the topic, trying not to be caught red-handed. In all of these fallacies, an unwarranted assumption leads the argument to an incorrect conclusion being drawn.

Key Fallacies of Presumption

These fallacies are like magic tricks: so long as we do not stop to think about the arguments, they look good. But they are never to be trusted. In each case the unwarranted assumption, once uncovered, reveals how weak is the argument. There are 10 key fallacies of presumption that we will look at below.

1. Accident

This occurs when a general rule or principle is applied to a special case in which, by reason of its special or atypical characteristics, the rule simply does not apply. This fallacy might be a misapplication of a moral principle, a rule from work, or a general pronouncement made by a family member or friend.

The unwarranted assumption is that the rule applies to all cases, without exception. But most rules and principles simply fail to apply across the board and so there are exceptions that make the rule inapplicable. The fallacy of accident occurs when this is not recognized.

Examples of Accident:
    a. The Bible says, "Thou shalt not kill," so it is wrong to kill in self-defense.
    b. My minister said to always tell the truth. Therefore, I should tell my Uncle Bob he has stomach cancer!
    c. "Be sure to return what you borrow," that's what my father said. As a result, I should return the axe I borrowed from my roommate, even though she's been threatening the UPS deliveryman.

In each of the examples the general rule does not apply. We do consider some killing to be acceptable, including self-defense. Ordinarily we do believe in honesty, but not without exception. Uncle Bob may not want to discuss his medical diagnosis with you. And we would not likely want to return an axe to a murderous roommate. We need to watch for unwarranted assumptions in applying rules and principles. Otherwise, we may commit the fallacy of accident.

2. Hasty Generalization

This occurs when a generalization or moral principle is drawn on the basis of too small a sample or an atypical case. Stereotypes and other poor inferences have been drawn about entire groups of people on the basis of either too little information or a group that is not representative. Hasty generalization often occurs because the sample size is too small. Therefore, the inference drawn is an incorrect generalization.

Examples of Hasty Generalization:
    a. Inez Garcia ran through five red lights taking her sick baby to the hospital last night. Therefore, we should all be able to run red lights whenever we want.
    b. Nick ate an egg roll he bought at a street fair in Seattle. He got sick as a dog. That just goes to show you—never buy any food at a street fair!
    c. Rob dated three women who were in a sorority, and they were airheads. Therefore, all sorority women are airheads.

Here we see the two different types of hasty generalization. In the first one, the generalization was the rule ("We should be able to run red lights whenever we please"). But it is based on a special case (an exception) where it is permissible. In the other cases, the inference was an observation about the population under discussion (food at street fairs, sorority women). The conclusion rests on a sample that is too small—hardly a convincing study. People draw conclusions and make recommendations on the basis of atypical or inadequate samples all the time. So we must be attentive. Check that no unwarranted assumptions have been made.

3. Biased Statistics

This fallacy occurs when an inference is drawn on the basis of a sample that is not diverse enough. That is, the sample is not representative of the target population. We see this in studies that exclude a certain age group, gender, ethnic group, and so on—and yet draw a generalization to a population which includes the omitted group.

> *Examples of Biased Statistics:*
> a. *Cyber Digital did a study of teenage boys in Detroit and found that 45 percent of them like computer games. Therefore, 45 percent of all Americans like computer games.*
> b. *Ninety-five percent of toddlers prefer a bottle of warm milk at bedtime. Therefore, 95 percent of all children prefer a bottle of warm milk at bedtime.*
> c. *A poll of KTBT FM found that 67 percent of community college students have a commute over at least 10 miles from home. Therefore, 67 percent of all students have a commute of at least 10 miles from home.*

In all of these cases, there is a shift from the sample population to the target population. That is the way to spot a case of biased statistics. Compare the sample group (teenage boys, toddlers, community college students) to the targeted population (Americans, children, students) to determine if it is sufficiently representative.

In the examples here, the samples are not diverse enough to support the generalizations drawn. It is not a question of size, as with hasty generalization. Here the issue is <u>diversity</u>. When it comes to sample studies, there are key factors to consider, such as race or ethnicity, class, gender, age, educational level, geography, religion. Depending on the focus of the study, some factors may be more instrumental than others in being able to infer to the targeted group.

4. Bifurcation (Also Known as "False Dichotomy" or "Excluded Middle")

This fallacy involves the presentation of an "either/or" situation when, in fact, there are more than two options. This occurs when a division of opposites is presented as complete and absolute (i.e., uncompromising contrasts). This omits what lies between the two extremes, creating the problem. For example, after the United States started bombing Afghanistan in reaction to the terrorist attacks, Osama bin Laden reportedly said: "These events have divided the whole world into two sides: the side of the believers and the side of the infidels" (CNN, 7 Oct. 2001).

Examples of Bifurcation:
   a. *New Hampshire state motto: Live Free or Die.*
   b. *If you don't know Bob Dylan, your knowledge of music is inadequate.*
   c. *"There is a great temperamental and ideological divide between those who believe in self-defense and those who believe in surrendering and begging for mercy" (Dr. William L. Pierce).*
   d. *America: Love It or Leave It.*
   e. *If you're not for freedom, you're for terrorism.*
   f. *From* The Good, the Bad, and the Ugly *(see www.imdb.com):*
      • *"There are 2 kinds of people in the world, my friend: Those with a rope around the neck, and the people who have the job of cutting." (Tuco Benedicto Juan Ramirez aka "the Rat")*
      • *"There are 2 types of spurs: Those who come in by the door, and those who come in by the window." (Tuco Benedicto Juan Ramirez aka "the Rat")*
      • *"You see, in this world there's 2 kinds of people: Those with loaded guns and those who dig. You dig." (Blondie)*

Not all "either/or" dilemmas are fallacious. For instance, either you are pregnant or you are not. Either you have a heartbeat or you do not (assuming you haven't had an artificial heart transplant!). Either you are deathly allergic to peanuts or you're not. Do not assume that someone who says, "It's either this, or it's that" is right. Check for other options.

5. Complex Question

This fallacy is in the form of a question in which two questions are rolled into one. The answer to the hidden, unasked question is assumed, thereby creating the fallacy.

Examples of Complex Question:
   a. *Do you usually eat garbage for breakfast?*
   b. *Aren't your friends worth your best chocolate?*
   c. *Have you always been a liar and cheat?*
   d. *Tell me, is celibacy the only way to find happiness?*

In all of the above, we have two questions, not one. Separate the two and examine them. For instance, we might ask if our friends even eat chocolate, before determining if they're worth the best chocolate.

At times, it may be an intentional attempt to trap the listener in a complex, incriminating question (like an ambush). Legislative bodies try to address complex question. Whenever anyone detected the fallacy of complex question, they would move to "divide the question." The question would then be divided up into two questions, removing the unwarranted assumption. For example:

The current process for the consideration of the "Account Allocations for the Next Fiscal Year" bill considers the budgets divided out and then the remaining budgets, and

WHEREAS: This forces representatives from many organizations whose budget recommendations are not contentious to wait through the separate considerations of the more contentious budgets, and . . .

4.13.3 After the author of the legislation has read the legislation for the second reading, the Chair shall ask the Senate if there are any motions to "Divide the Question" (Senate Bill 2001-2-031y, Government of the Student Body, Iowa State University, 26 Sep. 2001, *www.gsb.iastate.edu/legislative/bills/2001-2-031Y.htm*)

Here the student Senate Bill is trying to avert problems when uncontentious budgets are tied together with contentious ones—by separating them each budget is considered on its own terms.

6. Post Hoc (or Post Hoc Ergo Propter Hoc— "After This Therefore Because of This")

This fallacy asserts a causal connection that rests on something happening earlier in time. The fallacy goes like this: Because something precedes something else means that it must then cause the later thing to happen. No evidence given to support such a causal link. Any connection might be coincidental. It would be unwarranted to assume a causal connection.

For example, scientist Dr. Peter H. Duesberg came to believe that AIDS researchers had fallen into a causal fallacy in contending that the HIV virus is the *cause* of AIDS. This, Duesberg argued, was mistaken. He claims that HIV is the effect, not the cause of AIDS and sets out a detailed argument on virology to make his case (see "HIV Is Not the Cause of AIDS," at *www.duesberg.com/ch2.html*).

Examples of Post Hoc:
a. *Whenever the team is on a winning streak, Coach Sanders wears the same tie to each game. The Salmon Bellies won the last three games, so Coach Sanders' lucky tie must be working!*
b. *Alma's diet sure was amazing. She took OPS diet tablets every morning and then had a cup of coffee and a grapefruit for breakfast, a head of lettuce for lunch (no dressing!) and 6 ounces of cottage cheese for dinner. In two weeks she'd lost 12 pounds! Those OPS diet tabs really work miracles!*
c. *Paul had bacon and eggs and three pancakes for breakfast. Then he took the SAT exam. He scored in the top 20%. I am so proud of him. That just goes to show you: A good, hardy breakfast was the reason he did so well. Everyone should eat a big meal before an exam!*

In all of the above, the prior event is considered the cause simply because it happened earlier in time. But just because it occurs earlier (e.g., picking a certain color tie, eating diet tablets, having a hardy breakfast) does not necessarily mean it's the cause of some event (the team winning, losing weight, doing well on the exam). The connection needs to be established.

We also see post hoc arguments when people base their reasoning on "bad omens" or attributing success to a lucky charm or a ritual. Be careful. We don't have to give up mythology or religion to be critical thinkers. But examine arguments carefully, watching for assumptions and omissions.

Exercises

Directions: Name the fallacy of presumption below. draw from: accident, hasty generalization, biased statistics, bifurcation, complex question, and post hoc.

1. What tool did you use to pry open the window of the lab?
2. A poll was taken of 2000 yacht owners. Of the yacht owners, 79 percent of them said that the economy is doing just great and they will have an easy time when they retire. Consequently, 79 percent of all citizens think the economy is doing just great and they'll have an easy retirement.
3. The Bureau of Fish and Game released nine California condors into the wild. The next week the rain started coming down in buckets! That just goes to show you, the American Indians were right—the condor really *is* a bearer of rain. Those birds caused all this flooding!
4. At a conference on animal rights, two panelists said animal experimentation violates the rights of sentient beings. We can conclude that philosophers in general oppose animal experimentation because of the rights of sentient beings.
5. People should always stand up for their beliefs. Therefore, it's commendable that young people in Turkey are dying from hunger strikes to protest the conditions of Turkish prisons.
6. If we don't require a writing exit exam for college students, we might as well kiss off all our standards around a quality education.
7. Donna dated a law student she met in Ann Arbor. They went to see *Memento* and he fell asleep! That goes to show you—if you're dating a law student, you should forget about late-night movies.
8. Basically you've got these two choices: join the Army or work on the farm until you can save money for college.
9. A poll taken of women who watch CNN news found that 83 percent opposed expanding the "War on Terrorism" to Iraq, Iran, and North Korea. This suggests that only 17 percent of Americans are behind the Bush administration's war expansion plans.
10. Where did you hide the LSD you stole from the lab?
11. The policy of the Alaska Moose Bed and Breakfast is that guests must take off their shoes before entering. That means your 90 year old grandmother better not try to sneak it with those fancy shoes of hers on her feet. A rule's a rule.

12. Either we should relocate the toxic waste dump to Southern Nevada or we'll have to convince the taxpayers that we need a satellite station to send hazardous substances to outer space.

13. Have you always been a wild man?

14. Either you are for freedom—or you're for the terrorists!

15. In a TV poll of 700 Latino males, it was discovered that they prefer flan to fudge brownies for dessert. Therefore, all men prefer flan to fudge brownies for dessert.

16. Have you always been so dull-witted when it comes to mathematical equations?

17. Maria came into a nice sum of money lately, if you can believe that! You know, I think it's because she's been using Feng Shui, putting her apartment in spiritual order. She put a large pile of in the North corner of her living room. They say that's supposed to help bring good energy to your work life. It sure must have worked! I think you should try Feng Shui, too. Maybe you can improve your finances.

18. Either you believe money paves the road to happiness or you won't be sufficiently motivated to change the world.

19. Do you realize 97 percent of the 240 participants at the interfaith meeting said that prayer can bring world peace? That suggests that 97 percent of religious people think we can bring about world peace with prayer.

20. Kant was right to put honesty at the center of his moral theory. That means you are obligated to tell that phone solicitor your social security number and the list of people to whom you are financially indebted.

More Fallacies of Presumption

7. Red Herring

This fallacy occurs when an irrelevant line of reasoning is intentionally used to divert people away from the topic at hand. We see this when someone purposely shifts the subject of the conversation to avoid an incriminating line of questioning or to deceive someone. It's called a red herring, because a stinking little herring (fish) is an effective way to lead the hound dogs off the scent.

Examples of Red Herring:
   a. DR. TRAN: *Excuse me, Jeremiah, what's that answer sheet I see you peeking at during this exam?*

JEREMIAH: *Oh Dr. Tran, I heard that you got invited to speak at the American Philosophical Association meeting. What an honor, I am sure you must be totally thrilled. And of course, everyone knows what a brilliant mind you have.*

b. AMY: *Honey, what's this love letter from your secretary that I found in your pocket?*

MIKE: *Oh sugar, my sweet pea, you have made the most delicious pot roast I ever ate in my life—what ingredients did you put into this heavenly gravy? And how did you make such tender green beans to accompany this feast?*

c. JOURNALIST: *Mr. President, what do you have to say to the American people about the rising unemployment in this country?*

PRESIDENT: *You know, we must think positive: during my term in office, inflation has stayed constant and I have helped keep drugs off the streets!*

Most of us have seen red herring fallacies. People often jump around topics: Some families regularly communicate by going from one topic to the next and back to the first. But what marks a red herring is that the change of topic is done with the intent to deceive and divert attention from one thing to another.

8. Slippery Slope

In this case, an argument is made against something on the basis that, if it is allowed, it will lead to something worse which, in turn, leads to something even worse and so on (down the slippery slope). Behind this reasoning is the unstated assumption that the first in the causal chain leads to the second and that leads to the third, and so on.

An example of the slippery slope fallacy is in a full-page ad put out by R. J. Reynolds Tobacco Company that presents a series of questions: "Some politicians want to ban cigarettes. Will alcohol be next? Will caffeine be next? Will high-fat foods be next? Today it's cigarettes. Tomorrow?" The fallacy is that banning tobacco would not necessarily lead to bans on other substances. We would need to show that such bans would follow. The connection should not be assumed.

Examples of Slippery Slope:

a. *I tell you, Bert, if we support the legalization of marijuana, next thing it will be the legalization of cocaine and then heroin and pretty soon the whole society will be on hard drugs. So don't support legalizing marijuana.*

b. ANN MARIE: *I'm in favor of strict rules against cheating on exams.*

YOLANDA: *You are? If you punish students for cheating on exams, that will lead to punishing them for misquoting authors on essays, which, in turn, will lead to punishing them for spelling errors and finally punishing them because of one typo! It is clear that there should be no university policy against cheating!*

c. *My son tells me he would like to get a few rabbits as pets. But I will not allow it. If we start with a few rabbits, soon we will have hundreds of them everywhere and all our money will be spent on rabbit feed. Then he will want to get other animals too. I am not going to sacrifice my life savings for him to run a zoo.*

We can find an example of a slippery slope in a speech on gun control. William L. Pierce on a 1994 radio program *American Dissident Voices* argued as follows:

> The present campaign to disarm Americans will not abate. Neither the controlled media nor the government will back away from a goal of total disarmament of the civilian population. They won't reach this goal in a single step, but they'll continue taking steps until they do reach it.
>
> The target now is semi-automatic rifles. Later it will be all semi-automatic pistols. Then it will be other types of handguns. After that it will be all firearms which hold more than three cartridges. "That's all a sportsman really needs," they'll say. Then it will be all firearms except muzzle-loaders. Somewhere along the line, various types of ammunition will be banned. "Only a criminal would want a cartridge like this," they'll say. Before too many steps have been taken there will be compulsory registration of all firearms and firearm owners, in order to facilitate confiscation later.

The argument is that a negative chain of events will follow from something being put into effect. There is no attempt to prove that one situation actually does lead to the next one or that situation to an even worse one. Rather, the connection is incorrectly assumed and not proven. Many have been victims of parental slippery slopes. This occurs, for instance, when your parents say you can't stay out late because something bad will happen and that, in turn, will lead to something even worse and that worse thing will lead to something truly horrific. Down, down, down the slippery slope!

Note: Not all propositions that involve causal chains are slippery slopes. If it is demonstrated that situation A leads to situation B and so on, they are *not* committing slippery slope. The fallacy occurs when the chain is asserted, but not proven.

9. Straw Man Fallacy

This fallacy occurs when an opponent's position is presented as so extreme that it's indefensible. We are then steered toward another, more moderate or appealing, position, which is offered as the alternative. The image of the "straw man" (scare crow) is that of something so flimsy that it will go up in smoke if we put a match near it.

We saw the straw man fallacy in the 1994 California election when Tom Umberg, the Democratic candidate for attorney general, attacked Dan Lundgren, the Republican incumbent. He suggested that Polly Klaas, 12 years old, would not have been murdered if Lundgren had financed a computer tracking system for convicts. By painting his opponent in such an extreme manner linking Lundgren's position with Polly Klaas getting murdered, Umberg fell into a straw man fallacy.

Examples of Straw Man:
   a. *Don't even think about his position. Opposing the death penalty means letting criminals walk away from crimes scot-free and giving them the green light to murder anyone they choose!*
   b. *Students these days object to being searched for drugs. We must realize, however, that if we don't search them, then students will be peddling drugs at school and drug abuse will be rampant.*
   c. *Those animal rights people make me sick. If they get their way, medical advances in this country will come to a grinding halt.*
   d. *Two men I met at the racquetball court thought the proposal for a ban on pornography was a stupid idea; that it'd mean magazines or movies showing any bare skin at all would be censored! Sorry, but I don't want to live in a puritanical society—do you?*

With the straw man fallacy, the opposition is painted as much more extreme than it actually is. What usually happens is that the speaker's own position is offered as the preferred, reasonable alternative.

10. Begging the Question (Petitio Principii)

This fallacy consists of circular reasoning, whereby the speaker assumes what she or he is trying to prove. The conclusion is drawn on the basis of evidence containing a restatement of the conclusion itself. Because of this repetition, it is called begging the question. This fallacy has other names; for example Judge Aldisert in his book *Logic for Lawyers,* calls the begging the question fallacy, "Pulling the Bunny out of the Hat!"

Examples of Petitio Principii (Begging the Question):
   a. *People should get paid for studying for logic exams, because human beings deserve a salary for studying logic.*
   b. *Mahatma Gandhi must have been an honest person, because he would never lie to anyone.*
   c. *The belief in God is universal because everybody believes in God.*

The message here is this: Don't assume what you are trying to prove. What is concluded must come out of the premises and not be a restatement of them. A rehash is just that. The evidence must provide good reasons for drawing the conclusion. If the premises and conclusion say basically the same thing, we're facing a fallacy of begging the question.

Question-Begging Epithets.   One of the variations of begging the question rests on the use of highly slanted language. Here, biased language stacks the deck with language that is slanted in one direction or another. The result is that it is difficult to stay focused on the issue. Question-begging epithets are either a euphemism or a dyslogism (name-calling)—biased in a very positive (praiseworthy) way or biased in a highly negative (critical) way in terms of descriptions of people or situations. (See Chapter 3 on language.)

Can You Spot the Fallacies?

GEORGE: Hey Julio, what's up?

JULIO: Either you've got a potato for a head or you've heard the news, George! I got a part in the new film, *Temple Impossible*! You know, it's starring I.C. of the band *The Blind Mice*! I.C. says guys who lift weights are more likely to succeed, so I just bought a membership at Joe's Gym! You should join, too, you know! If you don't build up your biceps, girls won't find you attractive, and then you'll just be sitting around picking the dust mites out of your ears every evening! Join that gym today.

GEORGE: Have you always had menudo for brains? I joined a gym last November, you pie-head! If you don't pay more attention to what's going on in my life, I'll let the air out of your tires and we'll see how far you can drive in that new Mazda of yours! If you want to be with it, man, you'd not just join a gym, you'd consider taking steroids to pump up those muscles a little faster. Randy Smutts, who is trying out for the Olympics, used steroids for years! He's a monster!

JULIO: You know, that's not a bad idea, but I wouldn't listen to what Randy says. You know he's a member of the Harley Bikers Club. Plus, you know he's German—that's where Nazis came from! What a loser!

GEORGE: My mama said to never tell a lie. So I have to tell you, Julio, your new toupee looks like a possum! You really ought to just go for the glow. Forget the toupee—either you live free or you die!

JULIO: You know, my pint-sized friend, I heard two chicks on the subway say they prefer possum-heads to bald eagles! That just goes to show you, women like hairy men!

GEORGE: Don't sound like that pea-brain guy I saw on TV the other night who was discussing the psychology of baldness—he couldn't tie his shoelaces if you paid him. I take it you think you need hair to be all-American. Abraham Lincoln had a beard, so why don't you?

JULIO: Ho ho. Maybe I should get a beard, so I can get a monument dedicated to me! By the way, what's this I hear about you getting caught speeding last night? Got a ticket, did you?

GEORGE: Uh, urk. Hey, Julio, I heard you got that big award last week at work. What was that for anyway, Employee of the Week or something? You are something, man!

JULIO: Yeah, I should have gotten Employee of the Year. I deserve it. Not only did I spend my life savings on lottery tickets; that cousin of mine took my pet iguana and sold it at the flea market in Tijuana!!

GEORGE: Poor you. Well, gotta go, man. Catch you.

JULIO: Later to you too! Adios.

Question-begging epithets are all around us. For instance, suppose you called a man a "leech on society" instead of "a man burdened with misfortune" or "someone down on his luck." Your listeners could be swayed so strongly by the negative label ("leech on society") that they may unfairly and incorrectly infer that he is guilty of a crime. Similarly, to talk about a defendant with glowing terms, as a saintly, loyal citizen, makes it hard to examine the evidence without being prejudiced. In that sense, question-begging epithets have set down the groundwork for prejudging the case at hand.

Examples of Question-Begging Epithets (Euphemisms):
   a. *You should believe whatever our legislators say about patriotism, because they are hard-working American citizens, with an appreciation of the greatness of this country's history.*
   b. *Grandma Juarez definitely has good advice on tax reform, since she is a veteran of World War II and drives the Meals on Wheels bus.*

Examples of Question-Begging Epithets (Dyslogisms/Name-Calling):
   a. *Don't believe what those students say about philosophers, they are just a bunch of mealy-mouthed, pea-brained, two-bit hustlers, with no sense of the demands of the intellectual life.*
   b. *Don't listen to Professor Stewart's ideas for rebuilding the downtown core—he's an atheist and he once pleaded guilty to a cocaine possession charge! He's a bit too slimy for words!*

The fallacy here centers on the use of language. The language used in the argument has either a negative or positive bias (that is why it is called "loaded"). This prejudicial slanting makes it hard to be objective in examining the evidence and suggests a relevance that doesn't exist.

Exercises

Part One

Name the fallacy, drawing from *all* the fallacies of presumption.

1. Only those who have seen a moose can claim to know the wilderness. Visit Alaska today!

2. Do you always steal from your friends?

3. Most people prefer tortillas to bagels. A fall 2001 poll of Latinas at the National Educators Conference in Cincinnati, Ohio, found that nearly 87 percent considered tortillas superior to bagels for most cooking needs.

4. The Constitution guarantees freedom of speech. Therefore, people should have the freedom to post pornography on high school websites.

5. Winona Ryder should not be found guilty of shoplifting. She is a sweet person who is kind to others and made a real contribution to humanity by her fine performance in *Girl Interrupted*.

6. All you fine citizens of Philadelphia know this one truth: you must choose between security and freedom. Though you may be inclined toward freedom, don't forsake your security by outlawing assault rifles.

7. The college has a no-alcohol policy. Therefore, you probably won't be allowed to bring your rum-ball candies to the dance after the Super Bowl.

8. Professor Dingman was on her way to discuss her new film script with her agent when a meteorite shower pelted her car with marble-sized rocks.

The agent loved her script, so that meteorite shower must have been a sign of good fortune.

9. Assemblywoman Snyder said the journalist who photographed her throwing popcorn in the polar bear compound at the zoo is just a pathetic little mealyworm with nothing better to do than to cause trouble for respected politicians.

10. CHONG: I deserve an A, Professor Garry.
    DR. GARRY: I'm not sure why you say this, Chong. Clue me in.
    CHONG: My work warrants the highest grade a student can get, that's why.

11. My grandma said never tell a lie. That means I should tell the new high school principal that she needs to go on a diet. That woman has a serious weight problem—I'm going to give her a few ideas on how to knock off some of that flab of hers!

12. Either you think *The Simpsons* is the most insightful social commentary today or you are simply missing out on the best philosophy going.

13. "You're a scaremonger," Stossel scolded genetic engineering critic Jeremy Rifkin, "Why should we listen to you?" (See *Fairness and Accuracy in Reporting*, 17 July 2001)

14. Christina, if you keep drinking orange juice for breakfast, you'll get too much acid in your system. Too much acid means an ulcer can't be far behind and, next thing you know, you've destroyed your stomach lining! You'd be advised to cut back on that orange juice you've been guzzling.

15. How could a tax-paying citizen like Robert Downey ever mean to violate his probation? He is innocent.

16. We ought to oppose gun control. Gun control means a police state is around the corner.

17. If you don't like fried chicken and popovers, you won't want to live in Kentucky. *either you like or don't go Kent.*

18. Silvio says he loves me and he must be telling the truth, because he would never lie to someone he loves.

19. George Sanders is a nincompoop, so don't vote for him for governor.

20. It's obvious that men overwhelmingly prefer naps to exercise, because a 2002 poll found 93 percent of male patients at nursing homes said they'd much rather nap than exercise.

21. Alma Warner has been concerned about the increasing number of abortions in this country. Be careful about voting for her for governor. A vote for her is a vote for the mentality of those who bomb abortion clinics!

22. Airport security to Jennie's parents: "To ensure tight security at the Detroit airport so air travel is safe from terrorists, it is vital that every 10th person ready to board a plane is searched. Rules are rules. Therefore, we have to search your three-year old daughter, Jennie. Please have her step right over here!"

23. North Korea is thinking of building its nuclear arsenal, because they believe they need more high-tech weapons that have a nuclear capacity.

24. For the kick-off dinner for the Pre-Law Club they served moussaka from the Greek restaurant that recently opened on the Sunset Strip. It was so awful: It was too salty, the eggplant tasted like rubber, and there was hardly any meat in it. It just goes to show you, you can't depend on Greek food if you want a nice dinner.

25. Mike Milken couldn't possibly be guilty of financial wrongdoing. You know how nice he is to the people in his neighborhood and he regularly gives money to charity.

26. Dr. Meek said not to sleep with your newborn infant. He said if you take the baby to bed with you when she cries, it will lead to an abnormal relationship with her parents and then her sexual development will be totally unnatural. You certainly don't want that! So just pat her back when she cries.

27. Smitty Watkins would be good as mayor, since he'd be great as the top city official.

28. PROFESSOR: Pardon me, Reinaldo. Exactly, what are these test notes doing here in the exam?
    REINALDO: Oh, Professor Davidson, did I ever tell you how much I like your ties? You manage to find such colorful ties! Where do you shop?

29. If you let the little girl have a stick of gum, then she'll want gum every day and pretty soon she'll start swallowing it. Once she starts swallowing gum, her intestines will get all clogged up and she will have dreadful health problems. Don't give that child chewing gum.

30. Only if you have heard Pablo Neruda's poetry read in Spanish, can you call yourself worldly.

Part Two: Quick Quiz on Fallacies of Presumption

1. What is hasty generalization?
2. What happens in a post hoc fallacy? Explain and give an example.
3. Explain the fallacy of accident.
4. What happens in a red herring?
5. Explain why the slippery slope is aptly named.
6. How does hasty generalization differ from biased statistics?
7. What's an example of a complex question?
8. Why is bifurcation a fallacy?
9. Explain how we can spot question-begging epithets.
10. What makes a fallacy a straw man?

Part Three

1. Discuss whether or not Senator Hatch committed a fallacy (state your reasons why/why not):

   Raising the Minimum Wage Causes "Disemployment"
   [Some people] believe that an increase in the minimum wage is a quick, painless way to help the disadvantaged in our society. I can only wonder then why they have not offered raising the minimum wage to $15, $20, or $30 an hour. There is indeed an adverse effect on employment. For every 10 percent increase in the minimum wage, the disemployment effect was between 100,000 to 300,000 jobs. Disemployment means jobs not only eliminated, but also jobs that are never created in the first place. (See Senator Orin Hatch, *www.issues2000.org*)

2. Discuss Richard Doerflinger's comment about experiments to clone human embryos:

   They're really raising the stakes here," said Richard Doerflinger of the National Conference of Catholic Bishops, which opposes federal support for any kind of embryo research. "In two days, it's amazing we've had two announcements of drops down the slippery slope. We don't think there's a stopping point once you start down this road." (As noted by Rick Weiss, "Firm Aims to Clone Embryos for Stem Cells," *Washington Post*, 12 July 2001)

3. Can you spot the fallacies?

   The average person is afraid of snakes—which should make you think twice about getting a snake for a pet. A study was done of herpetologists—those scientists who study snakes. Of the herpetologists in the study, 74 percent thought snakes do not make good pets, given the way most owners treat them. Therefore, 74 percent of humanity would say don't have a snake for a pet! Are you always this suicidal anyway? Snakes are vicious, especially those cobras you keep admiring!

   My cousin, Ralph, had a pet cobra once and it ate some moldy banana bread that he left on the counter and the stupid cobra was dead! Ralph said that his life went downhill after that: He lost his job, his wallet was stolen while he was in line for a movie, and he started drinking again. I'm sure that cobra dying was the cause of it—talk about a curse! Plus, I hear snakes get the spooks and can attack you without warning.

   Most people think snakes are creepy, anyway. That's another good reason not to get a snake! When that many people agree on something, there must be truth to it.

   And don't forget, if you get a snake your Dad will kick you out of the house! Forget it! Besides, you are basically a good person, so you should have a good pet! I know Richard said you should get a snake; that they are intelligent and excellent exterminators of rats and mice—but you should know by now that his advice isn't any good. He's from the Arctic, where there are no snakes!

   Get a cat or dog instead of a snake. I heard Keanu Reeves has a cat and he seems happy enough. And Elvis didn't sing about hound dogs for nothing! In addition, if you get a snake you could pick up some tropical disease and then you could become sterile or get a weird disease like malaria. Next thing you know it, you've lost a leg from gangrene or an infection! That's the last thing you need. Forget snakes!

▨ Key Fallacies of Ambiguity

You pick up a magazine and read, "Prince Philip underwent surgery in a London hospital for a hernia. After being discharged, he warned that wild pandas face extinction within 30 years" (*Auckland Sunday Star,* as noted by *The New Yorker*). This is funny because of the juxtaposition of the report on his surgery and his warning about wild pandas.

Basically, this is a structural issue—as are all cases when two very different topics are juxtaposed, creating a confusing or humorous effect. You've just been hit with a linguistic fallacy. Fallacies of ambiguity, also known as linguistic fallacies, are so named because of an unclear sentence structure, grammar, or use of words. The result of the ambiguity is that an incorrect conclusion is drawn. Let's look at the different types of fallacies of ambiguity.

There are five main fallacies of ambiguity, with the flawed reasoning related to confusions created by such things as shifting meanings of words, misleading emphasis of a word or phrase, unclear sentence structure, or mistaken inferences from parts to wholes, or vice versa. Let's look at these types of fallacies.

1. *Equivocation*

This fallacy occurs when two or more different meanings of a single word or phrase are used in the same context. The resulting ambiguity leads to an incorrect conclusion being drawn. This is also known as a *semantic* fallacy. We often see equivocation in puns and jokes.

For example, in the Wit Women cartoon, a woman is telling her counselor that her alien mate is moaning for more space. The joke rests, like most puns, on the shifting meaning of a word. In the alien's case, "space" may mean more space to move around (like a bigger room), or it may mean outer space (like a different planet!). The equivocation on the word "space" is what makes the cartoon funny. (See Figure 4-1.)

A special kind of equivocation has to do with "relative terms"—which have different meanings in different contexts (like "tall" or "big" or "small"). We also see equivocation playing on the sound of a word, for example, "How do you make antifreeze? Steal her blanket." The word "antifreeze" sounds like "Auntie freeze," thus the joke.

Examples of Equivocation:
  a. *Ad for Lasik eye surgery:* You really *won't believe your eyes.*
  b. *Ad for movie* Cats and Dogs: **Critics are Lapping up the #1 Movie! Two paws up!**
  c. *Article on Luxurious bedrooms:* "Suite Dreams"
  d. *Line in weather report in the Boston Globe:* "Boston Baked Beings"

FIGURE 4-1

Examples of Equivocation Humor:

a. *Two lovers who had been apart for some time were reunited on a foggy day. One whispered to the other "I mist you" (playing on mist/missed).*

b. *The cheap eye surgeon was always cutting* corneas *(playing on corneas/ corners).*

c. *Two vultures boarded an airplane, each carrying two dead raccoons. The stewardess looked at them and said, "I'm sorry, gentlemen, only* one carrion *per passenger is allowed" (playing on carrion/carry on).*

d. *A chicken crossing the road is* poultry *in motion (playing on poultry/ poetry).*

e. *A group of chess enthusiasts checked into a hotel and were standing in the lobby discussing their recent tournament victories. After about an hour, the manager came out of the office and asked them to disperse. "But why?" they asked as they moved off. "Because," he said, "I can't stand chess nuts boasting in an open foyer." (playing on chess nuts/ chestnuts and foyer/fire).*

Lady Killer

Among many young women, smoking is viewed as stylish.
It is not. Smoking is deadly.
If you smoke, please consider stopping. For help, information and support,
please contact your local American Cancer Society.

AMERICAN
CANCER
SOCIETY®

GIVE SMOKING
A KICK IN THE BUTT.

With every puff, your health could be going up in smoke.
If you'd like to kick the habit but you need help, call your local
American Cancer Society.
It could be the first step to quitting for life.

AMERICAN
CANCER
SOCIETY

FIGURE 4-2

Can you spot the equivocation in these three ads?

Thanks
For
Making
Us Best
Pop Duo.

2. Accent

This fallacy occurs when, because of the way a word or phrase is visually or verbally emphasized, we are led to drawing an incorrect conclusion. This includes the repetition of a word or phrase to create a certain effect that leads to an incorrect conclusion. Think, for example, of ads where the word "Free" is accented but, in tiny print, we are told what we have to do or buy to get the freebie. Another way the fallacy of accent occurs is when someone misquotes someone or takes something out of context. When quoting someone, be careful that the quote represents the author's thought and intent. Taking material out of context can be very problematic, and even ludicrous at times.

Examples of Accent: emphasizing the word FREE=accent

a. FREE BOX OF CHOCOLATES *whenever you buy $200 worth of merchandise.*

b. *From* Weekly World News, *August 14, 2001:* **AMAZING DOG SPARKS RELIGIOUS REVIVAL** . . . *by walking 16 miles to church every Sunday!*

c. FLY TO FRANCE FOR $100—*not counting tax, surcharges, fuel fees, and miscellaneous charges.*

An example of misleading repetition is found in a Pillsbury ad once used for Hungry Jack Biscuits. The ad copy reads:

*Hello **Honey**! Introducing Hungry Jack **Honey** Tastin' Biscuits. Warm your family's heart with the golden flavor of **honey**. New Hungry Jack Biscuits have the same tender, flaky layers that Hungry Jack Biscuits are famous for, with a touch of **honey** flavor baked right in. Try our Hungry Jack Biscuits today and treat your family to the taste of **honey**. (Emphasis added)*

The word "honey" is repeated five times in the advertisement, leading us to think these biscuits contain honey. However, only if you looked at the bottom of the page and read the writing on the pictured container would you see this: Hungry Jack Artificial Honey Flavor Flaky Biscuits. Note the word "Artificial," which indicates that the impression that honey was in the biscuits was unfounded.

3. Amphiboly

This fallacy occurs because of an ambiguity created by the use of grammar or sentence structure. This is also known as a fallacy of *syntax*. Think of an amphibian—a creature that can live in two entirely different environments. The fallacy of amphiboly occurs when the sentence structure is confusing, leading to an incorrect conclusion being drawn. For example, "Soon after Sam and Ella got married they experienced food poisoning." Because of the odd sentence structure, it sounds like Sam and Ella's food poisoning was caused by their marriage!

Sometimes amphiboly results from two nouns preceding the verb or two nouns with an unclear reference afterward (as in "Baby George walked toward grandpa, his diaper falling to his knees"). Sometimes the fallacy results from a missing verb phrase—as in this twist on an example by Irving Copi, "Firefighters often burn victims." If the sentence structure seems awkward or funny, check for amphiboly.

Examples of Amphiboly:
a. *Title of article about Superior Court Judge, William R. Nevitt Jr. in the Daily Journal: "Former Helicopter Pilot Lands on Bench."*
b. *Marx Brothers line: I shot an elephant in my pajamas. (How he got in my pajamas, I'll never know.)*
c. *(Noted in the* Farmer's Almanac): *The concert held in the Fellowship Hall was a great success. Special thanks are due to the minister's daughter, who labored the whole evening at the piano, which as usual fell upon her.*

4. Composition

This fallacy occurs when it is inferred from what is true of the parts or members of something that it is true of the whole thing (or organization). The fact that something is true of the members or parts of something does not mean that it will be true of the whole. For example, there could be a football team where every member is a great athlete, but they do not work well as a team. Similarly, great musicians might jam together, but be unable to produce great music.

Examples of Composition:
a. *Mariah Carey, Madonna, and Sinead O'Connor are all great singers. I bet they'd be a dynamite girl group.*
b. *Since each and every one of us must die, that means the human race must one day come to an end.*
c. *Raspberries are in season and I just made some delicious chicken dumplings. Therefore, we should put those raspberries on top of our chicken dumplings—yum!*

5. Division

This fallacy occurs when we infer that what is true of a whole or organization is also true of its parts or members. This is the opposite of composition. There we went from what was true of each and every part and then argued it must be true of the whole. The fallacy of division occurs when it is argued that simply because something is true of a whole (or an organization) that it will necessarily follow that each part or member has that characteristic too. But this is fallacious.

The fact that the Edmonton Oilers were great in 2001 doesn't mean each player on the team was great that year. And even though the Boston Pops orchestra was in top form in 2000, the lead oboe player and first violin were not necessarily in top form that year. And even though Bob's fudge brownies were delicious, the eggs and baking powder he used may not have been delicious. What is true of the whole will not automatically be true of the parts or members. And it is a mistake to think so. Look at the reasoning of Bart Simpson in the TV show *The Simpsons*: "Uh, mam, what if you're a really good person but you're in a really bad fight and your leg gets gangrene and has to be amputated. Will it be waiting for you in heaven?"

Examples of Division:
  a. *The school board is inefficient. So, don't expect Irene Chan, the president of the school board, to do a good job.*
  b. *Housing prices have been on the increase for the last 10 years. This means we ought to be able to get a great price for our house if we put it on the market.*
  c. *The American Mathematical Society is highly regarded as an organization. Therefore, Dr. Pi, a founding member, must be held in high regard.*

Exercises

Part One: Can you spot the fallacies?

Zumaro and Mike were on their way to Oaxaca to buy a Huichol yarn painting when they ran out of gas. As the car died, it groaned and rattled. Zumaro and Mike were not happy about this turn of events. Let's listen in on their conversation:

ZUMARO: Mike, I can't believe we ran out of gas. Most people think to check their gas tank before a journey—why didn't you? (Tears in her eyes.)

MIKE: Please don't snarl at me, Zummie!! You don't know anything about cars, what woman does—so I don't have to listen to you nitpick my brain! (Wipes his forehead and kicks a tire.)

ZUMARO: If you knew about cars, you would have handled the situation Mike! Why can't you be like those guys in *Fast and Furious?* I heard one of the actors in the crowd scene say it pays to keep your car in good condition and he should know, watching all that action in the movie! (She blows her nose.)

MIKE: Sure, and why not throw your Dad at me too? Want a donut? (He whips out a nice strawberry jelly and hands it to her.)

ZUMARO: Yum! I love a man who knows a donut!! Have you always been so wonderful? Well, let's figure this out: We both took critical thinking! Either we get gas for the car right away or we could be mugged.

MIKE: I hope not, sugar lump. I don't deserve to have that happen to me. And I don't deserve to run out of gas either. Do you realize that I flunked the final for my Death and the Afterlife class? Plus, I bounced three checks last week, and my boss caught me taking an hour for my coffee break. I just have had it so bad lately! I deserve a break!

ZUMARO: Well I think you are the greatest, my honey bunch! Either I stay with you or I'm an idiot! (Looks into the donut box.)

MIKE: What can I say? (Hands her another donut, a chocolate glaze). These donuts are so greasy they could do a lube job! I love these little grease ball treats!!

ZUMARO: Hey, you know I ate five donuts last night before bedtime and you know what I dreamed last night? I had this nightmare that we'd have bad luck today. Can you believe it? That just goes to show you, donuts before bedtime cause prophetic dreams! I should eat them every night!

MIKE: Are donuts going to your brain, sugar pea? Prophecies or no prophecies— if you eat too many donuts, you'll get a liver glut from all the grease. Anyone with a liver glut is on the road to getting jaundice. Therefore, eating too many donuts is going to destroy your liver!!

ZUMARO: Pooh! I heard three guys at Powell's Bookstore talking about how people who eat a lot of donuts have more meaningful relationships. Those guys were wearing University of Illinois sweatshirts, so we should put some stock in what they have to say! (Reaches for yet another donut, a cinnamon swirl.)

MIKE: Ho! You can't prove that donuts make your life any better, so it must be false. Enough already! Hey, Zum, there's a tow truck!! Let's flag him down and get out of here!

The end.

Part Two

Directions: Name the fallacy of ambiguity below.

1. Restaurant ad: "Our omelettes are eggceptional!"

2. Airline ticket office sign: "WE TAKE YOUR BAGS AND SEND THEM IN ALL DIRECTIONS."

3. **GET AN EASY A IN LOGIC** provided that you study hard, get good grades on everything and participate a lot.

4. I know you didn't want to do a nude scene, Maricella. But if you get modest on me now, you can forget about trying out for the part of Rosa in the sequel to *Silence of the Sheep*. You decide, my fair one!

5. A discussion of beautiful women cited Angelina Jolie (best lips), Julia Roberts (best smile), Andie McDowell (best hair), Drew Barrymore (best eyes), and Janet Jackson (best midriff). Can you imagine how beautiful the woman would be if she had all these traits?

6. The White House is not nearly as large as you'd think, given all of its functions. Therefore, the Oval Office inside the White House must not be very large either.

7. From Peanuts Classics comic strip: "The name of the other team was Devil's Advocate. They always win," he said. "I hate to play Devil's Advocate."

8. Ad copy for the Boston Medical Professional Corporation:

SEX FOR LIFE!

ERECTION PROBLEMS? PREMATURE EJACULATION?
IMMEDIATE RESULTS (only one consultation required).

Licensed MD's specializing in men's health. Safer and more effective treatment than Viagra. Medication exclusively forumulated for premature ejaculation. Separate waiting rooms to ensure your privacy. Especially beneficial to patients with diabetes, high blood pressure, heart conditions, stress, etc., or those who would like to improve their sex lives.
Boston Medical Professional Corporation.
For a Better Sex Life Call: 800-337-7555.

---

9. Last night I saw the movie *Nuclear Mutants*. That movie is so bad it should be punished.

10. Maria Elena had been dancing for 12 years when she broke her leg.

11. The review I read in the *Lexington Pioneer* said *Planet of the Apes* is the best action movie ever made using primates in lead roles and starring Mark Wahlberg. That means we can safely conclude that *Planet of the Apes* is the best action movie ever made.

12. The Supreme Court is an honorable institution and, thus, it follows that Justice Thurgood Marshall must have been honorable too, given he served so long on the Court.

13. We should do what's right. What is right should be enforceable by the legal system. People have a right to die with dignity, therefore, physician-assisted suicide should be legal in this country.

14. On a restaurant menu: **OUR WINES LEAVE YOU NOTHING TO HOPE FOR.**

15. **MAKE BIG BUCKS WITHIN A YEAR** if you participate in the fetal brain transplant study. Call today: 888-NO-BRAIN

16. Ad for William Bounds Ltd. pepper mill (that grinds and crushes peppercorns): **We've got a crush on pepper!**

17. Shaq is a big man, even for a basketball player. Therefore, he must have huge feet and hands.

18. Sailors don't have to do any laundry: If they just throw their clothes overboard they'll be washed ashore!

19. WIN FREE RENT FOR LIFE if you will be our first subject in a brain transplant.

20. Jim had been lifting weights for 20 years when he dropped a barbell and crushed his big toe.

21. Ad for Crown Royal Whiskey after Lakers won the 2001 NBA championship: "Every Champion Deserves a Crown" (photo of basketball next to Crown Royal Whiskey bottle).

22. Sale on shirts for men with 16 necks.

23. (From the *Farmer's Almanac*): Frequent naps prevent old age, especially if taken while driving.

24. Portobello mushrooms are delicious. So is Camembert cheese. I bet they'd be exquisite to put together as an appetizer!

25. *Quick Easy Money* if you just proofread the *Oxford English Dictionary*.

26. WAITRESS: Cooks are so mean!
CHEF: Why do you say that?
WAITRESS: Because they always beat the eggs.

27. The Lakers have shown themselves to be the number 1 basketball team in the country. You can't win the NBAA championship over and over without being NUMBER ONE. Therefore, every single member of the team is the best, and I mean the best there is!

28. If you don't go to other people's funerals, they won't come to yours.

29. Don't be chicken. Try octopus for a change! It's delicious.

30. Name the fallacy at issue in the following campaign ad for politician Jackie Goldberg:

Cesar Portillo and Guns in School

Cesar Portillo sent out a "hit mailer" accusing Jackie Goldberg of voting against expelling kids who brought guns to school. This is completely untrue.

Portillo's evidence for this claim is a 1990 quote from Goldberg in a *LA Times* article about a School Board vote to require mandatory expulsion for bringing guns to school. Portillo quotes Goldberg saying, "This will not make campuses any safer." But Portillo fails to include the entire article proving that Goldberg voted *for* the tough expulsion policy, and stated that we had to do *even more* than simply expel students to make our schools safe.

Part Three

Directions: Name the fallacy below. These draw from all the fallacies we studied in this chapter.

1. A few ambassadors around the world cannot guarantee world peace. As a result, there's no point in appointing any more ambassadors to foreign countries.

2. Mel Gibson ate dog food in *Lethal Weapon,* so it must be tasty. Try some!

3. Sign on building: LEGAL GRIND: Coffee and Counsel.

4. Children should not be allowed out on Halloween. This is due to the fact that every year at least one person finds something like a razor inside an apple or glass placed inside a candy bar. It's a shame you can't trust anyone any more.

5. "The Indians of Milwaukee spread the rumor that they were going to invade the Milwaukee Yacht Club so they could have *Red Sons in the Sail Set,* but it was rumor and nothing more" (see Vine Deloria, Jr., *God Is Red: A Native View of Religion*).

6. We ought to allow stem cell research. Polls show that the majority of people support it.

7. The Constitution guarantees us a right of privacy for decisions about reproductive freedom. Therefore, gays should be able to use surrogate mothers to bear them a child.

8. Bill Clinton deserves to go down in history as a great president. He's a nice person and it's a shame he's had so much trouble with that affair with Monica. It's really created a hardship on his marriage and hurt his relationship with Chelsea. Poor guy.

9. Timothy McVeigh was supposedly—and I mean supposedly—executed for his part in the Oklahoma City bombing. But you know they did *no* autopsy! Without an autopsy, we cannot be sure he's actually dead. You can't prove to me he was really killed by lethal injection. I can only conclude one thing and one thing only: Timothy McVeigh is still alive.

10. Frances said that eating tomatoes is bad for you: If you eat tomatoes, your diet is too acidic. An acidic diet is simply too yang! And if you have a diet that is imbalanced in terms of the yang and yin elements, you are more prone to illness and cancer. Look at those stewed tomatoes piled up on your plate! Your health is in jeopardy. Stick to seaweed treats. Here, have some nori!

11. The intricate design of nature can only be due to the existence of God; because there could be no natural order and design if God did not exist.

12. No one has proven that jailing pregnant drug abusers is a societal problem; therefore it must be morally permissible to incarcerate pregnant women who abuse drugs. Lock them up!

13. DIANA: Hey Frank, what's that weird mark doing on the side of your neck?
    FRANK: Oh, Diana, did I ever tell you what a lovely voice you have? I bet you could get a record contract!

14. If you don't savor the taste of a green corn tamale, you can't call yourself a gourmet.

15. I can't understand why the coach was arrested for sexual harassment. He always helps out with the Little League and drives the church school bus for the Sunday school.

16. Sign in bar: SPECIAL COCKTAILS FOR THE LADIES WITH NUTS.

17. You would be advised to think twice before voting for Jim Bradley for governor. He's a vegetarian and someone like that will make sure the beef industry in this state is stripped of any lobbying power in the legislature!

18. VIOLET: You know Dan I just don't believe God exists.
    DAN: You better believe in God, or you'll go straight to hell!

19. Friedrich Nietzsche suffered from incurable syphilis. That means we shouldn't waste our time reading his work—it couldn't possibly have any value for us today.

20. CBN TV took a poll of patients in County General. They were all senior citizens living on a fixed income. They said that hospital food is grossly underrated. In fact, they agreed that, on the whole, most hospital food is delicious. Therefore, all American patients must think hospital food is delicious.

21. Aerobics exercise is great for your cardiovascular system. Therefore, Mr. Martinez should do it to help his recovery from his quadrupal bypass surgery last week!

22. Title of article on fashion: ***Dress Code Anarchy and the Right to Bare Arms.***

23. Did you hear about Martin trying to convince Carlos to stop drinking raw eggs in beer? Martin said it's bad for your health and might even cause kidney problems. But who is he to talk? He can dish out advice; but he never takes it!

24. Why did the cow stop giving milk? Because she was an udder failure!!

25. The reality is this Bob: If you don't stay in shape, no woman will find you attractive.

26. You know, Nancy, men are all alike; they all like to ogle naked women! Do you realize that I saw 15 men going into the strip club on Hollywood Boulevard—just in the time I was in my car waiting for the light to change. I tell you, it's a sad world we live in.

27. DR. CHAN: Hey, Rita, what's that I heard about you being an ex-con?
    RITA: Oh, Dr. Chan, did anyone ever tell you that you look like Bruce Lee? I bet you get stopped all the time and asked for your autograph.

28. Ad for Pol Roger Champagne:

    "My tastes are simple. I am easily satisfied by the best."
    —Winston Churchill

    Perhaps Winston Churchill owed his sparkling wit to the finer bubbles of *Pol Roger Champagne*. Simply the best.

29. Professor Whitman said that taxes are out of control, that the government is so wasteful, they can't handle the money they've got already. But why should we listen to her, did you know she used to be a member of S & L Watch? She'd certainly be biased.

30. Did you hear about the KSOP radio poll of female college students: they found 78 percent of the women polled think men should bear more responsibility for birth control. Therefore, all Americans think men should bear more of the responsibility for birth control.

31. Title of article on the tennis superstars Venus and Serena Williams: Venus Mars It for Serena.

32. Why does a dead dog weigh more than a live one?

33. Humans must be the products of environmental determinism, since no one has proved for certain that we have free will.

34. **Win a Free Flight to Hawaii** if you're willing to work 23 hours a day and have no social life.

35. Question asked of Diana Eck, noted in *Encountering God:* "Give me a quick yes or no: Is Christ the only way to salvation?"

36. Don't pay any attention to Senator Ted Kennedy's proposal to help those on welfare. You know he's a Kennedy and must have millions to his name! What could he possibly know about poverty?

37. Ad for prayer books: **Nun Better.**

38. Liposuction is the all-American way to become thin. Do it today!

39. Leo deserves a raise in his job as a computer technician, because he simply can't afford to pay for his son's soccer gear, his daughter's tap dance lessons, and his father's knee surgery on the salary he gets. And that's not even counting the money he's putting away for a family vacation to see the relatives in Saginaw, Michigan next summer. Give him a break!

40. Australia is the most beautiful country. We can conclude, then, that every town in Australia must also be beautiful.

Part Four

Directions: Name the fallacy below. Be on the watch. If it is *not* a fallacy, say so.

1. All I know, Robert, is you better fix the election there in Dade County, or you can think again about a career as a political consultant. I'll make sure your options are limited unless you work with us on this little voting problem here!

2. You really ought to help John hide some of his assets from the government so he doesn't have a big tax bill this year. You know what the golden rule says about doing unto others what you'd like them to do to you. If you helped him cheat on his taxes, you could probably count on him if you ever needed help in exchange.

3. DEFENSE ATTORNEY: "Tell me, Miss Raymond, you say you saw the defendant attack Mr. Busso at the Chicago Brew House at 8:00 p.m. on Saturday, July 12th?

   MARIE BUSSO: Yes, I did. He hit him with a tire iron three times.

   DEFENSE ATTORNEY: Well, tell me, Miss Busso. Isn't it a fact that you are a lesbian and that's why you were at the Brew House in the first place? Didn't you go there to pick up another woman?

4. Robert Thurman has written a lot of books on Tibetan Buddhism, but I don't know whether to believe what he says, since he's not an Asian.

5. Jena Bush deserves a break, even though she's been caught several times drinking underage. After all, she's the president's daughter and that's enough right there to be stressful. I feel so sorry for her, living in a fishbowl and all. It's ridiculous that the children of politicians should be subjected to such coverage by the media. The judge should just let her off with a warning.

6. Wow, you sure have a nice body, Steve. Come to my office tonight for a little stroking. If you don't, I'll make sure your boss in the maintenance department hears about you cutting out early last Friday.

7. In Canada, patients with cancer getting chemotherapy can use medicinal marijuana. Therefore, all of us should be able to smoke marijuana whenever we want.

8. No one proved that Elvis really offended people with his dancing, so any claims to that effect must be groundless.

9. Gwyneth Paltrow likes pink ball gowns; so any woman who needs an evening dress should get one too.

10. Why is it that girls are more linguistically advanced than boys?

11. Heredity alone makes someone into a criminal, since heredity by itself determines what a person becomes.

12. OFFICER: Hey, mister what's this foot I see sticking out of your trunk?

    MOTORIST: Oh, officer, I hear you were given an award last night at the LAPD command center. That's really great, I bet your mom and dad are so proud of you!

13. The Democratic Party favors strong unions. Therefore, Senator Strom Thurmond, a southern Democrat, will surely vote for the ballot measure to strengthen the Teachers Union.

14. Discuss the use of language by Carl Elliott, as quoted by *The New York Times* (2 Aug. 2001): "Bioethics boards look like watch dogs, but they are used like show dogs."

15. Radiated food must not be bad for your health. No one has proved it causes cancer—so it must be okay.

16. Loosely wrapped in bubble-wrap she carried a crystal vase.

17. Kobe Bryant, Allen Iverson, Vince Carter, Tracy McGrady, and Grant Hill are all great basketball players. If they were on a team together, they'd be dynamite.

18. Freedom of speech is a landmark of a democracy. Therefore, neo-Nazis should be free to verbally harass the Jewish family down the street.

19. It's a shame Julia Roberts and Benjamin Bratt broke off their engagement. Each one is so attractive you would have thought they'd make a great couple!

20. Neither chihuahuas nor beagles are large dogs.

21. For sale: Combination TV-VCR and futon.

22. Either you run the marathon or you are a hopeless failure.

23. Is Prince Andrew really considering starring in a Hollywood production?

24. Don't listen to John Travolta's view on religion. You know he's a Scientologist.

25. If we teach people to think clearly and logically, our country will be stronger. This is due to the fact that a strong country requires that its citizens have well-developed reasoning skills.

26. Only those who have smelled a grizzly bear in their tent have had to come to terms with their own mortality.

27. A large meal isn't fattening if you take small bites.

28. In a study of females 13 to 17 years old, it was found that 76 percent of them want to have a child before they are 24 years old. That just goes to show you: most teenagers want to have a kid while they're young.

29. California condors are nearly extinct. I saw a California condor at the wildlife sanctuary; therefore that poor bird is nearly extinct!

30. Immanuel Kant was a hypochrondriac. It seemed that he continually thought he had some illness or another when nothing was wrong with him. Perhaps we'd be advised not to bother reading Kant's work in philosophy—it'll surely be false.

31. Did you vote in the last presidential election?

32. ANTHEA: Excuse me, Jason, what's all this money doing here on your desk?
    JASON: Oh, Anthea, have I ever told you how much I love your hair? It is so shiny and smells so nice. Plus, it is so soft I can barely contain myself! What do you do to keep it so beautiful?

33. Bob makes rich fudge, so he must spend a lot of money on the ingredients.

34. Congress is a well-organized group; therefore Senator Feinstein must be a well-organized person!

35. Marilyn Monroe must have had a premonition that she'd be a screen goddess. You cannot prove I'm wrong, so I must be right!

36. You should pray every morning—any decent American would.

37. Roxanne told me to quit smoking cigars. She said they were hard on your respiratory system and made your clothes smell dreadfully. But I refuse to listen to Roxanne since she has been puffing on cigars since she was a teenager.

38. I believe in survival of the fittest. How do I know which one is the most fit? That's easy. It's the one that survives!

39. We all have the right to life, liberty, and the pursuit of happiness. This means that Warren has the right to do drugs if it helps him come to terms with the fact he did not make the Olympic team.

40. Richard had the worst week. His dog nearly choked to death on a curler it found in the street and it cost Richard $150 at the vet's; plus someone let the air out of his tires and he nearly crashed into a school bus. Richard deserves to get a scholarship to Purdue—that guy's life is a mess.

41. WILMA: Ricardo, why are you peering in that little box? Doesn't that belong to the bank? What's it doing here in the house?
    RICARDO: Wilma, my dearest sweet plum cake, how utterly charming you look in your new flamingo hat! Let's go out on the town!

42. You can ignore Blanca's evaluation of who's the best player in the NBA today. As a woman, it's highly unlikely she'd be very knowledgeable about basketball. You might be better off asking a man if you want to get a dependable assessment.

43. Can you imagine how great it would have been if Picasso and Van Gogh—only two of the greatest artists of the 20th century—could have done a painting together! They would have been dynamite!

44. At the city council meeting Sheriff Aramessian reaffirmed the fact that we should all obey the law. That means we shouldn't allow police officers to shoot off guns on public streets. If anyone else did that, they'd be locked up for sure.

45. Excerpt from an ad for Western Union "Money Zap" service to move money online:

CASE STUDY EXERCISES

Las Hermanitas
(The Sisters)

Norma Almaraz
Critical Thinking Fallacy Story

Fallacy Stories. The following are fallacy stories written by students in my Critical Thinking class. Read the stories and see if you can spot all the fallacies.

Lorena tells her sister, "If you go out to a club tonight you may end up enjoying it, and the next thing you know you will be going out every school night, your grades will drop, and eventually you will drop out of school and become a *borracha* and a nobody like the rest of the *familia. Por favor* Paula, you cannot go out to a club on a school night. You either listen to me or forget that you have a sister and a place to come home to. I will also tell Luis, your boyfriend, that you cheated on him last month," says Lorena firmly.

However, whatever Lorena is saying seems not to have any effect on Paula. She continues to sort out her going out clothes with excitement as she hums the melody, *"Tu O Nadie."*

"I am telling you this for your own good Paula, look what happened to your *hermano* Miguel; he started very good in school, he was the hope of the family, but he started going out dancing during school nights, he liked it and eventually he dropped out of school. That just goes to show you—*nunca* go out to a club on a school night," says Lorena.

Paula finally speaks up with a smile on her face, "What do you think about this skirt? Luis *me la compro* this weekend for me to wear tonight. It looks just like the one you are wearing. Do you have $20 I could borrow?"

Lorena furiously says, *"Por Dios* Paula, aren't you listening to me?"

Suddenly Paula reminds Lorena about the hard times she gave *Mama:* "Who are you to tell me not to go out, when you did the same thing after mother told you not to because you had to graduate from the university for the sake of the family! Leave me alone. Are you always going to be closed minded like the rest of the *familia?* For your information Lorena, every time Maria goes out to a nightclub on a school night she always scores 100 percent on the following test. So, if you want me to get 100 percent like Maria, and make the family proud, let me go out tonight and stop giving me a hard time."

Lorena is pacing back and forth in Paula's room, upset, frustrated, thinking what else to tell Paula to convince her to stay at home and study instead of going out to the club. Lorena says next, "Aside from almost destroying your future, in God's eyes you are also sinning because you are disobeying and disrespecting your elders and those you love the most. You know, there was a study done at UCLA that 90 percent of Latin women dropped out of school for going out dancing on school nights. Therefore, because you are a Latin woman Paula, you have the tendency to drop out of school."

Paula stops what she is doing and says, "It is cool to go out on school nights. Thousands of college students do it; I do not see anything wrong with it. Besides, you do not know anything about statistics, you did not even take a class on it, so leave me alone and stick to being a housewife and mother."

Lorena was astonished at Paula's response and started crying, *"Oh Dios Mio,* there must be a bad spirit wandering in this house. And it is he who is talking through you, because it cannot be you. My little *hermanita* telling me to stick to being a housewife and a mother!"

Paula sensed that she went a little too far with her statement, so she hugged her, "*Oh hermana*, I am so sorry for what I said. You just got me very upset with everything that you are saying; it does not make sense to me. I could understand your fear, and I promise—*te lo juro*—I will not drop out of school, become a *borracha*, or let the family down. Please Lorena let me go out tonight. I deserve to go out with my friends. I have had three major exams back-to-back for the last two days. Plus, my bird, *Pecas*, died, and my ex-boyfriend turned out to be gay! I deserve to go out tonight. *Que Piensas?*"

The end.

Translations:

1. Borracha = drunk
2. Familia = family
3. Por favor = please
4. Tu O Nadie = you or no one else
5. Hermano = brother
6. Nunca = never
7. Me la compro = bought it for me
8. Por Dios = for God's sake
9. Mama = mother
10. Oh Dios Mio = Oh my God
11. Hermanita = little sister
12. Hermana =sister
13. Te lo juro = I promise
14. Pecas = freckles
15. Que Piensas = What do you think?

Reprinted with permission of Norma Almarez.

A Day in the Life
Donita Valdez
Critical Thinking Fallacy Story

Julie never felt better in her life. She is one of the most popular girls in school and is dating the all-star quarterback. Just when she thought life could not get any better, Julie finds out that she has been accepted into UCLA. "Wow!" Julie shouted. "My parents will be so proud, maybe they'll buy me that new BMW. After all I heard that Brad Pitt owns a BMW, so it must be a good car."

"Not so fast," commented Britney. Julie's friend Britney always had something to say. "Do you think that your parents will be able to buy you a BMW?" "I mean they are Asian and most people who buy BMW's are European and rich." "Gosh Britney, What kind of remark was that?" Julie said sarcastically. "Your parents belong to PTSO and they are always asking for donations."

Just as Britney opened her mouth, Mike walked into the room. "Look what I got!" Mike replied excitingly. "Everyone seems to be getting body piercing, so I finally got my tongued pierced. There was a sign at the tattoo shop for FREE body piercing. I ran right in the shop to only find that there was a catch to it. The guy said I get a free piercing if I allow him to pierce any body part. I didn't want to risk it, so I ended up paying for the tongue ring." "Yuck!" snarled Julie. "How do you expect me to be seen with you in public now?"

"Hey Julie did I mention how beautiful you look today?" responded Mike. He was hoping Julie would stop complaining about the tongue ring. "Well I have to go to football practice now. I'll call you later Jules." Mike waved bye as he ran to practice. "I can't believe he got his tongue pierced. Next thing you know he'll get more body parts pierced. Then he'll go broke since his money will be wasted on piercing," replied Julie. "Calm down Julie!" assured Britney. "Maybe Mike needs it to feel better, after all his dog died last week and they lost the football game on Friday."

"Who are you to talk Britney?" replied Julie. "You broke up with Paul over his eyebrow piercing."

"Well either you stay with the all-star quarterback or break up with him and be sad!" Britney rolled her eyes at Julie. "Let's just go home. I have to talk to my parents about my acceptance letter," Julie replied sadly. She felt like Britney thought she was ungrateful for being upset over Mike. The next day at school Britney saw Mike collapse to the ground. She didn't stop to help him since she didn't want to get in trouble for being late to class. She felt bad, but saw campus security walking from Berkley building to Brand Hall. One of the girls in the hallway saw how Britney walked away.

"WOW! Britney was selfish to walk away, so she must be selfish in donating to the school canned goods drive," commented the girl. A few minutes later Julie showed up and ran to Mike. She yelled for help as students gathered around her. Mike was brought to the nurse's station to rest. Julie heard how Britney didn't bother to help Mike. Without hesitation, she ran over to Britney's class. "Have you always been this cold-hearted? I can't believe you saw Mike collapse and you didn't bother to help him," said Julie angrily. She pulled Britney outside of the classroom. "If you don't change your attitude, I'll tell your parents about that dent on their car."

"My dad caused that dent on the car. You can't prove that it was me, so I'm telling the truth," responded Britney. She felt like Julie was betraying her. I can't believe she brought up the car incident, she thought. "Well call me when you get your act together," replied Julie. She started to tear. She always thought Britney was her best friend and now she wasn't sure.

"Julie I had a logical reason. I didn't want to be late for class. You know that Mr. Smith is close to failing me and attendance might be the one thing to save my grade," Britney said sympathetically. "I mean who are you going to believe, me or those five dizzy girls that stood in the hallway? You can't judge me based on what you heard in the hallway. What people saw is different from what I thought. I'm shocked you didn't talk it over before coming to confront me. You assumed I was a cold hearted person."

Julie looked at Britney and began to hug her. She realized what she had done and felt bad. They apologized to each other and headed off to the nurse's station to check on Mike.

The end.

Reprinted with permission of Donita Vadez.

The Case of Mistaken Furs

Miriam Salgado
Critical Thinking Fallacy Story

MARGARIT MOUSE: Sonia are you going to talk at all during our picnic?

SONIA SQUIRREL: Well, if you insist, have you heard the news about Willy Wolf?

MARGARIT MOUSE: Have you always been a gossip? You squirrels are all the same, always talking about everyone else!

SONIA SQUIRREL: Don't get me started on mice. They are always trying to be the big cheese!! Do you want to know or not?

MARGARIT MOUSE: Fine, tell me.

SONIA SQUIRREL: The police have arrested Willy Wolf for having attempted to kill Rosy pig and destroying her house. Rosy has picked him out of a line-up and is going to testify against him in court tomorrow.

MARGARIT MOUSE: That awful wolf. How could he have done all those bad things to an animal as nice as Rosy? They are just wasting money having a trial for Willy, there is no way that anyone would think he is innocent. First of all, he is a wolf and wolves are notorious for picking on pigs. As if this wasn't enough, Willy is the Big Bad Wolf's nephew. Big Bad Wolf has tried to hurt many pigs: he's been arrested twice for assault with carving knife and roasting pan. That kind of hatred toward pigs runs in Willy's family!

SONIA SQUIRREL: How can you be so sure of Willy's guilt? He does have an alibi. He was with Jake the Snake the night that it happened.

MARGARIT MOUSE: Sonia Squirrel, are you nuts or something! You can't trust Jake—everyone knows that he is a low-life. Also, the movie star Arnold Armadillo says that all wolves are criminals, so it must be true! There is no doubt that Willy Wolf was the one who destroyed Rosy's house because he is one of the founders of the Tuesday Afternoon Demolition Club, whose members are destructive. Now are you convinced?

SONIA SQUIRREL: I don't care what you say—I don't think that Willy Wolf is guilty. Most of our friends also think that Willy has been falsely accused. Maybe Rosy is lying, did you ever think of that?

MARGARIT MOUSE: Gosh, how many facts do I have to give before you believe me? The majority of this town thinks that pigs are honest; therefore there is no way Rosy is fibbing. Also, you should tell everyone that Willy is guilty so the jury will be persuaded to send him to jail. This way Rosy can cash in on her insurance. She should have things go her way. After all, her house has been destroyed, two of her uncles are homeless, the third one is always mean to her, and her pet just died.

SONIA SQUIRREL: I just don't think that Willy Wolf would do something like that. I used to be good friends with him in grade school.

MARGARIT MOUSE: Either you think Willy is guilty or you're an idiot. All the signs point to him. Also, the night before it happened I had a dream in which Rosy's dead pet told me that Rosy would be attacked by a wolf. You can't prove that I didn't so it must be true!! Furthermore, the only wolf around here is Willy. Oh I almost forgot, I asked a few pigs if they were scared of wolves and they said yes. Therefore, this whole town is scared of wolves and we should put this one away in jail right away before he hurts anyone else.

SONIA SQUIRREL: Have you always said so much trash?

MARGARIT MOUSE: You better tell all your friends Willy is guilty or I'll tell the police you went over to Rosy's house dressed in a wolf's costume!

SONIA SQUIRREL: That won't work with me, Margarit. Anyways, the only person around here that owns a wolf costume is you. I still remember that you were a wolf for my Halloween party last year.

MARGARIT MOUSE: Yeah, but what's that got to do with anything?

SONIA SQUIRREL: You and Rosy weren't real good friends, especially since she stole your boyfriend. And you always said that one day you'd get even. Also weren't you headed toward Rosy's house yesterday carrying a big bag?

MARGARIT MOUSE: Sonia this lunch is fantastic, you are such a talented cook. Have you ever considered becoming a caterer? I have a friend who could help you get started. Let me go see him right now!

SONIA SQUIRREL: Okay!

The next day, just as Willy Wolf was about to be transported to the courthouse, an anonymous call was made to the police to go check out Margarit Mouse's house. When the police got there they found the wolf costume and blue prints of her plans to get revenge on Rosy pig. The police arrested the mischievous mouse and freed Willy.

The end.

CHAPTER FIVE

Analysis: The Heart of Critical Thinking

When you are philosophizing you have to descend into the primeval chaos and feel at home there.

—LUDWIG WITTGENSTEIN, *Culture and Value*

Analysis is not just done by scientists in a lab. It is an aspect of all of our lives, even on the most mundane or everyday level. Watching TV, for example, need not be a slide into oblivion if you use the opportunity to think about what's on the screen. Turning on *The X-Files* reruns, you find agents Mulder and Scully at odds over a series of deaths linked to unusually bold cockroaches. Agent Mulder suspects the cockroaches may be an alien species, whereas Agent Scully seeks a scientific explanation for the deaths. Glued to the TV, you, too, try to account for the mysterious deaths and begin to weigh the two explanations and contemplate alternatives.

To accomplish this, you need to develop the brain power to see what's at issue, gather and weigh evidence, sort relevant from irrelevant information, consider competing explanations, assess the cogency of the reasoning, and arrive at some conclusion if at all possible. To say the least, these are very useful skills. Having such skills at our fingertips is very empowering—both on the individual level and in terms of working together as a team.

At the heart of critical thinking lies the ability to analyze. Extracting key ideas, pulling out hidden assumptions, and setting out the structure of arguments are important aspects of analysis. It also helps to have a creative, expansive side where we generate ideas and turn over alternatives in our minds.

We see this when we try to see the big picture, set goals, brainstorm ideas, and set out a plan of action. It helps to keep this broader view in mind as we dissect arguments, organize the various components, inspect fine details, and see how it all works together. Otherwise it's easy to go astray or off on a tangent. Strong analytical skills make it much easier to stay on track and do the job right.

Attention to Context

To stay focused we need to be aware of the context. Issues and problems do not exist in a vacuum, but are embedded in people's lives and usually take place within a certain location and time frame. We need to pay attention to this. For example, it used to be that anyone wishing to get married had to get a blood test (for syphilis) for a marriage license. Because syphilis is a treatable disease and not the scourge it once was, this policy changed.

We can also see the significance of context in the following comments about the way Israelis would see a scene from the movie *Sleepless in Seattle*:

> Terror and war have shaped the lives of countless Israelis. For example, an Israeli screenwriter would never write a scene such as the one that appears in *Sleepless in Seattle* atop the Empire State Building when Meg Ryan searches through the backpack Jonah has left there. No Israeli would dare touch an unfamiliar, abandoned backpack, and no more than a few minutes would pass before someone would alert the bomb squad. (Akiva Eldar, "Dead End at Oklahoma City" *Freedom Forum Media Studies Journal*, Fall 1995)

Given the political tensions in the Middle East, we can see why an Israeli would be leery of an abandoned backpack. Being alert means we need our antennae out and make no unwarranted assumptions. It also means we need to decide what can reasonably be taken for granted.

In this chapter, we will go into analysis and become familiar with these various elements. We will do this by examining the issue of credibility, types of evidence, weighing evidence, analysis of a short article, and analysis of a longer article.

Assessing Credibility

In 1985, a case came to trial in Boston centering on a police detective striking a man who was suspected of soliciting a prostitute and who resisted arrest. Seven people spoke at the trial: Long Kuang Huang (alleged victim), Detective Francis Kelly, Bao Tang Huang (Huang's wife), Audrey Manns (prostitute), Paul Bates (construction worker—witness), Gretl Nunnemacher (defense witness), and Dr. Jane Silva (neurologist). Use the grid following the article (see box) to rate each speaker on a scale of 1 to 5 (5 being high, or very credible, 1 being low—not credible). Rate each one in terms of a credibility grid created by Mary Anne Saul.

Defense Witnesses Describe Chinatown Beating
John H. Kennedy

Defense witnesses in the nonjury trial of Long Kuang Huang yesterday drew a sympathetic portrait of the peasant farmer from China as perhaps a victim of mistaken identity just 10 months after he immigrated to the United States. Huang, 56, is on trial in Boston Municipal Court on charges of soliciting sex for a fee and assault and battery on Detective Francis G. Kelly Jr. last May 1 near the Combat Zone [seedy area in Boston with strip clubs and bars]. Attorneys are scheduled to give closing arguments this morning before Judge George A. O'Toole Jr. makes his decision.

In the final day of testimony, all the witnesses were called by Huang's attorneys, and included his wife. Some described the scuffle between Kelly and Huang, although their versions differed on details. The case has become the focus of charges by some Asian-Americans of police brutality. Kelly faces police department hearings on his conduct during the May 1 incident.

Bao Tang Huang, 52, whose testimony in Chinese was translated, said her husband could write his name in English, but did not speak English. His only experience with police was in China where officers wear white uniforms and do not carry badges, she said. Both grew up and lived in a "large village" of 300 people in the People's Republic, where Huang was a farmer. They have two sons, who came with them to Boston July 1, 1984. Huang has no formal education and has worked in restaurants in the Boston area, she said.

Earlier this week, prostitute Audrey Manns identified Huang in court as the man who spoke broken English to her, and who made it clear that he would pay her $30 to have sex with him. Kelly testified he followed them for two or three blocks before arresting Manns, and then Huang after an extended struggle, in front of 35 Kneeland St.

Kelly and Manns testified that Huang kicked and hit the detective several times before Kelly connected with a single punch to Huang's face in an attempt to subdue him. The detective also testified he identified himself as a police officer, both with his badge and by speaking to Huang.

Two defense witnesses yesterday said the detective connected with two punches to Huang's face, while Manns told the detective to stop.

Paul Bates, 39, was working on a renovation project at 35 Kneeland St. when he saw a woman in an "electric blue" outfit and "bright blonde" hair walk by with a man who looked Hispanic.

A short time later, Bates said he came onto the street and saw Kelly struggling with Huang. The blonde woman in the blue outfit, who he said was Manns, came over to the two. "She told him [Huang] to stop struggling, the other person was a police officer," said Bates. Bates said Manns told Kelly: "He's not the man. I wasn't with him. He was just walking down the sidewalk. I swear to God, Kelly." He said he later saw Kelly connect with two "short, chopping punches."

The version of another defense witness, Gretl Nunnemacher, differed somewhat from Bates'. She said Kelly slammed Huang against the side of the car "several" times, Kelly's fist started to come down but she said she didn't see it land. Then, said Nunnemacher, a blonde woman emerged from another car. "She said, 'Kelly, Kelly, what are you doing. Stop,' . . . she told me he was a cop." Dr. Jane Silva, a neurologist who treated Huang at the New England Medical Center, said Huang suffered a concussion with post-concussive symptoms—headaches, dizziness, listlessness."

Source: *Boston Globe*, 23 Aug. 1985. Reprinted with permission of the *Boston Globe*.

The Saul Credibility Grid

| WITNESSES | CREDIBLITY RATING | STANDARDS |
	LOW 1 2 3 4 5 HIGH	REASONS FOR YOUR RATING
L. Huang		
Det. Kelly		
B. Huang		
A. Manns		
P. Bates		
G. Nunnemacher		
Dr. Silva		

When making your list of standards (criteria), think about what makes the person seem credible. Proximity to the crime, ability to observe easily, conflict of interest, background information, professional training, cultural factors, and personal characteristics may all affect a person's ability. These factors act as criteria for credibility of witnesses.

Thanks to Ann Garry's Critical Thinking class at Cal State Los Angeles, there is more about this trial that we can examine (they tracked down subsequent articles on the case). These provided the basis for the following set of exercises.

Exercises

1. Prosecution witness, Harry Ayscough, helped the defense in the Chinatown case, above. He testified that Audrey Manns yelled, "He's not the one, that's not him," as Detective Kelly tried to arrest Long Kuang Huang.
   Answer the following:
   a. Do you think this testimony clearly indicates that Detective Kelly may have been arresting the wrong man?
   b. Is there any other conclusion that might be drawn from the testimony?

2. Does the fact that Audrey Manns testified that it was Huang who offered to pay $30 for sex and then violently resisted arrest create any conflict with your decision about Ayscough's testimony (set out in 1, above)? Discuss how you'd resolve a possible conflict in these pieces of evidence.

3. What significance should you give the fact that defense witnesses painted a sympathetic portrait of Long Kuang Huang and suggested that he might have been a victim of mistaken identity?

4. The case resulted in an unusual settlement:

> Huang received $85,000 from the city. Detective Kelly got $40,000 in back pay and overtime (he had been suspended without pay for a year), $55,000 in legal fees, and $20,000 in additional damages. In return, Kelly was to drop a suit against the police commissioner and Huang was to drop his $1 million civil rights suit against the Boston police. Joseph Mulligan, the corporation counsel, said, "We decided to package the whole enchilada and make it all go away." (See Steve Marantz, "2-Way Settlement Ends Police Suit," *The Boston Globe,* 15 July 1989)

In your assessment, does this seem like a wise decision in terms of its impact on police–community relations?

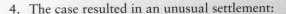 Cogency

When assessing an argument, one key concern is whether or not the reasoning is *cogent*. This means that the argument is convincing because of the quality and persuasive force of the evidence supporting the conclusion. A cogent argument is well reasoned and clearly structured so we can follow the argument, seeing how the evidence lays the foundation for the conclusion. This is a cogent argument:

> If you want superlative sound from your audio system but don't want speakers that could do justice to Stonehenge dominating your room, this should be music to your ears: Bookshelf speakers and three-piece systems performed just as well as—and in some cases better than—floor-standing speakers in our latest tests. And some fine performers cost only $100 to $200, so you can save money as well as space.
>
> That's a switch from years past, when big-box models were considered the only way to get outstanding sound quality . . . we tested 23 bookshelf speakers ranging in price from $100 to $650 a pair and five three-piece systems priced at $300 to $600.
>
> We compared these speakers to three floor-standing models, priced at $400 to $700. . . . The results demonstrate that smaller speakers more than hold their own. (See "Small Boxes, Big Sound," *Consumer Reports,* Aug. 2001)

The evidence is clearly set out, with the results of the tests cited to demonstrate the different units are comparable in quality. The conclusion is presented first, with the evidence offering strong support.

The task in setting out a cogent argument is this:

- Aim for a well-structured argument
- In which it is clear what is being asserted
- With sufficient evidence supporting that conclusion
- And relying on no unwarranted assumptions
- So that no alternative conclusion seems plausible.

Developing Analytical Skills

Arguments may occur in a variety of formats. Whether the evidence is presented in a film, video, TV program, radio show, chapter in a textbook, or a newspaper article, you need analytical skills to examine and assess what is being presented.

An effective analysis entails recognizing the focus (point, direction, position), pulling out evidence, seeing the structure of the reasoning involved, weighing strengths and weaknesses, considering alternative explanations, examining assumptions to root out those that are unwarranted, looking for omissions (missing pieces), and potential sources of bias or prejudice (e.g., loaded language, name calling).

To get a quick overview of an article, try to determine the focus, thesis, or position being argued, the overall structure or organization, relevant background information and evidence, strength of the reasoning, any weaknesses, whether there are crucial omissions or questionable assumptions, and whether the article is informative and/or convincing. This can be summarized as follows:

Key Points in Analyzing an Article

Subject: What is the focus of this piece? What is it about—what's the general topic?

The Territory: What territory is being covered here? What is the context for exploring the ideas or issues?

Thesis: Is the author arguing a particular position? What point is the author trying to make?

Ideas/Main Thrust: What are the main ideas or key points? What, in a nutshell, is the purpose of the article?

Approach: How much is directed to the central idea and how much is aimed at side issues or tangents? What is the style of delivery? How is this argument structured?

Assertions/Evidence: What kinds of assertions are made? In the case of an argument, what counts as evidence?

Fine Details: What examples, statistics, or other support is given to back up the key evidence or premises? Do the details presented work to develop the central idea or vision?

Cogency: Does the evidence work in part or in its entirety to support the thesis? Is the thesis/conclusion well supported by the evidence?

Clarity: Is the presentation clear and to the point? Are the key issues, ideas, or details of the story clearly presented?

Overall Impression: What is the overall impression in terms of a political message, social commentary, or personal vision? What are you left with, what sticks in your mind?

Persuasiveness: Are you persuaded by the argument? Is the case convincingly made? If not, what's missing, questionable, or off-track? If the article is expository rather than argumentative, was it informative or helpful?

Using the key points for analyzing an article, set out your analysis of the article below. In this article, Michelle Delio examines a new "toy" which allows the user to "execute" Marv, who sits in an electric chair, ready to be jolted. Then answer the questions that follow.

CASE STUDY

Death Row Marv
Kids' New Rage: Executing Marv

Michelle Delio

Wired magazine, Aug. 10, 2000

Flip the switch and a surge of electrical current slams into the figure strapped in the chair. He convulses. His hands tremble. His eyes glow red. His teeth clench. And then he utters his last words.

"That the best you can do, you pansies?"

No, it's not the nightly news from Texas. It's Death Row Marv, the latest plastic sensation from McFarlane Toys, makers of the Spawn and Austin Powers action figures. Marv is one of the main characters in the Frank Miller comic book series "Sin City." He's a big (7-plus-feet tall), ugly, dangerous, drunk, ex-con medicated into some semblance of sanity by his parole officer's psychiatrist girlfriend. But while trying to do his version of good, Marv eventually came to a bad end.

The toy, which comes complete with an electric chair, a wired helmet for Marv's head, and a switch that, when pulled, shoots the juice into the hapless Marv, had a first production run of tens of thousands, according to MacFarlane Toys. No sales figures are available yet, but Marv is feeling a big buzz in more ways than one. New York's Forbidden Planet comic store and Island Comics both have waiting lists with more than 30 names on them.

"Kids really love Marv," said Island's Rick Varo. "Teen-age girls think he's cute, which terrifies me."

Death Row Marv is also a big draw at Manhattan's Midtown Comics store located near Times Square. A salesman there who preferred to remain anonymous ("You never know who's looking for you," he said) noted that people have been dropping into the store on a daily basis just to jolt Marv a few times. "It's not just kids, either," he said. "We get guys in suits.

We get moms. Old people. They come in looking like they had a rough day, but after they juice Marv they leave with a smile on their faces. It's a happy kind of thing."

But not everyone is having a good time playing with Marv. Dennis Golkven, a child psychologist in private practice in New Jersey, says that the toy could be dangerous. "It teaches children that it's fun to hurt people," Golkven said.

Ten-year-old Jason Devors of Brooklyn, New York, disagrees. "Marv is not a person," he said. "He's just a toy."

Answer the following:

1. What do "toys" like Death Row Marv reveal about our society?
2. State the strongest argument you can for allowing Death Row Marv to be sold to children.

3. State the strongest argument you can in favor of banning or restricting toys like Death Row Marv.

Analyzing Arguments

There are different ways in which thoughts and ideas get expressed. This needs to be noted at the outset, so we can adjust our expectations and method of analysis accordingly. Here are the three major forms:

(1) *Assumed neutrality or objectivity:* In an expository essay, ideas and information are presented in as objective or neutral a manner as possible. The goal of an exposition is to relay information or to present all relevant sides or perspectives on a particular issue. In assumed neutrality, the author tries to present the material in as unbiased and balanced a manner as possible. There will still be a certain amount of cultural baggage and value-laden language, so we need to be attentive to that.

(2) *Argument:* In an argumentative essay, evidence is given in support of a particular position. The goal here is to be persuasive and our task in analyzing the work is to determine the strength of the reasoning.

(3) *Creative expression:* This is a creative work, such as a poem, play, or short story, where artistic means are used to explore a topic or present a point of view. The goal here is to creatively use images or stories to explore issues, ideas, feelings, states of mind, and so on. In addition to artistic works, one example of creative expression is brainstorming ideas. We see an example of this cleverly conveyed in the Matt Groening cartoon, "A Brief History of Anger." (See Figure 5-1.)

Authors are more likely to assume neutrality in expository writing, by means of descriptions, data, statistics, diagrams, tables, and the like. In this case, information and points of view are conveyed in as objective and balanced a manner as possible, taking into account the major points of view. We see this in balanced news coverage; for example, when guests present different positions on a politically or socially controversial subject. Each speaker offers a distinct perspective and the guests are in dialogue so we are able to compare and contrast the views being expressed. This also allows the points of contention to be clarified. There may or may not be an attempt at a point of resolution (a middle ground).

In the second case, that of an argument, the task is not simply to survey the territory around an issue or event. Instead, the aim is to set out a particular position (thesis), and back it up with supportive evidence. Assessing arguments is central to critical thinking. We often see arguments set out in the Op/Ed section of newspapers, where people set out their points of view and try to persuade us to one way of thinking about an issue.

Another example is when talk show hosts raise a topic for discussion and then enlist audience response. Here the host or a guest sets out a point of view and then fields the questions and comments from the audience. These shows are capable of considerable influence and can be far more persuasive than a dispassionate, more in-depth, inquiry. The very format of talk shows tends not to allow sustained arguments to be presented because of time restrictions or assumptions about the educational level of the audience. Also, the host is generally dependent on the

Source: From *Binky's Guide to Love* © 1994 by Matt Groening. All Rights Reserved. Reprinted by permission of HarperCollins Publishers, New York.

FIGURE 5-1   audience to raise points and ask penetrating questions. This does not mean the shows are not persuasive—quite the opposite. The very immediacy of the show and the emotional pitch can influence the audience.

In the third major type of format, a creative work, the goal is usually to develop a theme or explore an idea through imaginative means. We would not treat it as an argument per se, but we can still undertake an artistic, literary, film, or textual analysis. Determining the focus of an artwork may require a multilayered approach, such as examining the literal level (the narrative), the mythological or symbolic level, and the political or social level. In this assessment, it helps to look at the context and keep the bigger picture in mind when looking at the details. If we lose sight of the overall context, we may go off on a tangent, overlook evidence, or fail to spot problematic assumptions.

Exercises

In the excerpts below, decide whether the author assumes a neutral/unbiased stance or whether the author is arguing a position. If the passage contains an argument, state the conclusion—even if that conclusion is implied and not explicitly stated. Note also the key pieces of evidence.

1. "Now you can open any size jar or bottle with ease. Grip Tite incorporates a unique blend of flexibility and deep set gears to create a force that opens any jar or bottle so easily that you'll wonder how you ever got along without it. Gone are the days of asking for help on that stubborn jelly jar. Grip Tite is made from a unique blend of flexible man made materials. At only $6.97 you'll want to buy two and get the shipping and handling free" (Dream Products, Inc.).

2. "White America does not want Chicanos in power. Anglos fear Chicanos will treat them the ways Anglos have treated Chicanos and other minorities" (Irene I. Blea, *La Chicana and the Intersection of Race, Class, and Gender*).

3. "In a case that appears to broaden the prosecution of women who pass drugs to their infants through their bodies, a woman was sentenced here Monday to six years in prison because her breast milk, tainted with methamphetamine, had killed her baby daughter. In recent years, 160 women in 24 states have been charged with delivering drugs to their babies either during pregnancy or, through the umbilical cord, immediately after childbirth. But the case here in this town 40 miles southeast of Los Angeles is apparently the first in the nation based on the passing of drugs through breast milk" ("Mother Gets 6 Years for Drugs in Breast Milk," *The New York Times*, 28 Oct. 1992).

4. "For those of you remain unconvinced, we have started to catalog the many examples of proof that Tiger Woods is no mere mortal. . . . One of Tiger's most remarkable non-golfing abilities seems to be his power to both diagnose and instantly heal any injuries that he may sustain. At the 1999 Tour Championship Tiger purposely struck a large rock that was in front of his ball causing him GREAT pain. For the remainder of the round Tiger was not even able to complete his swing and was bent over in pain after every shot (he went one under par the rest of the way!). Immediately after the

round Tiger, completely unfazed . . . calmly stated that he simply had a "stinger" and that everything would be just fine. . . .

"Tiger's father, Earl, has confirmed that he and Tiger each possess the supernatural ability of mental telepathy. Earl made this statement on two separate occasions to *Sports Illustrated*. . . . Jesus gave his mother the gift of changing water into wine at a marriage feast. Tiger bought his mother a house in Tustin, California and gave his mother the keys to a new car after winning the 1999 Buick Invitational" (*www.tigerwoodsisgod.com*).

5. "While dining with the abductees [who claimed to be abducted by aliens], I found out something very revealing: not one of them recalled being abducted immediately after the experience. In fact, for most of them, many years went by before they 'remembered' the experience.

"How was this memory recalled? Under hypnosis. . . . Memory is a complex phenomenon involving distortions, deletions, additions, and sometimes, complete fabrication. Psychologists call this *confabulation*—mixing fantasy with reality to such an extent that it is impossible to sort them out. . . . Every parent has stories about the fantasies their children create. My daughter once described to my wife a purple dragon we saw on our hike in the local hills that day" (see Michael Shermer, *Why People Believe Weird Things*).

6. "Young women reading USC's *Daily Trojan*, UCLA's *Daily Bruin* and Hollywood trade papers are being asked to sell their eggs for insemination. Not everyone's eggs are wanted. . . . The agencies that advertise on campus all claim to help prospective parents select healthy donors, ages 21–30 or so. Shelley Smith, of the Egg Donor Program, says they do not solicit eggs from women who "need money to eat"—such women could be swayed by their need for food and shelter, she says. The USC financial aid office estimates a year at the school costs about $33,000. Smith says donors should be kind, intelligent and have the right reasons for entering the program. Smith also says donors should be attractive and intelligent. . . . The Egg Donor Program ad promises a $1,500 bonus to donors 'when you are chosen by a couple within the first month of being accepted by, and completing The Egg Donor Program'" (See Eyal Amiron, "Egg Donor Companies Target Some College Women, But not Others," *Los Angeles Independent*, 4 Oct. 2000).

7. "In the past thirty-five years, Boston, like other major cities in the United States, has seen some remarkable changes. In the years since the 1965 Immigration Act reformed a very restrictive quota system, immigrants from all over the world have come to make Boston their home. . . .

"In the nineteenth century, immigrants from southern and eastern Europe brought rich Jewish, Catholic, and Eastern Orthodox traditions. The new immigrants of the late twentieth century, however, have come from Asia, Africa, Latin America, and the Middle East as well as from European countries. In the ten years between 1980 and 1990, the Asian-American population of Boston doubled to 5.3 percent of the total and the Hispanic population increased to 10.8 percent. The African American population increased only slightly to 25.6 percent, while Boston's white population fell by 8 percent to 62.8 percent, even though the fast-growing Hispanic population is included in this group. Native Americans and people of other races comprise 6.2 percent of the population.

"Although these figures include only the city of Boston itself, a view of the wider Boston area would reveal similar changes. No matter how you look at it, the Boston of today represents a radically new racial, ethnic, and cultural reality" (*The Pluralism Project,* Harvard University, *www.fas.harvard.edu/ ~pluralism*).

Types of Evidence

Central to an analysis is assessing the evidence—the premises. For example, when Kathleen Tuttle says, "The majority of white people in America are not racist," she is not saying "No white person in America is racist." But because the *majority* is not the same as *all,* her claim is not universal in scope. Whether her claim is actually true is another matter.

There are different types of evidence. Some evidence comes in the form of facts or factual claims. Some evidence comes in the form of confessions or testimony (e.g., personal, eyewitness, or expert testimony). Some evidence comes in the form of statistical data, government reports, relevant policies or guidelines. And so on. Whatever the form it takes, evidence must be examined in a careful analysis. For the argument to be strong the premises need to provide sufficient support for the conclusion and, so, each piece of evidence should be scrutinized.

Claims of Fact versus Speculation

Facts are like stones on the path, giving us something firm to stand on. If a claim of fact were assumed to be false it would conflict with evidence known to be true. This would create a contradiction, which means the claim of fact must actually be true. Facts and factual claims do not permit a rival conclusion—any rival conclusion simply would lack support. For example:

AIDS and Donor Sperm: The AIDS virus can be transmitted through artificial insemination. Recent cases confirmed through scientific testing that a small percentage of women have gotten AIDS through a donor sperm they used when they were artificially inseminated years ago. At that time, AIDS tests were not routinely run on potential sperm donors.

Assuming it was *false* that cases confirmed that some women had gotten AIDS through a donor sperm in artificial insemination, there would be *no support* for the contention that AIDS could be transmitted through artificial insemination. The assertion about women getting AIDS through donor sperm clearly supports the conclusion that AIDS virus can be transmitted through artificial insemination. There is no doubt that this conclusion will follow from the evidence. This is not the case with speculation, however, which is much more nebulous.

Speculation

Speculation is a form of guesswork. When we assert something with little or no evidence, it's called speculation. Speculation has, at best, only partial support and is, basically, the argumentative version of going out on a limb. Speculation is not necessarily true; in fact it could be false and not conflict with known evidence or theoretical understanding. Speculation is not necessarily false—in fact it may prove to be correct. What distinguishes speculation is that the evidence given is insufficient to support it. In this sense, it is often based more on unsubstantiated opinion, hearsay, or a hunch.

Speculation often shows personal bias, even though it may be treated as common knowledge. It is important, when we analyze, to watch for speculation and not treat it as if what's being asserted is certainly the case. Consequently, speculating from one piece of evidence, however attractive, has its dangers. It is far better for us to stop and try to gather more evidence than to draw a hasty conclusion.

Let us look at some examples of speculation (indicated in italics) in the conversation between Andrea and Omar, below. See if you can see the dangers in going from the one observation to the speculative claim that is inferred:

ANDREA: Reuben has been exercising a lot lately. *He must want to join the Marines.*

OMAR: You may be right, but get this—I saw Reuben drinking wine with a beautiful stranger at the Café Madrid. *He and Maria and must be getting a divorce.*

Both Andrea and Omar are speculating about Reuben. Of course, he may want to join the Marines and his marriage may be on the rocks, but we could draw a rival conclusion from his recent exercising (e.g., his doctor told him to lose 25 pounds). And his marriage may be just fine (the beautiful stranger could be his cousin from Topeka). We must be careful about speculating, because it may lead us far from the truth and do more harm than good.

Here's speculation on a societal level: On a 1995 proficiency test of 156 examiners of fingerprints, one in five examiners made at least one "false positive" identification linking a mock crime scene print to the wrong person. Plus, fingerprint misidentifications do happen. Richard Jackson, for instance, was cleared of a murder conviction in Philadelphia in 1999 because three examiners had mistakenly matched his prints to those found at the scene (see Andy Newman, "Lawyers Question Fingerprinting's Reliability," *Daily Journal*, 28 June 2001). Given this situation, we might question the wisdom of allowing fingerprint "evidence" into criminal trials because of doubts about its reliability and speculate about how many of those in prisons may be victims of fingerprint misidentification. Of course, we don't know for certain if such misidentification actually is a serious problem and, so, our speculation conveys the uncertainty. It is important that we remember that fact.

Exercises

In the following, note when the reasoning seems *well supported* and when it is *speculative*:

1. Many children's cartoons contain acts of violence. Children are highly impressionable. We should monitor shows that may affect children. Therefore, we ought to monitor children's cartoons.

2. Many soap operas contain sexual themes and romance. Mario loves soap operas, so he must be obsessed with sex.

3. Most news programs focus on acts of violence, like murder and robbery. Therefore, Norm's suicidal tendencies must be due to the fact that he watches too much news.

4. Beth is an honest person. She recently refused to help her boyfriend get a copy of the history test, and last year she found a wallet on a bench and returned it to the owner. Not one of the $50 bills tucked behind credit cards in the wallet was touched.

5. Things are not always what they seem when it comes to politics. Facts can be twisted to suit the picture sought, speeches can be written to hide political problems and make the public feel everything's fine when it isn't. We might be better off with a healthy dose of skepticism. That means we should be skeptical about promises made by politicians.

6. Chong must be about to quit her job. I heard her complaining about a cup of coffee spilled all over her desk by one of her co-workers. She had to re-type the pesticide report she had just finished and missed happy hour with the gang. All that extra work made Chong mad as a hornet!

The Scope of a Claim

We need to be able to assess a body of evidence. Be attentive to the scope of a claim, to see exactly what it is meant to cover. "All" means more than "some" and vague generalities mean less than specific, detailed claims. For instance, when a radio executive claims, "Listeners prefer a sports piece right after the traffic report," she implies that *all* listeners prefer sports after traffic. However, it's not clear that this is true. For example, men may prefer to hear the sports after weather, whereas women may prefer sports after the business report or after the entertainment news. We have to be careful when universal claims starting with "all" are used and be willing to question such claims when we see them.

It's a question of scope. "*Everyone* who purchased a lottery ticket is eligible for the drawing for a new Taurus" covers much more territory than the claim, "*Some* people who purchased a lottery ticket are eligible for the drawing for a new Taurus. The term "all" covers the entire subject class; whereas "some" means only "at least one." These terms are considerably different in scope.

The significance of scope also applies to the use of "always" versus "frequently" or "often." "Often" is weaker than "always," for its scope is more limited. This means that a claim using "often" instead of "always" or "never" has less weight.

It helps, also, to think about the context. For example, in dealing with Aunt Pauline's lung cancer, the claim "Lots of people smoke" would not count as strong evidence without knowing more. It would be valuable to know that Aunt Pauline lived with Uncle Larry, a smoker, and that she worked in a smoke-filled airport bar. We could now consider whether secondhand smoke was the cause of her death. Specific details that relate to Aunt Pauline's health and possible causal factors of her cancer make it easier to evaluate alternative courses of action.

Credible Sources

Credible sources serve an important role in arguments. Suppose medical researchers claimed there was a causal connection between secondhand smoke and lung cancer. This could be very significant if the researchers were credible sources and had no conflict of interest (for instance, had not been bribed by an antismoking lobby). If solid statistical data established a pattern of health problems with secondhand smoke exposure, we would have more evidence to support the lawsuit. As we saw in the Chinatown beating case earlier in the chapter, assessing the credibility of witnesses and other sources can be very important. The outcome of a trial may turn on the credibility of the witnesses for the prosecution or defense.

Credibility of sources is also crucial in news coverage, as the following demonstrates. In June 1998, CNN broke a story claiming the nerve gas sarin (which is known to be deadly), was used by the United States against defectors in the Vietnam War. They based their report on what *seemed to be* credible sources. One source cited by CNN was retired Admiral Thomas Moorer of the Joint Chiefs of Staff. According to the report, he confirmed that sarin was used in Operation Tailwind (as the operation was known). However, the source evidently recanted his story:

> Moorer backed away from the CNN-Time report. He said in an interview that he had no firsthand knowledge of the gas being used anywhere in Southeast Asia. "I've never

seen a document indicating that it had been used or a document indicating it was going to be used," he said. (See Paul Richter, "Cohen Orders Probe of Alleged Gas Attacks," *Los Angeles Times,* 9 June 1998)

This shifting report and hedging on the part of Admiral Moorer causes us to wonder what exactly happened, if anything, to the American defectors and what to make of CNN's report. The question here is, "Is CNN right in their claim about the use of sarin and the presumed endorsement of doing so by the very highest levels of government?" If so, it would appear that Admiral Moorer originally told the truth and now is backing away from it. If not, then CNN went out on a limb and lacked the evidence to support their claims.

Of course, not all testimonials or "experts" *should* carry much weight. For example, actors and athletes are often hired to swear to the effectiveness of a particular product. Look also at trials where both sides bring in "experts" to bolster their case. We often see this in high-profile trials, where expert is pitted against expert in the hopes of convincing a jury that one side should prevail.

Jurors are regularly put in the position of having to assess the credibility of expert witnesses. Sizing up credibility is not always easy, which may account for the role of gut reaction on the part of some jurors.

Value Claims

Value claims may be used as evidence, but should be handled carefully. These may relate to character references and issues of credibility. Value claims are usually expressed in sentences that assert a judgment of taste, as in "Novels are always better artworks than movies." We also see value claims in moral judgments, as in "You ought not to watch so much television" or "People should exercise their rights in a democracy and vote." Value claims functioning as evidence will need to be scrutinized. These may relate to character references and issues of credibility. Personal values can influence a decision, so we need to be attentive to that fact.

Moral or religious values can also weigh heavily in a decision. For example, in a commentary on the movie *Godzilla,* Ryan Harvey argued that the directors ignored the creature's soul. In his scathing attack on the movie, Harvey said,

> So what do [directors] Emmerich and Devlin give us? A big iguana with squinty eyes, Jay Leno's chin and bad breath instead of flames. He's also a spineless wimp, dodging buildings, fleeing helicopters and hiding in the subways. The real Godzilla would never hide. . . . *Godzilla* didn't let TriStar down. TriStar let *Godzilla* down. (See Ryan Harvey, "Even Godzilla Movie's Gotta Have Heart," *Los Angeles Times,* 8 June 1998)

Harvey's argument indicates that the movie *Godzilla* failed because the directors neglected to give the monster a soul. He suggests that viewers need a creature to identify with, a monster whose fate we can care about while still feeling a vicarious fear of all that power.

Group Exercise

Assess the reasoning in a ruling by the California Supreme Court that a man who fathers a child with a woman married to someone else may be denied all legal parental rights. Set out your response, in light of the following:

1. Justice Joyce L. Kennard said that a man, "who fathers a child with a woman married to another man takes the risk that the child will be raised within that marriage and that he will be excluded from participation in the child's life."

2. In a 5–2 opinion, the court majority said that because Dawn was married at the time the baby was conceived and was living with her husband when the baby, Sam, was born, they were bound by state law that presumes a husband to be the father of his wife's children.

3. Jerome "Jerry" Krchmar, 41, lived with a woman in 1995 while she was separated from her husband to whom she'd been married for six years.

4. The woman, "Dawn," became pregnant within a month of living with Jerry.

5. After living with Jerry for four months, Dawn, moved back in with her husband.

6. Jerry took a parenting class and tried to negotiate child support.

7. Jerry filed a lawsuit before the baby was born to assert his parental rights.

8. Dawn and her husband refused to let Jerry see the baby, Sam.

9. Dawn's husband punched Jerry when the three people met for a blood test.

10. Jerry said, "I will never give up my son." (See Maura Dolan, "Court Denies Parental Rights to Unwed Father," *Los Angeles Times,* 7 Apr. 1998)

Statistical Evidence

It's an interesting thing about human nature: Most people don't like math, but are mesmerized by those who use it. One of the primary uses made of mathematics in argumentation is employing statistical studies. People often draw upon statistical studies to bolster an argument. Haven't you seen those commercials like, "Four out of five doctors surveyed prescribe Preparation K for the relief of polyps" or "Most dentists prefer Crescent mouthwash"? We need to ask ourselves, "How many doctors and dentists were actually surveyed?"

The use of statistics can be very effective, particularly when the studies are current. Besides the date of the study, the key concerns in assessing statistical studies are size and diversity. The sample size should be adequate and have sufficient diversity: the group sampled needs to be representative of the target population being studied. We have to be careful, though. If the sample size is not large enough, it may result in a *hasty generalization* (fallacious reasoning that occurs when a sample study is insufficient in terms of size, leading to an incorrect conclusion being drawn). If the studies fail to be diverse enough, the result may be *biased statistics* (fallacious reasoning that occurs when a sample study is not diverse enough and, thus, fails to be representative). Watch the percentage, also. The closer to 100 percent in a positive claim (X percent of A's are B's) and the closer to zero in a negative claim (Y percent of C's are not D's), the stronger is the claim.

Think of it this way: you are creating an ad campaign for cube-shaped pasta. You do a market analysis and find that 78 percent of men prefer cube-shaped to donut-shaped pasta, whereas only 45 percent of women prefer the cube-shaped pasta. If more women normally buy pasta than men, your job is to get women to change their minds. Plus, you'll try to convince the 22 percent of men who prefer donut-shaped pasta to try the cubes.

However, if the researcher found that 94 percent of children prefer cube-shaped to donut-shaped pasta, you could aim your advertising at this younger market. We know how fast food chains target ads to children with great success. So paying attention to the role of statistics in effective reasoning can be very helpful to developing critical thinking skills.

Exercise (Group or Individual)

Here's a medical mystery:

Finland, a country of 5.4 million is among the wealthiest, least polluted, and most health-conscious in the world. Yet it has the highest rate of diabetes in the world, including insulin-dependent diabetics. Of the more than 180,000 Finns with diabetes, 30,000 are insulin-dependent. In other countries researchers found that breast-feeding helped inhibit diabetes; but Finland allows mothers to stay home with full pay and benefits for nine months, resulting in more breast-feeding than in other developed countries. However, Finland uses nitrates and nitrites in their farming and in cured meats, which are widely consumed. Finns are among the biggest consumers of coffee in all of Europe. (See Carol J. Williams, "Researchers Struggle to Solve Mystery of Finland's High Diabetes Rate," *Los Angeles Times*, 30 July 2000)

Answer the following:
1. What can you infer from this information about Finland's problem with diabetes?
2. Speculate as to possible causes or solutions to this situation.

⊞ Circumstantial Evidence

This occurs when we have no hard evidence one way or the other, but the evidence points to the one conclusion. Circumstantial evidence works together in support of a particular conclusion that, in the absence of any reasonable alternative, seems highly likely. The key word here is "likely": no amount of circumstantial evidence can provide certainty. What gives circumstantial evidence its weight is the lack of an alternative explanation for the pieces in the puzzle. Circumstantial evidence has been strong enough to convict people of murder, even in the absence of a body!

In one of the longest criminal proceedings in Connecticut history, the prosecution's case rested on circumstantial evidence. Murray Gold was charged with the murder of his ex-wife's parents. There were no witnesses to the crime, no fingerprints, and the weapon (a Buck hunting knife) was never found. What they had against Gold was a motive (a "festering resentment" of his former in-laws whom he blamed for his divorce from his wife), a bloody shoe print with the imprint of a Cats Paw label on the heel (four pairs of shoes bearing Cats Paw brand names were found in Gold's apartment), and three pieces of plastic. Two forensics specialists say that the plastic, picked up in the bedroom of the murder victims, could have only come from a button replacement kit later found in Gold's apartment.

Those pieces of plastic were considered by the state attorney, Walter Scanlon, to be the key to the case (see William Hathaway, "Prosecution Rests Its Case in 4th Murray Gold Trial," *Hartford Courant*, 12 July 1986). The jury would have to decide if there is another explanation for the plastic being near one of the victims' bodies—for example, that the ex-wife or the police must have planted the plastic in the bedroom to frame the defendant.

Let's look at another example: In the late 90s, claims surfaced that Thomas Jefferson had had a 38-year-long involvement with a slave, Sally Hemmings. This rested, at least initially, on circumstantial evidence (later DNA evidence was introduced to show that Tom Woodson was not Thomas Jefferson's son). In a review of a book on the subject, Eyler Robert Coates, Sr., gave some valuable suggestions about how to handle circumstantial evidence. He says,

> The only way a study of such a mass of contradictory circumstantial evidence could be conducted fairly would be to take each piece of evidence and present the arguments for and against its acceptance, with a final summary of the best arguments for each separate piece. Ideally, this might be done by two persons, one arguing for and one against. A totally disinterested person might, with considerable effort, fill both roles. But that level of impartiality when dealing with such highly charged issues is almost humanly impossible. (See Eyler Robert Coates, Sr., "The Jefferson-Hemmings Circumstantial Evidence," *The Jefferson Perspective, www.geocities.com/CapitolHill*)

As Coates indicates, examining circumstantial evidence in as fair a manner as possible may require some effort. This needs to be kept in mind when we face such situations.

Conditional Claims

Evidence may be expressed as a conditional claim—an "If . . . then" claim. We see how a conditional claim can operate in this comment about actor–musician Russell Crowe:

> On the personal side, Crowe remains a rather reclusive personality. He has said that he would only live in L.A. if certain conditions were met, namely: "if Australia and New Zealand were swallowed up by a huge tidal wave, if there was a bubonic plague in Europe, and if the continent of Africa disappeared from some Martian attack." (*www.moviething.com*, 18 July 2001)

In order to live in Los Angeles, Crowe asserts several antecedent conditions must first occur—namely Australia and New Zealand being swallowed up by a tidal wave, a bubonic plague hitting Europe, and the African continent eliminated by a Martian attack. The fact the antecedent is so highly unlikely suggests that Crowe similarly sees as a dim prospect that he'd ever live in Los Angeles.

For any given conditional claim, the antecedent is not necessarily true. Often we are told "If A then B" and yet A never happens, or isn't likely to happen in the near future. For example, here are two examples of conditional claims with false antecedents:

- If I weighed 700 pounds, I could be a Sumo wrestler.
- If foreign workers had some basic rights concerning work conditions and benefits guaranteed to them in international trade agreements, they would not be as vulnerable to exploitation.

In the first case, I have no shot at weighing 700 pounds, regardless of how many donuts I eat. In the second example, if we knew what was required to make the antecedent true, we might be able to arrive at a true consequent. But the lack of certainty in establishing the antecedent means that the consequent cannot be assumed.

Analogies

Instead of giving straightforward evidence, an analogy, metaphor, or comparison may be offered as evidence. These sometimes colorful or vivid comparisons can make a great impression on the audience or reader. See if you can find all the analogies in the excerpt from a review of a book on spirituality that was in *Shambhala Sun* magazine:

> Spirituality is like Jell-O. It comes in every imaginable flavor, it's almost impossible to pin down, and your definitions of it will only last until it morphs into another shape. That's how the eminent sociologist of religion, Wade Clark Roof, explains the difficulty of defining our culture's love affair with things spiritual. Roof, who teaches

at the University of California, Santa Barbara, does come up with two clarifying categories in the slippery word of contemporary spirituality: seekers, who pursue meaning by sampling a smorgasbord of dishes, and dwellers, who feast from a single table. (See Anna-Liza Kosma, "Seekers and Dwellers," *Shambhala Sun*, May 2001)

Analogies often have persuasive power, so warrant a detailed study. We will do this when we delve into inductive reasoning. As we'll see, the strength of the analogy rests on the strength of the relevant similarities of the two things being compared. The stronger the relevant similarities, the stronger the analogy; but if there are significant differences in what is being compared, the analogy is weakened.

Here's another example. The term "virus" is now widely used in both medicine and technology. According to Ken Dunham, there are "valid comparisons between biological and computer viruses that support the origin of the term "computer virus" (see Ken Dunham, "The Great Analogy," *Securitydatabase.net,* 2 July 2001, *www. dbase.dmrt.net*). To decide if Dunham is right, we'd need to set out the comparison and look at the similarities and differences of biological and computer viruses and weigh the relative strength of each.

In order to assess the analogy, we would want to weigh the similarities and differences and then assess the quality of the comparison and, thus, the strength of the argument. It must be recognized, however, that analogies always contain a degree of uncertainty given there will be some differences in the terms being compared. Because of this, any conclusion drawn on the basis of an analogy only can be said to follow with probability. This means the argument has an inherent weakness (as do all inductive arguments) that we need to be aware of.

Cause and Effect Reasoning

Cause and effect reasoning occurs when someone asserts that something either causes or is an effect of something else. For example, if Uncle Al declared, "Secondhand smoke *caused* Aunt Pauline's lung cancer," we ought to examine the causal connection and eliminate other possible causes of lung cancer before we could consider secondhand smoke the likely cause. Perhaps Aunt Pauline lived near a factory spewing out toxic chemicals. Perhaps she had a habit of sniffing glue. Perhaps she used a strong chemical for scrubbing her floors and had poor ventilation in her house.

A causal claim may have merit, but it is crucial that alternative causes be dismissed first. Once they can be eliminated, a causal claim has more force. We can see this by the ways in which different theories about the origin of AIDS have been offered. Some argue that AIDS entered the human population through malaria experiments on prisoners and researchers, who injected mangabey (monkey) blood into the human subjects. Others argue that AIDS entered through oral polio vaccines given to about a million people in central Africa from 1957 to 1960 and was cultured from the cells of primates. Still others think AIDS can be traced to human consumption of primates' blood or exposure to the bodily fluids of chimpanzees.

And so on. Until it is obvious what caused AIDS/HIV to enter the human population, there will be a host of theories swirling around.

For example, when people argue that media violence causes viewers to become more violent, they are saying that the existence of the one (violence on TV or in movies) is directly linked to the other (violence on the part of viewers). It is a powerful claim and one that has raised a great deal of concern. Nevertheless, before we accord it much weight, we need to see what evidence underlies the cause and effect reasoning.

We see cause and effect reasoning behind arguments for censorship of film and TV. There are those who insist violence on the screen is causally linked to violent behavior. What follows from this is that to change the latter we must restrict the former. It has, for instance, been argued, "If we don't want people doing crazy things like setting subway toll booths on fire, then we shouldn't show such acts in movies like *Money Train*." In other words, those who believe violence on screen can cause acts of violence on the part of a viewer react with alarm to movies like *Money Train* or TV shows like *The Sopranos*, which has caused some pretty strong public commentary because of its casual depiction of execution-style killing. Such response comes out of a belief that the causal link between a movie and human behavior is strong.

Exercises

Refer to the different types of evidence (universal versus particular claims, use of sources, statistical studies, value claims, circumstantial evidence, conditional claims, arguments based on analogy, cause and effect reasoning) covered thus far. Identify the type of evidence presented and any questions you might have about its value in assessing the box office success of the film *Waiting to Exhale*.

1. *News Monthly* did a poll of 434 people at the USC versus Northwestern Rose Bowl (football) game and found that 86 percent of college women at the game thought the portrayal of black women in *Waiting to Exhale* was positive.

2. Some of the men in the *News Monthly* poll of 434 people attending the Rose Bowl game were offended by the portrayal of black men in the film *Waiting to Exhale,* but still liked the movie.

3. bell hooks, an African-American scholar of popular culture, criticized the portrayal of black women in the movie, arguing that the movie did not further the cause of black women in this country.

4. If the movie continues to gross figures at anywhere near the rate of the first few weeks after opening, *Waiting to Exhale* is going to have an impact on the way Hollywood approaches films with blacks in the lead roles.

5. Lots of people enjoyed *Waiting to Exhale*. In fact, my friend Rivien said is was great.

6. People ought to support films like *Waiting to Exhale*, since it focuses on African Americans and doesn't just have the actors playing police officers or gang members.

7. *Waiting to Exhale* is a lot like *Joy Luck Club*, in that it looks at women who are not white and presents them in nonstereotypical ways.

8. Men should enjoy *Waiting to Exhale*, since it shows how much women enjoy talking about men and how central relationships are to women's lives.

9. Ticket stubs to *Waiting to Exhale* were found on George's desk at work, along with a note that read, "Alice, I sure had a great time last night." George must have taken Alice to see the movie.

10. Everyone interviewed at the midnight showing of *Waiting to Exhale* on its opening night said it was a good movie.

Independent versus Interdependent Evidence

When it comes to analyzing evidence, you can see that we have to be aware of what sort of evidence is being presented and begin to assess it for strength. It's one thing to be able to see the structure of an argument so you know what is being claimed and what the various pieces of support are. This is the crucial stage of dismantling the argument. However, we aren't done yet. The next stage is that of examining the evidence we have been given. Here is a guide for weighing evidence.

Not all evidence is of equal value. Any one premise is potentially much more powerful than the other premises. It may be that one or more premises independently supports the conclusion. When one piece of evidence is sufficient in and of itself, we would say that that piece *independently,* or singly, establishes the conclusion. Suppose, for example, that we have a confession from the suspect, as well as DNA evidence. Either the confession *or* the physical evidence may establish guilt, assuming the confession is not coerced and is made by someone who is competent. In that case, any other evidence would be extraneous. However, not all criminals confess and not all physical evidence can seal a conviction. We often need to piece together all the evidence.

If we lack one definitive piece of evidence, then we have to look at the way our evidence works together. When this occurs, we say each contributing piece of evidence is *interdependent*. With interdependent premises, the evidence operates as a package deal. This is strongest when the evidence works together like interlocking pieces, holding up the conclusion. For example, if Ralph had no alibi, e-mailed

Jorge setting out his intention to steal Jorge's new Toyota Four Runner, and the cell phone calls Jorge received that day could all be traced to Ralph's home phone—all that evidence together builds the case against Ralph when Jorge's Four Runner is missing.

And when that evidence poses no clear conflicts or contradictions if we assume it is actually true we have *corroborating* evidence. With corroborating evidence it is harder to attack a case, because the foundation gains more strength. For example, because Ralph has no alibi and was known to have e-mailed threats to Jorge we'd say these two pieces of evidence corroborate each other. Similarly, if we knew that Jorge got a perfect score on his SAT, had strong letters of reference, and had just received a phone call from the university's financial aid office, then we have corroborating evidence that this could be news about the scholarship he applied for shortly before his car was stolen.

Exercises

The Three Strikes Law in California

On June 19, 2001, a California Appeals Court upheld the 25-years-to-life prison sentence given to a homeless man on parole. This was handed out under the guidelines of California's so-called three strikes law. According to this law, anyone committing a third felony would be given a mandatory 25-years-to-life sentence, regardless of the severity of the crime committed (so long as it was a felony conviction). The fact of the third felony being committed independently of the circumstances results in the sentence. On the other hand . . .

1. Assume you are a member of *Prisoners' Rights Now,* a group that takes on cases that appear to be unjust. They ask for your position on this case. <u>Share what you will say, after reading the following about this actual case:</u>
   - Yes, Kevin Thomas Weber did commit a felony in breaking into a Santa Ana, California, restaurant.
   - Yes, Weber did come in through a roof vent.
   - Yes, Weber might have taken more had he not been interrupted by a blaring burglar alarm.
   - But, still, Weber stole only four cookies.

2. Justice David G. Sills wrote in a unanimous opinion, "A safecracker who cracks an empty safe is nonetheless a safecracker." <u>Give a response to Judge Sills from any two of the following:</u>
   - The perspective of the owner of the restaurant.
   - The perspective of Weber's family.
   - The perspective of potential burglars who have two strikes against them.
   - Your own perspective.

▦ Weighing Evidence

In the process of trying to evaluate an argument, chain of arguments, policies, and decision making we need to have some systematic way of dealing with the evidence. That is, we need to see how to evaluate the strength of the evidence and prioritize it in terms of its role in supporting the particular goal. Here is a guide for weighing evidence:

Checklist for Weighing Evidence

Scope	Universal claims "All A is B" or "no A is B" are stronger than the particular claims "some A is B" or "some A is not B."
Relevance	Claims pertinent to the topic (focused on the issue) are stronger than general observations or vague "truisms"; set background information concerning the context to the side, unless it is necessary to make the argument.
Support	Examine the evidence to assess the quality of support and its role in the argument (Does any of the evidence independently support the conclusion? Are all the premises needed to make the case? Are any extraneous, unnecessary?). Use of credible sources, properly documented is stronger than speculation.
Testimony	Watch for the credibility of those giving testimony. Look out for any conflicts of interest, poor grasp of relevant information, poor observation skills, emotional problems, or inattention to details that could affect credibility.
Facts stack up	Relevance is the key here: The more indispensable a fact is to the case, the more weight it should have. Valuable facts may seal the case.
Circumstantial evidence	Key here is that there's no reasonable alternative explanation. Ask yourself if a rival conclusion is feasible.
Statistical claims	Be attentive to: • Date of study. • Size of study. • Diversity in terms of relevant variables or factors so the study is representative of the target population.
Conditional claims or hypotheticals	Watch for "if . . . then" constructions (If P then Q). Can we determine if the antecedent condition P is true? Is the consequent Q known to be false? Is this one link in a chain of conditional sentences?
Value claims	What is the force and impact of the claim? Who holds it? What are the consequences of not believing in it? Do ethics or religion color the way in which things are interpreted, or presented? Watch for evidence of personal bias that could prejudice the case.

Analogy or precedent	Analogies can never be put forward with certainty, and resist verifiability. Look for strength of similarities. Similarities must carry more cumulative weight than differences for the analogy (precedent) to hold. Similarities MAKE an analogy. Differences BREAK an analogy.
Omissions	Watch for "holes" in the reasoning. Ask if anything has been left out (whether intentionally or unintentionally).

Exercise

Part One: Weighing Evidence

1. It seems that the estate of the Bear family was broken into and the suspect is Goldie Locks. Sort through the evidence, categorizing it as good, bad, or interesting. Decide if the case against Goldie is strong enough to go to trial. Choose the five strongest pieces of evidence for the prosecution and the five strongest for the defense.
   a. Goldie's alibi could not be substantiated.
   b. Goldie eats porridge every other day for breakfast, but never on Mondays.
   c. The Bears eat porridge almost every day.
   d. Porridge stains were found on Goldie's blouse.
   e. Goldie's mother served porridge yesterday, but today made fried eggs.
   f. The Bears' front door was pried open, possibly with a tool.
   g. Goldie had a pocket knife in her purse.
   h. Some little girls are afraid of bears.
   i. No little girl should go wandering in the woods, where bears live.
   j. If Goldie broke into the Bears' house, she had to have had a tool or knife.
   k. The little Bear's chair was broken.
   l. A study of robberies in 2001 revealed that most robberies are committed during the day and by someone who is familiar with the victim.
   m. Goldie says she had never met the Bears.
   n. Mrs. Bear found muddy footprints on the sidewalk.
   o. Many people have mud on their feet and little girls often have muddy feet.
   p. A piece of wood that matches that of baby Bear's chair was found in Tom Thumb's backyard, next to Tom's truck collection.
   q. Goldie had mud on her shoes.
   r. The muddy footprints were approximately size 6 shoes.
   s. Goldie's mother said Goldie was a lovely child.
   t. Little girls are less likely to get into trouble than are boys.
   u. Dr. Zut, child psychologist, said children are innately curious.
   v. Both Tom Thumb and Goldie have size 6 shoes.
   w. Goldie has no criminal record.

    x.   Goldie's kindergarten teacher said Goldie had been well behaved and helpful to the other children when she was in her class four years ago.

    y.   Goldie showed no remorse and said, "I could care less about those stupid bears."

    z.   The crime took place on a Monday.

    aa.   Baby Bear had psychiatric treatment last year for chronic lying.

    bb.   Mrs. Bear said baby Bear's toy truck was taken during the robbery.

2. You are investigating possible defects in the Jeep Grand Cherokee (see Ricardo Alonso-Zaldivar 's two articles: "Cherokee SUV target of Fed probe," *Los Angeles Times*, 5 July 2001 and "Jeep Cherokee Blame Game Heats Up," *Los Angeles Times*, 23 Dec. 2001). Sort through the evidence, categorizing it as good, bad, or interesting. Choose the five strongest pieces of evidence for the pro side (buy the Cherokee) and the five strongest for the con side (shop around for another car).

    a.   Federal authorities are investigating a possible defect in Jeep Grand Cherokees that may cause the SUV to lurch into reverse.

    b.   Cases of lurching usually happened when idling with the gearshift in the "park" position, but have been known to happen when the engine is turned off.

    c.   More than 860 people have complained to the government or to DaimlerChrysler about "inadvertent rollaway in reverse" incidents involving Grand Cherokees.

    d.   Complaints involved 1995 to 1999 Grand Cherokees.

    e.   No deaths have been reported.

    f.   There have been 359 crashes and 184 injuries involving the lurching of the SUV into reverse.

    g.   The company has denied there being anything wrong with the vehicle.

    h.   Given all the Grand Cherokees sold, the number of incidents is small.

    i.   About 1.3 million of the popular SUVs are affected by the investigation.

    j.   The National Highway and Transportation Safety Administration (NHTSA) issued no recommendations for Grand Cherokee owners while it conducts the investigation.

    k.   The company does not believe there is any issue with the vehicle, but is cooperating with the investigation.

    l.   Dominick Infante, safety spokesperson for DaimlerChrysler, which builds the Grand Cherokee, said he had no information on any consumer complaints received directly by DaimlerChrysler.

    m.   Typically, manufacturers get far more problem reports than does the NHTSA, since many consumers are not familiar with the process of registering complaints with the federal auto safety agency.

    n.   Since 1999 Grand Cherokees have been redesigned, with a new type of transmission.

    o.   The Grand Cherokee is a very popular sports-utility vehicle.

    p.   A lot of customers really appreciate the choice of colors for the body and interior of the vehicle.

q. Jacquee Kahn of Los Angeles said her 1997 Cherokee rolled into reverse while she was filling it up at a gas station just before Christmas 1999, with the engine turned off; the open driver door crunched into a gas pump, bringing the jeep to a halt.

r. Kahn is now too terrified to drive the car.

s. The rate of park-to-reverse complaints for Grand Cherokees is more than five times greater than for any similar SUV made by a different company.

t. Customer Kahn said DaimlerChrysler did not take her complaint seriously, perhaps because she was a woman; they instructed her to reread her owner's manual.

u. The company examined Kahn's jeep and said it had no problem.

v. Many customers think the Grand Cherokee is the best looking SUV on the market.

w. An Oklahoma man said his Grand Cherokee lurched into reverse when his wife went to open a gate at the ranch; the jeep crossed a busy highway, went down a 40-foot slope and hit a tree.

x. The company has denied there was anything wrong with the Oklahoma man's car, suggesting it was the wife's fault—she is now afraid to drive the car.

y. Company official, Dominick Infante, said, "We do believe these incidents resulted from mistakes made when drivers shifted into park."

z. Sports utility vehicles are gas-guzzlers, but are fun to drive.

3. Set out your position as to whether or not it should be possible for Daniel Patterson to give his second kidney to his daughter, Renada, in light of the various pieces of evidence set out below. Be sure to sort through the evidence, weighing it for strengths and weaknesses:

a. Renada, 13 years old, was born with only one kidney, an unhealthy one.

b. For seven years, Renada was on dialysis three times a week, unable to go to school.

c. Renada's father, Daniel Patterson, is serving 12 years in prison for burglary and drug convictions.

d. Daniel Patterson had abandoned Renada when she was a baby, but donated one of his kidneys two years ago, when he turned out to be a compatible donor.

e. For two years Renada lived with her father's kidney, but often skipped her medication; his kidney (now hers) began to fail.

f. Renada needs a new kidney; her 38 year-old father wants to donate his remaining kidney (he still has three more years in prison).

g. If Daniel Patterson gives away his last kidney, he will require dialysis; that will cost the system $40,000 a year.

h. To take Daniel's kidney clearly puts him at risk.

i. 3100 patients are on a waiting list for a kidney in Northern California

j. Hank Greeley of Stanford's Center for Biomedical Ethics said that a father in most situations should be allowed to make a sacrifice for his daughter, though he said this made him nervous.

k. Arthur L. Caplan, director of the Center for Bioethics at the University of Pennsylvania is opposed to the surgery; he says, "You don't ever want to kill a person to say you saved another's life."

l. There has never been a live kidney transplant, says Caplan, where a person went from one kidney to none.

m. This would be Renada's third donated kidney (her body rejected the first when she was five).

n. There is a question whether Renada's body would accept another kidney from her father, since, when she didn't take her medicine required for the transplant before, her face became bloated, her stomach distended, and she hunched her back and felt ill.

o. Dr. Nancy Ascher, a professor of surgery, says, "Whether the organ was rejected because the medication wasn't taken, the body may have decided that this organ is incompatible and will do so again."

Part Two: Applying our Knowledge

There are many different forms arguments can take. Some are set out in a straightforward manner, with the conclusion clearly articulated and the evidence presented in its totality. But this need not be the case. Even advertisements present arguments that can be analyzed. This is true in spite of the case that ads often attempt to persuade the audience without ever commenting on the product itself (at least not explicitly). Look, for instance, at the MTV ad (see Fig. 5-2).

FIGURE 5-2
What can we conclude about MTV from this ad?

Exercises

1. Examine the MTV ad, "I'm itchy. Do I have MTV?" and then,
   a. Discuss whether or not you think this ad presents an argument.
   b. Share your thoughts on the effectiveness of the ad and how MTV has been so successful in reaching its audience.

2. Assume department store chain Nordstrom wants to tap into your critical thinking skills. Set out your position and go into detail (so you are giving them an argument) as to whether or not this will be an effective ad campaign: "We're all shoppers. We're all neighbors. We can't wait to meet you."

3. Read the article excerpt below about Taco Bell and the use of genetically engineered corn that is not for human consumption. Then answer the questions that follow.

   Genetically engineered corn that has not been approved for human consumption has found its way into Taco Bell taco shells sold in supermarkets, says a biotech watchdog group. The group, Genetically Engineered Food Alert, is calling on the Food and Drug Administration to recall the taco shells . . . The group says the corn . . . has characteristics that suggest it could cause allergic reactions, including nausea and shock. The FDA has had no reports of anyone becoming ill from eating the tacos and has not verified the claims. But a spokeswoman says the agency, with the Environmental Protection Agency, is "actively looking into the issue," and if the allegations are proved, the product will be pulled from the market.

   Larry Bohlen of environmental group Friends of the Earth, one of the members of the Food Alert campaign, says the group does not know of any health effects related to the tacos, but "the American public had no way of knowing whether an allergic reaction could be tied to" the biotech corn. Bohlen says only Taco Bell-brand shells sold in supermarkets have been tested, but "we're going to next test taco shells from Taco Bell restaurants." Kraft spokesman Michael Mudd says the company is having an independent lab test the taco shells. "The goal all of us share is the safest food supply possible," Mudd says. "As much progress as we've made, we have to continue to improve it."

   Lisa Dry of the Biotechnology Industry Organization says the FDA is planning to do its own testing of the taco shells, and results could be available within three days. "We don't actually know whether this corn actually did make it into these Taco Bell taco shells," she says. She questioned the accuracy of lab tests conducted by Genetic Id of Fairfield, Iowa. "This lab has in the past not had accurate results. The testing process is complicated." (See "Taco Bell Asked to Hold the Chalupas/Biotech Corn Found in Grocery Taco Shells," *USA Today*, 19 Sep. 2000)

   Answer the following:
   a. State the three strongest pieces of evidence *for* pulling the taco shells from Taco Bell's restaurant chains.
   b. State the three strongest pieces of evidence *against* pulling the taco shells from Taco Bell's restaurant chains (i.e., for allowing Taco Bell to continue using them at the present time).

c. Are there any questions you would need to have answered before you'd believe the corn should be pulled from the market?
d. What if any assumptions (note warranted versus unwarranted) are made in the article?
e. Which side did you find most persuasive? Say why.

Analysis of an Article or Argument

Once we feel comfortable handling evidence, we can tackle all sorts of arguments, great and small. Let's start first with the title, to see if it sets the stage for any interpretation that may follow. The way things are labeled or titled may shape the way in which they are perceived.

Notice, for example, the title of the article on the Chinatown case we examined earlier. In the title of the article, the altercation between Detective Kelly and Mr. Huang was called a "beating." However, inside the article it was called a "scuffle." There is quite a difference: a "scuffle" is generally considered fairly minor, where no one gets hurt. In contrast, a "beating" usually refers to something more severe, where someone is seriously injured.

The judge must decide whether this was a "scuffle," a "beating," or something else. The severity of Long Huang's or Detective Kelly's injuries would be a factor in coming to a decision. The language used to describe the incident shapes our understanding of what took place. Test this yourself: Find three to four news articles and rewrite the title from at least two different perspectives and see how things shift according to each distinctly different title. The thing about titles is that we want to be sure not to get misled, or biased, by a title that overtly or covertly influences the way in which we read the article. So we must be on the watch.

Structure

An analysis of an article involves looking at the way the article is structured, determining the author's position, frame of reference, and method of approach; examining the use of language; and checking for bias. It is important to be on the lookout for bias. There may be bias as shown through the use of language, which shows the values or position favored by the author, or the explicit or implicit expression of attitudes or values. There could be bias in the very way in which evidence is presented (e.g., the author skews the article in favor of one side). It could be that key evidence for one side is missing or distorted, ignoring or underplaying one side. This would then result in an imbalance in terms of a fair representation of both sides.

Basics

Central to an analysis is an examination of the key claims or arguments. Clarify what is being argued (the thesis) and then set out the premises. Then pull out and weigh the evidence. The argument may rest on such things as research data, statistics, physical evidence, causal claims, comparisons, testimony, personal statements, confessions, and anecdotes.

Examine the evidence carefully. We may be headed in the wrong direction if vital pieces of evidence are missing. Similarly, it is important to look at any assumptions we make. What we assume affects how we think and what we think about; it is important to discern whether our assumptions are warranted or unwarranted.

Your personal reaction is generally a separate issue from an analysis. You could incorporate reactions at the end; say right before the conclusion, to add a personal note to your essay. This is not formally part of the analysis. However, if your analysis leads to your reflections, then the personal angle could be relevant and its addition justified.

Staying Focused in Short Analysis Papers

In a short essay (less than five pages) be selective. Zero-in on the most important aspects; you cannot do everything. Nevertheless, if you are writing clearly and concisely, you can do a lot in a brief analysis.

The key aspects you'd want to include are (1) a statement of the article's focus or thesis, (2) key points and organization, (3) use of language, (4) strengths, (5) weaknesses, and (6) persuasiveness of the article. In some cases you might want to focus on one area, but generally try to give an overview of all six. We can summarize these six in the following table:

Ingredients of a Strong Analysis

1. Statement as to what is being argued or discussed.
   - Thesis or focus of the essay or article.
   - Include in your introduction your assessment of the article's persuasiveness.

2. How it is being argued or discussed.
   - Key points made and issues raised.
   - Could include how the argument or discussion is structured.

3. Relevant observations about the use of language.
   - Note value-laden, biased, or prejudicial language.
   - Watch use of metaphors and connotations of words.
   - Note when use of language is clear, concise, and accessible for the targeted audience.
   - Note degree of clarity in use of language.

4. Set out the STRENGTHS.
   - Note arguments that best support the author's thesis.
   - Note valuable points or insights in the expository essay.
   - Point out powerful uses of language, effective use of statistics or credible sources, pertinent examples, and well-supported details.

5. Set out the WEAKNESSES.
- Note any aspects that diminish the quality of the article.
- Note any contradictions or inconsistencies in the author's reasoning.
- Point out when statistics are used poorly or are out of date.
- Note any speculation or unsupported claims.
- Watch unfounded assumptions, or use of references (witnesses or "experts") that are not credible.

6. Assess article for persuasiveness.
- Watch for omissions.
- See if evidence is strong.
- Notice if language helps or hinders.
- Decide if weaknesses are too great.
- See if the argument is fully developed.
- See if illustrations and examples back up claims.
- Watch for questionable assumptions.
- Assess the cogency of the reasoning.

Proceeding with Your Analysis

Even in a short analysis, we should include these six aspects. If the author's use of language raises no questions or concerns in your mind, then you could omit discussion of the language. However, it is good to note that the use of language is unproblematic, and explain why. Always be on the lookout for loaded terms. Carefully examine the way an article is structured, to see if it gives a fair presentation of the issues under consideration.

First, you want to see what is the focus, issue raised, and/or position argued. Make sure it's clearly indicated. You must know the focus and the thesis before you can evaluate the argument. And you can only evaluate the argument when you have identified the conclusion and supporting premises.

Be careful here. Some writers do have a thesis, but you may not find the thesis until three, four, or five paragraphs into the paper. Such fishing expeditions may be necessary, so be ready. It also helps clarify the purpose of the article. Determine the intent (position paper, exposition, etc.). In a position piece, where a particular point of view is set out and defended, you must first clarify the thesis. Only then can you decide if the evidence presents a strong case.

Exercises

1. Set out the thesis and key claims in the following argument:

   Kimosabe must have eaten the sock. He's often a bad dog when left inside the house and he was alone all day long. The socks were out on the table. He's been known to eat socks left on the floor. The window was wide open, but I wouldn't think a stray cat or dog would come in and take a sock. Only a few other things are missing. So it's surely Kimosabe who ate the sock!

2. Set out the thesis and key claims in the following argument, then decide if it looks like a strong case:

1200 people are complaining of ailments since the El Al accident. The "black box" cockpit voice recorder disappeared from the evidence bin where firefighters insist they put it. Five hours into the rescue effort, after Dutch security police had cleared the crash site of emergency workers and the press, men in white-hooded fire suits were seen jumping from a helicopter into the smoldering rubble and carrying off debris in unmarked trucks. Police videotapes were erased before investigators had a chance to review them. Vital details of the cargo's hazardous contents (recently revealed to be the deadly nerve gas, sarin) were kept secret for years. The disaster took 43 lives on the ground and four more on the 747 Boeing jet. This whole thing looks to be either a monumental bungle or a cover-up. (See Carol J. Williams, "Dutch Probe '92 Jet Crash after News of Toxic Cargo," *Los Angeles Times,* 13 Oct. 1998)

3. Set out the thesis, key arguments, strengths, and weaknesses in this argument, which suggests that monkeys can think:

Animals do not have language and, so, people throughout history said they could not think because words are the means of thought. However, a study of two rhesus monkeys, Rosencrantz and MacDuff, suggests that animals can think in ways that do not involve language. The study shows monkeys can arrange things in serial order. Pressing panels on a computer screen, the monkeys showed repeatedly that they could touch in correct numerical order, displays containing one to nine objects.This isn't the same as being able to count from one to nine—rather they show they can recognize sets in the correct numerical order. The monkeys may also have the ability to think "one, two, three," but that remains to be proved, said Dr. Terrence, a psychologist studying the monkeys. One day this week, when Rosencrantz and MacDuff were not working, Dr. Terrence showed a video of them touching a sequence of panels displayed on a computer monitor. The monkeys seemed absorbed in their task, which they performed with ease. (See Nicholas Wade, "Study Suggest Monkeys Have Ability to Think," *The New York Times,* 23 Oct. 1998)

4. What are the three strongest pieces of evidence in the following argument that might be used to convince one of your friends or fellow students NOT to use steroids? Read the excerpt and then set out the three strongest pieces of evidence.

Performance-enhancing drugs and treatments have become a bigger problem than ever in recent years, both in the major U.S. team sports and in international competition. But although professional football has had success in cracking down on steroid use—other sports haven't. Baseball, with muscle-bound sluggers Mark McGwire and Sammy Sosa, does not test for steroids use. Some players say that as many as half a dozen players per team are using steroids. Some put the number even higher. Where baseball insiders say once only big, strong players trying to hit home runs used steroids, now steroids are also used by players who want a few more homers, and by pitchers, looking to add a few miles an hour to their fastballs. But the common thread is the pressure to excel at the expense of long-term physical and mental considerations.

Manfred Ewald, 73, oversaw the East German doping program that flourished in the 1970s and 1980s. He and his cohorts are accused of giving steroids to girls as young as 11—and intimidating those who raised objections, accusing them of "cowardice." The women now appearing in a Berlin courtroom endured a wide range of health problems. Some became infertile because of the steroids. Many endured excessive body hair, deepening of their voices, and liver, kidney, and menstrual problems. Machalett told the court that when she was 19, her liver failed—because of the mixture of steroids and contraceptive pills she had been taking. Much could hang in the balance. The more they know, the more the world knows—and today's athletes using steroids might think twice about risking liver damage and other long-term health problems. (Adapted from Steve Kettmann, "Doping Haunts E. Germany," *Wired News,* 25 May 2000)

5. Set out the thesis and key claims in the following argument:

"A rat is a pig is a dog is a boy," says Ingrid Newkirk, co-founder of the largest animal rights activist group, People for the Ethical Treatment of Animals. There's no question that's fringe thinking. But it's thinking that recently gained a dangerous toehold in federal regulation. . . . The biomedical research community opposes including rats, mice and birds under Animal Welfare Act regulation because, they say, research laboratories already are subject to guidelines on the humane care and use of laboratory animals issued by the U.S. Public Health Service. More regulations would only burden researchers with unnecessary, time-consuming and expensive administrative requirements, says Estelle Fishbein, general counsel of the Johns Hopkins University in a commentary in this week's *Journal of the American Medical Association.*

This is sound reasoning, certainly. But it's a timid and inadequate defense of the use laboratory animals in medical research. . . . Animal research may make some uneasy. But it's not done without good reason. Laboratory animals provide living systems for medical researchers to test out their ideas. Without laboratory animals, human beings would be the guinea pigs for medical researchers. Animal research has a tremendous track record, playing a key role in research resulting in the prevention and treatment of many diseases, including rabies, small pox, anthrax, rickets, tetanus, arthritis, diphtheria, whooping cough, cancer, rubella, measles and AIDS. (See Steven Milloy, "Laboratory Animal Farm," *www.foxnews.com,* 4 Apr. 2001)

6. Discuss the quality of the reasoning in the following ad:

Kids who eat breakfast perform better in school. We all grew up hearing how breakfast is the most important meal of the day. And in fact, studies from around the world show that kids who eat breakfast perform better during their morning school hours. So how do you get them to eat breakfast every day? By serving them their favorite cereal with milk. For more information on the importance of breakfast to kids and the nutrition of cereal, call us at 1-800-468-9004. Cereal: Eat it for life. (Photos of Fruit Loops, Corn Flakes, Frosted Flakes, Sugar Pops)

7. Consider this ethical dilemma: In 1991 educators in Visalia, California, admitted to deceiving students in order to make them more attentive to astronomy. Read the following and then answer the questions below:

   Educators admitted that they conned students into thinking that a stealth bomber would fly over so they would pay close attention to stars. Even a radio disc jockey joined the hoax by hosting a live evening broadcast, telling a shopping center crowd that the plane was heading their way. It wasn't, even though the KARM-FM disc jockey did a simulation of a countdown to the moment the plane was to have appeared overhead. . . . "The stealth sighting was just a way to keep people looking into the sky," said Loren Olson, program director for the Christian station. A school district spokeswoman shrugged off the con, which included press releases. (See "Bomber Hoax Shoots for the Stars," *Los Angeles Times,* 17 Aug. 1991)

   Answer the following:
   a. What is the best argument that could be made in support of the hoax?
   b. What is the strongest argument that you could make in opposition to this hoax on the students?
   c. What are the potential pitfalls in a school district using the media to participate in a con on the students?
   d. Write a memo (three to four paragraphs long) to Loren Olson expressing your opinion on the Christian radio station taking part in the hoax on the students.

8. State the conclusion and note two strengths and two weaknesses of the following argument on egg donation:

   It is not a pleasant way to make money. Unlike sperm donation, which is over in less than an hour, egg donation takes the donor some 56 hours and includes a battery of tests, ultrasound, self-administered injections, and retrieval. Once a donor is accepted into a program, she is given hormones to stimulate the ovaries, changing the number of eggs matured from the usual one per month up to as many as fifty. A doctor then surgically removes the eggs . . . there is little indication that most of the young women know what they are getting themselves into. They risk bleeding, infection, and scarring. When too many eggs are matured in one cycle, it can damage the ovaries and leave the donor with weeks of abdominal pain. (See Kathryn Jean Lopez, "Egg Heads," *The Human Life Review,* Fall 1998)

9. Analyze the following argument about Mother Nature:

   I once worked with a man who'd had much of his face ripped off during a grizzly mauling. Think Freddie Kreuger—and multiply by two. The horror of that visual aftermath was exceeded only by my frozen panic at coming nearly nose-to-nose with a bear in the backwoods. I was employed in an isolated camp in northern B.C. and on summer evenings used to jog along trails cut through the trees by D-8 Cats. On one occasion, I burst around a turn, and before I knew it, I was almost on top of a bear that was heading back into the brush.

   When I saw it, I froze. I stood there rooted to the ground, waiting for whatever was going to happen next. Fortunately, it was "only" a black bear. Better fortune still, it was a bear in a fairly good mood. It watched me with a kind of lazy wariness before clumping off into the forest. A warden later told me if it had been a grizzly in a snit, I would have been dinner in a pair of battered Nikes. The encounter taught me Mother Nature is really a dangerous bitch. (See Peter Stockland, "The Madness in Protest Tactics," *The [Montreal] Gazette,* 24 July 2001)

CASE STUDY

Wen Ho Lee and the FBI
Testimony of C.A.R.E.S. Before the President's Advisory Commission on Asian Americans and Pacific Islanders

Victor Hwang
July 24, 2000

After a respected scientist, Wen Ho Lee, was arrested held without bail because he was a suspected spy, civil rights groups rallied to protest the way in which Lee was being treated. The following testimony of Victor Hwang of the Asian Law Caucus was one of the many ways in which supporters expressed concern. Read the testimony and then set out how Hwang presents his case before the committee.

Good Evening Commissioners:

My name is Victor Hwang and I am the managing attorney of the Asian Law Caucus, the nation's oldest civil rights and legal services organization serving the AA/PI community.

Tonight I am here to represent the Coalition Against Racial and Ethnic Scapegoating (CARES), a national coalition of civil rights groups and individuals united to fight for justice for Dr. Wen Ho Lee and to work against racial profiling of all communities of color. Our coalition includes many organizations which I am sure are familiar to the Commission including the Caucus, Chinese for Affirmative Action, AALDEF in New York, APALC in LA, the ACLU, National Lawyers Guild, the national Organization of Chinese Americans, the national Japanese American Citizens League, the national Chinese American Citizens Alliance as well as many other groups.

You have heard from many speakers tonight regarding the grave injustice done to Dr. Wen Ho Lee. While I know that the actual prosecution of Dr. Wen Ho Lee is beyond the jurisdiction and scope of this Commission, there are numerous federal policies and practices highlighted by Dr. Lee's case, which I would urge the Commission to investigate and take action on.

First and foremost, I would urge the Commission to investigate and work to end the FBI's program and policy entitled "Kindred Spirit." According to the FBI, the Chinese government practices espionage in ways different from the Soviets and other nations. The Chinese are supposed to be more crafty, content with collecting information piece by piece like grains of sand. According to the FBI, the Chinese government targets and works with Chinese American citizens who are more willing than Americans of other ethnicities to betray the United States and benefit some ancestral homeland.

This "kindred spirit" presumption is what the FBI has used to justify their denial of due process and equal protection to all Chinese Americans in a way which harkens us back to the excuses leading up to the exclusion and internment of Japanese Americans. The federal government has continued to unabashedly advance this racist stereotype and racial profile in its court papers, in its search warrants, and apparently in its continuing investigations.

Whether or not a foreign country practices espionage in a certain way, this does not excuse the United States from its own guarantees of equal protection and due process under the Fourteenth Amendment.

I urge the Commission to look into the use of this "kindred spirit" philosophy.

Secondly, I urge the Commission to take up and follow through on the excellent recommendations and findings generated by the Department of Energy's own Task Force on Racial Profiling. This task force concluded that the Department of Energy practices have created a hostile working environment for its employees such that the number of APA employees has dramatically dropped. By way of example, I cannot fathom how Notra Trulock, the head of DOE counter-intelligence, was allowed to remain in his position at the Department of Energy after commenting publicly that "ethnic Chinese" should not be allowed to work in the sensitive parts of the lab. We need an independent agency to thoroughly examine the Department of Energy's policies, practices, and commitment to equality in the work place.

Finally, I would urge the Commission to work with an appropriate independent government agency to investigate the prosecutorial misconduct that has already taken place in the Wen Ho Lee case. I won't even talk about the issue of selective prosecution which has already been covered by the other speakers and well documented in the press. I want to address a different but parallel form of prosecutorial misconduct, which was engaged in suppressing the publication of certain FBI reports, which would have assisted in clearing Dr. Lee's name. In looking at this issue, I cannot help but think back to the suppression of evidence by General De Witt and the Department of Defense in justifying the exclusion and internment of loyal Japanese Americans during World War II. On behalf of CARES and on behalf of an agency, which under the direction of Commissioner Dennis Hayashi, fought to redress the wrongs done to Japanese Americans during World War II, I would urge this Commission to take action to ensure that the injustices of the past are not repeated in the future.

Thank you for allowing me the opportunity to testify.

Structure

Once you know where the argument is headed, you can see how it's structured. Often the focus or thesis is clear from the title or first paragraph. Your task is then to see how the issue is approached. If it is a descriptive or expository article, see how the article is structured and whether or not there is a balanced presentation.

Using a Flow Chart

One of the ways to discern the structure is with a flow chart. Draw boxes around each paragraph, number each paragraph and then set out a flow chart showing what each paragraph contains.

Here's How.   Go through the article, boxing each paragraph. Number each box (paragraph). On a separate sheet of paper (or there on the article), draw boxes for all your paragraphs joined by arrows going from one to the next. Then put a descriptive label of each paragraph (*brief* summary of the key points—think telegram). Do this for all your boxes/paragraphs. You now have a flow chart.

Why Bother.   Flow charts can be valuable in several respects. First, flow charts help us see how arguments are structured. Second, flow charts help us clarify in our own minds what, exactly, is going on in each paragraph. Third, flow charts help us see if a discussion is imbalanced or biased. They are especially useful for people who do not outline and/or have trouble standing back and seeing the whole picture. If you get lost in the sea of details, try a flow chart.

Exercise

Set out a flow chart for the article, "Just Say No" by Judge James P. Gray, in which he sets out an argument for the legalization of drugs.

Group Exercise

In an article in *California Lawyer,* Judge James P. Gray argues for the legalization of drugs. Analyze his argument, with each group focused on one task. Topics for the groups could be altered or omitted, depending upon the number of groups (usually it works best if groups have three to five members). Two groups can have the same topic:

- Group 1: Thesis and assumptions.
- Group 2: Key claims.
- Group 3: His use of language and values to make his point.
- Group 4: Strengths of his argument.
- Group 5: Weaknesses of his argument.
- <u>Everyone:</u> Persuasiveness of his reasoning.

Just Say No
An Orange County Superior Court Judge Calls for a Truce
in the War On Drugs

James P. Gray
California Lawyer, April 1, 2001

Our drug laws have failed. We've lost the so-called War on Drugs, and now it is time for a coherent and common-sense approach to the drug problem. I say this not as an ivory-tower idealist but based on my experience as a former federal prosecutor in Los Angeles, a criminal defense attorney in the Navy's Judge Advocate General Corps, and a trial judge in Orange

County since 1983. Because my judicial duties have required me to enforce this failed system, I eventually could not keep quiet about it any longer. . . . We must, as a country, investigate the possibility of change and be mindful of the following five points:

First, just because people discuss alternatives to our current drug policy, or even because they believe we should adopt one or more of these options, does not mean that they condone drug use or abuse.

Second, there is no such thing as having both a free society and a drug-free society. Put another way, dangerous as they are, drugs are here to stay, and we should work to discover how best to reduce the harm they cause in our communities.

Third, the failure of our present drug laws is not the fault of law enforcement. These dedicated people have an extremely difficult and dangerous job, and they are doing it much better than any of us have a right to expect. Law enforcement is no more at fault for the failure of drug prohibition than was Elliott Ness for the failure of alcohol prohibition.

Fourth, it is far easier and more effective to control a legal market than an illegal one. Under our current policy the only laws that are enforced about the use and sale of illicit drugs are those imposed by the drug traffickers. As such, we have seen a collapse of the rule of law with regard to quality control, sales to minors, and regulations of the marketplace. The better approach would be to bring those dangerous drugs back under the law.

And fifth, no matter what options we use, there will be some problems.

Drug prohibition has its own unique and harmful consequences as well. For example, when drug dealers shoot police officers, witnesses, innocent bystanders, or even each other; that is a drug-prohibition problem rather than a drug problem. Today, when the distributors of Coors and Budweiser have a problem with each other, they take it to court, but the distributors of illicit substances take their problems to the streets. Similarly, when drug users are forced to prostitute themselves or steal to get money to buy artificially expensive illicit drugs from the criminal underworld, that is a drug-prohibition problem much more that a drug problem. So, too, is the diversion of billions of dollars from the prosecution of violent street crime and fraud to the prosecution of hundreds of thousands of nonviolent drug sellers and millions of drug users a distinct problem of drug prohibition. . . .

Unfortunately, it is easy to become a demagogue about the issue of drug policy, "standing up for our children" by advocating ever more strict criminal sentences for drug dealers. . . . Fortunately, many people are beginning to agree that our War on Drugs is not working, but they still feel a deep frustration that no viable options have presented themselves. Former Secretary of State George Shultz succinctly voices this view when he says, "I have a zero-tolerance attitude, but I am still searching for the best way of implementing it." Well, there's some good news: We have viable choices between the two extremes of zero tolerance on the one hand and drug legalization on the other, and many of these options are working quite successfully in other countries.

These options include various forms of drug treatment, such as rehabilitation,both voluntary and involuntary, public and private. Other options include medicalization, which fundamentally puts drug-using people under the supervision of a medical doctor and his or her staff; using needle-exchange programs, which exchange without charge dirty needles for clean ones; drug maintenance, which allows prescriptions for an addict's drug of choice to be filled at a medical clinic so that the subject neither gets high nor goes through withdrawal but is maintained at an equilibrium level until he or she is ready to attempt to be drug free (this program is working very well today in Switzerland); and drug substitution, which substitutes one drug, such as methadone, for the subject's drug of choice, such as heroin. Many countries in western Europe, which are not as concerned as we are with puritan morality, take a much more practical, harm-reduction approach to their drug problems by combining these alternative methods-with successful results.

Another option, of course, is an even more strictly administered War on Drugs, zero tolerance—"only this time we will *really* get tough!" Unfortunately, we have been getting tougher and tougher for the past several decades, and yet every time we have done so it has made our problems worse. In fact, in my view, our current policy of zero tolerance has brought us the worst of all possible worlds: We have filled our prisons with the less-violent and less-organized drug sellers, thereby leaving this enormously lucrative market to those who are more violent and more organized. The result has been that the availability and purity of drugs have increased dramatically while the price has gone down. We couldn't have created a worse situation if we had tried.

The best option we have is federalism, the principle that guided the repeal of alcohol prohibition in 1933. When alcohol prohibition was repealed, each state pursued the policy that best met its needs, and the federal government was eventually limited to helping each state enforce its own laws. Of course, whatever option or combination of options we eventually pursue must and will include a major component for drug education. . . . [M]any people believe that this is the only component of our current policy that is actually working.

Finally, we must explore various methods of "deprofitizing," or taking the money out of selling these dangerous drugs. Of course these drugs are dangerous, but it is drug money that is causing the most significant harm. Methods to reduce the profitability of the drug trade include decriminalization, which basically means that, although the drugs remain illegal, as long as people stay within very clear guidelines, the police will leave them alone (this program is working quite well today in Holland, where drug use for both adults and teenagers is about half of

what it is in the United States); regulated distribution, which is the strictly controlled and regulated sale to adults of designated drugs, similar to the way alcohol is sold in most states; and legalization, which basically leaves the distribution of drugs to the marketplace, with all of its protections under the civil justice system, and uses the criminal justice system to govern people's behavior. Almost no one I have heard of actually favors the extreme system of legalizing drugs, and I certainly do not.

Voters appear to be well ahead of politicians in the area of drug policy. Why? Because politicians perceive that they will be labeled soft on crime if they take a more moderate approach. Even President Clinton did not talk about a possible change in drug policy until the final weeks of his term. Whose fault is this? We have no one to blame but ourselves. It is our government, and it is our responsibility to show our elected officials that it is all right to talk about the possibility of change.

To some degree, this is beginning to happen. When presented with initiatives about making marijuana available for medical purposes, voters in nine states as well as the District of Columbia have said yes, in overwhelming numbers. . . . Progress has also been made in other areas. In the past ten years we have seen a positive revolution in the way the criminal justice system treats nonviolent offenders who use mind-altering drugs. This is, of course, our drug courts, where drug users are treated compassionately as human beings who have a problem. But they are also held strictly accountable to satisfy the demands of the court's drug-treatment program. In many cases the results have been gratifying. . . .

(For example, does anyone seriously believe that it is any more helpful to put actor Robert Downey Jr. in jail for his drug abuse than it would have been to put Betty Ford in jail for her alcohol abuse?) . . . What was true for the dangerous and sometimes addicting drug of alcohol is also true for other dangerous and sometimes addicting drugs. Since problem drug users will find their way into our criminal courts anyway, why are we persisting with our failed policy of drug prohibition and punishment? . . .

Consequently, it is up to us as caring citizens, voters, and taxpayers to continue to make the government move toward a more rational, workable, and, as good fortune would have it, vastly less expensive national drug policy. This can be done simply by recognizing that we have viable alternatives to our failed War on Drugs. Waiting for those who have vested interests in the status quo to come around simply will not work. . . .

In my opinion, drug policy is the single most important issue facing our country today. But we can all help to make a positive change by simply recognizing that we have alternatives to our failed drug policies. Demand for dangerous drugs can be reduced through education, drug treatment, bringing the users closer to medical professionals, reducing incentives by taking the profit out of trafficking in drugs, and, very importantly, holding people accountable for their actions in the same way we do for people who cause harm by their use or abuse of alcohol. The best way to start is to remember-and to remind others-that just because we discuss or even use these other options does not mean that we condone drug use or abuse.

James P. Gray is a judge of the Orange County Superior Court. He is also the author of *Why Our Drug Laws Have Failed and What We Can Do About It: A Judicial Indictment of the War on Drugs* (Temple University Press, 2001).

Source: © 2000 Daily Journal Corporation. All *rights reserved. Permission granted by the* Daily Journal.

Analysis of Longer Articles

You may feel overwhelmed when asked to analyze an entire chapter or long article (over five pages). Don't be! Try a flow chart to block out the article or a brief summary of each paragraph. Once you get an overview, you are in a better position to do your analysis.

When you are writing 10, 20, or 40 pages—or more even, as with a thesis or dissertation—you need to go into greater depth. This is not that much harder, it just takes more time. This will call for more than six steps that we learned above.

For example, expanding our steps to include titles and subtitles, don't assume the title is representative of the work. An example of a misleading title is "Solid Cast, Direction in *Mr. Write.*" Going by the title, you'd think this was a positive review. However, in the first paragraph we find: "*Mr. Write,* unfortunately is *Mr. Wrong,* a stale, labored romantic comedy all too obviously adapted from a play that is at best fodder for whatever is left of the summer-stock circuit." The author, Kevin Thomas, may not have been responsible for the misleading title. Given that there is such a great discrepancy between the title and the opening paragraph, it makes us realize how important it is to look carefully at titles and not assume the title mirrors the article's content.

With that in mind, let us see what a more detailed analysis involves. We can set out the steps for a longer analysis as follows:

Tips for Analyzing Long Articles

1. *Titles and Subtitles.* Look at: frame of reference/point of view, language, bias, images, impact, effect, overall thrust, or direction. Your goal here is to detect the bias or implicit set of values of the author, and to see if the title is representative of the article's content.

2. *Language.* Look for: loaded terms (positive or negative), false-neutral terms, technical or scientific terms, connotations, language of description (adjectives, images created, symmetry in descriptions taking into account gender, race, religion, and so on). Note impact of race, gender, age, religion, ethnicity upon descriptions. Check for slanting, bias, or hidden value assumptions.

3. *Structure.* To get a sense of structure try any of the following: block out, outline, sketch without words, create a flow chart, construct paragraph blocks with labels, list the sequence of information (whose side is given first and last, and if it is a balanced presentation), note who has first and last word. Do a quantitative analysis (count premises and block out pros and cons), examine the use of quotes or statistics (amount, purpose, effect). An overview of the structure can help you decide if the author presents the material or argument in a fair and balanced way.

4. *Testimony.* Examine: credibility and potential conflict of interest versus impartiality of the person being cited (as a source, or used as a witness, as in a trial). Decide if the person/source in question is reputable. Check for possible bias.

5. *Factual Reporting.* There are three things to look at: Who is reporting, whether the report is sufficient, and whether the reporter is biased or unbiased. Check the frame of reference of the author, possible omissions or errors because of incompetence, lack of sufficient detail or failure to include diverse perspectives and finally any possible bias or conflict of interest.

6. *Literary Analysis.* This includes: themes; patterns; plot line and narrative structure; character development; diversity of perspective; description and attention given to different characters; connection between form and content; moral, spiritual, and social concerns; use of language; sentence style, structure, symbols and images (mythological or metaphorical).

7. *Socio-Cultural Frames.* Be attentive to social and cultural frameworks: treatment of social issues or moral problems, cultural baggage and biases, societal attitudes. Recognize the social and cultural context of the author and work (since it is not written in a vacuum).

8. *Use of Statistics.* Use of statistics signal us to look at: date of study, size and diversity of sample (Is sample representative of the target population?), strength of percentage in inferring conclusion, relevance of study to topic under discussion, assumptions or cultural attitudes embedded in study. Determine currency and relevance of the statistical study, and discuss any problems you perceive.

9. *Fallacies.* Any fallacious reasoning needs to be pointed out. Note any fallacies and determine the degree to which the author's work is affected by any such errors.

10. *Argumentation.* This is at the center of any detailed analysis and includes these steps:
    - Define the problem or clarify the thesis.
    - Separate background information from evidence.
    - Weigh evidence.
    - Assess support (e.g., credibility of sources and documentation).
    - Assess testimony, use of facts, and factual reporting.
    - Recognize and assess circumstantial evidence.
    - Recognize and assess statistical evidence.
    - Recognize and discuss any value claims.
    - Examine use of analogies, precedents, and metaphors.
    - Examine any causal or other inductive arguments.
    - Examine any deductive arguments.
    - If deductive, test for validity:
      (True premises → True conclusion) = *Valid* argument
    - If deductive, test for soundness:
      (Valid + Premises actually true) = *Sound* argument

Exercises

Part One

1. Discuss Arnie's reasoning:

   ARNIE: Eric and Lyle Menendez were convicted for murdering their parents. They are now in prison. I can't understand why they got life in prison. The poor guys—you know they must have been traumatized losing their parents at such a young age.

   GINA: I never thought of it like that, Arnie. You are such a sensitive person!

2. Read the following passage and then state the author's thesis and key points.

   As a member of the Justice Department panel that reviewed the Federal assault on the Branch Davidian compound near Waco, Tex., I found the Government's investigations seriously deficient. It was difficult to make the constructive recommendations we were asked to provide because the Government never gave us a candid account of what went wrong—why 75 people, including 25 children, died in the April 19, 1993, raid that ended in an inferno.

   That is why Congress's decision to hold hearings on both the original raid on Feb. 28 and the final assault is welcome. At the least, a thorough investigation should dispel bizarre conspiracy theories that have flourished in the past two years. But the hearings, which are set to begin on Wednesday, should also require law enforcement officials to tell the nation much more than they have so far and to acknowledge that they lacked justification for their military-style tactics against a compound filled with children. (See Alan Stone, "Time to Explain Waco," *The New York Times,* 17 July 1995)

3. Analyze the following argument on surveillance:

[C]ell phones have become the digital equivalent of Hansel and Gretel's bread crumbs. When a cell phone is turned on, it broadcasts an identification number to the closest antennas, which allow the carrier to chart its customers. It's a simple matter—known as triangulation—to track the signal as it arrives at different towers, then calculate the location of the phone based on time differences. The police have taken full advantage of this tracking trick, though—technically, at least—they need a court order to access the information. Earlier this year, Timothy Crosby, 40, was busted for raping and robbing a Brooklyn woman after the police located him by homing in on his cell phone signal. In November 2000, authorities pursued Kofi Apea Orleans-Lindsay for allegedly killing a Maryland state trooper during a buy-and-bust operation. Police used cell data to track Orleans-Lindsay to Brooklyn, where they arrested him. (See Adam L. Penenberg, "The Surveillance Society," *Wired,* Dec. 2000)

4. Select any advertisement (print ad) and treat it as an argument for the conclusion, "Therefore, you should buy this product (Coke, Nike shoes, Harley-Davidson motorcycle, and so on)." Give your analysis of the argument presented in the ad.

Part Two

On August 31, 2001, a Florida judge upheld a state law banning gays from adopting children. This is the first federal court ruling on the issue. Read the following about the case and then answer the questions that follow:

A federal judge in Miami upheld Florida's ban against adoption by gay men and lesbians, ruling Thursday that the state has articulated a "legitimate interest" in placing children in homes with a married mother and father. The decision leaves Florida as the only state that "flat-out prohibits gay adoption under any circumstances," while Mississippi and Utah have more-limited restrictions. . . .

In his 20-page opinion, U.S. District Judge James Lawrence King found that the plaintiffs had the burden "as the one attacking the homosexual adoption provision to negate every conceivable basis which might support it." "They did not meet that burden," he wrote, saying the plaintiffs "left unchallenged [the state's] assertion that the best interest of the child is to be raised by a married family. It is unnecessary for this court to evaluate whether [the state's] statements are correct" as long as they are "arguable." . . .

The Florida law at issue, adopted in 1977, is succinct: "No person eligible to adopt under this statute may adopt if that person is a homosexual." The state said the law reflects the state's moral disapproval of homosexuality, and it serves the best interest of Florida's children to be raised in a home stabilized by marriage between a mother and a father. King rejected the first argument, writing, "The court cannot accept that moral disapproval of homosexuals or homosexuality serves a legitimate state interest." But King did find a state interest in the second argument, noting that the state gives primary consideration for adoption to married heterosexual couples who can provide children with "proper gender role modeling and minimize social stigmatization."

"Plaintiffs have not asserted that they can demonstrate that homosexual families are equivalently stable, are able to provide proper gender identification, or are no more socially stigmatizing than married heterosexual families," King found. (See Gail Epstein Nieves," Court Backs Ban on Gay Adoption," *The Miami Herald,* 31 Aug. 2001)

Answer the following:
a. Set out Judge King's argument.
b. Evaluate his reasoning and explain whether you think his ruling was a wise one.
c. State your response to Randall Marshall of the American Civil Liberties Union (ACLU) who said, "We believe the statute is simply the irrational discrimination that is rooted in prejudice and hostility against gay people by members of our state Legislature" (see *The Miami Herald,* 31 Aug. 2001).
d. State your response to Rev. Lou Sheldon, Presbyterian minister who hailed the judge as having upheld the age-old paradigm of the family. "It takes one father and one mother, and the chemistry that the male and female create, to raise a child," said the Rev. Lou Sheldon. He added, "It's hard enough for a single parent, not to mention same-sex adults" (see John-Thor Dahlberg, "Judge Backs Florida Ban on Adoptions by Homosexuals," *Los Angeles Times,* 31 Aug. 2001).

Part Three

On the next page is an article written by an attorney, Michelle Scully, whose husband was killed in a rampage in a San Francisco high-rise. She wrote this article in an attempt to influence members of Congress who were about to vote on a proposed ban on assault rifles.

Read over her article and then <u>answer the following questions</u>:

1. What are the key arguments?
2. If you were opposed to the assault gun ban, what key arguments would you make in response?
3. Are there any other ideas you can think of that would support a ban against assault rifles?
4. How can we educate people to prevent more cases like the one Scully experienced or the use of guns in high schools, like Columbine, where students and faculty were killed or injured? Share your suggestions.
5. In the case of a number of the school killings, other students knew that the killer(s) talked about murdering their classmates or had other knowledge that the murderer(s) were about to vent their violent rage. What responsibility do these fellow students or friends have? Should they be held accountable for their failure to warn?

A Gun Widow's Request: Courage in Congress
Michelle Scully

Last July 1 began with my husband John and me driving to work together in San Francisco, making plans for a long Fourth of July weekend. We had been married just nine months, but had been in love for nine years. We were best friends and felt incredibly lucky to have each other as lifetime companions.

By 3 that afternoon, our plans for the weekend and our entire lives were shattered. A deranged man had walked into my husband's law firm equipped with two TEC-DC9 assault pistols, a .45-caliber pistol and more than 100 rounds of ammunition. Within minutes, eight people were dead, including my husband.

I was working in an empty office at my husband's firm when John came in to tell me that shots had been heard upstairs. We went into the hall, trying to leave the building, and saw a young man shot right in front of us. John and I attempted to hide in a nearby office, but were hunted down by this madman. My husband used his body to shield me from the flying bullets. When the shooting finally stopped, I opened my eyes to see my husband lying on the floor in front of me, blood coming out of his nose and mouth. He had been shot four times and fatally wounded in the chest. I had been shot in the right arm, and spent the next half hour sitting in a pool of blood, begging John to stay alive. He finally looked up at me and said, "Michelle, I'm dying. I love you."

I have not been the same since that moment. I now go through every day wishing there was some way that I could bring John back, because I can't stand the loneliness of living my life without him. I can't stand the pain on the faces of his parents, his sisters, his brother and his many friends. When John Scully died, a piece of everyone who knew him died too, because he touched everyone he met in a profound way.

I know there is nothing I can do to bring John back, so I have committed myself to preventing other John Scullys from dying. Unfortunately, it takes stories like mine to move the leaders of this country to action to take military-style assault weapons from our streets. These are not hunting or sporting weapons. They are weapons of war, designed to kill a large number of people in a short period of time. They have no place on our streets, in our schools or in our office buildings.

It would appear that the House of Representatives believes that assault weapons aren't a crime problem, having left this measure out of its debate about crime and out of its omnibus crime bill. While it's true that these killing machines may not be the most widely used weapons, they are 10 to 20 times more likely to be used in the commission of violent crimes than are conventional weapons. And assault weapons represent nearly 30 percent of the guns traced to organized crime, drug trafficking and terrorist crime.

My husband John committed the ultimate act of bravery by saving my life from a madman's bullets. Congress must only find the courage to pass a piece of legislation that will save lives and save others from the pain and loss that I will carry for the rest of my life.

Reprinted with permission of Michelle Scully.

Case Update

The Court Ruling: Can Victims Sue Gun Makers?

On August 6, 2001, it was reported that the California Supreme Court ruled on the lawsuit that stemmed from the massacre of nine people, including Scully's husband. Here a mentally disturbed man, Gian Luigi Ferri, entered a San Francisco high-rise and opened fire in a law office with two TEC-DC9s and a revolver. In addition to the eight people he killed, he wounded six people before committing suicide. In a 5–1 decision, the court ruled that victims cannot sue gun makers when criminals use their products illegally.

All but one of the justices basically adhered to the view, "guns don't kill people, people kill people." Only Justice Kathryn Mickle Werdegar disagreed with the majority view that the manufacturers bore no legal responsibility. She felt that the company, Navegar, was negligent in marketing the fast-firing weapon to the general public. In her view, until the law is changed, gun makers "will apparently enjoy absolute immunity from the consequences of their negligent marketing decisions."

As we saw, above, Michele Scully responded to the tragedy of losing her husband by taking a public stand against assault guns. She did not let her grief and anger prevent her from political action. This is an important dimension of critical thinking: At any moment our lives can be radically altered and demand us to think about the issues facing us and where we stand. In many cases, we may be called to a social or political response, as was Scully when she sat down to write her letter to the editor. In developing our reasoning skills, we are in a stronger position to reflect on what we see in the world and how effectively we can act. In this way, we are able to enter the public dialogue on the issues facing us in our lives.

CASE STUDY

Crossing the Moral Boundary
Mario Vargas Llosa

Eminent Peruvian novelist, Mario Vargas Llosa, looks at the issue of the global trade in women. He reflects on the French justice system charging one of its citizens who, while vacationing in Thailand, had sex with children. As discussed in the article below, the French system does not require such a crime to have taken place within its own boundaries.

It is this moral boundary that is reflected upon below. Read the article and write a brief letter (or statement) of response to Mario Vargas Llosa. Be sure to note at least one of his key points and respond to that (or those), along with sharing your own ideas and insights on the justice issue he examines.

A model employee of the French public transport authority, according to his chiefs and workmates, the Parisian bachelor Amnon Chemouil, who is now 48, discovered one of Thailand's tourist attractions in 1992. Not its tropical landscape or its ancient civilization and Buddhist temples, but cheap and easy sex, one of the country's flourishing industries. At the resort of Pattaya, near Bangkok, he could have sex with very young prostitutes. He vacationed there again in 1993 and 1994.

On his third trip, he met in a bar at Pattaya another sex tourist, Viktor Michel, a Swiss citizen, who encouraged him to seek out even younger girls. Mr. Michel took care of everything: found the procuress and a hotel room. The woman appeared there with a niece who was 11 years of age, and Mr. Chemouil paid $20. All the doings in the hotel room at Pattaya were recorded on video by Viktor Michel, and upon returning to Paris and his job in the public transport system, Mr. Chemouil received a copy of this cassette from his friend and added it to his collection of pornographic videos.

Some time later Viktor Michel found himself in trouble with the Swiss police, much less tolerant than the Thai ones. Searching his home for illegal pornography as part of an investigation into a pedophile ring, they found the video from Pattaya. Under interrogation, the video hobbyist revealed the circumstances in which the video had been filmed and Mr. Chemouil's identity. A report was sent to the French police, who put it in the hands of a judge.

Here I must open a parenthesis in my story, to declare my admiration for French justice. Many things function poorly in France and deserve criticism, but justice functions very well. French courts and judges act with an independence and courage that are an example for all other democracies. They have brought to light countless cases of corruption at higher economic, administrative and political levels, and have sent to trial—and in some cases, to prison—people who by their wealth and influence would in other societies be untouchable. In matters of human rights, racial discrimination, and subversion and terrorism, justice in France is usually characterized by efficacy and prompt intervention.

This was not, we may assume, the impression felt by the surprised Amnon Chemouil when he was arrested and taken before a court in Paris to pay for having violated the penal code of 1994 by sexually violating a minor. The French penal law is applicable to all offenses committed by a French citizen "within or without" French territory, and a 1998 law authorizes the courts to try "sexual aggressions committed abroad" even when the deeds are not considered crimes in the country where they were committed.

The trial of Amnon Chemouil, which took place this fall, set a precedent. It was the first time an offense of "sex tourism" had come before a court in one of the wealthy countries where this sort of tourism typically originates. Several organizations that oppose sexual exploitation of children appeared as plaintiffs, among them the United Nations Children's Fund (UNICEF), End Child Prostitution in Asian Tourism and a group in Thailand that was able to locate in Bangkok, seven years later, the aunt and girl of the story. The girl, now 18, went to Paris and testified, in private, to the judges, who also viewed a copy of Viktor Michel's video that was found in the search of Amnon Chemouil's house.

The accused, who said that in the eight months he had spent in prison awaiting trial he had experienced a mental cataclysm, admitted he had performed the acts in the video, begged the victim's pardon and asked the court to punish him. The sentence was seven years' imprisonment, instead of the 10 called for by the prosecutor.

Many conclusions may be drawn from this story. The first is that if France's example were followed by countries like Spain, Germany, Britain, Italy and the United States, which, with their high incomes, are among the principal practitioners of "sex tourism," then it is possible that the thousands of offenses of this type committed daily in the poorer countries—especially concerning the sexual exploitation of children—might at least diminish and that some of the perpetrators might be punished.

The precedent established by France is impeccable: a modern democracy cannot allow its citizens to be exonerated of legal responsibility if they sin cheerfully outside of national borders just because a foreign country has no juridical norms that prohibit the activity or because those norms are not enforced.

Hunger, the need for money, and extensive corruption and inefficiency in many poor countries have caused child prostitution to prosper spectacularly, with the indifference or open complicity of the authorities. As UNICEF and its allies testified at the trial of Mr. Chemouil, the dimensions of the problem are multiple and growing. We need not entertain very high hopes of its eradication, of course, because the poverty and misery that lie behind it constitute an almost insurmountable obstacle.

But the trial in Paris shows a positive side to the new bete noire of the incorrigible enemies of modernity: globalization. If frontiers had not been fading away and, in many fields, disappearing, Amnon Chemouil would never have appeared before the court that tried and sentenced him, and would surely have spent many more vacations in Pattaya. The rigid, straitjacket conception of national sovereignty is being transformed, leading to attempts at wider justice like the detention of Augusto Pinochet in England for his crimes against humanity in Chile, and now this trial.

Globalization is not only the creation of world markets and transnational companies; it also means the extension of justice and democratic values into regions where barbarism still flourishes.

Mario Vargas Llosa is a Peruvian novelist and winner of numerous awards, including the National Book Critics Circle Award, the Cervantes prize, and the Peace Prize of the German Book Trade. This article, which also appeared in *El Pais, Madrid*, was translated by James Brander.

Reprinted with the permission of Mario Vargas Llosa.

CHAPTER SIX

The Logic Machine: Deductive and Inductive Reasoning

It should be apparent that the most meticulous inspection and search would not reveal the presence of poltergeists at the premises or unearth the property's ghoulish reputation in the community.

—Justice Israel Rubin, Ruling a prospective buyer could recover his $32,000 down payment on a home that the owner claimed was haunted.

Suppose a real estate agent says the house you want to buy is haunted, pointing to a creaky staircase and the fact that two previous owners died accidental deaths. You go down the stairs and, sure enough, they creak. People in the neighborhood agree about the house's ghastly condition. Does this mean the house really *is* haunted? The evidence does not certainly show the house is haunted. We would need more evidence to be convinced.

In this chapter we will examine the two main kinds of arguments—inductive and deductive—and learn how to assess each kind. In an *inductive* argument the evidence alone is not enough for the conclusion to be certain, even if the premises are true. The evidence offers only partial support for the conclusion and, consequently, you cannot be certain that the conclusion is true. So, even if the evidence were actually true (that the stairs creak and two previous owners died in accidents) the conclusion that the house is haunted might still be false. It is because of this uncertainty that the argument is considered inductive.

On the contrary, the real estate agent could say, "All the houses in Charlestown, Massachusetts, are haunted. Obviously this house at 14 Hill Street is in Charlestown, so it must also be haunted." This argument is inherently different from the inductive one above. The evidence here, if true, would force the conclusion to be true. If all houses in Charlestown are haunted <u>and</u> the house at 14 Hill Street is in Charlestown, it would have to be true that the house is haunted. The evidence offers sufficient support for the conclusion. This type of argument is called *deductive*. The conclusion can be extracted from the premises.

Look, for example at the way the creator of the TV show *Criminal Intent* considered it a triumph of psychology over criminality. He referred to the lead character Robert Goren as an American Sherlock Holmes, "who uses deductive reasoning rather than brute force to nab his prey" (as quoted by *Entertainment Weekly*, 7 Sep. 2001). The intended parallel is that Goren, like Sherlock Holmes, regularly tests his deductive skills, as he draws inferences as to what might follow from the evidence.

What distinguishes a deductive argument is that the premises are claimed to be sufficient for the conclusion, that no further evidence is needed in order to draw the conclusion. In fact, of course, such claims are made (e.g., in criminal trials), without the evidence *actually* being sufficient. Nevertheless, when it is asserted or implied that this set of premises sufficiently supports the conclusion, we've got a deductive argument. If, however, a conclusion is drawn in spite of missing pieces or gaps in the set of premises, the argument is inductive.

Key Terms in Arguments

As you may recall from the first two chapters, an *argument* is a group of propositions, some of which (called the *premises*) act as supporting evidence for another proposition (called the *conclusion*). We could also put it this way: An *inference* is a conclusion drawn on the basis of certain evidence, though not necessarily supported by that evidence. Generally, the words "inference" and "conclusion" are interchangeable, as are the assertions "I infer" and "I conclude."

A *proposition* is an assertion that is either true or false. A proposition can always be expressed in the form in which something (called the *predicate*) is either affirmed or denied about something else (called the *subject*). Stated differently: The subject designates the referent and the predicate the class of characteristics the subject does or does not share. A proposition can be expressed in the following form:

Standard Form of a Proposition
SUBJECT   is/were/will be   *PREDICATE*

In other words, we are saying of something (the subject) that it is/was/or will have some characteristic being predicated—such as "*Ice Cube* (subject) is a *person who is both an actor and a singer* (predicate)." Note that the proposition is not always strictly expressed in the above form, but it could be rewritten in this format without changing the meaning of the sentence. Let us look at some examples.

Examples of Propositions
The history exam covered the Civil War.
Sweet potato pie is tastier than green fried tomatoes.
The Washington Post *broke the story on the Watergate break-in.*
The coyotes killed three cats in the neighborhood last month.

A proposition is called a *categorical proposition* if it can be expressed starting with the words All, no, some, or *x* percent (where *x* is any number other than 0 or 100).

Examples of Categorical Propositions
No bat has feathers.
Some house cats are the prey of coyotes.
Seventy-four percent of the Latinas in the Brand Institute poll indicated opposition to the so-called Star Wars missile defense system.

The Key to Distinguishing Propositions

The key to distinguishing a proposition is that it is asserting that some characteristic is being predicated of the subject. This can take a variety of forms, from sentences in the indicative to rhetorical questions. For instance, if someone says, "Did you know skunks eat rats?" they are asserting the proposition, "Skunks are rat-eaters." Similarly, if the justice of the peace (or minister, etc.) declares, "I now pronounce you, Joseph and Carmela, to be husband and wife," the claim is that "Joseph and Carmela are now married."

Think of it this way: however it is expressed, if someone is claiming that this (some subject) has some characteristic (predicate), then you're staring at a proposition. Note that it makes no logical difference whether this is expressed in the present, past, or future tense.

Matters of taste, opinion, and morality are often presented in the form of a proposition. For example, "No decent dinner is delicious without dessert." This looks like a universal claim to be applied for all time. However, it would be a bit preposterous of someone to really mean this. Unless the speaker is an egomaniac, she would probably be willing to add in the missing "in my opinion" or "to me." If not, there could be a problem. For instance, contentious claims like "People without nose rings are repulsive" or "Adultery is an unpardonable sin" can't be treated as simple propositions. This is because we can't clearly determine if they are true or false.

Rather, such contentious claims would have to be placed in a theoretical or ethical context and any attempts at assigning a truth-value would be context-dependent (i.e., relative to the framework in question). We could assume they are true for the purposes of assessing an argument, but we can't assume that they *actually* are either true or false.

Exercise

Directions: Indicate which of the following are propositions.

1. Get lost!
2. The parrot chewed a hole in the wall.

3. Chickpeas are members of the legume family.
4. Andy said the McGarrigle Sisters' music is fantastic.
5. If sharks are in the tank, it could be dangerous to stick your hand in the water.
6. Damn you!
7. There's not a man alive who wouldn't agree that you'd look cute as a redhead.
8. Where is my calculus book?
9. Either the tire has too much air in it or it doesn't.
10. Unless the plumber can fix it, we have a sewage problem.
11. Get a load of this, Colleen!
12. Congratulations—you are now an American citizen.
13. Eighty-seven percent of squirrels in the University of Alberta study preferred birdseed to table scraps.
14. What in the world did you do with your sock?
15. No one with a functioning taste bud can tolerate ketchup on fried eggs.
16. What's that—you passed your statistics final?
17. Some mathematicians are not fluent in Urdu.
18. If you don't want to watch *Beverly Hills Cop* again, then we can go bowling.
19. Yuck!
20. According to folklore, vampires are averse to daylight.

Deductive Reasoning

With deductive arguments, the conclusion comes right out of the premises. Think of all those movies you saw where the prosecutor tried to prove the case beyond a reasonable doubt. The claim is that the evidence is sufficient to seal the conviction, that any reasonable judge or juror should be able to conclude from the evidence that the conclusion follows.

Of course you know that prosecutors can claim all they want, but not all arguments are convincing ones. Plus, if you are a juror, you may not know if each piece of evidence is actually true. Your task is to decide whether, *if* that evidence were assumed to be true, the conclusion would follow and you'd have to convict the defendant. As a juror you simply are not in a position to ascertain the truth of all the evidence submitted. Your task, therefore, is to focus on the reasoning itself and decide if it holds together under close scrutiny.

So this tells us *one important thing* about deductive arguments: the focus is *not* on the truth or falsity of the claims, but whether or not the premises, on the surface at least, provide sufficient reason to draw the conclusion.

A *deductive argument* is an argument in which the premises are claimed to be sufficient for the drawing of the conclusion. This means there are no missing pieces; that the evidence is all there backing up the conclusion. In that sense, a deductive argument is a closed set. In other words, just like a crossword puzzle, the clues (evidence) should be sufficient to complete the job (draw the conclusion without resorting to any other references or resources).

Applications of Deductive Reasoning

Most mathematical proofs are deductive arguments. In mathematics, even arithmetic, deductive reasoning is pervasive. Think of geometry, where axioms and postulates are used to prove a theorem. You could only use those axioms and postulates; there is nowhere else you can go to get your reasons. It is a self-contained system; the conclusion comes out of the premises. Of course, if a postulate (= premise) is changed, the resulting mathematical system changes too.

For example, if we don't follow Euclid's fifth postulate (that two parallel lines will never intersect and are equidistant), then we get quite distinct theoretical systems. For example, think of drawing parallel lines on a globe or orange—they converge at both ends, or drawing parallel lines on the inside of a trumpet, where the lines diverge and would get farther and farther apart if the trumpet kept expanding.

Even examples from arithmetic demonstrate deductive reasoning. For example, to solve the problem 62 − 49, students in second grade are normally taught to borrow a 1 from the 10s place, much like borrowing sugar from a neighbor. However, as noted by Richard Rothstein in *The New York Times,* children in Shanghai are taught the reasoning behind borrowing so the process makes mathematical sense. In Shanghai schools, children are taught that 62 is the same as 60 and 2, 50 and 12, 40 and 22, and so forth. Once this is understood, the process of subtraction makes sense and isn't some magic act. Understanding the deductive reasoning involved allows students to move to more advanced mathematical topics.

Many arguments concerning moral and legal reasoning make use of deductive reasoning. For example, suppose someone said: "All monarchs are butterflies. All butterflies are insects, so all monarchs are insects." This argument is also self-contained. The conclusion, "All monarchs are butterflies" comes out of the two premises. You may take issue with the truth-value of the two premises but the argument is still a deductive one. Let us look at examples of deductive arguments:

Deductive argument example 1:

No pilot is afraid of heights.

Some football players are afraid of heights.

Therefore, some football players are not pilots.

The first premise asserts one of the characteristics of being a pilot; namely, not being afraid of heights. The second premise informs us that there are some people (football players) who do not have this characteristic. It is being argued that those two premises are sufficient for the conclusion, so the conclusion comes right out of the premises.

Deductive argument example 2:

No animal lover would mistreat a pet.

Anyone who mistreats a pet violates the fundamental guidelines of *People for the Ethical Treatment of Animals (PETA).*

So, no one who violates the fundamental guidelines of PETA is an animal lover.

Deductive argument example 3 (in the form of a modus ponens argument):

If you don't know how to cook, you won't know the recipe for hollandaise sauce.

Craig doesn't know how to cook.

Therefore, Craig won't know the recipe for hollandaise sauce.

In all of these examples, the premises are working together to support the conclusion, with no other evidence necessary for the conclusion to follow. That does not mean the argument is actually constructed so that the conclusion really does follow. However, in a deductive argument there is an implicit claim of certainty. The major kinds of deductive arguments are as follows:

Major Kinds of Deductive Arguments

1. *Categorical Syllogisms and Chains of Syllogisms:* These are three-line arguments (or chains of them), consisting of two premises and a conclusion, with all of the propositions in the form of categorical propositions.

   These propositions can be expressed in one of the four possible forms: "All A are B;" "No A is B;" "Some A is B; " and "Some A is not B." We will look at these in Chapter 15 when we examine syllogisms. For example,

   All romantics cry during sad movies.

   No one who cries in a sad movie can eat a lot of popcorn.

   So, no one who can eat a lot of popcorn is a romantic.

2. *Modus Ponens.* These are arguments of the form: "If A then B. A is the case. Therefore, B is true also." For example,

   If the dentist slips while operating, Wesley will need stitches.

   The dentist slipped while operating.

   So, Wesley had to get stitches.

   Remember the *fallacy of denying the antecedent* and the *fallacy of affirming the consequent* are mutations of modus ponens/modus tollens and not valid argument forms. (See Chapter 4 on fallacies to review.)

3. *Modus Tollens:* These are arguments of the form: "If A then B. B is not the case. Therefore, A is not true either." For example:

If there's a mural beside the road, the drive will be interesting.

<u>The drive was not interesting.</u>

So, there was not a mural beside the road.

4. *Disjunctive Syllogism.* These are arguments of the form: "Either A or B. Not A. Therefore, not B." For example:

Either that's a rainbow trout or a weird-looking salmon.

<u>That's not a rainbow trout.</u>

So, it's a weird-looking salmon.

5. *Hypothetical Syllogism.* These are arguments of the form: "If A then B. If B then C. Therefore, if A then C." For example:

If the lightning strikes the tree, George is in trouble.

<u>If George is in trouble, call 911.</u>

Therefore, if the lightning strikes the tree, call 911.

6. *Constructive Dilemma.* These take the form of: "If A then B, and if C then D. Either A or C is the case. Therefore, either B or D is the case." In other words, there's a choice between two options, where each option leads to some effect and you have to pick between either of the two options. This means, if you assume you'll pick one or the other option, then either of the two effects will happen. For example:

If the oil spills into the bay, the sea life will suffer, but if we can soak up the oil, the sea creatures won't be in jeopardy.

<u>Either the oil spills into the Bay or we'll be able to soak up the oil.</u>

Therefore, either the sea life will suffer or the sea creatures won't be in jeopardy.

We should note also that there are variations on the above forms. For example, here are two variations of modus ponens and modus tollens:

7. *Variations of Modus Ponens and Modus Tollens:*
   a. *Unless:* One variation is an argument of the form: "A unless B. B is not the case. Therefore A." or "A unless B. Not A. Therefore, B." For example, both of these are valid:

   David will return to Omaha State unless he transfers to Reed.

   <u>David did not transfer to Reed.</u>

   So, David returned to Omaha State.

   Beth will stay at Colby unless she transfers to Cal State Fresno.

   <u>Beth did not stay at Colby.</u>

   Therefore, Beth transferred to Cal State Fresno.

b. *Application of a Rule:* Another variation of modus ponens is in the form of the application of a rule to things that satisfy a set of criteria: "rule X applies to any cases with characteristics A, B, C, and D. Individual case P has characteristics A, B, C, and D. Therefore, rule X applies to case P. For example:

People will get a fine of $270 if they are caught driving in the carpool lane without a passenger in their vehicle.

Irene snuck into the carpool lane even though she was by herself and was seen by Officer Williams.

Therefore, Irene got a fine of $270.

Compounding the Terms of the Argument

Be aware that in all the examples above, a. and b. could each stand for a compound statement. A compound statement is one containing any of these words: "not," "and," "or," "if . . . then," and "if and only if." We can see this with the following example:

If $\boxed{\text{it's either an apple or an orange,}}$ then $\boxed{\text{it's a fruit and not a vegetable.}}$
That's $\boxed{\text{either an apple or an orange.}}$
Thus, it's $\boxed{\text{a fruit and not a vegetable.}}$

The above argument is of the same form as:

If $\boxed{\text{it's an apple,}}$ then $\boxed{\text{it's a fruit.}}$
That's $\boxed{\text{an apple.}}$
Thus, it's $\boxed{\text{a fruit.}}$

Although the terms of the first argument are compound, the FORM of the argument is still the same, as the terms in bold show us.

Validity

Valid is not the same as true in the realm of logic. Propositions can be true or false. However, we do not say of an argument that it is true or false. Instead we talk about validity (in the case of a deductive argument) or strength (in the case of an inductive argument). Let's start with deductive arguments and examine validity.

A *valid argument* is an argument in which the premises provide sufficient support for the drawing of the conclusion. That is, if we assume the premises were true and the conclusion could not be false, then the argument is valid. This has to do with the relationship between the premises and the conclusion. Validity is not about whether any statements are actually true or not—or whether the argument can be said to correspond to anything in the world. This is different than the way most people use the term "valid."

Some people think validity *is* the same as truth. It's not. Validity a question of structure—namely, whether the premises either separately or in combination sufficiently support the conclusion. This is a structural issue, not one about truth-values. Our goal is to see what happens if we *assume* the premises to be true. If we assumed they were true and the conclusion was forced to be true (it could not be false if the premises were true), then the argument is valid. If we could have true premises and a false conclusion, then the argument is invalid.

The key is that the connection entails *certainty:* If true premises force the conclusion to be true, then the conclusion certainly follows from those premises. For example, look at the following argument:

No bushwhacker has a refined sense of humor.
Buffalo Bill was a bushwhacker.
Thus, Buffalo Bill did not have a refined sense of humor.

We do not have to know anything about bushwhackers or Buffalo Bill for this to be a valid argument. If we assume the premises were true, the conclusion would certainly be true also. It could not be false when the premises were true. Let us look at another example. Suppose someone said:

No one who has a tattoo is inhibited.
Some Republicans are inhibited.
Therefore, some Republicans do not have tattoos.

If the two premises were true then the conclusion would follow. Remember, it is not important for validity whether or not the premises are actually true. The issue is the connection between the premises and the conclusion.

Watch for terms like, "must," "necessarily," "inevitably," "certainly," "entail," and "it can be deduced." These words often indicate a deductive argument. To make sure, ask: Do the premises provide sufficient support for the conclusion? The use of the phrase "I deduce that" or "It is certain that" does not mean that the argument is deductive or there is certainty. Sometimes people use the terms to bolster their argument, even though they have not made their case.

The Juror Model of Validity

To better understand validity, picture being a juror. There we are sitting in the jury box listening to the prosecution and the defense attorneys present their arguments, offering this or that piece of evidence, experts, and witnesses in order to try to convince us to conclude one thing or another. We have to assess the evidence, the witness testimony, the credibility of the experts and evaluate the strength of their reasoning without leaving the room.

In other words, we have to work with what is presented there in the courtroom. We can't run out the door and look at the crime scene (unless the judge permits all the jurors to do so under special conditions) and we can't go interview the neighbors to get a wider sense of what happened. Instead, we have to sit there in the courtroom and determine on the strength of the evidence whether or not there's a solid case being made.

On a jury we cannot know if the evidence presented in the courtroom is *actually* true or false. We must take on faith that the legal system is working, that people are telling the truth and that evidence is not being fabricated. Obviously these are not always true conditions and, at times, such serious problems force us to rethink or retry a case. But, as a juror, you can only work with the evidence given in the courtroom. Even if you know about the case, say through news coverage, you cannot bring any of that prior knowledge to bear upon your reasoning.

The task in a criminal trial is to decide if the prosecution has made its case. Is the evidence sufficient to convict, or is there a reasonable doubt that would make it possible to arrive at an alternative hypothesis? As a juror, your guide is, "If the evidence were true, does the conclusion then follow as true—or could it be false?" If it can conceivably be false, then the argument is invalid. If the conclusion follows directly from the premises, then the argument is valid. For example:

Valid argument example 1:
Either the lab destroyed the evidence or the defendant is lying.
The lab did not destroy the evidence.
Therefore, the defendant must be lying.

Valid argument example 2:
If the FBI fabricated photos, then the prosecutor has a problem.
The FBI fabricated photos in the Weaver case.
So, the prosecutor of the Weaver case has a problem.

Valid argument example 3:
All alien abductions leave the victim with some memory problems.
Samantha was the victim of an alien abduction.
Thus, Samantha will be left with some memory problems.

What makes all these arguments valid is that the premises are sufficient support for the conclusion. If the premises were true, the conclusion would have to be true. It is this element of certainty that marks an argument as valid.

Invalidity

An *invalid* argument is an argument in which the premises fail to adequately support the conclusion. We can tell an argument is invalid when the premises could be true and the conclusion false. Let's now look at examples of invalid arguments:

Invalid argument example 1:
Some drivers are drunk.
Some flight attendants are not drunk.
So, some flight attendants are not drivers.

If we assumed the two premises were true, it would not necessarily follow that "Some flight attendants are not drivers." The conclusion could be false while the premises were true. The conclusion, therefore, simply doesn't follow.

Invalid argument example 2:

No one with a heart condition should run the Boston marathon.
<u>Some photographers have a heart condition.</u>
Therefore, no photographer should run the Boston marathon.

Here the conclusion could be false and the premises true. The premises, therefore, fail to force the conclusion to follow.

Invalid argument example 3:

If you do not wear swim goggles, you could lose your contact lens.
<u>Rose lost her contact lens.</u>
Consequently, Rose must not have worn swim goggles.

Even if it were true that, without swim goggles you could lose your contact lens and Rose did lose her lens, it does not follow that she wasn't wearing swim goggles. For example, she might have lost her lens down the sink when cleaning them.

Exercises

1. Give a valid argument for the conclusion: "All big, burly men enjoy French literature."
2. Give a valid argument for the conclusion: "No one afraid of heights should take up parachute jumping."
3. Give a valid argument in the form of *modus ponens* that has as its first premise, "If you have a powerful car, you won't have trouble going over the Grapevine."
4. Give a valid argument in the form of the disjunctive syllogism that has as its second premise: "A Cessna is not a four-wheel vehicle."
5. Give a valid argument in the form of modus tollens that has as its first premise, "If there's meat on the sandwich, Carol won't touch it."
6. Complete the argument in the form of a constructive dilemma having as its first premise: "If there are mosquitoes in the tent, it'll be hard to sleep, but if there are no mosquitoes, then another insect is buzzing around."
7. Give an invalid argument for the conclusion, "The Lakers won the 2001 NBA basketball tournament." Explain why it's invalid.
8. Give an invalid argument for the conclusion, "All wolves are reptiles." Explain why it's invalid.

9.   Give an example of an invalid argument with all true premises for the conclusion: "Abraham Lincoln was a Republican." Explain why it's invalid.

10.   Give an example of a valid argument for the conclusion: "All dentists prefer rap music to country." Explain why it's valid.

Soundness

Once validity is determined, we can assess the soundness of an argument. It's at this point that issues around whether the evidence is actually true or false becomes significant. In other words, the question of *soundness* moves us out of merely looking at the relationship between the premises and the conclusion. Now's the time we ask whether or not the evidence is actually true and not just *if* it were true would the conclusion follow.

This moves us out of the jury box into the world of empirical reality. Sound arguments are important—who wants to have a good argument based on questionable claims, false statements, lies? No thanks! If we want our reasoning to be sound, then we want two things. We want it to be cogent (so our reasoning is strong, defensible, well structured, and gives sufficient evidence for the conclusion). And we want it to be grounded in truth. Otherwise we risk having a great-sounding argument that goes nowhere.

For example: "Men are now capable of bearing children. We need some more people living in the Arctic and embryo implants seem to be working to produce children. Thus, we ought to implant embryos in men and boost the Arctic population." However good an idea this may sound at face value, the fact that the first premise is clearly false means the argument has no legs. In other words, the reasoning may be strong in terms of the argument being valid, but it has no operational, functional, empirical value. The false premise sinks the argument. It is an unsound argument.

Assessing the Soundness of an Argument

We know when an argument is valid or invalid. And we now know that an inductive argument cannot be valid or invalid, but only more or less strong. The next thing to consider is whether the argument is a sound one. We can define a sound argument as follows:

An argument is sound if these two conditions are satisfied:

→ The argument is valid *and*

The premises are actually true.

To check soundness: First check for validity. If the premises were true, is the conclusion forced to be true (it couldn't be false)? If so, the argument is valid. If the premises really were true, the argument is sound. However, if either condition is not met, then the argument is unsound. Let us look at some examples of sound arguments:

Sound argument example 1:

All wombats are mammals.

All mammals are warm blooded.

So, all wombats are warm blooded.

This is sound because: First, the argument is valid. If the two premises were assumed to be true, then the conclusion simply couldn't be false. Second, the premises are also true. So both conditions for soundness are met.

Sound argument example 2:

If Sandra O'Connor becomes a Supreme Court justice, then there will be a woman on the Supreme Court.

Sandra O'Connor became a Supreme Court justice.

So, there is a woman on the Supreme Court.

This is valid because the premises are sufficient for the drawing of the conclusion and the premises are actually true. Since both conditions are satisfied, the argument is sound.

Sound argument example 3:

Either Quebec has seceded from the rest of Canada or it is still in the Confederation.

Quebec has not seceded from Canada.

So, it is still in the Confederation.

This argument is valid because, if we assume the two premises to be true, the conclusion could not be false. Since the premises *are* also true, this means the argument is a sound one.

Unsound Arguments

An argument is *unsound* whenever either or both of these conditions are met: (1) the argument is invalid or (2) the premises are not all true. The odds are that an argument will be unsound, because many arguments are invalid and often one or more of the premises are false. For example:

Unsound argument example 1:

If we legalize marijuana then alcohol consumption patterns may change.

We did not legalize marijuana.

So, the alcohol consumption patterns won't change.

This argument is invalid. If we assume the premises to be true, the conclusion could be false. There may be a number of reasons alcohol consumption patterns could change, not just one. Because the argument is invalid, it is unsound.

Unsound argument example 2:

All birds can swim.

All barn owls are birds.

So, all barn owls can swim.

This argument is valid, since the conclusion does follow from the premises. However, the first premise is not true, so the argument is not sound.

Overview

Remember, first check for validity. Assume the premises are true and see if the conclusion is forced to be true. If the conclusion cannot be false when you assumed the premises (evidence) were true, then the argument is valid. Otherwise, it's an invalid argument. Now move on to the question of soundness. Check to see if all the premises are actually true. If even one premise is false, then the argument is unsound. If both conditions are satisfied, the argument is sound. If one condition fails, then the argument is unsound. So if we have an invalid argument *or* a valid argument with at least one false premise, then we've got an unsound argument in front of us. We can summarize all this with a diagram:

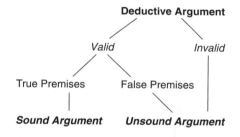

Exercises

Part One

1. Give a sound argument for the conclusion: "No cow is a reptile."

2. Explain whether or not this is a valid argument:

   All Olympic medal-winners are athletes.

   My brother Steve is an athlete.

   Therefore, my brother Steve is an Olympic medal-winner.

3. Give an example of a sound argument for the conclusion: "No lizard has feathers."

4. Give a valid but unsound argument for the conclusion: "Some cars are not dependable vehicles."

5. Give an example of a valid argument in the form of a hypothetical syllogism with first premise: "If Gary drinks too much espresso, he won't be able to sleep."

6. Give an example of a valid argument in the form of *modus ponens* that is unsound having this conclusion: "Tigers roam the streets of Atlanta."

7. Give an example of a valid argument in the form of *modus tollens* that is sound, having this conclusion: "Snakes do not have legs."

8. Give an example of a sound argument in the form of the disjunctive syllogism, with this conclusion: "Vitamin C helps prevent scurvy."

9. Give an example of an unsound argument in the form of *modus ponens*, with the first premise: "If hawks are birds, they will make nice pets." Explain why it is unsound.

10. Give an example of a sound argument in the form of the hypothetical syllogism.

11. Give an example of a sound argument for this conclusion: "Therefore, poisonous snakes do not make good pets." Explain why it is sound.

12. Give an example of an invalid and therefore unsound argument for this conclusion: "Therefore, chocolate ice cream is not fattening."

13. Give an example of an invalid and therefore unsound argument using this first premise: "If you can ride a horse, then you can do just about anything."

14. Give an example of a valid, but unsound argument for this conclusion, "Therefore, all vegetables are carrots."

Part Two

Directions: Test the following arguments to see if they are valid or invalid. If they are valid and fit one of the valid argument forms, then name the form.

1. If the temperature hits 100 degrees, Chicago is miserable. The temperature hit 100 degrees in the summer of 2001. Thus, Chicago was miserable that summer.

2. Anyone who eats a hamburger for breakfast is an eccentric. Anyone who is an eccentric is a deviant. It follows that anyone who eats a hamburger for breakfast is a deviant.

3. If you study hard, you will succeed in school. If you study hard, you will impress your friends. Therefore, if you impress your friends, you'll succeed in school.

4. Anyone who can shoot a musket while running is awfully nimble. Daniel Day Lewis is awfully nimble. Therefore, he shot a musket while running during the making of *Last of the Mohicans*.

5. Some birds are intelligent creatures. No intelligent creature should be forced to live in a cage. Chickens are birds. Therefore, no chickens should be kept in cages.

6. If you keep eating popcorn, you're bound to bust a tooth on a kernel, but if you don't keep eating popcorn you'll feel deprived. Either you'll keep eating popcorn or you won't. Therefore, either you'll bust a tooth on a kernel or you'll feel deprived.

7. People who ride Harleys are trained mechanics. Tom is not a trained mechanic, so he must not ride a Harley.

8. Any man who drives a convertible in a snowstorm is starved for attention. No one who is starved for attention would go without a warm scarf and beanie on his head. Therefore, no one driving a convertible in a snowstorm would go without a warm scarf and beanie on his head.

9. A rat is in the basement under the washing machine. If there are no rats in the basement under the washing machine, it's okay to do your laundry barefoot. Therefore, it's not okay to do your laundry barefoot.

10. Either there are squirrels in the attic or some other animal is making noises up there. There are no squirrels in the attic. Therefore, some other animal is making noises up there.

11. Anyone who is ambivalent about dancing won't want to go to a hootenanny. Phil doesn't want to go to a hootenanny. Therefore, Phil is ambivalent about dancing.

12. All cats are animals. All dogs are animals. Therefore, all cats are dogs.

Inductive Reasoning

An inductive argument is an argument in which the premises only provide some support for the drawing of the conclusion, but not sufficient support. In that sense, an inductive argument is like a puzzle with some missing pieces. So, there will always be an element of doubt in the argument. The conclusion can only be said to follow with likelihood or probability—never with certainty. In that sense, the conclusion goes beyond what is contained in the premises.

Every so often we come across inductive arguments that leave us scratching the tops of our heads in wonder, as, for example, when we read about unusual "cures" for AIDS or mind-boggling promises about a diet drug. And then there's the curious statistics we occasionally find cited. Look, for instance, at the following dream study:

According to a study that looked at dreams, "the further your politics lean to the right, the more likely you are to have nightmares." According to researchers it's three times more likely that you will have bad dreams if you are a Republican than if you are a Democrat. The results of this study are actually coming out of the University, within a stones throw from here—Santa Clara University in California. . . .

Dream researchers looked at more than four years of dreams dreamt by college kids from around the United States. The total number of subjects was 55, half were females, half males. Their political leanings were divided too, with half being very conservative and half being very liberal.

The results of the study [were] just presented in an annual meeting of the Association for the Study of Dreams. They found half the Republican's dreams were nightmares, compared to 18 percent of the Democrats. "What's striking is that the nightmares of people on the right were more nightmarish, they were bleeker, there was more hopelessness," says Kelly Bulkeley, the lead researcher on this study. (See New-Scientist.com, July 11, 2001, as quoted by Dr. Dean Edell, *www.healthcentral.com*)

As we might imagine, there are a few questions about the legitimacy of inferring from a study of 55 students to the general population. Not only is there a problem with the number of participants (too small), these are all college students (one age and educational level). Another question is whether these were *paid* participants (if so, who paid and could that have biased the result?).

Can you spot why the following are inductive arguments?

Inductive argument example 1:

Celine Dion is the Joan Baez of this generation. She has a powerful set of chords on her, just like Joan Baez who could bounce her voice off of a mountain in Northern California. She is a striking physical presence, just like Joan Baez who had big eyes, fine bones, and beautiful long hair at the peak of her beauty. She has a host of imitators, just like Joan Baez who put folk music on the popular map. Joan Baez was also an outspoken pacifist. So, I bet Celine Dion is against war too.

Well, let's look at this reasoning. What we have here is a list of similarities between the two singers: voice, looks, and imitators. Then a claim about Joan Baez's politics is carried over to Celine Dion, leading to the inference that she must also have shared the same political view on war. Even if the terms of the comparison were all true, there is considerable uncertainty whether the additional trait holds as well. There's a gnawing doubt we can't ignore about whether this leap is justified.

Inductive argument example 2:

The hantavirus is a biological agent targeting certain groups the government is out to get. Just look at the evidence. Where have there been outbreaks of the hantavirus? Not in Beverly Hills or Boca Raton! Fat chance. No, they've been in New Mexico and Arizona on tribal land, killing off Native Americans. In 1993 alone, the Center for Disease Control noted 150 cases in the four corners region of the Southwest (leading to the virus being nicknamed the "Navajo Virus").

Then the hantavirus showed up in South America. It's showing up in rural areas where more indigenous people live. If it were just a matter of being exposed to rodent droppings, there'd be a lot more whites coming down with it! It must be a conspiracy against Native Indians.

We can see, from the reasoning in this argument that the evidence rests on (1) geography and (2) victim profile. Because so many Native Americans have been affected, compared to other groups, plus the fact that the hantavirus hasn't shown up in wealthy cities like Beverly Hills or Boca Raton, the author infers that there's a conspiracy afoot. Is the evidence sufficient, though, for us to be sure of a conspiracy against indigenous people? Not on this evidence alone. Thus, the argument is inductive.

There are five major kinds of inductive arguments. These are as follows:

Major Kinds of Inductive Arguments

1. *Predictions:* In predictions, an argument is made about the future based on past or present evidence.

   Example:

   In light of the devastation in previous earthquakes, we can infer that an earthquake of magnitude 8.5 or greater in eastern Massachusetts will result in a large portion of Martha's Vineyard being swallowed up by the ocean.

2. *Arguments about the Past Based on Present Evidence:* In these arguments, an inference is drawn about what happened at some earlier point in time based on current evidence.

   Example:

   It doesn't look like all the Indians came over from Russia and Siberia. The fact there are Native American tribes in Alaska speaking Athabascan languages found in the Southwest and the southeastern United States point to an upward migration. The Cherokee, Navajo, and Apache all share a similar language with the Athabascan tribes in Alaska. Even now, they can communicate with one another in spite of the vast geographic distance.

3. *Cause and effect reasoning:* Here it is claimed that an event (effect) is based on one or more causal factors. Given the existence, then, of the causal factor(s), the effect should follow.

   Example:

   Hepatitis C is on the rise in the prison population in the United States. It is most likely the result of inmates sharing needles, spreading the disease.

4. *Arguments based on analogy:* This argument rests on a comparison, from which it is claimed that a characteristic true of the one term in the equation will also be true of the other. In law this usually involves the application of a precedent or legal principle.

Example:

Humans are physiologically closest to the chimpanzee. If we can use chimps to find a cure for Parkinson's disease or Alzheimer's, we'll surely be able to market the drug on humans. Therefore, this justifies using chimps in medical research.

5. *Statistical reasoning.* These arguments draw from sample studies or statistical reasoning, from which an inference then is drawn about either all or part of the targeted population.

Example:

Fifty-eight percent of people polled by the *Westview Daily* disapprove of embryonic stem cell research. Therefore, 58 percent of all Americans disapprove of embryonic stem cell research.

"All or Nothing" Reasoning

In the example of statistical reasoning, replacing 58 percent with 100 percent or 0 percent (all or nothing) would transform this into a *deductive* argument. The uncertainty is that we do not know what to make of the missing percentage. This missing piece creates the element of doubt and, thus, makes the argument inductive. If we replaced the 58 percent by 100 percent or zero, the uncertainty is then removed. Thus, the argument becomes deductive, not inductive.

The Wedge of Doubt in Inductive Arguments

In an inductive argument the premises could be true, but the conclusion will never follow with certainty. Remember, there is always some *wedge of doubt* between the premises and the conclusion. We can construct inductive arguments following one of the different forms of inductive reasoning. For example, let us construct premises for the conclusion, "Anna gargles with salt water to help her sore throat."

Inductive argument 1: Try one using an analogy.
Anna is a lot like her cousin Ruiz: both are college students and breed German Shepherds.
Ruiz gargles with salt water when he has a sore throat.
Therefore, Anna must also gargle with salt water for her sore throat.

Inductive argument 2: Try one using a prediction.
Every time Anna has had a sore throat in the past, she gargled with salt water.
Anna has a sore throat today.
Therefore, Anna will probably gargle with salt water to help her sore throat.

Inductive argument 3: Try statistical reasoning.

Seventy-eight percent of college students polled said they gargle whenever they have a sore throat.

Anna is a college student.

Therefore, Anna will probably gargle with salt water to help her sore throat.

Exercises

Part One

Directions: Name the different inductive arguments below. Explain what makes them inductive in light of the five main categories.

1. Yesterday was a lovely day for a picnic. Today is a lovely day for a picnic. It follows that tomorrow will be a lovely day for a picnic.

2. Seventy-one percent of people who phoned into KBST country music station prefer Patsy Cline to Buck Owens. As a result, 71 percent of Americans prefer Patsy Cline to Buck Owens.

3. There is a high correlation between smoking and both emphysema and lung cancer. Therefore, anyone who smokes will probably get either lung cancer or emphysema.

4. The movie *Manhunter* is a lot like *Silence of the Lambs.* Both focus on serial killers who target women. Both have detectives who spend an inordinate amount of time trying to get into the mind of the killer. Both detectives seem to be isolated from human companionship and seem obsessed on the one case to the exclusion of anything else. *Silence of the Lambs* has a female lead in the role of the detective; therefore, *Manhunter* must feature a female detective as well.

5. Robert Alton Harris must have had a terrible childhood, because he was such a disturbed man as an adult.

6. Edgar will love the teddy bear you got him for Christmas; he used to love teddy bears when he was a little boy.

7. Sixty-three percent of University of Michigan computer science majors prefer MACs to PCs. People who prefer MACs to PCs will really like the operating system, OS X. Therefore, Andrea, who is a University of Michigan computer science major will really like the MAC operating system OS X.

8. Cigarette smoking must cause people to become alcoholics, because a lot of people who are alcoholics have smoked at some point in their lives.

9. The ambassador to Greece usually loves the taste of spinach in spanako-pita. As a result she will probably enjoy the spinach soufflé they plan to serve at the Amnesty International function next week at the White House.

10. Lake Rudolph in Kenya must be the seat of human evolution, because that is where anthropologists like Richard Leakey found the oldest human bones to date.

11. The pharmaceutical company tested the antinausea drug thalidomide on primates and found it had no adverse affect on either the mother or the fetus. Therefore, they should be able to put the drug on the market without worrying about what it'll do to humans.

12. Inhalers made by Schering-Plough were listed as the probable cause for the deaths of 17 people from September 1998 to June 2000, a period when the recalled inhalers were on pharmacy shelves or in the hands of asthma sufferers. As a result, we should expect a recall of the Schering-Plough inhalers.

Part Two

Directions: Deconstruct the following inductive arguments (as we did in our first two examples). Set out the conclusion and discuss the nature and strength of the evidence and why the argument is inductive.

1. The following argument seeks to explain why poor people seem to suffer more medical problems than everyone else:

    Poor people have long been known to have more medical problems than affluent people of the same age, but a new study suggests that greater inequality in the distribution of income contributes to higher overall mortality rates and deaths from heart disease, cancer, and homicide. . . . The study found that for treatable conditions like tuberculosis, pneumonia and high blood pressure, mortality rates were higher in states where the income gap was wider. (See Robert Pear, "Researchers Link Income Inequality to Higher Mortality Rates," *The New York Times,* 19 Apr. 1996).

2. The following argument seeks to explain the rise in heat-related deaths in athletes:

    There were 103 recorded heat-related deaths in college and high school since 1960, but only five similar deaths from 1931–59. . . . According to the NCCSI charts, there were 17 heatstroke deaths from 1995 to 2000, as many as were recorded in 15 previous years. . . . Is the increasing quest for scholarships, money and superstardom—as one former NFL star thinks, pushing players beyond physical limits?
        Practices and procedures are being called into question in the wake of recent football-related deaths. Many trainers, coaches and former players wonder whether sports science can keep pace with players who are getting bigger and

faster by the year. . . . In his book, "The Junction Boys: How Ten Days in Hell with Bear Bryant Forged A Championship Team," author Jim Dent recounts how players, mouths frothing, literally crawled off practice fields to their Quonset huts. . . . Dent writes: "Bryant believed the fastest way to whip a team into shape was to deny the boys water, even in the brutal heat."

The thinking is incredibly Neanderthal by today's standards. Of course, players did die of heatstroke back then, but Goehring thinks there were two reasons why more did not. First, players were carrying less body fat. Goehring was a 185-pound lineman. He played both ways. "I couldn't play today," he says by phone. "I'd get killed." He also maintains players of his era were better equipped to handle the heat. "In those days, we didn't have air conditioning," he says. "All of us were acclimated to the heat. We worked tough, summer jobs where the heat was. I worked in a steel mill, worked in a blast furnace, and the heat was 110 degrees. You had a little asbestos suit around you, picking up samples of iron ore. So the heat wasn't that big of a factor. Today, golly bum, you never get out of the air conditioning. The body is a lot more suited to conditions that are comfortable." (See Chris Dufresne, "Cruel Paradox Of Camps: Old-School Training Programs Were More Rigorous Than Today's, but Heatstroke Fatalities Were Far Fewer," *Los Angeles Times,* 9 Aug. 2001)

3. The following argument centers on the rights of a doctor who invents a surgical technique:

Dr. Jack Singer, a Vermont ophthalmic surgeon who removes cataracts about 250 times a year specializes in an incision that removes the need for [sutures]. Dr. Samuel Pallin, an Arizona ophthalmic surgeon, claims to own the procedure for stitchless cataract surgery. He has a patent to support his claim that Dr. Singer and others who use the technique patented by Dr. Pallin should pay him royalties. Patents for techniques used to be very rare, but are now issued several times a week. However, the AMA says it knows of no doctor who has paid another one royalties. Dr. John Glasson, Chair of the AMA Council on Judicial and Ethical Affairs raised questions, saying, "How can anyone claim to own the way one turns one's knife when performing surgery?" Some claim that, no more can a painter own the way she holds her brush or a golfer own the way he handles a club, should it be possible for a surgeon to own a technique.

The AMA council fears that patents will restrict access to treatment, obstruct peer review of new therapies, add to the cost of health care, and be impossible to enforce. However, within the field of medicine patents are common and for decades medical techniques have been patented as the directions for using a device that was patented at the same time. Given this, Dr. Pallin asks, "How can the AMA rationally take the position that a pure method patent is unethical, while a combined method and device patent is not?" He also notes that the Hippocratic oath says nothing about intellectual property. (See Sabra Chartrand, "Why Is This Surgeon Suing?" *The New York Times,* 8 June 1995)

4. The following argument is in opposition to the Department of Energy's proposal to lower the standard of what is allowable in terms of selling radioactive metal:

The Department of Energy [DOE] has a problem: what to do with millions of tons of radioactive metal. So the DOE has come up with an ingenious plan to dispose of its troublesome tons of nickel, copper, steel, and aluminum. It wants to let scrap companies collect the metal, try to take the radioactivity out, and sell the metal to foundries, which would in turn sell it to manufacturers who could use it for everyday household products: pots, pans, forks, spoons, even your eyeglasses.

You may not know this, but the government already permits some companies, under special licenses, to buy, reprocess, and sell radioactive metal: 7500 tons in 1996, by one industry estimate. . . . They are pressing for a new, lax standard that would . . . allow companies to buy and resell millions of tons of low-level radioactive metal. The DOE is so eager to get radioactive metal off its hands that it has hired an arm of British Nuclear Fuels, called BNFL, to do the job. . . . The $238 million contract stipulates that the company may recycle for profit all the metals it recovers, including a large amount of formerly classified nickel.

When British Nuclear Fuels released 7000 metric tons of metal contaminated with low-level radioactivity for recycling into consumer goods in Britain earlier this year, it caused an uproar. A spokesman for British Nuclear Fuels explained his philosophy to the London paper *The Independent*. "It's recycling," he said. "If you have a cup of coffee, you don't throw the cup away, you reuse it." (See Anne-Marie Cusac, "Nuclear Spoons: Hot Metal May Find Its Way to Your Dinner Table; Dept. of Energy's Proposal to Recycle Radioactive Metal into Household Products," *The Progressive*, Oct. 1998)

Part Three

1. Construct an inductive argument for the conclusion below, using the form indicated:
   a. Using cause and effect reasoning support the conclusion: "Therefore, Maureen's melanoma could be traced back to sun tanning as a teenager."
   b. Using an analogy *or* a statistical argument, support the conclusion: "Therefore, *The Matrix* will go down as one of the greatest sci-fi films in history."
   c. Using a prediction *or* an analogy, support the conclusion: "Therefore, Jimmy Carter will be recognized as one of the great American statesmen of the 20th century."
   d. Using an argument about the past based on present evidence, support the conclusion: "Therefore, Einstein must have been mathematically advanced as a little boy."

2. Drawing from the different kinds of inductive arguments, construct two different kinds of inductive arguments for the conclusion that is given.
   a. James Joyce loved the sound of the French language.
   b. Harry Potter novels are the very embodiment of mythology.
   c. Brewer's yeast and yogurt mixed in a paste will do wonders for your complexion.
   d. Cell phones cannot possibly be related to brain tumors.
   e. Reading in dim lighting ruins your eyes.

3. Indicate which arguments are inductive and which are deductive:

I D   Eighty-nine percent of students get hungry when studying. Okima is a student, so she must get hungry when studying.

I D   Some Siberian huskies make great sled dogs. All great sled dogs have to work in dog teams. Therefore, some Siberian huskies have to work in dog teams.

I D   At no time did Dr. Lee indicate his allegiance to the Aryan Nation Defense League (ANDL). If he had sworn allegiance to the ANDL, he would not have risked exposure meeting the reporter to share files. But he did meet with the reporter! Consequently, you're mistaken to argue Dr. Lee is in cahoots with ANDL.

I D   Inebriation can cause a person to lose control of motor functions. Annette started drinking last night and by 9 p.m. she was dizzy and unable to walk a straight line. It must have been due to that can of beer she drank with her popcorn.

I D   No honest person would lie. All trustworthy people are honest. Therefore, no liar can be trusted.

I D   Tom Hanks must have been popular when he was a child, given that so many people like him now.

I D   No woman who wants an easy life should be a counterterrorist. Everyone in the CIA is a counterterrorist. Therefore, no woman who wants an easy life is in the CIA.

Assessing Inductive Arguments

Inductive arguments can never be said to be valid—they are assessed in terms of how *strong* or *weak* they are. Because the premises of inductive arguments never supply enough evidence to force the conclusion to be true, there is always an element of uncertainty, or probability, to inductive reasoning.

An inductive argument is neither valid nor invalid—we can only talk about validity with deductive arguments. The reason for this is that we can never guarantee the truth of the conclusion in an inductive argument. Even if the premises are all true, the conclusion might still be false. Consider:

Sixty-nine percent of high school students admire Nelson Mandela for his contribution to human rights.

Jaime is a high school student.

So, Jaime admires Nelson Mandela for his contribution to human rights.

Even if the premises were true, the conclusion could still be false. Jaime may be in the 31 percent of high school students who did not indicate that they admired Nelson Mandela for contributing to human rights. There is too much uncertainty to conclude that Jaime must admire Nelson Mandela. Think of it this way: If I ask you to go up in my Cessna plane with me and told you that you had a 69 percent chance of surviving the trip, you would not likely rush to go with me. However, the closer my percentage gets to 100 percent, the better your chances of survival.

There is no *one* specific method of assessing the strength of inductive arguments. Considerations vary according to the type of inductive argument. But one thing is common: There will always be a degree of probability involved. In all inductive arguments there exists a fundamental uncertainty about whether or not the conclusion follows from the premises. However, each inductive argument can be evaluated in terms of how strong or weak it is.

This, then, means an inductive argument is neither sound nor unsound. You cannot talk about validity or soundness with regard to inductive arguments. So never say an inductive argument is valid. Never say it is invalid. Never say it is sound. Never say it is unsound—these terms just do not apply.

Think of inductive arguments and deductive arguments like men and women. Some of the things you can discuss about men just do not apply to women and vice versa. For instance, you'd never say, "That man is either pregnant or he's not pregnant." It would be ludicrous to talk that way and we would think you were goofy if you did. This is the same with validity, invalidity, and soundness. These can only be talked about with respect to deductive arguments. Inductive reasoning is assessed differently; with induction we are looking for the relative strength of the argument. Let's look at an example from a legal case.

Avocado picker Allen Kimball, 33, was at the last tree to be harvested and saw a bunch of avocados near the top of the tree (see Donna Huffaker, "Amputee's Suit Alleges Neglect by Utility Firm," *Daily Journal*, 10 July 2001). Grabbing his aluminum-picking pole, Kimball climbed his aluminum ladder to pick the avocados. He did not see the Southern California Edison power lines until it was too late and 12,000 volts of electricity went through his body, igniting both arms and his right leg. He's had dozens of surgeries, including the amputation of most of both arms. He faces more surgery and will likely be confined to a wheelchair within 10 years. In his lawsuit against Southern California Edison, Kimball seeks $52.8 million. He says the company was responsible for the electric lines not being visible in the overgrown tree. The avocado tree was evidently two weeks overdo for a trim when the accident occurred. Kimball's lawyer says that Kimball is 15 percent responsible for the accident, because the lines were approximately 15 percent visible from the back yard where the tree was located.

Edison's attorney argued that Edison should not be held responsible for someone standing on an aluminum ladder with an aluminum pole 13 feet from the line. They said the wires cleared the branches by 6 feet (the state requires a "reasonable distance" such as 4 feet), so the wires were well within the legal guidelines. They claim Kimball got electrocuted because of his 10-foot aluminum pole hitting the wires and the mere fact that he didn't see the wires does not prove he could not see them. They argued that the only way to make it impossible to make power lines 100 percent visible is to chop down all the trees.

The question that must be decided is how to assign responsibility for Kimball's injuries. Kimball's own attorney suggests a 15/85 division (where he's 15 percent and Edison 85 percent responsible—thereby recognizing that Kimball himself bears some responsibility).

If we factor in the employer, however, this would have to change. Kimball was not picking avocados in his own back yard. He was doing it for his work. Surely it was his employer who sent him out with an aluminum ladder and an aluminum pole. A wooden pole would have protected Kimball against electrocution, but they are heavier. Thus employers prefer lighter poles and ladders, so workers can go at top speed. In trying to assign responsibility, there are a number of such factors that have to be considered. As we can see, a lot may rest on our being able to reason through such problems.

Group Exercise

Discuss the following argument using an analogy that rapper Joseph "Afroman" Foreman used. Note what's being compared, the similarities and differences of the two terms and if you think it's a good argument:

> Back in the day, a rapper playing guitar was like a nun wearing a bikini. You just didn't do it. But after I saw Wyclef Jean play, I knew it would be acceptable. I didn't have to be embarrassed and hide my guitar in the closet. (See Edna Gundersen, "Airwaves 'High' on Afroman's Funny Funk," *USA Today*, 20 Aug. 2001)

Exercises

Part One

Directions: Determine how strong you think the following inductive arguments are. Give reasons for your decision.

1. Of people who fly, 98 percent arrive safely. Governor Wilson is flying to New York. Therefore, he'll arrive safely.
2. Denzel Washington is a lot like Kobe Bryant. Both are African-American males, are talented people, are famous, and have a lot of fans. Kobe Bryant is a great athlete. That must mean Denzel Washington would be a great athlete too.
3. Approximately 250 of the 312 people attending the wedding reception suffered food poisoning. Ed and Jack attended the reception, so they probably suffered food poisoning too.
4. Steve usually makes barbecue chicken when the family gets together. Because we are going to his house on Thursday for Thanksgiving dinner, Steve's going to make us barbecue chicken.

5. In a study of women who tried out for the police department, the city found that 75 percent of them lifted weights and did aerobics. Therefore, 75 percent of all American women lift weights and do aerobics.

6. Some women who get liposuction have a few problems with their skin rippling. Therefore, liposuction causes skin to ripple in women.

7. Ben Affleck admitted that he has a serious problem with alcohol. He'll probably start a rehab program soon, because alcoholism can really mess up a person's life. (*celebritynews.about.com/library/weekly/aa080601a.htm*)

8. Scientists studying the pieces of pottery found in the archaeological site determined that of the 10,000 objects recovered, over 78 percent of them had some relationship to agriculture. They were either tools or receptacles for working the soil and raising crops. This suggests that the people who lived here were an agricultural, rather than a hunting society.

9. Eighty-two percent of the people who voted for Senator Collins reported in exit polls that they were Democrats. Charlene voted for Senator Collins, so she must be a Democrat.

10. Tom's phone number is one digit away from the pizza parlor's phone number. Last night he received 10 calls from people who wanted to order a pizza. Two nights ago he got 15 calls for pizza and three nights ago he got 12! I wish we didn't have to study at his house, because we are probably going to go nuts with pizza calls!

11. Circle all correct answers:
    a. A weak inductive argument is invalid.
    b. A valid argument always has true premises.
    c. An argument could be valid with false premises, provided that, if we assume the premises to be true, it would force the conclusion to be true.
    d. A sound argument is always valid.
    e. An invalid argument always has false premises.
    f. If you have true premises, you know the argument is valid.
    g. A sound argument must be valid and also have true premises.
    h. An inductive argument could be sound so long as the premises were true.
    i. An inductive argument is always unsound.
    j. An inductive argument could be valid, so long as the premises support the conclusion.

Part Two: Practice on Inductive and Deductive Arguments

1. Is this a valid argument? Is it sound? State your reasons.

   Everyone who studies logic enjoys horror films.
   Everyone who enjoys horror films likes the movie *Poltergeist.*
   Therefore, everyone who studies logic likes *Poltergeist.*

2. Indicate which of the arguments are inductive (I) and which are deductive (D):

    I   D   No one who eats squid is a vegetarian. Roland eats squid. So Roland is not a vegetarian.

    I   D   Fifty-six percent of the listeners who phoned in said that the death penalty is barbaric. So, 56 percent of teenagers think the death penalty is barbaric.

    I   D   The dinosaurs became extinct because evidence found in China last year suggested that an asteroid hit the earth during the time of the dinosaurs and sent up great dust clouds blocking the sun and causing very cold weather.

    I   D   All toxic substances should be handled very carefully. Dioxin is a toxic substance. So dioxin should be handled very carefully.

    I   D   Rhonda is just like her father—short, smart and determined. Her father dreamed of becoming a pilot, therefore Rhonda dreams of being a pilot too.

    I   D   Only a mean woman could put up with him. Only mean women hang out at Reggie's Bar. Cassandra hangs out at Reggie's Bar. Therefore, Cassandra could put up with him.

    I   D   Reading too many computer magazines causes a person to be depressed. Lauren reads computer magazines all the time, so she'll get depressed.

3. Set out a deductive argument for the conclusion, "Anyone who passes the calculus final exam should be able to pass the class."

4. Set out an inductive argument for the conclusion, "Most voters care about the world."

5. Circle all correct answers:

    a. A deductive argument is an argument in which the premises give some support, but not sufficient support, for the drawing of the conclusion.

    b. A deductive argument is an argument in which the premises are claimed to be sufficient for the drawing of the conclusion.

    c. A deductive argument claims that the conclusion follows from the premises with certainty.

    d. A deductive argument claims that the conclusion follows from the premises with probability.

    e. An inductive argument is an argument where the premises provide only some support for the drawing of the conclusion.

    f. An inductive argument claims that the conclusion follows with certainty.

6. Circle all the arguments below that are inductive:

    a. Georgia loves peach ice cream. Anyone who loves peach ice cream is a friend of mine. Therefore, Georgia is a friend of mine.

b. Seventy-five percent of women who love peach ice cream are wild and exotic. Georgia loves peach ice cream. Therefore, Georgia is wild and exotic.

c. No woman who loves peach ice cream is cruel to puppies. Georgia loves peach ice cream. So Georgia is not cruel to puppies.

d. Peach ice cream usually causes women to have a warm feeling inside. Georgia just ate some peach ice cream. So Georgia will probably have a warm feeling inside.

e. Everyone who loves peach ice cream lives a decadent life. Anyone who lives a decadent life forgets to vote. Therefore, everyone who loves peach ice cream forgets to vote.

7. Circle all the arguments below that are deductive. Remember the argument need not be valid, just deductive:

a. All football players are big and burly. Michael Jackson is not big and burly, so he must not be a football player.

b. Caffeine usually causes children to behave in unpredictable ways. That little girl is drinking some of her mother's coffee, so she'll behave in unpredictable ways.

c. All thieves are untrustworthy. Pablo Neruda is not a thief. So Pablo Neruda is trustworthy.

d. Seventy-five percent of Angelenos interviewed by NBC said they found the earthquake traumatic, but they will not leave the city. Allie Mac-Graw is an Angeleno. Consequently, she found the earthquake traumatic but won't leave Los Angeles.

e. Mack the Knife is awfully abusive to his dog. Abusive people were often abused as children. Therefore, Mack the Knife was abused when he was a child.

f. All munchkins are snapplepuffers. No snapplepuffer is a mork. Therefore, no mork is a munchkin.

8. Circle all the *valid* arguments below:

a. Everyone who goes barefoot risks being made into a laughing stock. Tarzan goes barefoot. Consequently, Tarzan risks being made into a laughing stock.

b. If he can't dodge bullets, he's not Neo. He's Neo. Therefore, he can dodge bullets.

c. Ninety-five percent of men who live in the jungle can swing from vines. Tarzan lives in the jungle, so he can swing from vines.

d. Batman is a lot like Zorro. He wears a funny-looking outfit and helps fight evil whenever he can. Zorro can do fancy tricks with his sword. Therefore, Batman can also do fancy tricks with his sword.

e. Everyone who dresses in a gorilla suit and drives on the freeway gets a lot of attention. Anyone who gets a lot of attention becomes terribly conceited. Therefore, everyone who dresses in a gorilla suit and drives on the freeway becomes terribly conceited.

f. Either you vote or don't complain. You didn't vote. So don't complain.

9. Explain whether this is an inductive or deductive argument:

In the early 1980s 11 people died of cyanide poisoning. Each victim had taken a Tylenol tablet and died within a few hours. There was no evidence that the cyanide had been added at the factory. Investigators suspected the jars had been tampered with and then placed on store shelves. At the time of the deaths, there was over $30 million worth of Tylenol on the shelves in stores throughout the United States. The company did not want anyone else to die of cyanide poison in Tylenol tablets. Until the source of the poisoned tablets was found, there was a risk that other people would die. Any time there is a serious risk to human life from a product, the product should be removed from the shelves and distribution stopped. Therefore, company officials concluded that the Tylenol should be recalled from the shelves.

10. Select two different arguments from either the Letters to the Editor or editorial section of a newspaper. Tape them to a piece of paper. Lay out the arguments, stating the premises and the conclusion.

   Answer the following:
   a. Are the arguments inductive or deductive? Explain.
   b. Are the arguments, if deductive, valid or invalid?
   c. Are there any sound arguments in your examples?

11. Here is a letter to the editor of the *Los Angeles Times* discussing the use of an analogy. Read the letter and decide if you agree with the author's argument that the analogy fails:

Letter to the Editor
Los Angeles Times

The publication of a highly inappropriate analogy, such as the one written by the National Director of the Anti-Defamation League and published in the *L.A. Times* on Saturday, March 30, 2002 ("Double Standards in Mideast"—Letters to the Times, 3/30/02) is offensive.

To equate the Israeli military response to Palestinian attacks with that of a firefighter to a fire set by an arsonist is an improper use of powerful images and words by making non-parallel comparisons. A firefighter's actions are neither aggressive nor violent, as this analogy would imply.

The firefighter does not interface with the arsonist, he only confronts the consequences of the arsonist's actions. A firefighter does not feed the flames he is fighting, whereas the Israeli military response stokes the fires which have been raging in the Middle East.

Given the richly deserved status of firefighters as heroes (especially since 9/11), selfless and apolitical in their actions, Mr. Foxman does them an injustice in his poorly drawn analogy. His equation of Palestinians with arsonists, meanwhile, is tantamount to defamation. It certainly does nothing to promote peace and tolerance, such as would befit comments from the Anti-Defamation League and contributes to the hyperbole surrounding the Mideast conflict. Surely not what the world needs more of, after witnessing the ongoing tragedy that is the Middle East.

Carla Nardoni

Part Three
Analyzing Inductive and Deductive Reasoning

1. Discuss Laker coach Phil Jackson's analogy in the following argument:

    Like life, basketball is messy and unpredictable. It has its way with you, no matter how hard you try to control it. The trick is to experience each moment with a clear mind and an open heart. When you do that, the game—and life—will take care of itself. (See Phil Jackson, *Sacred Hoops*)

2. After the September 2001 terrorist attacks on the United States, John Steinbruner, director of International and Security Studies at the University of Maryland, made the following remarks. Discuss his comments, focusing on his analogy:

    The main thing to keep in mind is that the main effect and main purpose is to induce a destructive response in the political system. Terrorism is an autoimmune disease—it is designed to get the political system attacked and do a lot of damage to itself. The U.S. government will struggle with overreaction and go to extreme measures. We don't know at this moment who did this. There will be theories and grave dangers of misjudgement of who is responsible. This may turn to the equivalent of Pearl Harbor. President Bush will need to develop an intelligent reaction to the issue. (See "Breaking News with John Steinbruner," *The Washington Post.com,* 11 Sep. 2001)

3. Deconstruct the argument below. Set out the conclusion and the premises. Note any inductive or deductive arguments that you see. Assess the strength of the reasoning.

    In 1980, the plaintiff became locked inside the trunk of a 1973 Ford LTD automobile, where she remained for some nine days. Plaintiff now seeks to recover for psychological and physical injuries arising from that occurrence. She contends that the automobile had a design defect in that the trunk lock or latch did not have an internal release or opening mechanism. She also maintains that the manufacturer is liable based on a failure to warn of this condition.

    Three uncontroverted facts bar recovery. First, the plaintiff ended up in the trunk compartment of the automobile because she felt "overburdened" and was attempting to commit suicide. Second, the purposes of an automobile trunk are to transport, stow and protect items from elements of the weather. Third, the plaintiff never considered the possibility of exit from the inside of the trunk when the automobile was purchased.

    The overriding factor barring plaintiff's recovery is that she intentionally sought to end her life by crawling into an automobile trunk from which she could not escape. This is not a case where a person inadvertently became trapped inside an automobile trunk. The plaintiff was aware of the natural and probable consequences of her perilous conduct. Not only that, the plaintiff, at least initially, sought those dreadful consequences. Plaintiff, not the manufacturer of the vehicle, is responsible for this unfortunate occurrence.

As a general principle, a design defect is actionable only where the condition of the product is unreasonably dangerous to the user or consumer. [A] manufacturer has a duty to consider only those risks of injury which are foreseeable. A risk is not foreseeable by a manufacturer where a product is used in a manner which could not reasonably be anticipated by the manufacturer and that use is the cause of the plaintiff's injury.

The purposes of an automobile trunk are to transport, stow and secure the automobile spare tire, luggage and other goods and to protect those items from elements of the weather. The design features of an automobile trunk make it well near impossible that an adult intentionally would enter the trunk and close the lid. The court holds that the plaintiff's use of the trunk compartment as a means to attempt suicide was an unforeseeable use. Therefore, the manufacturer had no duty to design an internal release or opening mechanism that might have prevented this occurrence. (See *Daniell v. Ford Motor Co., Inc.* (1984), as noted in Julie Van Camp, *Ethical Issues in the Courts*)

4. In discussing the Daniell case, above, philosophy professor Julie Van Camp asks, "If plaintiff were a 10-year-old child who suffered severe and permanent physical injury after *accidentally* locking herself in the trunk, should Ford Motor be held liable for damages?"
    a. State your answer to Van Camp's question. *Note:* Her question asks us to do some analogical reasoning and determine what, if anything, should change in the decision, if we changed a key detail of the case.
    b. Do you think the shift to "accidental" creates a crucial difference in the case? Discuss.

5. What if, instead of the adult plaintiff trying to commit suicide by locking herself in the trunk of the car, we had a plaintiff who jumped in the trunk and closed the door (thus locking herself in) to hide from a serial killer known to be roaming her neighborhood? She could not have foreseen such a use when she purchased the car, so does the decision above still apply in this case?

6. Discuss the reasoning in the excerpt below on Lyme disease. In 1999 the Center for Disease Control (CDC) recorded 16,273 cases. A controversy erupted:

    A study to be reported on Thursday in *The New England Journal of Medicine* is fueling a running disagreement among medical researchers over the unresolved issues in Lyme disease, a tick-borne illness that is endemic in much of the Northeast and in other pockets around the nation.

    The study, by Dr. Mark S. Klempner of Boston University Medical Center, showed that prolonged treatment with antibiotics was no more effective than placebos among those with persistent Lyme disease symptoms. Citing its importance to patients and doctors, the journal posted the study, along with two others and an editorial, on its Web site (*www.nejm.com*) a month before the scheduled publication date. The question is, "Why do a few patients who appear to have been treated successfully for Lyme disease have symptoms that come back strongly later?"

Both sides agree that antibiotics work in 90 percent of patients and that the disease never recurs in those patients, at least not from that tick bite. But among the other patients, symptoms either persist or come back after the standard treatment. Do the symptoms recur because the bacteria have been hiding out in the body, only to emerge again later? Or could the Lyme bacteria, even though they were wiped out by treatment, have brought on a secondary disease, a Lyme autoimmune disorder, in which the body's immune system attacks its own cells as if they were the Lyme disease organism?

Because the patients in Dr. Klempner's study were given a new round of antibiotics, the bacteria should have been killed, and the patients' symptoms should have gone away. Since that did not happen, proponents of the autoimmune theory say, the Klempner study is good evidence for their position. . . .

The Klempner study . . . found that extended treatment with antibiotics did not help people who believed they had persistent Lyme infection, a finding that suggested that their symptoms were unrelated to the bacteria. (See Philip J. Hilts, "Certainty and Uncertainty in Treatment of Lyme Disease," *The New York Times,* 10 July 2001)

7. Discuss the reasoning of the author, below, who takes issue with the reasoning by the Yale doctors and their followers on how to assess Lyme's disease. Stefanie Ramp asserts,

In part because Dr. Allen Steere, the physician credited with first identifying Lyme in Connecticut (but not the discoverer of the disease despite popular misconception), was on the Yale faculty at the time, Yale set the protocol for Lyme treatment (generally, a relatively short-term oral antibiotic therapy) and is still largely perceived as the beacon of Lyme wisdom. While everyone agrees that Yale doctors have done a great deal of valuable research on Lyme, many observers are now critical of Yale for clinging to its conservative opinions and jealously guarding its presumed founder's rights to the disease.

Despite an expanding body of contradictory evidence, most Yale-affiliated Lyme physicians continue to believe that chronic Lyme is not due to persisting infection and therefore refuse to sanction the long-term IV antibiotic therapy, which many doctors and patients have found effective in treating chronic Lyme. Since there's not enough solid research to support either theory, it's not so much the conflict of opinion that Yale critics take exception to. Rather, it's the arrogant close-mindedness of Yale doctors, who exclude every possibility, except those conceived by a Yale physician. (See Stefanie Ramp, "The Dirty Truth About Lyme Disease Research," *www.fairfieldweekly.com,* 1999)

8. Draw three to four inferences about the Lyme controversy, in light of the following quote from microbiologist Edward McSweegan:

Internet newsgroups regularly post wild criticisms of physicians and researchers who disagree with their claims and concerns. Research reports that run counter to the claims of Lyme activists are denounced and their authors accused of incompetence and financial conflicts of interest. Magazines and news organizations whose stories on Lyme disease are not sufficiently hysterical are barraged with e-mail complaints and urged to contact certain organizations for "the truth." Protests have been organized to denounce Yale University's research meetings and Lyme clinic because, according to the protesters, Yale "ridicules people with Lyme disease, presents misleading information, minimizes the severity of the illness, endorses inadequate, outdated treatment protocols, excludes opposing viewpoints, and ignores conflicts of interest."

Researchers have been harassed, threatened, and stalked. A petition circulated on the Web called for changes in the way the disease is routinely treated and the way insurance companies cover those treatments. Less radical groups have had their meetings invaded and disrupted by militant Lyme protesters. (See Edward McSweegan, Ph.D., "Lyme Disease: Questionable Diagnosis and Treatment," *www.quackwatch.com*, 30 June 2001)

9. Then there are the psychiatric views on Lyme disease. Read the follow and give your assessment of the reasoning:

Since the identification of the cause of syphilis in the early 1900s, psychiatrists have been aware that: (1) severe psychiatric disorders may be caused by a central nervous system infection; and (2) early antibiotic treatment may prevent permanent neurological damage. Syphilis was known as the "great imitator" because its multiple manifestations mimicked other known diseases. Today a new epidemic has emerged that has multiple manifestations and has been dubbed "the new great imitator"—Lyme borreliosis (Lyme disease). . . . Because Lyme borreliosis, like syphilis, has neuropsychiatric manifestations, psychiatrists are being asked to see these patients—often before they are diagnosed. Incorrectly labeling these patients as having a functional psychiatric disorder may result in a delay in initiating antibiotic treatment. . . .

Confounding accurate diagnosis is the fact that many of the prominent symptoms of Lyme disease share features with depressive illness, including irritability, fatigue, emotional ability, poor concentration, memory problems, and impaired sleep. Ruling out Lyme disease as a cause of these depressive symptoms can be difficult because currently available serological tests are inadequate, a third of all patients do not recall a rash or tick bite, and a long quiescent period may precede the late symptoms. . . .

While some doctors feel that depressive symptoms in the context of Lyme disease are evidence of continued disseminated infection, others believe that these represent a secondary emotional response to having a serious illness. Appropriate treatment if the former is true would consist of further antibiotics, which if the latter is true psychotherapy and/or antidepressant therapy would be the treatment of choice. Delayed additional antibiotic treatment due to an incorrect assessment of the disease process may enable an acute illness to develop into a chronic one. (See Brian A. Fallon, et al., "The Neuropsychiatric Manifestation of Lyme Borreliosis," *Psychiatric Quarterly*, Vol. 63, No. 1, Spring 1992)

CASE STUDY IN CAUSE AND EFFECT REASONING

The Provocation Defense and Gang Killings
"Provocative Act" Doctrine Rejected in Gang Killing

John Roemer
Daily Journal, August 28, 2001

An issue that brings together both cause and effect reasoning and arguments based on analogy is the question of assigning guilt in gang killings. Two cases provide examples for the sorts of inductive reasoning that goes into a legal decision of this kind. The dilemma is what to do when members of gangs are shooting at each other and (scenario 1) kill a bystander or (scenario 2) one gang member kills a member of a rival gang and, in retaliation, the rival gang murders a member of the gang that fired the first shot.

One issue that comes up is the question of cause. The direct *cause of something is that which leads to a particular effect without any intervening step. In contrast, the* proximate *cause of an event is the last causal factor in a chain leading to a particular effect. For instance, someone with cancer undergoing chemotherapy has a weakened immune system and then gets pneumonia and dies. The pneumonia is the* proximate *cause of the person's death, but clearly not the sole cause.*

Compare for example a child throwing a ball at a window, causing it to break (direct cause is the throwing of the ball) to a man carrying a tuna casserole slipping on a banana peel that a prankster just threw down on the sidewalk in front of the man, causing him to send the casserole flying in the air, going through a window, and breaking it (the casserole dish flying in the air is the proximate *cause of the broken window, the end of the sequence of causal factors starting with the prankster throwing down the banana peel).*

Read the following article from the law newspaper, the Daily Journal. *Then briefly state what was at issue and whether you think the de-cision in each case was a wise one in terms of addressing gang killings.*

SAN FRANCISCO—Gang killings in Santa Ana and Fontana led to distinctly different decisions by the California Supreme Court on Monday involving the "proximate causation" doctrine in murder cases and the state's controversial "provocative act" rule. Both unanimous decisions were written by Justice Marvin R. Baxter.

One ruling, *People v. Cervantes,* . . . appeared to be a win for defendants because it turned away an effort to expand the provocative act doctrine, which holds accountable for murder those whose non-lethal assaults lead indirectly to a killing. The other case, decided on the issue of proximate cause, was a victory for prosecutors in gang warfare cases. For the first time, in *People v. Sanchez,* . . . the high court approved dual murder convictions for two shooters when a lone bullet from one of them—whose identity cannot be ascertained—killed a single victim.

In the first case, the court unanimously reversed the murder conviction of Highland Street gang member Israel Cervantes. The justices, in overturning a Santa Ana appellate panel, declined to broaden the provocative act theory. Cervantes was convicted of first-degree murder even though his gunshot only wounded a member of the Alley Boys gang at a street birthday party in 1994. Friends of the victim retaliated by gunning to death Hector Cabrera, a member of Cervantes' gang, and prosecutors successfully invoked the provocative act theory to win a life sentence for Cervantes.

"Given that the murder of Cabrera by other parties was itself felonious, intentional, perpetrated with malice aforethought, and directed at a victim who was not involved in the original altercation. . . . the evidence is insufficient as a matter of law to establish the requisite proximate causation to hold defendant liable for murder," Baxter wrote.

The provocative act doctrine is most often used in cases where a defendant opens fire and someone else shoots back, killing a third party. Typically the deadly shots come from store clerks, police or other crime victims who react to a lethal emergency created by the initial shooter. But when the killers in the current case retaliated against another member of Cervantes' gang, they absolved Cervantes of responsibility for the death of their victim, Baxter wrote, citing a classic 1985 legal text, Horn & Honoré's Causation in the Law:

"The killers 'intend[ed] to exploit the situation created by [Cervantes], but [were] not acting in concert with him,' a circumstance that is 'normally held to relieve the first actor [Cervantes] of criminal responsibility.' In short, nobody forced the Alley Boys' murderous response in this case. . . . The willful and malicious murder of [the victim] at the hands of others was an independent intervening act on which defendant's liability for the murder could not be based." "The decision is good news for defense lawyers," said Philip M. Brooks, the Berkeley sole practitioner who wrote and argued the appeal before the high court. "Upholding this expansion of the doctrine would have completely changed the law," he said. . . .

And in Monday's other opinion—a case of first impression—the Supreme Court upheld the murder conviction of Julio Cesar Sanchez, a member of a Fontana gang named TDK (Diablo Klicka). That case came to the court as another provocative act case—but the justices decided it instead on the issue of proximate cause. The decision means that two shooters can be found guilty of a murder in which only a single bullet strikes the victim. Sanchez and codefendant Ramon Gonzalez of the rival Headhunters gang shot it out in 1996 on a Fontana street. A stray shot killed a bystander, and both shooters were convicted of murder under the provocative act theory.

Gonzalez did not appeal his conviction. The Sanchez guilty finding was overturned by a unanimous Riverside appellate panel, which concluded concurrent causation cannot be established in a single-fatal-bullet case. That was erroneous, the high court held. "The circumstance that it cannot be determined who fired the single fatal bullet, i.e., that direct or actual causation cannot be established, does not undermine defendant's first degree murder conviction if it was shown beyond a reasonable doubt that defendant's conduct was a substantial concurrent cause of [the victim's] death," Baxter wrote. He added, "It is proximate causation, not direct or actual causation, which, together with the requisite culpable *mens rea* (malice), determines defendant's liability for murder."

Defense lawyer Melvyn Douglas Sacks of Los Angeles called the decision significant. "It's a landmark for law enforcement in combating gang violence," said Sacks. . . . "The court may regard this as a step forward for society, but it's a step backward for the defense bar," he said. "It really stretches aiding and abetting. The other guy fired first and my guy never fired his weapon until after the victim was dead." . . . Justice Joyce L. Kennard, in a concurrence, discussed how the companion cases of *Cervantes* and *Sanchez* differ. "In both, the defendant was a gang member who discharged a firearm at someone belonging to a rival gang," Kennard wrote. "In both, defendant's conduct induced additional gunfire in which a third person died. But this court has concluded that these similarities are less significant than other circumstances distinguishing the two situations."

Proximate or legal causation was not established in *Cervantes* but was present in *Sanchez*, Kennard wrote, adding: "History sadly establishes that killings motivated by revenge may occur in cycles lasting many years and even generations. Although those whose conduct precipitates these vendetta cycles, and all who participate in continuing them, must bear moral responsibility for the ensuing bloodshed, the criminal law will not impose what in theory could be an unbounded liability for retaliatory killings, and courts must try to draw appropriate lines to mark the outer limits of legal causation in these situations.

"The court's decisions today in these two companion cases should begin to fix this line of demarcation separating mutual combat killings from retaliatory killings in the context of urban warfare between rival street gangs." Justice Kathryn Mickle Werdegar also concurred separately.

PART TWO

Going Out into the World

CHAPTER SEVEN

The Social Dimension

There's a black person on our street and we say "Hi," like he's a normal person.
—RESIDENT OF SIMI VALLEY, NOTED BY THOMAS L. DUNN

In the best of all possible worlds, social issues are easily recognized and re-solved. Many of them, however, start to look like they've settled down, when they pop up again. These sticky social conflicts are a bit like the story of Br'er Rabbit and the tar baby set in his path by Mr. Fox. After slapping the tar baby for not answering him, the pesky rabbit got stuck. The more he tried to extricate him-self, the worse things got, until Br'er Rabbit was completely trapped in the tar. Of course, this was just what the fox wanted.

Similarly, if we don't approach social problems with a clear mind, a good atti-tude, and an effective approach, we can get stuck, stuck, stuck. Think of all those festering social wounds that never seem to heal—like the Middle East conflict, the British–Irish problem, gang violence in the United States, the abortion debate, and the controversies around stem cell research and cloning.

Reasoning around social problems has roots that go far into our collective psy-che—our societal mindset. These roots are grounded in fundamental cultural val-ues, ethics, politics, and religious beliefs. We saw this at the 2001 G8 Summit in Genoa, Italy, where police killed a protester. As French president Jacques Chirac said before he was informed of the death of the protester, "One hundred thousand people don't get upset unless there is a problem in their hearts and spirits." The tensions around the global distribution of wealth are rising, and the path to reso-lution seems light years away.

Some social problems, as those faced at summits, are global in scope. Others, like the voting discrepancies in the 2000 U.S. presidential election are more na-tionally focused. Still other social problems get played out at the level of commu-nities, neighborhoods, and between individuals.

For example, in September 2001, there was considerable negative publicity about a novelist, Fay Weldon, agreeing to write a novel commissioned by the jewelry company, Bulgari. Evidently, as part of the bargain, she was to do a little "product placement," such as having characters wearing Bulgari jewels. An underlying concern was whether or not her agreeing to having a corporate sponsor of her novel was unethical or improper.

In a September 9, 2001, letter to the editor of *The New York Times*, the president of the Finnegans Wake Society dismissed all the kerfuffle. He said that Irish novelist James Joyce mentions the Guinness (ale) brewery many times in his novel *Ulysses*, even though he did not seem to profit from it. He did not mention the fallacy *argumentum ad hominem circumstantial*, but did point out the "the motive for the name dropping shouldn't matter; what matters is how good the book is." However true that may be, that's not likely to stop the criticism and questions about the social ramifications of her decision to do product placement in exchange for corporate cash.

▓ The Social Dimension of Everyday Life

Think of the range of social issues facing our lives. Some of these issues only indirectly affect us; others touch our lives. Most of us have had moments where a seemingly innocuous situation erupts, with wide-reaching consequences. Hurt feelings may heal after awhile, but some wounds don't heal easily if at all.

Have you ever betrayed a friend, or been betrayed by one? Have you ever driven drunk or ridden along as a passenger with someone who was "tipsy"? Do you have strong feelings about animal rights or vegetarianism? What should we do about children who smoke? Is our prison system just? Social concerns such as these are a part of our lives. Consequently, we need to be able to look at them, assess the policies and decision making associated with them, and determine how far we will go for what we believe in.

Think about all the aspects of an issue like honesty and ask yourself how it has touched your life. Have you ever lied for someone? Or have you been the victim of a lie? Have you ever seen a friend steal something and acted like it didn't matter? Have you ever cheated on an exam or helped someone else cheat? Have you ever seen what happens when lies are built on top of lies until there's an entire edifice of dishonesty? Once lies are set in motion, they have a way of snowballing. Let us examine how an issue like honesty can have both societal and personal repercussions.

CASE STUDY

Lies and Deception: The Joseph Ellis Case

On June 18, 2001, the *Boston Globe* published an article by Walter Robinson about a Mount Holyoke College history professor, Joseph Ellis. Ellis is a popular teacher and a Pulitzer Prize winner (for his book, *Founding Brother: The Revolutionary Generation*). Though he never served in Vietnam, Ellis regularly told his classes stories about his war years, painting a vivid picture about his supposed tour of duty in Vietnam. These fabricated anecdotes provided a backdrop to class discussion about the Vietnam War.

His lies expanded to other areas, such as claiming to have scored a winning touchdown in high school (no evidence he was on the team) and being an antiwar protestor after going to Vietnam (no evidence of either). In spite of the risks, Ellis became more public in his deception. His tales of war service came back to haunt him. According to Robinson,

Last year, he told *Globe* reporter Mark Feeney that he went to Vietnam in 1965 as a platoon leader and paratrooper with the 101st Airborne Division. . . . Ellis told Feeney that his Vietnam service also included duty in Saigon on the staff of General William C. Westmoreland, the American commander in Vietnam. And he later shared his observations about Westmoreland with David Halberstam, the author of the 1972 best-selling book, *The Best and the Brightest.* But an extensive public record review by the *Globe,* as well as the accounts of Ellis's friends from those years, contradict his assertions that he served in Vietnam. For his part, Halberstam said he has no recollection of ever meeting Ellis, and that Ellis was not a source for his book. (See "Professor's Past in Doubt," *Boston Globe,* 18 June 2001)

Initially Mount Holyoke president Joanne V. Creighton praised Ellis, saying he "earned a reputation for great integrity, honesty and honor." She also said, "We at the College do not know what public interest the *Globe* is trying to serve through a story of this nature," as if the newspaper was wrong to expose the lies and acts of deception.

However, as details became public, questions about Ellis's integrity, honesty, and honor multiplied. Ellis issued an apology through his attorney. He said, "Even in the best of lives, mistakes are made. I deeply regret having let stand and later confirming the assumption that I went to Vietnam. For this and any other distortions about my personal life, I want to apologize to my family, friends, colleagues, and students."

His publisher seems undeterred by the uproar: Ashbel Green, Ellis's editor at Knopf Publishing, says, "We intend to keep publishing him." But others have raised serious questions about the professor and about institutional policies around honesty. This has given rise to a public discussion on personal and professional integrity.

Group Exercise

Read the various responses to the news of Pulitzer Prize–winning author, Joseph Ellis's acts of deceit. (Groups can either look at all the observer's comments, or zero in on one of them.) Note the issues and concerns each observer brings up and what the overall picture is regarding notions of integrity.

Observations on Joseph Ellis's Lies and Deception

Observer 1: Peter Juran, Amherst senior who took Ellis's class.

It never would have occurred to me that he was being disingenuous. It seems incongruous that he would be living a lie like this. He has all the right credentials. There was no need for him to fabricate any of this. (As noted in the *Boston Globe,* 18 June 2001)

Observer 2: Edmund Morris, author of a book on Theodore Roosevelt.

Actually I feel no joy in Professor Ellis's discomfiture, only a profound sense of unsurprise. Well, *of course* he's woven the fabric of his life partly out of whole cloth and partly out of the shot silk of fantasy. Don't we all? Can any of us gaze into the bathroom mirror and whisper, "I never made anything up"? (Op/ed piece, *The New York Times,* 22 June 2001)

Observer 3: Stanford professor David M. Kennedy, 2000 Pulitzer Prize winner in history and former Yale classmate of Ellis.

We often need some perspective on this. I think what he did [lying to students] was professionally irresponsible and he has got to take the consequences. But it's not as if he misrepresented the nature of the Divine. (As quoted in the *Los Angeles Times,* 22 June 2001)

Observer 4: David J. Garrow, professor at Emory University School of Law in Atlanta and winner of the 1987 Pulitzer Prize in history.

"I can't imagine people taking the position that knowingly lying to your students in class is somehow less immoral than lying to your readers in print." According to the *Los Angeles Times,* Garrow said the case against Ellis was "open and shut" and Ellis should be banned from ever teaching history again if he doesn't remove himself voluntarily. (As quoted in the *Los Angeles Times,* 22 June 2001)

Observer 5: Christopher Hitchens, professor at the New School for Social Research.

Somehow there is a deep connection between Vietnam and Walter Mitty in our national psyche. The war begins with a lie about the Gulf of Tonkin—one of the biggest whoppers ever told the American public—and it carries on with a series of whoppers by Robert McNamara and others about the progress of the war. The entire undertaking was predicated on a web of falsehoods and delusions, which continue to this very day. (As quoted in the *Los Angeles Times,* 22 June 2001)

Observer 6: Jane F. Babson, historian and graduate of Mount Holyoke.

I am a historian and a graduate of Mount Holyoke College. I was educated there to believe that one did not lie about oneself in any way and that there was no excuse for those who did. I am ashamed of Prof. Joseph J. Ellis's lies to his class about his nonexistent service in Vietnam . . . and of the June 21 letter [to *The New York Times*] defending Mr. Ellis from Peter Viereck, professor emeritus of history at the college. What happened to my college's reputation as a place of integrity? (Letter to the Editor, *The New York Times,* 23 June 2001)

Observer 7: Ben Bagdikian, University of California–Berkeley professor and Pulitzer Prize winner in journalism.

Ellis's behavior "raises credibility questions about how he deals with historical fact, even though it seems to have no connection to his [Pulitzer Prize–winning] book. I think that someone who fakes his personal history in a significant way does not deserve to be honored as a historian. I don't think we should honor people who do that kind of fakery. . . . I would be very troubled if I were on the Pulitzer board." (As quoted in the *Los Angeles Times,* 19 June 2001)

Observer 8: Lance Morrow, *Time* magazine columnist.

I returned to a hero's welcome, the Prof. would remember. Mac Bundy threw me into Bobby Kennedy's pool. I did a cameo on "Laugh-In." I wrote a song called "Bobbie Magee and I," but Kristofferson stole it, the drunk—just changed the words a little. No, I'm afraid not. No excuse, no rationale will work—and especially not the foxy formulations some have attempted in Joe Ellis's defense, positively Gallic sleight-of-hand about the elusive interplay between truth and fantasy in the recounting of history. No: Ellis's lies were simply a disgraceful—and disgracefully stupid—business that betrayed his duty as a teacher and wrecked his intellectual credibility. (As noted in *Time,* 25 June 2001)

Observer 9: Robert Bowie Johnson, Jr., Airborne, Ranger, Infantry, Vietnam, West Point, Class of 1965.

Lies like yours permeate one's entire life and work. What I want is a heartfelt apology. This is the direction in which I expect the Supreme Spirit is already leading you. I want an apology to the memory of all those who gave their lives in Viet Nam, an apology to all who were physically, emotionally, and spiritually wounded there, an apology to all the aggrieved family members. And I want an apology to all those, nonveteran and veteran alike, who, unlike you, really did work hard in the antiwar movement, often sacrificing reputation, position, and wealth, to help bring that abominable war to an end. (Open letter to Joseph Ellis, *hometown.aol.com/viperash51/Meemir/story.html*)

Observer 10: Robert Kreiser of the American Association of University Professors.

It should be the responsibility of human beings to represent themselves as they are—and I suppose scholars have an additional responsibility, since we're members of a profession that has standards of behavior. (As quoted by Christopher Chow, "The Greatest Dishonor," *Accuracy in Academia,* 7 July 2001)

Exercises

1. On June 21, 2001, Mount Holyoke announced that Joseph Ellis would no longer teach his signature course on Vietnam and American culture. The college president promised a full investigation of the scandal. What advice or input would you give to the committee charged with investigating the case and determining what should be done about Prof. Ellis's behavior?

2. In a June 20, 2001 letter to the *Boston Globe,* Mount Holyoke president Joanna Creighton said "I, too, deeply regret the effect of his misrepresentation on students, colleagues and the public." Discuss her use of the term "misrepresentation" in her public statement.

3. In the June 20, 2001 letter to the *Boston Globe,* Mount Holyoke president Joanna Creighton said, "I presumed his innocence when I first heard of this matter." As well, "However, Prof. Ellis has since admitted, both publicly and to me privately, that he did misrepresent his military service."
   a. Assess Mount Holyoke president Creighton's statements.
   b. What would *you* have written, if you were the Mount Holyoke president responding to this case?

4. Former student Angel Kozeli said, "He seemed so genuine. Perhaps it was a fantasy he came to believe himself" (as noted by Christopher Chow, "The Greatest Dishonor," *Accuracy in Academia,* 7 July 2001). How should universities respond when instructors lie to their classes, bringing in fantasies they come to believe? Set out three to four recommendations for an academic integrity policy aimed at faculty.

5. On August 17, 2001, the *Associated Press* reported,

   A Pulitzer Prize-winning history professor who admitted he lied to his students about being a Vietnam combat veteran will be suspended for a year without pay, Mount Holyoke College said Friday. Joseph J. Ellis, 57, also must give up his endowed chair at the college.

   "I strongly rebuke Prof. Ellis for his lie about his military experience," Mount Holyoke President Joanne Creighton said. "The year away should give him and the college time for reflection and repair. This sanction is consistent with our honor code for students and its emphasis on education, reflection and ultimately restoration to an honorable place in our community."

   Answer the following:
   a. What do you think of Creighton's comments, given her earlier ones?
   b. Evidently, Mount Holyoke president Creighton made this decision herself. Do you think this was an appropriate response? If so, give your defense. If not, recommend what ought to have been done and state your reasons.

6. What would you do if you discovered that your professor lied to the class and shared supposedly true stories and scenarios to illustrate points, which turned out to be inventions? What would you do if it were *you* who found out the truth and that no one else knew that the professor was lying to the class?

7. What sort of policy should be in effect at colleges and universities to deal with dishonest faculty members? Do you think his one-year suspension without pay is appropriate punishment?

Broader Significance of Social Frameworks and Moral Reasoning

Some social conflicts and moral problems are ongoing. Think of euthanasia, the death penalty, world hunger, racism, and religious intolerance. These wide-ranging issues seem to defy resolution. On the other hand, some are resolved fairly quickly—for example, cases involving individual acts of plagiarism, sexual harassment, and violations of workplace ethics. The narrower the scope, the more likely is a resolution.

It is not always easy to apply ethical guidelines or legal rulings, especially to a controversial case. For instance, how near can someone get to an abortion clinic to handout protest literature? Someone had to figure that out.

Some ethical dilemmas vary with the political climate, as with abortion and reproductive freedom, animal rights, "illegal aliens," foreign aid, sexual ethics, welfare, prisoners' rights, and homelessness. Other dilemmas are caught up with ethnic and religious contexts, such as issues around reproductive technology, movie and music ratings systems, censorship of political literature, and norms around prostitution, nudity, and adultery.

One of the most volatile social issues facing us today is abortion. Katie Cannon, an Episcopal priest, once remarked that abortion is this century's civil war. It has certainly been a contentious issue. The fact that abortion is legal in the United States and Canada has not put a lid on the tensions around the issue. There are other aspects of the abortion debate besides the acceptability of an early abortion for a competent adult. Related concerns revolve around sex selection (e.g., Is it morally acceptable to abort a fetus because it's male or female?), the timing (e.g., Is late abortion morally acceptable?) and who's involved in the decision making (e.g., Should husbands have veto power on an abortion? Should parents be able to stop a minor?). Another issue is access to abortion (e.g., Should every county or every urban area greater than an agreed-upon size have to provide abortion facilities?). Then there are those who want to take the law into their own hands.

On the increase are threats or actual acts of "justifiable homicide," raising the question, Is it morally acceptable to use violence to stop an abortion? And with Internet providing a fast, cheap way to communicate across vast distances, organized violence, as well as reasoned dialogue, can take shape. Let us look at the case of a doctor who provides abortions under the threat of death and then look at his concerns in the article below.

CASE STUDY

9th Circuit's Decision
Makes Abortion Doctor Marked Man
Warren M. Hern, M.D.
The New York Times *and the* Daily Journal
April 23, 2001

Abortion Clinic Violence

According to the media watch group, FAIR: In December 1994, TV station NBC refused to air a segment of the program TV Nation. *In this segment Roy McMillan, director of the Christian Action Group said that assassinating Supreme Court justices would be justifiable homicide. The TV segment was subsequently aired in England by the BBC.*

The Christian Action Group's "Defensive Action Declaration" makes it explicit that violence in the name of stopping abortions is morally acceptable. The declaration is as follows:

Defensive Action Declaration

We, the undersigned, declare the justice of taking all godly action necessary to defend innocent human life including the use of force.

We proclaim that whatever force is legitimate to defend the life of a born child is legitimate to defend the life of an unborn child.

We assert that if Michael Griffin did in fact kill David Gunn [abortion doctor murdered in 1993] his use of lethal force was justifiable provided it was carried out for the purpose of defending the lives of unborn children.

Therefore, he ought to be acquitted of the charges against him.

www.ifas.org

This bears some resemblance to a declaration of war. Insisting their view is legitimate, the Christian Action Group asserts that it is both right and just to kill in the name of those beliefs. That it is unlawful does not appear to be a factor. The result is the followers seem closer to vigilantes than concerned citizens voicing opposition. Abortion providers like Dr. Gunn have borne some of the most direct consequences of the escalating tension around abortion. His death is proof that a determined minority is willing to take life to try to save life.

In October 1998, Dr. Barnett Slepian was killed when a sniper shot him through the kitchen window of his Buffalo, New York, home. An explosive device packed with nails killed a security guard and maimed a nurse at a women's clinic in Birmingham, Alabama. Nineteen women's clinics had butyric acid tossed at them and abortion clinics were subjected to scares involving a biowarfare agent, anthrax.

On July 11, 2001, a Canadian physician, Dr. Garson Romalis, was stabbed in the back while going into his Vancouver office. He survived this second attempt on his life—in 1994 he was the victim of a sniper shooting. Other doctors, nurses, and security guards of abortion clinics have been killed or injured in a range of attacks. Warren M. Hern, M.D., lives and works in the face of escalating violence toward abortion providers. Read his article, below, discussing the degree to which violence has touched his life and work. Then answer the questions that follow.

The news of James Kipp's arrest in France from the 1998 murder of Dr. Barnett Slepian reached me just as I finished performing an abortion for the last patient of the morning. My relief was tempered by the news of the previous day. A judgment against anti-abortion fanatics who want me and other doctors killed had been overturned by the 9th U.S. Circuit Court of Appeals in California.

The previous afternoon, as I sat by a window in my office talking with a reporter about the appellate court decision, I noticed that the Venetian blinds were slightly open. Without interrupting the conversation or thinking about it, I reached over to close the blinds. That has become my response when I find myself by an open window, I move away, draw the curtains, or close the blinds.

It's too dangerous for me to be in front of a window. Five shots were fired through the windows of my office in 1988. But I learned the need to be cautious most intensely in October 1998 as I watched in horror the reports of [Dr. Barnett] Slepian's assassination in the kitchen of his home in New York.

Whoever shot Slepian accomplished his purpose—to strike into my heart. It was an act of political terrorism, as have been the assassinations and attempted assassinations of 10 other attacks, also sometimes fatal, on other abortion doctors and several similar attacks, also sometimes fatal, on others who helped abortion doctors or were related to them. It is unusual for me to lift the coverings of windows in my home so I can see out. I have a nice view from my home of the famous Flatirons mountains that rise above Boulder, but it is a luxury to enjoy that view.

As my life is now, the windows cannot be uncovered at night. Sometimes I look into the homes of my neighbors and see them moving about and relaxing with their families. My office is a fortress of steel fences and bulletproof windows, and my home has become a hiding place from which I emerge and hope that I will not be the next assassin's target.

Kopp, a suspect in Slepian's assassination, has been arrested, but where is the next one like him? Who are all the people who helped him escape and hide? When and where will the next assassin strike? Will I get to live out my life?

This week's decision by the Court of Appeals was crushing. I am one of four physicians who are plaintiffs in this lawsuit against anti-abortion activists who have targeted us. We sued them under federal racketeering law and another law against inciting violence against doctors who perform abortions. We sat in that courtroom in Portland in 1999 for one month next in the people who wanted us dead. We listened to our lawyers present fact after fact to the jury, showing the terror that had been inflicted on our lives.

We listened to the self-righteous anti-abortion fanatics justify their use of speech in posters and on the Internet to terrify abortion doctors. My medical colleagues and I went into medicine to help people, and we do. But we became the targets of these despicable and dangerous people. Each of us doctors described to the jury how we had been stalked and portrayed as criminals by the defendants' "wanted poster" hit lists distributed as fliers and displayed in a 1995 news conference in Virginia. Later, this list was posted on the Internet.

We described how our lives had been warped permanently—in some ways ruined—by this harassment. Maria Vullo, our attorney, eloquently showed the pattern to the jury: poster, murder, poster, murder, poster, murder—all since 1993. Her colleagues pounded home the inescapable conclusion that the defendants purposely created a climate that said to people like Kopp: "Kill these doctors. Here's your list."

The federal jury of Portland citizens agreed with us that the anti-abortion posters and rhetoric were dangerous to us. Their verdict against the defendants was an important signal that our adversaries may not exploit our democracy's sacred freedom of speech in order to endanger others.

My name, along with those of other doctors, is in an Internet abortion hate list—called the "Nuremberg Files"—now found to be acceptable free speech by the appellate court's decision. Slepian's name has had a line drawn through it. Who's next?

Reprinted with the Permission of Dr. Warren M. Hern. This article appeared in both *The New York Times* and the *Daily Journal*.

Case Update   On May 16, 2002, the U.S. Court of Appeals ruled that abortion foes whose "Wanted"-style posters and websites targeted abortion doctors were engaged in illegal intimidation and that this was not constitutionally protected political speech. As Judge Pamela Ann Rymer wrote: "There is substantial evidence that these posters were prepared and disseminated to intimidate physicians from providing reproductive health services." She said, "Holding [the anti-abortion activists] accountable for this conduct does not impinge on legitimate protest or advocacy." They held that the anti-abortion activists were intentionally instilling fear so intense that the doctors felt that they had to wear bullet-proof vests. "Our Constitution has never protected violence, nor has it protected speech used to place someone in fear of violence," said Gloria Feldt, president of the Planned Parenthood Federation of America, in support of the ruling.

Dissenters felt this weakened freedom of speech. "The defendants here pose a special challenge, as they vehemently condone the view that murdering abortion providers . . . is morally justified," Judge Marsha S. Berzon wrote in one of three dissenting opinions. "But the defendants have not murdered anyone. . . . If we are not willing to provide stringent First Amendment protection and a fair trial to those with whom we as a society disagree as well as those with whom we agree . . . the First Amendment will become a dead letter."

As ACLU attorney Michael Simon put it, "There is significant disagreement here on an interpretation of the statute under the First Amendment." He added, "It is worthy of attention by the Supreme Court." (See "Ruling Curbs Abortion Foes' Tactics," *The Washington Post*, 17 May 2002). It remains to be seen if the Supreme Court will see such websites as the "Nuremberg Files" under the protection of the First Amendment, or as threats or acts of violence that exceed rights to freedom of speech.

Exercises

1. Set out the key arguments used by Dr. Hern to support his claim that Dr. Slepian's death was "political terrorism."

2. Set out Dr. Hern's concerns about the existence of an Internet abortion hate list. Are there other concerns that should be raised against the Internet being used to target abortion providers? State them.

3. Compare two pro-life websites with two pro-choice websites in terms of what is emphasized and the language used to discuss the abortion debate.

Social and Ethical Decision-Making Guidelines

When trying to assess social problems or ethical quandaries, it may be helpful to have some guidelines. This not only helps us get a handle on how we should approach controversial issues, but helps us structure a response.

Some preliminary work needs to be done before we can come up with an ethical decision we will not regret later. These are:

Decision-Making Guidelines
for Social and Moral Reasoning

1. *Define the Problem.* State, as clearly as you can, what is at issue. State it in its broadest terms, noting potential societal impact. And state it in its narrowest terms, noting the potential repercussions of the case at hand. Note how the very formulation of the problem shapes how we are going to solve it.

2. *Sharpen the Focus.* Clarify the parameters of the decision making. Know who is facing the dilemma, who is making the decision, who is most affected by the decision, what the options are, and what set of criteria will be used to make the decision.

3. *Clarify the Context.* Most decision making is contextual—where we look at a problem in terms of whose problem it is and how the different options would impact the lives of those involved. Set out the main context in which the problem arises.

4. *Gather Information.* Know the specific details of the case at hand. Set out all relevant evidence or information that can help make an informed choice. Don't be afraid to scout: Get on the Internet, running searches with key terms (alone or in combination). Hit libraries and don't be afraid to get the help of librarians or others who are savvy with research. Most people are happy to help.

5. *Clarify Key Concepts and Ideas.* Look at the relevant concepts that bear upon the social or ethical decision. Think of concepts as the framework of evaluation. Of course concepts like "justice," "freedom," "truth," "good," and "evil" are abstract terms, but they are understood—and applied—within a society and a culture. Be aware of how they are being interpreted. Don't assume those interpretations are fixed.

6. *Examine Assumptions.* Often invisible, assumptions can wreak havoc. A warranted assumption can be like a skeleton, helping keep the framework in place. An unwarranted assumption can be like a virus, run rampant through a system, bringing with it destruction.

7. *Identify Frameworks.* Look at the norms, beliefs, ethics, and political and ideological frameworks that shape the decision making. Watch for social norms, belief systems, ethical codes, religious attitudes, and political persuasions that frame ideas and shape interpretations. Watch for cultural influences and idiosyncratic approaches to framing issues.

8. *Shift Perspectives.* Get some perspective. Examine the problem from more than one perspective. Go into sufficient detail to see distinctly different ways of viewing the issue and assessing how the decision will impact others.

9. *Target Your Audience.* Who are you trying to convince? For what purpose? If you don't know who's in the audience, you will have trouble making your case. Knowing the audience allows you to make certain assumptions as well; for example, in terms of needing to define terms, documenting claims, citing sources, and so on.

10. *Formulate a Position.* Set out where you stand. Do this even if you stand undecided. Your indecision may be illuminating and help move us to a resolution farther down the line. Articulate as clearly as you can what your position is and why you hold it. See if you've got your evidence lined up to make your best case.

11. *Anticipate Criticism.* Consider the opponents' position and try to answer them. Knowing only your own side sets you up for an attack. It also suggests that the other side is not worth knowing (rarely true). Consider your opponent a friend, not an

enemy and try to give a sympathetic reading of the other side. Look for its merits and re-examine your own position to address your opponents' concerns.

12. *Set Out Your Argument.* You know where you stand, you've thought about the ideas and issues, you've done the research, you have formulated your position and gathered the support. As best as you can, set out your decision!

Group Exercise

The Hopi Codetalkers

President Clinton signed a bill at the end of the year 2000 which granted Congressional Medals to 29 living Navajo Codetalkers, but did not recognize Codetalkers from other tribes. For instance, the Hopi Codetalkers were honored by the local American Legion Post and other organizations, but have received no national recognition. On the national level, only Navajo Codetalkers have been recognized. Hopi Tribal vice chairman, Phillip Quochytewa, Sr., petitioned national leaders for recognition of the Hopi Codetalkers without success.

Directions: Read the following article by Debra Moon, journalist and photographer. Then set out the key arguments for the remaining Hopi Codetalkers being granted a Congressional Medal.

Hopi Culture Dictates a Different Face for Honor for Living Hopi Codetalkers

Debra Moon

Codetalkers during World War II were a small select group of the military. They had a job to do: get messages to the troops without the enemy knowing. They couldn't be captured, and they knew it. They had top-secret knowledge, and there was too much danger that the enemy could force it from them if they were captured. They took a vow to end their own life rather than be captured.

Some say we owe our success in World War II to them. They transmitted hundreds of error free messages that were responsible for taking out many Japanese artillery and machine gun positions, and monitoring Japanese troop movements, saving many American lives. After the job was over, they came home, and like so many veterans, found that they had to struggle for Veteran Services because of the bureaucracy surrounding the dispensing of services to our former military heroes.

Out of 300 original Codetalkers, a small percentage were Hopi, however, their role was as important as Navajo and other Native Americans who served during World War II with this mission. Fifty out of the original 300 [Codetalkers] are still living, and for Hopi, only three men are still alive. They are Franklin Shupla from Tewa/First Mesa, Floyd Dann from Moenkopi and Travis Yaiva from Bacavi. . . .

According to Cliff Balenquah, Hopi Tribal Council Representative from Bacavi and former Director of Veteran Affairs at Hopi, "They can't buy what they need with a medal," "They just want reciprocation, some very much needed Vet Services, like medical services, pensions, and disability benefits." But Balenquah testifies that these services are very hard for Hopi Codetalkers, and other vets, to obtain.

The three living Hopi Codetalkers agree with Balenquah. Since they are Hopi men, they never really wanted recognition. Hopi culture does not agree with bragging or even telling others the good things you have done. According to Balenquah, "Being paraded around is not the point, but like so many other times, the Federal Government has equated Native American with Navajo, the other tribes are not Federally recognized, although there were Codetalkers from many tribes, Hopi, Choctaw, Lakota and Cherokee to name a few."

Cliff Balenquah knows the system inside and out, literally. First of all, he is a Vietnam Veteran. He was also the first Director appointed by Hopi Tribal Council for the newly created

Office of Veteran Affairs on the reservation in 1990. He created a Veteran Outreach Office on the reservation also. . . . He worked diligently with Hopi Vets to fight for their rights and to assist them in a healing process from Post Traumatic Stress syndrome (PTS), a psychological and philosophical trauma often experienced by veterans of war. . . . Hopi Tribal Vice-Chairman, Philip Quochytewa, was instrumental in the formation of the original Hopi Office of Veterans' Affairs. He worked toward the creation of the office when he was a Councilman for the Tribe together with Wayne Taylor Jr., now Hopi Tribal Chairman, who at that time, was Vice Chairman. Quochytewa has taken up the Codetalker recognition issue with members of Congress. Although this action is well intentioned, it may not bring the desired results.

Veterans' benefits seem to be just another broken treaty, not only to Native American Codetalkers, to many veterans in this country. As spokesman, Cliff Balenquah, emphasizes, the Hopi would prefer to receive their honors in the form of an honored promise from the U.S. Government.

Reprinted with permission of Debra Moon.

Exercises

Figure 7-1 is a public service ad by the American Lung Association. Study this ad and then answer the following:

1. How would you describe this ad? Go into detail, being as precise as you can. Your aim is to clearly set out what you see being done in the ad.

2. What can you infer from the ad about the American Lung Association's intent? What do you think they are trying to tell us?

3. Create a public service ad (either a print ad, usually visuals, *or* a radio ad, with text only—limit to one page long) on a social issue that you care deeply about and that is one most others would tend to agree with you on, but need to be reminded of from time to time.

FIGURE 7-1

Public service ads, like
this one from the Ameri-
can Lung Association,
call us to examine issues
facing us as a society.

ODDS ARE THAT LOS ANGELES WILL SOON BE SETTING ANOTHER FASHION TREND.

It isn't so farfetched. The air in Los Angeles isn't only the dirtiest in the nation, it's the deadliest. Long-term exposure can lead to asthma, bronchitis and emphysema. As well as increasing the risk of death from lung and heart disease. But together, we can turn things around. For more information, call 1-800-LUNG-USA or visit www.lalung.org. And help us put air pollution out of style.

Photo: Jim Fets

✝ AMERICAN LUNG ASSOCIATION. *of Los Angeles County*

LET'S CLEAR THE AIR.

Exercises

Part One

Directions: Apply the decision-making guidelines to the following cases. Read about the case (which you can research to get more detail if you wish) and then answer the questions that follow.

1. Case 1: The May, 2001, death of 14 border crossers in the Arizona desert.

   The U.S. Border Patrol reported on May 24, 2001 that they had found more bodies of undocumented border crossers in the Arizona desert. The death toll hit 14 of people who attempted, and failed, to cross the desert into the U.S., planning to go to North Carolina to find work. Evidently smugglers ("coyotes") started the migrants on the tragic trek and abandoned the 25 migrants after five days. They were, at that point, about 30 miles from the nearest highway. They had little water and little chance of survival. Only 11 survivors made it out alive. Smugglers whose clients die can be prosecuted under a federal law that carries the possibility of the death penalty. Johnny Williams, Western regional director for the INS, said was reported to have blamed the fatalities on "leeches" who charge $1000 or more per client and sometimes abandon them en route. Cyril Atherton of the Border Patrol said, "It's rocks, sand, desert. It's nasty." (See Ken Ellingwood, "Two Bodies Found, Raising Toll in Migrant Tragedy to 14," *Los Angeles Times*, 25 May 2001)

Answer the following:

a. From INS regional director Williams's perspective, the tragedy can be blamed on "leeches." Assess the cause of the tragedy from any other perspective, such as that of a Mexican national seeking to go to North Carolina to work, the family of one of the victims, one of the survivors, or an employer in agribusiness who relies on migrant workers to produce crops, or an unemployed farm worker who sees the migrants as threats.

b. Given that people do try to cross the desert and enter the United States, what humane response might there be? Is there any way to avert another such tragedy, without necessarily changing the current policy on immigration?

2. Case 2: Ontario Canada's new welfare requirements.

The Canadian province of Ontario is taking a strong stand on welfare, due to the failure of a small group of welfare recipients to get off, and stay off, welfare. In a move some call "mean-spirited" and overly harsh, the government plans to make passing a basic literacy exam a requirement for receiving welfare. Furthermore, it will screen recipients for substance abuse (alcohol and drugs) and cut off benefits to any who refuse to get treatment. Officials contend that these measures are necessary to reach those who are the "hardest to serve" and who seem to have the greatest trouble getting and keeping work. They say that those who can't even read a simple business memo are shut out of the job market.

John Baird, Ontario's Minister of Community says, "If someone has a problem with literacy or addiction and refuses to get help, I don't know what else Ontario can do for them." The literacy program would help students learn to write memos, do basic accounting, and provide customer service. One welfare recipient said she wasn't worried about the literacy test; she was worried about finding day care for her four children. Michael Gravelle, an Ontario legislator and critic of the plan says, "I do not believe for a second that the goal here is to help these people. The real goal is finding another way of kicking people off welfare." (See Anthony de Palma, "Ontario's New Welfare Rule: Be Literate and Drug Free," *The New York Times*, 9 Aug. 2001)

Answer the following:

a. Assuming John Baird is right that there is a hard core of welfare recipients who seem trapped in the system—is Ontario's plan the solution?

b. Give three reasons why this plan might work and three reasons why it may fail. What, in your estimation, are the chances the program will really help change the hard core group that never seem to be able to get out of poverty?

c. Can you think of a workable alternative? Set out your idea of a different way to tackle the problem of illiteracy and substance abuse shutting people out of work and trapping them in poverty or welfare.

3. Case 3: Gays try to adopt a highway.

What are the limits to who can "adopt a highway" for litter clean-up? Among the groups who have adopted a highway Nudists (Florida), Friends of John Denver (Oregon), and the Ku Klux Klan (Missouri). But South Dakota has said no to the Sioux Empire Gay and Lesbian Coalition of Sioux City, South Dakota. State officials insist they can refuse the group on the grounds that it's an "advocacy group." Representatives from the group question this, given the state has allowed The Young Republicans and Animal Rights advocates, among others, to participate in the program. (See *www.datalounge.com*).

South Dakota Governor William Janklow says he'd rather abandon the program than to accede to their offer. The KKK disagrees with the governor. Ron Edwards, Imperial Wizard of the Imperial Klans of America said, "I hate to admit it, because I think being gay and lesbian is an abomination, but they have the same rights we do." He went on to say, "They'll win. We did." (As noted in the *Los Angeles Times*, 15 Aug. 2001).

The U.S. Supreme Court granted the KKK the right to adopt a highway in March 2001. On August 20, 2001 the Gay/lesbian group filed suit in federal court against the state's ruling. The issue, as yet, is unresolved.

Answer the following:
a. Set out the social issues and political concerns of this case.
b. If the state allows any group to "adopt a highway," does that implicitly legitimize that group's existence? Set out your thoughts.
c. What should be the criteria for being able to participate in a program like this? Should only groups be allowed to participate? If so, what sorts of groups?
d. In California individuals (e.g., Bette Midler) have adopted a highway. Should there be any limitations over *which* individuals can do this?

4. Case 4: Couple rejects twins—surrogate mother sues.

Meeting through the Internet, a San Francisco couple hired a British woman, Helen Beasley, to be the gestational surrogate mother for their genetic child. They supply the genetic material, she gestates the embryo, and hands over the baby at birth. The plan went awry when they found out she was going to have twins. Only wanting one child, they ordered Beasley to abort one. The surrogate, now 24 weeks pregnant, refused. She was stuck having to find another couple to adopt the twins (she did). The couple, Charles Wheeler and Martha Berman wants to be reimbursed for the $80,000 in expenses, arguing that she broke the contract. Berman did not want to have a boy, regrets creating the twins, and wants out of the mess.

Beasley has sued for damages. The director of the Organization of Parents through Surrogacy, Shirley Vager, blamed the do-it-yourself approach taken in this case, not the questionable ethics of surrogate parenting or whether this could be considered baby selling. She said there were 20,000 surrogacy births in the U.S. in the year 2000—of these, around 12 cases resulted in surrogates refusing to give up the child or contracting parents refusing the baby. (See John M. Glionna, "Twins Rejected, Surrogate Birth Mother Sues," *Los Angeles Times,* 11 Aug. 2001)

Answer the following:
a. What are the social issues and concerns arising from this case?
b. In light of the fact that there were 20,000 surrogate births in the year 2000, do you have any ethical or social concerns about the use of surrogate mothers?
c. At present there are no federal laws regulating surrogacy. It is purely a matter of state law: some states permit it, some don't. Some allow it but strictly regulate it; other states take a lax approach. Should there be a nationwide policy around surrogate parenting and related uses of reproductive technology? Set out your position.

Part Two

Barbara Mintzes is studying prescription drug advertising in conjunction with Health Action International. Read the following excerpt from a report of her findings and then answer the questions that follow.

Direct-to-consumer (DTC) advertising of prescription drugs is allowed in the U.S., where it has become increasingly common during the late 1980s and the 1990s, but not in other industrialized countries. How important is this form of advertising? In 1996 in the United States, expenditures for DTC printed advertisements for prescription drugs grew to more than US$700 million, and in both 1995 and 1996 the U.S. pharmaceutical industry spent more money on printed advertisements for prescription-only products to consumers than on printed advertisements aimed at doctors and other health professionals. About three quarters of this spending was on advertisements in consumer magazines. The entire expenditure on promotion was much greater—estimated at US$12.3 billion in 1996—with the largest proportion spent on the salaries of sales forces which still mainly target doctors.

Wyeth–Ayerst's prominent 1996 newspaper campaign for its antidepressant venlafaxine (Effexor), used three ads promising that life will get better for children and other family members too if a depressed parent or spouse seeks treatment—by implication with Effexor—with the statements "I got my mommy back" and "I got my marriage back." These statements promote magic solutions, the idea of a "pill for every ill," even when that ill may consist of complex emotional, family and relationship problems. These advertisements also failed to add that this antidepressant has not been found to be any more effective than less expensive alternatives. A U.S. magazine advertisement by SmithKline Beecham linked to its web site, "cafe herpes," played on consumers' emotions with a picture of a young woman saying: "I'll tell you about the shame, the pain, and a hundred broken dates—that's what genital herpes did to me before I found Famvir." Again, a drug solution is recommended for a social problem: social stigma—particularly for women who have contracted a sexually transmitted disease.

One consistent theme in direct-to-consumer advertisements in the U.S. is that consumers need to be anxious—that serious illness is lurking around the corner—and that drug treatment is needed to allay this anxiety. (See Barbara Mintzes, "Blurring the Boundaries," *Health Action International, www.haiweb.org/pubs/blurring*)

Source: Reprinted with the permission of Barbara Mintzes and HAI-Europe.

Answer the following:
a. What are Mintzes' strongest points?
b. What do her observations suggest about our society?
c. In light of Mintzes' argument and examples, do you think there should be restrictions on direct-mail advertising of prescription drugs?

Assessing Policies and Guidelines

As illustrated by the various cases in the above exercise, some issues cry out for policies and guidelines. If we allow one group to adopt a highway, for example, do we allow any and all others? Or do we allow only certain others, using some policy guidelines to sift and weigh which groups are in and which ones are out? And who decides, and on what set of criteria?

People often draw a distinction between what they do and what they would recommend others do. For example, alcoholics might argue from the standpoint of individual rights, but would not want their children to follow in their footsteps.

When we draw up policy guidelines, we are generalizing from our societal attitudes (and often norms), and our moral beliefs or principles. Once we say, "You ought to do such and so," we are giving a *moral prescription*. That is, we are setting forth a recommendation for how others should think and behave. Most people operate by a set of moral prescriptions. For example, many businesses and hospitals set out ethical guidelines.

To some extent, laws define acceptable modes of behavior, though laws do not necessarily set down ethical guidelines. Also, laws are not always respected. For instance, during the 1980s people in the Sanctuary Movement disagreed with the policy of the federal government regarding El Salvador, Guatemala, and Nicaragua. The government's attempt to catch and deport what they called "illegal aliens" and what the Sanctuary Movement called "refugees," resulted in people breaking the law out of their moral beliefs.

It is vital that we look at what we believe in and come to some understanding of what we would do in the name of those beliefs. The day may come in each of our lives when we must take a stand. What would happen, for example, if your college or university instituted strip-searches whenever they suspected a student of using or dealing drugs? Do you think that should be permissible? The following case examines a high school that routinely subjected students to strip searches and whether this policy violated students' individual rights.

Group Exercise

In an article on student rights, the American Civil Liberties Union (ACLU) claims that schools should not be able to routinely do intrusive strip searches of the students.

Read the article and answer the following:

1. Set out the key issues and concerns that were raised.

2. State the key arguments a proponent of routine strip searches might offer to counter the ACLU's position.

3. Decide whether or not high schools should be able to routinely run strip searches of students.

ACLU of Southern California Sues to Stop Intrusive Searches at High School
Tuesday, June 19, 2001

LOS ANGELES—Students at Locke High School here, who are routinely subjected to intrusive searches of their persons, papers, and belongings, took action today as plaintiffs in a lawsuit filed on their behalf in federal court by the American Civil Liberties Union of Southern California. The lawsuit, filed against various officials with the Los Angeles Unified School District, alleges that students' Fourth Amendment rights have been violated by the searches.

"Our society is moving toward treating every youth as a criminal suspect," said Ramona Ripston, Executive Director of the ACLU of Southern California. "Searches without reasonable suspicion are just one component in this trend—a trend that makes the false promise of providing safety in exchange for surrendering civil rights. The safety payoff never materializes,

but in the meantime, students' rights do get taken away."

"By instituting repressive security measures in schools, we educate our students to be residents of a police state, not a democracy," said Ripston. At Locke High School, students are subjected to two kinds of searches, neither of which is based on reasonable suspicion, according to the ACLU lawsuit. At the front gate of the school, some students who are late are chosen for searches. Students are scanned using a metal-detecting wand, and their jackets, book bags, pockets, and purses are searched.

A second form of search is conducted during class time, when students are randomly selected for a search in front of the class. Students report being taken to the front of the room and patted down in front of their classmates.

Elizabeth Perea, a junior at Locke, described one of the searches: "[A school official] . . . took the girls to the blackboard," said Perea. "We were told to face the blackboard. She told us to lift up our arms and open our legs. She patted down our pockets, ankles, and pant legs. She told us to untuck our shirts and to turn around. Nobody found anything on any of the students. Nobody explained why they were searching us. Instead, we each received a note afterwards explaining that we had been searched." Perea said that the searches humiliate and embarrass Locke students and waste time that could have been spent learning.

"The searches make me very uncomfortable," said Perea. "It is absurd. We try to stay away from violence and gangs, and either way we are treated like gangbangers. They should not search us during our education time. Plus, girls have private things in our bags, like for when we get our period, and that shouldn't be shown for everyone to see."

Parents also objected to their children being treated like criminals. Nathaniel Ali-Perkins, of the African-American Parent/Community Organization, charged that the searches damaged students' self-esteem.

"We believe the searches are dehumanizing and damaging to our children's self-esteem—and, overall, program them for failure," said Ali-Perkins. Moreover, the searches have failed as a security tool, the ACLU said. Not once in the eight years since the school district instituted its random search policy has a gun been uncovered as a result of a random search.

Source: Copyright © 2001, The American Civil Liberties Union. Reprinted with permission of the American Civil Liberties Union.

The Societal Context

At the heart of the most pressing issues we face as a society are moral problems. They tend to fall into categories like: the workplace, health care, social justice, the legal system, education, and economic issues. Many issues (such as civil rights legislation and the Equal Rights Amendment) have been raised within state legislatures or the Congress. Others have gone onto state ballots for us to vote on (such as physician-assisted death and taxation issues). Some of those are voted into law (e.g., Oregon voters legalized physician-assisted suicide). Still others have been resolved through the courts (as with the right to refuse medical treatment, abortion, and sexual harassment). Some are resolved on the level of churches, temples, and mosques.

One of the major issues facing us as a society—and one that has brought negative criticism from countries around the world—is our policy on the death penalty. First, let's get an overview, by examining the Department of Justice statistics for the year 1999 (see *www.ojp.usdoj.gov/bjs*). Here is where things stood as of that date:

Capital Punishment (1999)

In 1999, 38 states had capital statutes. More were executed in 1999 than any other year since the 1950s.

98 persons in 20 states were executed in 1999:

- 35 in Texas.
- 14 in Virginia.
- 9 in Missouri.
- 7 in Arizona.
- 6 in Oklahoma.
- 4 each in Arkansas, North Carolina, and South Carolina.
- 2 each in Alabama, California, and Delaware.
- 1 each in Florida, Illinois, Indiana, Kentucky, Louisiana, Nevada, Ohio, Pennsylvania, and Utah.

Of persons executed in 1999:

- 61 were white.
- 33 were black.
- 2 were American Indian.
- 2 were Asian.
- All were men.

Method of the executions in 1999:

- 94 were carried out by lethal injection.
- 3 by electrocution.
- 1 by lethal gas.

Prisoners under sentence of death in 1999 (increasing):

- 3527 prisoners (in 37 state and federal prison systems).
- 2 percent increase since 1998.
- All had committed murder.

Of persons under sentence of death in 1999:

- 1948 were white.
- 1514 were black.
- 28 were American Indian.
- 24 were Asian.
- 13 were classified as "other race."
- Nearly two in three had a prior felony conviction.
- 1 in 12 had a prior homicide conviction.
- Among persons for whom arrest information was available, the average age at time of arrest was 28; 2 percent of inmates were age 17 or younger.
- At year-end, the youngest inmate under sentence of death was 18; the oldest was 84.
- 50 women were under a sentence of death.

Exercises

1. Looking at the Justice Department's statistics, what can you infer? Draw three to four inferences from the above table.

2. One of the issues in the death penalty debate centers on the disproportionate number of people of color either executed or on death row, relative to their numbers in the population. Looking at the statistics, do you think those concerns have merit?

3. Numbers often mean more than statistics: The 2 percent of inmates no older than 17 years old who were arrested on a capital offense = approximately 70 people. This means 70 people who were minors at the time of their crime received the death penalty. Take a side (pro/con) and state your four strongest arguments for or against giving the death penalty to minors.

CASE STUDY

The Global Spotlight: The Timothy McVeigh Case

At this point, the U.S. policy on the death penalty has taken on global significance, with countries from around the world registering their protests to a practice many consider barbaric. When President Bush went to Europe shortly before the June 11, 2001 execution of Timothy McVeigh (convicted of the Oklahoma City bombing which killed 168 people) he was met with protestors along his route.

McVeigh was executed anyway—but not before there was a media spectacle around the proceedings and some pretty deep soul-searching about what direction we ought to be going in as a society. It was amazing what was included in the coverage; for example, we even got to find out what McVeigh ate for his last meal (two pints of mint chocolate chip ice cream). The *Associated Press* gave the fine details of the moments before his death after the IV lines were in and the first chemical started to flow: "McVeigh swallowed hard. His eyes moved slightly from side to side. His chest moved up and down and his lips puffed air out, as if he was trying to maintain consciousness" (*Associated Press,* "A View from the Chamber: McVeigh Dies Silently," 11 June 2001).

Exercise

1. On January 4, 1998, *The New York Times* published an article that focused on the last meals of condemned prisoners in the State of Texas. We were told some salient details, such as:

   Twenty-two men chose double cheese burgers, 15 opted for single cheeseburgers, 9 for hamburgers. Next most popular were steaks, typically T-bones, with 27 requests, and eggs (10 requests, most for scrambled). Most desired overall is a side of French fries (56 requests). Ice cream is the most popular dessert (21 requests), Coca Cola the most popular beverage (13, just edging out 12 requests for iced tea). And 24 inmates declined any last meal at all. (See "For the Condemned in Texas, Cheeseburgers Without Mercy," *The New York Times*, 4 Jan. 1998)

   Answer the following:
   a. Discuss the significance of one of the nation's most respected newspapers publishing this information.
   b. What can you infer about the paper and how they see their audience?

Issues around the McVeigh Case

Regardless of where you stand on the death penalty, the issue needs to be examined closely. In the McVeigh case, from the very beginning disturbing questions came up. For example, initially the bomber was thought to be an Islamic terrorist (and the media jumped on that bandwagon). When it was "just another American" they breathed a collective sigh of relief, with only a few calling us to examine the racism that lay beneath the surface. For example, see what you think about Josh Getlin's observations:

> Indeed, some believe America's initial perceptions of the Oklahoma City bombing—and its subsequent views of McVeigh—say more about innate racism than they do about domestic terrorism. Hours after the 1995 bombing, rumors began spreading that the crime had been carried out by Muslim terrorists. "Then we learned that it was McVeigh, and people suddenly saw the issue as less threatening, because he was a lone, crazed figure," said Todd Boyd, USC professor of film and pop culture.
>
> Nobody was ready to blame white culture for his crime, Boyd added, "but with other groups, it's as though one person does something and the entire group is seen as guilty. That's how racism functions in this country. . . . We chose to make him into a foreigner the way we initially suspected Arabs or others of the crime. And we had something of an exorcism in his deathwatch, because few of us wanted to listen to the things that Timothy McVeigh had said. (See Josh Getlin, "A Search for Meaning in the Spectacle," *Los Angeles Times,* 12 June 2001)

From the standpoint of at least some of the victims' families, McVeigh had surrendered his rights—to privacy, to be listened to, to stay alive. To appreciate the range of concerns, it is important to seek out the different perspectives and give them a fair hearing. You can easily access information about the McVeigh case and read statements from a host of commentators.

There are even those who insist McVeigh is still alive—that the very "execution" was faked (they cite the lack of an autopsy and the whisking away of the "body" as support for that theory). Such conspiracy theorists believe that McVeigh had government protection and the FBI intentionally avoided evidence pointing beyond McVeigh. The case has assumed a life of its own and has the makings of a sort of bizarre legend. As such, this reflects back on the society and what values, beliefs, fears, and fantasies are swirling about under the surface.

Let us examine one of those who spoke out about the death penalty and reacted to McVeigh's execution. Read the following letter and then answer the questions that follow:

Timothy McVeigh: Letter to *The Nation*

Susan Brison, Ph.D.
Philosophy Department, Dartmouth College
June 2001

I was outraged when, the day after Timothy McVeigh's execution, I read the following comments by family members of his victims:

"It was too easy for him. He just laid there. . . . He went to sleep. That was it."—Shari Sawyer

"Not like my mother, who was on the fourth floor and fell four floors. I thought I would feel something more satisfying, but I don't. So many people suffered and for him just to go to sleep is unfair."—Jay Sawyer, and

"I think I maybe expected more of a sense of closure or release or something like that. But it doesn't really provide as much as I thought it would."—Larry Whicher (whose brother died in the blast).

I live in Vermont, a state with no death penalty. As a U.S. citizen, I haven't officially executed anyone since 1963 and then I was just a kid, too young to know about, let alone protest, my country's action. I was too busy being a kid, struggling with learning the lesson that, even if the playground bully hits or taunts you and it seems only fair to hit or taunt him back, there are better ways of expressing moral indignation; that hurting those who've hurt you doesn't (or shouldn't) make you feel better; that it doesn't matter who's doing the punching, or why—you don't punch back, unless you have to, to defend yourself or someone else; that as much as you might like to, you just don't use violence in an attempt to even the scales, to make things right;

that this is how wars get started and feuds are perpetuated and, besides, there are more grown-up ways to handle conflict than to seek revenge.

On June 11, I once again, as a U.S. citizen, participated in an execution, the killing of a convicted mass murderer, Timothy McVeigh. This time, though, I'm old enough to feel some responsibility for it, even though I opposed it. I'm also old enough to have a kid of my own, a sensitive, empathic little six-year-old who nonetheless wants to strike back when he's been injured. It's only fair, he says. He did it to me, he says, first.

It's hard to know just what to say on these occasions, but I keep repeating: it's not going to make you feel better; in fact, you'll probably feel worse if you sink to the bully's level; you need to figure out how to express your anger in words, not violence; or, if all else fails, go tell a grown-up.

The problem is: when even the grown-ups are seeking the ultimate revenge—killing people and thinking it will bring "closure" and will somehow make things right—who's he going to tell?

Reprinted with the permission of Susan Brison.

Exercises

1. Write a letter (three to four paragraphs) to Dr. Brison in response to her comments above. Your letter should include any *two* of the following:
   a. What you see as her one strongest argument in support of her position.
   b. Your response to any one of her key points.
   c. At least one suggestion for how she can talk about the death penalty with her boy.

2. On the one-year anniversary of the Oklahoma City bombing the TV show *Muppets Tonight* was removed by ABC. It seems the show, aimed at young children, included a skit involving Sandra Bullock doing a parody of the movie *Speed* (about a city bus armed with a bomb that would go off if the bus's speed dropped below 50 mph). In the skit, a mad bomber threatens to

blow up the TV studio if the Muppets' ratings fall below 50 (see "Tonight's 'Muppet' Episode Withdrawn," *The New York Times,* 19 Apr. 1996).

Answer the following:

a. Would the children make the connection between the skit and the Oklahoma City bombing?

b. Do you think skits about bombing should normally be okay on children-oriented shows?

c. Was it appropriate for ABC to cancel the show?

Individual Accountability

At times we face agonizing dilemmas, even if we try to avoid them or if others try to protect us. *Moral agency* has to do with being capable of moral decision making, being seen as responsible for our actions, and being held accountable for those actions. Children, retarded people, comatose or unconscious patients are not usually viewed as competent and, therefore, not seen as moral agents. In our society, we draw the line between childhood and adulthood. This division under the law has been 18 years of age, though in some states adolescents are being prosecuted as adults (as we saw in the Department of Justice statistics on the death penalty). Some want to apply the death penalty to criminals who are 16, or younger.

A host of moral questions arise in confronting these issues. We ought not let the complexities prevent us from looking at the moral issues carefully. It is important to reflect upon the moral concerns we face as a society and to look at the various issues facing us in our individual lives.

Political involvement may be a response from a personal situation or broader social events and interests. Because of this, people join political parties, vote, take part in community organizing or in addressing social concerns. One of these ways is to call or write our political leaders. It is an important aspect of our democratic form of government.

If you wish to express your political concerns or contact a congressperson or a governmental office, you can easily access them by an Internet search. If you don't know the name of your senator, representative, or others you want to contact, you can still run a search (try typing in the name of your state plus the word "senator" or "politician" or the like). You can go to such websites as *www.house.gov* for a list of U.S. representatives or *www.senate.gov* for a list of U.S. senators. (See Appendix C for political addresses.) Once you get to the appropriate website, there will be links or contact information. This also applies to letters to the editor of newspapers: you can mail them in or e-mail them in. In either case, political involvement is one of the channels open to us in a democracy. It is not to be taken lightly.

Group Exercise

What Would You Do?
Wednesday, August 29, 2001, was a big day in the life of Ascension Franco Gonzales, a dishwasher from Hidalgo, Mexico, who was living in Los Angeles. While sitting at a bus stop, Gonzales saw an armored truck. As the truck drove by, the doors flew open and out fell a plastic bag containing $203,000. Gonzales picked it up and, fearing for his life, hid the loot. After an evening trying to figure out what to do, he called the police and handed in the money.

- What would you do if the $203,000 landed in front of you? Share your thoughts.

The Social Dimension of Integrity

We may think our decisions are our own, that they don't affect others. But often, private decisions become public matters. Look at Gonzales's decision to hand over the loot that literally landed at his feet. He could have snuck back to Hidalgo with his $203,000 and maybe have had a great life there living off his riches. Maybe so; but again maybe not.

Evidently one of the turning points for Gonzales was hearing a radio disc jockey wondering if there was anyone honest enough to hand in the missing money. Gonzales affirmed that he was such a man. Mind you, plenty of others think he blew a great opportunity. Weighing in with their opinions were:

- Reyna Hernandez, store employee, said, "I wouldn't have turned it in. I would have started a business."
- David Widom, social worker, said, "I think I would have turned it in. It's the honorable thing to do."
- John Snell, janitor, said, "I wouldn't let the temptation get me. I would resist."
- Johnny Shabaz, who thought Gonzales blew it not to take the cash, said, "He's crazy—the man's as crazy as a Betsy bug." (See Jocelyn Y. Stewart and Hector Beccerra, "Many Say They Would Have Kept Bag of Loot," *Los Angeles Times,* 30 Aug. 2001)

The mixed response to Gonzales's honesty and the fascination with his action in light of his situation (poor, dishwasher) reveal the social dimension of personal choices. For some it's the Ascension Franco Gonzaleses of the world that serve as role models and images of integrity. For others, as Gordon Gecko put it, greed is good. But incidents such as this one provide us with food for thought and call us to look at issues of free will, accountability, social responsibility, and virtue—and come to some sense of where we stand.

Political Messages and Manipulation

We've seen public ad campaigns for the American Lung Association, the stop-smoking campaigns, and public service ads by nonprofit groups. Such public service advertising extends even to warnings during the Cold War.

In the 1950s schools had students doing bomb drills and hiding under school desks, as if by doing so they'd survive a nuclear attack. The U.S. Civil Defense Agency put out posters to "educate" (cynics would say "brainwash") citizens to prepare them for an atomic war. One such example is a poster that pictured a little girl sitting at a desk with her head resting on her hands as if she were thinking to herself (see Fig. 7-2). The question is: What happens to us if the bomb drops? Underneath the photo are the fine details. The ad is directed to "Mummy," who is told—in one of the great understatements of all time—that an atomic war bears

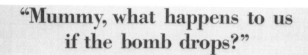

FIGURE 7-2
"Misinformation" campaigns are not new—just look at this public "service" ad from the 1950s.

some resemblance to natural phenomena. Specifically, "An atomic blast is something like a tornado, a fire and an explosion all rolled into one." Posted clearly in a boxed area is a list of "official disaster first-aid items," such as 4 triangular bandages, 12 sterile gauze pads, 1 oz Castor oil eye drops, and 2 large emergency dressings, among other minor items to help address the (obviously minor!) wounds you'd get in an atomic blast.

There are a number of unwarranted assumptions and outright deceptions behind this "public service" ad. Perhaps the most egregious is the implicit message that atomic war is survivable—that the child's wounds will just need a little field dressing. The fact that this lie was perpetrated on the general public stretches the moral imagination to the breaking point.

Exercises

1. Study the attempts to make the idea of atomic war palatable in the U.S. Civil Service ad "Mummy." Examine the visual message, as well as the verbal message of the ad and how the two work together to create a powerful effect. Summarize your findings.

2. Thinking in terms of a radio program as the vehicle of communication, create a public service warning for any *one* of these:
   • An Ebola virus outbreak in a Chicago suburb.
   • Uranium fragments resulting from bombing campaigns over Kosovo.
   • Tampered bottles of Tylenol that have already killed 11 people, with little assurance that others won't also be hurt or killed.
   • Firestone tires that may lead to blowouts and rollovers on SUVs.
   • A botched batch of designer heroin that can paralyze its users.
   • Anthrax hoaxes sent to abortion clinics.

3. Looking over your public service ad answer the following:
   a. Who was your targeted audience?
   b. What was your intended goal?
   c. How effective was your ad in reaching your goal, in your estimation?

Personal Autonomy

A central issue when examining decision making is whether or not we are free to choose and to what degree we will be held accountable for our choice. To be held accountable, we need to know that the person whose action is being scrutinized is (1) free to choose and (2) had the competence (so it is *informed* consent) to do so. It would be hard to hold you accountable for your actions if you were not free to make a choice. What if, for instance, you were coerced with credible-seeming threats? Or you were on a sugar high from all the Twinkies you consumed? Or you were overcome with anger and lost it? What if you were drugged into semi-consciousness? Accountability requires competence and free will. If one is absent, we may be reluctant to punish an offender.

We value our freedom. We see this in all areas of our lives. One of the most significant areas is the medical sphere, where most patients try to exercise control over their lives. For this, they need to be able to make informed decisions. It is now generally seen that patient autonomy must be reckoned with. For the most part, patients have considerable autonomy over what happens to their own bodies. Patients who are competent adults are free to choose a course of treatment that is medically unsound and may cease taking medicine altogether, even if that decision will bring about their death.

There are boundary issues around personal autonomy, as we will see in the cases below. These include such questions as: Do you have any rights to what happens to cells, blood, bone marrow, organs, or bodily tissues that you consent to have removed in the course of your medical treatment? If someone made a profitable discovery off of your tonsils, should you reap some financial rewards? What should set the limits of your own autonomy, your right to decide what you can do and what happens to your own body?

For example, should a patient be allowed to get a pig liver transplant, when we don't know if the pig virus PERV might mutate into some AIDS-like epidemic? Should societal concerns outweigh individual autonomy? Should a couple be allowed to hire a surrogate mother who agrees to hand over the baby at birth? Should people be free to undertake—or be subjects of—cloning experiments? Is this purely a matter of personal choice? These are hard questions. Tackling them poses all sorts of obstacles—both social and ethical.

Exercises

Read the following and then answer the questions that follow:

An Italian doctor and a U.S. researcher claim they will implant cloned human embryos in 200 female volunteers within the next few months, an effort that would mark the first known attempt at human cloning, and which is sure to complicate an already tangled debate in Congress over the procedure. . . .

The researchers have refused to say where they will conduct the work but that it would not be in the United States. Human cloning is illegal in much of Europe and would require Food and Drug Administration approval in the United States. Antinori told the Italian newspaper *La Stampa* that 1300 U.S. couples and 200 in Italy were being considered for the project.

Cloning is a process of producing a genetic twin of an existing organism. In mammals, it entails using DNA from an adult to create an embryo, which is then implanted in a surrogate mother and grown to term. Cows, goats and other animals have been successfully cloned, but the process often produces embryos that fail to grow or animals with diseases and deformities. (See Aaron Zitner, "Team Claims It Will Clone Humans," *Los Angeles Times,* 7 Aug. 2001)

Answer the following:

1. What assumptions lie behind the researchers' plan to implant 200 women with cloned embryos? State them and note those that seem warranted.

2. The article fails to tell us how the 200 women are to be selected. What questions would you ask the researchers about how the 200 women are to be picked?

3. What questions would you ask the 200 women who have "volunteered" to give birth to clones?

4. What issues and concerns should be addressed before deciding if cloning is morally permissible?

Challenges to Personal Autonomy

We tend to draw the line around the two aspects of autonomy: Are patients free to choose and are they competent? Our society does not grant children legal autonomy, because they are not thought to be fully cognizant of the moral dimensions of a case or able to fully grasp the issues so as to be considered competent to make an informed decision.

Prisoners have little autonomy. It is generally believed that prisoners have willingly—that is, through their own actions—given up the right to any full expression of autonomy. A fall 2001 decision to allow male prisoners to procreate (by artificial insemination) was a victory for male prisoners' autonomy. It was criticized by many, however, who argued that such benefits were undeserved and unwarranted. Female prisoners were not included, as it was argued that pregnant inmates created different issues for prison administrators.

CASE STUDY

Autonomy and Anthrax Vaccines

A related issue is the autonomy of members of the military. They didn't end up in the military because of criminal acts or punishment. Quite the contrary. They *elected* to join the military and to serve their country—and presumably did so willingly and with a clear mind. That said, should military personnel be able to refuse an-

thrax vaccines? No one could have imagined when this issue arose months before the bioterrorist attacks with mailed anthrax, that this issue would take on the significance that it has at this later date.

In 1999, the Department of Defense ordered that all 2.5 million military personnel be vaccinated against anthrax, regardless of duty station or responsibilities. Anthrax is a disease that preys on livestock, but is also one of the most deadly biological warfare agents ever developed. Members of the military were to be vaccinated under threat of court martial. The vaccine is administered in a series of six shots. The highest-ranking military officer and the first military physician to refuse the controversial anthrax vaccine filed a lawsuit on May 2, 2001, before the United States District Court for the District of Columbia.

Medical considerations.   According to Pentagon records, 1600 people have complained of adverse reactions. At one Air Force base, a number of people suffered ill effects from the vaccine:

The high incidence of unusual chronic health problems at Dover AFB include systemic signs and symp-

toms, such as vomiting, diarrhea, polyarthralgias, fever, splenic tenderness, cognitive problems, polymyalgias, weakness and numbness, and these problems can occur well after the usual reporting period for vaccine adverse effects.

Patients with preexisting autoimmune illnesses such as rheumatoid arthritis, lupus, multiple sclerosis, among others, are probably more likely to suffer a serious adverse reaction, as are those with neurologic disease, such as those who had polio in childhood. Stevens Johnson Syndrome, a severe allergic reaction in which there is loss of epidermis (skin) and the lining of the GI tract, was found in some patients as well as more classic allergic signs and symptoms.

Even more serious, many anthrax vaccine recipients report seizures with complete loss of consciousness. Respiratory distress and a variety of pulmonary illnesses have also been reported. (See "Anthrax Vaccine: Controversy over Safety and Efficacy," *www.gulfwarvets.com/anthrax5.htm*)

Exercises

1. After 9-11, the fear of an anthrax (or other biological) attack intensified the pressure to have military personnel have anthrax vaccinations. However low the percentage of adverse reactions (approximately .3 percent or around 1600 people), women are disproportionately represented among those suffering problems. Read the excerpt and then answer the questions that follow:

   "I spoke to, or examined the records of, a dozen military women who were perfectly healthy before the shots that they took," said Sheila Weller, senior contributing editor for *Self* magazine. "They got symptoms within weeks, sometimes days. And the symptoms were all autoimmune in nature, meaning they were linked to the family of diseases such as lupus and multiple sclerosis, in which the immune system attacks the body." Normally, women get autoimmune diseases 75 percent more often than men, and Pentagon records have shown that women do experience more temporary side effects from the anthrax vaccine. Women make up only 12 percent of anthrax recipients (the military is 85 percent male), but they make up 26 percent of adverse-effect sufferers. (See "Controversial Injections: Military women Uneasy About Anthrax Vaccine," *ABCNEWS.com*, 24 Oct. 2001)

Answer the following:

a. In deciding if any military personnel can opt out of the anthrax vaccine, what weight should be given to reports of gender-based difference, as mentioned in the above quote?

b. What, if any, weight should be given to the right to choose what constitutes an acceptable physical risk in terms of exposure to something that is not contagious?

c. Discuss what weight should be given to the manufacturer's assurances, as noted by ABC news: "In the research studies, the vaccine has, again and again, been proven safe, with no more side effects than any other vaccine, according to Dr. Tom Waytes, vice president of medical affairs at Bioport, the manufacturer of the anthrax vaccine. "There have been 18 studies looking into the safety of this vaccine . . . The final result is always the same: The vaccine is safe" (see *ABCNEWS.com*, 24 Oct. 2001)

d. What weight should be given to the fact that the Pentagon has also roundly refuted any claims that the vaccine may have caused serious illnesses, and has declared it safe?

2. Discuss if your position is in any way strengthened or diminished by the reported effects of the anthrax vaccine:

- Former Air Force security specialist Jenny Enoch was diagnosed in February 2000 with fibromyalgia. "I'm in constant pain," Enoch said. "I have chronic fatigue. I have serious concentration problems and memory loss" . . . "I was healthy and active, absolutely, prior to that third shot [of the anthrax vaccine]".

- Army pilot Ronda Breneman was noticed by superiors for her boundless energy and outstanding physical fitness. But weeks after her third shot for anthrax, she developed extreme gastroparesis, or paralysis of the stomach. She now lives in a state of chronic nausea, has lost 45 pounds, and has memory loss.

- Debbie Lipshield developed an intensive case of lupus within days after her shots. She's been in and out of hospital intensive care units, and is still in the hospital.

- Army Specialist Sandra Larson had her immune system collapse in a virulent case of aplastic anemia 3½ weeks after her sixth anthrax vaccination shot. She died two months later. (See "Controversial Injections: Military women Uneasy About Anthrax Vaccine," *ABCNEWS.com*, 24 Oct. 2001)

Ethical Considerations.   According to the Nuremberg Code, volunteers in an experiment must give their voluntary, informed consent. Because anthrax vaccines have never been used on a mass scale, their use by the Armed Forces is thought be an instance of medical experimentation. The entire stockpile of anthrax vaccine is owned by the Department of Defense. None has yet been made available for thorough, independent testing. There have been no completed studies of long-term side effects of anthrax vaccine and apparently no studies at all on women. Recent reports have appeared indicating that the Russians have developed anthrax strains for which it is claimed protective vaccines do not exist. All of these issues are problematic.

Ramifications.   Captain John Buck is a 32-year-old emergency room doctor at Keesler Medical Center who refused the vaccine. He claimed that the germ warfare vaccine is an experimental and potentially hazardous drug that was unlawfully forced on soldiers. He was court martialed in May 2001. A panel of 11 of Buck's fellow officers found him guilty after only 30 minutes of deliberation. His sentence includes 60 days restriction to Keesler Air Force Base, a fine of $1500 a month for 14 months and a written reprimand (see "In the End Discipline Had to Win," *The Sun Herald,* 24 May 2001). On the other hand, there is the view of the military about what is appropriate in such circumstances and why obedience is crucial. Marine spokesman, First Lieutenant Vincent Vasquez put it this way:

We in the Marine Corps don't have the luxury of deciding which order to obey and which to refuse. We obey all lawful orders, period. That's the issue here. It's our obligation to make sure our Marines go into a combat zone with every weapon at their disposal, and the anthrax vaccine is our best weapon against this deadly threat. (See Tom Gorman, "Marines' Refusal of Anthrax Vaccine Leads to Discharges," *Los Angeles Times,* 24 June 1999)

Exercises

1. Make the case for the members of the military having the *right to refuse* the anthrax vaccine, in light of the evidence above and any evidence you can find, for example, in research at the library or on the Internet. Note if the subsequent events of the war on terrorism and bioterrorism overshadow the individual's right to personal autonomy here.

2. Make the strongest case for members of the military being *required* to get the anthrax vaccine in light of the evidence above and any evidence you can find, for example, in research at the library or on the Internet. Note how the subsequent events of the war on terrorism and bioterrorism do or do not factor into your argument.

Group Exercise

Questions around the anthrax vaccinations multiplied in the fall of 2001, when anthrax-tainted letters and anthrax hoaxes closed down government offices, post offices, news stations, and other buildings. As of November 28, 2001, there were

23 cases of anthrax, of which 11 were confirmed as inhalation anthrax. Since the person(s) responsible were using the U.S. postal service, concerns finally arose as to the safety of postal workers in exposed facilities. After an outcry from the postal workers about their vulnerability and the lax response by the federal government to their safety concerns, secretary of Health and Human Services Tommy Thompson offered to give anthrax vaccinations to postal employees who might have been exposed.

Directions: Read the following response from the president of a New York postal union and then decide what questions you'd want answered before deciding whether postal workers should take the anthrax vaccine:

> "Is protecting postal workers who have been exposed to anthrax spores the priority of the CDC [Centers for Disease Control], or is experimenting with the health and safety of workers as guinea pigs the real reason for the distribution of the [DoD anthrax] vaccine? My members will not countenance another Tuskegee," warned William Smith, president of New York Metro Area Postal Union this week in a letter to Tommy Thompson, secretary of Health and Human Services. [The decades-long Tuskegee Syphilis study involved over 300 poor, black men in Alabama who were unwittingly subjects of an experiment which prevented them from getting treatment for their disease.]
>
> New York City postal union officials Thursday advised mail workers against taking the Department of Defense's vaccine for anthrax. . . . Thompson had offered the postal workers post-exposure doses of the controversial DoD anthrax vaccine as an extra measure of caution. Each member was given an informed-consent form to read and execute before acceding to the vaccinations. . . . Smith said he was "particularly disturbed by the statement made by a participant at the December 15, 2001, anthrax vaccine meeting at the CDC that 'it's also our duty to take advantage of the opportunity' [with the postal workers] to study the anthrax vaccine." . . .
>
> [Smith] complained that CDC's anthrax vaccine consent form did not fully describe the possible serious adverse reactions associated with the anthrax vaccine. Furthermore, according to Smith, the informed consent being offered the postal workers omits the complaints levied by military service. . . . "This statement is deliberately misleading, and cannot suffice as informed consent about the real and serious adverse reactions associated with this vaccine. To provide inadequate risk/benefit data to prospective recipients is medical malpractice." (See Dave Eberhart, "Postal Workers Warned Against Pentagon Anthrax Vaccine," *NewsMax.com,* 5 Jan. 2002)

The Impact of Science and Technology on the Social Dimension

As with the issues surrounding the anthrax vaccine, some of the dilemmas present today were unheard of a few decades ago. In fact, some of the concerns could inspire science fiction stories and horror films. Can't you picture yourself, blasted back to the 50s going to a drive-in movie to watch *The Night of the Living An-*

thrax on a double bill with *Batman and the DNA Dragnet Queen*? Fiction can't trump reality for sheer mind-boggling uses of science and technology. And many of those uses raise questions that warrant close examination.

Scientific progress and technological changes have brought with them many social dilemmas, such as cloning, stem cell research, surrogate parenting, egg donation and sales, embryo transfers and storage, harvesting animal organs for human transplants, fetal tissue brain transplants, genetic engineering of plants and animals, computer privacy in the workplace, hate speech on the Internet, and patient privacy (e.g., with medical records, DNA information, employer access, etc.). Technology has opened up a Pandora's box of ethical, legal, and social controversies. And we know it's not over yet.

It's amazing how many social issues come up that cause us to look at our fundamental values. For example, privacy issues around the use of computer technology abound. This is shown in the following:

> Hidden in the Microsoft Word document that carried the Melissa virus around the world last week was a seemingly innocuous serial number that helped Federal agents identify the computer responsible for the program. The incident dramatically illustrated technology's growing power for promoting both good and evil. The serial number itself—known in computer parlance as a global unique identifier—lies at the heart of a continuing controversy over tradeoffs between individual privacy rights and the common good.
>
> The dispute involving the Microsoft numbering system came just weeks after the company's partner, the Intel Corporation, announced that it was building serial numbers into each copy of its newest microprocessor, the Pentium III. The announcement touched off protests from privacy activists, who argue that such numbering spells the end of anonymity in cyberspace. (See John Markoff, "When Privacy Is More Perilous Than the Lack of It," *The New York Times*, 4 Apr. 1999)

Depending upon your vantage point, the world gets smaller while the knowledge base expands. With that, issues around social policy abound.

Group Exercise

The DNA Dragnet

How would you feel if your father or brother (or yourself, if you are a male!) were asked to submit to DNA testing in a rape case? How would you feel if you were raped and the likely suspect lives in your neighborhood and the police think a DNA test might catch him? As you might imagine, both questions raise interesting moral and social concerns. Such concerns are not academic, either, as DNA testing in crimes is now a reality. Read the following article and then answer the questions that follow.

DNA Dragnet in Search for Killer Raises Privacy Concerns

Jennifer L. Brown
Daily Journal
June 1, 2001

OKLAHOMA CITY—Police know who murdered Juli Busken. Not by name, but by the genetic code he left behind in the victim's car five years ago.

In their search for John Doe, police took blood from 200 men and compared their DNA to that of the man who left behind semen in Busken's car. There were no matches. Police plan to test 200 more men who either lived near the victim and have a criminal record of violence, resemble the police sketch or have been identified as a possible suspect.

There is a growing debate about whether innocent people should have to hand over their blood. Besides concern over unreasonable searches, even supporters of DNA testing say such large-scale genetic dragnets raise the possibility of police coercion.

For Busken's father, the answer is easy. Besides a rough sketch of someone who was seen with Busken before her death, a DNA match is about all he has to cling to in hopes of finding his daughter's killer. "If you don't want to give your DNA, you've got something to hide," said Bud Busken, who runs a golf course in Benton, Ark. "I'll stand by that until my dying day."

Busken, 21, had just finished her last semester at the University of Oklahoma when she was last seen on Dec. 20, 1996, and was about to drive home to Arkansas for Christmas vacation. Police believe she was abducted from the parking lot of her apartment building. Her body was found near a lake. The aspiring ballerina had been raped and shot in the head.

Cleveland County District Attorney Tim Kuykendall turned to the DNA testing last year.

Some of those tested gave DNA samples to exonerate themselves. Others were people associated with Busken, including fellow college dancers and even stagehands who worked at the university. Defense attorneys and civil libertarians call the sweeps an improper violation of the constitutional right to privacy.

A few such DNA dragnets have taken place in this country, but there's little precedent for determining their legality. Mass blood screenings are more common abroad, where the first was in 1987 in England when 5000 people had their blood tested after two teen-agers were raped and murdered.

Fred Leatherman, chairman of the Forensic Evidence Committee of the National Association of Criminal Defense Lawyers, said he knew of no legal challenges to block mass screenings in the United States. He predicted they would be challenged, calling them "a clear violation of the right to privacy."

Critics fear what happens to DNA samples after they're collected. Some suspect they would be used in future investigations by forensic scientists who sometimes make errors, or that they might end up in the hands of health insurance companies that could see which diseases a person is predisposed to develop. "This is just horrendous, appalling," said Doug Parr, a board member of the Oklahoma Criminal Defense Lawyers Association. "It smacks of the kind of police state tactics that this country has gone to war against."

Most of the 200 men tested so far gave their blood voluntarily, but prosecutors obtained search warrants in a few cases where people declined to provide the sample. One of those was Dennis Stuermer, 23, who said his reputation has been tarnished because Oklahoma City police forced him to give a blood sample. Stuermer's photograph ran on the front page of the state's largest newspaper after a woman in jail who knew his family said he might be Busken's killer.

In the months it took to get the results of the DNA test, his landlord tried to evict him, a boss threatened to fire him and a few personal relationships deteriorated. "I was scared to death," he said. "I didn't have anything to be scared of, but people were breathing down my throat." Attorney Doug Wall said he and Stuermer, who has no criminal background, may sue the police. "Police are basically saying, 'If we pop a needle into enough arms we're bound to get lucky sooner or later,'" Wall said.

Arthur Spitzer, a lawyer with the American Civil Liberties Union in Washington, said requiring people to give DNA samples without other evidence linking them to the crime would be an unconstitutional search and seizure. Attorney Barry Scheck, who co-founded The Innocence Project, a group that helps inmates challenge convictions with DNA evidence, said there are potential problems whenever so much testing is done.

Some people might feel coerced to give blood. "It's inherently coercive when a policeman comes to your door and says 'Give us a sample of your blood and if you don't give it to us, you're a suspect,'" he said.

Bud Busken believes if authorities found his daughter's killer, it might stop the emotional roller coaster he and his wife have been on since that day. "Our life is never going to go back the way it was," he said.

Exercises

There are a number of concerns raised by the DNA dragnet in the above article. Depending upon your perspective, the issue gets framed quite differently.

Answer the following:

1. From the frame of reference of the victim's family, what are the most important points raised in the article?
2. From the frame of reference of a male caught in the DNA dragnet, what are the most important points raised in the article?
3. Set out the strongest case you can for allowing such DNA testing for rape cases. Draw from the article to bolster your case.
4. Set out the strongest case you can in opposition to such DNA testing for rape cases. Draw from the article to bolster your case.
5. *Follow up:* Investigate the current status of DNA testing for criminal cases and share with the class (e.g., at the next class session) what you discover.

Know Thyself

In many cases, such as the one above concerning publishing abortion doctors' names on the Internet, the law has been the arbiter of ethical issues. Whether we like the decision or not, these sorts of issues grind their way through courtrooms and legislatures until decisions are put in place.

Of course, society doesn't always find a point of agreement. Unpopular laws and legal rulings are often relitigated with different cases, in hopes of a different result or at least some modification. Not all social conflicts, legal dilemmas, and moral problems are so wide ranging. Many take place on the turf of individual lives. Many times we have no one else to turn to when making a decision about a social or ethical issue.

Just think about all the ways such problems can hit home: If a girl left a wallet at the bus stop, would you run after her or would you pocket it? What would you do if a teacher made a pass at you? What would you do if your boss asked you to work for cash "under the table" to avoid tax forms? What would you say if a friend was shoplifting? What would you do if a friend in an abusive relationship asked you for help? Some ethical dilemmas are personal, some are societal or global. For example, what should be done about stem cell research? Maybe you know nothing about stem cells, much less why anyone would want to do research on them. Maybe you think your opinion doesn't matter. But maybe it does.

We are confronted with many social and moral dilemmas in the course of our lives. We must decide which ones warrant our reflection and response. Sure, we could just let things happen. Some of us act like passengers on a ship with others at the helm. On the other hand, others believe they really *can* make a difference and get in there and do their best. Of course, there are some of us who are marginalized and are operating with a skewed sense of what needs to be done and how to do it. Part of our responsibility to the community is to act as watchdogs to help us work toward peaceful resolutions to problems. That's not always easy, as we've seen in some of the cases in this chapter.

It pays to know what we believe in. Sometimes we have time to reflect on what we ought to do. Other times we have only a few minutes to decide what is right or wrong. But we have the rest of our lives to live with our decision. The cartoon by Ted Rall humorously drives that point home: we make decisions all the time (See Figure 7-3). Many of those decisions reflect back on ourselves, revealing what we value and who we are as individuals. It may seem attractive to sell out to the highest bidder, but there's always a price to be paid.

Reflecting on Our Own Morality

We stand to gain by undertaking a moral inventory. Socrates was not making idle chatter when he said, "Know Thyself." Most of us have no idea how strong our moral fiber is or how strong our depth of character. A test of moral strength can come at us when we least expect it. We never know when we will face a natural disaster, car accident, plane crash, bank robbery, or other sort of crisis. And yet, it's at such times that we look our own moral and social consciousness in the eyeball. Many people would save their own necks before reaching out to help others. Many others have given their lives to help a stranger. The question is, what kind of person are you?

Self-Inventory: The Personal and Social Dimension of Values   FIGURE 7-3

1. What five traits do you value most highly in a friend? Note what that tells you about your values and beliefs.
2. What could a friend do that would jeopardize your relationship? Note what this reveals about your values and beliefs.
3. What is your sense of your own integrity? Note what you think personal integrity entails in assessing yourself and others.
4. How important do you see community involvement and charitable work? Note what it tells you about the person who gets involved.
5. How important do you see voting, political participation, and social action? Note what it tells you about the person who gets involved.
6. What five character traits do you value most highly in yourself? Note what you think they reveal to others about who you are.

7. What is your most admirable trait? Do you think others see it too? What is your own "weakest link" in terms of strength of character? Note what would happen if these two traits switched places.

8. What personal story would reveal your commitment to justice or goodness in your own life?

9. Who do you admire among the people you actually know? Note the ways this person has made a difference to your life or to those around you.

10. Who do you admire as a public figure? Note the ways in which this person has contributed to the society.

11. What would you like to be remembered for? Note if you are doing anything to work toward that legacy.

12. What do you plan to have accomplished in the next 5 years and in the next 10 years that sets a direction for your life?

Exercises

1. Journalist Ellen Goodman cites a poll in *Fitness* magazine in which American women were asked which they would prefer: (1) live to be 90 years old or (2) lose 20 pounds permanently. Here's what she found:
    - Fifty-four percent of the sample chose weight over longevity. Better dead than fat.
    - The diet drug, Fen-Phen led to approximately 300 deaths.
    - Even after the danger was known, Goodman reports, the corporate officials at Wyeth–Ayerst, as well as the FDA, failed to take prompt action.
    - Approximately 7 million people took the drug and 45,000 developed serious health problems. (See "Still Dying to Diet, and Dying as a Result," *Boston Globe*, 17 June 2001)

    Answer the following:
    a. If you were on a jury, how would you assess responsibility?
    b. To what degree are people responsible for the risks they take, knowing over half would rather die sooner if they could be 20 pounds slimmer?

2. In each case below (a) give an argument in support the person's choice, (b) state three to four reasons against the choice, and (c) state how *you* think the situation should have been handled.

    Case 1: Deception
    One day combing his hair, Ron discovers a small lump on top of his head. A month later, while seeing his doctor about a twisted ankle, Ron asks the doctor to look at the lump. The doctor removes it and sends it to the lab. Two days later Ron gets a call from the doctor, who says it is melanoma, a serious form of skin cancer that can be fatal if it metastasizes. Ron and his wife decide not to tell their 20-year old daughter Lynn until they know more about his condition. Three

weeks later they tell Lynn, who is angry that she was not informed sooner. Was it right of Ron to delay telling their daughter Lynn about the cancer?

Case 2: Cheating

Mike and Frank have been best friends since grade school. Mike is an engineering major and Frank's major is Latin American studies. Both are in the same comparative literature class. Mike has fallen way behind. He has a chance to get an engineering scholarship, so he focused his attention on that. However, the term essay in comp. lit. is due in three days and Mike hasn't even started. Frank's essay is all finished. Mike asks Frank if he could borrow his essay, look it over and, changing the introduction, conclusion and a few key examples, modify it for his essay. Frank is a bit uneasy and voices concerns. However, Mike dismisses these worries, insisting that, with 62 students in the class, the teacher will not notice. Frank lets Mike use his essay. Was it right of Frank to let Mike copy his essay?

Case 3: Blowing the Whistle

A worker in a California pharmacy was developing customers' photographs when she came upon photos of a man with sawed-off shotguns, ammunition, and pipe bombs. She called the police. That California call led to the arrest of a college student on 122 weapons charges. The photo clerk in that case prevented a possible massacre at the nearby De Anza Community College. In a Nebraska case, however, things took a different turn. Beverly was working at a Nebraska discount department store developing photos when she saw a picture of a baby lying on a heap of marijuana leaves. She called the police too. But she was fired, not rewarded. Her boss, Stan, said they had to balance the respect for privacy of their customers with their obligation to stop criminal activity. Beverly is frustrated that her call to the police ended up getting her fired. Should Beverly have called the cops on the customer who had a stash of marijuana?

Case 4: Selective Abortion

Carla's friends, Nicole and Louis are expecting their third child. They already have two cute little boys, ages six and three. They come to Carla with their dilemma: they want no more than three children, they love their boys, but they also want a girl. Louis read about sex-selection procedures and showed the article to Nicole. If they get the fetus tested and find out that it's a boy, they can abort it and try again. They feel pretty strongly that they don't want three boys and really want their last child to be a girl. No one else knows they are expecting, so they won't have to worry about upsetting their families if they go through with this without telling anyone. They ask Carla for advice, because she has taken some ethics classes at college. Carla told them it was immoral to even think about picking the sex of their child; that they should take whatever God gives them. Was it right of Carla to give this advice (or any advice)?

3. What offends you? After the World Trade Center and Pentagon were attacked, Clear Channel, the nation's largest chain of radio stations, distributed to its disc jockeys a list of songs that might now be in bad taste (as noted by the *Los Angeles Times*, 18 Sep. 2001). These songs included those noted below. Look over this list and answer the questions that follow.

- Steve Miller: "Jet Airliner"
- Queen: "Another One Bites the Dust"
- Pat Benatar: "Hit Me with Your Best Shot"
- Bangles: "Walk Like an Egyptian"
- Kansas: "Dust in the Wind"
- Led Zeppelin: "Stairway to Heaven"
- The Beatles: "A Day in the Life"
- Nine Inch Nails: "Head Like a Hole"
- Bob Dylan: "Knockin' on Heaven's Door"
- Megadeth: "Sweating Bullets"
- Metallica: "Seek and Destroy"
- Jerry Lee Lewis: "Great Balls of Fire"
- Louis Armstrong: "What a Wonderful World"
- Peter, Paul and Mary: "Leavin' on a Jet Plane"
- Black Sabbath: "Suicide Solution"
- Simon and Garfunkel: "Bridge over Troubled Water"
- Third Eye Blind: "Jumper"
- Alice in Chains: "Down in a Hole"
- Hollies: "He Ain't Heavy, He's My Brother"
- Don McLean: "American Pie"
- Frank Sinatra: "New York, New York"
- Bruce Springsteen: "I'm on Fire"
- Ricky Nelson: "Travelin' Man"
- James Taylor: "Fire and Rain"
- Limp Bizkit: "Break Stuff"

Answer the following:

a. Do you see a pattern or theme in the choices of music deemed potentially offensive?

b. To what degree do you think music has the power to affect people—either positively or negatively?

c. Set out an argument either for or against the censorship of popular music on radio stations in times of national crises.

4. The beefed-up security at airports has resulted in numerous complaints about overly zealous or invasive searches. There have been reports that even women's eyelash curlers are among the items being snatched by security guards at some airports. Law professor Patricia J. Williams wrote about an encounter she had with airport security. Read the following excerpt and then discuss how we ought to balance airport searches with individual freedoms:

When I finally got to the airport I went through the abasements of security . . . I removed my shoes. I took off my coat. I held out my arms. A guard in a rakish blue beret bestowed apologies like a rain of blessings as she wanded my armpits. "You have an underwire in your bra?" she asked. "You mind if I feel?" It is hard to be responsive to such a prayer with any degree of grace. It is ceremonial, I know, a warding off of strip-search hell. "Not at all," I intoned, as though singing in Latin. Another agent was going through my bags. He removed my nail clippers from the intimacy of my makeup pouch and discarded them in a large vat . . . The agent put on rubber gloves and opened my thermos and swirled the coffee around. He removed the contents of my purse and spread it out. When he picked up my leatherbound diary . . . "My diary?" I said as evenly as I could. "This is getting like the old Soviet Union." . . . Anyway, I finally got to where I was going. And on my way back from Philadelphia, I wasn't searched at all. They stopped the woman just in front of me, though, and there she stood, shoeless and coatless, with the tampons from her purse emptied upon the alter of a plastic tray. (See Patricia J. Williams, "Bad Hair Day," *The Nation,* 25 Feb. 2002)

CHAPTER EIGHT

Desire and Illusion: Analyzing Advertising

And where do our sages get the idea that people must have normal, virtuous desires? What made them imagine that people must necessarily wish what is sensible and advantageous?
—FYODOR DOSTOYEVSKY, *Notes from the Underground*

There is a scene in the movie *Purple Rose of Cairo*, where Cecilia, the film's protagonist, has gone to see the same movie for the third or fourth time. She seems mesmerized by the story on the screen. The fantasy she is watching is much more pleasant than life with her abusive husband or her job as a waitress. Much to her surprise, Tom Baxter, one of the characters on the screen, sees her in the audience and steps out of the movie and into real life. Cecilia's life then takes quite a different turn, because she is faced with more choices than she ever imagined. Her life is transformed as she comes to exert much more control over the direction of her life. Sadder but wiser at the end, Cecilia comes to see both the seduction and the limitations of desire and illusion.

Advertising, like the fantasy life found so entrancing in *Purple Rose of Cairo*, frequently offers us an idealized world. This is a world filled with perfectly charming people having a great time. Their lives are free of disease. Their sexuality is untroubled by fear of AIDS or other sexually transmitted diseases—except for the new romantic advertisements for herpes medication, where the infected people are still frolicking on the beach or snuggling in a canoe. Their marriages are strong, not held together tenuously. Their relationships are loving, not indifferent or even violent. Their children are wonderful—not obnoxious or ill mannered. Their neighborhoods are dream worlds of well-manicured lawns and not war zones of drugs, violence, poverty, or decay. Who wants to have the ideal character step *out* of the ad and into our lives? It'd be far better to step out of our lives and *into* the ad. That's exactly what sucks us in.

We are a society of extremes. There is a wealth of opportunities, incredible choices of things to make our lives easier, and the means to communicate across vast expanses of space. And yet there is sorrow and need around us. This results in longing and desire. We yearn for more than we get—and what we get is not enough. Advertisers know this. Ads attempt to soothe our spiritual hunger problem and help us find a way to connect with those around us. And so, advertising addresses the need for gratification by tending to our desires and dreams.

As Michael Parenti points out consumption is no longer a means for life; it's a meaning for life. Ads don't tell us to "*Buy* Pepsi;" we are asked to "*Join* the Pepsi Generation." Similarly, ads don't tell us to buy a particular brand of cigarette; we are invited to "Come to Where the Flavor Is."

We don't have to feel needy, desperate, or lonely—there's a community for us, if we just buy a ticket (the product) and come on in. Such invitations abound. For instance, a Chandon wine ad says, "The grape varieties in Chandon require bright sun, cool mornings and Spring showers. We find these conditions are also excellent for most varieties of humans. *Come to Chandon and you will see.*" Look also at ads for Norwegian cruise line, which has as its advertising slogan, "It's different out here."

It would be quite remarkable to find someone who was unfamiliar with advertising. Ads are on the outside and inside of buses. Ads are pasted on billboards, buildings, and, at times, written across the sky. Ads package TV shows and are often found inside shows as product placements. We are surrounded by advertising. It is part of our cultural landscape.

Critical thinking helps us deal with the amount and kind of advertising in our lives. In this chapter we will look at key aspects of ads: assumptions, power and influence, and structural components (color, symbol, images, visual and verbal messages). We will also look at related issues—such as the lifestyle idealized in ads, the winner/loser mentality, the roles of sexuality and gender, for-profit versus nonprofit advertising, and the question of censorship.

Assumptions

Contemporary ads bear little resemblance to ads of the 40s, 50s, 60s, and 70s. Ads today are much more subtle and sophisticated. They assume a language of discourse not present in the past. And they routinely make assumptions about consumers' needs, desires, fears, and prejudices. A lot follows from this.

In their book, *Interplay of Influence: News, Advertising, Politics, and the Mass Media,* Kathleen Hall Jamieson and Karlyn Kohrs Campbell point out:

> People in ads have spacious kitchens, large lawns, expensive appliances, cars; they travel worldwide. Ads take for granted that the audience routinely buys soaps, deodorants, makeup, and cologne, and that the audience is not making a decision about whether to buy the product but rather is deciding which brand to buy.

It is a world where affluence is taken for granted and where buying now is preferred to buying later. Decisions therefore center on how to spend the money, not where it's going to come from or what is the best use of our money.

Exercises

1. John Berger argues that ads focus more on social relations than products, with envy being particularly important. He says,

   Publicity is about social relations, not objects. Its promise is not of pleasure, but of happiness: happiness as judged from the outside by others. The happiness of being envied is glamour.
   The spectator–buyer is meant to envy herself as she will become if she buys the product. She is meant to imagine herself transformed by the product into an object of envy for others, an envy which will then justify her loving herself. (See Robert Goldman, *Reading Ads Socially*)

   Answer these questions:
   a. Do you think Berger is right to think ads promise us <u>happiness</u>, not pleasure? Can you cite some examples for or against this claim?
   b. Using a collection of ads (at least five ads), make a case for or against Berger's thesis that envy is what ads are addressing in us.

2. What are the ways in which advertising plays on our emotions? Illustrate your position with five to six ads to support your claims. Be sure to attach your ads.

3. How pervasive is patriotism in advertising? Find at least four examples of ads that play on our sense of patriotism, using national symbols (like the bald eagle, national monuments, famous historical figures, military heroes, the flag) in order to hook us. Be sure to attach your ads.

4. Jamieson and Campbell note that "avenging guardians of the social order" inhabit the world of ads. These are the nosy neighbors, the socially superior guests who sniff out the smell of cats or cigars or who comment on spots on glasses, sweat rings on shirt collars, and dust on furniture.

   Answer the following:
   a. Do you think such "avenging guardians" are still present in ads? Find some ads (print or TV) inhabited by such social guardians and detail the role they play.
   b. What is the political significance of the avenging guardian of the social order? Do they keep us distracted by trivial issues, so we don't look at bigger issues facing us as a society? Or are they helpful figures?

5. In 1985, Michael F. Jacobson argued for a ban on alcohol ads. He argued:

   Despite industry's claims that ads are not targeted at heavy drinkers or youths, the Coors Lite ad tells viewers to drink "beer after beer and don't hold back . . . turn it loose." Harvey's Bristol Cream sherry teaches viewers to switch from traditional glasses to giant tumblers. Anheuser-Busch uses actor–athletes to show viewers that Bud Lite will bring out their best. The Wild Irish Rose wine ad, which depicts a Michael Jackson look-alike and break-dancing along with rock music, seems to be targeting grade school and high school kids.

Ads on radio are often disguised as popular music so they blend right in with the programming. Objective minds can hardly deny that the overall effect of the ads is to glamorize alcohol and foster the notion that drinking is the key to achieving personal goals. (See Michael F. Jacobson, "A Ban on Alcohol Ads Would Aid Society," *The Mass Media: Opposing Viewpoints*, David L. Bender and Bruno Leone, eds.)

Test Jacobson's claim: Try to determine if alcohol ads target a younger audience. Attach examples to support your position for or against his claim.

The Power of Advertising

Advertising does more than push a product. It also tells stories, provides social commentary, offers advice, and makes us laugh. More important, ads claim that our problems can be solved—where the solution is something we can buy. They also tell us that we deserve to be indulged; we have the right to pamper ourselves, given our stressful lives. These, then, are four key things to convey to the consumer:

Four Tricks of Effective Advertising

1. Shame → You've got a problem!
2. Optimism → Your problem can be solved.
3. Solution → You need *this* product.
4. Rationale → You have a right to solve your problem, regardless of cost.

Example of the Fab Four in Action:
GOAL: *How to Sell Delirious Perfume to a Skunk:*

1. Shame → You have body odor!
2. Optimism → Perfume helps!
3. Solution → *Delirious* perfume works wonders!
4. Rationale → You have a right to smell nice!

Look at the way this works: An ad for *Dove Promises* chocolates shows an attractive blonde woman curled up on a couch holding a chocolate egg while children are running in the grass in the background. The ad copy (text) says:

The Hunt Is Over

Introducing Dove Promises for Easter, to give or get by the basketful. Eggs of rich and lingering chocolate, each wrapped in an uplifting message. An indulgence too rich to be rushed.

You can't hurry Dove.

Off to the side is another chocolate egg beside its wrapper. The wrapper contains the "uplifting" message, "Family gatherings will bring Easter joy." However likely that is in reality, it certainly sounds attractive. It is this dream that we buy with Dove chocolates—and the transformation is thereby achieved. By the way, did you notice the last line of the ad copy, "You can't hurry Dove"? This mines the depths of our collective memory, calling up the song "You Can't Hurry Love" by the Supremes. The connection between Dove and Love, at least in some brains, is solidified. Basically the equation is this:

$$\text{Need} \rightarrow \text{Desire}$$

Our <u>need</u> for love can then be translated in the <u>desire</u> for a Dove chocolate.

Sin and Seduction in Advertising

There is a seductive quality to ads, something magical that draws us in. In spite of ourselves, we hope buying this product really can transform our lives, overcome our inadequacies, and make us feel better. The fact that envy, lust/desire, and greed are three of the Seven Deadly Sins does not escape the minds of ad agencies. Some ads play on the sinfulness of eating *those* chocolates, buying *this* car, owning *that* sound system. This taps into the rebel image.

The persuasive techniques range from obvious to subtle, ugly to the beautiful, hilarious to the serious, sexless to the oversexed. For example, a Chantelle bra ad has a close up of a breast in a lacy bra, with the copy "Our honeybee embroidery provokes ideas that are anything but sweet. It may be a detail but it's a Chantelle."

There's an enormous payoff to advertising, even if you never buy a thing. Advertising offers an escape from the troubles of life and the tragedies in the world around us. Some of it is creative and inspiring, some has social commentary, and some is amusing and entertaining. And much of it reflects on the societal context in which it lives and breathes.

It also has power. Dr. Alan Blum, medical professor and head of an antismoking organization, "Doctors Ought to Care," said, "The problem is we think we're smarter than the cigarette industry and that's not true." With large corporations behind them, advertising agencies can determine which images and icons have the greatest appeal. They build upon the collective belief in the folktales and myths that have become part of our culture—and, therefore, are difficult to uproot and analyze. However, we stand to learn by undertaking such an examination.

Advertising has complex artistic and mythological components. Look at the cast of characters in ads. There are winners and losers, villains and heroes, knights in shining armor and damsels in distress, the flabby and the physically fit, the social nerds and the social butterflies, and so on. Ads both shape and are shaped by the elements of our cultural landscape. In applying our critical thinking skills, we wouldn't want to ignore advertising.

Just think of the sheer quantity of ads the average person is subjected to on a daily basis. We often recognize corporate logos—such as those of Nike, McDon-

FORGET THE DOG.
MAKE SURE
YOU DON'T EAT
YOUR HOMEWORK.

Come to a school where the main courses are the main courses. At Culinard, we can teach you
to be a four-star chef in just 21 months. You'll slice. You'll dice. And when you get out, you'll
be able to find your way around the   vegetable market and the job market.

CULINARD
Develop a Taste for Success
BIRMINGHAM ALABAMA 205 802 1200

ald's, Mercedes-Benz, Honda, Coca Cola, and IBM. And we may remember advertising jingles long after a product slides into obscurity. Like it or not, advertising is part of our lives. With critical thinking skills, we can see how ads are constructed and analyze their effects (see Fig. 8-1).

Structural Components of Ads

There is a fascinating documentary called *Magic in the Sky*, produced by the National Film Board of Canada, that focuses on the introduction of TV to the Inuit people living in the Arctic. The Inuit had never been exposed to TV, much less advertising. Nevertheless, they were mesmerized, especially by soap operas. Even though 70 percent of the Inuit do not speak English (the language of the TV shows), this did not stop them from becoming TV addicts. The change on the Inuit society was dramatic. People were less inclined to visit their neighbors. Children stayed inside, glued to the TV set. No one wanted to sit around at night listening to the old folks telling stories. People were amazed by the images on the screen. Above all, they found TV ads riveting. Their lives were transformed in a way that undermines their native arts and their cultural values.

Most of us do not know what it would be like without advertising. And given the choice, most would prefer to accept the consequences of its presence in our lives. Still we ought not be oblivious to its power.

FIGURE 8-1
As this ad suggests, some stacks of homework are tastier than others. Even college administrators recognize this!

Group Exercise

There are two opposing views of advertising below. Read them both and decide which one is most defensible. Then <u>set out your defense</u>, which you'll share with the class:

View 1 (Ads Are Damaging to Society)

The world of mass advertising teaches us that want and frustration are caused by our own deficiencies. The goods are within easy reach, before our very eyes in dazzling abundance, available not only to the rich but to millions of ordinary citizens. Those unable to partake of this cornucopia [wealth] have only themselves to blame. If you cannot afford to buy these things, goes the implicit message; the failure is yours and not the system's. The advertisement of consumer wares, then, is also an advertisement for a whole capitalist system. (See Michael Parenti, "Advertising Has a Negative Effect on Society," in *Mass Media: Opposing Viewpoints,* Neal Bernard, ed.)

View 2 (Ads Do Not Harm the Society)

It is considered appropriate to attempt to persuade. This tells us something concerning our general assumptions about human nature. For why would we permit wanton persuasion to plague a helpless public? Simply because we believe that the public is not helpless, but armed with reason, guiles, and a certain savvy about how to make one's way in the market. If we are sometimes open to persuasion about frivolous products and services, it may be that we have become sufficiently jaded by affluence to let ourselves be seduced by clearly self-interested sources. (See Clifford Christians, Kim Rotzoll, and Mark Fackler, "Advertising Has Little Effect on Society," in *Mass Media: Opposing Viewpoints,* Neal Bernard, ed.)

Exercises

1. What are your two to three favorite ads (or ads you find appealing)? Describe each ad in as much detail as you can, explaining why you find it appealing. The ad need not be a current one.

2. What ad do you dislike the most (or find boring, nondescript)? Describe it in as much detail as you can and then explain where it falls short of your expectations. The ad need not be a current one.

3. What do you think we can learn about politicians from their ad campaigns? Explain and note how much trust is engendered by the ads.

4. Rate these advertising slogans (some old, some recent) in order of most powerful to least memorable:
   a. "I can't believe I ate the whole thing!" (Alka Selzer)
   b. "The True Definition of Luxury. Yours." (Acura)

c. "Only your hairdresser knows for sure." (Clairol)
d. "Betcha can't eat just one." (Lays Potato Chips)
e. "The skin you love to touch." (Woodbury soap)
f. "Even your best friends won't tell you." (Listerine Mouthwash)
g. "Don't leave home without it." (Visa)
h. "Got milk?" (California Milk Advisory Board)
i. "Be all that you can be." (US Army)
j. "You deserve a break today." (McDonald's)
k. "Nothin' says lovin' like something from the oven." (Pillsbury)
l. "Why ask why, try Bud dry." (Budweiser)
m. "Diamonds are Forever." (DeBeer)
n. "Image is nothing. Thirst is everything. Obey your thirst." (Sprite)
o. "An Army of One." (U.S. Army)
p. "Finger-lickin' good." (Kentucky Fried Chicken)
q. "I love what you do for me—Toyota!"
r. "All you add is love." (Ralston Purina Pet Food)
s. "Don't dream it. Drive it!" (Jaguar)
t. "We bring good things to life." (General Electric)
u. "The first time is never the best." (Campari)
v. "Have it your way." (Burger King)
w. "The Power to Be Your Best." (Apple Computers)
x. "Reach out and Touch Someone." (ATT)
y. "Coke is Life!" (Coca Cola)
z. "We try harder." (Avis Rental Car)

5. Looking over your ranking in 4, explain why your top three are the best and why your bottom three are the worst.

6. Do a study of advertising slogans (e.g., see *www.winspiration.co.uk/slogans .htm*). Note what you can infer about our society from ad slogans.

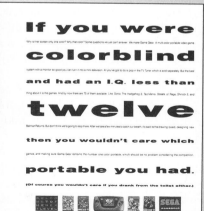

FIGURE 8-2
Wit and humor are powerful tools—and not just in advertising.

7. Examine the Sega ad ("If you were color blind") and *answer the following* (see Fig. 8-2):
   a. How does this ad work to persuade the viewer?
   b. Discuss the use of humor and its role in the ad's effectiveness.
   c. Discuss how the photo of the dog and the ad copy (the text) work together.

▦ Analyzing Ads

When examining an ad, we need to look at a range of concerns. These range from the values implicit in the ad to any stereotypical images, the use of language, verbal messages, and visual messages, among other key aspects. These are set out in the checklist below.

Advertising Checklist

1. *Values:* What values and beliefs does the ad convey? According to the ad, what's the best use of our time and money?
2. *Story:* If you think of the ad as telling a story, what story does it tell?
3. *Verbal Message:* Study the verbal message. What exactly is being said in the ad?
4. *Visual Message:* Study the visual message. What images, symbols, and visual impact are conveyed by the ad?
5. *Fallacies* (See Chapter 4): Watch for the fallacy of accent: Are certain words emphasized (made larger, repeated, set off by a different color) in order to mislead us? Watch for the fallacy of ad verecundiam: Is a celebrity being used to sell a product in lieu of solid reasoning? Watch for equivocation: Are there any shifts in the meaning of a word or phrase? Are there any plays on words or puns? Watch for ad populum: Does the ad play into a patriotic theme or join-the-bandwagon sentiment?
6. *Exaggeration:* Watch for false promises and exaggerated claims. What exactly does the ad claim the product will do? What is the nature of the guarantee? Do you see any puffery?
7. *Stereotypes:* Watch for stereotypes around gender, race, age, nationality, religion, economic class, and so on. Look at the various roles (such as dominant or authority roles, heroes and villains, helper roles, nurturer roles) presented in the ad.
8. *Diversity:* Who populates the ad? Does the ad reflect the society we live in? Note how gender, race, age, and economic class are represented and whether they typify the world we live in.
9. *Power and Class:* Watch for assumptions around power, class, and patterns of consumption. What is the economic class of those inhabiting the ad? Who are the targeted users of the product?

10. *Political Agenda:* Be aware of political or social messages. Ads often relay a set of attitudes, in the verbal or visual message. See if there's a hidden agenda in the advertisement.
11. *Prescriptions:* Look at the lifestyle presented. Ask yourself: Do I live (or want to live) like this; if so, at what cost? And what is the societal impact of this lifestyle?
12. *Sexuality:* Look at the ways sexuality, sexual orientation, sexual violence, and intimacy are handled, including turning men or women into sexual objects or using sexuality to sell the product.
13. *What Is Left Unsaid:* What is missing from this ad? Will using the product transform my life, as the ad suggests? Look at the ways ads overlook any number of societal or personal problems that may bear on buying or using the product.

Group Exercises

Pick three to four ads to study: you can use any ads in this chapter or bring in others. Then, examining the collection of ads, answer any *two* of the following:

• Study how the ads reflect the values of the dominant culture (beliefs, attitudes, social and moral values).
• Study how the ads reflect stereotypical ways of thinking regarding gender roles.
• Study how the ads reflect stereotypical ways of thinking regarding age, economic class, and education.
• Study how the ads reflect assumptions about societal expectations, world view, social roles and norms.
• Study how the ads reflect political realities (patriotism, loyalties, community ties, political allegiances).
• Study how the ads reflect racism or other prejudicial attitudes.

Power and Class

On the surface, ads may appear to be "just" about trying to sell some product. But, many who study advertising see much more going on. For example, Robert Goldman thinks ads are inherently political. He says ads are never ideologically impartial. In *Reading Ads Socially,* Goldman sets out these four warnings about advertising (see *Reading Ads Socially*):

Goldman's Assumptions in Advertising

First Assumption: You should think *this* about *that: Ads always have some political agenda.*

Second Assumption: $$ → Buy, buy: *Ads assume people are paid for their labor.*

Third Assumption: Poverty doesn't exist: *Ads hide class differences.*

Fourth Assumption: Need it? Buy it and find happiness: *Ads imply we can purchase happiness, a meaningful life, and an ideal world.*

Exercises

1. Looking at his assumptions, what do you think of Goldman's critique of advertising? Share your response.

2. Looking at any three or four ads, can you see if Goldman's points apply? Examine the ads for political agenda, assumptions, the ignoring of class differences, and presumptions about what money can buy. Be sure to attach the ads.

3. Focusing on one type of product (e.g., cars, clothes, alcohol) compare two ads targeting the wealthy to two ads targeting the working class. Go into detail on what you find that reflects economic class differences in our society.

4. See if you can find *one* ad that supports award-winning creative director Luke Sullivan's assertion that *simple = good.*

   At his Creative Club presentation, Sullivan explained that consumers are too busy, and sometimes too skeptical, to fall for a long, complicated, cluttered advertisement.

   "Go to the airport and watch somebody read a magazine," he said. "Take your client with you. The average reader will gloss over ads that are droll or complex, but simple ads will get attention," he said. "People don't have time to slow down to decode our clever ideas," he said. "People barely have time to read the editorial (content) in newspapers and magazines—and they're paying for the editorial!"

   "Compared with cluttered ads, simple ads are more memorable, effective, emotional and believable, and are easier for the consumer to notice," Sullivan said. And, as the old Volkswagen Beetle ads demonstrate, simple ads can be timeless. "Simple makes a good ad great," Sullivan said. (See Dave Simanoff, " 'Tis a Gift to Be Simple in Advertising, Sullivan Says," *The Bay Business Journal* (Tampa Bay), 21 Aug. 1998)

5. Discuss the text (ad copy) of the ads below that target members of the upper class (you could even compare with ones aimed at those in the lower-middle or working class):

   a. *Ad 1* (for International K9 Personalized Training and Sales)

      This dog can immobilize an intruder in 2.3 seconds. He's also Jack's pony [photo of toddler with large German Shepherd]. Call today for free information on how to have the perfect dog. Dog Sales & Training, Executive Protection, Self Defense Education and Bodyguard Services.

b. *Ad 2* (for Photo Stone)

Because some Moments in Life Deserve to be Set in Stone. PhotoStone™ turns your treasured photographs into distinctive works of art without altering the original prints! Printed on beautiful travertine marble, each piece is unique— just like the captured moment it reflects. Visit our web site or call for an order form today and celebrate those special moments for a lifetime.

c. *Ad 3* (for Quark Monitoring Equipment)

They may be your employees, but who do they really work for? Find out exactly where your employees' loyalties lie with one of our high-performance hidden cameras. This fully functional clock radio features a pinhole camera that records a crystal clear video image in virtually any lighting condition. Plus, it allows you to monitor office and home activities in real-time or record them for later viewing. We offer similar systems with covert faces convincingly disguised as smoke detectors, fire sprinklers, picture frames and many other home and office items. CIA tested. CEO approved.

The Verbal Message

In addition to looking at assumptions, it is also important to be able to dismantle the ad itself. This dismantling, or deconstructing, of ads involves:

1. Analyzing the verbal and visual messages of ads.
2. Examining the role of images, symbols, and the use of color to create an effect.

Let us look at these aspects, starting with the verbal message. This is created by the use of words and music, when sound is an option. This is the text of the ad. Some verbal messages have a powerful effect. This is most obvious when an advertising slogan becomes part of the cultural memory or sets in motion societal changes around attitudes and values.

Most ads have a greater visual message than verbal message, because people are drawn to striking images and vibrant colors. Some ads, however, rely on the use of words to create impact. This could be in the form of a story about the character, a testimonial about the product, or a commentary on events or issues in the society. When it works, the effect can be powerful. Look at the ad for *Time* magazine and how it relies on the verbal message for its effect (see Fig. 8-3).

Advertising jingles and slogans are part of the verbal message. Advertising jingles form an inherent part of the verbal message in TV and radio ads. It is often hard to forget them. Just think how many you can list off the top of your head ("Join the Pepsi generation," "Coke is life," "We are driven," etc.). These are often the heart of the verbal message. However, the verbal message goes beyond the

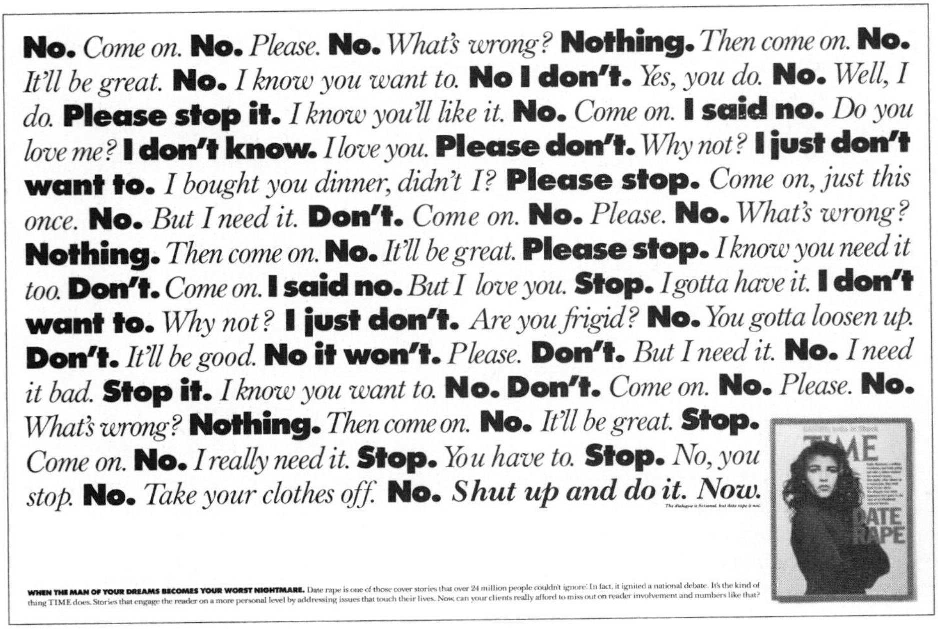
No. Come on. No. Please. No. What's wrong? Nothing. Then come on. No. It'll be great. No. I know you want to. No I don't. Yes, you do. No. Well, I do. Please stop it. I know you'll like it. No. Come on. I said no. Do you love me? I don't know. I love you. Please don't. Why not? I just don't want to. I bought you dinner, didn't I? Please stop. Come on, just this once. No. But I need it. Don't. Come on. No. Please. No. What's wrong? Nothing. Then come on. No. It'll be great. Please stop. I know you need it too. Don't. Come on. I said no. But I love you. Stop. I gotta have it. I don't want to. Why not? I just don't. Are you frigid? No. You gotta loosen up. Don't. It'll be good. No it won't. Please. Don't. But I need it. No. I need it bad. Stop it. I know you want to. No. Don't. Come on. No. Please. No. What's wrong? Nothing. Then come on. No. It'll be great. Stop. Come on. No. I really need it. Stop. You have to. Stop. No, you stop. No. Take your clothes off. No. Shut up and do it. Now.
The dialogue is fictional, but date rape is not.
TIME
DATE RAPE
WHEN THE MAN OF YOUR DREAMS BECOMES YOUR WORST NIGHTMARE. Date rape is one of those cover stories that over 24 million people couldn't ignore. In fact, it ignited a national debate. It's the kind of thing TIME does. Stories that engage the reader on a more personal level by addressing issues that touch their lives. Now, can your clients really afford to miss out on reader involvement and numbers like that?

FIGURE 8-3
For some ads the verbal message is prominent.

Fallon McElligott. Art Director—Bob Brinh. Copywriter—Phil Hamft. Creative Director—Phil Hamft. Reprinted with permission.

one-liner. Anything that is part of the ad copy acts as part of the verbal message. This includes the promises, the discussion of the product, background dialogue, or buzzwords placed around the product. These words form the verbal message and get filed into the linguistic recesses of our minds. We can study the verbal messages in ads. We can defend ourselves and not let the messages of ads imprint our minds like some kind of brainwashing.

We can also note when ads use humor or witticisms to become memorable. For instance, one of the 2001 award-winning ads featured in *Communication Arts* was a series of ads produced for Cyanamid for a product to kill corn nematodes (corn worms). These ads had prominent verbal messages, such as: "NEMATODES LIVE UNDERGROUND. THIS SHORTENS THEIR *TRIP TO HELL*" and "NEMATODES EAT FAR LESS CORN WHEN THEY'RE DEAD" and "IT STOPS NEMATODES FROM EATING YOUR CORN. *ACTUALLY,* IT STOPS THEM FROM DOING MUCH OF ANYTHING."

It is wise to examine the claims that are made or implied by an ad. For example, "Four out of five doctors recommend . . ." How do you know this is true? Has every single doctor in the country been asked for an opinion on headache remedies or cures for constipation? That is doubtful. In fact, it is not clear precisely what study was done on doctors' views of particular products—and who financed the study. All that needs to be true is that when five doctors were asked what product they recommend for such-and-such an ailment, and four of them suggest that product. The reader may assume that a respectable study using a representative (and large) sample of doctors has produced this claim. The assumption, however, could be erroneous and leaving the reader misled. So, watch what we assume when it comes to advertising.

Exercises

1. "So why isn't the Marlboro Man a soldier rather than a cowboy?" Share your response to the answer given by the president of Tech. Marketing Inc.:

   The mythical fighting man in our culture *is* a cowboy. He's our samurai. . . . You have to understand what smoking's all about. We as a society have abandoned tribal initiation rites, and cigarettes are a substitute; kids want to prove themselves and play the role of adults. When you rob people of something they want, marketers find a way to give it to them. (See Stuart Elliott, "Uncle Sam Is No Match for the Marlboro Man," *The New York Times,* 27 Aug. 1995)

2. Look at the ad for *Time* magazine (Fig. 8-3) and then answer the following:
   a. Does the ad convey the concerns around date rape?
   b. Why do you think this ad has received awards?
   c. Assume that you run an advertising agency. What might be an alternative way to present an issue on date rape for *Time*? Try to come up with two examples that are distinctly different than the one presented here.

3. One effective ad is, "Winston **tastes** good like a cigarette should." Another effective ad is for Camel cigarettes: "Genuine **Taste,** Never Boring." However, we don't normally eat cigarettes or refer to inhaling in terms of <u>taste</u>. Why do you think these two ads have been so effective? Go into detail.

4. Look at the way the Harley Davidson ad ("Paisley and Florals") addresses the type of person who would buy a Harley Davidson motorcycle (see Fig. 8-4). Discuss:

In some circles, paisley and florals have yet to catch on.

HARLEY-DAVIDSON OF NORTH TEXAS
190 OLD DENTON RD. CARROLLTON (214) 820 1777

Tilford, The Richards Group.

FIGURE 8-4   The target audience makes all the difference.

    a. The verbal message, including how the ad copy works to set a tone and persuade the viewer.

    b. The visual message, including how the photograph presents an image geared to impact upon the viewer.

    c. How the visual and verbal messages work together.

5. Find at least three examples of what you would consider great, memorable, or persuasive ad copy (verbal message). Note why you think they are persuasive.

The Power of Language: Analyzing Ads for Their Verbal Messages

Whereas ads with strong visual appeal tend to keep copy to a minimum, some ads, like the *Time* ad on date rape, rests their effectiveness on the verbal message. Some seek a balance of strong visuals and verbal impact. Whenever you remember the key line of an ad—as with Mitsubishi's "The Word Is Getting Around," Virginia Slims' "You've Come a Long Way, Baby," and Carl's Junior's "If it doesn't get all over the place, it doesn't belong in your face," ad agencies have scored a linguistic victory. When combined with catchy or dramatic use of music, the words potentially are carved onto the inside of your skull.

In decoding an ad, the examination of the verbal message is as important as studying the visual elements. Think of it like this: the ad tells a story. You have to read the ad carefully to ascertain all the fine details of the story and its possible effectiveness.

Sometimes the ad presents evidence that the product is of good quality, for example, by laying out reasons in an itemized way. Sometimes, the ad presents only the salient selling features of the product. Other times, the ad may rest its verbal message on explaining to you (the consumer) why this product is different and better than its competitors. Or the ad may not direct its attention to the product at all, but try to leave you with an impression, indirectly selling the product. For example, an ad may suggest that buying the product will result in a particular lifestyle or a membership into an elite group of people.

In addition to reading the ad for its narrative value, you should also do a word study. Carefully read the ad, watching for key words that will work to either emphasize the product's appeal or will hook the consumer by pushing the appropriate buttons. For example, words like sex, love, rich, mysterious, flavor, fun, pleasure, and satisfying carry weight. When they are repeated (sometimes over and over) in an ad, the loaded term acts like a drum beat, punctuating the ad's message.

Assessing the Verbal Message—Watch for:

- Characteristics or qualities of the product.
- Consequences of owning the product.
- Benefits of this product over rival products.

- A particular lifestyle that accompanies the product.
- Use of humor, diversionary tactics (such as shocking, insulting, or negative comments directed to the consumer).
- Social commentary that may or may not relate to the product.
- Use of statistics or statistical claims touting the benefits of the product.
- The testimony of ordinary people, so-called experts, or celebrities.
- Techno-lingo or pseudo-scientific terms to give weight to the ad's claims.
- Fallacies of reasoning or questionable claims.

Group Exercise

Each group should use the above list to study this ad text for its verbal message:

What does doing 125 killer squats have to do with spiking a volleyball 454 unreturned times in one season? To you, everything. Because sport training is all about training for your sport.

You wanted a hand in designing the shoe you'd use to do it in. You wanted it visually distinctive, yet stable (hmm—a lot like you . . .). Then you wanted it available to other women just as intense about training for their sports.

So how happy are you that the new Nike Air Trainer Patrol shoes are at the one store as committed to women's inner as well as outer strength as you've always been? In a word, "very." Because life is motion and anyplace else is a dink. **Lady Foot Locker.** Stop just long enough to come in.

Exercises

1. Select *one* of the following and write down your analysis of its verbal message, drawing from the elements listed above:
   a. "Tears are Antifreeze for the Soul. **Joop Jeans.** Just a Thought."
   b. "Power begets power. **Lagerfeld.** A fragrance for men."
   c. "**Now it's F-U-N to eat your words.** Duncan Hines Kids Cups ABCs are the fun new treat you'll enjoy baking with your kids. In minutes you have fluffy cupcakes covered with creamy vanilla frosting and crunchy alphabet candy. In a word, y-u-m-m-y. And easy as A-B-C. **Duncan Hines.** Hot Stuff!"
   d. "**God's Gift to Women.** 3 Musketeers Brand Miniatures. Delightful little squares of fluffy nougat wrapped in satisfying milk chocolate. Less than 1 gram of fat per piece. 5 grams of fat in a 7 piece serving. Oh the delicious arrogance of it all. **Big on Chocolate, Not on Fat!** 45% Less Fat Than the Average of Leading Chocolate Brands."

2. Select one of the following texts from the ads below. Study the text you selected and write down your analysis of its verbal message, drawing from the elements listed above:

   a. **Body & Mind.** Vogue Dessours understands every intimate detail that you desire in lingerie. We care how it makes you feel. We understand your need for beauty, comfort, sensuality and style. All are met in this alluring underwire stretch demi bra and stretch lace bikini from one of our many collections. **Vogue Dessous.** A feeling for your body."

   b. **4 Things Women hate:**
      1. Not-so-funny laugh lines.
      2. Disappearing eye shadow.
      3. Under eye circles and puffiness.
      4. Guys who won't commit.

      Triple-Action™ Eye Enhancer. The AHA eye cream that helps get rid of 1 thru 3. (With 4 you're on your own.) One breakthrough product, three beauty benefits.

      <u>Benefit one:</u> A dramatic reduction in the appearance of eye area expression lines, thanks to an alpha hydroxy acid formula that exposes younger-looking skin.

      <u>Benefit two:</u> As the perfect primer, it makes eye color waterproof and crease-resistant, helps keep it from fading.

      <u>Benefit three:</u> Special microspheres scatter light to camouflage undereye circles and puffiness. Use Triple-Action™ Eye Enhancer for six weeks and on average, here's what you'll see:
      • 23% reduction in appearances of fine lines,
      • 27% increase in firmness, 23% increase in moisturization.

      Buy Triple-Action™ Eye Enhancer and get a Powder Perfect Eye Color FREE. Pick a shade, any shade, and see what a difference the perfect primer can make. **Mary Kay.**

3. Select one of the following texts from the ads below. Study the text you selected and write down your analysis of its verbal message, drawing from the elements listed above:

   a. "**The advantage of being in control.** Taking matters into your own hands is an idea you wholeheartedly embrace. It lets you do what you want, when you want—while having as much fun as you want. That's the idea behind rack-and-pinion steering.

   Rack-and-pinion steering acts like a two-way transmitter between you and the front wheels of your car. Turn the wheel and the pinion (a gear) at the end of the steering column moves over a bar called (you guessed it) a rack to point your wheels in the right direction. Your car responds instantly. Accurately. Almost instinctively. It also sends the feel of the road back to you, letting you fine-tune your driving. That's what makes precision handling precise.

And, while nearly every Chevy we sell comes with the feel-good control of rack-and-pinion steering, including the Beretta GT, all of them come with the bottom-line value of a great Chevy price.

So try one, and take a turn for the better."

b. Note in the ad below, "sigint" = "signals intelligence" = communications intelligence = military satellites used for intelligence operations.

"Your mission's unique. You need a system that's unique. Whatever you need—sigint or maritime patrol capabilities or to update your fighter aircraft—we're more than ready, willing and able at Thomson-CSF to confront your requirements and come up with the right solution.

What makes us unique is the extensive experience of our Radars and Counter-measures Division built up over the years with a wide variety of international customers. Combined with the competence and expertise of many other specialist divisions throughout the Group. Together with the outstanding input provided by a number of key partners, all major players in their fields, worldwide. Thomson–CSF.

Your mission's unique. You need a supplier that's unique.

Thomson-CSF. Radars & Contre-Measures."

4. Study the following ad. First analyze the verbal message. Then, do a cultural analysis, focusing on societal or cultural assumptions about men.

"Impotence.

The facts. An estimated 10 to 20 million American males suffer from impotence.

- Up to 75 percent of all cases are physical in nature, not psychological.
- It is a treatable condition.
- It is not necessarily a function of aging.
- Experienced physicians, usually urologists, can provide safe, dependable treatments.
- Most men can be successfully treated.

Find out how you can join the tens of thousands of men who are now enjoying sexual relations with renewed confidence. Calling for your Free Information Kit from Upjohn is the first step."

▦ The Visual Message

We are a visual culture. We judge, buy, consume, or desire all sorts of things in terms of their visual appeal. Advertisers know this. We do not normally want to see things that are ugly or unpleasant—unless it is done with humor. We do want to see beauty and images of happiness, intimacy, and satisfaction. We like to see images of success, things working correctly, and problems being solved.

Let's look at the Perrier ad (see Fig. 8-5). This highly regarded advertisement is effective, at least in part because of the strong visual message. It is both visually striking and thought provoking. It plays with our cultural stereotypes by showing the couple in an old pickup with the empty Perrier bottles bouncing around the truck bed. Perrier is not just for rich people, but is something an ordinary guy and gal from the back roads of Texas would enjoy just as much. Look again at the ad and try to determine exactly what it has done to be recognized in the advertising world. Think also about the visual message and see what you can infer. Some ads, for example, go for the jugular by creating jarring, even disturbing visual images. Clearly these are *not* intended to help us escape into a fantasy world. Rather, they intend to use shocking or in-your-face advertising to take the consumer by surprise and create a kind of disequilibrium in their brains.

Benetton (clothing manufacturer) created an international furor with ads depicting illness, suffering, even death. Some of their notorious ads include such images as a bird drenched with oil, a dying AIDS patient, a prisoner on death row, a bloody uniform from a Croatian soldier, and a man's torso with a tattoo on his

FIGURE 8-5
Can you see how this ad for Perrier demonstrates the power of a visual message?

FIGURE 8-6
Compare these ads for Nike and Perrier with ads that rely on a strong verbal, rather than visual, message.

left arm that says "HIV positive." The images are unsettling. They have nothing to do with the product (clothes). But they do make a political statement—remember Robert Goldman's first assumption about the ideological aspect of ads.

Benetton is not the only company to use shock to jolt the audience. Diesel ads (JOOP Jeans USA) have come out with ad after ad that pushes the boundary of good taste. One diesel denim ad, for instance, features an elderly woman (in jeans) grabbing the crotch of an old man (also in jeans) who has nodded off on the couch.

In contrast to the Benetton and Diesel ads that jolt the viewer (presumably out of their complacency!), ads ordinarily present us with images of beauty, success, happiness, and pleasure. Connected with these images is a product. The idea is to get the consumer to draw the link between the images and the product; so we think getting the one will result in the other. This is a kind of variation on the movie *Field of Dreams,* where the motto was, "If you build it, he will come." With ads, the implicit message is, "If you buy it, they will come," where the "they" are desirable states of affairs.

The desire is for much more than mere ownership. We yearn for what the product represents and the lifestyle that accompanies it. Ads used to focus almost entirely on the product itself, spelling out what it could do for us. For example, with Pepsodent ads of the 50s and 60s ("You'll wonder where the yellow went . . ."), we had images of yellow teeth being magically transformed into gleaming white jewels. The payoff was that a member of the opposite sex (heterosexuality assumed) would now find you sexually attractive. It also implied that yellow teeth are the only things standing in the way of adoration. Attaining this was directly related to the use of the product.

Look at the Studebaker ad (Fig. 8-7): This ad is a classic example of presenting the product, rather than a mood or a lifestyle. In fact, this ad shows *only* a car; there are no people, plants, or animals populating this ad. There's nothing but an empty Studebaker. The underlying assumption is that the consumer wants only to focus on the product. At that time (1950s) ad agencies probably thought it would then be easier for the viewers to put *themselves* in the picture, rather than look at someone else in that Studebaker.

Things have changed. Now we would not want only the Studebaker, we want what the Studebaker will bring once we own it. Just look at the ad. Using a nuts-and-bolts approach, it states some key specifics about the car and informs us that this is a "Common-Sense" car. The phrase "Common-Sense" is repeated five times, so readers can have that point driven into their brain. Presumably, we would walk away thinking, "Gosh, it makes Common-Sense for me to go buy a Studebaker!"

FIGURE 8-7
Ads of the 50s testify to how much the world has changed. A pitch based on "common sense" is definitely a blast from the past!

Why do we call the 1965 Studebaker <u>the</u> Common-Sense car?

Because it's built so mechanically sound a man with reasonable driving habits can drive it for years without a major repair. Common-Sense.

Because the body style doesn't change every year. So you save money when you buy it. You save money when you trade it. Common-Sense.

Because it's functionally sized at both front and rear, with a full-sized 6-passenger living room in the middle. You can park it in incredibly short spaces. Drive over inclines, bumps, and dips with plenty of clearance for heads, headroom for hats and legroom for legs. Common-Sense.

Because either one of its two great new engines will take you as far on a gallon of regular gas as a gallon of gas is meant to go. Possibly a little farther.

Mind you, there's another car you might consider Common-Sense, too. It doesn't change body style every year, either. Just improves its insides from time to time, as we do. But, it's much smaller than ours. So small, in fact, that . . .

. . . some people affectionately call it a bug. Including the people who make it.

This technique of repetition has continued to the present, as recent ads demonstrate. As a critical thinker, you might ask yourself if such repetition has the power to hook people in.

Exercises

1. Looking at the Studebaker ad, why do you think there is a reference to the Volkswagen bug?

2. Do you think it works when an ad for one product refers to a rival product (the competition)?

3. Compare and contrast three recent ads for cars with this Studebaker ad. (Be sure to attach your ads!) Note all the similarities and differences you see.

4. Create text for an ad for the car of your dreams in which there is no photo or description of the car itself. Looking over the text of your ad (assume it's for the radio, then you don't have to worry about leaving out the visual message), explain (a) your targeted audience, (b) what you did to reach and appeal to that audience, (c) what verbal message you intended, and then evaluate the effectiveness/persuasiveness of your ad.

Use of Color and Symbols

One important visual dimension has to do with color versus black and white. Some ads, like the Harley Davidson ad, are entirely in black and white and the strong lines are part of the visual message. Other ads rely on color to create a mood or call up certain associations. Color can have a powerful effect on the audience. Many ads use symbols of patriotism, such as flag motifs, eagles flying majestically across the page, and the Statue of Liberty, national memorials or other historical monuments placed in the background. This is true even in times of peace—not just in wartime. Frequently this show of patriotism in ads gets reinforced with copy such as "America's number one pizza," or "The motor oil that Americans trust," or "The movie that Americans are all talking about."

All these symbols of patriotism signal to us how loyal we would be to buy this or eat that. It also makes us feel safe, at home in a world that is not always safe or homey. Remember, though, that such appeals to patriotism are usually examples of the ad populum fallacy we studied in Chapter 4. Watch the way such appeals are done to verify whether or not they are relevant. There are other uses of color and symbol that have nothing to do with patriotism or cultural traditions. Some ad agencies use vivid colors and images to create unique and distinctive ads that have popular appeal or emotional effect. Think, for instance, of the pink Energizer bunny, that became an advertising icon.

One of the most imaginative ad campaigns in current memory is that of Absolut Vodka (see Fig. 8-8). These ads have taken on a life of their own and have

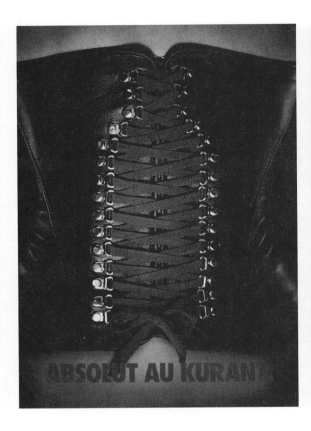

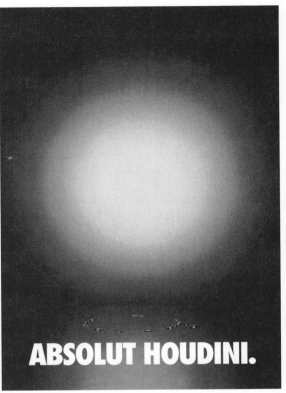

ABSOLUT HOUDINI.

Under permission by V&S Vin & Spirit AB.

FIGURE 8-8
"Absolut Country of Sweden vodka & logo, Absolut, Absolut bottle design and Absolut calligraphy are trademarks owned by V&S Vin & Sprit Ab. © V&S Vin & Sprit Ab."

evoked a powerful imaginative response within the artistic community and the general public. Absolut ads are not aimed at minors and the company has taken a strong stand against targeting those who are underage. Their ads do not use cartoon images or other "hooks" that might appeal to children. Neither do they employ themes or images such as references to blockbuster movies or popular music that target adolescents. Rather, these ads target adults.

The Absolut ads succeed because of their sophisticated, and at times even abstract, nature. They are closer to mental puzzles than sales pitches, as they challenge the limits of minimalism. It is in the myriad approaches representing the physical shape of the Absolut bottle itself that so distinguishes Absolut advertising.

In granting permission for the inclusion of these ads in this text, Seagrams & Sons, Inc., intend that they be used in conjunction with exercises for developing critical thinking skills. They are not presented here to condone, or even tolerate, the consumption of alcoholic beverages by minors. Rather, Seagrams & Sons, Inc., take seriously their social responsibility to restrict the Absolut advertising to people over 21 years of age.

Exercises

Part One

1. Focusing on color, find three ads as follows: one that is particularly striking or appealing in terms of the use of color or visual images; one that is visually disturbing or unappealing; and, finally, one that is boring or ineffective visually. Briefly explain why you judged them as you did.

2. Collect five to six print ads for the same type of product (e.g., cigarettes, perfume, cars, watches, etc.). Be sure your ads are in color, not black and white. Discuss the following:
   a. What ad is most effective in its use of color?
   b. What symbols, images, and themes are used? Which one is most effective and why?
   c. Looking at all the ads as a collection (rather than focusing on only one of them), what do they reveal about us as a society, in terms of cultural attitudes and values? Cite specific examples to back up your claims.

3. Do a study of the visual messages in movie advertising, noting what sorts of images and symbols are used. Do you see any differences in the advertising of blockbuster films from that of independent films? Share your observations.

Presenting a Lifestyle

If we examine an ad as we would any work of art, we go beyond the structural aspects of the work, to what it is actually saying to us as an art form. In other words, we can read an ad as we would read an illustrated story or social commentary. Whereas ads of twenty or thirty years ago raved about the product and what it could do, recent advertising is more contextual. That is, the product is *embedded* within a particular context, that of the lifestyle being presented. The product itself is placed within this lifestyle, but is not given a hard sell. This approach is not even soft sell, but more of an *indirect* sell, with a causal link drawn between the product and the desired lifestyle.

The indirect approach is, in that sense, a more risky maneuver on the part of the manufacturer. Such ads require an act of faith on the part of the ad agency. When they work, though, they can be enormously effective. In the Diet Coke ad (Fig. 8-9), the product is not even mentioned. The focus of the ad is a running monologue that goes hand in hand with a glass of Diet Coke that gradually disappears. The monologue starts with "I can't believe he dumped me" and proceeds to list the reasons why he was no Prince Charming (he belched the national anthem, he kissed like a mackerel, he gave an IOU for her birthday, he's hairy).

FIGURE 8-9
How much is assumed about the audience's knowledge of the product in this Diet Coke ad?

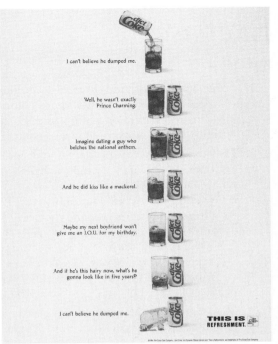

I can't believe he dumped me.

Well, he wasn't exactly Prince Charming.

Imagine dating a guy who belches the national anthem.

And he did kiss like a mackerel.

Maybe my next boyfriend won't give me an I.O.U. for my birthday.

And if he's this hairy now, what's he gonna look like in five years?

I can't believe he dumped me.

THIS IS REFRESHMENT.

There is no mention of the drink that, we assume, offers her gratification as she laments this disastrous relationship. The visual image of the disappearing beverage is all the statement a viewer needs to get the message that Diet Coke is her solace. The implicit message is that we, too, can find such comfort, even if we, too, have our own litany of troubles. No mention is explicitly made about the product: the sequence of images speaks for itself.

This chain of associations shows us how advertising has become much more subtle. It also shows us that advertising has succeeded in creating an art form and perhaps even a type of literary genre. That is, we "read" the copy and images of ads with a kind of familiarity and acceptance. We, then, can follow a story through a sequence of ads. In that sense certain products have become institutions. For many products, the logo/symbol or the slogan is all we need to set in motion a chain of mental (or emotional) associations. We then link the symbol/logo/slogan with that chain of associations analogous to the Coke = solace link made in the "I can't believe he dumped me" ad. There's a comfort in this and a kind of stability or security.

Winners and Losers in Advertising

At times it seems like we need to satisfy some list of qualifications in order to deserve the product, such as being cool enough or attractive enough to get access to the product being advertised. But, because we want to enter that parallel universe where people are having such a nice life, we are driven to get to that point of entry.

In these ads, there is a clear line between winners and losers. The winner–loser demarcation goes inside the ads, as well. An ad campaign for Foster Farm chickens illustrates this. The ad campaign shows two chickens trying to pass themselves off as Foster Farm chickens but the telltale evidence (such as a half-eaten bag of French fries) gives them away and they invariably get caught. They are failures— rejects—trying to be members of a club they can never join. We laugh at the ad's cleverness, but there is a way that the laughter masks the fear that, like the second-class chickens masquerading as the real thing; so, too, might we be second-class citizens pretending to be more than we are.

An ad agency could elect to exploit this notion of winners and losers. For example, an ad might present models of success or show people who do not fit society's definition of a winner. Look at the ads for Clarion ("Geek") and Kellogg's ("2 bowls")—(see Figs. 8-10 and 8-11). These ads have impact and tap into our deepest fears about success and failure. Why be a geek, when you can "strut your stuff"? Consider the mythology of the ads—the story of the ad, the images and symbols it uses, the overall effectiveness in relaying messages not only about the product, but about how we ought to live. How are these ads social commentaries?

FIGURE 8-10
Geek is not good.

FIGURE 8-11
2 is a lucky number:
Consider how the
visual and verbal
messages reinforce
one another here.

There's a new way to jump-start your healthy lifestyle. A leading university has discovered that eating Kellogg's *Special K®* and Kellogg's *Smart Start®* cereals can help you lose up to six pounds in just two weeks. Here's how:

✓ Start with a serving of cereal and skim milk with fruit for breakfast.
✓ Replace either lunch or dinner with the cereal meal.
✓ Have a third meal as you normally would.
✓ Snack on fruits and vegetables between meals.
✓ In two weeks, strut your stuff.

Consult your physician before starting any diet or exercise program. A registered dietician can help you plan a healthy diet. Results may vary. Average weight loss 4.2 pounds.

Exercises

4. Look at the Clarion ad ("Geek") and answer the following:
   a. What is the verbal message? What story does it tell?
   b. What is the visual message?

5. Look at the Kellogg's ad ("2 bowls") and answer the following:
   a. What is the verbal message? What story does it tell?
   b. What is the visual message?

6. Discuss how the two ads differ and which ad you find more persuasive (and why). Note also what each one reveals about societal values.

Sexuality and Gender in Advertising

Many ads use sexuality or sexual images to create an effect and sell a product (and an idea). Freud wasn't the only one who knew how powerful the sex drive is and to what extent we identify our sense of self and our choices in terms of body image. There is room for exploitation in this. For example, bodies of women are more likely to be portrayed in advertising than those of men, although men are increasingly becoming sex objects in mainstream advertising. Many ads use male and female sexuality to sell a product. For example, Calvin Klein's Obsession perfume ads caused a stir when they first appeared, because of the use of male and female nudity.

Sometimes the use of sexuality has only a remote connection with the product. For example, prominently displayed billboards in Los Angeles show a sexy woman in a swimsuit standing next to a car. The ad is for a company called One Day Paint and Body. The image of the sexy women triggers the fantasy that, with a nicely painted car, she (or someone equally as desirable) will be drawn to you. Only a new paint job separates you from finding such happiness, such pleasure.

One benefit of studying ads is to gain insight into our society. Through ads, we can discover prevalent stereotypes and folk wisdom—men are chefs, women are cooks, men mow lawns, women clean house, men show boys how to use power tools, women show girls how to use household appliances, both mothers and fathers tuck children into bed, more men than women drive their children to school, only mothers rub cold medicine onto children's chests, men like to drink beer with lots of other men, women like to drink coffee with one or two other women, phone calls are good things to get (especially with call screening to nix the telemarketers and unwanted others), women are worried about spots on glassware and are often troubled by vaginal yeast, men do not notice grease on their tools and sometimes struggle with impotence, both men and women are tortured by hemorrhoids and acid indigestion.

Do you think children's views of the world are affected by advertising? If so, how much? One way to find out is to look at the kind of ads directed toward children. For example, on the Kellogg's UK website (*www.kelloggs.co.uk*) is the following:

> **Coco Alert!**
> Oh no! Coco has gone to visit his granny and he's asked his gang to look after the Coco Pops. As soon as Coco left, Crafty Croc and his gorillas captured the gang! The gang needs your help to alert Coco. Go to the *www.cocopops.co.uk* website and send Coco a warning message now!

It is worthwhile to think about ads targeting children and how such activities found in the "Coco Alert!" ad work together to shape children's perceptions, values, and interests.

Exercises

Part One

1. You want to study contemporary North American society. All you can use in your study are advertisements. Gather at least 10 ads across a range of products. On the basis of your study, what can you infer about this society?

2. Given your same batch of ads you collected in 1 (or a new batch, if you are ambitious), what can you infer about our societal attitudes about *men*?

3. Given your same batch of ads that you collected in 1 (or a new batch, if you are ambitious), what can you infer about our societal attitudes about *women*?

Part Two

Directions: Answer *one* of the following, including the subparts of the exercise you select:

1. Gather five print ads on one theme; for example, cosmetics, perfume, cars, cigarettes, shoes, toys, stereo equipment, guns, and so forth. Answer the following:
   a. What patterns emerge from studying these ads?
   b. What overall message is there?
   c. Are there any aspects or messages that cause you concern? Go into detail.

2. Do a study of ads targeting children. Gather five print ads aimed at children or teenagers (specify which). Answer the following:
   a. What patterns emerge from studying these ads?
   b. What overall message is there?
   c. Are there any aspects or messages that cause you concern? Go into detail.

3. Find five ads that you think reflect our society, and do not create an alternate, perfect world.
   a. Discuss how the five ads work together to describe contemporary American society.
   b. Note how the ads portray any two of the following: class, race, gender stereotypes, relationship dynamics, family structure, values, and beliefs.

Using Ads with a Social or Political Theme

Given the potential to reach a wide audience and the power of persuasive advertising, nonprofit groups are turning to advertising to get their messages across. It is not surprising that advertising is used as a political or social tool.

Obviously politicians figured this out long ago, as we see in expensive and carefully orchestrated political campaigns. If we can sell people on the idea of buying a particular car, brand of soap, or cell phone, we ought to be able to sell them on one aspiring politician over another. Organized groups can reach the general public via advertising or a public service campaign. We are a society with people who speak their minds, express their political beliefs, and take action in the name of what they believe in. The advertising door has been opened to broader uses than selling products. Let us look at ads that carry a social message. Examine the two Rainforest Action Network ad (criticizing Chevron), the United States Campaign to Ban Landmines (UCSBL) ad, and the United Front ad (supporting affirmative action). (See Figs. 8-12 to 8-14.)

With the power advertising has had in transforming our society, it is not surprising that groups concerned about social, political, or environmental causes should turn to it to get their message across. It might be noted that antismoking ad campaigns have been effective in persuading people to either stop or to avoid

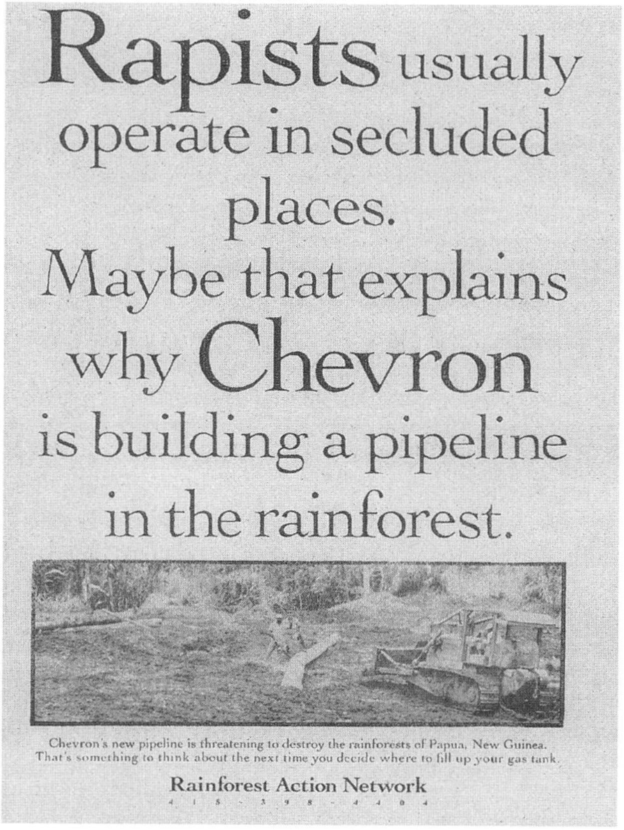

FIGURE 8-12

Rapists usually operate in secluded places. Maybe that explains why Chevron is building a pipeline in the rainforest.

Chevron's new pipeline is threatening to destroy the rainforests of Papua, New Guinea. That's something to think about the next time you decide where to fill up your gas tank.

Rainforest Action Network
4 1 5 - 3 9 8 - 4 4 0 4

FIGURE 8-13

Reprinted with permission of the U.S. Campaign to Ban Landmines (Banmines@phrusa.org).

FIGURE 8-14

Reprinted with the permission of Helen Cho.

starting smoking. It would be valuable to line these up next to a collection of pro-smoking ads put out by tobacco companies. R. J. Reynolds refused permission for inclusion of their ads in this textbook, given the primary audience of this book is under the age of 21. Consequently, you won't see their ads in this book, but you can readily find them and study them on your own. Or you could bring in a collection to this class and discuss them as a class activity.

Using the critical thinking skills we applied to consumer advertising, we can also examine public service advertising. Realize that you may see public service ads in print or on TV or hear them on the radio. This includes ad campaigns or public service announcements that focus on such topics as antismoking, drug awareness, health care, stopping domestic violence, family planning, environmental causes, human rights, and environmental causes.

Exercise

Part One

1. Looking at the Rainforest Action Network ad, the U.S. Campaign to Ban Landmines ad, and the United Front ad, state which ad you consider most powerful or persuasive and explain why. It doesn't matter if you agree with the political message—your task is to analyze effectiveness.

2. Study the public service ad for organ and tissue donation (Fig. 8-15), discussing both the visual message and the verbal message. Set out your thoughts on who is being targeted by the ad (give reasons). What would you do differently to target a totally different audience (e.g., in terms of age, class, race, etc.)? Go into detail on what would likely shift.

3. Answer *one* of the following:
   a. Write the text for a radio anti-drug campaign targeting amateur athletes who use performance-enhancing drugs or students who pop caffeine pills. After you write your ad, analyze its potential effectiveness.
   b. Pick a political or social issue that you care deeply about. Assume you are creating an ad for your side of the issue and your audience is radio listeners (so you do not need to do any visuals). Write (or create) an ad that would present your position and motivate a listener to act.

Part Two

1. Study the following public service radio commercial that was given recognition in a *Communication Arts Annual* edition on advertising:

   PATRICK REYNOLDS: Do you know what's in cigarettes? I can tell you right now the answer is no. Because the last thing tobacco companies want is for you to know how many poisonous chemicals there are in cigarettes.

FIGURE 8-15

"**Y**OU HAVE TO TALK IT OVER WITH YOUR FAMILY."

"My son, Daku, was driving a motorcycle when he was hit by a car and killed. In the hospital was the most difficult time of my life. But because we had discussed organ and tissue donation, it helped me, it helped my family, it helped everyone in making the decision to donate his organs and tissues. Every day I tell people, talk it over. Don't be afraid." For your free brochure about organ and tissue donation, call 1-800-366-SHARE.

Organ & Tissue
D O N A T I O N
Share your life. Share your decision.

 *Coalition on Donation*

And there are plenty. Stuff like formaldehyde, cyanide, in fact, some of the chemicals in cigarettes are so poisonous that it's illegal to dump them into landfills.

But apparently, tobacco companies think it's okay to dump them into our lungs. The worst thing is, they do it without telling you. Because you won't find a list of the chemicals anywhere on the pack or in their ads.

I'm Patrick Reynolds. My grandfather founded the R.J. Reynolds tobacco company. That means my family's name is on the side of more than seven billion cigarette packs a year. Why am I telling you this? I want my family to be on the right side for a change.

ANNOUNCER: A message from the Massachusetts Department of Public Health.

2. Examine the public service ad for smoke free movies (Fig. 8-16) then answer the following questions:

   a. How do you think the ad works to bring the issues around cigarette product placement in movies?

   b. Can you see why it has evoked some controversy? (You may want to do some Internet research on the impact this ad has had).

   c. Could this ad campaign serve as a model for bringing to the public eye other sorts of product placement or related concerns?

FIGURE 8-16
The Smoke Free Movies ad has sparked considerable response.

[ONE IN A SERIES]

How many people did it take to put Marlboros In the Bedroom?

Widely praised for its artful depiction of family tragedy, Todd Field's *In the Bedroom* is equally remarkable for gratuitously promoting Marlboro brand cigarettes on screen and in dialogue. Why would a cash-strapped independent do a favor for Philip Morris, which made $10 billion off tobacco sales last year?

Product placement is no secret in the movie industry, but even savvy ticket-buyers aren't privy to the details.

So if the stars of *In the Bedroom* (Greenestreet/Good Machine/ Miramax) chat about whether a "comfortable" new Subaru is a four-wheel-drive or an SUV, and the vehicle shows up in the next scene, all we can do is ask if somebody on the production made a deal.

And if a student hawking Kit Kat bars, shown in close-up, interrupts a ferocious scene between husband and wife, audiences can only wonder if it's paid advertising or a red herring.

But when star Sissy Spacek puffs the Marlboro brand on screen, and Miramax distributes a publicity still of her smoking, more serious questions arise.

▶ Did the gifted Sissy Spacek really need Marlboros to get into character as Ruth? As working-class Natalie, Marisa Tomei also smokes in one scene, but she's not required to endorse a brand.

▶ In "Killings," the taut 1970s short story that Todd Field expanded into this two-hour-plus feature film, author Andre Dubus noted Ruth smoking, but he saw no need to drop a brand name.

Sissy Spacek co-stars with a Marlboro in the critically-acclaimed "independent" film In the Bedroom. If we're supposed to ignore repeated brand references, why are they in the movie at all?

▶ A full generation later (the film is set in the late 1990s) the well-educated, upper-middle-class character played by Spacek would almost never smoke in reality. So much for naturalism.

▶ Smoldering, veiled, a Lady Macbeth filled with death wishes, whatever the writer-director had in mind, Spacek is much too skilled an artist to fall back on what Stella Adler called "cigarette acting."

Yet Ruth not only chain smokes, she broods over a Marlboro pack. In another crucial scene, she specifically asks a grocer for "Marlboro Lights."

Ruth's husband Matt (Tom Wilkinson), struggling to talk to Natalie, is interrupted once again—by a man off the street who demands a pack of "Marlboro Reds."

Is this sloppy writing, sophomoric symbolism, corruption or cluelessness?

Tobacco company files show they've offered hundreds of thousands of dollars to place their brands in movies and have long used stars to glamorize smoking.

Pressed by Congress, Big Tobacco said it halted Hollywood payola in 1989, yet on-screen smoking by lead actors has kept climbing. So long as no character sickens or dies from smoking, the giant tobacco companies don't care which characters smoke or what their "motivation" is. The marketing goal is simply to keep smoking visible.

Bottom line? *In the Bedroom* will dramatize smoking and glamorize the Marlboro brand by associating it with a star of Spacek's stature each time this "independent" labor of love hits a movie or video screen for decades to come.

With TV ads banned, Big Tobacco kills for this kind of promotional coup. The industry's 2001 death toll: 480,000 Americans, 4 million worldwide.

If filmmakers believe smoking is essential to tell a story, so be it. This isn't about censorship. But what a shame this otherwise admirable film poses moral questions it never intended. We urge U.S. filmmakers who portray smoking to:

1] ROLL ON-SCREEN CREDITS certifying that nobody on a production accepted *anything* of value from any tobacco company, its agents or fronts.

2] RUN STRONG ANTI-TOBACCO ADS IN FRONT OF SMOKING MOVIES. Put them on tapes and DVDs, too. Strong spots are proven to immunize audiences.

3] QUIT IDENTIFYING TOBACCO BRANDS in the background *or* in action. Brand names are unnecessary.

4] RATE EVERY SMOKING MOVIE "R." While this may identify smoking with maturity, it should give producers pause.

 SMOKE FREE MOVIES

Get the whole story at SmokeFreeMovies.ucsf.edu

Smoke Free Movies aims to sharply reduce the film industry's usefulness to Big Tobacco's domestic and global marketing — a leading cause of disability and premature death. This initiative by Stanton Glantz, PhD (coauthor of *The Cigarette Papers* and *Tobacco War*), of the UCSF School of Medicine is supported by the Robert Wood Johnson Foundation and the Richard and Rhoda Goldman Fund. To learn how you can help, visit our website or write to us: Smoke Free Movies, UCSF School of Medicine, Box 0150, San Francisco, CA 94143-0150.

3. Create a public service *radio* ad on any *one* of the following (be sure to include a brief statement explaining what you hope to achieve in your ad):

Alcoholism, domestic violence, drugs in schools, homophobia, animal rights, getting out the vote, eating a balanced diet, volunteering to tutor elementary school students, helping fight breast cancer, helping children learn to read, planting gardens to fight urban decay. (This means you only have to create a text—suggesting musical accompaniment is optional).

▦ The Question of Censorship

Advertising, like art, operates within a social context and has certain limits dictated by that social context. What is acceptable in television, film, and advertising changes with societal norms. Rear nudity (devoid of pubic hair) is acceptable in mass advertising, male frontal nudity is taboo. Female frontal nudity is occasionally acceptable (e.g., Reebok ad with nude woman presented in a cubist style). Showing before and after photographs of people getting liposuction is acceptable. Showing before and after photographs of people getting skin grafts for burns is unacceptable. Showing a picture of Rodney King being beaten by police officers was an acceptable ad for a TV news station. Showing the torture of an animal or a child would not be acceptable in any ad. Advertising has to steer within the boundaries of public taste and morality. Those boundaries are not fixed.

Some ads crossed the boundaries of public taste or caused controversy when they first came out. Some of the more infamous ones are: the ad for the Rolling Stones' album "Black and Blue All Over" (with photo of bruised-looking woman whose arms are tied over her head); Calvin Klein ads with anorexic models; the Benetton ads with political messages; the Nike ad showing runner Suzy Faber Hamilton, who must elude a chainsaw-wielding murderer by sprinting through the dark forest (though viewers can still run across the commercial, it was pulled from its high-profile Olympic slots). The latter wasn't the only problematic ad for Nike, as the following case study reveals.

CASE STUDY

The Nike "Air Dri-Goat" Ad Controversy

Some ads evoke more controversy than others. Some jolt us, some titillate us, some repel or disgust us, and some offend us. In the fall of 2000, a Nike ad elicited considerable *negative publicity. Read the background of the controversial Nike ad, along with the published response by the president of the Association of Disability Advocates.*

Answer the following:

1. Set out the key concerns raised by Frederick Shotz, president of Association of Disability Activists.
2. Do you think an e-mail and phone campaign directed at the corporation is an effective way to register concerns?
3. Share three alternative methods of raising concerns when advertising is perceived as harmful, hurtful, or socially irresponsible.
4. Share your response to Nike's public apology.

The Controversy

Background: The Air Dri-Goat ad contained a large photo of the Dri-Goat shoe against a red background and the following copy:

"Fortunately, the Air Dri-Goat features a patented goat-like outer sole for increased traction, so you can taunt mortal injury without actually experiencing it. Right about now you're probably asking yourself, "How can a trail running shoe with an outer sole designed like a goat's hoof help me avoid compressing my spinal cord into a Slinky™ on the side of some unsuspecting conifer, thereby rendering me a drooling, misshapen non-extreme-trail-running husk of my former self, forced to roam the earth in a motorized wheelchair with my name embossed on one of those cute little license plates you get at carnivals or state fairs, fastened to the back?"

To that we answer, hey, have you ever seen a mountain goat (even an extreme mountain goat) careen out of control into the side of a tree?

Didn't think so."

The ad ran in the fall of 2000 in the following national magazines: *Men's Fitness, Adventure Travel, Outside, Blue, National Geo Adventure, FHM, Stuff, Backpacker, Climbing,* and *Trailrunner.* In response to the protests Nike pulled the ad from 10 additional magazines in which this ad was supposed to run. Those publications included *Blue Ridge Outdoors, Sports Etc., Competitor, City Sports, City Sports NW, Metro Sports, Rocky Mtn Sports, Twin City Sports,* and *Windy City Sports.*

Nike Air Dri-Goat Ad: Call to Action

Frederick A. Shotz, President
Association of Disability Advocates

It's great that Nike has pulled the ad and written a brief apology. However that does not repair the damage done by this ad. Hundreds of thousands of people have seen this ad and many more will still see it before all of the copies of magazines carrying this ad end up in the trash. That means that hundreds of thousands of people will have been exposed to this offensive stereotype of people with disabilities who use wheelchairs. Every person who already carries negative stereotypes of people with disabilities and who sees this ad will have had that those negative beliefs reinforced and supported by the Nike ad. Picture the corporate human resources person who reads that ad on Sunday and then on Monday interviews a person using a wheelchair for employment. Will the ad color the perception of the applicant for employment? Will the ad decrease the chance of that person being offered the job? You bet!

The ADA was written and passed because people with disabilities face discrimination in this country. The ADA was not written to provide business to builders of ramps or to lawyers. The ADA was passed because of the negative and discriminatory attitudes held by the general public towards people with disabilities. When the Civil Rights Act of 1964 was passed one hope was that the law would, over time, help people to change their negative and discriminatory attitudes towards people of color. That same hope is embodied in the intent of the ADA. By people with disabilities having the opportunity to participate in all levels of society, over time, the negative and discriminatory attitudes of much of the general public will change.

I know of no research that can tell us how much attitudes towards people with disabilities have changed in the 10 years since the passage of the ADA. A few polls that have been conducted seem to suggest that we are making some progress. Thirty six years after the passage of the Civil Rights Act of 1964 there is still a great deal of work to be done in changing negative attitudes towards people of color. One of the focuses of groups such as the NAACP has been to have the negative stereotypes of people of color removed from entertainment and advertising. That focus is due to their conclusion that such stereotypes in entertainment and advertising perpetuate the negative attitudes towards people of color.

I believe that this Nike ad can undo any positive changes in the attitudes of people towards people with disabilities in those people exposed to this ad. The focus of this advertising campaign is the sports oriented segment of society including the "jocks" of our society. Efforts of the last 10 years to change the negative attitudes of this population group will easily be undone by this ad, which plays right into the attitudes towards people with disabilities in this group. Picture an ad that painted people of color as lazy, shiftless, and of criminal intent. Now picture that ad being focused on the segment of society most likely to have held that attitude in the past. Is there any question that many of those people would return to their prior attitudes with that kind of support of their prejudicial attitudes?

It is going to take far more than a short apology and an appearance on a disability oriented radio show (a show that is listened to by people with disabilities but not by the general public) to undo this damage. It is going to take an advertising campaign as large as this advertising campaign was supposed to be to repair this damage. My proposal is that the advertising agency that created this advertisement provide people with disabilities with an advertising campaign that presents a pro disability posture and a pro ADA posture. This work should be done for free as an apology to people with disabilities. The advertising developed by this ad agency should be as sophisticated as the ads they develop for Nike.

The next part of my proposal is that Nike pay for the placement of these ads in national magazines that have circulations equivalent to the circulations of the magazines in which the offensive ad has run. The pro disability, pro ADA ads should be placed in the number of magazines and for the number of issues that equals the run of this offensive ad. So, if the offensive Nike ad ran in 5 magazines for 3 months, 2 magazines for 2 months and 3 magazines for 1 month, and all magazines had circulation of 100,000 then Nike would run the pro disability, pro ADA ads a total of 22 times in magazines with average circulation of 100,000. Keep in mind that this is just an example, the number of runs of this offensive ad is not yet known nor is the circulation of the magazines in which it ran. Such an advertising campaign would equal the cost to Nike of running the offensive ad campaign. If we pick the publications to focus on populations likely to change their attitudes by exposure to these ads we can balance those with reinforced negative attitudes with people who have increasing positive attitudes.

The last part of my proposal is based on an idea first presented by Marcie Roth of the National Council on Independent Living. Marcie suggested a substantial donation to the Spinal Cord Injury Network. Considering that this offensive advertisement targeted people with spinal cord injuries I believe that Marcie's idea is excellent. Since Nike has withdrawn this offensive ad from 10 magazines for no less than one month in each magazine Nike has saved somewhere in the area of $250,000 based on an average cost of $25,000 per magazine per month. Since Nike was planning to spend this money promoting negative attitudes towards people with disabilities it seems only fair that they contribute this money to an organization that supports the people attacked in this offensive advertisement. . . . Whatever amount Nike spent and planned to spend on an advertisement that was degrading to people with disabilities and that supported negative stereotyping is the amount that Nike should commit to helping to improve attitudes towards people with disabilities and towards a substantial financial apology to people with spinal cord injuries.

If you agree with my position on this issue and if you believe that my proposal is reasonable then your support is needed. Nike needs to hear from hundreds if not thousands of us. Each one of us needs to tell Nike that we want them to pay for a pro disability advertising campaign equal to the anti disability campaign that they ran. Each one of us need to tell Nike that they need to apologize to people with spinal cord injuries by making a substantial donation to the Spinal Cord Injury Network. . . .

We must let Nike know that they cannot damage our progress in changing attitudes towards people with disabilities and then simply say I'm sorry and walk away from the damage they have caused.

Reprinted with permission of Frederick A. Shotz, President, Association of Disability Advocates

In all fairness, Nike did respond to the public outcry and issued a public apology:

Nike's Apology for the Air Dri-Goat Ad

Purely and simply, we made a mistake.

That ad should never have been approved, much less written, and we are examining our internal approval system to make sure such a mistake does not happen again. We offer a sincere apology to anyone who was offended by that ad and we have immediately pulled it from all publications that have not already gone to print.

We also are submitting apologetic letters to the editor to these same magazines. We are discussing both internally and with external advocacy groups some possible additional measures we can take to attempt to right this wrong.

As a company that has long honored and celebrated the athletic goals of people of all levels of ability, we are extremely distressed that this ad contradicts the spirit of the philosophy of our late co-founder, legendary track coach Bill Bowerman, who said, "If you have a body, you are an athlete."

It's also a contradiction of Nike's strong record on employing people with different abilities, which has included athletes as diverse as Casey Martin, Ric Munoz and others in our advertising. (Nike also outfitted the 2000 Australian Paralympic Team and provided uniforms to the US and Kenyan Paralympic Teams.)

We realize that regaining someone's trust is an often lengthy and sometimes impossible task, but hope you will allow us to make that attempt. Down to a man and woman, every Nike employee is personally embarrassed by this ad and we vow to learn from this mistake and grow both personally and professionally. Our internal Nike Employee Network for the Disabled also is providing important guidance.

For more information about Nike and our dedication to corporate responsibility we invite you to visit that area on *nikebiz.com*.

Source: www.nikebiz.com/media/n_drigoat .shtml

Analyzing Ideological Frameworks

The Caputi Technique: Charting the Flow

Jane Caputi, scholar of popular culture and women's studies, has developed a method of evaluating ideological frameworks. This technique requires that we study *both* the text and the ads that accompany (or surround) the text. For example, she recommends that we not just study the ads placed in a TV show such as *Everybody Loves Raymond* or *Friends* or *Saturday Night Live*. Instead study the combination of the ads and the show together. When we "chart the flow," we are mapping that juxtaposition of advertising images/message and the images/program/message of the TV show itself. How they work together, in sync, is, in Caputi's view, a window for viewing our societal attitudes, prejudices, fears, desires, and values.

This technique can be applied wherever ads appear in combination with a text, including magazine covers. For example, a *New York Times Magazine* cover for January 14, 1996 has photographs and descriptions of Tupac Shakur ("Rap star, convicted felon"), Suge Knight ("CEO Death Row Records), and Snoop Doggy Dogg ("Rap star, on trial"). Tupac Shakur is holding a large stack of money (bills). To the left is written: "It's 10 P.M. Do you know whose music your children are listening to? The godfather of gangsta rap, and his family values. By Lynn Hirschberg." Across the top is written *"The New York Times Magazine"* and above that, extending across the very top is written "The Triumph of Liberalism (No Kidding) by Roger Rosenblatt."

If we charted the flow of this magazine cover, we would have in mind the three figures—two rap stars and a CEO of rap records—along with the burning question about what are children are listening to, and (above it all) the statement on the triumph of liberalism. All this swirls together in our brain creating, according to Caputi, one impression. It is the way in which the juxtaposition of text, images, and advertising works together that concerns her.

Exercise

Read the following edited version of her article, "Charting the Flow." Then check this technique out for yourself: Get some magazine covers and/or study a TV show to determine if the ads work in conjunction—alongside—the "text" to create an overall impression, implicitly creating a message for the audience. If so, ask yourself what message that is and whether it has political/ideological elements to it.

Charting the Flow:
The Construction of Meaning through Juxtaposition in Media Texts

Jane Caputi, Ph.D.
Florida South Atlantic University

Contradictions between juxtaposed segments of television flow are not necessarily systematic in the sense of being willfully or consciously planned by programmers or sponsors (though on occasion one suspects conscious planning). However, they occur regularly, if individually, throughout the course of television programming. Almost everyone can cite particularly striking examples. (See Mimi White, "Ideological Analysis and Television," in Channels of discourse: Television and Contemporary Criticism," Robert C. Allen, ed.)

For instance, an interview, telecast in New York City, March 26, 1983, with a Black South African pastor who had been tortured three times by his own government, appealing for heightened American awareness of the international business props of the apartheid system, was interrupted by a "diamonds are forever" commercial from the South Africa deBeers Company. (See Farrel Corcoran, "Television as Ideological Apparatus: The Power and the Pleasure," in Television: The Critical View, *4th ed. Horace Newcomb, ed.)*

In its January 21, 1989 issue, *TV Guide* chided ABC for inattention: . . . On the season opener of ABC's *thirtysomething* there was a graphic fantasy scene in which a woman suffered a miscarriage. This was followed shortly thereafter by a commercial for an early pregnancy test. What *TV Guide* neglects to mention, however is that this episode of *thirtysomething* focused upon a character who was trying to develop her career as a journalist and therefore initially resisted her husband's pleadings for another baby. After the fantasy miscarriage scene, she changed her mind and took on her husband's desire as her own. The episode ends with marital lovemaking in hopes of conception. Despite *TV Guide*'s charge of impropriety, the pregnancy test ad that followed the miscarriage scene can be read as all too appropriate to the episode's sexist advocacy of childbearing and traditional nuclear family structure over the pursuit of a career. Rather than assume that the commercial was thus placed due to network inattention, we might entertain the possibility that the exact inverse was true.

In his influential study, "Television: Technology and Cultural Form," Raymond Williams describes the central television experience to be that of "flow"—that is, TV programs are surrounded by commercials and other audiovisual material (ads, trailers, etc.) which comprise an uninterrupted following of one thing by another (see *Television: Technology and Cultural Form*). Richard Adler [says]: "One result of this flow is a powerful tendency to blur the contents together, a result to some degree encouraged by programmer so that one program leads effortlessly into the next. . . . The goal of the programmer, of course, is to persuade us to stay tuned in for as long as possible" ("Introduction: A Context for Criticism," in *Television as a Cultural Force*, Richard Adler and Douglas Cater, eds.).

Yet flow simultaneously plays a more abstract and ideological function. As Williams contends, flow itself "established a sense of world" and reveals the "flow of meanings and values of a specific culture" (see *Television: Technology and Cultural Form*). Flow, moreover, can function to *construct* meaning through the juxtaposition of significant elements. . . . Williams writes that editing "is not only a matter of excision and selection. New positive relations of a signifying kind be made by the process of arrangement and juxtaposition" (see "Means of communication as Means of Production," in *Problems in Materialism and Culture Selected Essays*). Since Williams, many television analysts have incorporated some notion flow into their approach (see Gregory Waller, "Flow, Genre, and the Television Text," *Journal of Popular Film and Television*, Vol. 16. Spring, 1988). For example, Newcomb and Hirsch suggest that the most valid television text for study is not an individual episode, series, or genre, but

rather, they term the viewing strip—
"any given evening's televiewing" (see
"Television as a Cultural Forum," in
Television: the Critical View, 4th ed.,
Horace Newcomb, ed.). Budd, Craig
and Steinman take a different approach
and look at the flow pattern in one episode of "Fantasy Island," finding a
definite association between themes
and images of the narratives and those
of the commercials (e.g., one part of
the story stresses a mother's concern
for a child's happiness, soon followed
by a commercial for cereal which
makes children happy). Despite finding
strong associations throughout the
hour, these authors believe the connections to be unplanned, though reflective of the exigencies of commercial
television:

Ads become an inseparable part of the
repetitive flow of lack, enticement, and
pseudo-satisfaction. No conspiracy of conscious hidden manipulation by the network is necessary. The flow is possible because of the iconography of television . . .
its converging patterns of narration in programs and commercials. (See Mike Budd,
Steve Craig, and Clay Steinman, "Fantasy
Island: Marketplace of Desire," *Journal of
Communication*, Vol. 33, Winter 1983)

In other words, television stories are
based in dominant cultural values as
are the commercials themselves. As
such, they are linked ineluctably by
this shared worldview and will naturally complement and reinforce one
another. . . . Sometimes the juxtapositions are so well matched or so ideologically packed that, as with White, I
suspect programmer awareness of the
technique and conscious planning. . . .
Investigations could determine more

about various ways that messages can
be constructed via intertextuality
(theme, image, word, and sound), how
viewers actually receive and interpret
them, how conscious this stratagem is
in minds of both programmers and
viewers, how common the phenomenon is, and if it occurs more or less frequently in different sorts of presentation (e.g., the nightly news as opposed
to a sitcom, prime time or daytime).

To this end, I will cite several particular striking examples . . . For my
purpose, we might think of these types
of juxtapositions as "meaning strips,"
those moments in which the contiguity
of two or more disparate segments
works to create a new meaning. I have
chosen these particular examples for
two reasons. First of all, they address
issues of great social concern: electoral
politics, violence against women,
racism, and environmental practice.
Secondly, they illustrate diverse ways
that flow meaning can be constructed.

For example, the juxtaposed segments work together: 1) to emphasize
a political meaning of the primary
text; 2) to undercut, defuse, or mock a
political meaning of the primary text;
or 3) to create an explicit political
significance which otherwise would be
absent from any of segments taken
singly. . . . [T]hese principles also are
relevant to the progression of materials in magazine and newspaper presentations; thus I will extend my discussion of "meaning strips" to these as
well. Tony Schwartz one of the most
influential practitioners and theorists
of advertising, writes:

The critical task is to design our package of
stimuli so that it resonates with information already stored within an individual

and thereby induces the desired learning or behavioral effect. . . . The listener's or viewer's brain is an indispensable component of the total communication system. . . . In communicating at electronic speed, we no longer direct information into an audience, but try to evoke stored information out of them, in a patterned way. (See Tony Schwartz, *The Responsive Chord*)

Schwartz is referring to the resonance inducing stimuli contained in an individual commercial (e.g., an ad for Marlboro cigarettes that shows only a smoking cowboy, leaving it to the viewer to fill in the cigarette brand name). . . . Frankly, one could argue that a political message is most effective in this symbolic and intricately patterned form because it operates subliminally, in the realm of partial recall. . . .

The March 27, 1989 cover of *Newsweek* magazine shows a grocery bag filled with delicious foods, yet the bag is labeled "DANGER." That graphics announces an inside story, "How Safe Is Your Food?" The table of contents, on the right-hand side of a two-page spread, describes the recent events which inspired that cover story: "Terrorist threats to Chilean fruit followed hard on worries about pesticides-ridden apples and potentially contaminated corn . . ." Directly to the left of this statement, is a full-page ad for ICI, the "fourth-largest chemical company in the world." At the top, there is a picture of the Earth in space with the letters ICI written onto its face and underlined twice. Beneath it the copy reads: "Discover who we are,

and you will think the world of us." AN extensive summary of the corporation's diverse activities follow, as ICI details the various ways that it 'make[s] the world a little safer . . . healthier . . . durable . . . beautiful . . . efficient." The last section, recounting ICI's avowed efficiency reads in part: "We have the fastest-growing agrochemical business in the United States. Worldwide, we are the third-largest producer of crop-protection chemicals and the fourth-largest agricultural products company in the U.S."

Once again, we are confronted with what Corcoran calls the "uninterrupted processing of the inevitable social paradoxes," this time, however, not through television, but magazine flow. (See Farrel Corcoran, "Television as Ideological Apparatus: The Power and the Pleasure," in *Television: The Critical View,* 4th ed., Horace Newcomb, ed.) On the one hand, the right, fears are raised about chemical contamination of food through the normal use of pesticides. On the other, the left, a multinational corporation applauds itself for its role in the production of those very pesticides. A juxtaposition such as this arguably works to manage and defuse legitimate anger over food contamination through its evocation of the familiar myth of technological efficacy and supremacy. . . . Cultural analysts can use flow as an avenue to explore the parameters of contemporary ideologies.

Reprinted with the permission of Jane Caputi.

CHAPTER NINE

Voices of the Community: The News Media

It's immaterial. You're dealing with different times. We hold our public leaders much more accountable for their personal lives and actions than they did then.
—DAVID ROBB, spokesperson for the drug enforcement chief, commenting on the fact that President George Washington grew marijuana, as noted by the *Los Angeles Daily Journal*

In one of the great existential comedies, *Groundhog Day,* a news anchor is locked in a time warp—a real-life Mobius strip—where he must relive the same day, Groundhog Day, over and over again. He comes to realize that, if nothing else can change, he can change himself. And so dawns his awareness that he, Phil Connors, is free to make something of his life. We watch his transformation from sarcastic and self-obsessed to a person who is compassionate, generous, and thoughtful.

As Phil changes, his approach to the news does as well. And what at the outset was seen as the tedious job of a weather report centered on a "rat" (groundhog) is thereby transformed. As Phil starts to identify with the townspeople, his perception of the community tradition has much greater significance than mere filler on the nightly news. Once Phil becomes a participant, rather than a disinterested observer, he changes and his work as a news anchor changes as well.

Journalists form an important antidote to social chaos by reporting and analyzing newsworthy material and placing it in a social and political context. This is a vital role to play in our society. As journalist Frank Rich says, "A public estranged from the press is also disengaged from the institutions and newsmakers that journalists cover—and will understandably look outside the system for both information and leadership."

Thanks to newspapers, electronic access to information, libraries, and bookstores, we can stay informed about what's going on locally, nationally, and globally. The very fact, for instance, that we can experience world events via live coverage shows us how powerful the news media can be.

This power is not exercised in a vacuum, however. Sometimes governments seek to limit the power of the press. Coverage of wars and political conflicts tend to be restricted because of government controls in the name of national security. We cannot take the media for granted. We need to look at their role in bringing events into the public consciousness and in providing vital information and commentary for sustaining a free press.

News Coverage and Power

Being able to freely inquire into events, express concerns, and raise questions is liberating. If the media uses its power wisely, institutions can change—and even crumble. By covering political corruption or digging out newsworthy items that may have gotten buried in an informational glut, journalists do us all a great service.

The media subverts its own power, however, when it succumbs to corporate interests or political double-dealing. For example, in the 2000 U.S. presidential election, news stations were calling the election in some states where the count was too close to call. Such tactics are ethically unsound, because they may drive voters away from the polls and taint the political process. Furthermore, news anchors and journalists risk compromising their own role as observer and watchdog. As a result, we cannot blithely assume that all the news that's fit to print will actually reach us.

Tabloid-Style Journalism

Of course you aren't one of those people who pick up the *National Enquirer* of another tabloid and flip through it as you stand in line waiting to buy your groceries. You probably missed the latest on the Bat Boy ("Batboy Nearly Killed in Serious Accident! Breaks both Legs and Sprayed with Pesticides!!!"). And you weren't privy to the top stories in the *Weekly World News*, like:

$2 BILLION IN NAZI GOLD IS BURIED IN WYOMING!
NEW WAVE OF DEMONS RUNNING WILD IN AMERICA!!
YOU CAN BE ABDUCTED BY SPACE ALIENS ANYTIME YOU LIKE!
WHAT DO 90 OF THE CLINTON'S FRIENDS HAVE IN COMMON? THEY'RE ALL
  DEAD!
LET'S PUT A McDONALD'S IN EVERY CHURCH!
KAMIKAZE UFO ON COLLISION COURSE WITH EARTH!
YOU AND YOUR LOVED ONES CAN SURVIVE EBOLA . . . HERE'S HOW!
DEAR DOTTE: HOT-TUB HONEYS ARE STEAMING MY GLASSES!

Let's not fool ourselves, though. Periodically mainstream ("legitimate") news media have been known to succumb to tabloid-style journalism. In July 2001, for instance, the *Los Angeles Times* had a front-page story on male porn stars who use the male impotence drug Viagra to be "more effective" in their "work." Subsequent letters from readers expressed disgust that this article was given front-page status, instead of more significant issues.

Then there was the article, complete with photograph, of the attractive blonde woman on the front page of *The New York Times* detailing the saga of "the girl from Ipanema." We learn that the now 57-year-old Heloisa Penheiro is fighting to keep the name of her Girl From Ipanema boutique. We also learn that, just as in the song lyrics, it is still the case that when she walks "each one she passed went *ah*" (See Larry Rohter, "Still Tall and Tan, a Muse Fights for a Title," *The New York Times*, 11 Aug. 2001). Be on the watch for such "tabloidism." However entertaining tabloid-type articles may be, the time devoted to the sensational or titillating is time lost on other, potentially much more significant, issues.

Group Exercise

Read the following excerpt about a mystery man–like creature called "Big Foot," and then answer the questions below:

Stories have always been told about things that happened along old Mill Creek Road, the trail of bumps and switchbacks that winds up from the farms of southeastern Washington to the hushed and empty ranges of the Blue Mountains.

The large human-like footprints found along the creek. The sounds heard late at night outside the lonely cabins on the upper end of the road. The man who was riding his motorcycle and saw something in the brush, 10 or 12 feet tall, making a weird, high-pitched scream.

As far back as the 1920s, there were reports of a family of huge "man-creatures" skulking up near homesteads along the nearby Copper River. Six dairy cows were said to have been herded away by the beasts. One by one, the homesteaders left and moved back to town. But the stories persisted. As long as anyone remembers, it has been an item of belief for many here that Bigfoot walks the Blue Mountains.

"Up north here, we growed up with this thing. People would say, 'Look out for the wild man.' Man, how can you doubt it when you still got diapers on and they got a picture of you pointing at a Bigfoot track?" said Wes Sumerlin, a Walla Walla mountain man whose alleged sighting of two ape-like creatures about seven miles off Mill Creek Road last summer has led to hopes of the first scientific evidence of the legend.

Sumerlin and two colleagues came back with clumps of hair that Ohio State University researchers are testing for DNA comparisons. "The tests," said Oregon primate zoologist H. Henner Fahrenbach, "could legitimize, to my mind at least, the sightings, the footprints, everything. It would put one item of concrete evidence behind all the circumstantial evidence." (See Kim Murphy, "Science Is Hot on Heels of Bigfoot Legend," *Los Angeles Times*, 21 Jan. 1996)

Answer the following:

1. Why did this article rate the front page? Offer several hypotheses.
2. What did you learn about Bigfoot from this excerpt?
3. What did you learn about scientific knowledge of Bigfoot from this excerpt?
4. Who is the likely intended audience for this article? Explain.
5. What more do you need to know about Bigfoot to conclude it actually exists or once existed?

Exercises

1. Do a study of the ways in which one of your local TV stations covers *one* of the following. Note how the coverage of the topic reflects on our society. Select one:
   - Crime stories.
   - Human interest stories (ordinary people).
   - Treatment and coverage of celebrities.
   - National news.
   - International news.
2. Find an example of the news media at its *best,* showing how the press presents an issue in a fair and balanced manner or uses investigative journalism to unveil hypocrisy or corruption.
3. Find an example of the news media at its *worst,* showing how the press fails to give a well-rounded account of an event or forsakes professional integrity for shallow entertainment value.
4. Do a study of a newspaper or news station over two to three days and see if you can find any instances of *tabloidism.* That is, determine if any sensational or celebrity-driven news or non-news is given attention to the detriment of more pressing stories.

Serving the Community

Newspapers have the means to help a community function better for its members, for example, by acting as a networking center or a resource for helpful information.

Some newspapers or news programs have a section or columns devoted to voices from the community. Some have individual columnists or commentaries offering a range of points of view (e.g., liberal, conservative, etc.). By seeing the different ways events can be interpreted, we can sense how policies and decision-making may impact a particular community. This public service aspect of the newspaper helps remove barriers and build connections.

After the terrorist attacks on the World Trade Center and the Pentagon, the news media performed a vital function of providing information, helpful phone numbers, contacts for resources, community links for financial and other contributions to help victims, and so on. And as the days wore on and widespread despair and anxiety was evident, the news media listed reference numbers for counseling and printed articles on how to deal with stress. A number of steps were also taken to try to avert racial and ethnic attacks on and harassment of innocent people who "looked" Muslim or Middle Eastern.

Group Exercise

Each group should answer the following:

1. List 10 functions or types of coverage of news media (e.g., sports, weather reports).
2. Then list five to six ways to expand the role of the news media (e.g., include vacation tips for travelers or areas of the city to avoid after dark).
3. Try to come up with ideas for expanding or improving news coverage to better serve the community.

Watchdog Role of the Media

By turning its spotlight on an event, public figure, political issue, societal problem, or moral controversy, the press can relay relevant details and information to help us draw inferences as to what direction or policy would be preferable. This power of the press is not to be underestimated.

One important function of a newspaper is to serve as a watchdog over the institutions in the society. For instance, it was due to the careful work of Carl Bernstein and Bob Woodward of *The Washington Post* that the Watergate story broke when it did—an event that precipitated Richard Nixon's resignation as president. The news media also played an instrumental role in keeping questions about President Clinton's use of the presidential pardon before the public eye. Disclosing the questionable efforts to obtain pardons and the deal cutting that appeared to be involved resulted in a more negative assessment of Clinton's ethics and may taint his presidency.

Investigative journalists are often in the position of watchdogs. In the Spring of 2002, the news media tracked the Enron scandal, exposing corruption and mismanagement. They also brought to light governmental missteps regarding early warnings about the 9-11 terrorist attacks.

Journalist-watchdogs also examine events of the past. For example, the investigative work in the 80s and 90s of Eileen Welsome of the *Albuquerque Tribune* resulted in a Pulitzer prize for Welsome. Because of her dedicated research, she exposed to the public the radiation experiments that were conducted on American citizens by government scientists and doctors. This series of articles describing these experiments jolted the public into action. One consequence is that the federal government appointed a bioethics committee to study the experiments. The fact the experiments were so heinous led President Clinton to issue an apology to the research subjects.

You can go to the Pulitzer Prize website at *www.pulitzer.org* to read about other recipients of the prizes (journalism is just one category). Through this Internet site, you can also access the prize-winning articles so you can read them yourself.

Exercise

Directions: Set out the issues and concerns about the coverage of human radiation experiments, as raised by the following:

If you have any lingering thoughts that the government's failure to disclose radiation experimentation on humans was driven by misguided national security concerns, throw them in the nearest nuclear waste dump. At least some officials knew what they were doing was unconscionable and were ducking the consequences and covering their tails. A recently leaked Atomic Energy Commission (AEC) document lays out in the most bare-knuckled manner the policy of cover-up.

"It is desired that no document be released which refers to experiments with humans and might have adverse effect on public opinion or result in legal suits. Documents covering such work [in this] field should be classified 'secret,'" wrote Colonel O.G. Haywood of the AEC. This letter confirms a policy of complete secrecy where human radiation experiments were concerned.

The Haywood letter may help explain a recently discovered 1953 Pentagon document, declassified in 1975. The two-page order from the secretary of defense ostensibly brought U.S. guidelines for human experimentation in line with the Nuremberg Code [that set out guidelines for the protection of human subjects], making adherence to a universal standard official U.S. policy. Ironically, however, the Pentagon document was classified and thus was probably not seen by many military researchers until its declassification in 1975.

As these and a steady stream of similar reports confirm, for decades, the U.S. government had not only used human guinea pigs in radiation experiments, but had also followed a policy of deliberate deception and cover up of its misuse of both civilians and military personnel in nuclear weapons development and radiation research. (See Tod Ensign and Glenn Alcalay, "Duck and Cover (Up): U.S. Radiation Testing on Humans," *www.ishgooda.nativeweb.org*)

▥ Professional Standards

People tend to trust newspapers. Even when the news media falls short of our expectations or there are times we are critical of journalists, we generally approach newspapers as a source of truth, a repository of facts.

Occasionally those in the news media act impulsively, setting in motion rumors or unsupported claims that later require damage control. We see this when there is a misrepresentation of the facts, or a hasty conclusion drawn on the part of the journalist. For example, right after the Oklahoma City bombing, journalists printed speculation that the bombing was an Islamic terrorist attack. Here are some examples:

- "The betting here is on Middle East terrorists," declared CBS News' Jim Stewart just hours after the blast (19 Apr. 1995).
- "The fact that it was such a powerful bomb in Oklahoma City immediately drew investigators to consider deadly parallels that all have roots in the Middle East," ABC's John McWethy proclaimed the same day.
- "It has every single earmark of the Islamic car-bombers of the Middle East," wrote syndicated columnist Georgie Anne Geyer (*Chicago Tribune*, 21 Apr. 1995).
- "Whatever we are doing to destroy Mideast terrorism, the chief terrorist threat against Americans, has not been working," declared *The New York Times'* A. M. Rosenthal (21 Apr. 1995).
- "The Geyer and Rosenthal columns were filed after the FBI released sketches of two suspects who looked more like Midwestern frat boys than mujahideen." (Jim Naureckas, "The Oklahoma City Bombing: The Jihad That Wasn't," *EXTRA!*, 8 July 1995)
- "Both *The Dallas Morning News* and the *Fort Lauderdale News-Sun Sentinel* report today that the FBI and CIA have believed for months that Middle East radicals were plotting a terror onslaught aimed at the United States. The *News* said an internal FBI communique on Wednesday mentions theories that the Branch Davidians or the Nation of Islam might be involved—but concludes that 'we are currently inclined to suspect the Islamic Jihad,' a terrorist group with ties to Iran, 'as the likely group'" ("Terror in the Heartland: Who did it?" *The Atlanta Constitution*, 20 Apr. 1995)

Such claims were later retracted, when Timothy McVeigh and Terry Nichols were arrested. All those responsible for their racist conjectures were left with egg on their faces. As Ibrahim Hooper of the Council on American Islamic Relations said, "The reaction was so immediate and so harsh that when it turned around so quickly this country was slapped in the face with its own prejudice. It was so swift and so sharp it forced people to recognize their own stereotypes and their own bigotry. And that recognition is the first step toward change" (See Charles Sennott, "A New Cold War/Islam and the West," *Boston Globe*, 21 June 1995.)

After the terrorist attacks on the World Trade Center and the Pentagon, the news media was much more careful in speculating about the perpetrators. Furthermore, as information started coming out about suspected links to Islamic terrorists associated with Osama bin Laden, most news stations and newspapers were careful to warn people not to overreact and took steps to separate these acts from the members of the Muslim community who, for the most part, were quick to condemn the violence. These steps helped minimize harassment and violence against Muslims and people who appeared to be Middle Eastern living in the United States.

The press is obviously not above reproach. Part of the value of critical thinking skills is learning not to take things at face value. We need to have our antennae out. Even though we are the audience, we can still act as watchdogs to make sure those in the news media hold themselves to high standards. Assume, also, that there's a social conscience in the news media and audience response can make a difference. As an empowered audience, we have a role in helping sustain such professional ethics.

Exercise

Read the following from a report on race and the media and then answer the questions below:

Race and the Media

Berkeley Media Studies Group Report

Three quarters (76%) of the public say they form their opinions about crime from what they see or read in the news, more than three times the number who state that they get their primary information on crime from personal experience (22%). In a *Los Angeles Times* poll, 80% of respondents stated that the media's coverage of violent crime had increased their personal fear of being a victim. . . .

These survey results are consistent with communications research finding that the news media largely determine what issues we collectively think about, how we think about them, and what kinds of policy alternatives are considered viable. . . .

Most people have little or no personal experience with juvenile crime because adults commit most of the crime in the nation: about 89% of all crimes cleared by arrest are committed by adults.

The public depends on the media even more for its pictures of crime done by or to minority youth, because most of the public has no direct personal experience with crime by minority youth.

Eighty-six percent of White homicide victims are killed by other Whites, and overall, Whites are three times as likely to be victimized by other Whites as by minorities. The chances that a White adult will be the victim of a crime by a Black youth are quite small. . . .

Overall, the studies taken together indicate that depictions of crime in the news are not reflective of either the rate of crime generally, the proportion of crime which is violent, the proportion of crime committed by people of color, or the proportion of crime committed by youth.

The problem is not the inaccuracy of individual stories, but that the cumulative choices of what is included—or not included—in the news presents the public with a false picture of higher frequency and severity of crime than is actually the case. . . .

Professor Robert Entman documents that Blacks are most likely to be seen in television news stories in the role of criminal, victim, or demanding politician. Black suspects were less likely to be identified by name as were White suspects; were not as well dressed as White suspects on the news; and were more likely to be shown physically restrained than Whites.

In sum, Black suspects were routinely depicted as being poor, dangerous, and indistinct from other non-criminal Blacks."

Source: "Off Balance: Youth, Race, and Crime in the News," Berkeley Media Studies Group, *April 2001. Reprinted with the permission of Liz Ryan, Building Blocks for Youth Initiative.*

Answer the following:
1. What issues and concerns does this report convey?
2. What would you recommend to address the imbalance demonstrated by this study?

Presenting News in an Ethical Manner

We must guard against complacency. Our expectations of honesty provide a moral framework in which societal institutions operate. For newspapers to be a legitimate source of information, they must adhere to fundamental values around integrity.

If you pick up the newspaper and suspect deception, you'd rightly question the value of bothering to read it, other than to be entertained by the stories. Whatever benefit this may have for your leisure time, the traditional value of the newspaper to report on current events would be radically altered. Similarly, if you heard about deception on the part of the government, you'd want to know the details. In their role as watchdog, the media has a responsibility to reveal such deception and investigate it further when such issues are leaked to the press.

Exercises

Read the excerpt from "FBI Admits Photos of Idaho Shootout Scene Were Staged," below, and then answer the questions that follow:

> Two FBI agents testified at the murder–conspiracy trial of white separatists Randy Weaver and Kevin Harris that investigators did not tell defense lawyers that some evidence from the area where a U.S. marshal was killed had been taken away, then returned and photographed. Agent Greg Rampton said he did not disclose that the photographs of a bullet and other unspecified evidence were staged, even when he testified earlier this month. (*The New York Times*, 28 May 1993)

Answer the following:

1. What is implied in the quote, above, about the FBI handling of the case against white supremacist, Randy Weaver?

2. State the pros and cons of the news media exposing the government's use of lies and deception in order to achieve good overall consequences.

CASE STUDY

Is It Comical?

Rabbi C. Michelle Greenberg
Temple Sinai, Denver, April 2001

The Controversial Cartoon Strip
Easter of 2001 was eventful for reasons that went beyond the holiday itself. A controversy erupted around whether or not a comic strip was sufficiently offensive as to warrant being censored. The case centered on Johnny Hart's cartoon "B.C." The one that touched a raw nerve showed the Jewish Menorah slowly burning away to reveal a cross.

One of the many responses to this cartoon was a sermon by Rabbi C. Michelle Greenberg, who was not amused by the cartoon and expressed conerns about what she interpreted as anti-Semitism. Her sermon, as you will see, raises questions about cartoonist Hart's agenda and values. Read what Rabbi Greenberg has to say and then answer the questions that follow. (Note that you can see the cartoon at www.hollywoodjesus.com.)

Easter was a little different this year. Usually I forget entirely about it except for the occasional bunny on TV or the local kids rushing to find Easter Eggs. Perhaps CNN does a special on the Vatican and the *Wizard of Oz* always runs over and over this time of year. But this past Sunday, as I read the comics, I found a cartoon that evoked the feelings of a different age.

The Johnny Hart cartoon, B.C., has always been a favorite of mine. I look forward to his twisted definitions and the struggles of an oppressed. But this week there was a seven-armed candelabrum—a menorah as we were told to build it in Torah. The first image is a lit Menorah. In each successive bar, a light is extinguished while the captions quote the final words of Jesus on the cross. The three arms on either side of the candelabra disappear and we see a cross embedded in our Menorah. The final image shows blood dripping from the Menorah/Cross to the door of a home.

Quite a cartoon. Not very funny.

It reminds me of the propaganda of anti-Semitic regimes. Of Nazi Germany, of 15th century Italy, of Crusade era England. It looks like the literature that the KKK hands out. A most holy symbol of Judaism—a symbol older than the Star of David—was turned into a cross on the comic strip page.

The cartoonist, Johnny Hart, argues that it is not at all intended as anti-Jewish in any way. Nor is this cartoon meant to subvert the Menorah into a Christian symbol. Rather, Hart maintains, "I noticed one day that the center section of the Menorah—the sacred symbol of Judaism, bore the shape of the cross. I wanted everyone to see the cross in the Menorah. It was a revelation to me, that tied God's chosen people to their spiritual next of kin-the disciples of the Risen Christ."

The arguments in the newspapers, between politicians and among the clergy seem to fall into a few different categories: the right of free speech and the opposition to censorship, the impact on Jewish/Christian relations and whether the Jewish symbol has been subverted in an anti-Semitic manner.

I am not concerned about the issues of free speech here. Clearly individual news organizations made choices whether or not to print the comic and most ran columns discussing the impact of Hart's views within that genre. I am opposed to censorship by government organizations. I am not opposed to self-censorship. Hart was asked to cancel this comic because it is easily construed as anti-Semitic and hurtful to many people, Jews and non-Jews alike. That he chose to run the cartoon has nothing to do with censorship, rather it has everything to do with the cartoonist's beliefs and agenda.

Interestingly, many Christian clergy have condemned the cartoon for a number of reasons. It does not accurately depict the last words of Je-

sus. It is a simplification of holy ritual held on Good Friday night during which candles are extinguished one at a time during a hymn. It implies that Christianity exists only because of Judaism. It leads readers to believe that anti-Semitism is common and acceptable.

What concerns me most of all is the cavalier manner by which a Jewish symbol was used to evoke the image of Jesus. The Menorah is replaced by a cross. At any time this is insulting and denigrating. At Easter it is particularly wrong. During this Christian Holy Week in past years, many of the most violent attacks, pogroms and massacres have been perpetrated against the Jewish people. The liturgy in many churches is replete with both explicit and implicit negative messages about the Jews. To create this cartoon, Johnny Hart certainly seems to buy into this ideology. And now, he teaches it to a comics page audience that is made up of a disproportionate number of children. It is irresponsible. It is wrong.

Sadly, I have heard many people poo-poo the reactions of many of us against the cartoon. Some of my own colleagues have called even the slightest concern an over-reaction. They argue that the seven-armed candelabrum is merely that, it is not at all a menorah. I would love for that to be so, but it is not. This cartoon teaches that Jews should become Christians.

I worry.

I had the honor of speaking at the Interfaith Hospitality Network dessert earlier this week. These many many volunteers from all faiths work together to house, feed, clothe and support homeless families as they get back on their feet. They do good work. They do holy work. They make a difference. They are also a faith-based charity.

We discussed the current plan that would put government monies into faith-based charities that demonstrate they are doing legitimate work. Believe me, we were all for the free money. But each of us, Jew and Christian, was concerned about the decision makers. The likely recipients. The "fringe" faiths. And a very interesting comment was made: we are a liberal organization that does good work. We should apply for these grants whether or not we support the government role in religious charities because we know we will do what is right with the money. We should work now to organize our proposals so we, not the fundamentalists, will receive the money.

Fight them on their own turf?

It has certainly been an interesting week. We Jews support free speech, creativity, different expressions of ideas and beliefs. We are wholeheartedly committed to *Tikkun Olam,* healing the world. Many of us are committed Jews because of organizations like the Interfaith Hospitality Network, the youth group Bowl-a-thon raising money to send sick children to camp, we are here because our movement created Mazon, a multimillion dollar charity that collects money from Jewish events to give to the needy through-

out the world. We love religion. We embrace it. And we are being pushed into a most interesting public battle.

The lines between religions and government, between religion and media, between religion and being a basic secular American have always been blurry. Fifty years ago the Jewish outcry against this comic would never have been so loud or clear. We have come far. Let's make sure we don't slip backwards.

It has been an interesting week. Fortunately, we will have a bit of comic relief coming soon. A new cartoon "Wildwood" will begin running nationwide. The hero Bobo is a big warm-hearted bear who was recently the leader of a rock band. He is now a bicycle-riding minister with a congregation full of animals in a magical forest.

Enjoy.

Reprinted with the permission of Rabbi C. Michelle Greenberg.

Exercises

Part One

Among the issues facing newspapers that carry the "B.C." cartoon was whether this particular one belonged in the religion section of the newspaper (in light of its religious content) or rather should be omitted altogether (in light of its potential offensiveness to Jews and others).

Answer the following:
1. If you were a newspaper editor, what would you do?
2. Do you think cartoons ought to be subject to censorship? If so, what should guide the decision making around what to leave out and what to allow?

Part Two

Directions: In response to the furor around the cartoon, Rabbi C. Michelle Greenberg of the Temple Sinai in Denver spoke on the issue, as set out above, in the Case Study. State her key concerns and write your response (three to four paragraphs).

🔲 A Free Press

We can only succeed as a free country and a democracy if citizens are informed and have the ability and right to think for themselves. This means the right to access information and to have the critical thinking skills to reason about what you see and hear. A free press is vital as a source of information, ideas, and insights. The recognition of this value goes back at least as far as the 5th century, B.C., when Plato set out his thoughts on the ideal society.

In *The Republic,* Plato discusses the democratic form of government (see Part IX of *The Republic,* which can be accessed online in its entirety). Plato considered democracy an imperfect, inferior society, compared to an aristocracy or military-run government. Plato thought the ideal society would have intellectual elite—philosopher–guardians—as the ruling class. He thought those with knowledge obtained through rigorous years of education and physical training would be the ideal rulers. The aristocracy would fall into the hands of the military when they became greedy for power. In turn, the army state (called an "oligarchy") fell to a democracy when the common person (working class) became greedy for power and economic gain.

He thought democracy would bring moral decay and erosion of the social order and children would run amok, dominating their parents. This moral decay, Plato predicted, would lay the seeds for a tyrannical overthrow of the democracy. He thought that in the face of moral disorder, people would be seduced by a tyrannical ruler (Hitler types) who offered easy answers to hard questions.

Do you think Plato was right? You can probably point to some examples of moral decay and social chaos. However, there are many channels for addressing societal problems. For example, we can strengthen the educational system, address poverty and health care, and confront the sorts of injustices that plague us. And we can make sure the news media has a strong presence in the society. We can help make that happen.

In Plato's day there were no daily newspapers, radios, TVs, or websites bringing us information 24 hours a day, seven days a week. We, on the contrary, can access information and ideas quite easily. But Plato was right to worry about the vulnerability of the democratic form of government. We need to be vigilant about ensuring access to information and ideas about what's going on in our world and how we might address the problems facing us as a society.

Ownership and Control

We only need to read a futuristic novel like *1984* or *The Handmaid's Tale* to feel the fear of tyrannical control of information or censorship of artistic and political expression. In both of these novels the abuse of power was on the part of government, underscoring the importance of the free exchange of ideas and the protection of individual rights.

The exposure to a variety of opinions and different frames of reference is one way to stop from being too narrow minded and dogmatic. We gain mental flexibility by being receptive to alternative points of view. Newspapers and news programs can help unveil the different facets of an issue and provide us valuable access to information and ideas. To do this effectively, however, journalists must be free to express ideas—even controversial ones. They must be able to go beneath the surface and examine different facets of the issue.

After the Gulf War was over, for example, a few journalists lamented about the failure of the press to provide an unbiased look at the war. For example, Anthony Lewis pointed out the lack of objectivity of the press during that war, saying:

> For the most part the broadcast networks simply transmitted official images of a neat, painless war. Or worse: put a gloss of independent corroboration on those false images. And they were false. The officials told us belatedly that only a tiny percentage of all those explosives rained on Iraq were actually like the images we saw; bombs neatly zipping down the chimneys of military targets. . . .
>
>   Nor could most Americans have understood, from their press, that the allied bombs destroyed the civilian infrastructure of a modern society. . . . There was scarcely a mention either of Iraqi deaths. . . . To most of the press it was as if Iraqis did not matter—as if they were not fully human. (See Anthony Lewis, "To See Ourselves," *The New York Times,* 6 May 1991)

There also can be conflicts over competing interests. That is why it is so crucial that the news media seek to present balanced coverage and offer a range of perspectives on the social issues we face as a society.

Exercises

After the September 11, 2001 attacks on New York City and Washington D.C., the U.S. government took steps to limit access to information and, thus, raised questions and concerns about freedom of speech and freedom of the press. Read the following statement on freedom of the press by journalist Frank Rich in *The New York Times,* then answer the questions below:

> We learned this week that if we can't bring Osama bin Laden to justice dead or alive, the White House can still slap him with that most American form of capital punishment—kicking him off network television. . . . This may be a war "pitting the world's mightiest industrial nation against a cave dweller," as George Will has put it, but the cave dweller, we keep being rudely reminded, is no caveman. Through McLuhanesque ["medium is the message"] savvy, brazen timing and a cunning message, he upstaged the president of the United States on the day he sent American troops into battle. . . . Even so, America's New War, as CNN has branded it, is already whipping up one of the cold war's most self-destructive national maladies—a will to stifle dissent. . . . But there is much we don't know about what his administration is up to, and its determination to keep us in the dark and to stifle any criticism makes the minimal amount of dissent more alarming than reassuring . . .
>
>   The point of much of this dissembling, like the attempt to banish Mr. bin Laden from TV, is simple enough: what we don't know won't hurt us. At his press conference, Mr. Bush gave a progress report on the war to date—and found solid advances

on every single front, without a single setback, not even a minor one, of any kind. Asked if the American people had to make any sacrifices for the war effort, the only one he could come up with was longer lines at the airport. In other words, all the news is good news. Decide for yourself if that makes you feel safe. (See Frank Rich, "No News Is Good News," *The New York Times,* 13 Oct. 2001)

Answer the following:

1. What are the main points Rich makes to support his position?
2. What was the strongest point he made about freedom of the press?
3. How would an opponent of Rich's position respond to him? (It may help to find an article supporting restrictions on the press in times of national crises.)

Ideas and Freedom of the Press

The expression of ideas and reasonable access to information is one element of our educational system and the role of the press in our lives. Because of this freedom, we function better as a society. That is, exposure to ideas helps us develop our own intellectual and creative potential. It also helps us learn about others and be more tolerant of potentially conflicting worldviews and ways of doing things.

The free expression of ideas, however, is not an unbridled outpouring devoid of a sense of morality. There is no justification for racist diatribes and hate speech. We need not lose sight of justice, but we need to affirm the importance of presenting a range of ideas. Without an open inquiry that allows for the expression of diverse perspectives, we condemn ourselves to tunnel vision.

CASE STUDY

Free Press versus the Iranian Government

In the summer of 2001, there was an outcry against repressive actions against the press in Iran, asserting that:

An unprecedented attack has started against the press in Iran. Some 43 newspapers, weeklies, and other publications have been ordered shut by the judiciary. We condemn the closing of the newspapers and the jailing of their editors and writers. We support freedom of expression for all. We condemn suppression

of the people's rights and voices in all shapes and forms. (see www.payvand.com)

In response to the government's action, a letter campaign was launched. Form letters were distributed in hopes that people would fill out the letter and mail it in protest to the Iranian president. Read the letter and then answer the questions that follow.

His Excellency
Hojjatoleslam Seyed Mohammad Khatami,
President of the Islamic Republic of Iran
The Presidency
Palestine Avenue
Azerbaijan Intersection
Tehran, Islamic Republic of Iran

Your Excellency:

As you are well aware, an unprecedented attack has started against the press in Iran. Some seventeen newspapers, weeklies, and other publications have been ordered shut by the judiciary. Unfortunately, as you also know, such actions run contrary to the Constitution and civil legal code of the Islamic Republic of Iran in more than one area.

Overwhelming legal backing for the press, their rights, and freedoms, has been enshrined in the Constitution of the Islamic Republic of Iran, and its laws—a Constitution which is the fruit of the struggles of the Iranian people against dictatorship during the Islamic revolution of 1357.

As concerned Iranians abroad, who maintain no affiliations with groups seeking the overthrow of the current system of government of Iran, and respect the choice of the people of Iran as exemplified in countless popular elections over the past 20 years, we respectfully call upon your excellency to safeguard the Constitution and laws of this ancient land. We are extremely concerned about the future course and fate of the free press in Iran, and urge you to take action on their behalf.

Source: www.payvand.com.

Exercises

1. Give your assessment of the letter above to the president of Iran.

2. Note that the frame of reference is *Iranians abroad*. Do you think the letter would have more impact if it were modified to include "concerned citizens of the world" or other groups? Share your thoughts and ideas.

3. What are the likely benefits of a letter campaign such as this one?

4. Can you suggest some ideas for other steps that could be taken to address the steps taken against the Iranian press?

5. Because it is usually easier to criticize the policies of other countries, than those that shape our own society, do an Internet search and see what issues around freedom of the press face our society today. State those issues and concerns, citing the sources you find.

Dangers of Controls

How does the ownership and operation of the media by big corporations, like AOL Time Warner, Disney, and Viacom change what rates as "news" and how it was presented? Linguist and social commentator Noam Chomsky sees the potential danger of the media falling under the power of the government or corporate interests. He thinks the media are influenced, if not manipulated, by corporate and political interest groups. His advice? We need to be vigilant about being an attentive and critical audience. In other words, we need to make sure our critical thinking skills are operating at full speed.

At times, the news media have been used to shape public opinion by inflating one event to the detriment of others. Some thought this was the case in the handling of the Clinton–Lewinsky scandal, the Jon-Benet Ramsey murder case, the Chandra Levy (missing intern) case, and many other events. Discussions of media coverage characterized these with such terms as "media circus," "media zoo," and "feeding frenzy."

One concern of media analysts is the question of influence. The very idea of the "fourth estate" is that an educated citizenry depends upon a free press. We must, therefore, ensure that journalists are not coerced or otherwise pressured to push a given perspective. That's why issues like the freedom of the Iranian press, as seen in the case study above, become international issues.

Although the overwhelming majority of news organizations worldwide and nationally are privately or stockholder owned, there are public news sources, like NPR and PBS (in the U.S.), the BBC (Britain), the NHK (Japan) and the CBC (Canada). These public media help protect us from corporate or governmental interests controlling news coverage—both in the choice of focus and in the depth of analysis. Privately owned papers can also provide us with relatively unbiased news coverage. However, with both privately owned and public news media, we must be attentive to potential problems and conflicts of interest.

Balanced News Coverage

One way to achieve a balance of news coverage and perspectives is through exposure to a range of publications. For example, we can read newspapers of different political, social, and religious persuasions. We can seek out a wide range of commentaries on world events. We can keep an open mind. What's front-page news in one area may be relegated to a corner of page 24 in another city's newspaper.

We can also seek sources that present the interests of different cultural groups and social organizations. Watch for the potential influence of gender, age, class, sexual orientation, race, and ethnicity on topics and coverage. This may appear because of author bias, editorial bias, or assumptions about audience bias (i.e., assumptions about the audience that colors what is covered and how it is covered).

Fortunately, people with access to the Internet now have newspapers the world over at their fingertips. This means we can easily read newspapers and news summaries from the next city, the next state, the next country, the next continent, and almost every country imaginable.

This fact radically alters the ways in which we can become informed about current events, and do so on a scale unthinkable 5 or 10 years ago. Here are some guidelines for balanced news coverage.

Six Factors for Balanced News Reading

Political	→	Seek diversity of political viewpoints.
Economic	→	Seek diversity in terms of financial or class interests (who stands to gain or lose).
Frame of Reference	→	Seek diversity of perspectives (gender, race, class, and so on).
Conceptual	→	Seek diversity in ways problems are defined and solved (ground rules, use of language, assumptions, biases).
Ethical	→	Seek diversity of ethical and religious viewpoints (values and beliefs).
Cultural	→	Seek diversity of opposing viewpoints (worldview, social traditions, group identification).

Exercises

1. Study the way the news media handles key events in the lives of public figures. Select *one* of the following topics and then one example within that topic area:

   - *Historical Event:* Study the media coverage of an important historical event, such as the fall of the Berlin Wall, the bombing of the World Trade Center, humans walking on the moon, the breakup of the Soviet Union, the cloning of the sheep Dolly.
   - *Wedding:* Study the media coverage of a high-profile wedding, such as the marriage of Princess Diana and Prince Charles in England.
   - *Death:* Study of the ethics of the media behavior over the death of one of the following: Selena Quintanilla-Perez (1995), Jon-Benet Ramsey (1996), Princess Diana (1997), Florence-Griffith Joyner (1998), or John F. Kennedy, Jr. (1999), Pierre Elliot Trudeau (2000), George Harrison (2001).
   - *Trials:* Study the media coverage of an infamous trial, such as the Yates trial, McMartin trial, O. J. Simpson trial, *Abner Louima* vs. *NYPD*, or the Timothy McVeigh trial.

2. Obtain the front section of three different newspapers. You can find them at the library, newsstand, or on the Internet. You can run a search by the name of the newspaper or to an Internet news site such as *emedia1.mediainfo .com/emedia*. Use recent (non-tabloid) newspapers, preferably from at least two different geographic regions.

   Answer the following:

   a. Studying the three newspapers, how do they rate on the six factors of balanced coverage (see list above)? Compare and contrast the three papers.

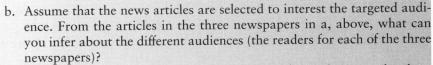

b. Assume that the news articles are selected to interest the targeted audience. From the articles in the three newspapers in a, above, what can you infer about the different audiences (the readers for each of the three newspapers)?

c. What are possible reasons for the overlap (if any) between the three newspapers? Note similarities and differences (e.g., the same lead story, national vs. international news, etc.).

d. Looking at list of articles in the three newspapers, draw some inferences about the journalistic goals or guidelines set for individual staff writers.

e. What are the pros and cons of a local newspaper using news services such as Reuters and the Associated Press as a major source for articles?

CASE STUDY

Where's the Beef in McDonald's French Fries?

Just when you thought you could eat a French fry without eating an animal by-product, the oil hit the fan in spring 2001. It centered on McDonald's use of beef fat in oil used for its French fries. The news brought an outpouring of complaints from vegetarians and others who felt duped by McDonald's. They argued that the failure to <u>explicitly</u> state its use of beef extract in its French fries was a serious no-no.

Examine the excerpt below about McDonald's use of beef extract in its French fries and then answer the questions that follow.

SEATTLE—Facing a class-action lawsuit from angry vegetarians, McDonald's this week confirmed that its French fries are prepared with beef extract, a disclosure the company said is not new. Although the fast-food giant has been saying since 1990 that its fries are cooked in pure vegetable oil, company spokesman Walt Riker said Wednesday that McDonald's never said its fries were appropriate for vegetarians and always told customers that their flavor comes partly from beef. A class action suit has been filed for "emotional distress" caused to vegetarians, some of

them vegetarian for religious reasons, who thought McDonald's fries were in line with their strong feelings about not eating meat.

The list of French fry ingredients that McDonald's offers at its franchises and on its Web site includes potatoes, partially hydrogenated soybean oil and "natural flavor." The list does not mention that the "natural flavor" comes from beef. To discover that, one would have to contact a McDonald's customer-satisfaction representative. Harish Bharti, the Seattle lawyer who filed the suit against McDonald's Tuesday, said the confirmation that the company uses beef extract to flavor its fries validates his case.

Bharti argues that a reasonable person who heard that McDonald's fries are prepared in "100 percent vegetable oil" and read the list of ingredients would assume the food is suitable for vegetarians. (See Eli Sanders, "McDonald's Confirms Its French Fries Are Made With Beef Extract," *Boston Globe,* 4 May 2001)

Answer the following:

1. Would you say the author is sympathetic to the concerns of vegetarians? Explain.

2. The article later notes that Walt Riker, a McDonald's spokesperson, was asked why

they did not specify that beef extract was used. He replied, "It's a good question. We're sensitive to all our customers' needs and concerns. We try to be as forthcoming and user-friendly as possible. We'll review it. We'll take a look at it." He added that using "natural flavor" as a synonym for beef extract is within federal Food and Drug Administration guidelines. If you were the reporter, what questions might you then ask Riker about this comment?

3. How would the article likely differ if the author were a press agent for McDonald's? Set out your ideas.

Sharpening Our Antennae

You pick up *The New York Times* and there on the front page is a photo of the Dalai Lama, the Buddhist leader of Tibet. You see his face quite clearly. It is in profile, with his right hand on the arm of a woman facing him. You see her less clearly, given that we see little more than the cheek of Rigoberta Menchu, Guatemalan Nobel laureate. The article's title is: "Nobel Winner Accused of Stretching the Truth." You may not know that the Dalai Lama received the Nobel Prize in 1989 and that Rigoberta Menchu received it in 1992. But you do recognize *his* face in the photo.

If you make it to the third paragraph, you discover that the stink is about Menchu's "autobiography," now asserted to be untrue. In other words, it is *she*, not he, accused of stretching the truth. So why was there a photo of the Dalai Lama there at all? If you were a cynic, you'd think someone had it in for him, as his photo is directly under the words "accused of." That image will imprint the brain of all those readers who are just skimming the newspaper. From the Dalai Lama's or a Buddhist's point of view, the inclusion of that photo with this article was, at best, a lamentable error.

Thanks to our heightened critical thinking powers, we are watching for such "errors," slips, misleading photos, and juxtapositions of image and text. This allows us to spot things that can go astray and lead to the wrong conclusion on the part of a hurried reader or someone just glancing at the front page.

Individual Responsibility

At times the press turns its eyes on a crisis, world event, or human-interest story and we get an avalanche of articles on it. All of a sudden, seemingly out of nowhere, an issue has a run of press attention. We are then inundated with articles about what's going on, what politicians think we should do, what the military involvement is likely to be, and so on. Sometimes the issue is truly of global proportions, as in the terrorist attacks in September 2001. Other times, the issue, looked at later, is relatively trivial or overblown. It rises into the public eye and then it falls back, into oblivion.

What we have to do is become informed and stay politically active. In other words, by taking individual responsibility for keeping up on world news and current events, we can be more powerful members of our democracy. This entails going beyond a headline—knowledge of events; instead we need to read in-depth news coverage and commentaries. And we need to ensure that we expose ourselves to a range of perspectives, so we get a broader understanding of events and their impact on people's lives.

There are three major ways a reader can use newspapers as vehicles for social action. One is through letters to the editor. Another is through a commentary (e.g., an op/ed piece in the editorial section of the newspaper). The third is through press releases (usually sent out by an institution or an organization).

In the case of a letter to the editor, you, the reader, can express your own point of view on a current issue or your reaction to news coverage of a particular event. With op/ed articles, individuals submit to the newspaper an article usually arguing a position, with the goal of persuading others to hold the author's thesis or to benefit from the insights the author shares on a particular topic. With a press release, an organization can bring events and news to the public eye by sending a prepackaged article on the event or speaker, in hopes the newspaper will pick it up and publish it.

By working in community—whether as members of a social group, political party, or religious congregation—we can let our collective concerns be expressed and have a voice in the direction our society takes.

Exercises

Shortly after the World Trade Center and Pentagon attacks, <u>rumors</u> flew through e-mails that the news station CNN had aired decade-old footage of Palestinians celebrating in the streets and presented it as if it were current. The person originating the rumor (a Brazilian university student) quickly retracted it (widely published). But the incident points to the potential role of the individual in holding the news media accountable for fair coverage. Read the excerpt from the CNN public statement and then answer the questions below:

(CNN asks that you copy and e-mail this statement to whomever asks about it.)

There is absolutely no truth to the information that is now distributed on the Internet that CNN used 10-year-old video when showing the celebrating of some Palestinians in East Jerusalem after the terror attacks in the U.S. The video was shot that day by a Reuters camera crew. CNN is a client of Reuters and like other clients, received the video and broadcast it. Reuters officials have publicly made the facts clear as well. The allegation is false. The source of the allegation has withdrawn it and apologized. (*www.cnn.com/2001/US/09/20/cnn.statement*)

Directions:
1. Investigate what you can find out about this case and summarize your findings.
2. What would you suggest someone do who has questions about the veracity of news coverage or who has found evidence that deception or misinformation has been utilized?
3. Suppose a news station looked out the window and saw some Palestinians celebrating the U.S. disaster, but there was no camera available. Do you think it would be ethically permissible to use old footage of Palestinians celebrating in the streets as a replacement? Share your thoughts.

Analyzing the Newspaper

When undertaking an analysis of the newspaper, you want to be sure to do an overview of the whole, as well as going into detail on particular articles. Your first move is to get a sense of the entire newspaper, which we'll discuss in the next section. Then, you want to go into individual articles in detail, while noting the way the article functions in the larger context of the entire newspaper and of the society.

The first step in analyzing the news is to become informed. Start by taking apart a newspaper or online news site piece by piece. First, get an overview. Look at it as a whole document and then look at the specific elements, so you get a sense of how it works.

Pick up several newspapers or go to their websites and survey the various articles. Determine how many columns in the front section were by the staff reporters and how many were purchased from news syndicates like the Associated Press, Reuters, *Los Angeles Times, The New York Times,* and so forth. This shows us how many sources are used to supply the news. It also helps us see a newspaper's emphasis (local, regional, national, international) and its range (hard news, entertainment, personal interest, self-help, community services, etc.).

Style and Content

One question to ask is what makes something news—and newsworthy? How do newspapers inform us, while keeping us interested? There is a delicate balance: If the newspaper were dull or dry, the potential audience would be limited. But if a newspaper neglected newsworthy world and local events in favor of the bizarre, the unusual, the freakish, the celebrity story, or wrenching personal interest stories, it edges away from being a "news" paper and toward being a tabloid.

News articles are not necessarily neutral or objective pieces of journalism and to assume otherwise puts us at risk of being manipulated by the media and their corporate or political sponsors. Read the news article both for style and content. Study the way the article is presented.

Try to discern the author's thesis or personal slant. Note the types of evidence (if any) cited. Watch the use of quotes or expert testimony. And so on. Whenever you pick up a newspaper, survey the front page, reading each heading and subheading. Get an overview of the front section by seeing how much is world news, how much is state or local news, how much is timely (within the last 24-hour period), and how much is attention-getting "non-news" (filler or human interest). In examining a news article in terms of style and content, you may find it helpful to use this checklist:

Checklist for Analyzing Style and Content

1. *Structure:* How is the article set out? Note where the thesis is presented and the way in which the author makes his or her case.
2. *Language:* Does the author use any loaded terms, technical terms, bias, or prejudicial language?
3. *Symbols and Images:* What sort of picture do you get from this article? Is the style forceful and hard-hitting, or is it subtle—even folksy? Try to characterize the approach.
4. *Analogies and Metaphors:* Does the author use a comparison to make a point? Analogies and metaphors can carry a great deal of weight, so watch for them.
5. *Use of Testimony or Expert Witnesses:* Any reliance on what others have to say about the issue? If so, how is that done? Are those who give testimony or expert "advice" well qualified to be doing so? Note the credentials of those who are cited.
6. *Personal Slant:* Does the author write from a personal, or subjective, perspective? On the subjective/objective scale, where would you place this article? Is it written in the first person, or from a "neutral" stance?
7. *Descriptive/Prescriptive:* How much does the author spend describing a state of affairs, going into detail on the specifics of the case? To what extent does the author impose his or her own set of beliefs, or assumptions, telling more about what ought to be the case, rather than what is the case?
8. *Cultural Baggage:* Is there evidence that this article is culturally embedded; that is, reflective of a certain time and place? How much does the author draw from the culture (social or political scene, music, art, literature, movies, TV, religion) within the article?
9. *Recognition of Audience:* Does the author write for a specialized, or learned, audience? Or is the article geared to anyone who can read? How much is presumed on the part of the reader by the author?
10. *Omissions:* What does the author include and what does the author exclude from the article?

Exercises

Part One

1. Discuss these headlines:
   - Article headline: "Beyond Multiculturalism, Freedom?" (*The New York Times*, 29 July 2001).
   - Article headline: "Voters Know, but the Politicians Just Don't Understand" (*Los Angeles Times*, 11 June 1998).
   - Article headline: "Lives on the line: Donated skin is being processed into cosmetic-surgery products. Meanwhile, shortages can leave burn victims at lethal risk" (*The Orange Country Register*, 17 Apr. 2000).
   - Article headline: "Miami Makes Sloppy Case Against the Seminoles" (*The New York Times*, 14 Oct. 2001).
   - Article headline: "Perdue campaign video likens Barnes to a rat" (*The Atlanta Journal-Constitution*, 22 May 2002).

2. Discuss these headlines:
   - Article headline: "Pulp friction in the North End: Lemonade stand causes a little stir" (*Boston Globe*, 22 June 2001).
   - Article headline: "Alien Criminals Face Charge for Re-Entering U.S." (*Los Angeles Daily Journal*, 21 June 2001).
   - Article headline: " 'Because Caribou Don't Vote' " (*Globe and Mail* [Toronto], 2 Aug. 2001).

3. Read about the case and then answer the questions that follow:

   On August 8, 2001, *The New York Times* had a front-page article on a proposal to shift the standards in legal ethics, allowing lawyers more leeway to reveal client confidences in order to prevent fraud, injury, or death. The American Bar Association's House of Delegates, the policy-making body of the ABA, voted to approve a proposal that would allow lawyers to discuss confidences whenever there is a reasonable expectation of death or serious bodily harm.

   Answer the following:
   a. Suggest three possible titles for such an article.
   b. Share your thoughts on the *actual* title of the article and what it suggests concerning what the article is about: "Lawyers Open Door to Telling Clients' Secrets."

4. Using the checklist discuss the extent to which the author asserts his own opinion in the following excerpt:

   My political hope, which I believe to be realistic, is that we are on the verge of a new era of reform, a new Progressive Era. A time of reform will require three large changes in our national life. First, it will demand a new civility in politics, defined not as an avoidance of conflict or difference but rather as a debate at once vigorous, honest, and mutually respectful over what new circumstances require of us.

Second, it will require a new engagement with democratic government and an embrace of the idea that in a democracy, government is not the realm of "them" but of "us." Democratic government is the realm of self-rule, not an arena of coercion or prescription.

As Paul Helmke, the Republican mayor of Fort Wayne, Indiana, put it, "Government isn't the solution. Government isn't the problem. Government is us. It's what we make of it. It's what we do with it." (See E. J. Dionne, Jr.'s "Faith, Politics, and the Common Good," *Religion and Values in Public Life*, Winter/Spring 1998)

Part Two

1. Compare and contrast the two descriptions, both from the same newspaper within one day of each other:

Description 1:

"I have not a clue about late Beethoven!" the pianist Mitsuko Uchida said with a little giggle. "But then, who *has* got a clue?" The remark seemed disingenuous, coming from one of the world's foremost concert pianists. . . . Sitting in a quiet corner of the Carlyle Hotel restaurant, hair flowing to her shoulders, wearing her customary black slacks with an Issey Miyake top in the palest shades of orange and grey, she spoke in an odd mixture of rapid-fire Japanese-style delivery of English, an occasional German "Ja" and Yiddish. When she laughed, she covered her mouth like a 19th-century Japanese aristocrat, a riveting gesture with her small but muscular hands. (See Dinitia Smith, "Plumbing the Mysteries of a Pianists Art and Power," *The New York Times*, 8 Apr. 1997)

Description 2:

Outside, it was the kind of soupy spatter of a day that keeps the rest of the country from moving here. Inside, Bill Nye, the Science Guy—the hipper, hyper Mr. Wizard of the 1990s whose frenetic children's science show has a television sudience of more than three million viewers in the United States and Canada. . . . In person, Mr. Nye, 41, is slower, calmer, his voice deeper. And his comic routines vary from high-pitched Three Stooges–style humming, as he grills salmon on his deck in the rain, to the classroom schtick of asking, "This—what? Anyone?" (See Carey Goldberg, "Pondering Fire, Infinity and a Head of Lettuce (Cool!)," *The New York Times*, 9 Apr. 1997)

2. Using the checklist analyze the excerpt below:

Edward and Sophie landed in Edmonton shortly after 5 p.m., looking freshly pressed. Edward was wearing a grey suit and blue dress-shirt, Sophie in a mint-green dress and jacket and carrying a pony-print handbag. Sophie, tucking her hair neatly behind her ear, smiled modestly for a small group of cameras as Edward chatted with Lt.-Gov. Lois Hole and Jack Agrios, chairman of the local organizing committee for the World Championships in Athletics.

While the Edmonton International Airport was abuzz with talk of their arrival, many aboard their plane didn't even know they were traveling with royal company. . . . Graham Stringer said they hurried into the plane's first row moments before takeoff, after a last-minute security check that put the flight slightly behind schedule. Stringer sat just a few seats behind the two rows occupied by the couple and their entourage, close enough to notice Prince Edward reading what looked like a pile of meeting agendas, and to form an opinion of Sophie's fashion sense. "Sophie Rhys-Jones looks a lot like Diana, really elegant, dresses very well," Stringer said.

When the couple arrived at the Westin Hotel, where they will occupy a whole floor during their stay in Edmonton, more than two dozen spectators were watching. . . . Inside the hotel, World's volunteers and guests greeted Prince Edward and Sophie as manager Tony Dunn handed the Countess a small bouquet of roses and orchids. (See "Edward, Sophie Add Touch of Glamour: Fellow Air Canada Travelers Were Floored To Hear They Flew with Royalty," *The Edmonton Journal*, 3 Aug. 2001)

3. Using the checklist analyze the excerpt below:

"Free trade is threatening us and our way of life," said Jose Pedro Mariano, 59, his face weather-beaten from years of working his cornfields nestled beneath the Pico de Orizaba volcano in the state of Puebla. Mariano looks out at the 20 acres that his grandfather fought for during the Mexican Revolution and wonders whether he will be able to sell all of his harvest this fall. As a result of the North American Free Trade Agreement, more U.S. corn is flooding the Mexican market. This may be good for big industry and states like Illinois, but small Mexican farmers like Mariano are feeling the pressure.

And trade between Mexico and Illinois is only likely to grow. On a mission to expand trade, agriculture issues have been a major topic of discussion between Illinois Gov. George Ryan and Mexican President Vicente Fox. They last met during Fox's visit to Chicago in July. Illinois officials were in Mexico last week to talk about ethanol and how the state can share technology to help Mexico develop a sugar-based ethanol industry for its own consumption.

In turn, Illinois could explore new markets for its corn products. "Finding ways to use these products—an alternative use for sugar and alternative uses for our corn—that's what we're all after," said Joseph Hampton, director of the Illinois Department of Agriculture, after a recent meeting in Mexico City. "We're looking at things we think are win-win." (See Teresa Puente, "Squeezed by U.S. Corn: Mexican Farmers Fault NAFTA for Low-Cost Imports," *Chicago Tribune*, 3 Aug. 2001)

4. Select an article from this week's news and pull out 3 paragraphs from the article. Then analyze the excerpt using the checklist.

Use of Language by the News Media

In discussing style and content language is a big issue. The words we use can make a great deal of difference in the readers' understanding of an issue or an event. The use of a word or phrase can shape the meaning of an entire passage.

For example, all of these refer to the same person: Laura Bush, Mrs. Bush, the first lady, the president's wife, George's wife, Barbara's daughter-in-law, and Jena's mother. However, they do not all function the same in a sentence. Calling the first lady by her first name suggests a kind of informality. Using terms like "the president's wife" or "George's wife" define her in terms of her husband. Depending upon the context any one of the references to Laura Bush may be appropriate, but we must realize that each term carries different connotations.

Similarly, referring to Prince Edward of England in the exercise 2, above, as "Edward" suggests a kind of informality or acquaintance that does not accurately reflect the very real distance between royalty and the average person.

Accountability

The way we use those words can shade an interpretation or slant the piece from one extreme to another. This is pretty obvious when racist or sexist language is used, because such language is loaded and can have an explosive effect on a reader.

An infamous case in the early 90s brings this home. This is the case of Jimmy Breslin, a Pulitzer-prize winning journalist who wrote for *New York Newsday*. Fellow *Newsday* journalist Ji-Yeon Yuh took issue with one of his columns; she sent him an e-mail that he had denigrated professional women and was "spewing sexism." Some felt Yuh misinterpreted Breslin's sense of humor and, therefore, could not appreciate Breslin poking fun at his wife in one of his columns. However, even his defenders were shocked when Breslin called her a "bitch," a "yellow cur," and "slant-eyed." When Breslin failed to show that his subsequent apologies were not sincere, he ended up with a two-week suspension.

Sometimes it is editors, not reporters, who must issue an apology. For example, on January 29, 2002, the editor of *The Battalion,* Texas A&M University's student newspaper issued a public apology. This resulted from a controversial cartoon that appeared January 14, 2002, which several student groups found to be racist. It featured a black mother reprimanding her son for his failing grades. The characters were drawn with exaggerated facial and body features resembling African-American stereotypes. Several student groups participated in a protest to give their opinions of the cartoon and its impact. In a response to the public outcry, editor Mariano Castillo wrote an apology, excerpted below:

> The editors and staff of The Battalion apologize to readers both in and outside the Texas A&M community that the Jan. 14 cartoon offended so many. . . . The Battalion hopes to dispel the misconceptions and accusations of being racist, and we are open to the reminder that racism is still a problem at A&M. We recognize that the cartoon was insensitive through its stereotypes. If we had it to do over again, we would not approve this cartoon for publication. (See Courtney Morris, "Cartoon Sparks Protest," *The Daily Texan* (the student newspaper at the University of Texas at Austin), 19 Mar. 2002)

Exercises

1. What should be the boundaries of freedom of speech when it comes to what a journalist or political cartoonist puts into print?
2. What sort of words and actions on the part of a reporter or news anchor warrant a public apology? Set out a set of guidelines.
3. Is there any difference between what should be permitted in newspapers and what should be allowed on the Internet?

The Distinct Role of Sports in the News Media

The subtitle here could be "Human Interest + Athletics." Sports coverage has a unique role in the workings of the news media. It used to be that newspapers had a section aimed at women—one with horoscopes, fashion, recipes, gossip columns, and the like. But this is no longer the fixture it once was; now such items are not necessarily all corralled in together. In contrast, sports coverage remains a staple of print, radio, and TV news.

The language, the images and descriptions, and outpouring of emotion in sports coverage gives it a kind of distinction and narrative power that other news typically lacks. There are a number of reasons for that. One is the unique role of athletes in our society. With strength and athletic finesse, with actions magnified for all to see and each move subject to instant replays, the athlete is a pivotal cultural icon. Turn on the news or open the sports pages and you can see it.

It's not simply a male thing, either. Though sports tend to be male dominated, it attracts both males and females as participants and viewers. The fascination with sports crosses age, gender, race, and political lines, and knows neither geographic nor linguistic boundaries.

Analyzing Sports Coverage

We can learn a lot about our society by turning our attention to sports. Often much more dramatically than other forms of journalism, sports coverage has the potential to reveal:

- Cultural values and beliefs.
- Notions of heroism.
- Gender roles and expectations.
- The evolution of language.
- Ethical and social norms.
- Contemporary mythology.

Think of it this way: Can you imagine teachers, doctors, lawyers, engineers, or composers getting an entire section of the newspaper and a chunk of virtually every news program devoted to their every move? If it were merely an issue of entertainment, athletes and professional teams could be replaced by comedians, singers, or actors. If it were simply to show what the human body is capable of, we could just look at body builders, yogis, and physical fitness buffs.

The reality is that sports, and sports coverage in the print media, radio, and TV, form an integral part of our culture. Therefore, when we apply our critical reasoning skills to examining sports, what we discover offers us a window on society. Through a look at sports coverage, we can learn about the media, our culture, and ourselves.

With such fertile ground for digging, we need the right tools. Using a variety of techniques, we can tackle sports coverage and develop our own ability to reason at the same time. This we can see in the checklist below.

Sports Coverage Checklist

1. *Examine the reasoning*—zero in on arguments, assess the strength of evidence cited in support of the conclusion.
2. *Analyze and evaluate*—check for warranted versus unwarranted assumptions, potential sources of bias or prejudice, stereotypical thinking, and the use of images and symbols.
3. *Watch for visual and verbal messages* in the presentation of information and the use of images/photographs.
4. *Check the use of language*—watch for loaded terms, biased language, asymmetrical descriptions, repetition, metaphors, and poetic expressions to convey an idea.
5. *Notice inductive and deductive lines of reasoning*—watch especially for use of analogies, reliance on statistical studies, cause and effect reasoning.
6. *Be on the alert for fallacious reasoning*—in particular check for the fallacies of ad populum (appeal to the masses), ad verecundiam (irrelevant testimonials of famous figures in place of solid evidence), ad hominem (personal attack), ad hominem circumstantial (discrediting by social or political affiliation), and question-begging epithets (slanted language biasing an interpretation).
7. *Be aware of the frame of reference*—check to see what other perspectives might be taken on the situation and how things would change if other voices were heard.
8. *Watch for cultural or ethnic sensitivity*—Examine the values and worldview implicitly presented, narrowing or broadening our understanding of the people or issues involved.

Cultural Values and Beliefs

Sports coverage in general is value laden. That is, a set of values and beliefs is threaded through articles about sports, radio and TV coverage of sports events, and even in peripheral ways, such as the use of athletes and sports references to sell products. For example, sports pages often include advertising for strip joints, "gentlemen's clubs" (nude and nearly nude dancing spots), and X-rated videos — as well as ads directed to men's body image (such as ads on cosmetic surgery, baldness, and male sexual dysfunction).

We can see how values are manifested in the way we view sports. In particular, we can examine the different elements — the athletes, teams, coaches, fans, sponsors, owners, support staff, mascots, cheerleaders, bands, and other team enhancers.

Try to determine what does or doesn't count. Notice how much attention is given to individual players, teams, winning and losing, competition, brushes with the law, violence in sports, the fans, and so on. Study the way people are described and look at the narrative dimension (e.g., see athletes as characters in a story).

Examine the use of language, colorful descriptions, nicknames, and other ways of referring to athletes. Watch for both overt and subtle differences in the coverage of sports figures and events. Try to look around. Approach as if it were the first time you've heard about sports, teams, players, and how they relate to the social fabric. Think of all the values that get reflected in sports coverage and what this tells us about our society (our attitudes, prejudices, fears, fantasies, goals, dreams).

The links between the society and sports form a wide-reaching web. To examine the interconnections of this web, look at the broader social context. We need to consider the different spheres that tie into this superstructure, and see what values and beliefs underlie each sphere.

Use of Language in Sports Coverage

The words we use reveal a great deal about our attitudes, values, interests, and prejudices. Sports coverage is often lively and colorful. Often journalists and sportscasters use a plethora of metaphors and even wild terms to describe a player's move, to refer to individual athletes, to draw comparisons between teams.

The language of sports is often expressed in more of a narrative style than traditional journalism. Sports news is usually packaged as a story with powerful images and terms used to convey ideas. Such writing tends to be more clearly subjective, with the author's own voice adding a stamp of uniqueness. Because of sports' entertainment value, we find descriptions that would be unacceptable in other types of news coverage. We must, therefore, watch for uses of language that are eulogistic (euphemistic) or dyslogistic (i.e., creating either a positive or negative slant to the story). Watch also for language that plays on our emotions and team loyalties. Be on the lookout for the use of stereotypes and language that plays into societal attitudes.

Keep in mind that the use of language is not a neutral affair. Words and images shape our thoughts and fuel our imaginations. They can bring us to our feet and inspire us to action. Furthermore, because many sports journalists are highly opinionated, their use of language can have a considerable impact on the audience.

Whatever you read, whether a seemingly innocent article on the Boston marathon or a commentary on the NBA play-offs, watch the way language is used.

To summarize, be attentive to the following uses (and pitfalls) of languages: loaded terms, use of technical language or lingo, use of colloquial (street) language, use of puns and other kinds of humor, asymmetrical descriptions of male versus female athletes, racist or other prejudicial language, name calling, hate speech, images and symbols used to create an effect, testimonials, personal revelations, and anything that sticks out as unusual or peculiar.

Exercises

1. Late, great sports writer Jim Murray showed the potential effectiveness of using metaphors in an article he wrote about a boxing match between Marvin Hagler and Thomas "Hit Man" Hearn. This match has been called one of the greatest of boxing history. Hagler, the winner, called it "the highlight of my career." Set out how he uses language to create an effect:

It was like watching Bambi being mugged, Little Red Riding Hood devoured by the wolf, a cat drowning. You had to cover your eyes. The Hit Man got hit, all right. Like a lot of guys in this bust-out town, he took a hit when he should have played what he had. Stood pat. Instead, he went for the bundle. He crapped out, rolled a 2. Hagler faded him . . .

It's like watching a baby walk into traffic, a canary leaving its cage when the cat's around. You want to say, "No, no, Thomas, not there! Thomas, you come back this very instant! Thomas, you listen to me, do you hear?!"

Thomas pays no attention. Thomas is like the kid climbing up a steep roof after a balloon, oblivious to the fall. (See Jim Murray, "Hearns Must Have Taken Fight Plan From the Titanic," *Los Angeles Times*, 16 Apr. 1985)

2. Here is an excerpt from an article on the August 1, 2001, heat stroke related death of Korey Stringer, Minnesota Viking football player. Read this and discuss the way the issue and ideas are presented. Note also how the sentiments of the author are expressed here:

If there was a moment that provided any hope at all in the disturbing aftermath of Minnesota Viking lineman Korey Stringer's death, it came when teammate Randy Moss put his head down and cried. . . . As he tried to describe his now-realized fears that Stringer would leave his 3-year-old son behind . . . he started bawling.

What was good about it? Because it was so contrary to the football code book. Football players aren't supposed to break down and cry. They aren't supposed to display emotion or show any sign of weakness. That's part of the code. The code needs to change. Elite players should not feel the need to prove themselves by continuing to run drills in ridiculous heat. It should be OK to stop. Because these pointless deaths need to stop.

Reports said that Stringer, 27, pushed himself during the heat and high humidity of Tuesday's practice. . . . He vomited at least three times during Tuesday's practice but fought all the way through, then summoned a team trainer. Later, he was rushed to the hospital with a body temperature of more than 108 degrees. He was pronounced dead at 1:50 a.m. Wednesday. . . .

"You have to practice," Nelson said. "But you don't have to die doing it." . . . When people compare football training camps to military boot camp, it's not much of an exaggeration. Washington State running back Dave Minnich spent four years in the Marines, and he said: "They're a little bit the same." (See J.A. Adande, "Time for the Code to Go Silent," *Los Angeles Times*, 2 Aug. 2001)

Examining Assumptions

In undertaking an analysis, it is important to look at any assumptions that lie behind the reasoning that is in operation. When the assumptions are warranted, the reasoning is strengthened. But when the assumptions are unwarranted, the entire argument is weakened and can be brought down.

In a sense, assumptions are like stilts holding up a house (the argument). If the stilts are strong (by resting on truth or strong probability), the house can stay standing even in a vicious storm. However, if the stilts are rotten or full of termites—that is, resting on falsehoods, irrelevant data, or dubious links—the house will crumble.

For example, it is a warranted assumption that talent alone will not allow an athlete to attain the highest levels of achievement. It is an unwarranted assumption to think that white men can't jump well enough to win a slam-dunk competition or women who fail to make the Olympic track team can't win a gold medal in bobsledding. If we assume race is a necessary factor in athletic skill, our argument will flounder. If we assume talent is not the only consideration in predicting success, we're heading in the right direction.

CASE STUDY

Drugs and Sports

The society has a schizoid way of separating public from private behavior. This makes it easier to think of the "private" behavior as an aberration—leaving professional persona intact. Fans may also find it hard to hold athletes to a higher moral standard than they apply to themselves. This is particularly true when it comes to behavior that doesn't relate to being a success as an athlete.

However, when runner Ben Johnson was stripped of his gold medal in the 1988 Seoul Olympics after a positive drug test (indicating steroid use), reactions to him were decidedly negative. Furthermore, the incident sparked changes in the laws around drug use in sports. Here, Johnson's sins were at the heart of his behavior as an athlete.

At the present time, use of performance-enhancing drugs is widespread. Doctors writing in the *Journal of the AMA* report that more than 1 million elite and recreational athletes use performance-enhancing drugs. In a recent survey of 195 top athletes, over 50 percent said they would take a prohibited performance-enhancing drug that would bring about their death from side effects if they could be assured of winning every competition for the next five years without being caught (see Janet Goshu and Ann Endo, "To Your Health: Steering Away from Steroids," *The Daily Yomiuri* (Tokyo), 17 Oct. 1998).

Athletes employing performance-enhancing drugs are not always, if at all, aware of the risks they are taking. In fact, little is known about the long-term effects of some supplements, such as creatine, purportedly used by both power hitters Mark McGwire and Sammy Sosa. Plus there is an element of coercion when coaches, doctors, and fellow teammates pressure athletes to use drugs and over-the-counter supplements. For example, Willy Voet, the physiotherapist of the French Festina cycling team in the Tour de France, was quoted as accusing team doctor Eric Ryckaert of injecting riders with banned drugs (see "Virenque Accused of Taking Drugs," *The Irish Times*, 24 Sep. 1998).

One question is what role the media ought to play in reporting on drug use on the part of athletes. And what do we do about pressure placed by teammates, coaches, owners, or sponsors to use performance-enhancing drugs? It's not that journalists have ignored the problem. Some express criticism, for instance: "We're giving McGwire standing ovations, but I wonder what we're celebrating: the work of a hero or the spectacle of a hero fashioning his own destruction—for our pleasure" (see William C. Rhoden, "Baseball's Pandora's Box Cracks Open," *The New York Times*, 25 Aug. 1998). Even with criticism such as this, the media, like the public, is conflicted on the use of drugs in professional sports and where lines need to be drawn.

Exercises

1. What stance should the media take on drug use in professional sports? Set out your thoughts and three to four recommendations.

2. Discuss one of the following quotes about drugs and sports and offer three recommendations for how the news media should approach the subject:

   a. Sepp Platter, President of FIFA, the World Soccer Federation: "Professional athletes are forced to take performance-enhancing drugs by the huge pressure to perform" (see Doug Rollins, "Competition and Drug Abuse," *www.humanistsofutah.org*)

   b. Cliff Floyd, an outfielder for the Florida Marlins, told the *Times* he believes at least 40-percent of MLB players have used steroids. . . . Colorado Rockies strength coach Brad Andress told the *[New York] Times* that Floyd's estimate is too high, though. Andress figures that about 30-percent of professional baseball players have used steroids at some point in their careers. Two other sources also spoke with the *Times,* but requested to remain anonymous. A West-coast GM said he believed at least a third of pro ballplayers are active steroid users, while a veteran

All-Star outfielder told the paper that he thinks that two-thirds of the top players in the National League are currently using some kind of steroid (see "Juiced," *baseball.about.com,* 14 Oct. 2000).

3. Discuss the extent and quality of sports coverage of steroid and other drug abuse, in light of the following comment by an ex-MLB (major league baseball) trainer:

> The average MLB player makes in excess of two million bucks a year. Steroids and the confidence that comes with them can be the difference between working at Wal-Mart and being among the richest people in the world. When you're a teenager, the long-term risks don't seem real, but the money and fame does. (See Gary Huckabay, "Steroids in Baseball," *www.baseballprospectus.com/news,* 4 May 2001)

4. Run an Internet search to discover the way the news media covered the September, 2001 decision by the NFL to ban the herbal supplement ephedra (related to the heat-stroke deaths of a number of athletes). The Food and Drug Administration has since said about 80 deaths have been associated with ephedra (see ESPN NFL, *espn.go.com/nfl/news/2001*).

Social Context

To understand an issue or an event in history, we need to root it, socially, culturally, and historically. This is as true of the use of drugs and supplements as any other aspect of professional sports. Only by placing the issue in context can we see what baggage is being carried along with it and what parameters must be used in assessing its significance.

For example, it wasn't very long ago that team loyalties were a fixture of the social fabric. Professional athletes and their teams went together like spokes and wheels. When hockey star Wayne Gretsky left the Edmonton Oilers for the Los Angeles Kings, it was a national crisis for Canada. It was bad enough that Gretsky was leaving the Oilers, but it was unthinkable he would leave Canada.

Somewhere along the line team loyalties began to erode, because of free agency and other factors. As a result of free agency, individual players can vie for the most attractive packages and leave for greener pastures when the time comes. Similarly, owners have been accused of putting economic success as a goal more worthy than team loyalties.

Societal attitudes have factored into these changes. And yet these changes have had an impact on our values and beliefs. So we need to look at the particular, examine its social roots, and trace the influence of the broader culture. One of our tasks as critical thinkers is to look at the big picture and see how the various (economic and other) forces shape the direction of events. We can examine how these forces are perceived by the media and by the public.

Sports Stereotypes

Embedded in cultural attitudes are myths and stereotypes. This is as true in sports as in other aspects of our society. Think of all the stereotypes that are part of our culture and their role in our collective mentality. We know from chapter one that stereotypes can act as an obstacle to clear thinking. This is as true in sports as the rest of society.

We can tell a lot about such stereotypes in the nicknames athletes used to get. No longer prevalent today, it was common in the past. Some examples from professional sports are:

- *In Football:* Eugene ("the hitting machine") McDaniel, "Mean" Joe Green, Dick ("the animal") Butkus, Raghib ("the rocket") Ismail, Fred ("the hammer") Williamson, and the Fearsome Foursome (L.A. Rams), the Purple People Eaters (Minnesota Vikings), the Steel Curtain (Pittsburgh Steelers).
- *In Baseball:* Babe ("The Sultan of Swat") Ruth, "Pistol Pete" Reiser, "Hammerin' Hank" Aaron, the Bronx Bombers (New York Yankees), the Gas House Gang (The St. Louis Cardinals).
- *In Basketball:* Wilt ("the stilt") Chamberlain, Hakeem ("the dream") Olajuwon, Julius ("Dr. J") Irving, Robert ("the chief") Parrish, Earvin ("Magic") Johnson.

The picture from such vivid nicknames is that athletes are larger than life, powerhouses of strength, and with an almost inorganic and indestructible might.

We still find sterotypes about athletes—for example, boxers are easily manipulated by trainers, left-handed tennis players have powerful serves, football linemen are dumb, black basketball players jump higher than white ones, African runners have more endurance, and hockey players are brutes. Tiger Woods has pretty much taken care of the stereotypes around golfers. Venus and Serena Williams have blown away some of the sterotypes around female tennis players. Calvin Murphy and Allen Iverson challenged stereotypes around basketball players having to be tall to be successful.

Then there are myths. There's the myth of the lovable athlete who helps poor, disadvantaged children and the myth of the dedicated athlete, like Rocky, who never gives up and one day comes out on top. There's the myth of the underdog who comes up from behind and surprises everyone. There are myths about perseverance being more important than talent. There are myths about jinxing pitchers (e.g., to talk about them having a perfect game will jinx them). Then there are myths and superstitions players have about what to do when they are on a winning streak (such as wearing the same socks, doing things in a certain order, lucky bats or sports gear, and so on).

Be on the lookout for myths and stereotypes around sports—and try to determine what they tell us about our society and the value we place on our athlete-heroes.

Group Exercise

Share your thoughts on the connection between our sense of heroes and sports figures:

- What are the three or four main characteristics of a hero in our culture?
- Name three people generally regarded as heroes.
- What are the three or four main characteristics of a sports "superhero"?
- Name three sports figures generally regarded as superheroes.

Exercises

Save one week's worth of sports pages from the newspaper *and* watch at least one week's worth of sports programs on the nightly news. Cut and paste the most significant articles you draw from and include with your answers, as an appendix (at the back) of your discussion.

Answer the following:

1. What myths and stereotypes (about athletes, about men and women, about fans, about the audience, etc.) are found in the sports coverage?

2. What do sportscasters and journalists <u>assume</u> on the part of the audience in terms of sports knowledge and interest? (Remember: An assumption is something taken as a given, as if it were a fact, without giving any evidence to support this). List any such assumptions and note which are warranted and which are unwarranted.

3. What does the sports coverage on TV and in the newspaper tell us about our society? Assume you are an anthropologist studying the society and all you have to go on are the sports pages and sports news coverage on TV.

Heroes and Role Models

Think of the functions heroes serve in our society and why we need to have them. For some, athletes are clearly role models, whether we like it or not. Others disagree. As Paul Daugherty put it,

> It is amazing, . . . that anyone can still equate strength and speed with grace and virtue. It's astounding that we still expect jocks to perform like Superman and behave

like Clark Kent. Old cliches never die. Some don't even fade away. I suppose at some long-ago point in time, it made sense for kids to look up to athletes with the same glazed admiration reserved for mothers and fathers and teachers and clergymen. That time is pretty much done. . . . Athletes are not role models. If anything, athletes need role models. Athletes act illegally, immorally and with selfish abandon. That is to say, they act like most of the rest of us. Yet we insist on holding them to a higher standard of conduct. (See Paul Daugherty, "It's Misguided to Label Athletes as Role Models," Scripps Howard News Service, 10 Aug. 1993)

Daugherty goes on to say, "Athletes aren't role models. They are heroes. There is a difference." Daugherty may be right, but, for most people, our heroes *are* role models. We want our sports heroes to be subjects of adulation, capable of standing for more than physical finesse and team smarts. That is why the line between hero and role model is blurred.

Like it or not, they often serve as role models and are expected to dispense folk wisdom accordingly. For instance ex–Dallas Cowboy Troy Aikman, the only quarterback in NFL history to win three out of four Super Bowl games, said, "In many ways, the worst season for me was also the best season for me. Going 1–15 allows me to keep in perspective how hard it is to win—and I don't care how good you are." Aikman suggested we keep a sense of perspective on events and stay aware that, no matter what our talents may be, we don't always come out winners. His advice functions as folk wisdom.

And so it is for sports superstars: their insights on sports are offered as metaphors for life, pearls of wisdom meant to guide us along our paths. This is what heroes do for us, leading the way and offering their guidance as they go. With such power and significance, it is no wonder that the nightly news devotes time to sports coverage.

Sports and Morality

It is interesting to consider the assumptions and values we hold about sports. For example, we assume that winning the gold is considerably more meaningful than winning the silver or the bronze. We assume that a certain amount of violence is acceptable on and off the playing field. And so on. You add to the list.

These assumptions and values shape a set of prescriptions about what we expect to see. They also tell us what we consider permissible behavior by individuals and teams, what we should tolerate on the part of fans, and what sort of relationship we want athletes to have with the general public.

For every Yoda, there is a Darth Vader; for every hero, there is a villain. So too is this true in sports. Many sports stars become idols, worshipped by an adoring public. But that is not to say sports figures have to be perfect—hardly. We tolerate a certain amount of deviation from moral goodness. For example, the society puts up with some alcohol and substance abuse, unprofessional behavior on the court or field, and domestic violence on the part of athletic superstars. We tolerate moral weakness, particularly if there's an expression of remorse or steps are taken to get help so they can address their "shortcomings."

Babe Ruth's drinking problems and womanizing was tolerated, so long as he was still capable of success as a player. The public tolerated Michael Jordan's gambling weaknesses, Mike Tyson's rape conviction, and Daryl Strawberry's alcohol and substance abuse. Public response to the widespread steroid use by basketball and NFL players has been fairly tepid.

This tolerance may relate to our collective desire that our heroes not be found to be lacking the moral qualities we hold most dear. It may also show our awareness that even superstars are human and, at least to some degree, not that different from the rest of us. Of course, there are limits—times when the public has to assess athletes as public figures. For example, when the news broke about Magic Johnson's HIV status, in that one week there were 259 news articles, 18 front-page stories, more lead stories on network news (8) than all other news around major AIDS events combined in the 11-year period 1985–96 (see "Covering the Epidemic," *Columbia Journalism Review,* July/Aug. 1996).

Politics and Sports

Every so often, controversies arise in sports or with regard to individual teams or athletes. It's unusual, but not impossible for issues around religion or politics to affect the way in which an athlete is perceived. For example, a few years back then Dodger shortstop Greg Gagne got both positive and negative publicity around his being a born-again Christian. Let's look at a particular case that continues to have repercussions about the connections between sports and politics, as well as individual liberties versus societal values. The case below concerns the boundaries of freedom of religion and what should be done when religious practices enter the sports arena. As critical thinkers, we want also to see the way in which the news media responded to the incident. One of our tasks is to determine what factors played a role in the news coverage. You decide if the coverage was in any way influenced by the fact that the athlete was Muslim (as opposed to being a Christian, Jew, Sikh, Hindu, etc.).

CASE STUDY

The Basketball Player and the National Anthem

On March 12, 1996, Mahmoud Abdul-Rauf, a Denver Nuggets basketball player refused to stand for the national anthem. Arguing that it went against his beliefs as a Muslim, Abdul-Rauf said, "I don't criticize those for standing; don't criticize me for sitting." It didn't go over with the public or with the NBA. The NBA fined him and suspended him indefinitely—until such time that he agreed to stand for the national anthem (which he did the next day).

Abdul-Rauf's refusal to stand for the national anthem evoked a national outcry. This tells us something about our values around sports. We expect our heroes to respect and honor the fundamental elements, including the symbols and rituals, of our society. Saluting the flag and singing the national anthem represents our commitment to this country and its underlying system of beliefs. One of the many responses to this case was that this was a question of religious freedom. As argued by Lupe Chavez in a letter to the USC student newspaper, the *Daily Trojan:*

In addition to protection under the First Amendment, Abdul-Rauf is protected by civil rights laws, which state that no person should be discriminated against or forced to do something against their religion. Why have we fought for freedom if all people are not to be guaranteed equal rights? (Letter to the editor, *Daily Trojan,* 28 Mar. 1996)

In response, Stand R. Escalante disagreed with Chavez and asserted that the NBA contract should prevail:

Assuming Abdul-Rauf enjoys this right, we can definitely conclude that he waived any such rights in exchange for valuable consideration, by virtue of his NBA contract. Let us examine the facts: Abdul-Rauf agreed to abide by the terms of his contract, in exchange for which the Denver Nuggets agreed to compensate him handsomely. Part of the contract obligates him to abide by the NBA rules. A subset of these rules requires all NBA players to stand during the playing of the national anthem as a sign of respect. The rules do not obligate him to espouse or compromise certain beliefs, nor do they obligate him to become a poster boy for "Stars and Stripes" magazine. They simply obligate him to stand during the anthem as a measure of respect. (Letter to the Editor, *Daily Trojan,* 3 Apr. 1996)

Exercises

1. Assess Escalante's reasoning in his above comments about Abdul-Rauf's refusing to stand for the national anthem. Note the strengths and weaknesses of his argument.

2. How might an advocate of Abdul-Rauf's position respond to Escalante? Set out three key points that might counter Escalante's claims.

3. Read the comments of El-Hajj Mauri' Saalakhan below and then share your response:

   Br. Mahmoud [Abdul-Rauf] generated controversy in March 1996, when he quietly declined to participate in the nationalistic ceremony that precedes each game in the NBA. Controversy was not his aim; he was merely following the dictates of his conscience. As the Prophet is reported to have said to a companion who had come to ask about righteousness: "Consult your heart," the Prophet said. "Righteousness is that about which the soul feels tranquil and the heart feels tranquil, and wrongdoing is that which wavers in the soul and moves to and fro in the breast, even though people again and again have given you their legal opinion [in its favor]."

Mahmoud's conscience dictated that given all of the socio-political issues connected with such ceremony, participation in it might not be appropriate for a conscientious Muslim. The Messenger of Allah (pbuh) is also reported to have said: "Avoid those things which make you doubt. . . ." And this is what Mahmoud attempted to do. A confirmation of sorts of the brother's misgivings—regarding what appeared to most people on the surface as an innocent and harmless ritual— was the issue taken by an influential voice in U.S. policy making circles.

In an article published in the February 21, 2000, issue of the *National Review,* Daniel Pipes places Mahmoud Abdul Rauf on his short list of American-born Muslims, who, in his opinion, represent "a threat to the American way of life!" (See El-Hajj Mauri' Saalakhan of the *Lexington Area Muslim Network,* 8 Apr. 2000)

4. Discuss the following reaction to Abdul-Rauf's actions and to what degree you consider this a representative view:

   To us here at the Pit, we feel anyone making that kind of money should be damn happy he is living in the greatest country on the planet, and if he wants to join his friends over in the Middle East where he'd probably be killed in some war, that's just fine with us. (See *www.laughpit.com*)

5. Compare the news coverage of another sports-related case involving religious practices (such as short-stop Doug Gagne's attempt to inject his religious practice into the sports arena by trying to lead the team in prayer) with the Abdul-Rauf case. This may involve library research, going to news websites, running Internet searches (e.g., try "religious + conflict + sports") to find some examples. Share what you discover as a result of your research.

CASE STUDY EXERCISE

Mahmoud Abdul-Rauf's Suspension for Refusing to Stand for the National Anthem: A "Free Throw" for the NBA and Denver Nuggets, or a "Slam Dunk" Violation of Abdul-Rauf's Title VII Rights?

Kelly B. Koenig
Washington University of Law Quarterly
Volume 76 Number 1 Spring 1998

Argument Analysis: The Abdul-Rauf Case
In the article excerpt below, the author examines the case from a legal standpoint, arguing in favor of Abdul-Rauf's right not to stand for the national anthem. Read the article, pulling out the key arguments. Set out the key claims and then whether or not you found the argument convincing.

Introduction

In 1965, Sandy Koufax, a Jewish baseball player, refused to pitch in the first game of the World Series because it fell on a holy day, Yom Kippur. In 1967, numerous state boxing commissions stripped Muhammad Ali of his boxing license and of his heavyweight title when, as a result of his Muslim beliefs, he refused to step forward for the draft during the Vietnam conflict. More recently, in 1996, the National Basketball Association (NBA) suspended then Denver Nugget Mahmoud Abdul-Rauf without pay when he refused to abide by a league rule that requires "players to line up in a dignified posture for the anthem." Abdul-Rauf claimed that his Muslim beliefs precluded him from participating in the National Anthem because the Koran forbids participation in any "nationalistic ritualism." Moreover, Abdul-Rauf believed that the American flag and the National Anthem connote tyranny and oppression.

Religion and athletics have often conflicted in amateur sports as well as in the professional realm. . . . For example, at Memphis State University, several football players alleged that the coaches instituted a "no pray/no play rule." . . . The university . . . settled this issue by reprimanding the coaches for violating state education rules on religious activity. It is not uncommon for athletics and religion to conflict. . . . As a result, it is necessary to evaluate how much a professional athlete can allow his or her religious beliefs, practices and observances to affect his or her employment. Does the law require private athletic employers to accommodate an athlete's religious beliefs, and thus allow him or her to refrain from standing for the National Anthem? . . .

Historical Background of Abdul-Rauf's Claim

On March 12, 1996, Mahmoud Abdul-Rauf, a basketball player for the Denver Nuggets and a Muslim since 1991, announced that the NBA rule requiring players to "maintain a dignified posture" during the playing of the National Anthem prior to each game violated his religious beliefs. For most of the 1995–1996 basketball season, the Denver Nuggets, with NBA consent, allowed Abdul-Rauf to remain in the locker room during the anthem. In mid-March, fans began to notice that Abdul-Rauf was not standing for the anthem and, as a result, called Denver radio talk shows to voice their outrage. In light of this outrage, the Denver Nuggets changed their position. Although the Nuggets tried to resolve the matter, Abdul-Rauf was adamant in his decision to refrain from participating in the National Anthem.

Abdul-Rauf, a devoted Muslim, believed that the Koran prevented him from observing any "nationalistic ritualism." Furthermore, Abdul-Rauf believed that the American Flag and National Anthem symbolize oppression and tyranny. Standing for such a symbol, according to Abdul-Rauf, interfered with his loyalty to Islam. The NBA suspended Abdul-Rauf without pay on March 12, 1996, a move that cost him more than $30,000 per game. After a one game suspension, however, Abdul-Rauf agreed to stand and pray silently as the anthem played in the arena. . . .

Abdul-Rauf's sincerely held religious belief did not preclude him from fulfilling the essence of his employment duties. His primary duty was to play basketball. Once the National Anthem ended, Abdul-Rauf entered the arena and arrived at the Nuggets' bench prepared to play. Thus, the substitute employee factor is not a relevant component of Abdul-Rauf's accommodation analysis. . . . Specifically, the NBA could have allowed Abdul-Rauf to refrain from participating in the National Anthem or it could have, as it did, required him to stand for the National Anthem. Unlike accommodating the Seventh-

Day Adventist, the Worldwide Church of God member or the Orthodox Jew by switching shifts to give the employee his or her Sabbath off, there were no similar alternatives available to accommodate Abdul-Rauf.

Based on these first two factors, accommodating Abdul-Rauf's religious beliefs would not be a difficult requirement to inflict on the NBA and Denver Nuggets. . . . In most cases, there are only two or three interested parties involved, including the employee, the employer and possibly a substitute employee. In the context of professional sports, however, . . . Fan reactions to athletes adhering to a particular religious practice can have a significant impact on the financial success of a team or sport. Specifically, fans can demonstrate their objections by choosing to refrain from attending the sporting events, watching games on television, and buying team merchandise. By doing so, fans are capable of directly lowering ticket sales and profits. . . .

It is important to evaluate how fan reactions may impact Abdul-Rauf's potential case. Once Abdul-Rauf's routine of remaining in the locker room during the National Anthem hit Denver Radio shows, numerous callers angrily noted that Abdul-Rauf had been willing to accept American prosperity. . . . They expected a quid pro quo from him with regard to respecting the National Anthem. Moreover, by March 14, 1996, just two days following his suspension, the Denver Nuggets received more than two hundred phone calls from irate fans threatening to boycott games as long as Abdul-Rauf remained with the team. Many fans threatened to cancel their season tickets. Moreover, the league itself feared that [this might] . . . translate into a reduction in support from advertisers and television networks. . . . Even if the NBA and the Denver Nuggets accommodated Abdul-Rauf's religious belief, the evidence suggests

that they would have incurred significant financial losses.

Fan Factor as an Undue Hardship
. . . The NBA and the Denver Nuggets have a strong argument that the fan factor would cause them undue hardship if forced to accommodate Abdul-Rauf's religious belief. The significant impact of the fan factor is unique to professional athletic employment. . . . [A] professional athletic employer will often be able to avoid accommodation based on a fear of both fan outrage and the loss of advertisers' support. . . . As a result, it is likely that if fans voiced outrage and threatened to refrain from attending games, the NBA and the Denver Nuggets would have a strong argument that they would have incurred an undue hardship if required to accommodate Abdul-Rauf.

Proposal
. . . First, athletic employers cannot be sure that angry fans will carry out their threats and refrain from attending games or purchasing team merchandise because of a player's religious beliefs and observances. Second, employers cannot be sure that advertisers will withdraw or alter their relationships. . . . [U]ndeterminable financial losses should not be allowed to override an employee's right to adhere to his or her religious beliefs. Therefore, the Denver Nuggets should have been forced to accommodate Abdul-Rauf's religious beliefs until they could quantify their undue hardship as a result of the fan factor. . . . [In] situations such as Abdul-Rauf's, where the employer is unable to calculate financial losses or even to demonstrate that losses would occur as a result of accommodation, the fan factor alone should not be enough to create an undue hardship for the employer. Moreover, an athletic employer forced to hire or negotiate with a replacement employee should not be treated

differently from any other private employer who faces a similar situation. . . .

Conclusion

. . . It is appropriate then, that courts ensure that athletic employers are not able to use the fan factor to hide the ball from the athlete-employee. Rather, all private employees, from famous and affluent athletes to modest assembly line workers, should be treated equally. . . . In short, all private employers must play the ac-commodation game on the same court. Likewise, all private employees must have an equal chance to catch the ball and to pursue their religious beliefs.

Note: To access the footnotes and to see the entire article, please go to the Washington University Law Quarterly *(www.wulaw.wustl .edu/WULQ/76-1/761-23.html). Reprinted with the permission of the* Washington University Law Quarterly.

CHAPTER TEN

The Seductive Screen: Film and TV

In principle I am now for censorship in the medium. I have to accept that I belong to the ranks of the menacing.

—ANTHONY BURGESS, author of *A Clockwork Orange*

At times screen characters seem larger than life and the real world dull and less substantial by comparison. What we see on screen affects our thoughts, values, and the very way we perceive and solve problems. Our entire culture, even our language, has been shaped by TV and film. Most people watch TV and movies more often than they read. The consequences for the society are dramatic in terms of dissemination of information and culture.

In the past, people read, told stories, sat around campfires sharing tall tales, and had nightly story-telling rituals at children's bedtime. Now the average person reads little, rarely sits around campfires, and mostly shares family stories at family holidays, weddings, or funerals. But that doesn't mean we have lost touch with mythology, morality, and social issues. The stories unfolding on the screen are often deeply connected to stories and myths embedded in our cultural history.

We can apply critical thinking to these two media—and look at the underlying meaning, patterns, stereotypes, and both implicit and explicit messages about how to live and think. We need to see if there are links between what we see on screen and the ownership and control of the media (the power structure). This involves assessing and constructing arguments, drawing inferences, examining film reviews, analyzing films, and looking at the issues around the societal impact of film.

"The movie is the total realization of the medieval idea of change, in the form of an entertaining illusion," says Marshall McLuhan in *Understanding Media*. He says the business of the filmmaker is to transfer the viewer from one world to another so that those undergoing the experience accept it subliminally and without critical awareness. Producer Edward Zwick says, "There are no truths, only stories. In my life, art has meant narrative . . . only narrative can reach us in a kind of limbic place where learning begins" (see "The Campaign Celebration," *Harvard* magazine, Vol. 102, No. 6, July–August 2000).

Some "entertaining illusion" provides the viewer with an escape from reality. Some take us into realities we only pictured in nightmares. Some movies show us wimpy, milquetoast men who acquire extraordinary strength and power or female heroes who reduce grown men to pulp. Some have an otherworldly dimension, some are creepy, whereas some are downright nasty, brutish, and cold. At times heroes and villains are clearly distinct; other times the line is blurred. There are villains that make such an impact that they are resuscitated in sequel after sequel. Even flesh-eating convicts who manage to ingratiate themselves as alter egos of detectives and FBI agents become cultural icons.

Group Exercise

In the summer of 1998, the American Film Institute published their list of the top 100 films. The top 10 were: *Citizen Kane, Casablanca, The Godfather, Gone With the Wind, Lawrence of Arabia, Wizard of Oz, The Graduate, On the Waterfront, Schindler's List, Singin' in the Rain.*

Does anything strike you about this list? Only one of these (*Schindler's List*) was made within the last 10 years. In a bow to the present decade, list what you consider the top 10 films made in the last 5 to 10 years. Then do a quick assessment:

1. Did the films have an overriding social message?

2. What sorts of things do we look for in calling a film a work of art?

3. What makes a film a <u>classic</u>?

Exercise

What can you infer about men and women and their film interests looking at the following poll results? State your conclusions:

2001 International Movie Database Users Poll

Top 10 Movies Voted For by Male Users

Rank	Title
1	*The Godfather* (1972)
2	*The Shawshank Redemption* (1994)
3	*Shichinin no samurai (Seven Samurai)* (1954)
4	*The Godfather: Part II* (1974)
5	*Memento* (2000)
6	*Citizen Kane* (1941)
7	*Casablanca* (1942)
8	*Star Wars* (1977)
9	*Schindler's List* (1993)
10	*Dr. Strangelove or: How I Learned to Stop Worrying and Love the Bomb* (1964)

Top 10 Movies Voted For by Female Users

Rank	Title
1	*Pride and Prejudice* (1995) (mini)
2	*The Shawshank Redemption* (1994)
3	*Schindler's List* (1993)
4	*La Vita è Bella (Life is Beautiful)* (1997)
5	*The Usual Suspects* (1995)
6	*The Godfather* (1972)
7	*Wo hu cang long (Crouching Tiger, Hidden Dragon)* (2000)
8	*Moulin Rouge* (2001)
9	*The Sixth Sense* (1999)
10	*Memento* (2000)

Note: Only regular voters could vote.
Source: *www.imdb.com*, 12 Aug. 2001.

▦ The Interface between Film and Reality

Films may leave an impression, whether we like it or not. Images can be extremely powerful, as we know from the study of advertising in Chapter 8. According to bell hooks, media images have so much power that they distort reality and encourage children to seek solace in fantasy (see *Reel to Real*). As we see in *The Republic,* Plato expressed a similar idea much earlier. He argued that children are highly impressionable and, thus, we must guard against their exposure to works that might leave a lasting impact. He thought that images, music, and stories create so powerful an effect it can't be eradicated.

Think about it. There are horror movies that mutate into nightmares. But there are also scenes, characters, and even dialogue that make a mark. Think of lines like "Hasta la vista, baby," "Go ahead, make my day," "You can't handle the truth," "Show me the money," and "Here's looking at you, kid." These phrases have been incorporated into our thoughts and speech.

If film were not such a powerful medium, there would not be so many questions raised about its potential social impact. Social commentators like Ed Guerrero, Cornel West, Kathy Maio, and Michele Wallace have been concerned about the treatment of women and people of color in film. Such concern motivates film commentators to also examine audience reaction to assess the social impact of a film. For example, audiences cheered during *Set It Off* and *In The Bedroom,* men expressed disgust in *Wild Things* at one woman making a pass at another one; women watching *Thelma and Louise* openly hooted and screamed, and black women cursed out loud and yelled at the screen during *He Got Game,* when the lead character, a black man, got sexually involved with a white woman.

Exercises

1. In *Understanding Media* Marshall McLuhan says, "The movie is not only a supreme expression of mechanism, but paradoxically it offers as product the most magical of consumer commodities, namely dreams."
   a. Do you agree with McLuhan that movies offer us dreams?
   b. Cite three examples of films that show we can (or, alternatively, cannot) escape from class roles and gender and ethnic stereotypes.

2. What is the social significance of horror films? Set out three or four ideas explaining why audiences flock to films like *The Exorcist, The Shining, Nightmare on Elm Street, Poltergeist,* and *Night of the Living Dead.*

3. What factors help create a surprise hit on either TV or film? (Think, for instance, of films *Speed, The Full Monty, Legally Blonde, Fast and the Furi-*

ous, and *Babe* and of TV shows *Alias, Friends, CSI, Malcolm in the Middle, Six Feet Under, Sex and the City,* and *The Sopranos*).

4. Why are some films box office duds? If a film executive asked for your advice on why some films are total failures at the box office, what would you say? Share your thoughts.

Key Concerns: Applying Critical Thinking to Film and TV

The following checklist sets out some key concerns. Add those of yours to this list:

Checklist: Film and Television

1. *Frame of Reference*
   - From whose perspective is the story told?
   - Are there any other relevant perspectives?
   - What would change if we shifted the frame of reference?
   - How does the frame of reference shape our perceptions of the story?

2. *The Mythological Dimension*
   - Are there links to earlier myths, fairy tales, folk tales, universally shared stories?
   - What major archetypes (such as heroes, villains, trusty sidekicks, damsels in distress), characterizations, and patterns are presented?
   - What mythic elements like the hero's journey and obstacles are in the film?
   - What sorts of universal messages, symbols, and images are in the film?

3. *The Social Dimension*
   - How are factors of race, gender, age, nationality, class, and education expressed?
   - What vision of society or community is being presented?
   - How is the family is presented?
   - What social issues are explicitly or implicitly addressed?
   - How are issues like sexuality, relationships, and psychological conflicts presented?
   - What are the political messages of the film?
   - How do issues of economic class inform our interpretation?

4. *Ethical and Spiritual Dimension*
   - What values and beliefs are expressed?
   - Are there any religious messages or religious symbols?
   - Are there any value conflicts presented?
   - Would a shift of perspective affect the values portrayed?
   - Is there integrity in characterizations of individuals and communities?
   - How are the issues of good versus evil dealt with?

5. *The Justice Dimension*
- What is expressed or implied about justice vs. injustice?
- How is the law presented (e.g., law-abiding citizens vs. vigilantes, well-ordered society vs. lawless anarchy, honest vs. corrupt politicians, trustworthy vs. nontrustworthy lawyers and police)?
- Are there any stereotypes in the portrayals of characters?
- Who has power and is that power used in a just way?
- Are the race relations realistically portrayed?
- What concepts of justice, compassion, and fairness are expressed?

6. *Philosophical Dimension*
- What philosophical ideas and issues are raised?
- Are there any metaphysical concerns—such as the nature of the universe or the individual's place within a larger context?
- How is the existential dimension examined—such as the search for meaning, authenticity vs. inauthenticity, despair, facing death?
- How are concepts such as free will, personal identity, social responsibility, or other philosophical themes treated?

In using the checklist, select the key items that apply to the specific film/TV program, drawing from each of the six categories. Film theorists usually add a seventh component; namely the filmic aspects like cinematography, color, sound, music, film editing. They were omitted here because, without special training, assessing those areas has little value beyond mere opinion. That said, let's look at the six categories:

Frame of Reference

The vantage point or what is also called the frame of reference influences interpretations and can either reinforce or challenge how we think. This is the answer to the question, "From whose perspective is the story being told?"

Consider some examples: *Schindler's List* tells the story of the Holocaust from the frame of reference of the victims, not the oppressors. *Heavenly Creatures* tells the story from the frame of reference of a troubled girl who takes part in a murder. *Memento* tells the story from the frame of reference of a man who must reconstruct his past with a seriously deficient memory. *Sixth Sense* tells the story from the frame of reference of (as we discover at the end) the ghost of a dead psychologist. Very different stories would be told if we saw the Holocaust through the eyes of a Nazi, if we saw the troubled girl through the eyes of the murdered mother, and so on. Being aware of the unseen perspectives is crucial.

The Mythological Dimension

The mythological dimension is found in both TV and film. For instance, heroic journeys; struggles with demons and monsters, gladiators, knights, and other mythic figures; Egyptian mummies; curses; vampires; nightmares; and fantasies keep showing up in TV and film. Myths help us find our way in the world. Facing our fears and the darkness within are part of that mythological history.

Consider one mythic feature—the underworld. This is a fixture of action and sci-fi films. Time after time the protagonist ventures into an abyss, a cavernous realm, deep space, an underworld, a cave, or cellar before monstrous obstacles can be overcome. *Alien,* for example, has an ominous scene where some of the crew enters the alien's breeding ground. Indiana Jones has to confront his own fears in a pit filled with snakes. In *Cliffhanger,* the heroes face a cave filled with bats. In *Demolition Man,* we see an entire group of people (rebels) living in a subterranean world under the city, and the hero of *Ghost* acquires key skills from an under-worldly ruler of the subway system. In *Ghostbusters II,* the heroes are lowered into the cavernous sewer system and barely escape falling into the river of pink sludge moving under New York City.

Like myth, like film. Healers and shamans of myth must pass through the valley of death or otherwise confront their own demons and deal with the spirits of the dead. Modern-day heroes must also. The hero often has an evil counterpart or adversary (e.g., Roy in *Blade Runner,* Hannibal Lecter in *Silence of the Lambs* and *Hannibal,* the Scorpion King in *The Mummy Returns,* and Darth Vader in *Star Wars*). Some characters are jolted to a higher state of consciousness (*Regarding Henry, Dry White Season, Accidental Tourist, With Honors*).

Mythological Aspects to Characters

Consider the treatment of men and women on the screen. There are mythological aspects in the characters men portray, such as:

- Macho-heroes (*Diehard 1* and *2, Collateral Damage, True Lies, Rambo, Terminator 2: Judgment Day, Predator, Dirty Harry, Blade 1* and *2*).
- Clever heroes (*The Insider, Mission Impossible, Don't Say a Word, The Firm, The Conversation, Seven, Stargate, Patriot Games, Columbo, Outbreak, X-Files, Manhunter, Law and Order, The Bone Collector, Entrapment*).
- Martial arts heroes (*Crouching Tiger Hidden Dragon, Seven Samurai,* most films of Jackie Chan, Bruce Lee, Jean-Claude Van Damme).
- Bumbling or funny heroes (*Forrest Gump, L.A. Story, Being There, Raising Arizona, Beverly Hills Cop, Born in East L.A., There's Something About Mary, Meet the Parents, What About Bob?, Duck Soup, Pink Panther, Get Shorty, The Bandits*).
- Heroes with a cause (*In the Heat of the Night, Independence Day, Gandhi, Malcolm X, Cradle Will Rock, Mississippi Burning, To Kill a Mockingbird, Geronimo, Matewan, Talk Radio, Powwow Highway, Sixth Sense*).
- Heroes facing racism/racial tensions (*Higher Learning, Jungle Fever, Mississippi Masala, Dry White Season, Boyz N the Hood, Do the Right Thing*).
- Heroes with aliases or disguises (*Superman, Brother From Another Planet, Star Man, True Lies, Batman, Witness, F/X, Spider-Man*).

- Heroes transformed by circumstances (*A Beautiful Mind, Wings of Desire, Groundhog Day, Shawshank Redemption, The Doctor, Training Day, Dances with Wolves, Thunderheart, Wall Street, Cast Away, Jerry Maguire, Witness, Il Postino*).
- Villains (*Star Wars, Boys From Brazil, Aliens, Terminator, T2 Judgment Day, Matrix, The Perfect Murder, Ghost, Cool Hand Luke, Apt Pupil , Betrayed, The Gift*).
- Male buddies (*Men in Black, Batman, Lethal Weapon, Rush Hour, Showtime, O Brother Where Art Thou?, Smoke Signals, Blues Brothers, Butch Cassidy and the Sundance Kid*).

There are also mythological aspects in the characters women portray, such as:

- Heroic female figures (*Matrix, Erin Brokovich, Fargo, Terminator, T2 Judgment Day, Coma, Blue Sky, The Music Box, Silence of the Lambs, Fargo, Alien, Thunderheart, Beloved, Mississippi Massala, Qiu Ju, Crouching Tiger, Hidden Dragon, Lone Star, Sister Act, X-Files*).
- Nurturing or supportive figures (*Amelie, Testament, The Deep End, Stuart Little, Sixth Sense, October Sky, Ghost, Tumbleweeds, Poltergeist, Mi Familia/My Family, Soul Food, Bagdad Cafe*).
- Muses or sources of inspiration (*Harold and Maude, Alice, Desperately Seeking Susan, Lord of the Rings, Cold Comfort Farm, Matrix*).
- Heroic women transformed by circumstances (*Central Station, Girlfight, Dark Angel, Alias, The Accused, Buffy the Vampire Slayer, What's Love Got to Do With it?, The Official Story, Last of the Mohicans, The Song Catcher*).
- Dead or missing mother figures (*Cinderella, Star Wars, The Little Mermaid, The Teenage Mutant Ninja Turtles, Never Ending Story, The Princess Bride, Beauty and the Beast, Mulan, Pocahontas, Fly Away Home, The Secret Garden, Crossing Jordan*).
- Villains/witches/hags (*Snow White, Little Mermaid, Willow, Wizard of Oz, The Witches, Robin Hood, Prince of Thieves, 101 Dalmatians, Mommy Dearest, One Flew Over the Cuckoo's Nest, Misery, Fatal Attraction, Single White Female*).
- Sirens—Young, nubile witches (*Disclosure, Fatal Attraction, Basic Instinct, Queen of the Damned, The Hand That Rocks the Cradle, Working Girl, Total Recall, True Lies, Wild Things, Spawn, Species*).
- Troubled women, women in distress, victims (*Wait Until Dark, Girl Interrupted, Carrie, The Accused, Dead Calm, Kiss the Girls, Frances, The Birds, Psycho, Two Women, Unlawful Entry, The Terrorist, Single White Female, Silence of the Lambs, The Cell, Exorcist, Beloved, Enough*).
- Buddy figures (*Thelma and Louise, Julia, Beaches, Outrageous Fortune, Charlie's Angels, Set it Off, Boys on the Side, Fried Green Tomatoes, Waiting to Exhale, La Vida Loca, Ghost World*).
- Girls of power (*Spy Kids, Wizard of Oz, Fly Away Home, Anna to the Infinite Power, Anne of Green Gables, Princess Mononoke, Mulan, Aliens, Selena*).

Exercise

Add any categories and examples you consider missing from either or both of the two lists above. Then, in two or three paragraphs, discuss what you infer about societal attitudes around class, gender, race, religion, and ethnicity, from the ways in which both male and female heroes are presented.

The Social Dimension

It is important to consider the social dimension of film. We can use our critical reasoning skills to examine social issues, such as social structures and political systems, the way individuals deal with a societal framework, the portrayal of families and relationships, the way social problems are solved, and the employment of violence to "resolve" conflict.

Here's how families fare: Mothers are usually missing or dead in children-oriented films (e.g., *The Secret Garden, Fly Away Home, Star Wars, Lara Croft: Tomb Raider, Indiana Jones,* virtually all Disney films). Occasionally there are fiercely protective mothers, especially in films directed to adults (*The Deep End, T2 Judgment Day, Aliens*). Fathers tend to be loving, dependable, and strong, but some films present husbands and fathers in a negative light (*The Piano, The Stepfather, October Sky, American Beauty, What's Love Got to Do With It?,* and *Radio Flyer*). TV shows of the past like *Little House on the Prairie, Leave it to Beaver,* and *Father Knows Best* present idyllic families with wonderful fathers and doting, submissive mothers. More recently, there are some nuclear families (e.g., *Everybody Loves Raymond, The Sopranos, Beverly Hills 90210*), but there are also single-parent families (*Third Watch, The Practice, ER*) and even dysfunctional families (*Six Feet Under*). Then reality TV gave us *The Osbournes,* where we got to watch a celebrity family. Why such a hit? Former NBC exec Warren Littlefield says, "The Osbournes to me are a hugely relatable family, and they're famous and a little crazy, but human and identifiable." (See Alex Kuczynski, "In Hollywood, Everyone Wants to be Ozzy," *The New York Times,* 19 May 2002).

We need to observe how TV and film families and relationships are structured and unearth assumptions and attitudes. We need to look also at who gets marginalized. Rarely are there elderly lead characters. Equally rare are film treatments of illness, death, or disability—and those themes tend to be romanticized. TV and film take place within a societal and cultural context that affects both what is produced and what is affected by those productions.

If the real world reflected the screen world, here's what we'd find: There would be many more boys than girls; vastly more whites than people of color; lots of male buddy-partnerships in work; fewer mothers; more attentive fathers; significantly more men than women; many prostitutes and strippers; an astonishing number of serial rapists and murderers; a scattering of gorgeous women, many of whom are victimized; almost no one who is old, frail, or has disabilities other than blindness; many alien creatures; robots; and human-looking zombies, mutants, androids, cyborgs, and vampires. The society would be ridden with violence and conflicts resulting in a vast amount of gun-related violence, bombs, explosions, men leaping across rooftops, people falling through glass ceilings or large windows, phones that don't work, an inept or corrupt police force, lots of lone heroes who prevail in the face of extraordinary odds.

Concerns about the social impact of film abound; even senators and presidential candidates have voiced concerns. For example, philosopher Sissela Bok's book *Mayhem* centers on the societal impact of film—pleading for a change toward a more socially conscious approach. Ex-Senator Bob Dole finds some movies "friendly to families," while others are "nightmares of depravity." His examples of films that support family values are *The Lion King, True Lies, The Santa Clause, The Flintstones,* and *Forrest Gump.*

Dole accused Hollywood of promoting violence, rape, and casual sex in music and movies and said that "the mainstreaming of deviancy must come to an end, but it will only stop when the leaders of the entertainment industry recognize and shoulder their responsibility." He felt that a "line has been crossed—not just of taste but of human dignity and decency." He specifically criticized *Natural Born Killers* and *True Romance* as "films that revel in mindless violence and loveless sex." Dole said, "Televisions and movie screens, boom boxes and headsets are windows on the world for our children." He contends that, "our popular culture threatens to undermine the character of the nation."

More recently, *New Republic* writer Gregg Easterbrook echoed these concerns. As stated in *Voice of America:*

GREGG EASTERBROOK: This is the 1996 movie, *Scream,* a Disney movie, it contains roughly a dozen scenes of helpless people being butchered, screaming. This is a movie very popular, beloved by critics, promoted by the Disney corporation, and now broadly defended as the sort of thing that teens should be allowed to see in the name of freedom of speech.

NATURAL SOUND FROM MOVIE: Movies don't create psychos, they make psychos more creative. . . .

GREGG EASTERBROOK: It's full of jokes, but the fact that you make something full of jokes doesn't excuse glorification of violence. There's a dozen scenes in this movie showing people being butchered while people tell jokes. Is that entertainment? (*www.voa.gov/ thisweek /sampler /scree.html*)

On the other hand, there are others who consider violence part of our lives and an acceptable part of our entertainment. There was considerable speculation after the terrorist attacks on New York City and Washington, D.C., that Hollywood would be forced to undergo a radical transformation, that viewers would not tolerate the levels of violence that have been typical in recent years. Partly in response to this question, writer Andrew Klavan said:

After a violent atrocity, there is always a rush to declare that movies were partly to blame because they desensitize us to violence. But after Sept. 11, our collective response to the horror showed that the vast majority of people know the difference between movies and reality and react accordingly.

Many people remarked on how the video images of the terror on television looked incredibly like a Hollywood movie. But I haven't heard of anyone who reacted as if it actually were a Hollywood movie. We didn't sob when the building blew up in *Die Hard;* we didn't join the army when the aliens destroyed the White House in *Independence Day. . . .*

Violence, along with sex, is a part of entertainment because it is part of human experience. I happen to love action films, Mr. Schwarzenegger's in particular. It would do my crusty heart good to see the Terminator vanquish a terrorist right about now. Indeed, Mr. Schwarzenegger's oversized screen persona will strengthen my faith in the real Schwarzeneggers who have to fight our battles for us—so much greater than the screen image because they are so much smaller, so much braver because they are so mortal and fragile and afraid. (See "At the Movies, Losing Our Fears," *The New York Times,* 5 Oct. 2001.)

Exercise

Share your thoughts on the sentiments expressed below:

RICHARD BELZER: I believe that indiscriminate violence or excessive violence in film and television not only affects young but older people, too, and I think it desensitizes people and is dehumanizing, but I don't think it's the role of the government to discern at what point is violence dehumanizing. I think that's the discretion of producers and creative people to exercise their own taste, for parents and educators and critics and people in the arts to, if something does get created that is virulently dehumanizing, then people can speak out about it in the appropriate forums.

GREGG EASTERBROOK: I'm not in favor of censorship and no sensible person is. But there is a difference between saying that and saying everything should be shown. The sensible position is to ask Hollywood and especially companies like Disney to voluntarily stop promoting this kind of thing, not to attempt to censor it, you couldn't anyway, simply for Hollywood to ask themselves, what do they want their own children seeing? (*www.voa.gov/thisweek/sampler/scree.html*)

The Ethical and Spiritual Dimension

TV and film expose us to a set of values and beliefs—and some reflect the values of the dominant society. Screen treatments of moral decision making may also have a prescriptive effect. Some people think the impact is limited, that we are bombarded with many potentially conflicting influences. Others believe that the impact of TV and film is great; that both values and behavior are shaped by what we see.

Lawsuits over the perceived influence of TV and film illustrate the societal debate over this. TV shows and films said to have inspired acts of violence include *Murder in the Heartland, The Basketball Diaries, Taxi Driver, Kojak, The Deer Hunter, Born Innocent, MacGyver, The Program,* and *Child's Play 3.*

When assessing films for their ethical impact, watch for demonstrations of values and beliefs in the action, the characterizations, the language used, the images presented. Look also for subtle ways values and beliefs are presented. It is also beneficial to look at any spiritual and religious images, symbols, and messages. There is not always agreement as to what images and symbols mean. As we'll see on pages 414 to 416, one reviewer of *Sixth Sense* saw strong religious symbols and images, whereas others failed to mention any. Controversies over films like *The Lion King* and *Pokemon* illustrate how films can touch a societal nerve.

Film and TV often present struggles of good versus evil. Some show battles on a global or cosmic scale. For example, science fiction and action films frequently have a mythological or epic dimension to them. Films can both guide and inspire us. They have the power to reinforce moral complacency or can steer us down the right or wrong path. Movies like *Gandhi, Kundun, The Music Box, Schindler's List, Malcolm X, The Official Story, El Norte, In the Heat of the Night,* and *Dry White Season* present us with models of human goodness and show us people struggling with ethical decisions about good versus evil and trying to stay true to their own personal integrity. On the other hand, *A Simple Plan, Diabolique, The Postman Always Rings Twice,* and *Body Heat* show people unraveling or cornered by their own dishonesty.

▦ The Justice Dimension

Issues of justice are expressed in film in the treatment of the law, the legal system, and legal concepts, the portrayal of crime and punishment, reparations, and revenge. The political framework needs to be recognized and unpacked; the political dimension of TV and film may or may not be overt. For example, *The Rainmaker, A Few Good Men, To Kill a Mockingbird, The Official Story, 12 Angry Men, The Fugitive, Set it Off, Stand and Deliver, Erin Brokovich, Traffic, Witness for the Prosecution, Chinatown, O Brother Where Are Thou* present us with situations around justice versus injustice. *Return to Paradise, Dead Man Walking, Midnight Express,* and *Shawshank Redemption,* are powerful indictments of the justice system and penal institutions.

We need to be especially attentive to racist and stereotypical portrayals, a preponderance of female victims, and an imbalance of blacks, Latinos, Native Americans, Asians, and Germans portrayed as villains, pimps, dope dealers, deviants, or servants. We should watch for religious intolerance in the stories and characterizations. For example, *True Lies, Aladdin, The Siege,* and *Not Without My Daughter* were found particularly offensive to Muslims and Middle Easterners. All too many villains involving international incidents have been Middle Eastern, Asian, or Germanic. And far too many villains in localized cases of crime, mayhem, and murder have been Latino or African American. If we think there is any way such images and portrayals influence our perceptions of those around us, then justice has not been served.

Class issues on the screen are also interesting, particularly because they are usually missing. A few exceptions are *Journey of Hope, Germinal, Matewan, City of Hope, Born in East L.A., The Commitments, Joy Luck Club, Alice, The Full Monty,* and *Angela's Ashes.* We'd never know how much poverty there is or that most working people struggle to make ends meet. To judge by what we see, most people have very short workdays, plenty of cash, and lots of spare time. Most have few, if any social obligations or others to care for. Most seem to have little, if any, money worries. Most live in nice homes and nice neighborhoods, except for attractive single women who are preyed upon by murderous rapists, marauding bands of gangs in the downtown area and "poor" neighborhoods, and an awful lot of strip joints where men do business or detectives discuss crimes. If we are worried about our brains being imprinted by the screen, we should pay close attention to the materialism and sheer consumption we see.

Overall, we can get a sense of the justice dimension of screen portrayals and shows if we set out the concepts of justice and injustice implicitly or explicitly presented and determine if the portrayals of individuals and groups are realistic, skewed, prejudicial, idealistic, romanticized, and so on. Be careful to note who wields power and how decisions are made—and by whom. Examine the symmetry versus asymmetry in power relationships and in decision making. Furthermore, we should consider the potential impact of such justice-related issues in our collective mindset.

The Philosophical Dimension

Films frequently grapple with ideas and questions of meaning. We should watch for philosophical concepts and themes that are raised in films. For example, *Being John Malkovich, Total Recall, Memento, Gattica, Blade Runner, Blue, The Usual Suspects,* and *The Matrix* all raise metaphysical issues about what it means to be human, what traits form the basis of our sense of personal identity, how states of consciousness can be shaped or manipulated by outside forces, and how memory can be accessed, distorted, or reconfigured.

Some movies touch on philosophical themes like freewill vs. determinism, the search for meaning, what our place in the universe is, how to live in community, and how to confront life/death issues. For example, think of *Mystery Train, Purple Rose of Cairo, All of Me, Wings of Desire, Groundhog Day, Mississippi Massala, Blood Simple* and such films as *Invasion of the Body Snatchers, Frankenstein, Apocalypse Now Redux, Gods and Monsters* that show individuals facing cataclysmic bodily and/or mental turbulence.

Among the philosophical issues that focus on individuals are such existential themes as authenticity versus inauthenticity, and how characters confront such boundaries as death, dread, despair, and alienation. For example, think of the personal anguish over life-changing decisions in such movies as *Secrets and Lies, Testament, Every Mother's Son, Casablanca, Casualties of War, The Accused, Testament, Crimes and Misdemeanors, The Music Box,* and *Sophie's Choice.*

See how films grapple with questions about what we can be said to know, and what differentiates us from machines, cyborgs, androids, and animals. Articulate the worldview presented by or embedded in the film or TV show.

Group Exercise

Do a study of TV cartoons or a recent children's film. (e.g., *Monsters, Inc., Shrek, Ice Age, Toy Story 1* and *2, Spy Kids, Princess Mononoke, E.T., Mulan, Rugrats, Pokemon, Little Mermaid, Beauty and the Beast, The Lion King, Pokemon, The Simpsons*). Discuss any *one* of the following:

- The central dilemma and its resolution.
- The power dynamics between children and others.
- Male/female roles and stereotyping.
- Parent/child relationships.
- The nature of the hero.

Exercises

Part One

1. Study the portrayal of heroes:
   a. Draw up a list of male heroes found in both TV and film. Note what distinguishes them as heroes—their actions, personal characteristics, community positions, and so on.
   b. Draw up a list of female heroes found in both TV and film. Note what distinguishes them as heroes—their actions, personal characteristics, community positions, and so forth.
   c. Compare your lists, noting any patterns. Draw some inferences about what your lists tell us about the society.

2. Recently there have been films with African-American male heroes (such as *Ali, Passenger 57, Drop Zone, Pelican Brief, Kiss the Girls, The Siege, Men in Black, The Bone Collector, Independence Day, Blade*). How do the race and gender of their characters affect our sense of them as heroes?

3. Disney's *Snow White* and *Cinderella* are relatively unthreatening films for children. In contrast, Tim Burton (director of *Nightmare Before Christmas*

and *Planet of the Apes*) added a frightening, almost ghoulish touch to *James and the Giant Peach*. What would you do to make a film or TV show of a fairy tale or popular children's story with a political twist or as a social commentary? In three to four paragraphs, sketch out your approach or ideas. State which story you are using as a base.

4. Discuss the portrayal of women in any two prime-time TV shows and to what extent the portrayals are (a) positive, empowering; (b) negative, disempowering; and/or (c) realistic versus unrealistic.

5. Discuss the portrayal of men in any two prime-time TV shows and to what extent the portrayals are (a) positive, empowering; (b) negative, disempowering; and (c) sensitive to real-life issues.

6. bell hooks says the black maid in *Purple Rose of Cairo* broke through race, class, and gender boundaries when she put a pompous (white) man in his place with, "You better calm down—you've been up there on the screen flickering too long."

   Answer the following:
   a. Discuss ways stereotypes about men and women, as well as groups, are broken down because of film and TV.
   b. Cite any examples you can from recent movies or TV shows.

7. Pick two TV families (each from a different TV show) and compare and contrast the treatment of the family on television.
   a. Note the similarities and differences.
   b. Note any cultural stereotypes about the "typical" family. Look at such aspects as race, class, education, and family dynamics.
   c. Look also at the portrayal of the mothers and fathers.

8. How has TV dealt with sexuality? Answer *one* of the following, citing specific examples from TV shows:
   a. Do a study of a show that is aimed at both teenagers and adolescents and assess how realistic you think it is.
   b. Should TV show teenagers dealing with such issues as sex, birth control, sexually transmitted diseases, AIDS, and abortion?
   c. Given the widespread fear of AIDS, is it wise of producers to show so much unprotected sex on the screen?

9. Answer *one* of the following:
   a. List three to five films you find empowering or inspirational and explain why you picked these. Choose one from your list and go into detail.
   b. In TV shows like *Buffy the Vampire Slayer, Alias,* and *Dark Angel,* we see young female protagonists with superhuman strength and agility. What do these shows tell you about our society?

10. List three to five films that suggest there is hope for our society, that we can live together, that people are capable of acts of generosity and that people do have a sense of justice. Choose one of your five and go into detail.

Part Two

1. Does TV accurately portray the impact of racism, poverty, and oppression on the life of an individual? Make your case, citing examples.

2. Answer *one:*
   a. Give an argument for or against the claim: "TV should show a gay couple or an interracial couple raising a child, since it would reflect something that goes on in our society."
   b. Give an argument for or against the claim: "Children should be shielded from TV shows that present gays and lesbians in a sympathetic way."

3. When it comes to disabilities, we usually find the mystery tale (e.g., *Blink, Jennifer 8, Wait Until Dark*) where beautiful blind women outfox killers. Or we may find (as in *Scent of a Woman* and *At First Sight*) blind men with an attitude find compassionate, lovely young women who liberate them. Discuss the implications about our attitudes around disability from portrayals on screen.

4. What would be different if a film were presented from another character's frame of reference? Select either a classic or contemporary film *or* a prime-time TV program and explain what would be different if there was a shift in the frame of reference.

The Role of the Reviewer

Directors tend to have a love–hate relationship with reviewers. Although a good review can boost a picture, it doesn't guarantee success. Similarly, a movie can be panned by critics and become a big hit nevertheless. For example, when *Blade Runner* came out, the reviews were dismal; yet it is now one of the most written-about films of all time.

Reviewers have a tricky job: They need to make their judgment clear to the reader, give a sense of the story line, and set out reasons for their rating. This must be done succinctly and in a readable and engaging way. Because the review presents the film critic's assessment of the film, we need tools of analysis to see what the critic is saying and why. As we discussed in Chapter 2 on argumentation, we need to set out and weigh the evidence, make sure the conclusion has sufficient support, consider alternative hypotheses, and watch for omissions, unwarranted assumptions, and biased or prejudicial language.

It may help to walk through a review of a movie, *Mission Impossible*, that most of us have seen or can do so easily. Read the following excerpts from the review, looking at the way the reviewer makes his case. Key parts are in italics to clarify the structure.

Review Highlights of *Mission Impossible*

Mission: Impossible has lots going for it—a charismatic star in Tom Cruise, Brian De Palma's sleek, elegant direction, a first-rate cast, a superb suspense sequence, lots of action capped by a breathtaking stunt at the climax. And all the gadgetry, special effects and stunning production design that a $64-million budget can buy.

Yet at any given moment in super-secret agent Cruise's mission . . . *it is impossible to say with any confidence what's going on.* So you should approach this like the most convoluted Chinese kung fu movie: *Let it wash over you and don't try to figure anything out.* Proceed in the reasonably safe assumption that good will surely triumph over evil and that everything eventually will become clear, or at least fairly so. (See Kevin Thomas, "Superb Stunts and Suspense Stay in an 'Impossible' Story," *Los Angeles Times,* 21 May 1996)

In a nutshell, these two opening paragraphs convey Thomas's argument about the movie. In the rest of his article, he goes into detail about the movie. In his opening, we are briefly told the movie's strengths, the key weaknesses, what we can assume, and the implication that, as long as we are not too demanding, we will enjoy the movie. This introduction has a lot packed into it.

Key Elements of a Film Review

Reviews are an interesting form of argument: They have to tell a story so as not to lose the audience and they have to present a position that is backed up by evidence and examples. Reviews generally contain the following elements:

Key Elements of a Film Review

- A brief plot summary.
- An evaluation or rating.
- Key evidence and assumptions.
- Detail laying out the argument.
- Concluding remarks reiterating the rating.

Our task is to evaluate the strength of that evidence. For reviewers to do a good job, they need to make their case. So, in analyzing the review, examine it as an argument and evaluate it. See if the evidence offered lends sufficient support for the conclusion the reviewer has drawn.

Note that you can easily access film reviews and film criticism through websites like *www.imdb.com, filmlinc.com, www.filmcriticism.com, www.lib.berkeley .edu/MRC,* and *allmovie.com.*

Exercises

Part One

1. Draw all the inferences you can from the comments excerpted below reviewers made about *City of Angels:*

Reviewer 1 (Mark Peranson of the *Toronto Star*):
As an angel, Cage acts like he's hooked on methadone; after his fall, he's briefly a charming lout who very much conveys the joy of being alive. But [Meg] Ryan's character is pure Hollywood construct—the "doctor of the people" who bikes to work and makes house calls. . . . Despite overhead shots of LA and a powerful use of integrated special effects, the film aims as high as an empty Harlequin romance.

Reviewer 2 (Roger Ebert of the *Chicago Sun–Times*):
When there's a trend toward humility and selflessness, then we'll know we're getting somewhere on the spiritual front. That time is not yet. *City of Angels* hits the crest of the boom in angel movies—and like most of them, it's a love story. Hollywood is interested in priests and nuns only when they break the vow of chastity, and with angels only when they get the hots for humans. . . . Still, as angel movies go, this is one of the better ones, not least because Meg Ryan is so sunny and persuasive as a heart surgeon who falls in love with an angel. This is one of her best performances, as Dr. Maggie Rice.

Reviewer 3 (Shawn Levy of *The Oregonian*):
A melodramatic love story with a strong dose of New Age spiritual hooey, it has three seemingly insurmountable obstacles to overcome: Meg Ryan plays a heart surgeon; it's a Hollywood-ized remake of Wim Wenders' poetic 1988 masterpiece *Wings of Desire;* and Meg Ryan plays a heart surgeon in it. . . . The best thing by far is Cage. He's a genius of screen acting, able to give himself so wholly over to a part that he dissolves. His eyes are so calm and empathetic, his gaze so steady, his heart so plainly on his sleeve that he simply overwhelms you with earnestness. Late in the film, when he arrives on earth, he plays with unbridled comic gusto like a genie uncorked from a bottle. It's such a tremendous performance that he even makes Ryan look substantial.

Reviewer 4 (Shane Ham of *Journal X*):
Seth (Nicholas Cage) is an angel who is jealous of humans because they have five senses. He goes around Los Angeles doing the requisite chores for God, but he keeps notes on people, watching their moves and listening to their thoughts, and longs to be one of them. One day, while waiting to escort a man who dies on the operating table, he is entranced by Dr. Maggie Rice (Meg Ryan), a hot-shot heart surgeon who just happens to be as cute as Meg Ryan. Before long, Maggie is living her own personal episode of Stalked by an Angel, as Seth follows her everywhere and watches her do everything, including bathing. . . . Occasionally funny, occasionally touching, *City of Angels* seems as if it was made to be viewed by an audience with the perceptions of God himself: it takes eternity to get to the inevitable.

2. Study the review below of *Fargo*, and then discuss how Desson Howe makes his case:

The Coen Brothers' *Fargo*, a satirical, macabre saga set on the frigid plains of the American Midwest, works like a charm. A really weird charm, that is. . . . And throughout the hypnotized Midwestern atmosphere of this movie-picture a cross between Garrison Keillor's *A Prairie Home Companion* and George A. Romero's *Night of the Living Dead*—Frances McDormand enjoys the comedic role of her career.

In the story, which is loosely based on real events, Minnesota car salesman Jerry Lundegaard (William H. Macy) travels to Fargo, N.D., where he hires thugs Carl (Steve Buscemi) and Gaear (Peter Stormare) to have his wife (Kristin Rudrud) kidnapped. . . . The abductors get away with their hostage, but leave a bloody scene behind them. This brings in Police Chief Marge Gunderson. . . . Gunderson conducts her first murder investigation with remarkable, and comic, aplomb. At the crime scene, with bodies littered around an upturned car on the snowy plains, she performs her job with the chirrupy nature of a crossing guard. . . .

There's a nutty regionalism at work: A surrealistic statue of Paul Bunyan, for instance, greets visitors to Gunderson's little town; the goofy locals never seem to blink and pepper every sentence with a "Yaaaah." Into this, the Coens expertly weave the grotesque, as the kidnappers' desperate plight forces them to take bloodier measures.

But after watching this . . . I couldn't help wondering about Joel (the co-writer/ director) and Ethan (the co-writer/producer) Coen. . . . Their stories [are] basically boxes within boxes. . . . But the secret, the point, or the ultimate punch line becomes ever smaller. . . . Do these guys ever step outside themselves? Do they have a worldview, a feel for humanity? . . .

It's worth seeing *Fargo* if you have the taste for this kind of irony, but please, also mutter a short prayer for the filmmakers to step outside once in a while and breathe a little oxygen. (See Desson Howe, "In Cold Blood in Cold Climes," *The Washington Post*, 8 Mar 1996.)

3. Study three different reviews of any *one* of the current blockbuster movies of the week. Go into detail comparing and contrasting the three reviews of your movie.

4. Write a movie review of a movie you have seen in the last year, using the key elements of a film review (p. 411). Avoid reading any reviews of the film, so you can explore your own ideas and insights.

Part Two

1. Set out the argument and note any assumptions in the following discussion of film director Spike Lee:

In an interview after the release of the film [*Do the Right Thing*], [Spike] Lee said that he was constantly amazed at people indignant over the destruction of property, but ignoring the black youth's death. Lee was initially concerned to interrogate the conditions that could lead to wanton killings of black youth, spurred on by the Howard Beach killings in which white youth gratuitously assaulted black youth, leading to one of their deaths. Thus, Lee seems to believe that violent protest is a legitimate response to the senseless killing of blacks, as would, presumably, Malcolm X himself. In a book on the making of *Do the Right Thing*, Lee remarks: "The character I play in *Do the Right Thing* is from the Malcolm X school of thought: 'An eye for an eye.' Fuck the turn-the-other-cheek shit. If we keep up that madness we'll be dead." (See Douglas Kellner, "Spike Lee's Morality Tales," in Cynthia A. Freeland and Thomas E. Wartenberg, eds., *Philosophy and Film*.)

2. Set out the argument and note any assumptions in the following from film critic, Kathy Maio:

If male filmmakers cared what I and other feminists thought about their work (and they most assuredly do not), I'd almost pity their predicament. They face what amounts to a no-win situation. If they leave women out of their movies, or use us only as trivialized support characters, damsels in distress, or beautiful objects of their male lust, they get blasted for their sexism. If they use us as major characters, we still love to pick holes in their portrayals of women, and we blast them anyway. Of course, all this blasting is done for good reason. It seems as though it matters little whether it's a bimbo bit part or a dramatic lead, male filmmakers can't seem to keep themselves from saying nasty things about women. (See Kathy Maio, *Popcorn and Sexual Politics*)

Part Three

1. What traits do you think should be in a film seeking to be representative of the American character? List films that illustrate those traits.

2. What films best reflect the reality of your life or those closest to you? What qualities do you see in the films you selected?

3. Use the key elements of a film review to discuss a movie that made a positive impression on you. Write for an audience who is not acquainted with the film, explaining why the film deserves to be seen.

4. Do a study of three film reviews (find these at film sites on the Internet or in film journals).
   a. Briefly characterize (or set out) the key points of each review.
   b. Write a response or a short letter (two to three paragraphs) to *one* of the reviewers about the review. Be sure to share some of your own feedback on his/her argument and a few of your own ideas about the film.

CASE STUDY

Reviews of *The Sixth Sense*

Read the following excerpts from reviews of The Sixth Sense *and answer the following:*

1. Share your thoughts on what the reviews reveal about the focus, interests, and values of the individual reviewers.
2. Draw some inferences about the weight that should be given to the writer/director's comments about what the film means.

Review 1

Some movies do the twist. They stand or fall on their endings. They have no content except the last big reversal. They twist the night away. So when I say that the ending of writer–director M. Night Shyamalan's "*The Sixth Sense*" knocked me out of both socks, and I loved that pure moment of revelation, you must bear in mind that—hard as it is to recall now—for the first hour and a half it depressed me. . . . The movie is a maximum creep-out. It's invasive. It's like an enema to the soul as it probes the ways of death—some especially grotesque in a family setting. You leave slightly asquirm. You know it will linger. It becomes a clammy, chilly movie building toward a revelation that you cannot predict. As I say: I cannot tell you. You'd hate me if I did. I can only say, don't look now, but look sometime. (Stephen Hunter, *The Washington Post*)

Review 2

As *The Sixth Sense* winds towards a conclusion, shedding uncertain layers to reveal intelligence, it becomes ever sadder. Despite knowing that some good has emerged from this cinematic therapy, it's hard not to feel the void's bone-chill. Then, with a genuine last minute unveiling, Shyamalan both binds the film together and heightens your emptiness. At that exact instant you want to watch it again, to catch the tracks that appear so clear in retrospect; not for the scary moments, but for the scenes in-between. Sure, sophisticated use of effects provides the former, but Shyamalan knows that he's not here to create a cookie-cutter horror story—his desire is to investigate the power of healing and redemption. There are loose ends and unconvincing lines to be sure, but few enough to ensure that *The Sixth Sense* provokes thought rather than derision. (Damian Cannon, *Movie Reviews UK 1999*)

Review 3

Thus, *The Sixth Sense* serves to replace the psychological pain, and we leave the film believing that perhaps the apparitions will cease as he reestablishes communication with his mother. Malcolm, satisfied with his success in treating Cole, then learns to accept his own fate and achieves peace of mind as well. Although the tagline of the film is "Not every gift is a blessing," the film should definitely appeal to those who have had difficulty accepting a loss of an important family member, dead or alive. The music

and sound effects keep up the tension in what is otherwise a rather slow-moving story that is clearly designed to comfort those of all ages who fear death. (*Political Film Society Film Review*)

Review 4

About the only reason it's important that *The Sixth Sense* is set in Philadelphia is that it is, as a grade school history teacher helpfully reminds us, "one of the oldest cities in America," and thus home to a lot of dead people—which, in case you've forgotten, little Cole can see. In a way, it may be a good thing that the movie takes so long to reveal this, since the delay leaves you less time to realize that there's nothing else to *The Sixth Sense,* apart from a trick ending and one decent scene between the boy and his mother (played by the misused Toni Collette). The entire plot of the movie goes like this: Boy sees dead people, boy is upset about seeing dead people, boy learns how to deal with seeing dead people. No plot twists, no complications, no nothing. It might take some kind of extrasensory perception to explain what fills *The Sixth Sense*'s 114 minutes, because I certainly can't explain it. I know I sat in a movie theater for two hours, but I'll be damned if I can tell you what happened. (Sam Adams, *City paper.net,* Philadelphia)

Review 5

The film works because we all think about the afterlife heaven and hell. It is amazing that in a film like this, filled with so many symbols of death and life, our film critics are reluctant to talk about the spiritual aspects. I have yet to read one review that discusses the blatant spiritual symbolism found in this movie. Our culture demonstrates a great curiosity about spiritual things and yet our film critics are reticent to discuss these issues when reviewing film. . . . You will be amazed by the questions this film will initiate. Another great topic this film deals with is our own truth. "And the truth shall set you free," Jesus said. I believe at the core of this film is the importance of truth-telling within a relationship. I know there will be some who will fault this film for its "communication with the dead" which they are sure to point out as wrong. . . . The film is a fantasy, but the story is filled with important truth and crucial life issues. Don't be afraid to deal with the afterlife, spiritual things, and the issue of truth-in-relationships. Allow this film to be one of the ways God opens your thinking to new dimensions within your life. (David Bruce, *Hollywoodjesus.com*)

Observations of Writer–Director M. Night Shyamalan

The Sixth Sense is frightening, disturbing and horrific in the tradition of films like *Rosemary's Baby, Repulsion* and *The Omen*. It's reality-based fright. It comes from the fears of real people, real children and real adults; fears of loss, the unknown, of having a sixth sense about what lies beyond and fears of not understanding those intuitions. Ultimately, it's about learning how to communicate those fears, whether it's communication between a doctor and the patient, a husband and a wife, a mother and a son or between ourselves and loved ones who have passed on. As we all have seen, not communicating with, or keeping secrets from people we love can destroy marriages, careers, families and even lives. That in itself is horrifying. (As quoted by David Bruce, *Hollywoodjesus.com*)

CASE STUDY

Assessing Arguments in Film Reviews: *The American President*

It helps to see a film review by taking it apart and writing it out like the argument it really is. Our focus will be a (negative, critical) review of *The American President* by John J. Pitney, Jr. He argues that movies such as *The American President* show us that Hollywood thinks voters are stupid (see John J. Pitney, Jr., "Hollywood Sneers at the People," *Los Angeles Times*, 26 Nov. 1995). He makes his argument in 10 premises.

John J. Pitney Jr.'s Argument

Premise 1: The American President concerns a chief executive (Michael Douglas) who is progressive yet practical. He says that gun control is hard to pass because people do not understand the link between guns and gun-related crime.

Premise 2: After he falls in love with an environmental lobbyist (Annette Bening), an evil senator (Richard Dreyfuss) turns the unthinking masses against the good President by making nasty comments about his new lady friend.

Premise 3: The President's approval ratings tumble, and the White House staff bemoans the people's willingness to believe anyone with a microphone.

Premise 4: At a climactic moment, the domestic policy advisor (Michael J. Fox) compares Americans to nomads who need a drink of water but get a glass of sand.

Premise 5: The President bitterly replies: "They drink the sand because they don't know the difference."

Premise 6: The image of a dumb, deluded electorate is hardly original with this movie; it is one of the film industry's moldiest clichés.

Premise 7: Many other films treat the electorate like idiots; for instance in *Mr. Smith Goes to Washington* (1939), ruthless thugs smash the young Smith with false charges and vicious news stories and the gullible public goes along.

Premise 8: In *Citizen Kane* (1941), Orson Welles plays a legendary newspaper publisher who can whip his readers into a war frenzy with far-fetched stories about Spanish galleons off the Jersey coast and thinks he can tell people what to think.

Premise 9: In *The Candidate* (1972), an idealistic Senate contender runs an issue-based campaign against a stodgy incumbent (with the stereotypical dark suit and short white hair) and seems doomed to lose until he starts speaking in platitudes and wins over the voters with mushy statements.

Premise 10: Political films show contempt for the people.

Conclusion: Hollywood thinks that the voters are stupid.

Group Exercise

This exercise can be done by each group or it can be subdivided, so each group answers only one of the questions. Read over Pitney's argument and then decide:

- Is Pitney correct in his characterizations of the films he cites as treating voters with contempt? (If no one in the group has seen any of these four films, go on to question 2.)
- Assuming Pitney's characterization of the movies is correct, is his sample of four political films sufficient to show that Hollywood thinks voters are stupid?
- What are the strengths of his argument?
- What would an opponent need to do to disprove Pitney's claims?
- Can you think of any counterexamples (Hollywood movies that don't treat voters with contempt)? If so, would this disprove Pitney?

Assessing Arguments about Films

An assessment of an argument about a film entails the following steps:

Key Guidelines for Assessing Arguments on Films

1. *Check the Factual Claims.* Are the claims made actually true? (Do not assume the speaker is necessarily correct.)

2. *Check any Assumptions.* Determine if they are warranted or unwarranted. Unwarranted assumptions should be recognized and carefully examined.

3. *Check for Exaggeration.* Are the claims made inflated or slanted to one side or another, when in fact another interpretation is possible?

4. *Check for Omissions.* Has the reviewer left out relevant details that would offer another perspective or lead us to a different conclusion than the one being drawn?

5. *Check for Fallacious Reasoning.* If a sample is used, is it sufficient in number and a representative sample? Note: If the sample group is too small, the speaker may have committed the fallacy of hasty generalization. If the sample group is biased toward one point of view or group, then the speaker may have committed the fallacy of biased statistics.

6. *Check the Strength of Reasoning.* Decide if the conclusion is sufficiently supported by the evidence given. The evidence lays the foundation for the conclusion and it is important that this foundation is a solid one.

With these guidelines in mind, let's return to Pitney's argument. First, consider the claims of fact. He says *The American President* presents voters as dumb and deluded, that they "believe anyone with a microphone." Pitney doesn't talk about the end of the movie, or what happens after the president is bitter about the gullibility of the public.

We need to know: Did the "unthinking masses" come to see that the "good president" was *really* a good president and they were wrong to believe his critics? Are voters "unthinking" if they are receptive to those who make nasty comments about presidents or the women in their lives? Does listening to gossip imply a dumb or deluded mind?

Second, examine his assumptions. Pitney assumes a familiarity with the other films he cites (*Mr. Smith Goes to Washington, Citizen Kane,* and *The Candidate*). Depending on the audience, this assumption may or may not be warranted, because many of his readers may not have seen these movies.

Third, watch for exaggeration. It's a temptation to inflate key points for an extra boost. Assuming it is true that the public initially fell for the nasty comments about the president's new lady friend, does that mean they are "unthinking masses" or "a dumb, deluded electorate"?

Fourth, make sure nothing important has been omitted. Omissions often lead us to mistaken conclusions. In Pitney's case, he fails to take into account the whole picture—he stops at the president's bitter reply to his domestic policy advisor's comment about nomads getting sand instead of water to drink. We need to consider what happens after this. Decide if Pitney develops the implication that the public is deluded, or whether the movie goes in a different direction. Also, consider if he ignores anything about the other films cited.

Next, watch for fallacious reasoning. If we think about all the films that come out of Hollywood, it is unlikely that only four of them make judgments about voters (through portrayals of voters, comments, or indirect references). Pitney's collection ought to be a *representative* sample if we are going to draw conclusions from it. If not, his reasoning is not well founded.

Last, examine the connection between the premises and the conclusion. And don't overconclude. The conclusion should not say more than is warranted by the evidence. Consider whether Pitney's citations of four films made between 1939 and 1995 warrant the conclusion "Hollywood thinks voters are stupid."

Group Exercise

Break into small groups and answer one:

1. Do politically oriented films such as *Wag the Dog, Primary Colors,* and *Bulworth* present citizens as being as idiotic as Pitney's study found? Discuss how a film other than *The American President* presents voters and the general public.

2. Has the TV show *The West Wing* presented an alternative view of the citizenry? Discuss.

3. How do professionals other than politicians (think of lawyers, doctors, teachers, nurses, etc.) fare in movies?

Exercise

What can you infer about the Vatican's Pontifical Council for Social Communications in light of the following:

Having a sympathetic religious character does not guarantee a blessing from the Vatican. *The 10 Commandments* was absent from the list. Such literal movies "are kind of dead and unconvincing dramatizations," said Henry Herx, director of the United States Catholic Conference Office for Film and Broadcasting, which provides weekly movie and television reviews and ratings for the church's news service. . . .

In the council's list [of great movies] Mr. Herx said he discerned a trend or two, like a leaning toward films that show religious people demonstrating their faith through social action, rather than simply personal piety. One of the films the Vatican cited is Elia Kazan's *On the Waterfront,* in which Karl Malden plays a priest determined to expose racketeers on the docks.

The list also marks the rehabilitation, in the church's eyes, of at least three Italian films: in addition to *Open City* it includes Federico Fellini's *La Strada,* . . . and *The Bicycle Thief.* . . . A generation ago, the Catholic Film Office's predecessor, the Legion of Decency, warned moviegoers about those three films, rating them as "morally objectionable," because they portrayed social themes in gritty or even brutal terms. (See Gustav Niebuhr, "How the Church Chose the Best Films Ever," *The New York Times,* 7 April 1996)

The Prescriptive versus Descriptive Debate

A central concern when examining what we see on the screen is what the film tells us about life and any insights we can glean about human nature. Some people think art, and thus film, is *prescriptive,* in the sense that it sets down social and ethical guidelines for us to follow. For example, people who worry about the effect of film on children and teens subscribe to the view that TV and film can inspire "copycat" behavior on the part of the viewer.

On the other hand, some people think art (and thus film/TV) is *descriptive,* in the sense that it reflects, or describes, our society. They would argue that, if a film or TV show touches a nerve, it's because the nerve was already there in the first place, pulsating away in our body politic.

We must be careful, however, not to bifurcate. That is, perhaps films and TV shows not only can be said to be prescriptive and descriptive, but there could be other options. That is, what we see on the screen may be a catalyst for some action. It may be descriptive of some actions, people, or communities. But it could also have other functions in the human psyche. For example, film and TV often help us understand psychological and spiritual truths. They convey myths and meaning not clearly originating from the individual director or producer. There may be political undercurrents afoot that they unconsciously incorporate, for instance, while consciously describing another reality altogether.

This connection between art, life, and interpretation is an interesting one. In an article on James Cameron's film *Terminator 2,* Kirk Honeycutt tells the following story:

> James Cameron likes to point out that the world's most famous videotape—the footage of motorist Rodney G. King's beating by Los Angeles police officers—actually contains two segments.
>
> Amateur cameraman George Holliday shot scenes on the set of the Arnold Schwarzenegger action epic, *Terminator 2,* at a location two blocks from his Lake View Terrace home, before capturing the beating.
>
> "That, to me, is the most amazing irony considering that the LAPD are strongly represented in *Terminator 2* as being a dehumanized force," says Cameron, the film's writer–director. "What the film is about, on the symbolic level, is the dehumanization we do on a daily basis." (Kirk Honeycutt, "Terminator's Generator: James Cameron Says He Uses Violence to Make a Point," *Los Angeles Times,* 5 July 1991).

For Cameron, the movie reflects our lives and the dehumanization that is all around us—that is, it is thus descriptive. Later in the article Honeycutt cites reaction to *The Terminator;* for example, Richard Corliss (*Time* magazine) considers it descriptive: "The Terminator is a hip retelling of the Annunciation." Janice Hocker Rushing and Thomas S. Frentz see it as prescriptive: "*The Terminator* is a potent wake-up call to face the demonic proportions of the technological shadow we have loosed upon the world. The humans in *The Terminator*'s future are fully awake to their predicament" (*Projecting the Shadow: The Cyborg Hero in American Film*). Susan Jeffords argues that both *The Terminator* and T2 *Judgment Day* are descriptive *and* prescriptive; that they both center on issues of masculinity. She asserts:

> *The Terminator* films offer male viewers an alternative to the declining workplace and national structure as sources of masculine authority and power—the world of the family. It is here, this logic suggests, that men can regain a sense of masculine power without having to confront or suggest alterations in the economic and social system that has led to their feelings of deprivation. (Susan Jeffords, *Hard Bodies.*)

Theories of Interpretation

As we saw in the various reviews of *The Sixth Sense,* if we examine a film using a religious perspective, we see one thing; if we use a political or social perspective, we see another. And so on. Conceptual frameworks are like mental headgear— lenses for the mind's eye—coloring what we focus on and how we interpret what we see. Commentators often refer to theories of interpretation using such frameworks by the German word, "hermeneutics." (Now you'll know what they're talking about when you come across this word!)

The framework we use to do an interpretation shapes our understanding. Let's take a classic of its genre, *Die Hard,* and see how this works. We will use six interpretative models: mythological, social, ethical, justice/political, philosophical, and psychological. The latter framework allows us to bring in a Freudian approach, which is often found in film commentaries (especially in French film criticism). Let's start with a brief overview of the film and then look at different frameworks that could be used in interpreting a film or a TV show.

CASE IN POINT: *DIE HARD*

Plot Summary

Die Hard is an action film about a terrorist takeover of a high rise in Los Angeles, where the terrorists are German and the hostages are employees of an international corporation. Only one man, John McClane—an NYPD officer thought to be a bit of a renegade—can stop them. However, he is vastly outnumbered and lacks the arsenal of weapons the terrorists have at their disposal. Among the hostages is his wife, Holly, from whom he has been estranged because of marital problems he has come to Los Angeles to address. With the exception of a psychologically wounded but

good-hearted black LAPD officer, Sgt. Al Powell, who befriends him but is powerless to give much more than moral support until the very end, McClane has only his own wits and physical strength to draw from. The movie is that story.

Framework 1: Mythological Interpretation of *Die Hard*

Examining *Die Hard* as a myth, we have the hero or prince, the villain and his evil sidekicks, helper figures, the princess (the estranged wife, Holly), and the community (the hostages) the prince rescues. The hero, McClane, is called by the force of circumstances to save the princess (his estranged wife) and restore order. He did not go into this intentionally; he is a bit of a fallen angel (drinking problems, suspended from the New York police force). However, he must rediscover parts of himself and develop his own inner strength.

Along the journey, our hero faces obstacles of mythic proportions. He sheds blood walking on glass, which represents his getting in touch with his heart. He is willing to sacrifice himself so that others may live. He goes down the elevator shaft, symbolizing the descent into darkness. In the darkness, McClane confronts evil spirits and must be willing to face his own death. He plunges into the abyss (over the rooftop, where he hangs by a thread). It's definitely the dark night of the soul for him.

Before the hero can win the heart of his beloved, he must prove himself worthy. He must show that he is good, selfless, loving. There is no compromise with the devil; that much the hero knows. He also knows that no one else can take his place—like it or not, he has been called by destiny to go forth on this journey. McClane proves he is up to it.

Framework 2: Social Interpretation of *Die Hard*
Here we look at stereotypes, racism, sexism, religious or other sorts of group bias, expressions of power, unwarranted assumptions, symbols and images that reinforce or challenge the status quo, and social impact. *Die Hard* presents us with an all-American (white) male hero named John and Nazilike villains with names like Hans. The psychologically scarred black buddy figure (who is healed as the movie progresses) and a black limo driver down in the garage are outside the action; the Asian CEO is killed; and the woman Holly is silenced. She dares not speak so as not to be used to flush out her husband, McClane. She is also silenced in more subtle ways. Having resumed her birth name, Holly Gennero, she ends up willingly relinquish-

ing her name (and a part of her identity) as a result of her eagerness to be together again.

Some of the stereotypes are: the hero (courageous, honest, good at heart); the villain (cold, cunning, vicious, uncompromising); the loving wife (selfless, dependent, caring, supportive, protective); the news anchor (selfish, ruthless, obnoxious); the police, fire department; and other social institutions (worthless except to clean up); the buddy–sidekick (devoted, supportive, likeable); Germans (cold, analytical, technologically adept, good at planning and execution); Latina housekeeper (maternal, caring, easily manipulated, weak).

Framework 3: Ethical Interpretation of *Die Hard*
To examine a movie using an ethical framework we should look at these elements: the concept of good (and examples of it in the film), the concept of evil (and examples in the film), trust, caring, forgiveness, sin and redemption, justice, revenge.

Die Hard presents good versus evil as an either/or situation. The hero is unquestionably good; the villains are thoroughly evil. McClane, even with a shady past and a need to clear his record, is still a sympathetic figure. The terrorists deserve to die (or so it seems) and, thus, McClane's shooting to kill rather than maim is presented as the correct thing to do. The presentation of evil in *Die Hard* is fairly straightforward. The terrorists are unequivocally evil. The audience is not expected to identify with or care for the terrorists.

The notion of justice is simple and straightforward. There is good, there is evil, there is loyalty to family and country, self-reliance is crucial, and if the societal institutions won't or can't uphold what is right and good, then the individual must be willing to do so, regardless of personal risk. Do not tolerate those who have no regard for the values we hold dear. Be cunning and strong to confront those who are evil. Stand up for what is right and be willing to look death in the eye.

Framework 4: Justice/Political Interpretation of *Die Hard*

The film, from this perspective, presents a kill-or-be-killed situation of Darwinian proportions. The un-American, can't be negotiated with, have-no-respect-for-life terrorists aren't receptive to dialogue. The hostages are unarmed and unable to escape. Both a hostage and a TV anchorman put others at risk for their own personal gain. This is not an image of people working together. The police are ineffective—they give no credence to our hero McClane's call. An attempt to bring out the fire department similarly fails. He is on his own inside a monolithic building facing well-armed opponents who have no respect for American values of justice.

We have, then, an updated Lone Ranger tale: A New York cop hero faces great odds to overcome evil. Limited support is offered by two men on the outside, a limo driver down in the parking garage and Sgt. Powell, the LAPD officer with emotional baggage of his own who drove to the building to investigate McClane's call. Powell especially provides moral support while McClane is battling the forces of destruction on the inside.

The journey is perilous. This is not an argument for gun control; there are bad guys out there and we need all the weapons at our disposal to arm ourselves against them. It's a brutish world; and it demands that our heroes be willing to be brutes in order to set things right again.

Framework 5: Philosophical Interpretation of *Die Hard*

In approaching *Die Hard* using philosophical frameworks, we want to consider how the film helps us better grasp the big questions of life, the existential situation of this one man, alone in his quest to set things right, and alienated from his peers—the fellow cops, other than the black, unarmed, cop, who is similarly alienated. He faces the absurdity of terrorists who have no respectable values (as Holly said, they are simple thieves). They cannot be reasoned with, they won't negotiate, and are untrustworthy anyway. He is an outsider, a nonconformist, a rogue with an attitude who doesn't follow rules that appear to make no sense. He lives in the face of his own possible death. He is willing to die for his beliefs.

McClane undergoes a personal transformation in the course of stopping terrorists from killing dozens of hostages. Doing some serious values clarification, he grasps the importance of his family, and reaffirms his commitment to fight for what is good. He realizes that he has behaved inauthentically in the past but gets back in touch with his own integrity. We watch him apply problem solving and critical thinking skills to put a stop to the terrorists and to save the hostages.

Framework 5: Psychological Interpretation of *Die Hard*

Examining the film through a psychological (say Freudian) angle, the terrorists represent the violent, uncontrollable parts of the psyche that must be watched by the moral conscience. Without firm guidelines, all hell will break loose, as shown in the film. The terrorists symbolize those parts of ourselves that we have failed to face. Out of the depths, no matter how deep we bury our psychic garbage, come monsters (terrorists) that surface and cause destruction.

John McClane, symbolizing the good, but stern, hero/father (the Ego), has to regain control over the errant parts of his out-of-control passions (his unconscious, the Id). The bloody feet he gets in doing so represents the loss of innocence that the hero must undergo in order to assume power (and to experience full sexuality). That he tears his clothes along the way, revealing his masculinity/muscles shows that sexuality is fully a part of our becoming our own person. His estranged wife rediscovers her beloved, reawakens her own desire, and reunites with him at the end.

Exercises

Part One

1. Do you think films that use vivid scenes of violence, like *Natural Born Killers, Seven, Manhunter, The Cell, Hannibal, Clockwork Orange,* are descriptive (realistically portray the society)? Are they prescriptive (try to influence how things should be)? Are they both? Is there a third way to interpret them?

2. Why have there been so many films about vampires? Write three to four paragraphs setting out your theory about what vampires symbolize; that is, what they tell us about our society.

3. Respond to the concerns raised by Princeton University Professor Karen Beckman, who wrote in the *Journal of Criminal Justice and Popular Culture (JCJPC):*

   Why does our society long to look at the bodies of dead women? How are we, as viewers and readers, implicated when we watch or read repeated scenes of female torture? Why do serial killer movies generally not show the murder of women, focusing instead on the dead bodies left at crime scenes? These questions seem crucial to any analysis of the genre in a socio-political context. ("Review of Philip Simpson, PsychoPaths: Tracking the Serial Killer through Contemporary American Fiction and Film,"*JCJPC,* Vol. 8, No. 1, 2001)

4. Film commentator, Susan Jeffords argues that issues around masculinity (and physicality) are central to films like *Die Hard*. She says,

   It wasn't just the jobs or social obligations that brought these men to betray their own feelings and families. It was, in an odd way, their very bodies themselves, these heroic exteriors that made it possible for them to do what other people could not. (Susan Jeffords, *Hard Bodies: Hollywood Masculinity in the Reagan Era*)

   Answer one *of the following:*
   a. To what extent do American films reflect a cultural attitude about male and female bodies? Discuss, drawing from recent films to support your points.
   b. What would you characterize as the dominant view of masculinity and femininity? Illustrate your points by giving examples from recent films.
   c. What would be examples of male strength and power in recent films? What do they tell us about cultural attitudes around male sexuality?
   d. What would be examples of female strength and power in recent films? What do they tell us about cultural attitudes around female sexuality?

Part Two

1. Answer *one* of the following:
   a. Using any three of the frameworks of interpretation, do a study of one of these: *Do the Right Thing, Shrek, Last of the Mohicans, The Music Box, Brazil, Lone Star, Cold Comfort Farm, Shawshank Redemption, In the Heat of the Night, Scream.*
   b. Do a study of the American western (draw from at least two westerns), from any *two* frameworks.
   c. Do a study of *The Matrix* or any other recent sci-fi film drawing from any three frameworks.
   d. Do a study of the first 10 minutes of four different movies, drawing from any of the various frameworks.

2. Looking at either TV or film, answer *one* of the following:
   a. Compare and contrast the female buddy film (like *Thelma and Louise, Set It Off, Boys on the Side, Beaches, La Vida Loca, Outrageous Fortune*) with that of the male buddy film (like *Lethal Weapon, Showtime, Rush Hour 1* and *2, Butch Cassidy and the Sundance Kid, Men in Black*).
   b. How should class struggles and/or poverty be presented? Watch any one of these to see how they deal with the issues around economic class: *The Full Monty, Brassed Off, Germinal, Trading Places, The Commitments, A Million to Juan, Angela's Ashes, Norma Rae.*
   c. Discuss the treatment of substance abuse (e.g., *Blow, Traffic, High Art, When a Man Loves a Woman, Leaving Las Vegas, 28 Days, My Private Idaho, Trainspotting*)
   d. Discuss the treatment of children and/or family (e.g., *Soul Food, Fly Away Home, A Walk in the Clouds, It's a Wonderful Life, Crooklyn, Beetlejuice, The Adams Family, What's Eating Gilbert Grape?, Daughters of the Dust, Eve's Bayou, The Brady Bunch Movie, E.T., Hope Floats, My Life, Free Willy, Mi Familia/My Family, To Sleep With Anger, The Ice Storm*).
   e. Discuss any two philosophical issues such as justice, good versus evil, freedom and responsibility, alienation, personal identity that are raised in one of these films: *Ghost World, Bagdad Cafe, Repo Man, Goodfellas, Unforgiven, Brother From Another Planet, One Flew Over the Cuckoo's Nest, Witness, To Live, Apocalypse Now Redux, The Piano, Opposite of Sex.* Alternatively, focus on a TV show, such as *The Pretender, Buffy the Vampire Slayer, The Sopranos, Sex and the City, Six Feet Under, Alias, Friends,* or *The Gilmore Girls.*
   f. Do a study of the portrayal of friendship on screen (e.g., *Monsoon Wedding, Cold Comfort Farm, Il Postino, An American Quilt, Fried Green Tomatoes, Stand By Me, Boyz N the Hood, I Know What You Did Last Summer, Waiting to Exhale, Lethal Weapon 2, Independence Day, Clueless*).

▦ The Thematic Approach to Film and TV

To undertake a thematic study of a movie or a TV show, you could look at one of the following sorts of issues: despair, self-identity, alienation, good versus evil, freedom, the human costs of greed or lust, racism, justice, family disintegration, to name a few. These are all thematic approaches that could be taken to examine a film.

For example, we could study the movie *Falling Down,* using violence as a theme. One aspect of the study might be to compare *Falling Down* with other films in which personal disintegration and violence are predominant. Or we might focus on the issue of despair, studying how the lead character William Foster (a.k.a. D-Fens) deteriorates as the movie progresses and how his sense of his own identity starts to crumble. We could study his alienation from his wife, his daughter, the strangers he comes upon on his journey, and himself.

When doing a thematic approach, our goal is to be single-minded. Stay focused on the central theme and go into depth, citing examples to back up points. For example, you could approach *Falling Down* as a study of escalating violence or a contemporary tale of alienation. Don't get sidetracked by other themes like male sexuality, female stereotyping, or the loss of childhood unless they are directly relevant. See how the theme unfolds from the start of the movie to the very end. Examine the evidence (the film/the TV show) to find anything, large or small, that ties in to our theme. Be careful not to make any assumptions or to rule out any possibilities that may prove valuable in our study of the film.

Aspects of a thematic approach in analyzing a film or TV show are: setting out the theme; characters; relationships among characters, dialogue, music, images and symbols; cinematic elements, settings, and the development of the story line. As much as possible, show the particular theme can be seen in the myriad aspects of the film, drawing from scenes and illustrating by way of example.

CASE STUDY

A Thematic Approach to *Babe*

Babe *was a surprise hit and a film that touched a lot of people's hearts. See, for example, the comments of philosopher Susan Bordo who found the movie an inspiration (see* Twilight Zones). *The film is not only endearing; it also lends itself to multiple interpretations.*

Let's approach Babe *using a particular theme, say social transformation. We want to show how the theme of social transformation is devel-* oped in the movie. To accomplish this goal, we'll bring in the various elements that may illustrate how the theme is developed in the movie.

Theme.   Social transformation in *Babe.*

Characters.   Looking at social transformation, we will study the protagonist, Babe, and how his character develops throughout the movie. Starting as a scared little pig crying for his mother, Babe ends up saving the day and winning the championship (taking the prize away from well-trained sheepdogs) by using persuasion rather than force. In the case of this theme, we'd focus most of our attention on the character of Babe and the impact he has on the lives of others.

Relationships between Characters.   With our social transformation theme, we could examine Babe's relationship with various animals at the Hoggett farm (Rex and Fly, the two dogs; Ferdinand, the duck; Maa, the sheep matriarch; and Duchess, the cat), as well as Babe's relationship with the farmer Hoggett and his wife.

Dialogue.   Looking at social transformation, we find key pieces of dialogue. For example, when Babe sees that biting sheep doesn't work to herd them, he realizes that talking to them and treating them with respect is far preferable. Another example would be the way honesty and values are conveyed from one episode to the next. We could also look at the three mice that function as commentators—like a Greek chorus reporting on the events.

Music.   The central song of the film reinforces the sense of empowerment and transformation brought about by and to Babe. The farmer's song and dance could be studied, as well as the sing-song commentaries of the three mice (tying this into the dialogue).

Images and Symbols.   Various images and symbols reinforce a social transformation theme. For example, Duchess acts as a kind of guardian or gargoyle figure watching over the house. The image of Babe and the duck crossing the cat's path and suffering a fall from grace (symbolized by both the paint and the yarn),

are key parts of the movie. This fall presents an obstacle that Babe—and the farmer Hoggett—must overcome for Babe to be an effective figure of change. The symbols of both the fax machine Hoggett is given and the dollhouse rejected by the bratty child remind us that, outside the magical world of the Hoggett farm, there are nasty elements and a world undergoing a radical change from the pristine realm we see here.

Color and Other Cinematic Elements.   From the dark world of the hog factory at the opening of the movie to the beautiful, charming world of the Hoggett farm, we are presented with a startling shift. The shadow of the slaughterhouse, death, destruction, and evil is a sharp contrast with the light. The use of color in key scenes, such as the blue and yellow footprints after Babe and Ferdinand enter the house and the red blood on Babe's snout when Maa was killed—these all reinforce the scenes' significance and the role Babe is playing in the course of events.

Settings.   The different settings—the hog factory, carnival, Hoggett farm, and sheepdog competition—help reinforce the theme of social transformation. Moving from mother's breast to the outside world, the carnival to Hoggett's farm (and there the barn, the yard, the house), and then to the contest grounds visually support the character development of Babe from suckling pig to championship "sheep dog."

Development of Story Line.   The movie has a *Rocky* theme to it. This is the story of the oppressed (mother dies and he is sold to the farmer, potentially to be eaten). Babe, however, rises above the circumstances to triumph. From downtrodden to a leadership position, Babe is cheered by all and respected even by those who initially rejected him.

Group Exercise

Film Study

Select *one* of these films. Each group will watch and study a film. Any of these are good choices: *Blade Runner, Pretty Woman, Ghost World, The Matrix, The Commitments, Raise the Red Lantern, Gods and Monsters, The Time Machine, Zoot Suit, Lord of the Rings, Ghost Dog, Smoke.* Each group should study the film using the framework below and should then share their conclusions with the class:

- Group 1: Sociopolitical analysis of the film.
- Group 2: Psychological analysis of the film.
- Group 3: Mythological analysis of the film.
- Group 4: Race/class/gender analysis of the film.
- Group 5: Ethical analysis of the film.

Exercises

Select one of the following claims and set out the strongest argument you can, using examples from movies to illustrate your points:

1. "The western hero rarely becomes domesticated. He lives between the sagebrush and civilization, between the desert and the den, belonging to neither world. He is like a lone, quiet god come from out of time as an answered prayer to those within time" (Geoffrey Hill, *Illuminating Shadows: The Mythic Power of Film*).

2. "Well, as the preacher man told us at the end of *Pulp Fiction,* the tyranny of evil does not disappear just because we change the channel. . . . But as the poet Amiri Baraka reminds us, 'Cynicism is not revolutionary.'" (bell hooks, *Reel to Real*)

3. "Female killers are few and their reasons for killing significantly different from men's" (Carol J. Clover, *Men, Women, and Chain Saws: Gender in the Modern Horror Film*).

4. "The reality of rape is rendered invisible by the many novels and films, such as *Gone With the Wind,* which romanticize and mystify it" (Tom Kuntz, "Rhett and Scarlett: Rough Sex or Rape? Feminists Give a Damn," *The New York Times,* 19 Feb. 1995).

5. "Black sexuality in the 1980s was either constructed as something entirely perverse or more often, absent in mainstream cinema" (Ed Guerrero's *Framing Blackness; The African American Image in Film*).

⧈ Violence on the Screen

On one hand, people decry the amount of violence and, on the other hand, they rush to see it. *Basic Instinct* with its ice pick sex murderer was a blockbuster. The two *Terminator* films propelled Arnold Schwarzenegger to fame and fortune. *Pulp Fiction, Natural Born Killers, Wild Bunch, Mean Streets, Apocalypse Now,* and *Taxi Driver* are commonly viewed as great films. *Silence of the Lambs,* a movie about a serial killer who skinned his (female) victims, won the Academy Award for best picture and was resuscitated in its sequel *Hannibal.* As one ad put it, "You don't have to go to Texas to see a Chainsaw Massacre." You need only go to the theater and see it on the screen.

Many films show graphic murders, heads being decapitated, throats slashed, bodies being impaled, and women being raped and murdered. This is no longer reserved for movies; a 2001 episode of the TV show *The Sopranos* focused an entire show on the rape of one of the key female characters.

Not much is sacred. Little is off-limits. From *Silence of the Lambs* it was a short leap to *Boxing Helena*—from skinning women to chopping off their arms and legs. And it was a shorter leap beyond that to *Hannibal*'s cannibalism and the ritualized torture in *The Cell.* Sex with children may be the only taboo, though the movie *Pretty Baby* skirts that line. Cruelty to animals is usually avoided, though *The Godfather* showed a decapitated pet horse's head tucked in bed. The scarcity of taboos has caused some people to demand that we rethink our notions of acceptable violence.

Key Questions about Violence on the Screen

- How much is too much?
- Does screen violence desensitize us to actual acts of violence?
- Does screen violence lead to copycats, who commit violence?
- Should pornography and the portrayal of graphic rape and violence to women and children be off-limits?
- What, if any, censorship should there be? Using what set of criteria? And under whose control?
- Will censorship of violence lead to censorship of ideas?

Systemic Violence, Collective Violence

Many Native Americans find scenes of the cavalry engaged in a mass killing of Indians painful to watch, a reminder of the betrayal and violence Indians experienced. Images of blacks being lynched may internalize the oppression of African Americans. Jews may find it disturbing to watch graphic films on the Holocaust. Young Asian, Latino, and African-American males may be demoralized by gang-banging stereotypes that fill the screen. Women who see rapes, sexual murders, or torture of young women may be drained, depressed, or enraged.

Filmmakers often justify their choice of subject matter by citing a "supply and demand" argument. As long as people will pay to see violence, they will make it.

If you don't like it, don't watch. It is as simple as that. The trouble is that it is not that simple. Sometimes an audience has no idea of the objectionable or disturbing graphic content of a film (even if they saw the trailers). Few viewers know how or where to voice their concerns.

Group Exercise

Princeton University professor Karen Beckman examines how horror films involving serial killers raise serious questions about the violence against women on the screen. Read the article and set out her thesis and key claims. Then decide if the concerns warrant limitations around what is permissible to show on-screen.

Dead Women and Serial Killers:
Autopsy and Cinematic Spectatorship

Karen Redrobe Beckman, Princeton University
August 2001

Like horror movies in general, the serial killer genre privileges women in the victim role. At the most basic level, we can read the violence against women that is repetitively staged in these movies as symptomatic of a sadistic and misogynist culture that takes pleasure in the torture and eradication of female bodies. But how are we as spectators implicated in this violence against women? What kind of "pleasure" do these films offer to male and female spectators alike?

Horror movies delight in the spectacle of the torture and death of female bodies in particular. Numerous critics have noted the way horror movies cause the body to experience sensational jolts—to experience at a bodily level the emotions of terror, panic, even hurt.[1] But we might

regard the serial killer movie as less "sensational" than other forms of horror film, perhaps because this genre tends to focus less on the victim's terror and frenzy as she is pursued by the monster/killer, and more on the spectacle of her dead body after the terror is over. Serial killer movies seem slower and more meditative than horror films, largely because they are less interested in the experience of dying, in the victim's experience of terror, focusing instead on the image of the (often female) corpse.

Serial killers make their presence known by leaving a trail of dead bodies in their wake—police and "ordinary people" discover these bodies in trashcans, lakes, parks, apartments—and the camera lingers on the spectacle of these discoveries. But the corpse disappears into a police body bag only to reappear on the pathologist's table, and it is this table which stands at the center of the genre.

The camera repeatedly aligns itself with the figure of the detective/forensic scientist, and through the audience identification this alignment constructs, the genre encourages cinematic

[1] For examples of this line of argument, see Linda Williams, "Film Bodies: Gender, Genre, and Excess," *Film Theory and Criticism: Introductory Readings,* eds. Leo Braudy and Marshall Cohen (New York and Oxford: Oxford University Press, 1999) 701–715; Carol J. Clover, *Men, Women, and Chain Saws: Gender in the Modern Horror Film* (Princeton: Princeton University Press, 1992).

spectators to linger over the dead (female) body as if it were their job to do so. The presentation of the corpse in the context of the autopsy invites an attitude of calm contemplation, where the horror of the victim's murder is subordinated to intellectual inquiry.

Detective and audience alike must wrestle with the problem of how to read this body in such a way as to reveal both the identity of the killer and the "type" to which the dead body belongs. That is, the corpse on which we gaze is presumed to be doubly inscribed with identities that marginalize the importance of the individual identity of the victim. S/he matters only in so far as we can read the killer or his future victims in the physical matter of her corpse. Like the victims themselves, the killer's identity becomes defined by the readable traces on the bodies of his victims, blurring the boundary between victim and murderer in complicated ways.

As the detective and audience stare at the "puzzle" of the corpse, they must learn to write the serial killer narrative out of the "clues" this body leaves behind, must learn to understand the pattern of the plot, to read the pattern of bodies of which the corpse is just one example. In short, the detective must think like the serial killer, and we are encouraged to do the same.[2] This writing of the plot by the ostensible "good guys" on the basis of forensic evidence further breaks down the moral clarity of the film—we are no longer sure of the moral integrity of the detective if he can successfully enter the mind of the serial killer.

But the detective's "writing" also reverses the temporality of events in problematic ways. Instead of the corpse being the ultimate "goal" or end-point of the serial killer narrative, the detective's narrative *begins* with the dead body of the victim. Ironically this dead body seems to *produce* and even *precede* the serial killer narrative that produced it. The woman is dead before the narrative that kills her has even been written.

Though this reversal of the sequence of events within the serial killer genre may seem insidious in the way it blinds us to the agency of the killer, the life of the victim, her individuality, and her suffering as something that was not, at least for her, simply typical, these films also provoke us to consider our role as spectators in interesting ways. The OED defines "autopsy" as "the dissection of a dead body," but the first definition it offers is "seeing with one's own eyes."

As detectives spin serial killer narratives out of the spectacle of the female corpse, they frequently become uncomfortably aware of their own participation in and proximity to the violence of the serial killer himself. In so far as we, the spectators, are encouraged to identify with the figure of the detective, this genre opens up a space for us to reflect upon the "autopsies" we perform ourselves every time we linger on the spectacle of death in cinema, forcing us to consider the relationship between violent murder, post-mortem dissection, and the simple act of looking.[3]

Permission granted by Dr. Karen Beckman, Princeton University.

---

[2] For a detailed discussion of the doubling of the serial killer and the detective/criminal profiler, see Philip L. Simpson, *PsychoPaths: Tracking the Serial Killer Through Contemporary American Film and Fiction* (Carbondale and Edwardsville: Southern Illinois University Press, 2000) 70–112. The pursuit implied by Simpson's title reveals just how strongly readers and viewers of this genre take the responsibilities of the detective upon themselves.

[3] Other important studies on the serial killer genre include: Judith Walkowitz, *City of Dreadful Delight* (Chicago: University of Chicago Press, 1992); Jane Caputi, *The Age of Sex Crime* (Bowling Green: Bowling Green State University Popular Press, 1987); Mark Seltzer, *Serial Killers: Death and Life in America's Wound Culture* (New York and London: Routledge, 1998).

▦ The Question Of Censorship

With the rewards of profit or industry acclaim, it is not surprising that filmmakers go for blood and gore—or sex—to draw in audiences. But ethical questions remain. Producers often claim the audience sets the limits of acceptability.

At this point, most of us are used to seeing violence on the screen. The question is what effect this has had on our collective mentality and morality. Have we become desensitized or psychically numb? Has screen violence contributed to violent crime in the society?

After the murder of a toddler by two 10-year-old boys, there was an outcry in Britain against the violence in film, especially Hollywood movies. Because some thought the boys had been influenced by a horror film, *Child's Play 3,* the British pushed for a change—and got it. Consequently, many films have to be cut before being allowed in the country. Some films (like *A Clockwork Orange, The Exorcist, Texas Chainsaw Massacre, Reservoir Dogs, Mikey, Bad Lieutenant*) have not been allowed in at all, because they are seen as too offensive.

Exercises

Part One

1. Suzanna Andrews says, "When it comes to naked bodies, movies have a double standard: women first and foremost; men under wraps." Discuss this and decide if this double standard is at all justified.

2. A study on television addiction cited by Daniel Goleman in *The New York Times* ("How TV Becomes an Addiction") points out that "As a group, the compulsive watchers were more irritable, tense and sad than the others, and felt they had little control over their lives." Assuming the study has merit, should we limit how much television children should watch?

3. Screenwriter Jeff Silverman once said "Guns on screen leads to guns off-screen." Share your reflections on the prevalence of guns on the screen and what, if any, impact you think this has on our social consciousness.

Part Two

In an article in *The Hartford Courant* (Connecticut) newspaper, journalist Deborah Hornblow cited evidence from two films in distribution that there is reason for optimism and cause for hope. She cites evidence on the screen that we are evolving in terms of being a more tolerant society. Read her article below and answer *one* of the following:

1. Write Deborah Hornblow a letter (three to four paragraphs) setting out her thesis and the three strongest pieces of evidence and the degree to which you

found her article persuasive. Share with her at least two ideas and insights of your own about what you see on the screen that addresses issues of tolerance.

2. Set out Deborah Hornblow's thesis and the three strongest pieces of evidence and then write three to four paragraphs comparing or contrasting her insights on *Rush Hour 2* and *Planet of the Apes* with two other recent films.

Hollywood Delivers The Message Of Racial Harmony

Deborah Hornblow
The Hartford Courant, *August 12, 2001*

Just as Page 1 headlines have been trumpeting the coming together of urbanites and suburbanites, blacks and whites, to rid Hartford of drug violence, the Hollywood dream factory is manufacturing hopeful and long overdue images of racial and ethnic cooperation and coexistence. Well, glory day.

On the surface, Tim Burton's "Planet of the Apes" and Brett Ratner's "Rush Hour 2" have little in common. "Planet" is a remake of Franklin Schaffner's classic 1968 sci-fi flick based on the Pierre Boulle novel in which men find themselves in a hostile new world where humans are slaves and apes are masters. In "Rush Hour 2," a sequel to 1998's surprise box office smash "Rush Hour," the great physical acrobat and martial arts fighter Jackie Chan and mouthy cut-up Chris Tucker are reteamed in a shaggy-dog cop saga involving an international ring of counterfeit-money launderers. So where's the link?

Ape costumes and police badges aside, the main message delivered by both "Planet of the Apes" and "Rush Hour 2" is one of racial and ethnic tolerance. If neither film amounts to a classic or even a great picture, both are entertaining diversions worthy of applause for conveying visions of one-world harmony in mainstream cinema.

"Planet" confronts issues of contemporary ethnicity directly, early on invoking the words of Rodney King, "can't we all just get along," which are voiced in rather comical fashion by one of the apes, Paul Giamatti's orangutan Limbo, a weak-willed slave trader who traffics in humans and serves as the film's comic relief.

"Rush Hour 2" deals with the themes more off-handedly. The main action focuses on the predictable work of good guys catching bad guys and creating excuses for Chan's spectacular fight choreography. But the subtext here is pure ethnicity. To start, there is the glorious fact that the film is carried by two minority actors, Chan and Tucker, a circumstance that remains too much of a rarity in Hollywood. The film's other principals are also minorities:

Agent Isabella Molina is played by Roselyn Sanchez, an actress of Puerto Rican descent. Asian actress Zhang Ziyi, one of the stars of Ang Lee's "Crouching Tiger, Hidden Dragon," issues more high kicks in the role of the cold-blooded Hu Li, and John Lone, also of Asian heritage, appears as underworld kingpin Ricky Tan.

The "Rush Hour" formula, which will doubtless spawn more sequels, is a hopeful contradiction of traditional studio logic. The far more common formula for major Hollywood studio releases involves teaming a leading ethnic actor—Jennifer Lopez, Morgan Freeman, Danny Glover, Angela Bassett, Yun-Fat Chow—with one of Caucasian persuasion. It's Hollywood hedging its box office bets and creating cast lists that could be Bennetton commercials. (Think "Out of Sight," "The Bone Collector," the "Lethal Weapon" series, "Anna and the King," "Glory," etc.)

The unanticipated success of both the original "Rush Hour" and last year's "Crouching Tiger" may have forever rearranged tired Hollywood preconceptions about what will and will not sell to mainstream audiences. Beyond its casting coup, "Rush Hour 2" gleefully traffics in ethnic stereotypes and cultural history, using both as sources of mirth. In one scene, Tucker's Det. Carter claims, "Lionel Ritchie ain't been black since the Commodores." He threatens to "bitch-slap [Chan's Det. Lee] all the way back to the Ming Dynasty," a line reprised when Lee promises to "bitch-slap [Carter] back to Africa."

Carter suggests to Lee that the way to solve the crime is to "follow the rich white guy."

In one of the film's most comically pointed scenes, Det. Carter distracts a largely white and well-heeled casino crowd by making race an issue and demanding to know why he was given different chips than all the white players. Carter is ostensibly making the ruckus to prevent security guards from pursuing Lee into the casino's back rooms, but he is also saying what is. The monologue is the sort that gives "Rush Hour 2" an unexpected and welcome import. Carter continues the antics by rolling a seven for "his man" Nelson Mandela and all the years the South African leader spent in prison. It is an absolutely giddy moment of retribution and fair-squaring boiling to the surface.

The appeal of the comedy, written by Jeff Nathanson from characters created by Ross LaManna, is that each character openly deals with his or her ethnic baggage and transcends the whole messy lot. "I hate this fortune-cookie [stuff]," says Ricky Tan, before getting even with a business partner.

Most touching of all is the scene in which Chan's Lee thinks he has lost his loud-mouth American colleague in an explosion. Driving in his car, Lee listens to Carter's music on the radio. He begins moving his head, snaking it to the left, snaking it to the right, and back again, just as Carter would have done. The movements grow bolder, and a smile creeps across Chan's face, breaking through like a vision of what harmony brings.

The coexistence of races in "Planet of the Apes" is far more tentative and unstable, despite the contemporizing touches brought to Broulle's 1963 novel by screenwriters William Broyles, Lawrence Konner and Mark Rosenthal. In the early (and most memorable) scenes of Burton's ambitious but flawed remake, Mark Wahlberg's stranded astronaut finds himself hunted down and captured by apes (never to be called "monkeys"). The first words he hears spoken in this new place are: "Get your hands off me, you filthy human."

(In what amounts to an insider's payoff, the line is voiced by Michael Clarke Duncan, the towering actor whom filmgoers last saw as the black spiritual guru in the odious drama "The Green Mile." His character ultimately submits to state-sanctioned execution as a favor to his white pal, Tom Hanks' prison warden. Hearing Duncan utter the misanthropic line in "Planet of the Apes" amounts to something like divine retribution.)

If Wahlberg's Leo Davidson is alienated in his new home, he forms an almost immediate and fortuitous bond with the ape called Ari (an intelligent role beautifully acted by a scarcely recognizable Helena Bonham Carter). The daughter of a senator wears a coat made by one of her human slaves—an intricate tapestry that she calls proof of the existence of a human culture. At her father's dinner table, surrounded by militaristic hard-line apes, most notably Tim Roth's seething, man-hating Thade, she courageously argues for equality and peaceful coexistence. "It's disgusting the way we treat humans," she says in one of the film's noble but too didactic moments. "It demeans us as much as it does them."

But if Burton's remake confronts themes of species co-existence and even inter-species relationships, it takes only baby steps toward its own bold thinking. Ari and Leo develop a romantic attachment at first sight, but the film shies away from dealing with questions of crossbreeding. As insurance against confronting the issue, a blond human female called Daena (a rather wooden Estella Warren) is Ari's rival for Leo's affections, but the romantic triangle is never resolved. Yes, Leo does kiss Ari before the film's end, but he treats Daena likewise. The readaptation of the "Apes" material stops at in-

troducing the idea and leaves the audience to wonder at the ramifications. "Planet" also culminates in a rather convenient deus ex monkey moment and ends with a cheeky but regressive surprise, but its message is resoundingly clear. Hatred and oppression of one race or another is self-defeating, ignorant and narrow-minded.

The colder realities that too often govern race relations in our lives have been chronicled in numerous films, from Spike Lee's thrillingly angry "Do the Right Thing" to "Guess Who's Coming to Dinner," "Mississippi Burning" and "In the Heat of the Night."

It is refreshing to see new films in which minority status is no object, and races coexist in harmony. Perhaps, finally, Hollywood is getting a dream.

Reprinted with Permission of The Hartford Courant *(Hartford, Connecticut).*

CHAPTER ELEVEN

Web Sight: Critical Thinking and the Internet

The Internet is probably the greatest forum for the exchange of ideas that the world has ever seen. It operates across national borders, and efforts by the international community or any one government to regulate speech on the Internet would be virtually impossible.

—THE ANTI-DEFAMATION LEAGUE

A mythic being central to the Laguna Pueblo Indians is Spiderwoman, who is so powerful that she can *think* things into being. She spins a web of stories that can transform the world. Language becomes prayer, ceremony, and ritual as she weaves the web linking people to ceremonies and to the earth. It is a positive force: "Their evil is mighty but it can't stand up to our stories."

We reaffirm this powerful link between people every time we access the Internet. For example, we reach out into the universe when we use e-mail, access a dial-up, text-based library catalog, or use a URL to call up a website. Each "www" that we type reminds us that we are inextricably bound to one another in the World Wide Web. We are globally as one, tied by a web that allows us to traverse thousands of miles in a matter of seconds or minutes. It is truly an astonishing resource.

The Internet has fundamentally changed our lives. It has the potential to democratize knowledge, by making available a seemingly limitless range of possibilities for research and the communication of ideas and information. It has no geographic boundaries: It doesn't matter if you live in a penthouse or a shack, the boondocks or a bustling metropolis, a fleabag motel or a swanky suite, a yurt on top of Mount Tamalpius or out of the backseat of your car in Fresno. It truly is a *worldwide* web. Whether you are in New York City or Montreal, Tijuana or Taiwan, Cape Dorset or Guadalajara, you can go online and access products and services, phone numbers, addresses, and directions from one place to the next, and a wealth of information. The Internet has the potential to level the playing field, by allowing us to expand our knowledge base and communicate across virtually all borders and boundaries. The exponential growth of its use is staggering: in 1994, there were approximately 10,000 web servers; in 1999, there were an estimated 10 million web servers and 146 million people connected to the Internet (see James Gillies and Robert Cailliau, *How the Web was Born*).

It is important to remember, though, that this is true only as long as you have a reliable telephone line and electricity. And access to a computer. Witness the lack of Internet use by Africans and Appalachians alike. Once we can address these obstacles and create global access to the Internet, the resulting resource will be revolutionary in its scope.

Just think of all we can access through the Internet. We can locate people and businesses, research with library databases, access professional journals, take a virtual tour of an art museum, and create a map from point A to point B. We can research photos at the National Archives, access military records, read the entire first edition of Marx's *Das Kapital* in either German or English, converse with specialists on health issues, compare the film scripts of *Alien* and *Aliens*, examine political commentaries on virtually any topic you can name, and delve into the archives of newspapers. If it's communication we desire, we can enter a chat room and discuss current events, movies and concerts, local blues artists, or virtually any topic under the sun.

Within our reach is a vast network linking us to religious organizations, political and social action groups, job opportunities, and medical services. Of course, there are also links to Aryan Nation, white supremists, and other extremist groups. And then there are the links to quacks offering up a panoply of health remedies, hucksters selling worthless products, not to mention pornographers, and dubious characters who would like to meet some nice young person to molest.

Imaging the Internet

That's the thing: the language used to describe this resource is very revealing. Think of terms like World Wide Web, Internet, and cyberspace. All three (webs, nets, and spaces) have physical correlates that are instructive to contemplate. The Web may seem fragile, but is a well-constructed series of links with almost limitless possibilities. The Internet really *is* a kind of net. Just like fishing nets that pull in battered old shoes as well as a nice rainbow trout, the Internet offers garbage as well as treasures, useless junk as well as valuable information, and access to weirdos, as well as to experts. In spite of attempts to set down some limits—such as protections for children who may be vulnerable to predators—much of the Internet is wide-open territory.

In that sense, cyberspace really is a kind of space. People, as well as corporations, have staked out territory, attempted to set down guidelines, and enforce rules of conduct. Some have made claims about who owns what in cyberspace. Given the vastness of the enterprise, it is virtually impossible to control its growth, regardless of any attempts to rein it in. The result is a universe of ideas, information, products, services, texts, contacts, commentaries, speeches, images, audiovisual aides, movies, music, historical documents, political tracts, advertising, personal bios, family albums, and more.

It's a bit like the Wild West, with few laws and almost no way to enforce them. It's so easy to erect a website or sign up for an e-mail address that setting down controls and keeping some semblance of order is exceedingly difficult. Plus, there is a lack of central authority. No one has to "certify" your page. There are neither Internet publishing bodies nor police, as are generally accepted in "real life" societies. This leads to conundrums such as how to deal with differences in different nations' laws—for example, the illegality of Nazi material in Germany, whereas it is merely tasteless in the United States.

And, when it comes to the vast wealth of information, data, research material, articles, and the like, the sheer glut of what's out there is staggering. The fact that so much is available does not mean it is easy to find. Navigating the Web can be frustrating and difficult. To a great extent, we are on our own. The host of search engines and techniques may or may not get us to where we want to go. This can lead to confusion and hair pulling over the time it takes to access good material. As T. Matthew Ciolek wrote in his article, "The Six Quests for the Electronic Grail":

> [The Web] can be said to resemble a hall of mirrors, each reflecting a subset of the larger configuration. It is a spectacular place indeed, with some mirrors being more luminous, more innovative or more sensitive to the reflected lights and imagery than others. The result is a breathless and ever changing "information swamp" of visionary solutions, pigheaded stupidity and blunders, dedication and amateurishness, naivety as well as professionalism and chaos. (See *www.ciolek.com*)

True, there is a sense of being in an "information swamp" at times—Ciolek is right about that. Just in terms of sheer quantity, it's sometimes difficult to find our way out of the swamp. And, for the most part, there is no guide to orchestrate order to the chaos or lead us through the mazes we encounter along our path.

Given there is an inherent untidiness to the Internet—a kind of anarchy, even—we need to acquire tools to navigate the system. That is, librarians can help us steer our way, but there is no one source we can access that will put things in order for us. Rather, we have to rely on our own problem-solving skills and ability to follow leads (and links) to find what we are looking for.

There are other issues around the Internet that are interesting as well. As critical thinkers, we want also to examine Internet-related issues around freedom of speech, privacy rights, intellectual property, and questions around where lines need to be drawn in terms of what should be accessible.

Exercises

1. What point do you think Michael Skube is trying to make in the following:

   The more we venerate information for its own sake, the less we cultivate what needs cultivating. And the less we honor what deserves greater honor in the culture generally. It's commonplace that Americans have always been enamored of technology and its machines. The computer is only one more contraption, marvelous in obvious ways but still something that needs plugging in and, too often, rebooting. I own a pair myself. . . . We change gears, run out of gas and, sometimes, park our dreams. As with the car, so with the computer. (See Michael Skube, "Culture: The Tyranny of Information," *Los Angeles Times,* 19 Aug. 2001)

2. Set out directions to someone who has never used the Internet how to search for the following:
   a. A particular professor at a specific university (e.g., Dr. Alfred Newman at Mad University).
   b. An essay written by a particular author (e.g., "Still Crazy after All These Years" by Zooey Wild).
   c. How to get to the website of a newspaper (e.g., the *Chicago Tribune*).
   d. How to get the requirements for a philosophy major at a particular university (e.g., at Oxford University in England, University of Texas at Austin, Santa Monica College).
   e. Directions from the Detroit Metro Airport to the University of Michigan Law Library (in Ann Arbor, Michigan).
   f. The latest edition of *wired.com.*
   g. Five different film reviews of a movie (e.g., *Ghost World, Memento, Il Postino, ET*).

3. Explain to a beginner at using the Internet how to find articles on a complex topic with three to four terms (e.g., *Marines* who refused *anthrax vaccinations* and faced a *court-martial* (note Marines = first term, anthrax = second term, vaccination = third term, and court-martial = fourth term). *Hint:* Don't forget the usefulness of the + sign and the − sign in running a search. Be aware, however, that different search engines/databases use different mechanisms. Some include all terms automatically, for example.

4. Using your Internet research skills, find out what you can about how to avoid a Web hoax (fake websites that look like the real thing—e.g., *martinlu therking.org* which was created by a white supremacy group). Write a summary of what you find on Web hoaxes and any suggestions to avoid getting trapped by them.

5. What do the following statistics tell you about the role of the Internet in the life of a student? Note if there are any surprises in this list:
   - 71% of middle school and high school students with Internet access said they rely on electronic technology most in completing a project.
   - 24% said they relied most on libraries.
   - 73% of students 12–17 years old (= 17 million) have access to the Web.
   - 96% of teachers said use of the Internet was essential to communication.
   - 18% of students said they knew someone who cheated using the Internet. (See "Internet Helps With Homework," Reuters, as cited in the *Los Angeles Times,* 2 Sep. 2001)

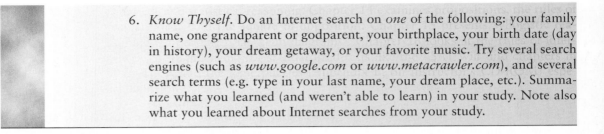

6. *Know Thyself*. Do an Internet search on *one* of the following: your family name, one grandparent or godparent, your birthplace, your birth date (day in history), your dream getaway, or your favorite music. Try several search engines (such as *www.google.com* or *www.metacrawler.com*), and several search terms (e.g. type in your last name, your dream place, etc.). Summarize what you learned (and weren't able to learn) in your study. Note also what you learned about Internet searches from your study.

Web Hoaxes

The Web lends itself to practical jokes and hoaxes, given the ease of constructing and dismantling bogus sites. Some also play on people's gullibility and curiosity, for example, the Online Pregnancy Test (*www.mypregnancytest.com*) or the Clones-R-Us site (*www./www.d-b.net/dti*). Fortunately for the truly dupable, Clones-R-Us does offer a legal statement to clear the air, including:

- "DreamTech does not exist in this dimension; this site is a spoof site, intended to simulate one possible manifestation of reproductive cloning technology, and stimulate thought on the pros and cons of reproductive cloning."
- "DreamTech attorneys cannot be held liable for any physical or mental anguish which may or may not have been caused by reading legal documentation in tiny typeface." (See *www.d-b.net/dti*)

Here are some of the many examples of fake websites, parodies, and spoofs. These sites range from the morally repulsive to the bizarre to the amusing to the hilarious. The many fake sites that are pornography sites are out there, but are not listed below:

Web Hoaxes, Parodies, and Spoofs

- *www.martinlutherking.org* (professional looking, but a white supremacy site).
- *www.onion.com* (parody, silly articles that some have thought real and cited them).
- *www.funnycrap.com* (spoof site, creates fake sites).
- *www.whitehouse.net* (cartoon), others lead to porn sites; the real thing.
- *www.whitehouse.gov* (see the link to kids).
- *www.whirledbank.org* (alternative version of www.worldbank.org, has logo "Our Dream is a World Full of Poverty").
- *www.gatt.org* (counterfeit version of *www.wpo.org* [The World Presidents' Organization is a global organization of more than 3300 individuals who are or have been chief executive officers of major business enterprises]— *www.gatt.org* is highly critical of the World Trade Organization).

- *www.adbusters.org/spoofads* (spoofs of advertising).
- *www.improb.com* (publishes the parody, *The Annals of Improbable Research*).
- *www.improb.com/airchives/classical/cat/cat.html* (now infamous article "Feline Reactions to Bearded Men").
- *zapatopi.net/afdb.html* (aluminum foil Beanies).
- *lme.mankato.msus.edu/akcj3/bmd.html* (The Burmese Mountain Dog site).
- *online.coled.mankato.msus.edu/ded/webcred/Fredericton.html* (Visit Exciting Frederickton site).
- *www.ihr.org* (historical review—front for Holocaust revision).
- *www.cafeherpe.com* (commercialized health care site—pushes their product).
- *www.globalwarming.org* (says global warming is a hoax).
- *www.gwbush.com* (fake Bush site; real one: *www.georgewbush.com*).
- *homepages.udaytonedu/~ahern/rurindx.htm* (a site for a fictitious country with games and simulations used at University of Dayton). (See Paul S. Piper's "Better Read that Again," *SEARCHER: The Magazine for Database Professionals*, Sep. 2000); Kathy Schrock's "Guide for Educators," *school .discovery.com/schrockguide;* and "Medical and Legal Information on the Internet," *SEARCHER: The Magazine for Database Professionals*, Oct. 2000).

Deceit and Trickery with Domain Names

Web hoaxes and parodies aren't the only potholes on the Internet. What about the debate over domain names? Someone can have a business or organization with the same or similar name as a more famous one.

For example, People for the Ethical Treatment of Animals didn't like it that People Eating Tasty Animals having the domain name *peta.org*—and sued to get it! Another example: the Islamic Society of North America, one of the biggest Islamic groups, does *not* own *www.isna.org*. This website is run by the Intersex Society of North America!

This gets into the phenomenon of "cybersquatting"—where someone buys up the name of some well-known company and then demands money to give it up. As noted by Susan Thea Posnock,

> Though the Internet presents a powerful new channel, it also enables individuals to encroach upon magazine brands, by registering domain names with the intent to sell the URL back to the publishers at a high cost or lure customers to their own sites. . . .
>
> Publishers say the best way to avoid cybersquatters is to strike first by registering domain names early. "We typically don't write the business plan or get the money approved without securing the URL," says Ann Wilkins, vice president, Internet Strategy and Development, Penton Media.
>
> Penton has been aggressive in securing names, Wilkins says. For example, the company secured some 20 domain names related to the concept of a site for educating design engineers. "Be proactive," she says. "Register more than less, relative to the brands that you foresee developing." She says the company has approximately 250 domain names registered, with close to 10 percent currently not in use. (See "Conquering Cybersquatters," *Folio: The Magazine for Magazine Management*, Spring 2001)

We might ask ourselves of such cybersquatting: Is it devious and misleading? Or are people just gullible to assume *whatever.com* will be the website they seek? It certainly has created havoc for companies, groups, and individuals. In 1999 in tacit recognition of the greedy or malevolent acts by some cybersquatters, Congress enacted the Anti-cybersquatting Consumer Protection Act. This act allows publishers to take civil action against anyone with bad-faith intent to profit from use of an identical or confusingly similar domain name.

Exercise

Select a few spoof or hoax sites from the list above and study them. Try to figure out the source (author or group) of the site; the purpose of it; whether there are links that take you to the "mother site," revealing the agenda behind the site; and what issues and concerns the site raises.

Hoax Busters.   Helpful resources are hoax buster sites and scam buster sites. In an article in *Searcher* magazine, Paul Piper notes a number of such sites, including:

- *www.nonprofit.net/hoax/hoax.html.*,
- *www.fraud.org/welmes.htm* (a consumer fraud center, including Internet fraud),
- *www.scambusters.org*,
- *ciac.llnl.gov/ciac/CIAHoaxes.html* (U.S. Department of Energy site that lists hoaxes).

Helpful to know about when confronting problems with hoax sites are the American Library Association (*www.ala.org*) and the U.S. Department of Energy (*ciac .llnl.gov/ciac/CIAHoaxes.html*). In addition, there are several websites with advice on how to avoid fake sites, namely:

- Virtual Chase, a guide to legal research on the Internet (*www.virtualchase .com*).
- Wolfgram University's links and references on evaluating Websites (*www 2.widener.edu/Wolfgram-Memorial-Library/webevaluation/webeval.htm*).
- American Association of Law Libraries' Checklist for Evaluating Websites (*www.bc.edu/bc_org/avp/law/lawlib/aallwg/criteria.htm*).

Dirty Tricks

Yes there are hoax sites. Then there are the dirty tricks. As anyone who uses the Web regularly knows, sometimes you click a link and end up at a pornography site. This is an example of what's been called "user manipulation." J. D. Biersdorfer cites a case in September 1999 where people trying to get to 25 million popular Web pages were intentionally rerouted to pornography sites they then got trapped in—and could only escape by shutting down. In that case, the FTC (Federal Trade Commission—go to *www.ftc.gov*) filed an injunction against those who were responsible.

But that's not the only dirty trick. Manipulators of the Web have also been known to disable the "Back" button, keeping you stuck at the site so you'll look at its content and ads. Then there's metatagging. A metatag is a place in the HTML code where information about the site is listed. By putting in popular terms (like "sex") in the metatags will guarantee more surfers to that website. (See J. D. Biersdorfer, "Trapped in the Web Without an Exit," *The New York Times,* 7 Oct. 1999.)

Metatags are certainly not inherently evil. They were designed to better match computer users with the sites they seek. Some search engines rely on metatags to offer a description of the site. It is when Web designers include irrelevant words that users are deceived. Metatagging can be used for deceptive and sneaky purposes. For example, Bierdorfer notes that companies could imbed names of the rival so if someone searches for the rival company, they get the manipulator also. If you've ever gone hunting for sites on controversial issues like abortion, you find this metatagging going on here too. Searches for pro-choice sites bring up pro-life sites. Of course, some supposedly "pro-choice" sites turn out to be sites where the woman's choice should be to be a mother and not get the abortion at all.

Applying Critical Thinking Skills to the Web

Life can be very funny. Even when it comes to computer viruses, things can take a humorous turn. Take the example of the "naked wife" virus that evidently ran amok in May 2001. While the worm was chomping its way through victims' computer files, governmental officials were gnashing their teeth trying to find a way to warn people. Evidently they became victims of their own forethought. The very warnings they tried to send bounced back, censored, censored, censored. Here's the scoop:

> A recent example [of literal meanings that are frequently wrong or confusing] is the "naked wife" virus that spread rapidly through cyberspace a few months ago. The Department of Energy found it couldn't send out a warning about the virus because its prudish computer software interpreted "naked wife" literally—and censored the warning. (See K. C. Cole, "Moving Beyond the Boundaries of a Literal Meaning," *Los Angeles Times,* 14 May 2001)

According to CNN, the bug masquerades as a Macromedia Flash movie, using the subject line "Fw: Naked Wife." The e-mail message states that: "My wife never look like that! :-) Best Regards," and then adds the name of the sender (see *www .cnn.com/2001/TECH/internet/03/06/nakedwife.virus/#1*). The worm spreads by e-mailing itself to addresses listed in the user's Microsoft Outlook address book, clearly wreaking havoc.

Exercises

1. If the term "naked wife" couldn't be used by the Department of Energy (DOE) to send a warning, how might we alert the public about this virus? We may need to know whether it was the word "naked" that was objectionable, the word "wife" that caused the glitch, or the complex phrase "naked wife." It may be interesting to know if "naked husband" would have caused a similar reaction in the government's software. So what could the Department of Energy do to get around the software censorship? Offer some ideas and suggestions.

2. In September, 2001 warnings circulated through e-mail regarding a kind of bioterrorism involving packages mailed to people containing a so-called "Klingerman virus" which was supposed to resemble severe dysentery. Share your thoughts on the Center for Disease Control's response:

   The Centers for Disease Control and Prevention (CDC) has recently received several inquiries concerning an e-mail message about people who have been infected with "Klingerman virus" after opening gift packages delivered to them in the mail. According to the e-mail message, a number of people became ill with a viral infection after handling a sponge contained in a package marked, "A gift for you from the Klingerman Foundation."

   The e-mail is a hoax. There is no "Klingerman virus," and the information in the e-mail notice is untrue. If you receive an e-mail message about "Klingerman virus," please do not forward it to others.

   Although the e-mail message is a hoax, if you are concerned about the contents of a package you receive in the mail, contact your local post office. It is a criminal offense to send potentially hazardous agents through the mail for the purpose of deliberately causing harm to human health. When such an incident occurs, the local emergency response system should be activated by dialing 911 in most communities; in communities without 911 systems, local law enforcement authorities should be notified. The local FBI field office and local and state public health authorities also should be notified. (See *www.cdc.gov/ncidod/klingerman_hoax.htm*)

Applying Critical Thinking Skills

Whether we surf the Web or dogpaddle our way through a few websites, we need to be able to think critically about what we see and read. Not only do we have to deal with images, symbols, and text, but we also have to deal with advertising, dirty tricks, hoaxes, spoofs, being manipulated and sent to a pornographic hinterland or an advertising stranglehold that traps us in its lair (at least until we shut down). And that's not even considering computer viruses arriving through e-mail attachments or e-mail advertising that comes out of nowhere.

Critical thinking skills are not just handy—they are essential to accessing information, evaluating websites, and analyzing the material obtained on the sites.

The range of critical thinking skills that apply to use of the Internet, can be set out in the tabl:e below.

Applying Critical Thinking Skills to the Internet

Analysis: Analytical skills are crucial to evaluate websites, to assess the credibility of authors and resources, to sort and weigh evidence, and to evaluate the strength of the reasoning in Web documents.

Deductive Reasoning: Deductive reasoning skills are needed to use the operating "rules" of the Web (e.g., using URL's and search engines, setting up websites, links, and hyperlinks), to access information within a particular site, saving and classifying resource material, and to assess the quality of reasoning.

Inductive Reasoning: Inductive reasoning skills are needed to draw inferences from search results, to assess search engines and websites, to work with statistical reasoning and analogies, to compare various websites, to synthesize information, to evaluate cause and effect reasoning, and to make predictions on the basis of Web documents.

Fallacies: The Internet is no more immune from fallacious reasoning than any other vehicle by which ideas and information are expressed. In particular, be on the lookout for the fallacies of accent, ad hominem, ad hominem circumstantial, ad misericordiam, ad verecundiam, and question-begging epithets.

Problem Solving: Problem-solving skills are a must for Internet use and especially for Web-related research. Be prepared to experiment with search engines, search techniques, search terms, navigating through poorly constructed websites, and dealing with hoaxes and dirty tricks.

Question Techniques: Being able to formulate different types of questions is crucial for using the Web. We need to be able to ask certain types of questions aimed at eliciting specific responses. We need also to be able to ask questions to help access information, ideas, images, and Web documents.

Argumentation: In using the Web to research, set out arguments, or evaluate documents, we need to be able to deconstruct arguments and sort through the evidence. We need to assess credibility of authors and website publishers, identify warranted versus unwarranted assumptions, prioritize evidence, recognize positions being asserted, and any omissions that need to be addressed.

Use of Language: Whatever mode the expression takes—reflections, theories, policy statements, arguments for or against some claim, political tirades, news commentaries and so on—we have to be able to examine the use of language and evaluate it. This is as true on the Web as anywhere else language is being used.

Visual Messages/Verbal Messages: The visual message of a website warrants examination also—particularly when graphic images and symbols serve a persuasive function (to sway, repulse, delight, disgust, titillate, and so on). Similarly, the verbal messages provide us with specific content we can analyze for its own sake, separate from graphics or images that may have a powerful emotional effect.

Using Diverse Perspectives: We need to be flexible and open minded about how we investigate issues, do research, evaluate websites, and assess the documents and information we get via the Internet. Shifting frames of reference and approaching from more than one perspective helps open up new ways of seeing and thinking about issues and ideas.

The News Media: Online news rarely contains as much as the print version, although it has the advantage of listing related links. Watch for what is highlighted and be prepared to search further for material and through connecting links. See also Chapter 9 on the news media.

Advertising: Critical thinking skills used to assess advertising are particularly useful, since Web advertising seems to pop out of nowhere. Some ads are almost impossible to stop and some are traps. Be aware too that ads are often disguised or can easily be mistaken for the real thing (e.g., links on a news page that appear to be articles, but are really advertisements). Plus, articles are sometimes really infomercials and, thus, highly biased and aimed to persuade the reader toward one position or the other.

Film and TV: To some degree film and TV shows can be accessed through the Internet. We can also access film and TV commentaries, scripts, reviews, news items, archives, stars' bios and the like. The Internet is a vast resource for researching film and TV and all our critical thinking skills for evaluating these media apply here.

Exercises

1. Using the list above, analyze any *one* of these websites:
   - The British Mycological Society (*www.britmycolsoc.org.uk*).
   - The American Nursing Association (*www.ana.org*).
   - Revlon (*www.revlon.com*).
   - Barbie (*www.barbie.com*).
   - Porsche (*www.porsche.com*).
   - Kelloggs U.K. (*www.kelloggs.co.uk.*).
   - News for Nerds (*slashdot.org*).
   - Coca Cola Company (*www.cocacola.com*).

2. Using the list above, analyze *one* of these museum sites:
   - Museum of Science Boston (*www.mos.org*).
   - Getty Museum (*www.getty.edu/museum*).
   - National Museum of the American Indian (*www.nmai.si.edu*).
   - California African American Museum (*www.caam.ca.gov*).
   - Canada Technology and Science Museum (*www.science-tech.nmstc.ca/english*).

3. Using the list above, analyze a website of *one* of the following hate groups noted by the Southern Poverty Law Center: Christian Identity, Racist Skin-

head, Ku Klux Klan, Neo-Nazis, Neo-Confederate Movement, American Front.

4. Compare and contrast the website of the Democratic National Committee with that of the Republican National Committee.

5. Analyze one TV news site (e.g., *pbs.org, abcnews.com, cnn.com, nbc .com*, etc.).

6. Compare and contrast a small-town newspaper website with that of large urban newspaper, such as *The New York Times* (*nytimes.com*), *Washington Post* (*www.washingtonpost.com*), *Atlanta Journal–Constitution* (*www.ajc .com*), *Los Angeles Times* (*www.latimes.com*), and *Chicago Tribune* (*chicagotribune.com*).

7. Find a website in one academic area (e.g., sociology, psychology, history, chemistry) and note how easy it is to navigate and access information and documents.

8. Compare any two websites on any topic in medicine (such as smallpox, AIDS advances, lasik eye surgery, finding an egg or sperm donor, alternative treatments for teenage acne, etc.) or law (such as legal services for the poor, positions by professional law groups on social issues, legal research sites, etc.). Focus especially on their use of graphics and assess the overall organization of the two sites.

▦ Web Analysis

You know those sci-fi films where the ship lands (or crashes) on an alien planet? Sometimes, as in *Contact,* the alien planet is wonderful to behold and a great place to visit. Other times, as in *Alien* and *Aliens,* the alien planet is a place to escape from, sooner the better! So it is with travel in cyberspace.

There are a lot of helpful, even fantastic, websites out there. But, as we travel to the outer reaches of the cyber galaxy, we may unknowingly land in hostile territory where we get trapped. We could land on a website graveyard filled with dead links, dead ends, and nonexistent "contacts." Or we could land on a website junkyard, piled up with useless trivia, outdated relics, or once valuable treasures that are no longer relevant. Fortunately, our critical thinking skills can help us steer our way through all this and hopefully get us to a website that either meets our objective or provides valuable leads so we can continue our quest.

In addition to our own reasoning powers, the American Library Association (ALA) has produced helpful guidelines for evaluating websites. As we know for those websites with strange inhabitants, anyone can publish almost anything on the Web. There is no Internet editor or cyber cop to weed out the oddities, the fringe, the threatening, the unpopular, the cheesy. That has both advantages and

Five Criteria for Evaluating Web Pages

**1. Accuracy   2. Authority   3. Objectivity
4. Currency   5. Coverage**

1. *Accuracy:*
   - ☐ Who wrote the page and how can you contact them?
   - ☐ What is the purpose of the document and why was it produced?
   - ☐ Is this person qualified to write this document?
   - ☐ Who is the author and who is the Web-master?
   - ☐ Does the author provide a way to be contacted?

2. *Authority:*
   - ☐ Who published the document?
   - ☐ What is the domain of the document? (Is it self-generated, a private company, an organization, an academic institution, a governmental agency? Check the URL.)
   - ☐ Is there an institutional affiliation listed?
   - ☐ Does the publisher list any qualifications?
   - ☐ Can you figure out the author's credentials or credibility?

3. *Objectivity:*
   - ☐ What goals or objectives does this Web page meet?
   - ☐ How detailed is the information?
   - ☐ Does the author express any opinions?
   - ☐ Is the Web page a mask for advertising?
   - ☐ Do you detect any bias?
   - ☐ Is this Web page like an infomercial on TV?
   - ☐ Why was this written and who is the intended audience?

4. *Currency:*
   - ☐ When was it produced?
   - ☐ When was it updated?
   - ☐ How up to date are the links (if any)?
   - ☐ Are there any dead links are on the page?
   - ☐ Is any of the information on the page outdated?

5. *Coverage:*
   - ☐ Are the links (if any) evaluated?
   - ☐ Do the links complement the document's theme?
   - ☐ What function do the visual images (or sound/videos) serve?
   - ☐ Is there a balance of text and images?
   - ☐ Is the information presented cited correctly?
   - ☐ Does the page require any special software?
   - ☐ Is there a cost to obtain information?
   - ☐ Is there an option for text only, or a suggested browser for better viewing?
   - ☐ Are there links to more detailed documents or related resources?

Source: Adapted from the American Library Association Guidelines.

---

disadvantages. One advantage is that it makes it less likely that tyrannical governments exist without a channel for opposition. That is, the Internet not only provides access to information it also allows networks to form and alliances to build. It also means we are pretty free to search for a wide range of documents. We can also go through archives that might otherwise be eliminated because they are narrow in scope or of interest for only a small number of people.

On the other hand, we cannot assume that everything we find on the Web is legitimate, well researched, or credible. Most documents have not been subjected to a peer review, a professional organization, or an editorial staff. And most are not held to any standard of excellence. This means we have to learn to evaluate sites and determine the value and legitimacy of the material we find. Let's look at the ALA recommendations and then we'll try to apply them to a range of websites.

Exercises

Directions: Using your critical thinking skills and the adapted ALA guidelines, answer the questions below.

1. What is the ideal university website? Set out your ideas as to what should and should not be on a university website (e.g., phone numbers of offices and staff, cafeteria menus, course schedules, courses required for each major, average SAT score, retention rate, campus safety, and so on).

2. Evaluate the Web page of a university other than the one you attend.

3. Evaluate a website on any *one* of the following historical topics: the Zoot Suit riots, the Holocaust, the underground railroad, the civil rights movement, Vietnam War protests, the Battle at Wounded Knee, the internment camps in WWII, the fall of the Berlin Wall, the United Farm Workers and the grape boycott, the Suffrage Movement or the temperance movement, the Human Genome Project, or the Parti-Quebecois separatist movement in Canada.

4. Evaluate two websites focused on the significance of the life or the death of *one* of the following: John F. Kennedy, Pierre Trudeau, John F. Kennedy, Jr., Jon-Benet Ramsey, Princess Diana, Mahatma Gandhi, Martin Luther King, Jr., Elvis Presley, Marilyn Monroe, Frieda Kahlo, Selena, Andy Warhol, Emily Carr, Mother Theresa, Malcolm X, Zora Neale Hurston, Bruce Lee, Sojourner Truth, Matthew Shepard.

5. Find a good website on any *one* of the following "how-to" topics: collecting sports memorabilia, cooking shellfish, ostrich farming, baking a chocolate soufflé, painting with glazes, caring for an exotic pet, polishing an antique car, repairing broken glassware, or training a parrot to talk.

6. Evaluate a website on any *one* of the following controversial topics: cloning, egg donation, homophobia, legalization of marijuana, the death penalty, surrogate parenting, electric shock therapy, xenotransplants, paying human subjects, prisoners' rights, physician-assisted suicide, or animal rights.

7. Compare and contrast two websites that focus on *one* of the following figures: Leonard Pelletier, Amelia Earhart, Lizzie Borden, Jane Goodall, Nelson Mandela, Cesar Chavez, Wilma Mankiller, Arthur Asche, Simon Wiesenthal, Medgar Evers, Geronimo Pratt, Delores Huerta, or Thich Nhat Hanh.

8. Compare and contrast any two websites that focus on *one* of the following topics: the case against the tobacco industry, addressing anorexia in teenagers, drug abuse in the music industry, pitfalls of intelligence testing, ethical or political concerns with statistical methods in clinical research, the Japanese influence on animation, the effects of gospel music on rhythm and blues, the antiwar movement in the late 1960s and the 1970s, prosecuting Nazi war criminals, the success of the Greenpeace movement in protests against the sealing industry, applications of Greek mythology to U.S. politics, or the Navajo uranium miners' attempts to get redress.

▦ Web Research: Defending or Attacking a Claim

You've procrastinated as long as possible, but you are running out of time and that essay deadline is looming. And you are too late to go to the library; all you have is your computer for a research tool. Well, it may not be as good as a library, but there's a lot out there on the Web. There are two key questions here, though:

Will you access good information?

This is a search question.

Can you distinguish higher-level from lower-quality websites and documents?

This is an evaluation question.

We need to look at both of these questions. The first one involves being able to search the Web. For that, you need to know how to use search engines, when to try more than one search engine, and other ways to access reference material. That can take time, so that needs to be factored in as well. Also, we need to apply problem-solving and questioning techniques to optimize searches. The second question brings in the range of critical thinking skills set out earlier in the chapter (see "Applying Critical Thinking Skills to the Web," p. 445).

Whether you are a seasoned veteran of Internet research or a novice, there's still a lot to learn and, as more and more websites are developed, there are an increasing number of sites out there in the cybergalaxy. Below are 10 pearls of wisdom of Web research that we should all keep in mind as we navigate cyberspace.

Exercises

1. Choose any *two* government websites; such as: the FBI website, *www.fbi .gov;* the NASA website, *www.nasa.gov;* Internal Revenue website, *www. irs.ustreas.gov;* the Center for Disease Control website, *www.cdc.gov;* and the U.S. Postal Service website, *www.usps.gov.*
   a. Compare and contrast the quality of the resources.
   b. Compare the relative ease of navigating the sites.
   c. Give your overall impression of the two websites.

2. Pick any *two* celebrities (e.g., movie stars, athletes, famous authors), and then compare and contrast the best website you found for each of your two figures.

3. How are people honored? Select *one* area (the Pulitzer Prize, the Nobel Prize, the Caldicott Medal, Academy Awards, Emmy Awards, NBA Hall of Fame, etc.) and then evaluate the awarding organization's website.

Ten Pearls of Wisdom of Web Research

1. *Research Takes Time:* Allow time to follow links and links within links to investigate the resources out there. If you do, you may find far more than you ever imagined possible.

2. *Think Like a Fox:* Maybe you'll win the lottery, maybe not. Maybe you'll find great stuff after your first search, maybe not. Be prepared to try different search engines and different ways of formulating questions or search terms.

3. *Be Imaginative:* Be crafty when phrasing search terms. If one doesn't work, try another. Try different search engines and electronic databases, approach the topic through various avenues, and consider different perspectives. You may hit the jackpot with one of them.

4. *Libraries Are Good Things:* Use library websites and resources. Try local library resources (e.g., *lapl.org*), university library websites, the Library of Congress, and so on. These have a wide range of resource tools, links, and helpful databases for accessing a wide variety of sites including online dictionaries (e.g., the Oxford English Dictionary is available online at many university and public libraries' websites). And don't forget the Librarian's Index to the Internet (*www.lii.org*) and the American Library Association website (*www.ala.org*).

5. *Don't Reinvent the Wheel:* Investigate professional organizations. Remember laws and legal decisions are available on line (e.g., U.S. Supreme Court site, *www.supremecourtus.gov*, the U.S. Supreme Court multimedia database, *oyez.com,* and the legal database, *findlaw.com*), as well as statistics, government documents, photo archives, historical papers, music and film reviews, and other hard-to-find resources.

6. *Know Your Friends:* Publishers' websites are good places to scout for documents; government sites can be a treasure trove, as can national archives, newspapers online, online journals, and metasearch engines.

7. *Consider Unlikely Suspects:* Go to sites that seem tangential. These may not directly relate to your search, but may provide a back door to the topic, or to links and resources that take you where you want to go.

8. *Network:* One research channel is to communicate with those who are in the know: E-mail professionals, organizations, or other online contacts if you have questions or concerns that their expertise can help. Remember to be as precise as you can in your request. Many are generous with their time and will answer and offer some leads or give you feedback.

9. *Ask Questions:* It helps in navigating search engines and using search tools to be able to formulate your search as a question. In this way, you can be clear in your own mind what is the focus of your search and how to narrow down the topic should the need arise. Plus, at a website, you may need to clarify what you seek or have to rephrase or narrow down the search. Additionally, contacting reference persons or giving feedback to a site may demand good, clear questions. Questions help us stay focused.

10. *Keep an Open Mind:* Be receptive to new ideas and fresh perspectives. Try a variety of approaches. Think of your research as tackling an intellectual puzzle. Rigidity of thought is rarely useful, whereas mental dexterity and emotional detachment can expose the dimensions of a problem, and even the solution. The answer to our prayers may be staring us in the face, but we need to be perceptive and receptive to different ways of seeing the world.

▦ The Internet and Intellectual Freedom

One nice thing about the exposure to ideas is that it makes us think! Of course, we don't always come across ideas we agree with. And we don't always come across ideas that are noble or worth preserving. Some ideas are disturbing, disgusting, or detestable. On the other hand, some ideas are cathartic, inspiring, or groundbreaking. Some ideas have truly changed the world.

Access to ideas and information is necessary for a democracy to flourish—and we cannot take this for granted. Just look at the ongoing issues around works of fiction. In the last 30 years a number of novels have been banned from libraries or schools, including *Death of a Salesman* (Arthur Miller), *The Color Purple* (Alice Walker), *Brave New World* (Aldous Huxley), *A Clockwork Orange* (Anthony Burgess), *The Diary of a Young Girl* (Anne Frank), *Forever* (Judy Blume), *Harriet the Spy* (Louise Fitzhugh), *1984* (George Orwell), *Of Mice and Men* (John Steinbeck), *One Flew Over the Cuckoo's Nest* (Ken Kesey), *The Shining* (Stephen King), *Slaughterhouse Five* (Kurt Vonnegut, Jr.), *That Was Then, This Is Now* (S. E. Hinton), *To Kill a Mockingbird* (Harper Lee), *Ulysses* (James Joyce). (For a fuller list and discussion, see the American Library Association website at *www.ala.org.*)

Many of these works are considered classics of fiction. But objections were raised for a variety of issues (depending upon the work) such as profanity, undermining race relations, graphic language, immoral tone, lack of literary quality, violence, irreverence, explicit sexual content, demonic possession, vulgar language, Communist sympathies, and teaching children to lie, talk back, and curse, among others.

And yet, many of these works are also celebrated. For example, though *To Kill a Mockingbird* was been accused of "undermining race relations," the novel was selected in August of 2001 as the *one* book that people in Chicago should read and discuss. Presumably, the fact that the Pulitzer Prize–winning novel does examine race relations was not seen as a detriment. It was expected that tens of thousands of people would participate (see Stephen Kinzer, "Chicagoans Are Reading the Same Book at the Same Time," *The New York Times,* 28 Aug. 2001).

The American Library Association (ALA) is actively trying to stop the censorship of ideas or information that individuals or groups find objectionable or dangerous. Let's see what they have to say:

> The free expression of ideas as embodied in the First Amendment is a basic human right. As American citizens, we have the right to read what we want to read, hear what we want to hear, watch what we want to watch and think what we want to think. Intellectual freedom is the right to seek and receive information from all points of view, without restriction, even those ideas that might be highly controversial or offensive to others.
>
> As a personal liberty, intellectual freedom forms the foundation of our democracy. It is an essential part of government by the people. The right to vote is not enough— we also must be able to take part in forming public opinion by engaging in open and vigorous debate on controversial matters. Libraries allow people to be well-informed so they can make the decisions our Constitution says are ours to make. (See *www.ala.org*)

Incidentally, not all librarians agree with this and have protested the ALA's unwillingness to discuss this issue at all. Many librarians have spoken up against this position. It is controversial. One of the arguments goes like this: What about the fact that libraries "discriminate" in what books and videos they purchase for their library? One criterion for selecting what to buy is <u>quality</u>. Does the filtering process that libraries use in purchasing materials for the library have no parallel in the cyberworld? Libraries don't stop this material from being published—they just don't make it accessible from their library.

CASE STUDY

Cyberpornography and Libraries

One of the issues around the use of filtering software for computers in public libraries is the censorship of pornography. Some, as we saw above, hold the view that filtering software is inherently against the right to access information and ideas. They consider any form of censorship to be wrong-headed, as it has the potential to take us down a slippery slope, leading to the censorship of literature or unpopular ideas. It is out of such a framework that the ALA is fighting attempts to "protect" children by requiring filtering software in library computers.

On the other hand, many librarians and others argue that human filters have been in place since public libraries first opened. They note that we ordinarily set limits around what is socially permissible and have had no problems ejecting people out of libraries if they crossed the boundary of decency or acceptable behavior. Arguing in favor of such limitations with the help of filtering software is Leonard Kniffel. In an editorial to American Libraries, *he made the following argument. Read it and then answer the questions that follow.*

Chicago librarian Laura Morgan has filed a grievance with the Equal Employment Opportunity Commission against the Chicago Public Library, alleging that because public Internet terminals at CPL are unfiltered, the library has subjected her to a hostile work environment created by patrons displaying graphic sexual images on library computers and printing them on library printers. The easy availability of pornography on the Net, says Morgan, has created an epidemic of behavior problems that, under the cloak of intellectual freedom, the library refuses to address.

What sets Morgan's case apart from others that merely argue for the use of filtering software is the charge of sexual harassment. . . . Morgan's charges that library users are employing the Internet to intimidate, taunt, and humiliate employees are far less easy to dismiss, and her assertion that the library has not taken her fears seriously is disturbing. She maintains that it is almost exclusively men and boys who surf the library computers for sex thrills, and it is women and girls who must suffer the hostility their activity poses.

There has never been and probably never will be universal agreement among librarians over the effectiveness of filtering software. Many libraries use it in combination with policies and staff training to control the behavior of users. But it has always been unacceptable to exhibit sexual behavior in public. Such behavior related to the Internet makes it no different from other intolerable behavior. Unless libraries establish and enforce acceptable-use policies, they will be increasingly vulnerable to charges such as Morgan's, charges that the library administration has ignored the legitimate concerns of its employees. (See Leonard Kniffel, "Editorial: You Can't Have Sex In The Library," *American Libraries*, Vol. 32, Mar. 2001)

Answer the following:

1. State Kniffel's thesis and key arguments.
2. What are his strongest points?
3. State the two to three strongest points an opponent of filtering software would make to Kniffel.
4. Do you think patrons using library computers have the right to print pornographic photos and images?

Exercise

In the year 2000, issues around censorship of books still raged.

- Read over the list of the books most challenged, along with the types of challenges for the entire decade 1990–1999.
- Then share your ideas about the degree to which books found to be offensive raise similar concerns about the World Wide Web. *Note:* Concerns that are Web related but not necessarily an issue with books.

The Most Challenged Books in the Year 2000:

1. *Harry Potter* series, by J. K. Rowling, for occult/satanism and antifamily themes.
2. *The Chocolate War,* by Robert Cormier (the "most challenged" fiction book of 1998), for violence, offensive language and being unsuited to age group.
3. *Alice* series, by Phyllis Reynolds Naylor, for sexual content and being unsuited to age group.
4. *Killing Mr. Griffin,* by Lois Duncan, for violence and sexual content.
5. *Of Mice and Men,* by John Steinbeck, for using offensive language, racism, violence, and being unsuited to age group.
6. *I Know Why the Caged Bird Sings,* by Maya Angelou, for being too explicit in the book's portrayal of rape and other sexual abuse.
7. *Fallen Angels,* by Walter Dean Myers, for offensive language, racism, violence, and being unsuited to age group.
8. *Scary Stories* series, by Alvin Schwartz, for violence, being unsuited to age group, and occult themes.
9. *The Terrorist,* by Caroline Cooney, for violence, being unsuited to age group, and occult themes.
10. *The Giver,* by Lois Lowry, for being sexually explicit, and occult themes and violence.

Between 1990 and 1999, of the 5718 challenges reported to or recorded by the Office for Intellectual Freedom):

- 1446 were challenges to "sexually explicit" material.
- 1262 to material considered to use "offensive language."
- 1167 to material considered "unsuited to age group."
- 773 to material with an "occult theme or promoting the occult or Satanism."
- 630 to material considered to be "violent."
- 497 to material with a homosexual theme or "promoting homosexuality."
- 397 to material "promoting a religious viewpoint."

Note: Other reasons for challenges included nudity (297 challenges), racism (245 challenges), sex education (217 challenges), and antifamily (193 challenges).

Source: www.ala.org.

Censorship of the Internet

It's interesting to consider the censorship of the Internet alongside censorship of books. Obviously there are many similarities, but there are some key differences too. One key difference is how easy it is to access Internet sites in the privacy of your own room. Thus, unsupervised children may come upon (or seek out) material that parents would not normally allow them to access and libraries would not likely contain (e.g., pornography and hate speech). The question is whether those differences are sufficient to suggest a different policy for the Internet than for novels and other books.

Group Exercise

Taking into consideration the proliferation of pornography, hate sites, and access to potentially offensive documents, *answer the following:*

- State the three to four strongest arguments for and against censorship of the Internet.
- Assume a mediation model. You can't have all or nothing when it comes to censorship, so what would you agree to let in? And what would you consider essential to be banned from the Internet? Make a decision.
- State the strongest justification you can for what could be *on* and what must be *off* the Internet in terms of *one* of these: (a) private users; (b) use of adults at public sites (cyber cafes, libraries, colleges, and universities); (c) use of minors at public sites (schools, libraries, cyber cafes, etc.).

CASE STUDY

The FBI Wiretap System, Carnivore

The FBI has an Internet wiretapping system called "Carnivore" that has been described as a PC Robocop. Like a pig sniffing for truffles, this Carnivore system uses a "packet sniffer" during criminal investigations to sniff out data for the FBI. For instance, Carnivore can be used to harvest information from e-mail messages (both ingoing and outgoing) much like tapping a phone line to trace the origin and destination of a suspect's calls. However, Carnivore can do much more: supposedly it can capture and archive all traffic through an Internet service provider. Read the following excerpt and then answer the questions that follow:

The new system, which operates on off-the-shelf personal computers, takes advantage of one of the fundamental principles of the Internet: that virtually all such communications are broken up into "packets," or uniform chunks of data. Computers on the Internet break up e-mail messages, World Wide Website traffic and other information into pieces and route the packets across the global network, where they are re-assembled on the other end.

FBI programmers devised a "packet sniffer" system that can analyze data flowing through computer networks to determine whether it is part of an e-mail message or some other piece of Web traffic.

The ability to distinguish between packets allows law enforcement officials to tailor their searches so that, for example, they can examine e-mail but leave alone a suspect's online shopping activities. The system could be tuned to do as little as monitoring how many e-mail messages the suspect sends and to whom they are addressed—the equivalent of a telephone "pen register," which takes down telephone numbers being called without grabbing the content of those calls. (See John Schwartz, "FBI's Internet Wiretaps Raise Privacy Concerns: New System Tracks Suspects Online," *The Washington Post*, 11 July 2000)

Answer the following:

1. What do you think are the best reasons for Carnivore's existence?
2. What do you think are the major concerns about Carnivore?
3. Do an Internet search and see what pro-Carnivore advocates have to say. Share the highlights of your search.
4. Do an Internet search and see what critics of Carnivore have to say. Share the highlights of your search.
5. What should be done about this system that has the capabilities to scan private information and collect data on people (suspects and nonsuspects)?

▩ Carnivore and National Security Issues

Shortly after the 9-11 terrorist attacks on the United States using commercial aircraft, concerns were raised about computer privacy. Fears were expressed that the FBI would seek to expand the steps taken with Carnivore, as noted below:

"I heard former President (George H. W.) Bush saying we've got to prepare to give up our civil liberties," said Erwin Chemerinsky, a constitutional law professor at the University of Southern California Law School in Los Angeles. "All of that sentiment is very dangerous at this point in time. I think there's going to be a real effort to give government more surveillance authority," he added. . . .

"When I heard (of) this (attack), I thought people are just going to trample the Bill of Rights into the dust," said Lance Cottrell, president of *Anonymizer.com,* which allows people to surf the Web anonymously. (Reuters, "Experts Say Digital Privacy May Suffer Amid Attacks," 13 Sep. 2001)

However, terrorists in this case left a paper trail—they used credit cards, real names, and rental car receipts. Nevertheless, the wider issues that involve computer privacy vs. government surveillance continue to be unresolved.

Conflicting Views of the Internet

Los Cybrid is made up of artists Monica Praba Pilar, John J. Leaños, and Rene Garcia, who have let out a battle cry against technology and information society. As reported by Angel Gonzalez:

"We're against the fervor of the digital revolution," says Leaños, referring to the promises of prosperity, equality, direct democracy and multi-culturalism heralded by the Internet gurus of the last decade. "The Net is controlled by the military and the multinationals. They are the ones who benefit." . . . According to the Cybrids, the Net is where global capitalism has flourished the fastest and benefited the most, thanks to its newly acquired ability to spy on users.

The new economy doesn't solve inequalities, but rather perpetuates them along the lines of racial divide. The presence of technology comes through policing, surveillance, INS databases and all kinds of information collected to maintain control over citizens, especially those of color, according to Pilar. "Privacy is not an individual, but a social problem," she says. (See Angel Gonzalez, "A Disturbing, Latino View of Tech," *Wired Digital,* 27 June 2001)

Certainly not everyone agrees with Los Cybrids' view of technology or global capitalists. But, as we saw from the anti-World Trade Organization sites, many do worry about the gap between the rich and the poor—and the ways in which such uses of technology as we see in the Internet may be fueling that division. It is a legitimate concern, especially if we consider how powerful a tool the Internet can be.

On the other hand, the Internet can also be used to fortify resistance, strengthen channels of communication, and share information—and do all this quickly and efficiently. And, although it provides channels for megacorporations to expand their horizons, we also find websites allowing those in far-away places to survive. Think, for example, of the Benedictine Monks doing illuminating manuscripts on Web pages (see, for example, the Vatican website at *www.vatican.va*). Or think of the Tibetans trying to sustain their culture, religion, and language (see, e.g., the government of Tibet in exile at *www.tibet.com*). Or think of all the Native American tribes whose websites are hubs of information (see, e.g., *www.cherokee-nc.com, www.tlingit-haida.org,* and *www.navajo.org*). Or think of all the indigenous artists trying to sustain their traditional arts and crafts by selling beadwork, weaving, and sculpture through a website.

The Internet and Community

Nancy Pearl, a Seattle librarian, had the idea for a city to sponsor the "read-one-book-together" plan. She feels that such a project strengthens community because "It's based on the noble idea of community. My noble idea was that people would come together who would never come together any other way. Literature brings them together because a book touches them" (quoted in *The New York Times*, 28 Aug. 2001). She may be right in her speculation. A shared experience can certainly draw people together—even if only for a short time—to exchange thoughts and ideas. Such shared events can build community and empower people to work together for social change.

Potentially as powerful as shared reading experience is the channel for dialogue that has been opened by the Internet. This channel has both positive and negative aspects. Surely the dark side is that hate groups can proliferate, given the almost otherworldly or underground quality to the Internet; namely, the ease of spewing hate in the privacy of one's own bedroom with a potentially global audience. It's frightening to think how much harm just one determined individual can do with such a tool.

And yet, there is this amazing positive side. This tool allows people to communicate without ever hearing the other's voice or seeing the other's handwriting. As Amy Harmon put it, "many of those who make an effort to take advantage of what it [the Web] has to offer say that the cultural impact of the Web lies not in its would-be alternative media outlets, but in the way it facilitates contact between individuals who would otherwise never have the benefit of each other's experience." Steven Johnson echoes Harmon, saying, "Maybe it turns out that what the Web is good for is connecting people" (as quoted by Amy Harmon, "Exploration of the World Wide Web Tiles from Eclectic to Mundane," *The New York Times*, 26 Aug. 2001).

The potential for the "noble community" Nancy Pearl sees with books is there too with the Internet. In that sense, it is a liberating and powerful way to bring people together to build community and help one another. We saw this immediately after September 11, 2001. Not only were chat rooms a channel for people to process their grief and outrage, but those with needs and services also found the Internet a valuable resource. For example,

> The website for the QVC shopping service devoted its home page to resources on blood donation. Travel site *OneTravel.com* offered to donate 10 percent of earnings to New York firefighters. Online clothing retailer *Bluefly.com* sent online notices offering displaced companies the use of vacant office space. Ken Seiff, the company's chief executive, received several responses within hours. The American Psychological Association posted tips on managing traumatic stress, while the American Academy of Pediatrics had advice on counseling children. At an online prayer forum, individuals

posted personal prayers for victims and emergency workers. (See "Web Becomes Global Support Forum," The Associated Press, 12 Sep. 2001)

This use of the Internet to help others in a time of such crisis must be heartening to those who envisioned the Internet as a channel for networking and for a sense of a broader community working together for common goals. As we'll see in the exercise below, one of the ways we can build community and help others is through the sharing of information and expertise.

Group Exercise

The U.S. State Department estimates that there are 60 to 70 million land mines in nearly 80 countries. Equally mind-boggling is that one kills or maims victims an average of every 22 minutes. According to the United Nations 30 to 40 percent of these victims are children. In an article on innovative uses of online courses, Bonnie Rothman Morris tells the following story. Read it and then discuss the questions that follow:

> A medical worker in San Miguel, a city in eastern El Salvador, Mrs. Monge de Quintanilla toils daily at the Salvadoran Rehabilitation Institute, making and fitting prosthetic limbs for up to eight amputees daily, most of whom are victims of land mines. She acquired her skills as a prosthetist a decade ago through a military program during the war in El Salvador. . . . In June she started an eight-month distance-education course intended to train her in the latest prosthetic techniques. She is one of 23 prosthetists in El Salvador, Nicaragua and Guatemala who are taking the pilot program, which was developed by the Center for International Rehabilitation, a three-year-old organization in Chicago that works to help victims of landmines. . . .
>
> When the relief workers leave, the health problems remain for amputees, especially children, who need to be monitored, fitted and refitted with new prosthetics. "People with disabilities need a lifetime commitment," said Dr. William Kennedy Smith, director of the Center for International Rehabilitation and president of Physicians Against Land Mines.
>
> The lessons for the prosthetics course were developed at the Northwestern University Prosthetic Orthotic Center. (See Bonnie Rothman Morris, "Online Course Lets the Isolated Bring Their Medical Skills Up to Date," The New York Times, 30 Aug. 2001)

Directions to groups:

1. Discuss the potential for using the Internet to help address other societal problems or tragedies.

2. Suggest online courses, other ways of disseminating medical or other expertise, and any innovative ideas you have to help those areas of the world that are short on money, resources, or personnel and yet face serious issues like the one Mrs. Monge de Quintanilla is trying to alleviate.

Exercises

1. Do you believe a live video feed of the inside of a jail would deter would-be criminals? Sheriff Arpaio of Phoenix, Arizona is convinced that using the World Wide Web will deter crime. It is his hope that the *only* visit you make to his jail is a virtual visit.
   a. Set out your position on the claim, "24 hours a day live video of a jail will help deter criminals."
   b. Go to Jail Cam at *www.crime.com* and see for yourself. Do you think this website will help would-be criminals rethink their lives and go straight? Look at the site and evaluate its merits, given this goal.

2. Select *one* issue, such as homelessness, poverty, access to health care, prisoners who claim innocence and seek DNA testing to make their case, teachers who are addressing literacy problems in the inner city, people whose English language skills are poor trying to access health care or education for their children, battered women and children trying to rebuild their lives, teenagers struggling with substance abuse or alcohol, children with learning disabilities trying to make it through public schools. Then:
   a. Write down all you think is being done to address this issue in our society.
   b. Are you optimistic or pessimistic about how much we are doing to try to make a difference? Set down your thoughts.
   c. Using *only* the Internet, see what is being done to address the issue you selected. Summarize your findings.

3. Select *one* of the following groups: The police, fire department, local churches, medical professionals, lawyers' groups, teachers' groups, actors, musicians, airline employees, members of the military, and so on. Then:
   a. Set out your ideas about what the group you selected is doing in terms of community-outreach or is otherwise involved in service toward the community.
   b. Try several searches to see what you find about the group you picked. Summarize the results and share whether or not you were surprised at your findings.
   c. See what you can find on your group using community-networking websites such as *www.scn.org* and *www.bev.net*. Note that you can read about public libraries' role in providing community information at *www.si.umich.edu/Community*).

4. In light of the excerpt below set out your three strongest arguments for or against allowing prisoners to use the Internet:

The Internet has given a platform to death-row inmates and other American prisoners to plead their cases and seek pen pals, sparking outrage among many families of victims and creating a new debate about the rights of the growing number of prisoners. While no American prison allows inmates access to the Internet, prisoners use third-party services, usually for a fee, to reach out to a potentially huge audience. . . .

Beau Greene, who is imprisoned in Arizona, appears on a website in a picture, cradling a fluffy cat and asking for penpals. . . . Mr. Greene, 32, does not mention that he was convicted in 1996 of killing a slender, 58-year-old musician, Roy Johnson, by bashing the man's head against rocks. When the victim's daughter, Jennifer Johnson Lopez, discovered the website, she said she was horrified that the killer . . . was able to use the Internet to escape his feeling of confinement. "I was disgusted," Ms. Johnson Lopez said. "He said he missed companionship. I thought, "Serves you right."

Victims' rights groups complain that it is humiliating for victims and their families to see prisoners popping up on websites. And the groups also complain that some people browsing the Internet might begin correspondence with violent criminals or fall for their stories without knowing the real details of their crimes.

In the face of such criticism, officials in New York and Arizona have enacted policies or laws that forbid prisoners to use third-party Internet service providers. Washington and other states have debated similar measures. But in the view of many civil libertarians, these measures infringe on the First Amendment rights of inmates. (See Dirk Johnson, "Using Internet Links from Behind Bars," *The New York Times*, 1 Aug. 2000)

5. *You decide:* Convicted murderer Mumia Abu-Jamal (who says he was framed) has a number of websites supporting his release from jail (his legal appeals have thus far been denied). Read the following, examine some of these pro-Abu-Jamal websites for yourself and then share your thoughts on how the Internet can (and should?) be used for political and personal causes.

The Internet has also become a tool in championing the causes of individual inmates, such as Mumia Abu-Jamal, who defenders contend was wrongly convicted of killing a police officer in Philadelphia in 1981. At least a dozen websites carry details about the case and history of Mr. Abu-Jamal. One of the largest sites, operated by a private anti-death-penalty group in New York called Refuse and Resist, describes the inmate as "a prominent radio journalist" being punished because he "allowed the angry and anguished voices of the oppressed onto the airwaves." It features a photograph of Mr. Abu-Jamal, smiling and raising a clenched fist.

A page on the website, under a headline reading *The Frame-Up,* calls the police account absurd and says that witnesses in Mr. Abu-Jamal's defense were harassed by law enforcement authorities. The site invites people to join marches around the country on Mr. Abu-Jamal's behalf. It also encourages website visitors to print and distribute the posting to other potential supporters. (See Dirk Johnson, "Using Internet Links from Behind Bars," *The New York Times*, 1 Aug. 2000)

6. What should be done to protect young people from sexual predators on the Internet? We keep reading about teenagers and children who are lured by a sexual predator posing as a "friend" in online chat rooms. Law enforcement agencies have stepped up Internet patrols, in light of the rising incidents.

Read the following comments and then offer your suggestions about how to stop Internet predators of teenagers and children:

"There is no silver bullet," said Bob Weaver, the assistant special agent in charge of the New York Electronic Crimes Task Force, which is run by the Secret Service and harnesses the efforts of 45 law enforcement agencies. "Traditionally, law enforcement in general has a stovepipe approach," he said. "The primary focus is on arrests, prosecutions and convictions. Now you're getting into education. Now you make a difference. You're going to catch the kids before they have a problem."

Since 1995, the task force, which deals with all forms of technology-related crime, has patrolled the Web in search of child pornography users and suspected pedophiles. In January, the task force added a prong to its approach, lecturing about the dangers of cybercrime to Boys and Girls Clubs. The program may be expanded into the public school system, Mr. Weaver said.

Some pupils are told the story of an investigator in New Jersey who tracked down a girl he met online using the scant information she had given him, then warned the girl and her parents that others could do the same. "Some of them sit there and they're amazed," said Robert M. Sciarrone, a special agent in charge of the program. "We tell them not to give out personal information." (See Elissa Gootman, "Stepping up Protection for Youths on Internet," *The New York Times,* 21 Aug. 2001)

7. Nelson King quotes a man, John, who says of the Internet,

As a place to go for information, I wouldn't let a novice go near it. Only people who are skilled at organizing information and have enough experience to cull out the B.S. can wander around in the quagmire of search-engine results without completely losing a sense of what's real, what's useful, and what's not. (See Nelson King, "A Chance Encounter," *ComputerUser,* Sep. 2000.)

Note that John goes on to compare teachers telling their students to use the Internet for a research paper to parents who let their kids watch eight hours of TV a day to keep them quiet.

Answer the following:
a. Do you think John is right to be so critical of the Internet? Share your thoughts.
b. Is John's analogy a strong one? Discuss.

▦ Netspeak

Thanks to the Internet, we now have a new form of language—one in which abbreviations and an array of new terms and phrases has altered communication styles (e.g., RUOK (Are you O.K.?), CUL8R (See you later), smiley faces, symbols in the place of words and letters, and so on). Language specialist, Dr. David Crystal, asserts that, "The Internet is a genuine third medium of communication."

(Number one is speech; number two is writing; and number three is computer-mediated discourse). (See Anne Eisenberg, "Pooh-Poohing the Purists, a Scholar Revels in Netspeak," *The New York Times*, 13 Dec. 2001)

He considers computer-speak (alias Netspeak) to be fundamentally different from both speaking and writing. Among its unique qualities is the ability to have a discussion (in a chat-room) with 20 people, resulting in a hybrid of speech and writing. And, contrary to the claims of many anxious parents and teachers, Crystal contends that the Internet is not spawning a generation of illiterates. He believes it is developing into a splendid new medium that shows how very inventive and clever people can be.

Crystal disagrees with those who worry that English will be ruined by its casual treatment on the Internet. He says,

"Children know that you use crazy, geeky language on e-mail and on mobile phones, and then they are sensible when they are writing for the teachers." He adds, "If I leave out the punctuation in an e-mail, you don't say, 'Crystal doesn't know his grammar.' You say, 'Crystal's in a hurry.' Similarly, people looking for a job will construct their e-mail quite differently than they would if chatting with friends." (See Anne Eisenberg, "Pooh-Poohing the Purists, a Scholar Revels in Netspeak," *The New York Times*, 13 Dec. 2001)

Group Exercise

How do you think the Internet affecting the way we use language? Share your thoughts and then try to come up with a list of netspeak lingo that you or your friends use in e-mail or in chat rooms.

Hate Speech on the Web

The Web is no more immune from hate speech that any other vehicle of communication that does not have strict controls in place. The very existence of hate-filled websites has created a controversy around freedom of speech and freedom of information. Many think we ought to err on the side of freedom, letting the audience decide for themselves where the axe should fall in terms of what is legitimate and what isn't. On the other hand, there are those who view with alarm the rise of hate sites and think the very ease of access and use of the Web means those who are most vulnerable (such as children) may become victims.

What should we do when children are involved in producing or sustaining a website that has as its very purpose the glorification of one group at the cost of others? What should we do when we find websites targeting members of different racial, religious, or other groups? What should we do about websites that send out a call to arms or to acts of violence (e.g., as found in some of the extreme anti-abortion sites)?

For example, in 1999 an Internet service provider shut down an antiabortion website that an Oregon jury considered a threat to abortion providers. The creator of the website planned to set up video cameras at abortion clinics in five U.S. cities and in England and Japan to monitor activities. The website also included names and addresses of abortion providers. Three doctors whose names appeared on the list were killed. A federal jury ruled that the website, called "The Nuremberg Files" was a threat to abortion providers and awarded $107 million in damages. This was struck down on appeal, however, and The Nuremberg Files site was considered to be allowable under First Amendment protections (see chapter 7 for more on this issue). The U.S. Supreme Court has agreed to hear the case.

In addition to websites that are directed at issues like abortion and use strong graphic images and calls to action, at least as problematic are websites that reveal strong biases or prejudice. Furthermore, these websites are not just aimed at adults; some target children as well. For instance, in an article on a white supremacy website called Stormfront, *USA Today* reported:

> WEST PALM BEACH, Fla.—Twelve-year-old Derek Black . . . looks like the typical tech-savvy preteen he is. Yet the thing that makes his father proudest is that Derek runs a website for kids—promoting white supremacy and racial hate. "Couldn't ask for anything more," says Don Black, who keeps a framed photo of Derek dressed in a Confederate soldier's uniform above his desk in his home office. In 1995, Black, 47, created what is believed to be the Web's first hate site, *Stormfront.org*. Today he boasts that it has become the most-visited white supremacist site on the Net. Derek runs the site's children's section, working closely with his dad.
>
> More than 5,000 unduplicated visitors come to Stormfront daily, and several hundred a day (344,000 in two years) have visited the children's pages, where puzzles and games are mixed with animated Confederate flags, sound files of white-pride songs, an inflammatory article about Martin Luther King Jr. and a personal statement from Derek asking visitors to stop sending him hate mail. (See Tara McKelvey, "Father and Son Team on Hate Site. *USAToday.com*, 10 Aug. 2001)

At the "kids" link of the Stormfront website is an image of an American flag morphing into a Confederate flag, along with games, music, and other links to appeal to children.

One of the issues with Internet hate sites is how influential they could be on vulnerable or receptive minds. In an interesting twist on the Twinkie defense (where Dan White blamed eating Twinkies and getting a sugar high as the reason he went berserk and murdered Harvey Milk, an openly gay man who was elected to the San Francisco Board of Supervisors), a mass murderer recently blamed the Internet for the rampage.

Richard Baumhammers drove through Pittsburgh picking out people of color on the street to shoot at, killing five. He blamed the rampage in part on Internet hate mongers, who fueled his psychosis. The judge, however, rejected this defense. Baumhammers received five death penalties and at least 112 years in prison for other charges (as reported Sep. 7, 2001 by the Associated Press).

Exercise

In response to the prevalence of hate sites on the Web, the Southern Poverty Law Center (SPLC) decided to fight back. Known for their assertive and often innovative approaches to fighting racism and injustice, the SPLC decided to try a counteroffensive involving advertising spots. Read the following excerpt and then share your response. Be sure to include whether you think this approach will make a difference in addressing the problem.

> Hate groups and white supremacists on the Internet may soon find some in-your-face ads urging tolerance and racial harmony appearing near their racist chat rooms and clubs. And the messages come from one of their chief antagonists: the Southern Poverty Law Center (SPLC). "We hope to take the Web back, and take it away from these haters," says Morris Dees, head of the center in Montgomery, Ala., that today is launching a website called *Tolerance.org*.
>
> But it is the ads, starting in about three weeks; that may represent the newest response to Internet hate. Yahoo, the Internet's No. 1 portal, has agreed to provide SPLC with $3 million worth of ad space over three years. The center hopes other Internet firms will match the effort. . . . In this case, someone using Yahoo to find Ku Klux Klan information or to visit neo-Nazi chat rooms might encounter ads for *Tolerance.org*. . . . Typical ads might say: "Bias doesn't just happen. What are you teaching your kids?" Or, perhaps, "The struggle for civil rights is history. Then why does discrimination occur every day?"
>
> University of Pennsylvania media professor Joseph Turow, who specializes in Internet advertising, says he had not heard of using this kind of targeted Internet advertising "as a way to respond to political controversy. But I think, in this case, it sounds like a terrific idea. It's a creative approach." (See Patrick McMahon, "Tolerance Ads to Infiltrate Websites of Hate Groups," *USA Today*, 2 Apr. 2001)

CASE STUDY

Poisoning the Web: The Internet as a Hate Tool

The Anti-Defamation League

Poisoning the Web: Hate Speech
The Web has become a powerful tool of extremist groups. They can reach a vastly wider audience with significantly less cost than has previously been the case. It used to be that they'd stand on the street handing out leaflets or they would spread their message at clandestine meetings in out-of-the-way places. Not any more.

Under the auspices of the First Amendment, groups have been able to use the Web to spread their message of hatred and violence. They usually target blacks, Jews, gays and lesbians, abortion providers, and others whose lives are deemed of little value. Groups like the Southern Poverty Law Center, the Anti-Defamation League, and many other civil rights groups and peace-oriented organizations have raised concerns about the harm being done thanks to the proliferating hate websites.

Whereas some think we need to draw limits around what is allowable; others think Web censorship will end up hurting everyone by restricting free speech and the sharing of ideas.

Directions: *Read the article below from the Anti-Defamation League and then write a three to four paragraph response, nothing the issues and concerns raised in the article and whether or not you were persuaded by the reasoning here.*

For years, hate groups have created written materials of every kind to spread their propaganda, including books, glossy magazines, newspapers, flyers and even graffiti. As communication technologies advanced, these groups have kept up. First, they used standard broadcast-band and short wave radio, audiotape, videotape and public-access cable TV. More recently, bigots of all kinds recognized the Internet's power and rushed to use it to rally their supporters, preach to the unconverted, and intimidate those whom they perceive as their enemies.

Even before *Stormfront* appeared on the Web, extremists had begun exploiting other ways to use the Internet, and these practices continue today. Lively conversations take place on numerous extremist Internet Relay Chat channels, such as #Nazi and #Klan. The USENET, a collection of thousands of public discussion groups (or newsgroups) on which people write, read and respond to messages, attracts hundreds of thousands of participants each day, both active (those who write) and passive (those who simply read or "lurk"). Newsgroups have been compared to community bulletin boards. Haters of all sorts debate, rant, and insult their opponents on newsgroups with titles such as *alt.politics.white-power* and *alt.revisionism.*

Electronic mailing lists (or "listservs") flourish as well. Such lists are like private "bulletin boards" available only to subscribers. While some lists keep their subscription information confidential, most are easy to join. Postings to some of these lists are moderated (i.e., monitored by the list operator who applies certain standards of acceptability), but others are entirely unregulated.

In fashioning their lists, extremists and racists create an "electronic community" of like-minded people. Before the Internet, many extremists worked in relative isolation, forced to make a great effort to connect with others who shared their ideology. Today, on the Internet, bigots communicate easily, inexpensively, and sometimes anonymously with encrypted E-mail, extremists have found a secure forum in which to exchange ideas and plans. Hundreds of fellow extremists. Online, extremists reinforce more easily each other's hateful convictions.

Extremists also use E-mail, which allows them to communicate with one another directly, their missives ostensibly hidden from public view. In fact, E-mail is not truly private: computer-savvy individuals can intercept and read private messages. Some users, nervous about eavesdroppers, now use cryptographic programs. Cryptography converts written material using a secret code, rendering it unreadable by anyone who does not have the means to decode it. With encrypted E-mail, extremists have found a secure forum in which to exchange ideas and plans.

E-mail can also be used to spread hate propaganda. With a mailing list and a message, hate mailings can easily reach the mailboxes of large numbers of people. Enterprising haters have managed to mass-mail hate materials to tens, hundreds, or even thousands of unsuspecting people without revealing their identity.

Though purveyors of hate make use of all the communication tools the Internet provides, the World Wide Web is their forum of choice. In addition to its multimedia capabilities and popularity with Internet users, the Web allows bigots to control their message. Organized haters complain about civil rights activists who critique their manifestoes in USENET newsgroups and other interactive forums. In contrast, haters can refuse to publish critical messages on their websites, just as a TV station can refuse to broadcast another station's opinions over its airwaves.

Furthermore, it is impossible for someone surfing the Web to know if any particular organization, other than one with a national reputation, is credible. Both the reputable and the disreputable are on the Web, and many Web users lack the experience and knowledge to distinguish between them. Increasingly, Web development tools have made it simple for bigots to create sites that visually resemble those of reputable organizations. Consequently, hate groups using the Web can more easily portray themselves as legitimate voices of authority.

Source: *www.adl.org*. Reprinted with the permission of the Anti-Defamation League.

CHAPTER TWELVE

Specialized Tools:
Problem Solving, Question
Techniques, and Writing Skills

One morning, upon awakening from agitated dreams, Gregor Samsa found himself, in his bed, transformed into a monstrous vermin. He lay on his hard, armorlike back, and when lifting his head slightly, he could view his brown, vaulted belly partitioned by arching ridges, while on top of it, the blankets, about to slide off altogether, could barely hold. His many legs, wretchedly thin compared with his overall girth, danced helplessly before his eyes. "What's happened to me?" he wondered. It was no dream.

—Franz Kafka, *The Metamorphosis*

Remember that movie classic, *Terminator*? The Terminator is a cyborg that comes back in time to kill a woman, Sarah Connor, so she won't give birth to the future Savior. Reese, the human who travels back to help stop the Terminator, tells Sarah: "It can't be bargained with! It can't be reasoned with! It doesn't feel pity, or remorse, or fear. And it absolutely will not stop, ever, until you are dead!" She is, justifiably, terrified. We follow her attempts to evade the Terminator and stay alive. There is a nail-biting scene in a motel where Reese leaves Sarah by herself while he goes to get material to make a pipe bomb. Sarah calls her mother to let her know she's okay.

Unbeknownst to Sarah, she's telling the motel's location to the Terminator. Not only is it a killing machine, it can perfectly mimic voices. Sarah made a serious unwarranted assumption in presuming that voice was her mother's; as a result she needs to brush up on her problem-solving skills. If she wanted to contact her mother and reassure her, what would be the best way to do this without setting herself up for more trouble from that murderous cyborg? That's an issue for us to think about.

As you know from *T2: Judgment Day,* her son, John, also had a phone call with the cyborg on the other end of the line. When he phoned home to talk to his stepparents, the now-protective Terminator was there to try to stop the newer, more advanced T1000 model cyborg. The Terminator advises him to ask a trick question and, thus, discern if he is really talking to his stepmother or if the T1000 is faking her voice. Cleverly, John asks about his dog "Wolfy" (not the dog's real name). The T1000 may be highly advanced, but it's not that advanced. And, thus, the truth came out. Nothing like a well-placed question to crack the case!

That's what we will be looking at in this chapter; namely problem solving, question techniques, and then writing skills. Here's why these are valuable: If you can't solve the problem of how to change a flat tire, you could be sitting by the roadside for an awfully long time. If you can't find the right question to ask your doctor when he tells you that you've torn a ligament from trying to change the tire yourself, then you may not know your prognosis. And if you can't write a letter to the tire manufacturer about your brand-new tire having a blowout for no apparent reason, you may not be able to get redress as soon as you'd like. Let's start with problem solving.

Problem Solving

We are not always in a position to jump right in and start something. Often we must consider alternatives, select an option, and draw up a plan of action first. However, we are often unsure that we've considered all the alternatives, picked the best option, or have a workable plan. And unfortunately, being good at reasoning will not prevent us from making mistakes. But taking care in assessing problems and selecting options can help prevent disaster.

Problems can range from small to big, from what to do if we hear squeaking noises in our living room walls to what to do if a loved one betrays our trust. Problems range from pressing to distant. For example, you have only a few seconds to decide what to do if there is a wasp in the car, you are driving 65 miles per hour on the freeway, you are in the fast lane, and there is a child in the back seat deathly allergic to wasps. What should you do? On the other hand, some problems are not time-urgent. For example, you may have years to plan your retirement. Most problems have more than one solution. Most solutions have varying degrees of satisfaction. Some problems are true dilemmas, where we have two distinctly different options. And some problems are catch-22 situations, where each option is problematic and, so, the choices must be carefully examined.

Consider this historical example of problem solving: In the mid-19th century, people in London were dying by the hundreds from cholera, then a mysterious disease whose origins were unknown. John Snow, a British physician, stopped the spread of the disease. He figured out that the source was the water supply. In one simple action—removing the handle from the Broad Street water pump so residents could not obtain the tainted water—he contained the deadly epidemic (as noted by Marlene Cimons, "Lessons Taught in the Origin of AIDS," *Los Angeles Times,* 23 Dec. 1999). It should be noted that, not only did Snow solve the problem scientifically, but he took swift action as well. In many cases, problem solving has both intellectual and practical levels. As a result we need to be able to work with ideas and concepts, and take action when it's called for!

Critical thinking entails many levels of thinking and many approaches. Some might be considered higher order, others lower order. But all orders have their place. Part of our goal as learners is to use the right tool for the right task and to explore new paths that allow us to expand our repertoire and our skills at thinking and reflecting.

Not All Decisions Are Good

Remember the failed laundry detergents (see Chapter 2) that were duds for a variety of reasons? Well, it is a fact of life that not all problem solving is going to be successful. Some are well-intended bad decisions—as when we sincerely try to arrive at a good solution to a problem, we think we have it, and it's one big disaster.

Some decisions can't be taken back at a later date. We see this with the development of the nuclear bomb, cloning, the invention of the wheel, and having wisdom teeth yanked out. Some decisions can be rethought and changed or modified. We see this with ongoing modifications on computers and other electronic products, methods for storing data, strip mining, the building of dams, the use of cobalt radiation, medical experimentation on children, the use of the electric chair for executions, silicone breast implants. Some decisions can be rethought entirely so the original (deficient) solution can be ameliorated or erased. We see this with ineffective or unjust laws that are repealed, court rulings that are reversed on appeal, divorced couples who remarry, students who change their majors and then change them back again.

When we are in the middle of problem solving, we have to think of both short-term goals and long-term consequences. We also have to think about what we are bringing into the decision making that we don't want to compromise—such as a set of values, a sense of our own integrity, policies that need to be followed, processes that we want to keep in place, and so forth.

Exercises

1. Is it wise of parents who try to infect their children with chicken pox by exposing them to others? Read the following and then share your thoughts on their decision:

   Connie Shoemaker doesn't try to give goody-bags to the kids who attend parties at her house. She tries to give them chickenpox. Shoemaker and other parents skeptical of the relatively new vaccine for the disease are throwing "chickenpox parties," inviting healthy children to mingle with infected ones so the youngsters will catch chickenpox and gain lifetime immunity. "It's a natural way to deal with the problem instead of introducing more chemicals into kids," Shoemaker said. . . . Last month, Shoemaker sent her three children to the house of a friend whose child was infected with chickenpox, hoping they would catch the highly contagious virus. They did, and since then, Shoemaker, who lives in Butler about 30 miles north of Pittsburgh, has thrown three of her own chickenpox parties.

Two weeks ago, Tammy Swanberg, 38, took two of her children, ages 3 and 5, to one of Shoemaker's chickenpox parties. As of Wednesday, they had not developed any symptoms. "I think that vaccines can have their place, but sometimes I think our society just abuses them," Swanberg said. Some of those who choose intentional infection are leery of vaccines in general or cite religious reasons. . . . About half of all states now require the chickenpox vaccine for schoolchildren. (See "Leery of Vaccine, Some Parents Hold 'Chickenpox Parties' to Infect Kids," *www.foxnews.com*, 19 Oct. 2001)

2. Discuss the following case of governmental decision making at the FBI siege at Waco, Texas that resulted in the death of 80 people, including 21 children:

[I]ncendiary devices were used by government agents at Waco. "This is not an assault," said the voice of a government official at the scene as an M-60 tank tore off the wall of the Branch Davidians' home and shot tear gas in their faces. To protect the 25 children inside from child abuse, U.S. federal agents harassed the Davidians and their children at night with massive floodlights, blaring recordings of screaming, slaughtered rabbits, and loudspeakers blaring Nancy Sinatra singing *These Boots Are Made for Walking*. Though allegations of child abuse were never proven, and the Davidians had fewer guns per capita than the average Texan, Janet Reno authorized the agents to saturate the house with CS gas, a gas that is banned by international law as chemical warfare and which medical literature warns may cause children inhaling it—"fulminating chemical pneumonia and death." Before ordering the attack, Reno was informed that gas masks wouldn't fit the children. (See Sarah McCarthy, *World Net Daily*, 31 Aug. 1999)

3. Discuss the following case of decision making on the part of the Pentagon to send planes over Bosnia in 1997 to jam broadcasts and put in their own political programs to be broadcasted in that country:

The United States announced Thursday that it has dispatched to Bosnia electronic warplanes (three Air Force EC-130 planes) that can jam the vitriolic, anti-West radio and television broadcasts of hard-line Serbs and replace them with alternative programming. The planes were sent to Bosnia, the spokesman said, because followers of indicted war crimes suspect Radovan Karadzic had reneged on promises to eliminate violence-inciting broadcasts and air opposition voices. . . .

Dispatch of the aircraft follows weeks of debate among international officials on how far to go in cracking down on the Bosnian Serb Radio and Television network, SRT. . . . Some international officials were wary of exerting censorship that interferes with freedom of speech. But repeated distortions by SRT, the officials said, were trying international patience and justifying extraordinary action. . . . The elite EC-130 aircraft, which were used in similar psychological operations in Haiti and Somalia, were ready to transmit "a fair and balanced report of news and information" to Bosnia, the Pentagon spokesman said. (See Tracy Wilkinson and Stanley Meiser, "Planes for Jamming Broadcasts Head for Bosnia; Balkans: U.S. Dispatches Aircraft Aimed at Blocking Vitriolic Programming of Hard-Line Serbs," *Los Angeles Times*, 12 Sep. 1997)

Problem-Solving Model

Often problem-solving can be divided into discrete steps. Psychology professor Robert Sternberg has developed a useful model. It involves discrete steps and works best on problems that can be fairly clearly delineated. The model can help us get a better handle on the question. With an overview of the territory, we can then develop a macroplan or policy. In this way we can address the issues that are interrelated.

Realize that some problems fall into neat categories and we can package them up quite tidily using a linear model. Some problems, however, resist the divide-and-conquer mentality, such as moral dilemmas and family disputes. Generally these are messy and defy tidy categorization. However, subjecting even a messy moral dilemma to the problem-solving model may be useful, because you may get ideas about the nature of the difficulty or ways solutions might be found. We might find, for example, that the problem resists an all-or-nothing sort of solution; that mediation or negotiation toward a compromise is the way to go.

Problem-Solving Model: A Seven-Step Solution System

Step 1: Define the Problem
↓
Step 2: Set Criteria & Standards
↓
Step 3: Gather Evidence
↓
Step 4: Sort and Weigh Evidence
↓
Step 5: Aerial Surveillance—Form a Picture & Set out aHypothesis
↓
Step 6: Critical Examination—Compare Old and New Data
↓
Step 7: Draw an Inference

Stages of the Problem Solving Model

Stage 1.   Define the problem.   In the first stage, we want to define the problem or articulate goals. It usually helps to clarify relevant contexts or frameworks, as most problems are context-dependent or at least better grasped if the context is made clear.

Stage 2.   Set out the criteria framing the decision making.   This will include such things as the terms of a contract, acceptable evidence, standards of evaluation, expert qualifications, and standards for weighing evidence and for arriving at a final decision. Philosopher Sandra Harding sees two aspects of this stage:

1. *Clarify Context of Discovery:* Determine the framework within which the problem is named and how evidence will be sought and weighed.

2. *Clarify Context of Justification:* Determine the framework within which the proof or argument and its evidence will be assessed or justified.

Our goal in this stage is see what criteria we'll use to guide the way toward a solution. If we don't know where we are going, it is hard to get off the ground. If we don't know what tools we plan to use along the journey, we could be spinning our wheels in the sand. Do not underestimate the importance of the first two stages.

Stage 3.   Gather evidence.   Conduct research, compile data, and generate ideas. To generate ideas we could brainstorm, research similar cases, examine precedents, conduct interviews, and explore different sources and perspectives. Include diverse perspectives to provide a more well-rounded view and allow a wider range of evidence.

We shouldn't be limited by assumptions and habitual ways of doing things. Keep a receptive mind and be observant. Do not be discriminatory at this stage. Amass all the relevant information, no matter how trivial or seemingly minor. Make no assumptions at this stage: We cannot assess until we have done the groundwork.

Stage 4.   Sorting and Weighing.   Keep only that which fits the criteria. Put aside, but don't toss out, the information that does not fit. To do this, determine which criteria are relevant and which are irrelevant or less useful to our task. Look for direct as well as indirect links.

There are three aspects of this stage

1. *Clarify What Is Relevant in Light of the Set of Criteria.* The set of criteria may already be fixed (e.g., admissibility in a court of law) or open to interpretation (e.g., questions of personal taste). Clarify exactly what it is you are doing, what counts as valuable evidence, and what factors should influence the selection process.
2. *Sift Relevant from Irrelevant Information.* Depending upon our criteria, we can sort evidence into the categories: relevant, irrelevant, and "not sure." Hold onto what's relevant, put aside the irrelevant, and shelve the "not sure" as potentially worthwhile. Once it is clear what counts as relevant, sifting evidence is not usually difficult. If you run into problems, review the set of criteria.
3. *Weigh Strengths and Weaknesses.* Once we've determined the criteria and found the relevant evidence, we can prioritize it in terms of its supportive value. It helps to review the model for weighing evidence (see Chapter 5 on analysis) and determine which information is most directly tied to the specific topic and how key pieces of evidence work together.

If we reach a dead end with a potential lead, we can return to the "questionable" list and investigate it. What initially appears to be a great lead may end up a dud. We are then back at the drawing table, looking at information we thought unimportant the first time we examined it.

Stage 5.   Aerial Surveillance.   Get an overview by piecing together the data and evidence gathered. To do this, it may help to look at the structure; language; social framework; assumptions; omissions (if any); and patterns and themes. We want to arrive at a general idea sufficient to draw well-supported inferences. *Ask:* Can we see the big picture? Is there a working hypothesis we can formulate?

YES, big picture is clear

- Check context and assumptions.
- Look for a path to the solution or resolution.
- Form a hypothesis.

NO, big picture is unclear

- Examine what we have and determine what we need.
- Is there any missing evidence or overlooked information? If so, look for more pieces of evidence. Don't assume the "obvious" is obvious. Turn over stones!
- Could this be a false lead or dead end? If so, look for more pieces of evidence. Try at least one different approach. Rethink assumptions. Be imaginative and open to new avenues of exploration.
- Still stuck? Try a new approach or try a different perspective on the problem. Put yourself in several distinctly different frames of reference.
- Reconsider how you defined the problem back in stage 1. Try a new formulation.

Stage 6.   Comparison of New and Old Data.   Try any or all of the following:

1. *Go back to the ground floor.* Look over evidence and try another frame of reference, a different way of looking at the problem. It often helps to look at the same information from more than one perspective.
2. *Rearrange the evidence.* Rethink our weighing process and make sure we did not either undervalue something that was relevant or overvalue something that's irrelevant or minor.
3. *Try to find an analogy or precedent.* The use of an analogy often clarifies both the case at hand and the possible solutions.
4. *Rethink assumptions.* Are some of the assumptions weighing us down? Do the assumptions force us into a mentality that blocks a workable solution? Do our assumptions reflect an outmoded way of viewing the world? Is there an unconscious bias that impedes our problem-solving skills?

Stage 7.   Draw a Conclusion.   At this stage we are ready to pull it all together. Be careful not to make any unwarranted assumptions or ignore what's right before our eyes. Be on the alert. We do not want to be tripped up, much less by the obvious!

Applying the Model

The usefulness of the model becomes clearer once we see it in motion. Let's examine several examples using the problem-solving model, starting with the caning case.

Case in Point: Taking a Stand on Caning as a Method of Punishment.   The professor asks, "Should the United States follow Singapore's example and institute caning (paddling someone's bare behind with a dampened wooden cane, known to tear off skin and occasionally cause the person being caned to go into shock) in order to address such crimes as painting graffiti, defacing public buildings, and going on 'joy-rides' in stolen vehicles?" You need to take a stand and make your case. See if the problem-solving model can help. Let's go:

Stage 1: Define the Problem.   Decide where you stand. Let's say you want to argue *in favor* of caning, that you are sick of what has been going on and think it's time to paddle some fannies. So you opt for a "pro" argument on caning for minor criminals.

Stage 2: Set Criteria and Standards.   So how will you be able to convince someone that caning is defensible? Well, you may need to show that it is fair—that it is a just form of punishment in light of the crime. How else will you need to convince your audience? That's what you need to figure out for the criteria to be clear.

Ask yourself: "What standards must be met to be able to convince someone to my point of view? What do I want to be sure to cover in making my case?" In this case, you'll probably want to include these: fairness, appropriate punishment for the nature of the crime, value of public shaming techniques, teaches the "criminal" a lesson, possible deterrent effect on others.

Stage 3: Gather Evidence.   This will involve research. Investigate how caning is used in Singapore or internationally. Find out its effectiveness in addressing minor crimes. Obtain information to assess this method of punishment, its effectiveness, and why it is better than the alternatives. Because caning may cause discomfort, but not usually any lasting physical harm, you may be inclined to favor caning.

Stage 4: Sort and Weigh.   Now we have to deal with all that information. This involves sorting, weighing, and clarification. Determine what counts as "success" and what counts as "failure" when it comes to punishment.

If we used the death penalty, we could eliminate the criminal altogether. However, if the method of punishment should somehow "fit the crime," we need to decide on an appropriate punishment for painting graffiti. Only then can we assess the different solutions that have been proposed. See what worked, what didn't, and how strong a case you can make.

Stage 5: Look at the Big Picture and Form a Hypothesis.   Here you need to look at assumptions and values. Is it correct to assume that all crimes should be punished? Is the age of the offender relevant? If so, should children who paint graffiti be caned? What is the cutoff in terms of age—15, 14, 10 perhaps? Was the caning wrong if the offender turns out to be a "hardened criminal" who paints graffiti at every chance he gets? Are you assuming that caning deters future crimes? What if it doesn't? Are all those convicted of a crime, in fact, guilty? Can we assume that what is attractive in theory will work in practice?

Your argument depends on how strong a case you can make. Historical data may be necessary to prove that punishment is an effective deterrent. You'll need to show that any assumptions made are warranted. Once you see what values underlie your argument, you are in a position to articulate and defend those values—or rethink them if the values seem indefensible.

Make sure you have good evidence, such as statistical data supporting corporal punishment's effectiveness for minor transgressions or the deterrence value of caning. Good quotes by credible sources (experts) usually strengthen an argument. Examples do not prove your case, but may illustrate a key point and, therefore, could be valuable.

Stage 6: Comparison of New and Old Data.   You have collected the evidence you intend to use. Now examine it from a different perspective; this will help you detect any holes, weaknesses or omissions.

For instance, what if *you* were accused of painting graffiti and you were innocent? It's your word against the officer's, and the members of jury look at you and shake their heads. What then? And what if you really did do it, you guilty scoundrel? Do you deserve to be put into shock getting skin whacked off your rear end? On the other hand, what about the blight of graffiti in inner cities and the frustration of business and home owners who are tired of having their property defaced. It helps to look at punishment from the perspective of the offender and then compare it to the perspective of the victim or the community most affected by the act. The range of perspectives gives us a more nuanced sense of the issues and concerns.

Reexamine the set of criteria and values you brought to bear on the case. On what grounds would an opponent attack your argument? Have you answered any potential criticism as strongly as you could? Did you overlook anything vital? Could you use an analogy to strengthen your argument? Does your argument show any bias (e.g., are you targeting a particular group)?

Stage 7: Draw Your Conclusion.   Now that you have your argument in favor of caning set out, look it over. Is it as strong as you could make it? List the strengths of your argument. If possible, diminish any weaknesses you spot. Read it out loud to see if it "rings true" or is as powerful as it seems to be when eyeballing it. Patch any holes and that's it!

Exercises

Directions: Select *one* of the problem cases below. Run through the problem-solving model on the following, setting out the stages.

1. Should we allow genetic hybrids? This is when the DNA from one species is mixed with another in order to produce a hybrid species with enhanced traits. Take a stand on this case:

About 150 goats that have been bred with a spider gene are to be housed on 60 acres of a former Air Force base in Plattsburgh, N.Y. Montreal-based Nexia Bio-technologies, Inc. said up to 1500 genetically-altered goats may eventually live at the facility. The goats have been bred with a spider gene so their milk provides a unique protein. The company plans to extract the protein from the milk to pro-duce fibers called "BioSteel" for bulletproof vests, aerospace and medical supplies. Spider silk has a unique combination of strength and elasticity with an ultra-light-weight fiber. The agreement included an up front payment for the university, fund-ing for research and development expenses plus royalties on the sale of silk-based products. (See "Biotech Company to Produce 'BioSteel' Milk," Associated Press, 18 June 2000)

2. Read about the following case and then answer the questions below:

Abbott laboratories developed a narcotic lollipop intended to calm down children before surgery. A group of doctors asked the federal government to bar the nar-cotic lollipop. They argue that the narcotic, *fentanyl,* is too dangerous for children and that the lollipop could create new problems for doctors. Some doctors suggest that a tranquilizer would be preferable, since it doesn't have the same risks as the narcotic. The FDA asked Abbott to set up a training program to insure anyone us-ing the lollipop will be familiar with its dangers and its proper use. They said that doctors now make up their own, unregulated, sedatives to calm children and the FDA prefers one that can be given in controlled doses and under federal control. (See Mike Goodkind, "Help Your Child Relax to Reduce Pain and Recover More Easily after Surgery, Says Anesthesiologist," *med.stanford.edu/center/communica-tions,* March 1999)

Answer the following:
a. Should the FDA ban the narcotic lollipop? Go through the steps of the problem-solving model to decide how this issue could be solved.
b. What further information is needed to make a decision?
c. If you had to vote on this issue, would you allow the narcotic lollipop to be distributed? Explain how you reached your answer.

3. The use of animals for organ transplants (called "xenotransplants") in hu-mans is already a reality, with pigs being thought the most likely source for compatible organs. And why not? You decide. Read the following and take a stand, using the problem-solving model:

Today, despite fears that pig-to-human transplants could unleash a deadly new virus, the dream is closer than ever to reality. In August, a long-awaited safety study conducted by Nextran's chief competitor, Imutran Ltd., of Cambridge, En-gland, found no evidence of active infection in 160 people who had been treated with pig tissue for a variety of conditions. The findings come as the companies are laying the groundwork to begin testing transplanted organs in people. Sometime within the next few years, and possibly as soon as the end of next year, either the British or the Americans will grab the brass ring: approval from a regulatory agency, either the United States Food and Drug Administration or its equivalent in Britain, to perform the world's first animal-to-human transplant using a heart or a kidney from a genetically engineered pig.

Nobody expects cross-species transplants to be successful overnight. But with time, xenotransplantation could solve the most pressing crisis in medicine—the organ shortage. It could also make the companies very rich. Unlike human organs, which are donated, pig organs will be sold, and in a climate in which demand far outstrips supply, the seller will name the price. By greatly expanding the donor pool, pigs could make transplants possible for tens of thousands of people who, because of the current rationing system, never even make the list, not to mention those in some Asian nations, where taking organs from the dead is culturally taboo. Imagine a therapy as revolutionary as penicillin and as lucrative as Viagra rolled into one. (See Sheryl Gay Stolberg, "Could This Pig Save Your Life?," *The New York Times,* 3 Oct. 1999)

4. Here's the scenario: You just got a call from a lawyer (the "I" in the excerpt below). A doctor (call him Dr. Sims) who is having second thoughts called him for advice. Given this is the call, what will you recommend in terms of a policy for these sorts of cases? You may choose to answer *one* of his questions. Go through the steps to clarify how to prepare yourself:

Four years ago, I got a call from an infertility specialist who was in the midst of a procedure. He was just about to transfer an embryo created by a childless couple's egg and sperm to the woman who had volunteered to carry the baby for them. But he suddenly had second thoughts. "I've got an embryo from a couple in a catheter," he told me hurriedly. I pictured him, catheter in one hand, telephone receiver in the other. "I'm about to implant it in the surrogate, who is the husband's sister," he explained, and wanted to know if it would violate his state's ban on incest. If he decided not to go through with the implantation and the embryo died, he asked, could he be found guilty of murder? (See Lori B. Andrews, "Embryonic Confusion," *The Washington Post,* 2 May 1999)

Process of Elimination

In the process of problem solving, we may have to use a process of elimination. Sometimes this is obvious and straightforward, for example, when we can easily assess what might or might not warrant closer examination. Sometimes it's a hit-and-miss proposition, entailing repeated attempts to narrow down the body of evidence or relevant factors in order to arrive at a solution.

In a process of elimination (e.g., of possible causes of an event or probable suspects in a crime) we use our deductive, and sometimes inductive, reasoning skills. Let's look at a case in which researchers attempted to use a process of elimination to solve a medical mystery. Though a number of radically different hypotheses were offered, the mystery remains unsolved. Read about the case and see what direction you think the investigation should have taken.

CASE STUDY

The Gloria Ramirez "Mystery Fumes" Case

The case centers on a 31-year-old woman, Gloria Ramirez, brought into a Riverside, California, hospital emergency room on February 19, 1994. ER nurses and doctors noticed a strong smell similar to ammonia after her blood was drawn into a presterilized syringe. A number of medical professionals complained of the fumes. Besides the patient, 23 of the 37 ER staffers reacted to the fumes. A nurse, who said Mrs. Ramirez's skin had an "oily sheen " smelled the blood-filled syringe, complained of an ammonia-like odor and fainted. After Dr. Julie Gorchynski picked up the syringe and sniffed it, she collapsed. Both have had lung problems since then and the bones in the doctor's knees are dying from lack of blood circulation. Gloria Ramirez died. The hazardous materials (hazmat) team arrived within two hours to investigate. A test of the ER for poisons was inconclusive. As reported,

An autopsy was also inconclusive. Led by Riverside coroner Scotty Hill, a team of pathologists conducted the examination inside airtight contamination suits. They collected blood and tissue samples, as well as air that had been sealed in Ramirez's body bag. . . . The official cause of Ramirez's death: cardiac dysrythmia as a result of kidney failure, which had been brought on by her cervical cancer. Hill had identified no identifiable toxic substance that might have played a role in her death or in the illnesses of those present in the Riverside General ER. (As noted by ParaScope at *www.parascope.com*)

The story received considerable media attention. (See, for example, The [Cleveland] *Plain Dealer*, 22 Feb. 1994 and 24 Feb. 1994; *Los Angeles Times*, 23–26 Feb. 1994; *Chicago Tribune*, 23 Feb. 1994.) William Hamilton of *The Washington Post* reported on the extent to which the case baffled experts:

Anita Rockewell, a Loma Linda spokeswoman, said Gorchinski's blood tests indicated evidence of poisoning by a class of chemicals called organophosphates, which are used in pesticides and poison gas. However, Peter H. Kurtz, senior medical coordinator for the California Department of Food and Agriculture, and an expert on the chemical group, discounted organophosphates as a cause. "Personally I think it's premature to start guessing," he said, adding: "I know of no organophosphate chemical in use today that would cause the kinds of things reported in that hospital." Malathion, a pesticide commonly used against the Mediterranean fruit fly that has been a scourge of California agriculture, is a member of the chemical group. But Kurtz said tremendous concentrations of it would have to be present to have caused Gorchinski's symptoms. "The whole thing is bizarre," he said. (See William Hamilton, "Patient's Toxic Fumes Baffle Experts; Investigators Hope Autopsy Will Explain What Killed Woman, Felled Medical Team," *The Washington Post*, 23 Feb. 1994)

Several hypotheses were offered: one that Ramirez must have taken DMSO, an herbal remedy and a chemical reaction from DMSO killed her (the family denies she ever took DMSO). Another hypothesis was that the mostly female ER staff suffered from "mass hysteria," though later this speculation was rescinded. The attorney for the ER physician who was in intensive care for two weeks following her exposure to the fumes, Dr. Gorchynski, disputes the DMSO theory. He suggests that the hospital negligently failed to clean excess residue from toxic chemicals used in the hospital.

Another theory was that there was an illicit methamphetamine (meth) lab at the hospital and that Mrs. Ramirez had inadvertently been given a meth precursor in the IV she received shortly after arriving. "Those smells and symptoms are classic to meth-fume exposure," says Tom Net-wal, a forensic chemist who analyzes drug lab materials for the Colorado Bureau of Investigation. "All that would be consistent with a drug laboratory." That theory is still advocated in some circles, particularly given the missing evidence and the hush-hush way the case was handled by authorities. Charles Cox, the Cal-OSHA (Occupational Safety and Health Administration) district manager, is quoted as saying,

I believe there was an intermediate product, not full meth, that was being manufactured in the hospital and then transported out to be completed elsewhere," Cox says. "I think very quickly into the investigation county officials figured out there were some hospital workers running their own business on the side. I don't think anyone in the hospital knew about it at the time other than those involved. But as a result of this incident, they found out what was going on and decided to cover everything up. It is the only plausible scenario to explain what happened. (See "Anatomy of a Fuming Woman," *New Times,* 15 May 1997)

Said to be one of the most elaborate autopsies in history, Mrs. Ramirez's autopsy was conducted with the utmost of precautions:

Inside the ivy-covered Riverside County Coroner's Office, a special chamber was constructed so the four men dealing with the body would be sealed off from the rest of the world. They would wear Level A protective suits—space suit like gear normally used by specialists cleaning up toxic spills. Oxygen would be pumped to the autopsy workers through umbilical cords. In the event the main oxygen supply failed, they had emergency air canisters tucked inside their suits. Outside the chamber, four members of Riverside County's hazardous-materials team watched the autopsy via video monitor. They too wore protective suits and were assigned to rescue those inside if problems arose. Three fire trucks were nearby, their crews ready to leap into action. (See "Anatomy of the Fuming Woman," *New Times,* 15 May 1997)

The case has never been solved. But the doubts linger about how it was handled and what could explain the actions of Cal-OSHA and hospital personnel with respect to the case.

Ramirez's brother-in-law, David Garcia, said at the time. "I think the county has already found out how she died and wanted to make sure we did not find out" (*New Times,* 15 May 1997). At the family's request, the body was eventually returned to them for burial, although Mrs. Ramirez's heart was missing and never found. The case has been closed—unsolved—leaving many unanswered questions behind.

Solving Cases with Seemingly Minor Evidence

It is fascinating to think that crimes have been solved with only minor pieces of evidence. By a process of elimination all reasonable alternatives are removed, leaving only one as the solution. It requires careful attention to details, though, as you will see.

The solution may lie in as small a detail as a staple. In a case noted in the *Association of Firearms and Toolmark Examiners Journal* (*AFTE*), a woman had been receiving threatening letters. There were no fingerprints or handwriting in the letters, only words from printed material that was then cut and pasted onto a plain piece of typing paper. One letter had two pages, stapled together. The investigators focused on the staple to try to solve the crime.

The staple was removed and examined microscopically, which revealed that the staple had a particular marking where it bent. Twelve Swingline staple guns were obtained for testing and each left specific and unique marks on their staples from the amount of pressure used. Because there were several suspects, the police got search warrants and obtained the staplers of the suspects. Through a process of elimination, it was determined that one suspect's stapler made markings that microscopically matched the one found on the threatening letter. They were then able to pinpoint which stapler was used and, therefore, the case against the suspect was strengthened.

Deductive reasoning is essential for crime solving. We saw this in the case above and we can see it in the criminal investigation into the following murder. A bullet, for all practical purposes, travels in a straight line unless it is deflected by an intervening object. Powder and residues are emitted and follow the bullet and, if found, can be used to determine the distance from the muzzle of the gun to the target. Physical evidence reconstruction can be used to make or break a story.

Exercises

Directions: Read the following case and then answer the questions below:

A boy was shot and killed by his stepfather. The boy had stepped between the stepfather and mother, who had been arguing. The stepfather says the boy had a knife. The stepfather left the room and returned with a .22 revolver. The stepfather explains that he picked up the revolver because he was afraid what the boy might do to his mother. He claimed the boy came at him with the knife and, to stop him, he fired into the floor and then into the door. The boy kept coming. The stepfather shot into the boy's leg and, when he didn't stop, he shot into his arm and then his chest. He continued to fire, not knowing where he was striking the boy, who kept coming at him. (Adapted from a case noted by the *AFTE Journal,* Vol. 23, No. 1, Jan. 1991)

Answer the following:

1. Does the stepfather's story seem credible?

2. What alternative explanations might there be for the events preceding the boy's death?

3. What could disprove the stepfather's claim that the boy was coming at him with a knife and he fired at the boy to protect himself?

4. Here is the physical evidence at the crime scene: The bullet in the floor had threads on it from the boy's pajama bottoms. How does this affect the believability of the stepfather's story?

5. Here is more physical evidence: The boy's leg was lying so that the right thigh wound was directly over the bullet. What can you conclude from this new piece of evidence?

6. Investigators concluded that the bullet was fired after the boy was down and not moving anymore. The man claimed the boy was threatening him with the knife, but physical evidence showed that the knife had blood on it, while the boy's palms were clean. This suggested the boy did not have a bloody knife in his hand, but that it was placed there after he died. Do you think the physical evidence is sufficient to convict the stepfather? Make your case, given what we know.

Questioning Techniques

Questions are extremely important things to understand. A trick question can fool us into revealing things that may be hurtful or incriminating. An obscurely worded question can hide the real intent of the author/speaker and be used to manipulate people.

Our answers to questions, like those on essay exams and writing assignments, can make all the difference in what we get out of a class and the grade we receive. For example, perhaps the professor wanted a detailed discussion involving comparison and contrast, while you (fool!) thought the professor just wanted us to regurgitate information found in the encyclopedia.

Getting a Handle on Questions

Questions can range along the objective–subjective spectrum. For example, the question may be an "objective" fact-based question devoid of personal interpretation. In this case, our personal response would be so inappropriate as to seem like a comedy routine. For example, the instructor asks, "What is x, if $5x + 4 = 29$?" Your task is to solve the equation and very clearly mark your answer, $x = 5$. Opinions and feelings are not normally expected to be included in the answer, although we may be asked to outline the process of solving the equation.

Some professors even ask students to submit a list of possible quiz questions or questions for the final exam. When this happens, students have some input into shaping the course material and requirements. Knowing about questioning techniques can be very useful.

This all entails a fair amount of critical thinking skills. It may, thus, be helpful to understand the types of questions we may run across. This can be pictured as a spectrum or spiral, where we move from questions that are at a distance and ask us to be dispassionate, detached fact finders, to questions that ask us to draw from our values and beliefs in setting out our answers. In a nutshell, questions range along a spectrum that focuses on the factual or objective, at one end, to the most subjective or reflective, at the other.

Different Types of Questions

Recall: Draws on memory, useful for assimilating large amounts of data, generally considered a "low-level" thinking skill, tests our knowledge of what is the case, such as facts. For example: What rule describes the process . . . ? What is the definition of . . . ? What are the different kinds of . . . ?

Descriptive: Draws on observational skills, useful for clarification, calls upon a certain kind of precision and ability to separate description from inference. For example: What is the visual message in this illustration? Describe what you see happen when oil is mixed with milk. Describe the setting for a novel.

Dialogical: Is basically hypothetical, but requires us to bring together potentially divergent areas or thinkers and see connections—and do so in the form of a dialogue. For example: Write a dialogue between Martin Luther King, Jr., Gandhi, and *you*. What advice would you give Oedipus? You are stuck in an elevator with a staunch opponent to physician-assisted death. What would you say to each other?

Application: Here we apply a theory or concept to specific cases, related areas of discourse, or even other disciplines. For example: Distinguish autobiography from fiction and from journalism. Why didn't drafters of the Constitution mention the word "fetus"? What would Cesar Chavez think of Andrew Carnegie? How would a Freudian interpret *Sleeping Beauty*?

Conceptual: Draws upon knowledge of key terms and concepts and asks us to think on a more abstract level. For example: What are the key aspects of honesty? Does a belief in free will allow for an insanity defense? What are all the different ways we understand the word "love"?

Theoretical: These are as abstract as conceptual questions. They are geared to help us think about the way things—or systems—work by looking at how they are arranged and what sorts of boundaries exist. For example: Why are irrational numbers studied separately from rational numbers? How do you test the theory of evolution? Prove cats cannot fly.

Analogical: Comparing and contrasting two distinct things helps clarify characteristics of both. For example: How do political theories differ from scientific theories? Compare and contrast Shakespeare and Milton.

Hypothetical: Draws on inferential skills and ability to imagine consequences or potential states of affairs, and synthesize a body of material. For example: If you assumed the laws of gravity did not hold, what major problems would we face? What will computers be like in the 21st century? What would be different if Native Americans or African Americans wrote the U.S. Constitution?

Persuasive: Draws upon skills of assessment, ability to weigh evidence, and techniques of persuasion, using sound reasoning. For example: Defend or attack the censorship of high school newspapers. Give your strongest argument against mandatory AIDS testing. What is the best case to be made for the elimination of the grading system?

Evaluative: These, like value questions, rely upon a context of attitudes, norms, values, beliefs, but do not necessarily draw upon any specific set of normative values or religious beliefs. In an evaluation, an assessment is made on the basis of a set of criteria. For example: Assess the choices facing King Lear. Do you think the rap singer Eminem is obscene? What criteria did you use? Could a good forgery be considered a work of art?

Value Questions: These may involve a persuasive element, but draw upon knowledge of a larger value framework, such as a religious or an ethical belief system. These may involve moral judgments. For example: What is the best argument for banning handguns? Do you believe we should always "turn the other cheek" when responding to acts of violence? Set out a policy on concealed weapons.

Meta-Cognition or *Watching Your Own Thinking Process:* This draws upon observation skills, reflective skills, and the ability to abstract what we do in order to see how we do it. For example: How did you solve that math problem? What is the best process for talking someone out of using drugs? By what means did you assess the testimony of these speakers?

Personal-Reflective: Here we are into the core of the subjective response, which draws upon the stand we take and reflects on why we believe one thing as opposed to another. For example: What piece of music most reflects your life experience? What are your deepest fears? Write a myth about heroism.

Getting a Handle on Expectations

Some answers to questions require a subjective or personal response, such as interpreting a novel or a work of art. In those cases, the answers are not clear-cut, unlike mathematical problem solutions. Furthermore, some questions require us to state a moral or social position; for instance, How do you make a case for or against minors being required to get parental consent for an abortion? If the question asked *only* for your own position, you could focus on the side you picked, so long as you gave a credible argument.

On the other hand, more is required if we were asked: "Give your position on minors being required to get parental consent for an abortion. Now *support* your argument, drawing from at least two of the authors we have studied in this class. Finally, *criticize* your argument, drawing from at least two of the authors we have studied in this class." In this case, we are asked to (1) think about the issue, (2) articulate a position, (3) defend our position, (4) support our argument using specific authors, (5) show that we know the other side by using other authors, and (6) show that we can reply to an opponent.

Exercises

1. Here's a case reported by Bob Herbert in *The New York Times*. On May 16, 1994, the prime minister of India, P. V. Narasimha Rao, and his entourage checked into the Four Seasons Hotel in Boston. Thirty-six rooms were booked for Mr. Rao and his 50-plus attendants. There were U.S. Secret Service Agents assigned to protect Mr. Rao, who was scheduled to speak at Harvard University on May 17th. There was only one glitch: The prime minister's office requested that only white people wait on him, carry his bags, clean his room, and serve his food. The Four Seasons agreed to this request, though, once it became public, made extensive apologies and called their decision "very, very stupid and unforgivable and painful."

a. Drawing from the questioning techniques, ask five distinctly different questions about this case. Be sure to label your types of questions.

b. Aside from any question used in a, above, create questions that would fit each of the following categories: recall, application, conceptual, analogical, persuasive, value.

2. Here's another case. Eponyms—such as *Alzheimer's* disease and *Parkinson's* disease—are a form of recognition, generally to the scientist who made the discovery or whose work transformed the field. Do you think it is ethically sound to name a medical condition after someone who has behaved despicably? Here's a troubling case:

[A] common condition of unknown cause that affects the joints, eyes, urethra and skin and is known as Reiter's syndrome, named after a German doctor, Hans Conrad Reiter, who reported a case in a military officer in 1916. The eponym was adopted in English language journals in the early 1940's. But by then Dr. Reiter had become an early disciple of Hitler. And now, new attention to his career shows that his involvement in Nazi atrocities was deeper than previously known. Two arthritis experts at the University of California at Los Angeles have added further evidence of Dr. Reiter's role as a Nazi who helped plan and approve "human experiments" in concentration camps.

   Writing in the current issue of *The Journal of Clinical Rheumatology*, Dr. Daniel J. Wallace and Dr. Michael Weisman, renewed calls made over the last quarter of a century to drop Dr. Reiter's name from the syndrome. Dr. Reiter may have earned the highest marks for his teaching and service to the community, the doctors said. But, they asked, "Should a war criminal be rewarded with eponymous distinction?" (See Lawrence K. Altman, M.D., "The Doctor's World: Experts Re-examine Dr. Reiter, His Syndrome and His Nazi Past," *The New York Times*, 7 Mar. 2000)

a. Drawing from the questioning techniques, ask five distinctly different questions about this case. Be sure to label your types of questions.

b. Aside from any question used in a, above, create questions that would fit each of the following categories: descriptive, theoretical, persuasive, reflective, and evaluative.

3. Are male characters on TV poor role models? At least one writer thinks so. Read the excerpt and then answer the questions that follow:

Men in a growing number of comedies are depicted as rude, crude, sex-crazed, sexist, childish and blindly egotistical. The curmudgeonly title character of *Becker* (Ted Danson), a middle-aged doctor, says things like: "If you want to know about women, you don't ask a woman. If you want to know about meat, do you ask a cow?" When a patient tells him that an injection hurt, Becker replies, "Grow up, will you?" On *Friends*, Joey eats steak with his fingers at Ross's wedding reception. On *Dharma and Greg*, Greg (Thomas Gibson), a respectable married lawyer, can't have his wife (Jenna Elfman) work at his office because every time he looks at her, his legal training and his self-discipline vanish and he has to have sex with her, right there on the desk.

Prime time gives us grown men who can't stop giggling in church, bawdy male magazine publishers married to women half their age and men who stick Montblanc pens up their noses in order to meet women in the emergency room. Anyone who watches television regularly could get the impression that one of the two sexes on this planet is not only dimwitted and uncouth but darned proud of it. . . .

So what do the programming experts decide? Rather than developing or buying series that might appeal to those fascinations with ability, victory versus defeat or good versus evil, they give us shows about men watching football and wrestling. And doing little else. Now little boys across America want to grow up to be just like them. (See Anita Gates, "Men on TV: Dumb as Posts and Proud of It," *The New York Times*, 9 Apr. 2000)

Answer the following:
a. Assume you have the chance to meet the author, Anita Gates, and want to understand her position in more detail. What four questions would you ask her?
b. Looking over each of your four questions, what category does each question fall into?

▦ Writing Techniques: Essays

To become a better writer, the most important thing you can do is to write. The next most important thing is to read good writing. The very act of writing, writing, writing, changes everything. For some, writing is more terrifying than encountering the zombies from *Night of the Living Dead*. But don't despair: You can become a more proficient writer if you apply yourself.

In developing our writing techniques we want to be comfortable with the following: writing hints, fine points about writing essays, key things to look for in assessing writing, and answering exam questions, such as on the LSAT, where we are presented with a choice between two options. Here are some keys for becoming a better writer. We'll go into each one, so we can get a handle on ways to transform our writing. We can learn to structure our writing so it is clear, coherent, and convincing.

It takes time and commitment to be a good writer. Writing can be frustrating, but we should not give up. Some people are born with a talent for writing. The rest of us have to learn and practice. Good writing is within our reach given time and commitment. With that in mind, let us look at what is involved in developing our writing skills.

Key Writing Hints

1. *Write as frequently as you can.* Even 10 minutes a day helps you relax as a writer, develop your own style, and awaken your "inner voice." If you cannot write every day, try to write on a frequent basis.

Writing Hints

- Write every day or as often as you can.
- No more rush jobs.
    - → Pace yourself.
- Use outlines and brainstorming.
- Get a first draft as soon as you can.
- Approach project and research with gusto.
    - → No lazy lumps.
- Clarify goals and make a plan.
- Visualize the structure of your paper.
- Keep thesis/focus narrow.
    - → Don't try to do too much.
- Think depth, not breadth.
- Keep introduction and conclusion clear and concise.
- Detail, detail, detail!
    - → Back up all your claims.
- Aim for well-defended, cogent reasoning.
- Read your work aloud.
- Watch for originality and personal stamp
    - → Be distinctive
- Affirm your own voice and style.
- Document correctly and give credit to others' ideas
- Set aside draft, get some distance, and then look it over.
    - → Scrutinize your work.
- Be humble: Don't expect perfection.
- Be proud: Set high standards of excellence.
- Don't beat it to death—know when to stop.

2. *Don't wait until the last minute.* Rush jobs are just that. Quality work, research, thinking, and writing all take time. Most writing requires a second or third draft, so factor that into the equation. Preferably allow at least three to four days of "breathing time" between a finished essay and its due date. We may have trouble seeing even glaring errors after we have just completed a work. We need this distance from it to spot the strengths and weaknesses.

3. *Use an outline.* Try the cluster type when you are in the idea stage of writing, brainstorming about the topic and the direction to take. Try a rough linear outline to set out your points and key claims. An outline does not kill spontaneity. Rather, it helps ensure you cover all the major aspects.

To use a cluster outline, try this:

- Write down the general topic area of your paper and draw a circle around it.
- Brainstorm and jot down key words that come from thinking (very quickly) about your general topic. Draw a circle around each of these key words.

- Brainstorm and jot down key words that come from thinking about each of the group of words you generated. Draw a circle around each of these key words.
- Brainstorm ideas and key words that come from the last group of words you generated. Draw a circle around each of these ideas and key words.
- Look at the cluster map you have created to see themes and connections. Jot any of these down and draw circles around these themes and connections.
- Look over your cluster map and see if you have any workable ideas for use in your writing.
- **Now you are ready to work up an outline for your paper.**

To develop your essay outline, try this:

- Brainstorm ideas; for example, use a rough outline, such as a cluster outline, to bring out ideas and get rolling.
- Write for 10 minutes, with your outline as a general guide, just writing freely so you can get some sense of where you want to go in your paper.
- Write a linear (conventional) outline. This helps structure your research as well as shape ideas.
- Research your topic and see if your initial plan or idea is actually achievable. You may need to modify it or narrow it down.
- After you have done a little reading and thinking, write a more detailed outline. This helps you set a structure.
- **Now you are ready to polish your outline.**

4. *Now write a first draft.* Have fun with it, relax, try different styles, and do not be too hard on yourself. What you want to do is get something down on paper. Having your ideas in written form, however roughly sketched out, makes all the difference. Then you can look at them, mull them over, and see how they work to support your thesis. Think about what further research is necessary. Gather your evidence, quotes, statistics, and examples.

5. *If more research is required, get started.* Don't allow your perceived need for research, facts, quotes, ideas, and useful tidbits to become a reason *not* to write. Some people spend so much time on research that they neglect the writing. Avoid that. Also some people think they are not smart enough to write. Avoid that, too.

6. *Document as you go.* Yes, it does take time to write in the details as you whip out your drafts. Give proper citation for quotes and the ideas of others that you incorporate in your work. If you don't, it can come back to haunt you later. If you document as you go, your work will be complete in terms of citations. Think of it as a form of housekeeping that helps keep you organized and is a great time saver in the long run.

7. *Clarify goals.* You have your first draft there in your hands, complete with your bibliography and footnotes. Before you proceed further, do a little reality check. Exactly what are you trying to accomplish? In one sentence,

what is the intent of this paper? If you cannot say it simply, perhaps you, yourself, are not clear. Your reader cannot climb into your brain, so your writing has to stand on its own.

8. *Watch for detail.* As you study your first draft, keep an eye out for the level of detail you use. On a blank piece of paper, sketch out the key ideas or intention of each paragraph of your paper. Each paragraph is like a piece in a puzzle: It should fit snugly and should be obvious if it is missing. If you can remove a paragraph without noticing its absence, then throw it out. Your goal should be to produce a quality work.

   Ask: Is the evidence I offer strong? Is anything missing that I need to add? How would an opponent attack my paper? How can I answer the opponent's criticism? Check if you did what was proposed in the introduction. Stay on task, and do not wander off.

9. *Make sure thesis is clear.* We should be able to say exactly what the focus is and what we are attempting in the paper. If it is not clear to you, it won't be clear to anyone else. To check this, read your paper aloud to yourself or to another person. After hearing your opening paragraphs, your listener (even if you are the listener!) should be able to see where you're going. Keep the opening paragraphs clear, concise and simple. Avoid sentences that are too long or cumbersome. And after hearing the conclusion, your listener should know what you were trying to accomplish. See how you achieved this.

10. *Make a good first impression.* Start with a strong introduction. End with a strong conclusion. The introduction and conclusion set the framework of the paper, allowing the readers to know where they are going and where they have been. They also help draw the readers in by establishing enthusiasm and a connection to you.

   Do not get into the main ideas or evidence in the introduction or conclusion. Save that for the body of the paper. In your introduction, set out the general area under consideration, the specific issue to be examined, the position to be defended (in the case of a persuasive piece), and, briefly, how you will proceed. Have a clear thesis statement. For instance, General Black failed to address the root causes of racism during the Civil War. As we will see, this is shown in his ideology, his policy planning, and his relationship with the rural communities.

   Your examination of another person's argument (as, for instance, in the op/ed section of the newspaper) is not an "objective" one. You are viewing it through your own perspective and have your own set of values and reactions to the issues. This perspective is relevant. It should, therefore, be noted when you discuss whether or not you were persuaded by the author's reasoning.

11. *Examine the body of the work to check for strong arguments and clearly articulated points.* Make sure all your claims are well supported. Check for assumptions or questionable claims. Watch your use of language and make sure key terminology is explained. Don't just say it; show it. Don't insist;

prove. All the paragraphs in the body of your essay should build upon one another.

12. *Read your work aloud.* Your masterpiece is taking shape. Reading aloud helps you catch wordy sentences, sentences that go on forever, or incomplete sentences. At this stage, the problems tend to be minor and are usually easily addressed. If you spot any major problems, it's better to tackle them now than later.

13. *Double-check documentation.* Make sure all sources have been cited properly, all quotes documented, using a style manual that your professor finds acceptable. Do not invent your own system of documentation. There are excellent style manuals available.

14. *Allow time to look over your draft.* Set it aside for a few days or even a few hours to get some distance. Emotional attachments can cloud our ability to spot errors. A little detachment helps an assessment.

15. *Write a second draft.* Write your second draft, putting in all the vital details you gathered or later see as necessary. Try to write carefully, paying attention to your research, thoughts, and ideas. Get a friend to proofread for spelling and typing errors. Watch also for style problems. Read your second draft out loud.

16. *Don't flog a dead horse.* Know when to stop. You don't want to lose the energy and voice of your work. Don't be merciless with yourself!

Exercises

1. Outline a finished essay that you have already written. (Go through it paragraph by paragraph and sketch out an outline, based on the essay in front of you.) Then:
   a. Examine your outline to see if it indicates a well-organized and nicely structured essay. Look at it with a critical eye.
   b. From your outline alone, state your thesis and the key arguments you make in support of the thesis.
   c. Given your outline, would you do anything different with your essay to change it? Explain why or why not.

2. Write an introduction to your own autobiography. Then look over your introduction and assess it: What are you trying to do? What issues did you raise?

3. Pick any recent comic strip or political cartoon and write a page discussing what idea(s) the strip/cartoon is trying to convey and whether or not you think it works.

4. Examine any old essay (preferably your own). Then write a constructive criticism or assessment intended to (a) relay encouragement and (b) give no more than three to four pieces of constructive criticism. The goal is to help, not crush the sensitive writer's spirit!

Organization

Planning and organization are valuable tools for developing writing skills. Both take time, but once a plan is in place the time can be used quite constructively. You will be amazed at how much can be accomplished in an hour or two. It is sort of like painting a room. If you get paint and a brush and do not spend much (or any) time on preparation, it usually ends up taking much longer. Sometimes we think the time we take in taping windows or moving furniture is a waste. However, once the spills start and paint splats are all over the place, the cleanup gets very time-consuming and frustrating. This is like writing.

Be prepared when you sit down to write your essay. If not, then the "cleanup"—in the form of rewrites, gathering more quotes, going back and finding those references, trips to the library, Internet research, and making sure you did not screw up the documentation—will be time-consuming and frustrating.

Planning and Structure: The Nitty-Gritty

- *Research.* When research is appropriate, it clearly strengthens the case. Vague generalizations, hearsay, and so-called common knowledge do not make a solid case. Become familiar with libraries, databases on the Internet, professional journals, search engines, and websites. Examine the websites of professional organizations (American Medical Association, American Bar Association, etc.) to get links or leads to information on specialized topics or resources.

- *Root your quotes and examples.* Don't leave quotes floating in space—tie them to your work. Discuss all examples and quotes, rather than just plopping them in the paper. The quote or example is an illustration of what *you* are trying to say. Show their relevance, so the reader can best grasp your points.

- *Watch your language.* Do not make judgments ("stupid," "ridiculous," etc.) unless you can establish that judgment is well founded. Better yet, make your case by a carefully reasoned argument. Ultimately, nothing beats strong evidence as a tool of persuasion.

- *Use analogies carefully.* Steer clear of analogies unless you have a strong case. An analogy can be very persuasive, if it is good. A weak analogy, however, can seriously damage your argument. (See Chapter 13.) Use an analogy only after assessing its strengths and weaknesses.

- *Avoid tangential stories.* The "this is like such and so" is only a wise move if it is *really* like such and so. Your personal or fictional accounts are like analogies—if they are good, they are powerful. Weak or irrelevant stories detract from your work.

- *Use a clear structure.* Be conscious of the structure of your essay. Visualize it. Do you make your best argument first? Or is the best saved for last? Consider what structure best suits your intentions. Before your final draft, study your essay and note its strongest and weakest points. Then decide how to structure your essay for the most impact. Use an outline. Even in essay exams, an outline can be a valuable time saver and ensures you don't forget key points.

- *Look at transitions.* Use paragraphs. You should have at least two per page; paragraphs that are too long are hard to read and show that you did not structure your thoughts. Each paragraph should be connected—this is what transition sentences do.
- *Look at sentence style and length.* Do not always use long or always use short sentences. Vary the length. If you have three long sentences, make sure the next one is a short sentence. If you do not understand how important this is, read your paper aloud. When you vary the length of the sentences it both sounds better and is easier to follow.
- *Use I or we.* The impersonal subject, like the passive voice, is a mask that writers hide behind. Own your thoughts and include your reader, whenever appropriate. Normally, you should write your paper using "I"—not "one," "you" or "we." Be careful what gets swept under the linguistic rug. The rule is this. Say "I" when it is your own thought, say "we" when you are including everyone else. Say, "I think the president is brilliant," not "We think he is brilliant." However, there are times when we *are* included, as with, "We will look at the reasons for this argument in the following."
- *Always read your work aloud.* You will be amazed how this will help you find major and minor problems. Reading a paper aloud helps you find such weaknesses as sloppy sentence structure, bad transitions, weak writing, and insufficient detail.
- *Explain any technical terms.* This includes scientific words, concepts, philosophical words, or field-specific words. Establish a connection with readers so they know how you are using your terms. You don't want your writing to be dry and lifeless. On the other hand, you don't want it to come across as a letter home. Achieve a balance between the two.
- *Be attentive to appropriate length.* If the teacher asks for five pages and you only have three, go back and expand. Go into more depth and fill in more details. Look for the key points and discuss them more fully. If your paper goes beyond the maximum suggested, cut it down.
- *Keep adjectives to a minimum.* Nouns usually stand better on their own, so use adjectives sparingly.
  Compare: President Bush plans to have an impact on foreign affairs in the 21st century.
  With: Bush is a great and inspiring president who plans to have a lasting impact on foreign affairs in the 21st Century.
  If you like adjectives, use them. Just don't overdo it.
- *Use a dictionary.* If you make more than one or two spelling errors a page, you need help. Your paper is simply not quality work with spelling or grammatical errors. Most computers have spell checkers you can use. Also, dictionaries can be accessed online, as well as in print form (own and use a dictionary!).
- *Give credit whenever it is due.* If you quote or paraphrase someone, give proper credit. If you get an idea from someone, even a friend, give credit. The failure to credit sources is *plagiarism.* It is one of the most serious academic offenses. People's careers have been blighted, if not ruined, by acts of intellectual dishonesty, as we saw in the Joseph Ellis case in Chapter 7.

- *Use a style manual.* Style manuals tell you more than how to do proper foot-notes. They also give you useful stylistic advice. Avoid pain and suffering by properly documenting your work and having a nice presentation in terms of style.
- *Proofread your work.* Consider every first draft a *first* draft, and not a finished masterpiece. Do not settle for an imperfect essay. Aim for higher quality. Your values, your integrity, your thinking are represented in every written work you hand in.
- *Do your best.* Proofread, retype if necessary, rewrite if necessary. Get a friend to look at your writing. Try to tell your friend what you were trying to achieve. If you do your best you will feel pride and satisfaction. Your writing will also improve. Each time we push ourselves to greater heights, we learn.

Exercises

1. Answer any *one* of the following:
   a. Write one page on an exchange you had with a complete stranger that, in retrospect, touched you in some way. Your goal in your one-page es-say is to convey to the reader what happened and how it impacted you.
   b. Write one page on an exchange you had with a family member or close friend about a moral issue, such as honesty, betrayal, confidentiality, fair-ness, or generosity. Your goal is to present your position as strongly as you can. It is not necessary to go into detail about any precipitating event.

2. Answer *one* of the following:
   a. The school board wants your ideas on what we should change to make our educational system better. Looking at the schools in your own neigh-borhood—such as those you attended or are currently attending—what would you recommend? Write two to three pages. Your essay should have an introduction and a conclusion and briefly go into your key ideas.
   b. Write a letter to the editor of a local or national newspaper on an issue you care deeply about. Your goal is to make a gripping, powerful argument. (Read a few first, in order to get an idea of how others have written opin-ion pieces like the ones you find in the op/ed section of newspapers).
   c. Write a letter to the communications director of a large corporation whose ads you find particularly disturbing (or boring, or sexist, or presumptu-ous, etc.). Be sure your letter is positive and constructive so that it will be taken seriously. You can go to the Internet or a library reference book to find names and addresses if you later want to mail off your letter!
   d. Write a letter to a director of a prime-time TV show discussing *one* thing about the show you particularly like. If possible, also share two to three ideas for making the show more relevant or more socially conscious.

Tips for Readability

Write with the assumption that your reader is interested and appreciates the fact that you speak simply and from the heart. Go into detail and present your thoughts clearly, concisely, and in a way that sparks interest. If your essay bores you, it will probably bore your readers. Find something interesting in your topic area and zero in on this. Once you have completed your essay, take the time to look it over and make sure it satisfies the following major areas.

Quick Review of an Essay: Short List of Writing Tips

1. The introduction should set out the topic area, specific focus of the paper, your thesis, and method of approach. Clarify where you are headed and how you plan to get there.

2. Set out your case and develop ideas in a careful, consistent, and coherent way. Write clearly and make sure your reasoning is cogent. Give evidence for your position. Use details, quotes from credible sources, or examples. Support your claims. If you make a judgment, back it up with reasons and examples.

3. Use quotes judiciously and only as much as necessary. Think of the quotes as nuggets that boost your argument, but weigh it down if the nuggets become boulders. Discuss all quotes or otherwise integrate the quote into your paper. This makes for smoother writing and tells the reader that you are using your sources to strengthen (not pad) your paper.

4. Express your own ideas and make sure *you* are in the paper. Your own insights and ideas are important. Put yourself in the essay. Don't paste together a bunch of quotes as if they would replace your own thoughts on the issue. Your own uniqueness in terms of ideas and style gives life—individuality—to the essay.

5. Make sure research, quotes, statistics, illustrations, examples, and references are well used. Be sure statistics are current. If they are out of date, do not use them, or qualify their application. Make sure material from other sources is well integrated with your own expression.

6. Watch style. Express yourself clearly and concisely. Don't be too wordy. Go into detail. Back up your claims. Make sure points are clear. Avoid repetition, except as a springboard for going deeper. Check for smooth transitions, so paragraphs are not a series of leaps over the abyss.

7. Scrutinize the quality of your arguments. Show why alternative positions were rejected. Anticipate both your critic and the opposing side. If you anticipate an opponent's argument, the essay will come across as more thorough and well researched.

8. Watch that expository essays show balanced inquiry and not a diatribe. You are not expected to be completely neutral, but you should be fair to both sides. You do not have to hide your position, but do not flaunt it in an expository essay.

9. A conclusion can provide a summary of key points or reflection on what we can learn from the discussion. The conclusion ties together the most perti-

Essay Check List

	Low				High
Introduction	1	2	3	4	5
Conclusion	1	2	3	4	5
Well-structured paper	1	2	3	4	5
Reads well, good transitions	1	2	3	4	5
Thesis clearly stated	1	2	3	4	5
Use of evidence	1	2	3	4	5
Cogent, well-reasoned paper	1	2	3	4	5
Anticipates opposition	1	2	3	4	5
Sufficient amount of detail	1	2	3	4	5
Avoids loaded terms/biased language	1	2	3	4	5
Shows originality and insight	1	2	3	4	5
Spelling/typos	1	2	3	4	5
Use of research material	1	2	3	4	5
Documentation (footnotes, sources)	1	2	3	4	5
Bibliography	1	2	3	4	5

nent points of your paper. It is rarely wise to introduce a new point in the conclusion, because this risks undermining your entire essay. If you must raise a new point at this stage, make sure you have a good reason for doing so. End strong. It is your last chance to communicate with your reader, so use it.

10. Before you hand it in, reread your paper and rate its quality. If you give it a low rating, rewrite, polish, or otherwise strengthen your essay. Use the essay checklist in the above table to assess your work.

Essay Exams with a Choice of Two Options

In some essay exams, such as the LSAT, test takers are given a choice of two options. You have 30 minutes to make a decision and give the best argument you can. In most cases, it is not that one option is the "right answer" and the other option "wrong." Rather, the test usually measures how well the student can defend the choice made. Here, the trick is to make a decision, give the strongest case for that decision and show why the alternative choice should be rejected.

Here are some guidelines for students asked to give an argument for a particular decision. They can also serve as guidelines the readers can use to examine the writing sample or essay. Knowing how you will be judged can help you better formulate your answer.

Guidelines for Defending a Choice between Options

1. *Organize your answer in terms of given criteria.* Announce the decision first, then support with evidence and argument.
   Evidence is the facts about the person given in the sketch.
   Argument is the conclusion or inferences you can reasonably derive from the facts.

2. *Argument can be both positive and negative.* The best arguments have both positive and negative elements:
   Positive: support your position.
   Negative: point out weaknesses in the opposing view.

3. *Criteria may not have equal weight,* or you may assign them different weights. Use only the criteria stated, because any added criteria could be used against you.
   Remember: The criteria operate as a *closed set.* Use the criteria in making your case. And no other criteria should be used in arriving at your decision.

4. *Stay focused and aim for clarity and precision.* In stating and defending your position, stick to the question and go into detail. Don't go off on tangents.

5. *Have a strong opening and closing, with the body of the essay setting out your argument.*
   Remember: Your introduction should state your position and, briefly, how you get there. Elaborate on your reasons, going into detail in the body of your essay. End with a conclusion that shows how your elaboration got you there. End your essay by restating your conclusion, summarizing the strongest points that support it.

6. *Use outlining technique* in your argument.
   It helps to itemize points as in, "the three most important aspects of this job are (1) _____, (2) _____, and (3) _____."
   Then show how your choice of options meets these criteria more closely than the other (competing) option. This technique helps the reader follow the argument and thus makes the argument more persuasive.

7. *Synthesize material; don't just repeat it.* In writing a good answer, show that you have read the facts carefully.
   Apply what you know: Show the relevance of the information you are given in making your case. Combine related facts into broader categories that relate to the criteria used as the basis for your decision.

8. *Spelling is important.* Written expression is a primary tool and if your tool is dull then you won't have the impact. Spelling errors are a form of dullness. Work on this, if spelling is not your strength.

PART THREE

The Logic
Connection

CHAPTER THIRTEEN

The Big Three of Induction: Analogies, Causal Reasoning, and Statistical Arguments

Harvey's ghosts have mischievous or evil facial expression, [whereas] Columbia's ghost appears bewildered.

—JUDGE PETER K. LEISURE, dismissing Harvey Publication's suit against Columbia pictures that the *Ghostbusters'* ghost looked too much like Casper's friend, Fatso

If you saw the movie *Ghostbusters*, you would remember the ghost that wreaked havoc and caused an enormous amount of destruction—so much so that a team of three armed with an array of weapons struggled to contain it. In trying to figure out if this ghost was a rip-off of the cartoon series Casper (the friendly ghost) of the past, Judge Peter K. Leisure had to line them up and compare them. Exactly what similarities did they share? Are there any killer differences? The judge had to go into the thicket of analogical reasoning. Artistic integrity and an awful lot of money rested on his being able to render a decision.

Harvey Publications, the creators of Casper, claimed the *Ghostbusters'* ghost (in the movie's logo) too closely resembled one of their creations, their ghost Fatso. The judge had to decide if there was too great a resemblance in the two ghosts, creating harm and violating the rights of Fatso's creators. Stop for a minute and think: What are the generic features of a ghost? Draw up a list before reading on!

Judge Leisure decided that no company can copyright the generic outline of a ghost but they *could* copyright facial features and certain other aspects of a drawing. To him, most ghosts had knotted foreheads and jowly cheeks (making them generic features). The question was how close the *Ghostbusters'* ghost was to the Harvey ghosts, especially Fatso, in terms of key (copyrighted) features. Judge Leisure found that, whereas Fatso had a mischievous or evil facial expression, the other ghost just looked bewildered. Judge Leisure had to study ghosts (or drawings of ghosts) and induce common, generic characteristics and then decide which characteristics or features could be copyrighted. In other words, he had to have clearly articulated reasons for his decision.

As it turns out, he dismissed the suit, given the differences between the two ghosts (remember differences can break an analogy). Sure there were similarities, but they were not sufficient to support the conclusion that the *Ghostbusters'* ghost was just a variation of the Harvey ghost, Fatso. In seeing the two ghosts you would not automatically infer that they were from the same poltergeist family.

Judge Leisure was using his powers of induction. As you remember from Chapter 6, an inductive argument never offers certainty. The evidence, at best, gives but partial support for the conclusion. In this case, there were a few similarities (such as the rounded features and bulbous nose of the two ghosts). However, there is always a wedge of doubt (because of the missing pieces) between the premises and the conclusion. In the ghost wars of Fatso versus the *Ghostbusters,* the differing expressions raised doubt in the mind of the judge. A look of bewilderment, the judge surmised, is distinctly different from a mischievous, or even evil, expression. Because of this uncertainty—this wedge of doubt—the case against Columbia pictures was past history as the analogy hits the dust.

In this chapter, we will focus on the three major kinds of inductive arguments. We will first examine arguments based on analogy. We will then turn to cause-and-effect reasoning. Finally, we will look at statistical reasoning and learn how to assess two common forms, the statistical syllogism and the inductive generalization.

Arguments from Analogy

Arguments based on an analogy are one of the most important kinds of inductive reasoning. Analogies can be found everywhere from politics to religion, and in all aspects of our lives. For example, rhythm and blues singer, Maxwell, said, "I like for my music to sound the way I like my women to look" (as noted by Steve Jones, "Maxwell Says He's Ready 'Now' to 'Get to Know Ya,'" *USA Today,* 20 Aug. 2001). Note what exactly is being compared to what—not to mention the similarities and differences. That's what we have to examine in order to analyze Maxwell's reasoning.

An analogy consists of a comparison between two things in which, on the basis of certain similarities, a principle or characteristic of the one term is then applied to the other term and asserted as true in that case as well. Think, for example, of terms like "mother board" that suggest a human, gestating presence in computer hardware. Such an analogy affects how we see other computer operations.

In law these take the form of precedents (previous cases decided by a court of law or made into law by a legislature). Think how powerful the analogy drawn between obeying the law and baseball has become. Namely, with the "three strikes" law the rules of a game became the model for addressing repeat offenders—except in the case of criminals striking "out" doesn't mean go sit in the dugout until the next inning. It means 25 years to life in prison—a much wider sense of "out" than ever imagined in baseball.

We also see analogies in literature, poetry, mythology, and religion. For example, "It is harder for a rich man to get into heaven than for a camel to go through the eye of a needle." Such analogies have power. Philosopher Douglas Hofstader says, "analogy is the driving force behind the way I think," recognizing its value to creativity, as well as critical reasoning. (as noted by *Wired* magazine, Nov. 1995)

Form of an Argument from Analogy

A is like B in terms of p, q, r characteristics

<u>A also has characteristic "z."</u>

So, B has characterististic "z" also.

Analogies can be very persuasive. For many, the fact someone has drawn a comparison implies that the comparison must be correct. But this is not necessarily true, for there may be relevant *differences* that make the principle or characteristic inapplicable. Our task is to see if the combined strength of the similarities outweighs that of the differences. In that way, we can assess how strong the analogy actually is.

For example, "Education cannot prepare high school students for marriage, even with the requirement that students carry dolls to class to approximate caring for children. Educating about marriage is like teaching someone to pilot a plane without ever leaving the ground. Until you're up in the air, you have no idea what's involved in flying." In this case, an analogy is drawn between marriage and piloting a plane. To assess the strength of this analogy, we'd have to list what's similar between teaching about marriage and teaching about flying and then list the differences. Of course, there are some significant differences (e.g., marriage involves a relationship, is not potentially life-threatening if you fall asleep, and so on).

The Persuasive Force of an Analogy

Whether the comparison is strong or weak, an analogy potentially carries great persuasive power. Therefore, it is unwise to let an analogy slide by without examining it. Let's look at some examples.

Example 1 of an analogy:

There is a famous analogy used by Garrett Hardin in an article on world hunger. He presents this scenario: Think of our nation as a lifeboat with 50 people and 10 empty seats. There are one hundred people (from underdeveloped nations) in the water, trying to get in our lifeboat. To take them all on, we would sink. If we take a few (how could we choose?), we'd lose our safety margin of the empty seats. So, we should not rescue any. This, Hardin argues, is why we are not in a position to help nations with world hunger. We need to preserve our own resources for future use and, thus, should not deplete them by trying (ineffectively, given the numbers) to help. (See Garrett Hardin's "Lifeboat Ethics: The Case Against Helping the Poor.")

Example 2 of an analogy:

Another influential analogy is one used by James Rachels in an article on active versus passive euthanasia. He presents two scenarios that he uses to contrast killing versus letting die. In the first case, Smith stands to gain a large inheritance if anything happened to his 6-year-old cousin and, so, Smith drowns the child one night in the bathtub and then makes it look like an accident.

In the second case, Jones, who also stands to gain if anything happened to his 6-year-old cousin, sneaks into the bathroom intending to drown the boy. But, before he can make his move, his cousin slips, hits his head, and falls face down in the water and dies "accidentally" as Jones watches.

Rachels then compares Smith's murder of his cousin with Jones's failure to intervene to save him. As far as Rachels is concerned, both are equally morally culpable and there is no significant moral distinction between the two scenarios. He then applies this to active versus passive euthanasia, making the same argument. (See James Rachels's "Active and Passive Euthanasia.")

Assessing an Analogy

If you allow the analogy off the ground, the argument is generally successful. If, however, the weight of the differences of the two terms is greater than that of the similarities, the analogy falters. That is, the argument is not as powerful if the differences outweigh the similarities. Every time you see an analogy you should ask, "What are the similarities? What are the differences?" The use of an analogy should start alarms ringing in our brain:

That's an analogy → Hold it right there!
　　　　　　　　　→ Stop and check it out.
　　　　　　　　　→ Weigh the similarities and differences.

What makes an argument based on an analogy inductive is that the evidence is partial. In an analogy, the premises only provide some support for the drawing of the conclusion; given there are differences in any comparison, there will always be holes in the argument. The result is that the conclusion does not (and cannot) automatically follow from the premises. If the premises are true, the conclusion that follows when an analogy is used will not certainly be true—the conclusion could be false. This is why an argument from analogy is inductive, not deductive.

Think of it this way: no matter how similar you may be to your mother or father, there are still some differences. Therefore, even though you can draw up a long list of similarities, there will nevertheless be differences that introduce some uncertainty into the comparison.

Most of us have been compared to a family member (positively or negatively). This reasoning is inductive because we are supposed to draw a conclusion on the basis of the asserted similarity. "Sonja, you are just like your mother! Your mother always makes delicious lemon meringue pie, so you should too!" Now Sonja may be like her mother in some respects. But that does not mean she is like her mother in *every* respect. They are not clones, so there will be some things about them that are not identical. Sonja may be a good baker, like her mother. But it is not certain. The fact of a resemblance does not automatically mean that the two are identical.

The Fallacy of False Analogy

Occasionally someone sets out a *false analogy*. This is a fallacy in which two terms are being compared for the purpose of making an inference resting on that comparison—and yet there are no real similarities at all, other than trivial ones. For example, here's a false analogy: "Michigan minus bowling would be like Pythagoras without his theorem." It's a brain-twister to think of any real similarities between Michigan without bowling and Pythagoras without his theorem. If there are no nontrivial similarities, then the analogy simply fails. Be on the lookout for false analogies and be careful, when setting out an analogy, that you can point to some shared characteristics between the terms of the comparison.

Analyzing Analogies

We can tackle analogies we run across by assessing the strengths of the comparison. Follow the steps, carefully laying out the analogy so you can then decide how strong it is.

Steps to Analyzing an Analogy

1. *Clarify the terms of comparison.*
   Note exactly what is being compared to what.
2. *Write it out like an equation setting out the comparison.*
3. *State the principle or characteristic attributed to the one term that is being applied to the other term.*
4. *List the similarities.*
5. *List the differences.*
6. *Survey the two lists.*
   Add any omissions to your lists.
7. *Weigh similarities and differences.*
   Determine the relative strength of the similarities compared to that of the differences. Some similarities or differences may be more important than others, so prioritize them in terms of relative importance.
8. *Assess the analogy.*
   Analogies, like all inductive arguments, fall along a spectrum ranging from dismal to strong. In a <u>strong analogy</u>, the similarities significantly outweigh the differences. In a <u>weak analogy</u>, the strength of the differences outweighs the similarities. Ask yourself: Is there a killer difference? Check to see if there is a difference so great that it would outweigh any similarity. If so the analogy fails. In a <u>false analogy</u>, there are no relevant (nontrivial) similarities at all.

Don't Forget:

- **Similarities MAKE an analogy**
- **Differences BREAK an analogy**

<h1 style="text-align:center">Group Exercise</h1>

John Balzar contends that receiving a grade of a "B" is not anything to be ashamed of, that we don't all have to get an "A" to feel like we've accomplished something. Using the steps listed above, assess his analogy to tales about seeing a moose:

> If Mark Richards up near Eagle, Alaska, tells you he saw a world-class moose, you will know it was the kind of bull that could clear-cut a forest with its antlers. On the other hand, an average moose walking by his cabin is still plenty big. If the kids earn an A in school, it's cause to celebrate, not merely something to be expected. Receiving a B is not a dishonor. Uncle Bob makes no special claim about his Yukon River meat-loaf, but everyone looks forward to a slice of it and there is never any left over.
>
> My dictionary describes average as "the usual or normal kind." Just do the math. It's self-evident. And I'm with my friends in the Far North who say let's relax about it, really. In fact, as I look around these days, normal sounds better all the time, even if you have to go all the way to the Arctic Circle and dodge moose to find it. (See John Balzar, "The Law of Average-ness," *Los Angeles Times,* 10 June 2001)

First Application

To get a sense of how this is done, let's examine some analogies and assess their strength. The first analogy we will look at is an analogy often cited in the abortion debate.

Analogy 1: Analogy of Fetus to an Acorn   In her article, "A Defense of Abortion" Judith Jarvis Thomson uses a number of analogies (see *Philosophy and Public Affairs,* Vol. 1, no. 1, 1971). Her first argument based on an analogy is this: "The development of a person from the moment of conception is similar to the development of an acorn into an oak tree." Let us examine this analogy using the 7 steps.

Step 1: Clarify What Is Being Compared to What.   In this case, it is:
   The development of the fetus into a person is being compared to the development of an acorn into an oak.

Step 2: Set Out the Terms of the Analogy.   These are:
   fetus/person ≡ acorn/oak.

Step 3: State the Principle Being Asserted.   The principle is:
   There is no clear line that separates a fetus from a person.

Step 4: List the Similarities.

1. In both cases we are talking about living things.
2. The fetus and the acorn are both early forms of the respective organisms.
3. The existence of the more mature organism (person/oak tree) depends upon the growth and development of the earlier form.
4. Both fetus and acorn can be destroyed or damaged by poor nutrition (soil), lack of nurturance, or other means.
5. Neither fetus nor acorn has clearly delineated stages of development.

Step 5: List the Differences.

1. The fetus grows inside mother's body, whereas the acorn grows away from and is separate from the oak tree.
2. The time it takes to develop (fetus to person, and acorn to oak) is different.
3. Quantity: An oak tree produces many more acorns than a woman does fetuses.
4. Societal values: The society values fetuses more highly than acorns and most persons more highly than most oak trees.
5. A fetus relies upon mother's body to be nurtured and its life sustained, but an acorn has no such reliance on the oak tree.

Step 6: Survey the Two Lists.

Look at the similarities: We've covered the category (living things), age parallels, dependence on the "mother" organism, need for nurturance and nutrition, and lack of clear stage delineation. Is there more we could add? Well, we might add that both (barring destruction) potentially grow into the same type of organism (human/tree) from which it came.

Now look at the differences: We've covered the internal vs. external factor, differences in maturation times, quantity, social worth, differences in source of nurturance. Anything else we could add? Well, some might point to the appearance issue (fetuses could be said to more closely resemble humans than acorns resemble oak trees).

Step 7: Weigh the Similarities and Differences.

The differences seem stronger, particularly numbers 1 and 5 and maybe even 4. There are no strong similarities, though the strongest are probably numbers 2 and 5.

Step 8. Assessment.

Given this weighting, it would seem that the analogy is not very strong. Note that it is not a false analogy, where there are at best trivial similarities. In this case there are some similarities. However, the differences loom larger and, consequently, the analogy does not appear to be very powerful. As a result, the principle being claimed that there is no clear line separating fetuses from persons has not been clearly established by using the analogy that fetuses are like acorns.

Second Application

It may help to go through another analogy to imprint the steps firmly on our minds. The second analogy is also from Judith Jarvis Thomson, but is more unusual than the first analogy.

Analogy 2: "People-Seeds" Analogy

Thomson presents the analogy as follows:

> Again, suppose it were like this: people-seeds drift about in the air like pollen, and if you open your windows, one may drift in and take root in your carpets or upholstery. You don't want children, so you fix up your windows with fine mesh screens, the very best you can buy. As can happen, however, and on very, very rare occasions does happen, one of the screens is defective; and a seed drifts in and takes root. Does the person-plant who now develops have a right to the use of your house? Surely not— despite the fact that you voluntarily opened your windows, you knowingly kept carpets and upholstered furniture, and you knew that screens were sometimes defective. ("A Defense of Abortion")

Step 1: Clarify What Is Being Compared.

In this argument, Thomson is comparing the use of screens to prevent a people seed from blowing into your house to using contraception to prevent pregnancy.

Step 2: Set Out the Terms of the Analogy.

Defective screen/people-seed ≡ defective contraception/fetus.

Step 3: State the Principle Being Asserted.

Thomson is asserting that the failure of contraception resulting in pregnancy ought not make us feel morally obligated to bear the child, that an abortion is morally acceptable.

Step 4: List the Similarities.

1. Both contraception and screens are intentionally trying to prevent something from happening.
2. Both contraception and screens have the potential for error; neither one is foolproof.
3. Both people-seeds and fetuses are earlier stages of the person and will lead to personhood, given appropriate conditions.
4. Both have long-term consequences if allowed to go to personhood.
5. In both cases, the result is undesirable (the mother/dweller of house did not wish to become pregnant/have a people-seed growing in the carpet).

Step 5: List the Differences.

1. People-seeds float about in the air, fetuses do not.
2. In one case there is a father whose wishes may bear upon the decision, in the other case there is not.

3. A people-seed grows in a carpet and does not depend upon the house dweller, whereas a fetus grows inside the mother and depends upon her body for nurturance.
4. You could sell your house or move away and avoid the problem, not so in a normal pregnancy.
5. People-seeds require no personal risk in their development, whereas the pregnant woman undergoes risk in pregnancy.

Step 6: Survey the Two Lists.

Look at the Similarities: We've addressed the fact that both are undesirable and that steps are being taken to prevent the people seed/human embryo from gestating, both methods of obstruction can fail, both have developmental and long-term consequences. Is there more we can add? Well, we could add that both might result in unforeseen difficulties for the house owner/mother and perhaps even some physical risk (people seed may develop into a psycho, the pregnancy could be an ectopic or other high-risk pregnancy).

Now Look at the Differences: We've addressed the fact that fetuses are not external to the mother, there is not necessarily a parallel to the father in the people seed case, and escaping from the people seed is much easier escaping from than from the fetus. Anything else we could add? Well, we might add that there could be hundreds of people seeds that take root in your house (say in a big windstorm)—no pregnancy could compare in sheer numbers of developing entities.

Step 7: Weigh the Similarities and Differences.

Looking over each list, the strongest similarities seem to be numbers 1, 3, and 5. The strongest differences seem to be 3, 4, and 5 and maybe 2. The additional difference we noted does not necessarily mean the consequences would be worse if we had hundreds of people sprouting in the carpet compared to one fetus that becomes a child (the significance of this difference may be hard to quantify).

Step 8: Assessment.

This analogy seems stronger than our last one. Namely, the similarities are not irrelevant or insignificant and the differences are there but not overwhelmingly strong. The difference of the relative risk to each seems strongest, as that is a bottom-line type of difference. Given the overall weight of the similarities is stronger than that of the differences in this analogy, we can infer that the analogy has persuasive value and may carry weight in Thomson's argument that abortion be allowable under certain circumstances.

The Persuasive Aspects of Analogies

Depending how you rank the similarities and differences, the persuasive value of the analogy varies. This means there's a subjective element to any analogy. After listing similarities and differences, the weighing of them is not neutral. Rather, your own set of values will factor in when deciding the strengths of the different claims, especially those relating to a set of beliefs.

Be prepared: Some analogies are highly inflammatory and offensive. It is common to see analogies used in racist, sexist, and ethnic slurs. Subsequently, we need to have the facility to dismantle hateful analogies when we see them. For example, journalist Bob Herbert writes about the vitriolic language used by a radio personality, Bob Grant. Herbert asserts that Grant made the following use of an argument from analogy:

> He would wonder aloud "if they've ever figured out how they multiply like that. It's like maggots on a hot day. You look one minute and there are so many there, and you look again and, wow, they've tripled!" (See Bob Herbert, "A Different Republican?" *The New York Times,* 29 June 2000)

We need to be able to assess the use of an analogy. This can be laid out as follows:

Assessing the Use of an Analogy: Structuring the Analysis

1. What is at issue? What principle or conclusion is being drawn from the analogy?
2. Exactly what is being compared? Set out the terms of the analogy.
3. What are the relevant similarities and differences? List them both.
4. Critically examine the lists, weighing them to see the strength of each side (similarities and differences).
5. How would you attack the analogy? (What are its weaknesses?)
6. How would you defend the analogy? (What are its strengths?)
7. If this is an analogy you intend to use, see if you can modify it to minimize weaknesses and boost strengths.
8. If this is an analogy you are evaluating, make note of the relative strengths and weaknesses and decide if the analogy is successful—or fails to be persuasive.
9. Remember: Similarities make the analogy and differences break the analogy.
10. You are now are in a position to question whether the conclusion (the principle being drawn) can be said to follow with credible support.

Group Exercise

In his memoir, *Parallel Time,* Brent Staples writes about the problems he ran into as an African-American man attending college in a mostly white neighborhood in Pennsylvania. Discuss how he uses an analogy to convey the experience of encountering people who were afraid of him in the excerpt below. Use the steps set out above:

> I'd been a fool. I'd been grinning good evening at people who were frightened to death of me. I did violence to them by just being. How had I missed this? I kept walking at night, but from then on I paid attention.
>
> I became expert in the language of fear. Couples locked arms or reached for each other's hand when they saw me. Some crossed to the other side of the street. People

who were carrying on conversations went mute and stared straight ahead, as though avoiding my eyes would save them. This reminded me of an old wives' tale that rabid dogs didn't bite if you avoided their eyes.

Exercises

Part One: Setting Out Analogies

1. How do you take apart an analogy? List the steps in order.

2. Discuss the issues and ideas raised in the following:

   What makes the perfect political anecdote? "Most importantly, it has to be a tear-jerker," says government professor Larry Sabato of the University of Virginia. A pitiful tale involving a child or young person is especially useful. "Just look at the victories of Mothers Against Drunk Driving," suggests Sabato. . . .

   John and Lucinda Borden, parents of twin boys who were adopted as embryos, testified in front of the same subcommittee. "Mark and Luke are living rebuttals to the claim that embryos are not people," Lucinda Borden said. "Which one of my children would you kill?" added her husband. "Which one would you choose to take?" (See Hans S. Nichols, "Making Policy by Political Anecdote," *Insight on the News*, 20 Aug. 2001)

3. Set out the terms and list the similarities and differences in the following:

   The criminal justice system is like a mirror in which society can see the face of the evil in its midst. But because the system deals with some evil and not with others, because it treat some evils as the gravest and treats some of the gravest evils as minor, the image it throws back is distorted like the image in a carnival mirror. Thus the image cast back is false, not because it is invented out of thin air, but because the proportions of the real are distorted. . . .

   If criminal justice really gives us a carnival-mirror image of "crime," we are doubly deceived. First, we are led to believe that the criminal justice system is protecting us against the gravest threats to our well being when in fact the system is only protecting us against some threats and not necessarily the gravest ones. We are deceived about how much protection we are receiving and thus left vulnerable. But, in addition, we are deceived about what threatens us and are, therefore, unable to take appropriate defensive action. The second deception is just the other side of the first one. If people believe that the carnival mirror is a true mirror— that is, if they believe that the criminal justice system just reacts to the gravest threats to their well-being—they come to believe that whatever is the target of the criminal justice system must be the gravest threat to their well-being. (Jeffrey H. Reiman, *The Rich Get Richer and the Poor Get Poorer*)

4. Set out the terms of the analogy below and list the similarities and differences:

   Affirmative action allows successful Blacks to play a cruel hoax on and advance at the expense of less fortunate Blacks. This is . . . why I so vehemently oppose it. . . .

At best, affirmative action is like rearranging the chairs on the deck of the Titanic. (William [otherwise anonymous], "Thoughts of a Black Conservative," America Online)

5. Set out the terms of the analogy below and list the similarities and differences:

Terminator 3 director, Jonathan Mostow speaking about Arnold Schwarzenegger: "Obviously, I'd be lying to say it wasn't daunting working in his shadow. The bar has been set very high." There's still Schwarzenegger to provide authentic Terminator wisdom, says Mostow. "I feel like I'm making the Bible and I'm getting to work with Moses." (See Rachel Abramowitz, "Rage Against the Machines: 'T3's' Rocky Road," *Los Angeles Times,* 11 Mar. 2002)

6. Set out the terms of the analogy below and list the similarities and differences:

When we take refuge we commit ourselves to the Buddhist path. This is not only a simple but also an extremely economical approach. Henceforth we will be on the particular path that was strategized, designed and well thought-out twenty-five hundred years ago by the Buddha and the followers of his teaching. . . .

This particular journey is like that of the first settlers. We have come to no-man's land and have not been provided with anything at all. Here we are, and we have to make everything with our own bare hands. We are, in our own way, pioneers: each is an historical person on his own journey. It is an individual pioneership of building spiritual ground. Everything has to be made and produced by us. Nobody is going to throw us little chocolate chips or console us with goodies. (See Chogyam Trungpa Rinpoche, "The Decision to Become a Buddhist," in *Shambhala Sun* magazine, May 2001)

7. Discuss the following use of analogies by philosopher Ludwig Wittgenstein (in *Culture and Value*):

Tradition is not something a man can learn; not a thread he can pick up when he feels like it; any more than a man can choose his own ancestors. Someone lacking a tradition who would like to have one is like a man unhappily in love.

Part Two: Analyzing Analogies

Go through the steps to check out these analogies and assess their strength.

1. Marriage without love is like driving a car without brakes.
2. "Words are like bullets—they can be used to kill." (Planned Parenthood)
3. "Racism, like the bite of a rabid animal, can infect a victim with the deadly disease of its madness." (Lloyd L. Brown)
4. "They should not allow stem cell research [that uses early human embryos]. It's no different than the experiments the Nazis did during World War II on the Jewish prisoners." (Comments at a discussion on stem cell research)
5. "Now, in the 1990's, I see substantial similarities between the cocaine epidemic and slavery. Both are firmly grounded in economics—at the expense of a race of people. There was, and is, money to be made. It would be foolish

to lose sight of this truth" (Rev. Cecil Williams, "Crack is Genocide 1990's Style," *The New York Times*, 15 Feb. 1990).

6. "The Lakers lined the Boston Celtics up against the wall and shot them Sunday. Finally. The battleship finally ran down the rowboat. . . . It's over. It wasn't a game; it was an execution. The Celtics should have been blindfolded. What took so long? It was such a messy application of capital punishment, any judge in the land would have commuted the Celtics' sentence" (Jim Murray, "Hearns Must Have Taken Fight Plan From the Titanic,"*Los Angeles Times*, 16 Apr. 1985).

7. "The education crisis is kind of like violence on television: the worse it gets the more inert we become, and the more of it we require to rekindle our attention" (Benjamin R. Barber, *A Passion for Democracy: American Essays*).

8. "To take an absurd example to illustrate why people should have a property right in their own tissues, suppose [billionaire head of Microsoft] Bill Gates' barber saves a lock of his hair and clones him, suing Gates for child support. The answer shouldn't be that Bill Gates has no recourse because he has no property rights in his tissue" (Lori Andrews, *Body Bazaar*).

9. "Most Californians view illegal immigrants as unwanted house guests. One very effective means of getting rid of such guests is to set your house on fire and burn it to the ground. This is Propositions 187's solution to illegal immigration. . . . No decent Californian should support it" (Ron K. Unz, 1994 Republican primary challenge to Governor Wilson).

10. "Some people say that by studying parallel processing, parallel hardware, parallel this and that, we develop a whole new paradigm for thought that will make us think differently. That's a really weird claim. It seems no more likely to me than that it will alter the mechanisms of our digestive tract. We can't modify those things! There's a fine line between what it means to have your thoughts shaped and having your thought processes shaped." (See Kevin Kelly, "By Analogy," *Wired* magazine, Nov. 1995.)

Part Three: Constructing Analogies

1. Give an analogy to argue for or against the use of women in combat positions in war. Set out the terms of your analogy.

2. Set out an analogy to argue for or against legalizing marijuana. Set out the terms of your analogy.

3. Give an analogy to argue for or against going to a pass/fail grading system. Set out the terms of your analogy.

4. Give an analogy to argue for or against banning smoking in public buildings. Set out the terms of your analogy.

5. Give an analogy to argue for or against white supremacists being allowed to pass out leaflets in public high schools. Set out the terms of your analogy.

6. Give an analogy to argue for or against physician-assisted death. Set out the terms of your analogy.

7. Wittgenstein, who wrote about the connection between language, thought, and reality, said of philosophy, "Philosophers use a language that is already deformed as though by shoes that are too tight." Construct an analogy or two that expresses your love or frustration with studying philosophy.

Analogies and Hypothetical Reasoning in the Law

One of the key issues faced by lawyers and judges is whether a legal precedent applies, that is, how well the letter of the law will apply to a particular case. A great deal hinges on the relevant similarities and differences of the precedent case to the case at hand. To assess this, we have to consider the amount of variation from the standard (norm or precedent-setting case) to the individual one being litigated. That is not always easy.

In order to help prepare a student for the practice of law, one teaching technique is to use a hypothetical case (alias *Hypo*). In hypothetical law cases, a scenario or story is presented, with the task of deciding how it is to be evaluated given the existing laws and precedents. This is an important application of analogical reasoning, requiring lawyers and law students to be both astute and imaginative in assessing the hypothetical cases.

By analyzing the specifics of the Hypo in relationship to the legal standard, students can then determine how the law should apply in the hypothetical case. Let's see how this is done. Drawing from an article by Sociology Professor Colleen Fitzpatrick in the *Journal of Criminal Justice Education,* we will look at some Hypos around prosecutorial decision-making of rape cases.

Directions: Read the article below that presents five rape scenarios and accompanying questions. Then discuss what would be involved in answering the questions (i.e., how you would arrive at an answer of whether or not the DA should prosecute). Go into detail and elaborate on any *one* of the scenarios (pick one).

Hypothetical Rape Scenarios as a Pedagogical Devise to Facilitate Students' Learning about Prosecutorial Decision Making and Discretion

Colleen Fitzpatrick
Journal of Criminal Justice Education, *Spring 2001*

Scenario 1.
Marilyn, a 22-year-old single woman, is at home asleep. She is awakened by the sound of her unlocked bedroom window being opened. A man enters the bedroom through the window. The man approaches Marilyn who is awake

enough now to scream, but the man gets a knife to her throat before she can do so. She still tries to break away, gets a cut across her face as a result, then submits to the man who forces his penis into her vagina and then her anus. Was Marilyn raped? Would you, as DA, prosecute?

Scenario 2.

Every Wednesday for the past year of her new marriage, Evelyn's husband, Paul, goes out with the "boys" for a night of bowling and drinking. Upon his return around 2 a.m., he strips off his smoky clothes and hops into bed with Evelyn. Inevitably feeling amorous toward his wife, Paul—smelling of smoke and booze—has sexual intercourse with Evelyn. On this particular Wednesday night, Evelyn decides enough is enough. When Paul comes home, gets into bed, and approaches Evelyn, she pushes him off and tells him she doesn't want to have sex tonight. Apparently not wanting to break his successive Wednesday night streak, Paul uses his strength and weight (but no hitting or striking) to have sex with Evelyn. Was Evelyn raped? Would you, as DA, prosecute?

Scenario 3.

After three rapes on the Mountain University campus, the campus police have advised coeds to avoid walking a dark path between the library and a dorm. All three rapes occurred along that path after the women were dragged into the bushes lining the path. Campus police told women the path was unsafe until recently budgeted lights could be erected and operating. One half hour before the library closed, Helen realized her boyfriend would be calling her dorm room in ten minutes. This being her only chance to talk with him this week, Helen, who is fully aware of the rapes and the police warnings, decides she can only get to her room in time by taking the path. Halfway to the dorm, Helen is pulled off the path and into the bushes where she is forced to have sexual intercourse with a man wielding no weapon but strong

enough to keep his hand over Helen's mouth. Was Helen raped? Would you, as DA, prosecute?

Scenario 4.

Nicole just finished moving into her new apartment. The friends helping her have left and she is feeling wide awake and a bit lonely. She decides to go to a nearby bar for some drinks and to check out the scene in her new neighborhood. At the bar, Nicole sees two men she had met a few weeks earlier through a mutual friend. The three hit it off and within a few hours all three "have caught a really good buzz." Nicole leaves the bar and accompanies the two men to their nearby apartment. She drinks more and, as best she can recall, passes out in the apartment. The next morning, Nicole recognizes the taste of semen in her mouth and feels semen dripping from her vagina. She has no memory of consenting to any sex act but also doesn't remember fighting or resisting sexual advances by either man. She firmly believes the sexual acts were performed against her will. Was Nicole raped? Would you, as DA, prosecute?

Scenario 5.

Ted and Charlie were out celebrating Ted's 21st birthday. After several birthday shots at various bars in town, Charlie suggested they go visit Connie—a local prostitute. Connie answered their knock on her door, but told them she was not working this evening since she had just finished an exceptionally busy weekend. Charlie said that since it was Ted's birthday she should at least allow them to come in for a drink or to do a quick line of coke. Connie let the two in her apartment, joined them in sharing some cocaine, then told them to leave. Charlie and Ted said they would leave right after she came across with a birthday lay. Connie refused, but Charlie pushed her onto the sofa, stripped off her clothes, and despite her physical and verbal protestation, forced her to have sexual intercourse. Ted then took his turn, but at this point Connie put up no resistance and simply told

them to both get out as soon as Ted had finished. Charlie tossed $50 (twice the amount
Connie charged Charlie on his last visit with
her) onto the table and they both left the apartment. Was Connie raped?—by Ted?—by

Charlie? Would you, as DA, prosecute?—Ted?
Charlie?

*Reprinted with the permission of Colleen
Fitzpatrick.*

Legal Precedents

One of the most powerful uses of analogies is in the law. The use of a precedent
can have a definitive effect on an argument, positively or negatively. Being able to
convincingly argue a precedent can transform the law. Failing to do so has stymied
even the best of us. A case is often applied to other, similar, cases, though there
may be crucial differences. Let's see how a case can act as a precedent.

Potential Precedents

Anyone who has told their parents that they should be subjected to the same set
of rules that are applied to their brothers and sisters (e.g., "Joe got to stay out until 3 a.m., why can't I?") has argued by precedent. When we argue using a precedent
we are employing an analogy. We are implicitly asserting that there are sufficient
similarities to allow for the principle of the one (the precedent-setting case) to apply to the situation at hand. The question is how this is done.

To block the use of a precedent—to break the analogy—we must point out the
key differences between the two cases, so the earlier decision cannot be applied. If
there are no significant differences, perhaps there are extenuating circumstances
that should be factored in to boost the analogy. One way this is done is to find *another* analogous case that supports the defense. If the earlier decision were not a
favorable one, then this process would be reversed. The opposition would focus
on the differences and the defense on the similarities.

A previous analogous case that has become law is called a *precedent*. Earlier
decisions that set precedents may be favorable or unfavorable to a later case, depending on the position argued. Lawyers often have to deal with such analogies
(potential precedents). They must either prove an earlier case is analogous, or the
differences are so great that it doesn't apply. Whether or not the earlier case acts
as a precedent is a matter of similarities or differences. This proceeds as follows:

Potential Legal Precedent:

1. *Research.* Study the case being litigated. Seek out the details of the case and
   determine what legal alternatives exist.
2. *Examine Potential Precedents.* Find cases that are similar. Find potential
   precedents that: (a) have strong similarities to show applicability and,
   (b) have rulings favorable or useful to the current case.
3. *Show the Analogy Holds.* Show that strength of similarities merit the application of the principle from the precedent to the present case. The lawyer
   can then assert that this new case warrants the same decision.

The Law and Analogies

Presenting Case	Case in Question (Note Key Elements)
↓	↓
Analogous Case(s) = potential precedents	Similar earlier cases having an acceptable decision.
↓	↓
Legal principle	Decision from earlier cases.
↓	↓
Application	Draw a similar legal principle to presenting case.
↓	↓
Assertion	**Decision Applies To Presenting Case.**

CASE STUDY

Campbell v. Acuff-Rose Music
Excerpt from the Opinion of the U.S. Supreme Court

The 2 Live Crew Case
Let us look at a U.S. Supreme Court case where both sides drew from precedents to support their arguments. This is Acuff-Rose Music, Inc. *v.* Campbell *that centers on a 2 Live Crew version (parody?) of Roy Orbison's song, "Oh, Pretty Woman." Acuff-Rose sued The 2 Live Crew (the members and its record company) for copyright infringement and interfering with potential profits. The 2 Live Crew argued their "parody" was protected under the doctrine of "fair use."*

The Order of Events
"Oh, Pretty Woman" was written and recorded by Roy Orbison and William Dees in 1964. In 1964 rights to the song were assigned to Acuff-Rose and they registered for copyright protection. Luther Campbell, lead vocalist and songwriter of The 2 Live Crew wrote a version of "Oh, Pretty Woman" in May 1989. Campbell claims he intended to create a parody as an attempt "through comic lyrics, to satirize the original work."

On July 5, 1989, after the release of the album, Linda Fine, general manager of Luke Records, informed Opryland Music Group and Acuff-Rose of "Two Live Crew's desire to do a parody" of "Oh, Pretty Woman" and noted that the popularity of 2 Live Crew ensured substantial sales. Gerald Tiefer of Opryland Music Group/Acuff-Rose informed her that they wouldn't permit the use of a parody of "Oh, Pretty Woman." This refusal did not stop 2 Live Crew from continuing to sell the album, "As Clean as They Wanna Be." Acuff-Rose brought suit in June, 1990.

Defendants submitted an affidavit from Oscar Brand, writer of works he calls "parodies." Lyrically, Brand found "Pretty Woman" to be consistent with a long tradition of making social commentary through music. African-American rap music, Brand stated, uses parody as a form of protest and often substitutes new words to "make fun of the 'white-bread' originals and the establishment. . . ." Brand considers 2 Live Crew's version to be an attempt to show "how bland and banal the Orbison song seems to them." Acuff-Rose presented an affidavit of musicologist Earl V. Speilman, who said there is "a significant amount of similarity" between the two songs; so a listener without musical training could tell "Pretty Woman" was modeled after "Oh, Pretty Woman."

The case went all the way to the U.S. Supreme Court. Following is a key excerpt from the verdict. (You can access the entire opinion on the Internet).

The germ of parody lies in the definition of the Greek *parodeia*, . . . as "a song sung alongside another." Modern dictionaries accordingly describe a parody as a "literary or artistic work that imitates the characteristic style of an author or a work for comic effect or ridicule," or as a "composition in prose or verse in which the characteristic turns of thought and phrase in an author or class of authors are imitated in such a way as to make them appear ridiculous." . . .

[T]he nub of the definitions, and the heart of any parodist's claim to quote from existing material, is the use of some elements of a prior author's composition to create a new one that, at least in part, comments on that author's works. . . .

Parody needs to mimic an original to make its point, and so has some claim to use the creation of its victim's (or collective victims') imagination, whereas satire can stand on its own two feet and so requires justification for the very act of borrowing. . . .

Here, the District Court held, and the Court of Appeals assumed, that 2 Live Crew's "Pretty Woman" contains parody, commenting on and criticizing the original work, whatever it may have to say about society at large.

As the District Court remarked, the words of 2 Live Crew's song copy the original's first line, but then "quickly degenerate into a play on words, substituting predictable lyrics with shocking ones . . . [that] derisively demonstrate how bland and banal the Orbison song seems to them." . . .

[T]hat the 2 Live Crew song "was clearly intended to ridicule the white bread original" and "reminds us that sexual congress with nameless streetwalkers is not necessarily the stuff of romance and is not necessarily without its consequences. The singers (there are several) have the same thing on their minds as did the lonely man with the nasal voice, but here there is no hint of wine and roses." Although the majority below had difficulty discerning any criticism of the original in 2 Live Crew's song, it assumed for purposes of its opinion that there was some.

We have less difficulty in finding that critical element in 2 Live Crew's song than the Court of Appeals did, although having found it we will not take the further step of evaluating its quality. The threshold question when fair use is raised in defense of parody is whether a parodic character may reasonably be perceived.

Whether, going beyond that, parody is in good taste or bad does not and should not matter to fair use . . . cf. Yankee Publishing Inc. v. News America Publishing, Inc. ("First Amendment protections do not apply only to those who speak clearly, whose jokes are funny, and whose parodies succeed").

While we might not assign a high rank to the parodic element here, we think it fair to say that 2 Live Crew's song reasonably could be perceived as commenting on the original or criticizing it, to some degree. 2 Live Crew juxtaposes the romantic musings of a man whose fantasy comes true, with degrading taunts, a bawdy demand for sex, and a sigh of relief from paternal responsibility.

The later words can be taken as a comment on the naivete of the original of an earlier day, as a rejection of its sentiment that ignores the ugliness of street life and the debasement that it signifies. It is this joinder of reference and ridicule that marks off the author's choice of parody from the other types of comment and criticism that traditionally have had a claim to fair use protection as transformative works. . . .

Parody presents a difficult case. Parody's humor, or in any event its comment, necessarily springs from recognizable allusion to its object through distorted imitation. Its art lies in the tension between a known original and its parodic twin. When parody takes aim at a particular original work, the parody must be able to "conjure up" at least enough of that original to make the object of its critical wit recognizable. . . . Using some characteristic features cannot be avoided. . . .

It is true, of course, that 2 Live Crew copied the characteristic opening bass riff (or musical phrase) of the original, and true that the words of the first line copy the Orbison lyrics. But if quotation of the opening riff and the first line may be said to go to the "heart" of the original, the heart is also what most readily conjures up the song for parody, and it is the heart at which parody takes aim.

Copying does not become excessive in relation to parodic purpose merely because the portion taken was the original's heart. If 2 Live Crew had copied a significantly less memorable part of the original, it is difficult to see how its parodic character would have come through.

This is not, of course, to say that anyone who calls himself a parodist can skim the cream and get away scot free. In parody, as in news reporting, . . . context is everything, and the question of fairness asks what else the parodist did besides go to the heart of the original.

It is significant that 2 Live Crew not only copied the first line of the original, but thereafter departed markedly from the Orbison lyrics for its own ends. 2 Live Crew not only copied the bass riff and repeated it, but also produced otherwise distinctive sounds, interposing "scraper" noise, overlaying the music with solos in different keys, and altering the drum beat.

Suffice it to say here that, as to the lyrics, we think . . . that "no more was taken than necessary," . . . [Moreover] there was no evidence that a potential rap market was harmed in any way by 2 Live Crew's parody, rap version. The fact that 2 Live Crew's parody sold as part of a collection of rap songs says very little about the parody's effect on a market for a rap version of the original, either of the music alone or of the music with its lyrics. . . .

We therefore reverse the judgment of the Court of Appeals and remand for further proceedings consistent with this opinion.

Exercises

1. Set out Justice Souter's key argument (in the box above) that affirmed that The 2 Live Crew's version "Pretty Woman" was allowable as a parody under the fair use law.

2. Discuss how the Court compared the two songs and reasoned that The 2 live Crew song "Pretty Woman" was a parody of "Oh Pretty Woman."

3. Since that decision, the book *The Wind Done Gone*, a takeoff (parody?) on *Gone With the Wind* faced a similar challenge. The novel is a retelling of the 1936 saga *Gone With the Wind* from the perspective of a slave, a half-sister of Scarlett O'Hara. The estate of Margaret Mitchell, author of *Gone With the Wind*, sued on the grounds that the book violated copyright protections. Research this later controversy (e.g., there are articles via the Internet) and write two to three paragraphs comparing it to the case, above, on the 2 Live Crew's parody of "Oh Pretty Woman."

4. Think of all the Disney films using or retelling tales and myths, such as *Pocahontas, Little Mermaid, Snow White, Beauty and the Beast, Aladdin.*
   a. Do you think there are any objections to Disney drawing from (cannibalizing?) earlier works?
   b. Does the fact that Disney's is a filmic version of a <u>fictional</u> work make a difference?

5. You've been hired by the producers of a new film, *La Casa Is Blanca.* It is an updated and stylized version of *Casablanca,* the film classic, but is now set in Mexico in the early 1980s. The movie features a dashing, handsome Latino helping refugees escape the repressive conditions in Guatemala and Nicaragua. The producers of *Casablanca* are unhappy. They argue that this new film is *not* a parody. Rather, it is a story of heroism and romance with some similarities to the original *Casablanca.* Discuss the issue and concerns you will face in getting *La Casa Is Blanca* released.

6. In two to three paragraphs respond to Dan Gilmore who says,

   Cultural works and inventions don't spring from an utter vacuum. They are the product of other people's ideas and works. Practically every melodic theme in music comes from older works, for example.

   Snow White was in the public domain before Disney got around to using her to make money. Victor Hugo must be spinning in his grave at the way Disney has turned the *Hunchback of Notre Dame* into a ridiculous cartoon—but Disney can do this, can create new ways to look at cultural icons, because the public domain exists. (See "Copyright Tempest over '*The Wind Done Gone,*'" *Siliconvalley.com,* 24 Apr. 2001)

Cause-and-Effect Reasoning

The second major kind of inductive argument is cause-and-effect reasoning. It may be hard to think of cause-and-effect arguments as inductive, because causal relationships are often presented as if they were certain. Nevertheless, there are uncertainties in causal reasoning.

It is also possible to confuse correlation with cause. Just because there may be a correlation between two events does not mean they are causally connected. For example, one pattern that has held for a number of years is that the direction of the Dow Jones Industrial Index predicts whether the AFC or the NFC will win the Super Bowl, but there is no causal connection between them.

Basics of Cause-and-Effect Reasoning

Cause-and-effect arguments present us with probability, not certainty. It is claimed that the stated condition will result in a particular effect. How likely it is becomes the issue. We often see cause-and-effect arguments in reasoning about health and disease.

For example, your doctor says, "It is probably a virus that is <u>causing</u> you to feel weak and tired all the time, because the antibiotics I prescribed didn't do anything. It's not bacteria, so it must be a virus." The doctor is not absolutely certain what is causing your problem. In eliminating one possible cause, she figures a virus is the likely culprit. Prognoses are, similarly, inductive; in fact they are predictions based on the given facts of the case, along with what is known about analogous cases.

Causal reasoning is particularly important in fields like medicine and scientific research, where empirical studies are an integral part of the research and theorizing. The fact that such reasoning is inductive does not mean it isn't taken seriously. The degree of probability may have an enormous impact on decisions people make. Following are some examples of causal claims.

Examples of causal claims:

- Gulf vets with a host of strange symptoms "link" their ailments to vaccines intended to protect them against biochemical warfare.
- Workers at an atomic weapons factory who made uranium metal for nuclear bombs died at significantly younger ages and suffered a higher incidence of lung, intestinal, and blood cancers than the American population as a whole, according to an analysis of their medical records.
- An Oxford University researcher theorized that AIDS might have entered the human population in a bizarre series of malaria experiments done between 1920 and the 1950s in which researchers innoculated themselves and prisoners with fresh blood from chimpanzees or mangabeys. Both chimpanzees and mangabeys are known to carry a virus similar to HIV2.

Exercises

Part One

Directions: List possible causes of the effect or event mentioned.

1. Your neighbor's burglar alarm goes off and continues for over an hour. You bang on their door, but get no response, although both of their cars are on the street. Thirty minutes later it is quiet.
2. At 7:40 a.m. you go out to start your car and there is only a grating sound.
3. One evening you are sitting in your living room, watching TV, and you hear a loud sound in the direction of your back yard. You look out and realize there is a helicopter aiming a bright light at your yard and at the two neighbors' yards south of your house.
4. Over 300 people are on a flight from Montreal to Los Angeles. They stop in Chicago to refuel and bring on food. After landing, 158 people complain of dizziness, nausea, and vomiting. Upon investigating, the airline discovers everyone who felt ill had eaten the chicken Kiev.

5. Ramona lives in a working-class neighborhood and attends an urban college where most students are commuters. She works part-time at a copy shop. One day Ramona left her class and discovered a deep scratch mark the entire length of her car.

Part Two

1. Read the two cases below and then answer the questions that follow:

Case 1:
In the early 1980s in Woburn, Massachusetts 14 children came down with leukemia. (This case was the basis for a book and movie called *A Civil Action*.) The families of the sick children got their water from the town wells G and H. The major industry near the neighborhood was the W.R. Grace Company. Barrels of the company's chemical waste were located near wells G and H. Grace employees testified that they had dumped the chemicals behind the plant into the ground or saw others do so. The Aberjona River was also located near the wells.

Case 2:
Fifteen thousand banana workers who work with pesticides and who are now sterile are suing companies (Dow Chemical, Shell Oil, Standard Fruit Co., Chiquita Brands, Inc.) that manufacture and use a chemical DBCP (dibromochloropropane, a pesticide). Their lawyer asserts: "DBCP was developed by Dow and Shell to combat microscopic worms that attack banana plants. It was widely used in 1968. Banana workers who applied the chemicals had no protective clothes or gloves. The chemical was banned in the U.S. in 1979, but shipped to Central American countries, even though it was thought to cause sterilization. Eight thousand Costa Rican workers are apparently sterilized and they blame DBCP, which they worked with." (For a discussion see *Multinational Monitor*, July/August 1990)

Answer the following:
a. What is the most likely cause of the effect cited?
b. What are three alternatives to the probable cause you cited in a?
c. What are two to three ideas for investigating further to determine the cause?

2. Read about a report on TDA in breast milk and then answer the questions that follow.

A scientist, Dr. David Black, discovered a cancer-causing chemical, TDA, in the breast milk of women who had breast implants covered with polyurethane foam. He reported that the hazard to infants was "minor" and said women exposed to secondhand smoke passed on a greater amount of carcinogens to babies through their breast milk. Surgitek, the manufacturer of the breast implant, disputed his report, though Surgitek had hired Dr. Black to undertake the study. Dr. Black's colleague, Mark Faulkner, is reported to have said, "When we got the results off the machine, my spine chilled." (Sandra Blakeslee, "Doctor Links Implants to Cancer Agent in Breast Milk," *The New York Times*, 2 June 1991)

Answer the following:

a. Assuming that Dr. Black's study can be duplicated and is, therefore, verifiable, is his information sufficient to tell women with the foam-covered implant not to breast-feed their babies?

b. What further information should we obtain before setting down policy recommendations on these implants?

c. List the strengths and weaknesses of Dr. Black comparing the risk of the carcinogen in foam-covered implants to that which comes from exposure to secondhand smoke.

Part Three

1. Set out the issues and concerns raised by the excerpt on dioxin below. Draw up a list of questions you would like answered before you could conclude that tampons using chlorine products are safe for women:

> Dioxin, which has been called the most toxic substance ever created by humans, is a class of halogenated aromatic hydrocarbons. The most potent is one of the contaminants present in Agent Orange, the defoliant used extensively during the Vietnam War, and which is thought to be the cause of a variety of health problems experienced by veterans of this war. The effect of dioxin on human health is still being debated by scientists. . . .
>
> Recently, some attention has been drawn to the presence of dioxins in tampons. Dioxin is a by-product of the chlorine bleaching process used to bleach tampons. In 1992, a congressional committee examining the public health risk of dioxin came across FDA reports which had previously not been made public. In these studies, there were trace levels of dioxin found in commercially produced tampons. There were memos discovered which indicated that as far back as 1989, scientists at the FDA believed that the risk of the presence of dioxin in tampons was high, and that further studies testing such levels needed to be done. The FDA never pursued this issue. Instead, they relied on data provided by U.S. tampon manufacturers. . . .
>
> Currently, the tampon industry faces surprisingly little regulations from the FDA (menstrual products are considered medical devices, and as such, fall under the FDA's regulation). Both the industry and the FDA have failed to protect women from negative health effects in the past; in 1980, 38 women died from tampon-related toxic shock syndrome. There was a class action suit filed against the manufacturers of Playtex and Tampax tampons, alleging that companies knew of the increased risk of TSS posed by super-absorbent rayon fibers used in most tampons today for more than ten years. Given this history of overlooking or downplaying the risk to women from menstrual products, as well as the marginalization of many other women's health issues, it seems reasonable to assume that an objective analysis of the presence and effects of dioxin in these products is needed, and the regulatory mechanisms and guidelines for this industry need to be evaluated and reformed to better protect women's health. (See Beth Ann Filiano, "Dioxin and Women's Health," Columbia University School of Public Health, 3 Dec. 1996, *www.webnet/terrafemme/dioxin.filiano.htm*)

2. Read about a case of an altercation outside a store, resulting in a lawsuit against the city, then answer the questions that follow. Here's the case:

A white man is suing the city because police failed to respond to his seven calls to 911 (emergency). An angry crowd gathered outside his store after he ran out of stereo speakers that were on sale. It seemed he only had five such items in stock. He offered to order more, but the crowd accused him of exploiting them (they were all Filipino) and started screaming. He claimed they made threats. The crowd dispersed after a half hour and no damage was done to his store. Nevertheless, the store-owner is suing the city for $1 million dollars. He insists the police's failure to respond put him at risk and he has suffered a nervous disorder ever since.

Answer the following:
   a. If you were on the jury—what more would you need to know before you would consider the man deserving of any settlement?
   b. What more would you want to know before you would rule in favor of the city?
   c. What are the pros and cons of throwing out the case for insufficient evidence?

3. You have been hired to represent 10 states that are to be compensated by the federal government because of their incineration of poisonous chemicals, including sarin and nerve gas. In light of the excerpt below, what questions do you want to direct to the U.S. governmental agency overseeing the burning of the deadly chemicals? The report was issued by the General Accounting Office and can be accessed online, if you'd like to read it, go to *www.gao.gov.*

As the Army begins to step up its effort to destroy its stockpiles of chemical weapons, a new Congressional report says thousands of people who live near three chemical depots face an unnecessarily high risk in case of an accident in incinerating the gases. . . . The Army has already destroyed about 7000 tons of chemical agents on Johnston Atoll, south of Hawaii, and at Tooele, Utah, complying with a 1985 law that spelled the end of the chemical weapons stockpile. There was a small leak of gas at the Tooele incinerator in May 2000, but there have been no serious injuries in the process.

But as the destruction program moves toward the far more populated area of Anniston next year, local officials and residents have been critical of the federal government's emergency planning. Emergency officials in Calhoun County, the site of the Anniston Army Depot, have refused to accept the government's recommendation that 35,000 residents who live too close to the depot to evacuate should plan to tape their houses with plastic sheeting if a major leak occurs. . . . The federal government had agreed to equip 28 schools and other buildings [in Alabama] with overpressurization devices that would keep outside air from entering and allow the buildings to be used as shelters in case of an accident. . . .

The official in charge of the Alabama chemical depot urged Governor Siegelman [of Alabama] not to delay the opening of the incinerator, noting that the rockets containing the deadly chemicals—sarin and VX nerve gas—had begun to deteriorate. "It is the stockpile that poses the danger to the public, not the incinerator," said Lt. Col. Bruce E. Williams, commander of Anniston Chemical Activity. "The incinerator is the solution. Delaying the destruction of the rockets does not serve the community's interests—it just delays the removal of the problem." (See David Firestone, "Report Faults U.S. Planning in Burning Chemical Arms," *The New York Times*, 17 Aug. 2001) *Update:* On March 28, 2002, Alabama Governor Siegelman's spokesman said the governor was confident FEMA would work with the state to provide safety gear.

False Correlations

As we know from our study of fallacies in Chapter 4, sometimes people draw causal connections between events that are unrelated. We see it in post hoc reasoning where an inference is drawn that something causes another thing to happen just because it happened at an earlier time. Of course, the fact that one thing precedes another does not necessarily mean they are related. To think they are is to draw a *false correlation*. To assert such a relationship requires more evidence than the temporal sequence of when the two events happened. Rather, we need to show that there are causal—not just temporal—links between them.

We can see this at work in the following example, an unpublished study on the links between abortion and the drop in crime. In an attempt to explain the drop in crime in the 90s, researchers pointed out that it could be related to the legalization of abortion in 1973. Here's how: "Many women whose children would have been most likely to commit crimes as young adults instead chose to abort their pregnancies. Because of that, a disproportionate number of would-be criminals in the 1990s were not born in the 1970s (as cited in "Study Links Dip in Crime to Abortions," *Los Angeles Times*, 9 Aug. 1999).

Consider the conclusions researchers drew, however. The fact there is lower crime could be due to the fact that fewer would-be criminals were born 20 years earlier. But that could be a false correlation. Perhaps there is a drop in crime because the society has changed, or perhaps because the educational system is better, or maybe because of the deterrent effect of current sentencing laws. It may also be due to a rise in women breast-feeding their babies, making them more psychologically stable. And on, and on. Without more evidence linking abortion laws to crime statistics, the presumed correlation leaves a lot to the imagination.

▦ Arguments Based on Statistical Studies

People frequently rest their argument on the basis of some statistical data or study. We need to know how to properly use statistical studies to recognize the strong arguments and not be fooled by the weak ones.

For instance, suppose someone said, "A study of 150 men at a Dallas university revealed that 54 percent had used recreational drugs; therefore, we can conclude that 54 percent of Americans have used recreational drugs." Is this good reasoning?

- If you said, "No," pat yourself on the back.
- If you said, "Yes," fear not, you can be helped, so read on.

A statistical study has several factors: One, a targeted population about whom we want information and, two, the sample group we intend to study as a a microcosm of the larger group. In certain sorts of statistical studies, such as medical experiments, psychological testing, or pharmaceutical studies, research protocol may call for a control group. This group is used to compare relative responses, for example, to a medical treatment or drug regimen, in order to eliminate other factors. In such cases, members of the control group are usually given some sort of placebo (e.g., a "pill," like candy, that has no medicinal value) to prevent the subjects from knowing whether or not they are in the control group or the experimental/sample group.

Once we gather evidence from the sample study, we'll generalize to the larger, targeted population, allowing for a certain "margin of error." The margin of error recognizes that the inference from the smaller, sample group to the targeted population is a bit iffy. The study sample may or may not be representative of the whole. In statistical studies, there are always uncertainties, even in the most elaborate, well-crafted cases.

Words of Advice

Realize that, if you really want to learn statistics, you need at least a semester course. This is extremely valuable, whatever your career goals. However, we can get a general overview of statistical studies. This is what we will try to do here.

Three Key Aspects of a Statistical Study

Date	→	What is the date of the study? Is it still relevant?
Size	→	How big was the sample group?
Diversity	→	How diverse is the sample population? Is it representative of the target population?

Importance of Date

A statistical study done 10 years ago may be out of date. Even the results of a study done five years ago could be worthless. Try to find current research for your data.

Think of AIDS research. A great deal has happened in the last 10 years. Recent studies are more likely to be reliable than ones done in the past. Also, think how much has shifted in terms of DNA research. And what about media research? Or research on methods of communication? Ten years ago, most people did not have VCRs. Forty years ago many people had no television sets. Personal computers are relatively recent additions to most homes. But their presence in our lives has had a tremendous impact. And think how much has changed since we got e-mail. We can communicate with people around the globe in a matter of minutes, or even seconds. This is far more powerful than telephones, because we can ship documents, letters, essays, and the like around the world as attachments. It has the potential to transform free access to information in the same way we see with the Internet.

Consequently, when we examine statistical studies, we want to pay attention to the date they were conducted. Consider their relevance, as well as any potential obstacles that may decrease their currency.

Importance of Size

Next, is the issue of sample size. If we have only a small sample population and generalize to an entire city, our results would be of negligible value.

For example, a study of 25 people in a city of 500,000 would have limited value. In fact, the fallacy of hasty generalization occurs when the sample size is too small. This happens, for instance, when people make generalizations about a type of ethnic food on the basis of one or two meals. A good study requires a large enough sample to avoid the problem of insufficient evidence.

Importance of Diversity

Last, is the issue of the diversity of the sample. The sample should be representative of the population in question. This means it should have sufficient diversity, preferably with that diversity comparable to the diversity of the target population.

Two Major Ways to Get Sufficient Diversity in a Sample Study

1. *Representative Sample.* A representative sample is obtained by trying to match the sample group with the target population. Try to keep a balance of the major aspects to consider (like gender, age, race, religion, education, class, geography).
2. *Random sample.* A random sample is *not* obtained by carefully orchestrating a sample group taking into account the relevant factors (like age, gender, nationality, class). In a random sample, each member of the target population has an equal chance of being studied. We get a random sample by using some numerical means (like every third person is polled, every sixth driver is stopped, every tenth voter is interviewed) with a sufficient quantity. Hopefully then we can generate enough diversity to reflect the target population.

For example, in the mid 80s, a study of the San Pedro, California, police found that officers pulled over people suspected of being drunk. The group had a striking absence of white or wealthy drivers. In the face of suspected prejudice (unwarranted assumptions), the police department instituted a change. They opted for random sampling, pulling over every sixth driver. Using this technique, *everyone* had an equal chance of being checked. The result was that those tested ranged across all racial groups, ages, and economic levels.

CASE STUDY

Men versus Women: Whose Listening?

Do women and men use the same parts of their brains, or the same amount of brainpower when they listen and think? Long a topic of conversation is the question of whether the biological differences between men and women affect our cognitive skills. Recent research has thrown a few logs on the fire.

A study at the Indiana University School of Medicine discovered that men listened only with one side of their brains, whereas women used both sides. Read each report and then answer the questions that follow.

1. State the key findings set out in each report.
2. Discuss the way the testimony of the researcher contributes to the overall message of the report.
3. Note some inferences that might be drawn on the basis of the report.
4. After you've examined each report, briefly compare the three reports and note key differences.

CNN Report on 28 Nov. 2000:

It's no surprise for many women—new research suggests men listen with only one side of their brain, while women use both. But scientists involved in the study cautioned the findings don't offer concrete evidence that women are better listeners than men—a question lead researcher Dr. Michael Phillips calls too "dangerous to ask" at this point in his research.

"Our brain findings on listening do not mean that either men or women do it better or worse, they just appear to do it differently," said Phillips, a neuro-radiologist at the Indiana University School of Medicine, Indianapolis.

In his study of 10 men and 10 women, Phillips said brain scans showed that men lis-

tened to language using mostly the left sides of their brains, while women appeared to use both sides. . . . "We're not really suggesting anything about ability or performance of the task," Phillips said. "But what we have shown here is that the processing is different. . . . It may mean that men and women's brains are different." (See Troy Goodman, "Do Men Really Just Listen with Half a Brain? Research Sheds Some Light," *CNN.com*, 28 Nov. 2000)

Chicago Tribune report on 28 Nov. 2000:

[S]tudies have suggested that women "can handle listening to two conversations at once, a sort of cocktail-party phenomenon," said Dr. Joseph T. Lurito, an assistant radiology professor at Indiana University School of Medicine. "One of the reasons may be that they have more brain devoted to it."

In Lurito's listening study of 10 men and 10 women, presented today at the Radiological Society of North America's annual meeting, sophisticated brain scans called fMRI—functional magnetic resonance imaging—showed that men mostly used the left sides of their brains, the region above the left ear long associated with understanding language. But somewhat surprisingly, Lurito said, the study suggested women use both sides.

The findings might seem humbling for the all-male research team, and Lurito acknowledged they were "feeling a little uneasy because we could be set up here." The results, however, don't necessarily mean women are better listeners, he argued. Another interpretation, Lurito suggested, "is that it's harder for them," since they apparently need to use more of their brains than men to do the same task. (See Lindsey Tanner, "Study: Men Use Less Brain in Listening than Women," *Chicago News Tribune*, 28 Nov. 2000)

***Los Angeles Times* report on 29 Nov. 2000:**
The new study is the latest addition to a growing catalog of research suggesting that the mental divide between the sexes is more complex and more rooted in the fundamental biology of the brain that many scientists had once suspected.

"As scientists, we're figuring out what normal is, and more and more often it seems that normal for men may be different than normal for women," said Indiana radiologist Dr. Micheal Phillips, co-author of the study. "That doesn't mean one is better than the others." . . .

Some of those differences appear to evolve throughout a lifetime. The brains of aging men

and women have significant structural and functional differences, recent research reveals. Men's brains are larger but are more damaged by the aging process; women's brains seem to work more efficiently and appear to age more successfully. . . .

"Our research suggests language processing is different between men and women, but it doesn't necessarily mean performance is going to be different," said Indiana radiologist and co-author Dr. Joseph T. Lurito. "We don't know if the difference is because of the way we're raised or if it's hard wired in the brain. We will never be able to figure that out completely." (See Robert Lee Hotz, "Women Use More of Brain When Listening, Study Says," *Los Angeles Times*, 29 Nov. 2000)

Fallacious Use of Statistics

There are two types of fallacies that frequently show up in statistical reasoning. (See Chapter 4 on fallacies for a fuller discussion). It is wise to be on the lookout for them, as you will certainly come across them at one time or another. These two fallacies are as follows:

- *Hasty Generalization.* → If the size is simply too small, a generalization from it could result in the fallacy of hasty generalization. These are commonly seen in stereotypical reasoning based on a sample of one or two. If the sample size is not sufficient, avoid drawing a generalization.
- *Biased Statistics.* → If the size is sufficient, a random sample will likely result in a sample representative of the target population. For example, in studies of human behavior, such issues as gender, race, religion, class, age, education, and geography might be factored in to fulfill the diversity quotient. The failure to do this results in the fallacy called biased statistics.

Group Exercise

The following "health tips" rest on research using statistical studies. Discuss the issues and concerns for each health tip and what questions we'd want answered before concluding that the tip should be a guideline for good health. Which of the tips are most credible, most believable? List them from 1 to 6, most credible to least credible tip and say why. Note any reasoning you find questionable:

Health tip 1:
Painkillers given to women during labor increase fivefold the likelihood of the child growing up to be a drug user. New research undertaken at Gothenburg University suggests that exposure in the womb to high-dose medication may be an important and preventable risk factor for later substance abuse. (See *Metro,* 19 Oct. 2000, as noted by *www.globalideasbank.org*)

Health tip 2:
Recent research suggests that vegetarian mothers are more likely to give birth to girls. Pauline Hudson, a pregnancy expert at the University of Nottingham, also found that vegetarian mothers had a significantly lower risk of giving birth to premature, under-weight, or stillborn babies. High magnesium, potassium and calcium levels were also shown to have an effect on gender, producing more boys, although there is no evidence to suggest that a vegetarian diet is deficient in these elements. (See *London Times,* 7 Aug. 2000, as noted by *www.globalideasbank.org*)

Health tip 3:
Some genetic learning disorders in people appear to be caused by a defect in their metabolism of essential fatty acids, found in salmon, tuna, trout, sardine, and mackeral. Researchby B. Jacqueline Stordy and Malcolm J. Nichol showed that children with both the inattention and hyperactivity/impulsivity forms of ADHD displayed signs of fatty acid deficiency. After 3 months, the group receiving the LCP [fatty acid] supplement displayed significant improvements in the average scores for cognitive problems, behavior problems and anxiety. (See *www.drstordy.com*)

Health tip 4:
Smoking is bad for your gums: Results of a new study indicated that teenage smokers are nearly three times as likely as their nonsmoking peers to have gum disease in their mid-20's. According to the authors of the study, the longer teenagers smoked, the greater the extent of gum disease. (*Community Dentistry and Oral Epidemiology,* April 2001, as noted by *www.coloradohealthnet.org*)

Health tip 5:
Ecstasy users could be ruining their long-term health. The recreational drug ecstasy could damage users' body clocks, making them feel permanently jet-lagged, scientists have said. Research carried out by Dr. Stephany Biello, a psychologist at Glasgow University, suggests that ecstasy disrupts the sensitive clock mechanism in the brain by damaging cells that contain serotonin. Serotonin carries messages between nerves and is thought to play a role in regulating sleep patterns in humans as well as their mood, memory, perception of pain, appetite and libido. The damage caused in humans could be permanent as research indicates that once a serotonin pathway is damaged it can never repair itself. (See "Ecstasy 'Ruins Body Clock,'" *news.bbc.co.uk,* 24 June 2000)

Health tip 6:
A study by doctors at the University of Maryland has found that people who fail to raise a smile in stressful or uncomfortable situations may be more likely to develop heart problems. The researchers interviewed 150 people who had either suffered a heart attack or had undergone bypass surgery. Their attitudes were compared with

150 healthy people of the same age. Participants were asked how they would react to a number of uncomfortable everyday situations. These included arriving at a party to find somebody else wearing the same outfit and having a waiter spill a drink over them at a restaurant. The researchers found that people with a history of heart problems were more likely to get angry or hostile rather than laugh or use humour to overcome the embarrassment of the situation. People with previous heart conditions were also less likely to laugh even in positive situations. (See "Laughter 'Protects the Heart,'" *news.bbc.co.uk*, 15 Nov. 2000)

Confronting Problems in Statistical Studies

What should you do if a study has problems? For instance, did you wonder about health tip 6, above? If someone who had a heart attack is less likely to laugh, what should we infer? We may conclude, as in the tip, that the person's heart attack was the *result* of failing to laugh enough. However, it may be that the heart attack was *due to* an excessive amount of laughing and, thus, the victim has no desire to take up laughing to the degree prior to the cardiac arrest.

Alternatively, perhaps the heart attack victim finds a great deal hilarious afterward, but finds a few topics (e.g., death, heart failure, doctors, hospital gowns) not at all funny, thus lowering the patient's laugh-quotient and throwing off the statistical study. Without more information, it may be unwise to conclude that we should bring comedians into hospital cardiac wards. Statistical studies cannot always be taken at face value.

We might also question a study done of only 10 men and 10 women. Was that a sufficient sample size? What race or ethnicity were the men and women? Can we assume that a small size is adequate and leaving out race and ethnicity is not a problem? These are questions we might want answered.

It may be that we are faced with a study that has some problems, so we need to decide what to do next. If we cannot retake our study (no time to get a larger sample group or more diverse sample group) but we want to ensure that our argument is as strong as it can be, what can we do to draw a conclusion about all students?

When the study is in doubt, basically we have these choices: (1) throw it out (in the event of serious concerns) or (2) examine the study's margin of error. Every study contains a margin of error. Because the inference from the sample study to the target population contains a wedge of doubt, this ought to be reflected in the conclusion.

That is, instead of going from x percent of the sampled group to x percent of the target population, a margin of error should be added to the conclusion. This would mean that your conclusion would change to "x plus or minus z percent of A's are B's," (where z is some little number, usually 5 or lower).

The Margin of Error

The smaller the margin of error z, the better. In well-orchestrated studies like those we see in the Gallup Poll, the margin of error is usually 2 or 3 percent. A margin of error over 5 percent may indicate a less reliable study. Mathematician Matthew Delaney considers a 5 percent margin of error hard to achieve and, therefore, it may be unrealistic to think a study can achieve this level of accuracy.

Remember the margin of error means the range goes from $-z$ percent to $+z$ percent, which is a range of $2z$. This means if your margin of error is 3 percent, then the range is 6 percent and a margin of error of 5 percent will give a range of 10 percent, which is significant range. For example, 32 percent plus or minus 5 percent means the range goes from 27 percent to 37 percent—a range of 10 percentage points!

Two Forms of Statistical Arguments

There are two prevalent forms of statistical arguments: (1) statistical syllogisms and (2) inductive generalizations. Let's look at each of them.

Form of a statistical syllogism:

x percent of A is a B.

p is an A.

Therefore, p is a B.

A statistical syllogism involves two premises. The first claims that a percentage of the subject class has some predicated characteristic. Then we are given an individual member of the class and conclude that (here's the inductive aspect of the reasoning) what was said of class A then applies to the individual member. Of course, the wedge of doubt is whether the individual member is in the x percent of A, or in the remaining $100 - x$ percent of A that don't have the predicated characteristic B. Here are some examples.

Statistical syllogism example 1:

Eighty-six percent of women in Louisiana like shrimp creole.

Natalie is a woman living in Louisiana.

Therefore, Natalie likes shrimp creole.

Statistical syllogism example 2:

Sixty-five percent of cats prefer birds to mice for dinner.

Prince is a cat.

Therefore, Prince prefers birds to mice for dinner.

The strength of a statistical syllogism is directly proportionate to the percentage. The closer to 100 percent in an affirmative claim, the better the argument. Basically, 85 percent and up is pretty strong, the higher the better. But the lower the percentage, the more questionable is the truth of the conclusion.

The second major kind of statistical reasoning is called an inductive generalization. In this case, we infer that what is true about the sample group is true of the targeted population as a whole. The wedge of doubt here comes in the leap from the sample (about whom we know some statistical data) to the targeted population of which the sample merely represents. As we know, the sample may not exactly resemble the whole group, so it is uncertain whether something true of the sample is really true of the larger group of which it is a part.

Form of an inductive generalization:

x percent of A's polled (or sampled) are Bs.

Therefore, x percent of all As are Bs.

In an inductive generalization we generalize a sample group to the target population. We then infer what was true of the sample group will also be true for the target population. Here are some examples.

Inductive generalization example 1:

Forty-eight percent of men polled outside the discount rug store in San Luis Obispo said they thought the president was doing a good job.

Therefore, 48 percent of American men think the president is doing a good job.

Inductive generalization example 2:

Seventy-three percent of the people in the Taos radio poll said the United States should not invade Haiti.

Therefore, 73 percent of people in Taos think the United States should not invade Haiti.

In a strong Inductive Generalization, watch for date, size, and diversity. Be sure the poll is recent, the size not too small, and the sample group representative of the target population. The issue of diversity (that the sample represents the larger group) is crucial.

A Word of Advice

Be aware that there is a lot more to statistics than the two inductive arguments discussed here. A thorough knowledge of statistical methods is vital for anyone going into math, business, psychology, sociology, economics, or clinical studies. Moreover, not all arguments using statistics are inductive. For example,

A toss of the coin will result in a 50 percent chance of getting heads.

Joe tossed the coin.

So, there's a 50 percent chance Joe will get heads.

This argument is deductive, because the premises are sufficient for the conclusion and there is no wedge of doubt between the premises and the conclusion.

If you are familiar these two inductive arguments based on statistics, you will be able to handle these two common forms. These two forms, the statistical syllogism, and the inductive generalization, are arguments frequently encountered. The exercises below will help you analyze these two forms of argument when you come across them.

Exercises

1. Here is an inductive generalization:
   <u>Seventy-nine percent of men in the bank poll prefer beer to wine.</u>
   Therefore, 79 percent of men who work in the bank prefer beer to wine.
   a. What would you need to know to determine whether or not this is a good inductive generalization? (What are the criteria?)
   b. What could you do to strengthen the argument, if you cannot take the poll again?

2. Discuss whether the following arguments are strong statistical syllogisms:
   a. Eighty-two percent of all women love sports cars.
      <u>Evangelina is a woman.</u>
      Therefore, Evangelina loves sports cars.
   b. Ninety-five percent of mechanics have mood swings.
      <u>Harry is a mechanic.</u>
      So, Harry has mood swings.
   c. Sixty-seven percent of air traffic controllers have problems with stress.
      <u>Gilbert is an air traffic controller.</u>
      So Gilbert has problems with stress.
   d. Eighty-one percent of computer technicians have well-groomed hands.
      <u>Yassir is a computer technician.</u>
      So, Yassir has well-groomed hands.
   e. Sixty-two percent of electricians prefer incandescent to fluorescent lighting.
      <u>Leah is an electrician.</u>
      So, Leah prefers incandescent to fluorescent lighting.
   f. Seventy-four percent of gardeners prefer mulch to fertilizer.
      <u>Tim is a gardener.</u>
      So, Tim prefers mulch to fertilizer.

3. Give an example of a strong statistical syllogism and explain why it is strong.

4. Give an example of a fairly strong, but not extremely strong, statistical syllogism.

5. Give an example of a weak statistical syllogism, explaining why it is weak.

6. State if this a good inductive generalization (explain):

   A telephone poll was taken in Oakland at noon on a Wednesday in April of 1994. Sixty-three percent of the people in the poll said they thought illegal aliens should be deported, even if they have families in the United States. The conclusion was then drawn that sixty-three percent of the people in Oakland must think illegal aliens should be deported, even if they have families in the United States.

7. Give your assessment of the value of the poll results of this study:

   Prof. Stramel did a poll of college students at Santa Monica College. Because he sample group had a disproportionately large number of Asian Americans in it compared to the number enrolled at the college, he calculated a margin of error of 8 percent.

CHAPTER FOURTEEN

Handling Claims, Drawing Inferences

It is absurd. The protons are positive and the electrons are negative, and, of the two, I am sure that the electrons are nicer. I hate a positive proton. They think they know everything. It is "This is so" and "That is so," until you want to smack them in the face. With the world in the state it is in today, nobody can be as positive as all that.

—ROBERT BENCHLEY

Feeling sluggish with your fever, you head off to the UCLA Medical Center to get some blood drawn. You don't imagine there'll be much to the form you are required to sign in order to get the blood test. It looks like the same old six and seven, until the next to last paragraph. Tucked into the paragraph labeled "Teaching and Research Institution" you find the following that you are being asked to assent to: "I further understand that the University of California, including UCLA Healthcare, may review and use medical information and specimens for teaching, study, and research purposes, including the development of potentially commercially useful products."

Your head bounces off the ceiling, as you leap up from your chair. As you pat the goose egg forming on the top of your skull, you try to decide: "Do I sign this and forego all commercial rights to my DNA—or do I forget about this blood test for now and pay for my own blood test elsewhere?" It's times like these you're glad you studied critical thinking. We need to know how to handle claims. Otherwise, we may come across assertions and be unsure of what exactly is being said and what in the world they mean. Also, we need to know what we are asserting when we make claims and what others might justifiably infer on the basis of our claims.

To see why this is useful, consider two court cases of the last decade. On August 10, 2000, the conviction of Sandy Murphy and Rick Tabish for the murder of Las Vegas millionaire Ted Binion was called into question. It seems that juror #10,

Joan Sanders, submitted to the court a potentially-explosive sworn affidavit. She admitted that, "I changed my vote to guilty when it was told to me by the other jurors, 'if you are in the house when a person dies, and do nothing to assist, that is murder.'" (See "Affidavit of Joan Sanders,"*www.courttv.com)*. In another case, actress Kim Basinger was sued for breaking the contract over the movie *Boxing Helena*. The verdict in favor of the producer was reversed by the appellate court—because the court ruled that the jury instructions were simply ambiguous. Here's why: The jury instructions used the phrase "and/or" in asking the jury to determine whether it was Kim Basinger personally or her corporation, Mighty Wind, that entered into the contract.

We don't have to be trapped by logic to learn it. Knowing the tools of logic helps us work within systems already in place. It's sort of like x-ray vision: A firm grasp of logic gives us the ability to see how arguments are structured, to organize that reasoning, and to dismantle it so it can be evaluated. This is both useful and empowering. What we will do in this chapter is go deeper into analysis and critical thinking skills by examining the different types of claims and learn techniques for handling those claims.

▦ Propositions

A proposition, or claim, asserts something is or is not the case. These are all propositions: "The car rolled out into the street," "Chicago is in Illinois," "John Lennon was a Beatle." Propositions are not normally expressed as questions or exclamations, unless those are rhetorical forms of an assertion.

In classical logic, moral claims (like "You ought to eat spinach" or "Assault guns should be illegal") were not treated as propositions, because of the difficulty in assigning a truth-value. That does not mean such claims are just a matter of opinion. But you cannot normally say they are "true" or "false" with the same degree of certainty attached to empirical claims.

Different Kinds of Propositions

Ultimately, moral claims were allowed into logic, with the understanding that there may not be an agreement over truth or falsity. We proceed by assuming the truth-value and then seeing the role a moral claim will play in the argument. Since any proposition can be assigned (or have an assumed) truth-value, there are exactly three kinds of propositions.

The Three Kinds of Propositions

- *Tautologies:* Propositions that are always true—or true by definition.
- *Contradictions:* Propositions that are always false—or false by definition.
- *Contingent Claims:* Propositions that are not necessarily true or false, but are dependent on what is going on in the world to determine the truth-value. This would include claims for which the truth-value is unknown.

Examples of tautologies:
- Either you did or you did not hear a seal bark.
- If B. B. King is the king of blues, then B. B. King is the king of blues.
- It is false that my car has gas but it does not have gas.

Examples of contradictions:
- Nelson Mandela is a Canadian and yet he is not a Canadian.
- Bananas are fruit, but bananas are not fruit.
- It is false that, if my car does not have gas then my car does not have gas.

Examples of contingent claims:
- It is raining in Portland.
- My name is Geronimo.
- If that is a beautiful sunset, Ansel is taking a photograph.

Most claims are contingent, since the context may vary, along with the parameters that determine whether the claim is true or false. For example, the claim, "It's roasting outside," is contingent because it may be true on one day, but not the next. Most of what we say is relative to a particular time and place and, so, such claims are contingent. We need also to be able to handle claims where the truth-value is unknown. These are sentences whose truth-value simply cannot be determined, for example, because we do not have the means or knowledge to ascertain if they are true or false as in the claim, "There is intelligent life existing on planets other than earth with more highly developed means of communication than we have." The evidence is not in yet on that one.

Propositions of unknown truth-value are not useless, but there are some limitations. We can use the propositions and draw inferences, but we cannot make any claims about the soundness of the argument (because that would require us to know the claim is actually true). These are relatives of contingent claims, but here we simply lack enough information to determine the truth-value.

Structure of Propositions

A proposition is either simple or compound. A *simple* proposition is one that is at the atomic level—that is, it does not contains any of the logical connectives "and," "or", "not, "if . . . then," or "if and only if." A proposition that contains any of the five logical connectives is considered *compound*.

Examples of simple propositions:
- Kimosabe wolfed down a beef burrito he found on the street.
- Swiss cheese has holes in it.
- Twenty-five percent of headache remedies have caffeine in them.

Examples of compound propositions:
- Kimosabe wolfed down a beef burrito and its paper wrapping.
- Either Kimosabe wolfed down a beef burrito or I was mistaken.
- If Kimosabe wolfs down a beef burrito, then he won't eat his crunchies.
- Kimosabe did not eat the shoe.
- Kimosabe eats paper if and only if there is food on it.

The Five Types of Compound Propositions
1. *Conjunctions:* Propositions of the form "A and B."
2. *Disjunctions:* Propositions of the form "Either A or B."
3. *Negations:* Propositions of the form "Not A."
4. *Conditional claims:* Propositions of the form "if A then B" or "B only if A."
5. *Biconditional claims (Equivalence):* Propositions of the form "A if and only if B."

Let us look at each of the compound propositions below.

Conjunctions

These are propositions of the form "P and Q," where P and Q are each called *conjuncts*. A conjunction is a proposition that asserts two things are true at the same time. This means the conjunction is true only if both conjuncts are true. Otherwise, it is false.

Examples of conjunctions:
- John plays guitar and Paul plays bass.
- Both broccoli and carrots are vegetables.

Alternative Constructions of Conjunctions.   A proposition does not have to contain "and" to be a conjunction. It could have alternative words or phrases that function the same as an "and," so be on the lookout. When you spy an alternative, toss it out and replace it with "and" so we have a uniform way of setting up propositions. Otherwise, it's just too easy to make mistakes. In the list below are some terms that can be replaced by "and." If you think of others, add them to the list.

Alternatives to "and":

However	Although
But	In addition
Also	As well/As well as
Moreover	Furthermore
Additionally	Plus

Disjunctions

These are propositions of the form "P or Q," where P and Q are each called *disjuncts*. A disjunction is a proposition that claims either one or the other, or both.

Examples of disjunctions:
- There is Ellen or someone who looks a lot like her.
- Either ghosts or burglars are in the attic making noise.

Note: Disjunctions in logic are inclusive. The " Either/or *or both*" makes the claim an "inclusive or." This means a disjunction is true if either one *or both* of the two disjuncts are true. This contrasts with the everyday use of "either/or" which usually is treated as an exclusion not allowing both disjuncts to be true at the same time; for instance, we see the exclusive "or" used in restaurant options. To the question, "Do you want soup *or* salad?" if you say, "Both!" you'll probably be hit with an extra charge.

Negations

These are of the form "not P." A negated proposition has the opposite truth-value of the original statement. A negation of a proposition is true only if the proposition itself is false.

> ***Examples of negations:***
> *The negation of:*   Galileo is the governor of Ohio.
> It is not the case that Galileo is the governor of Ohio.
>   → Galileo is not the governor of Ohio.
>
> *The negation of:*   Chocolate is not a health food.
> It is not the case that chocolate is not a health food.
>   → Chocolate *is* a health food.

If the original statement is negative, then the negation of it will be positive. In the second example, the double negative leads to a positive. This will be discussed further below.

Special Constructions of Negations.   Two special forms of negations are the "Neither/nor" and "Not both." Basically, with a "neither/nor" claim both options are eliminated (i.e., "Not this *and* not that"). With "not both" one of the two options is eliminated (i.e., "not this *or* not that"). We will learn how to handle these later in the chapter, along with other types of negated propositions.

Conditional Claims

These are of the form "If P then Q," where P is called the *antecedent* and Q is called the *consequent*. A conditional claim is true in every case except when the antecedent condition P is true and the consequent Q is false. Sometimes the "then" is omitted, so add it for clarification.

> ***Examples of "If . . . then" claims:***
> • If Vicky goes to Saskatchewan, then she'll take Ben.
> • You'll feel stuffed if you eat too many tamales.
>   *Rewrite as:* If you eat too many tamales, then you'll feel stuffed.
> • Stan will go to Ottawa, if he can get plane tickets.
>   *Rewrite as:* If he can get plane tickets, then Stan will go to Ottawa."
> • Being able to climb Mt. Hood is sufficient to make Gary happy.
>   *Rewrite as:* If he is able to climb Mt. Hood, then Gary will be happy.
> • A sufficient condition of Fred's gaining weight is to eat an entire pizza.
>   *Rewrite as:* If he eats an entire pizza, then Fred will gain weight.

Alternative Constructions of Conditional Claims.   Other forms of conditional claims include "P only if Q," "Q is necessary for P," "A necessary condition of P is Q," "P unless Q," and "Without P, then Q." We will look at the "unless" and "without" forms later in the chapter.

The "Only If" Construction.   Propositions of the form "A only if B" assert that, "If B does not happen, then A won't happen either." In other words, "A only if B" can be rewritten "If not B then not A" or "If A then B."

Restructuring an "Only if" proposition

P **only if** Q   P happens only if Q does.
→ If **not** Q then **not** P   If you don't have Q, you won't have P
→ If P then Q   So, if P occurs, so must Q.

Examples of "Only if" claims:
The parrot will go in his cage only if he's forced.
→ If he's not forced, the parrot will not go in his cage.
→ If the parrot went in his cage, then he was forced.

Watering the pear tree is necessary for it to bear fruit.
→ If we don't water the pear tree, then it won't bear fruit.
→ If it bears fruit, then we watered the pear tree.

Helpful Hints about Conditional Claims.   There are two parts to a conditional claim "If P then Q"—the antecedent P and the consequent Q. Be aware that the antecedent may not be listed before the consequent. Locate the "If" and the antecedent immediately follows. The *consequent* is what is said to follow from the antecedent condition. It is located after the "then". Be careful, though, because the consequent is sometimes expressed *before* the antecedent. For example, "We will dance all night, *if* the band plays until dawn." The consequent is "we will dance all night." When this occurs, rewrite the sentence in the form of an "If . . . then" claim and locate the consequent after the "then."

Handling Alternative Constructions of Conditional Claims.   "P if Q," "only if Q, then P," or "P only if Q," can all be rewritten in the "If . . . then" form. Be sure to make the necessary adjustments and add negatives when required. Below are some suggestions that should help clarify this:

Laying Out the Structure of a Conditional Claim

If <u>that is my pet bird, Wellie,</u> **then** <u>he will come down from the tree.</u>
      ↓   ↓
     Antecedent   Consequent

Example of Locating the Antecedent and Consequent.   If we have a conditional claim, make sure it is in the "If . . . then" form and then you can easily locate the antecedent and consequent. We can see how to do this in the following proposition:

We'd better call 911 **if** someone is hurt in the accident.
Rewrite as:

If <u>someone is hurt in the accident</u> **then** <u>we'd better call 911</u>.

           ↓   ↓

       Antecedent   **Consequent**

Once we have restructured it as an "If . . . then" claim, reading the antecedent and consequent becomes much easier. The antecedent then can be found between the "if" and the "then," whereas the consequent is the proposition that follows the "then."

Equivalence (Biconditional Propositions)

Two propositions are equivalent if they assert the same thing. The resulting proposition is called a *biconditional.* "P is equivalent to Q" is the same as "If P then Q, and if Q then P." When that occurs, you can say "P if and only if Q."

Any two equivalent propositions have the same truth-value; they are either both true or both false. It is impossible for A to be equivalent to B when A is true and B is false (or vice versa). *Note:* The term "equivalent to" can be expressed as an "if and only if" (sometimes abbreviated as "iff").

Example of a biconditional:
That Robert is addicted to cocaine is equivalent to his being physiologically dependent on it.
→ Robert is addicted to cocaine *if and only* if he is physiologically dependent on it.
→ If he is physiologically dependent on it, then Robert is addicted to cocaine, and if he is addicted to cocaine, then he is physiologically dependent on it.

We have now covered all five logical connectives. If a proposition contains none of these connectives, it is a simple proposition. If it contains at least one logical connective, it is called compound.

Categorical Propositions

For certain types of analysis, employing categorical propositions is most helpful. It enables us to quickly determine if an argument is valid. (See especially the next chapter, Chapter 15, on syllogisms). As you may recall, valid arguments are ones in which the premises provide sufficient support for drawing the conclusion. Here are the four different forms of categorical propositions:

The Forms of Categorical Propositions

All P is Q.	This is called an "A" claim.
No P is Q.	This is called an "E" claim.
Some P is Q.	This is called an "I" claim.
Some P is not Q.	This is called an "O" claim.

You probably wondered where we place claims like, "Charlie is a good ole boy" and claims like "Fifty-four percent of toddlers prefer hot milk at bedtime." Propositions containing proper nouns as the subject are considered A or E claims, relative to being positive or negative. Propositions of the form "x percent of A is B" (where x is neither 100 nor zero) are treated as I or O claims, relative to being positive or negative.

Examples of categorical propositions:
- A claim: All burnt muffins are inedible pastry.
- E claim: No burnt muffin is a tasty treat.
- O claim: Some burnt muffins are not good breakfast food.
- I claim: Some burnt muffins are good substitutes for hockey pucks.

The Quantity of a Proposition.   The quantity of a proposition answers the question, "How much?" In other words, the quantity refers to how much of the subject class is said to have something predicated of it. The possible answer is "universal" or "particular" (i.e., all or some of it).

Quantity is Universal Or Particular

Universal: "All P is Q" and "No P is Q."
Particular: "Some P is Q" and "Some P is not Q."

A and E   → **Universal claims**
I and O   → **Particular claims**

The Quality of a Proposition.   The quality of a proposition answers, "Are you asserting something *is* or *is not* the case?" You are either affirming that it is the case, so the quality of the proposition is positive, or denying it, so the quality of the proposition is negative.

Quality Is Positive or Negative

Positive: "All P is Q" and "Some P is Q."
Negative: "No P is Q" and "Some P is not Q."

A and I   → **Positive claims**
E and O   → **Negative claims**

Examples of Universal Claims:
All football players are burly.
Anyone who can paint with watercolors is talented.
→ A claims are universal and A claims are positive.
→ This proposition is <u>universal positive</u>.

No wind instrument has strings.
→ E claims are universal and E claims are negative.
→ This proposition is <u>universal negative</u>.

Universal Positive Propositions.   There are many ways to say "all" or none; to indicate we are referring to all the members of the subject class.

Every	Any
One hundred percent	If . . . then . . .
Without exception	The entire
Whatever	Whenever
Whoever	Whichever
Whomever	However (when used as "all the ways")

Universal Negative Propositions.   Propositions that are universal negative can take a number of different forms. Replace these with "no" and treat as E claims:

None	Zero percent of . . .
Not any	If . . . then not . . .
All . . . are not	Not a one is
Nary a one is . . .	Not even one
Whatever . . . is not . . .	Whenever . . . is not
Whoever . . . is not . . .	Whichever . . . is not

Be careful: "Not every . . . is . . ." is *not* the same as "No . . . is . . ." or "None." "Not every" is equivalent to "Some . . . are not. . . ." For example, "Not every musician is talented" is equivalent to "Some musicians are not talented."

Special Constructions of Universal Claims.   A proposition that has a proper noun as the subject is treated as a universal claim.

   Examples of propositions with proper nouns as subjects:
   Shan is an artist who can operate an airbrush.
   → Treat as a universal positive claim.
   → Classify as an A claim.

   The Statue of Liberty is not in Rhode Island.
   → Treat as a universal negative claim.
   → Classify as an E claim.

Particular Claims.   These are propositions that can be expressed in the form of "Some . . . are/are not. . . ." These include the following:

   Examples of particular claims:

Most . . . are/are not . . .	A few . . . are/are not . . .
Lots of . . . are/are not . . .	Many . . . are/are not . . .
Much of . . . are/are not . . .	A bunch of . . . are/are not . . .
Several . . . are/are not . . .	Almost all . . . are/are not . . .
Not all . . . are . . .	More than a few of . . . are/are not . . .
Not every . . . are . . .	At least one of . . . are/are not . . .

Special Constructions of Particular Claims.   Most important, a proposition of the form "*x* percent of P's are Q's" where *x* is neither 100 percent nor 0 percent would be treated as a particular claim. Even if the percentage is 99 percent it's not *all* and, therefore, cannot be considered a universal claim.

Examples of particular claims with statistical quantifiers:

- "Fifty-nine percent of acrobats are bicyclists" is a particular positive proposition, and would be classified as an I claim.
- "Eighty-two percent of phone calls are not solicitations" is a particular negative proposition, and would be classified as an O claim.
- "Ninety-six percent of librarians are helpful people" is a particular positive proposition (an I claim).
- "Seventy-five percent of restaurant cakes are not as delicious as a homemade pie" is a particular negative proposition (an O claim).

Exercises

Part One

Directions: State the quantity and quality of the categorical propositions below and identify the proposition as A, E, I, or O.

1. All chocolate is a sinful food.
2. No dog is an animal that likes lettuce.
3. Some skunks are not animals that like mornings.
4. All fish are creatures with scales.
5. Some snakes are not poisonous reptiles.
6. Some macaws are sociable birds.
7. No raccoon is a native of Baffin Island.
8. All the mammals in Ruth's backyard are deer.
9. Some radiologists are not people who are scared of dentists.
10. No Shakespearean actor is a person who needs memory lessons.
11. Some wombats are vicious beasts when angered.
12. All diners who eat their peas with a knife are folks who like cornbread.
13. Some people who sing at the top of their lungs are courteous drivers.
14. All dogs are animals capable of eating slippers.
15. Some diners are fond of chimichangas.
16. Aki is an awfully well behaved pup for his age.
17. No well-behaved pup is a dog that shreds couches.
18. Some animals that shred couches are disobedient cats.
19. Some couch-shredders are children.
20. All photographers are people who like the unexpected.

Part Two

Directions: Rewrite the propositions below in categorical form and then state the quantity and quality.

1. Not all islanders know how to swim.
2. Most fish are relaxed in the water.
3. Lots of ice skaters have strong leg muscles.
4. A few baseball players chew tobacco.
5. Any Sumo wrestler likes a back rub.
6. Not all football players are fearful people.
7. Badminton players are not bodybuilders.
8. Most hawks have powerful beaks and piercing eyes.
9. Any woman who takes up snorkeling has a good sense of humor.
10. Several karate students were injured in the park.
11. A couple of hikers got frostbitten last night.
12. Whenever you go surfing watch out for jellyfish.
13. Some rock climbing is dangerous.
14. Almost all dancers are graceful.
15. Very few roller skaters are self-conscious.
16. Not a one of the burly men ate the tortilla soup.
17. Some of the frostbitten hikers wore slippers to bed.
18. A few of the badminton players threw tantrums on the court.
19. Not every islander tolerates rambunctious boys.
20. Just about all horror movies disturb a sensitive woman.
21. Many a Sumo wrestler enjoys edamame beans and Miso soup.
22. Most people who drive a car with a V8 engine put milk in their tea.
23. None of the dim sum was left in the dish.
24. Ginny Lou was not happy with the lumpy grits on her plate.
25. None of the snorkeling women got tangled up in the coral reefs.

Symbolizing Propositions

To analyze an argument, we need to see its structure. Logicians prefer a symbolic language using variable (letters of the alphabet) and logical connectives. The result is a kind of logical x-ray. It makes the structure explicit and provides a handy shorthand method so sentences and arguments can be examined easily and quickly.

LOGICAL CONNECTIVES	SYMBOL	EXPRESSION	ALTERNATIVES
and	&	P & Q	$\wedge$ and $\bullet$
or	$\vee$	P $\vee$ Q	none
if . . . then . . .	$\rightarrow$	P $\rightarrow$ Q	$\supset$
if and only if . . .	$\equiv$	P $\equiv$ Q	$\leftrightarrow$
not	$\sim$	$\sim$ P	none

Note: "P if and only if Q" could also be expressed "P is equivalent to Q," with the connective then referred to as equivalence.

Translations.   When symbolizing a sentence, mark all the *logical connectives.* Symbolize simple propositions with capital letters (A, B, C, etc.). Pick a letter that corresponds with a key word in the proposition in question; otherwise it's going to be hard to look at the finished translation and double check it for accuracy.

Steps to Translating a Proposition

Symbolizing a Proposition.   Translate the following proposition:

If I run out of gas, **then** my car will stop.

Step 1: Unpack the structure.   We do this by examining the hierarchy of the connectives. This proposition's structure is straightforward, because there is only one connective. The structure is:

If (I run out of gas) **then** (my car will stop).

This is a conditional claim, with antecedent "I run out of gas" and consequent "My car will stop."

Step 2: Assign Variables To Component Propositions.   Replace the antecedent and consequent with variables (A, B, C, etc.). These are: "I run out of gas" and "my car will stop." Let variables—letters of the alphabet—stand for the propositions.

Assign: R = "I'll run out of gas"
S = "my car will stop."

Be careful: Assign a different variable for one and only one proposition at a time. Never use the same variable for two different propositions, or the resulting translation will be incorrect. Pick something obvious.

Step 3: Replace Component Propositions with the Assigned Variable.
Rewrite as: If R then S.

Step 4: Put Symbols in Place of All the Logical Connectives.   In this case, the $\rightarrow$ goes in the place where the "then" is located.

Translation: R $\rightarrow$ S

Translating Another Proposition

Let us translate the sentence: "If I eat sausages and potatoes, then I'll either get sick or fat."

Step 1. Unpack the Structure.   We have:

If (I eat sausages <u>and</u> potatoes) **then** (I'll either get sick <u>or</u> fat).

Note: the main connective in **bold** is the "if . . . then. . . ." The antecedent is "I eat sausages and potatoes" and the consequent is "I'll either get sick or fat." Because both the antecedent and consequent are compound propositions, we have to mark those logical connectives too. They are underlined above.

Step 2. Assign Variables to Component Propositions.

Assign: S = "I eat sausages"   P = "I eat potatoes"
G = "I'll get sick"   F = "I'll get fat"

We are now ready to substitute the variables into the proposition:

If (I eat sausages and I eat potatoes) then (either I'll get sick or I'll get fat).

Step 3. Replace Component Propositions with the Assigned Variables.

Rewrite as: If (S and P) then (G or F).

Step 4. Replace Connectives with Their Symbols.   We are almost done! All we have to do is put in symbols for the connectives and that's it.

Translation: $(S \,\&\, P) \rightarrow (G \lor F)$

Punctuation and Precision

Being sloppy with punctuation can be a disaster. If we are not precise with the punctuation, we may end up with a proposition that can be misinterpreted. In turn, we may end up with a translation saying something different than the original proposition. Because of this, we need to learn precision. Don't despair, though, because precision is a useful trait to have. Precision is not a snooty matter at all. In fact, it may prevent a crisis.

Think of it this way: Do you want a sloppy brain surgeon cutting into your cerebellum? Do you want a pilot who is not very precise with the controls when you are 33,000 feet up in the air? Do you want your car mechanic using imprecise calipers when adjusting your car's brakes? Absolutely not!

So we should be careful with punctuation and try to be as precise as we can. As a convention, start with parentheses, then use square brackets, then use curly brackets. For example,

$$P \lor [Q \rightarrow (R \,\&\, S)]$$

This expresses the proposition of the form:

Either P or, if Q then, both R and S.

This is the form of the claim:

> Either rats are in the walls or, if there are squirrels in the walls, then, they are awfully large and make high screeching sounds.

The superstructure of this proposition is a disjunction. The first disjunct is P and the second disjunct is "If Q then both R and S." We now have a convention that allows all of us to use the same packaging and easily read complex propositions.

Exercises

Directions: Translate the following sentences using variables and logical connectives. Use the letters indicated as your variables.

1. If I eat that sausage, I'll be poisoned. (E, P)
2. Both termites and butterflies are insects. (T, B)
3. It is not true that moths are carnivores. (M)
4. If another snail gets in my garden and chomps holes in the violets, then I will show no mercy. (S, C, M)
5. If Emmy Lou Harris cancels the concert, then Jody will be unhappy and take solace in music by the Soggy Bottom Mountain Boys. (E, J, S)
6. Either the grasshoppers ate the begonia or something weird is going on. (G, W)
7. If the medfly returns and the city sprays pesticides, then we are in trouble. (M, G, T)
8. Wellington will get sick if he eats that sow bug. (W, S)
9. Either the cat was stolen or was carted off by the coyotes last night. (S, C)
10. If the files are sent and the computer crashes, we'll be in trouble. (F, C, T)
11. Chicken soup and vitamin C help fight a cold. (S, V)
12. If mosquitoes are in the room and keep up buzzing, Carlos won't be able to sleep. (M, K, C)
13. Brazilian flamethrowers and violets are in bloom, but the poppies look dead. (B, V, P)
14. Chemistry is a useful subject, if you plan to be a doctor. (C, P)
15. If both Angie and Raphael quit fighting, then we can eat dinner. (A, R, D)
16. If Tina does more typing, her eyes will bulge and become bright red. (T, B, R)
17. If Anita sprays insecticide, the aphids will die, but if she wants to avoid toxic chemicals, she'll kill them by hand. (S, D, W, K)
18. He is a famous movie star, but Georgina forgot his name. (M, G)
19. Although Ralph was not an android, he was unusual. (A, U)

20. It is not true that if Vera does not smoke, she won't get lung cancer. (V, L)

21. If Ernesto takes either physics or statistics next semester, he'll cut back on his part-time job at the courthouse. (P, S, C)

22. Either both Bruce and Ryan are wearing their costumes to the party, or they will stay home and make popcorn balls. (B, R, S, P)

23. If Ernesto takes both physics and anthropology next semester, he'll quit his racketball lessons. (P, A, Q)

24. Anita will either yank out the ivy and plant primroses, or she will dig up the wilted Peruvian lily and replace it with a potato vine. (I, P, D, R).

25. Only if Anita yanks out the ivy will Gary help her with the primroses. (A, G)

26. Only if Gary helps with the primroses will Anita be able to clear space before lunch. (G, A).

27. Ryan falling on the new potato vine was sufficient to make Anita unhappy and Gary frustrated. (R, A, G)

28. Evan planted loquat seeds in the yard, but Connolly showed no interest in gardening. (E, C)

29. If both Paul and Evan go to Chicago, then Laurel will be able to work only if she gets help with the baby. (P, E, L, H)

30. If the morning glories spread to the fence and overtake the roses, then we'll have to cut them back; but if they don't get invasive, the morning glories will do fine in the garden. (S, O, C, I, F)

Rules of Replacement for Ordinary Language

Here are some techniques for treating different sentence structures that we commonly encounter. We will be looking at 12 different rules for replacing one claim with a logically equivalent form.

Rules of Replacement for Ordinary Language

1. *Only.* "Only" functions as an exclusion narrowing down the territory of the predicated class. Any proposition of the form "Only P is Q" can be rewritten: "If not P, then not Q." This is also equivalent to "All Q is P." Propositions of the form "Only P is Q" are symbolized as follows:

Forms of "Only P Is Q" $(\sim P \to \sim Q) \equiv (Q \to P)$
Only P is Q.
→ If it's not P, then it's not Q.
→ If it's a Q, then it's a P.

Example 1 of "Only":
Only Americans eat hamburgers.
→ If they are not Americans, they won't eat hamburgers.
→ All people who eat hamburgers are Americans.
Translation: ~A → ~H (form 1)   or   H → A (form 2)

Example 2 of "Only":
Only skinny women can be models.
→ If she's not skinny, she can't be a model.
→ All models are skinny.
Translation: ~S → ~M (form 1)   or   M → S (form 2)

See how the exclusion works? In the first example, the use of "only" narrows down those who eat hamburgers to Americans—everyone else is excluded. In the second example, "only" limits those who can be models to skinny women; everyone else is excluded.

2. *The Only.* Another exclusion is "The only." Here it is the subject being restricted; not the predicate as above. Any proposition of the form "The only P is Q" can be rewritten: "If not Q then not P." This is also equivalent to "All P is Q." Propositions of the form "The only P is Q" are symbolized as follows:

Forms of "The only P is Q"   (~ Q → ~ P) ≡ (P → Q)
The only P is Q.
→ If it's not Q then, it's not P.
→ If it's a P, then it's a Q.
→ All P's are Q's.

Example 1 of "The only":
The only woman for Romeo is Juliet.
→ If she's not Juliet, then she's not the woman for Romeo.
→ If she's the woman for Romeo, then she's Juliet.
Translation: ~J → ~W (form 1)   or   W → J (form 2)

Example 2 of "The only":
The only outer gear the count owns is a cape.
→ If it's not a cape, it's not outer gear the count owns.
→ All the outer gear the count owns are capes.
Translation: ~C → ~O (form 1)   or   O → C (form 2)

See how the exclusion works? In the first example, "The only" limits women for Romeo to Juliet; all other women are excluded. In the second example, "The only" limits outer gear the count owns to capes; everything else is excluded.

The Connection between "Only" and "The Only." We can change an "Only" claim to one that starts with "The only." If we focus on the object, we can see how they relate. Look at this example first:

"The only woman for Romeo is Juliet" *is the same as:*
"Only Juliet is the woman for Romeo."

Do you see what happened? In both cases, the object of Romeo's affection is Juliet. And this can be expressed using either "The only" or "Only," but the terms are switched. In other words:

"The only P is Q" *is equivalent to* **"Only Q is P."**

So we can move back and forth between them, but need to switch the order of the terms, P and Q, in doing so.

3. *Unless.* Propositions of the form "P unless Q" can be expressed as either a conditional claim or a disjunction. As a conditional claim it can be written, "If not Q then P." The restricted condition Q is the one thing that can stop P from happening. In other words, if you don't have Q, then P occurs. The second way to write "P unless Q" is in the form, "Either P or Q." To get to this second construction, just toss out the "unless" and replace it with "or" (or "Either/or") and you are done.

> **Forms of "P unless Q"** $(\sim Q \rightarrow P) \equiv (P \lor Q)$
> P unless Q.
> $\rightarrow$ If not Q then P.
> $\rightarrow$ Either P or Q.

> *Example 1 of "unless":*
> We will go on a picnic unless it rains.
> $\rightarrow$ If it does not rain, we will go on a picnic.
> $\rightarrow$ Either we went on a picnic or it rained.
> *Translation:* $\sim R \rightarrow P$ (form 1)   or $R \lor P$ (form 2)

> *Example 2 of "unless":*
> Unless Joe stops the car, he's going to hit the moose.
> $\rightarrow$ If Joe does not stop the car, he's going to hit the moose.
> $\rightarrow$ Either Joe stops the car or he's going to hit the moose.
> *Translation:* $\sim M \rightarrow J$ (form 1)   or $M \lor J$ (form 2)

Alternatives to "Unless."   An alternative to unless is <u>without</u>. It is treated exactly the same as unless, so would be rewritten in either form (the conditional, or the disjunction). So, you would translate "Without ice cream, pie is bland," as "If you do not have ice cream, your pie will be bland."

4. *Sufficient.* "P is sufficient for Q" asserts that Q will happen whenever P occurs. In other words, "P is sufficient for Q" is equivalent to "If P then Q." This is symbolized $P \rightarrow Q$.

> **Form of "P is sufficient for Q"** $P \rightarrow Q$
> P is sufficient for Q.
> $\rightarrow$ If P then Q.

Example 1 of "sufficient":
Traveling to Montreal is sufficient for seeing maple leaves.
→ If you travel to Montreal then you will see maple leaves.
Translation: $T \rightarrow S$

Example 2 of "sufficient":
Getting free airfare to Tokyo would be sufficient for my going there.
→ If I get free airfare to Tokyo, I will go there.
Translation: $F \rightarrow G$

Alternatives to "Sufficient." Another phrase that functions the same as "sufficient" is *provided that.* So, you would translate "I'll take flute lessons, provided that you take up the electric guitar" as "If you take up the electric guitar, then I'll take flute lessons."

5. *Necessary.* "P is necessary for Q" asserts that Q won't happen without P. That is, if you don't have P, you won't have Q. So if you have Q, you must also have P.

   Forms of "P is necessary for Q" $(\sim P \rightarrow \sim Q) \equiv (Q \rightarrow P)$
   P is necessary for Q.
   → If not P then not Q.
   → If Q then P.

   Example 1 of "necessary":
   Oxygen is necessary to stay alive.
   → If you do not have oxygen, you cannot live.
   → If you live, then you had oxygen.
   Translation: $\sim O \rightarrow \sim L$ (form 1)   or $L \rightarrow O$ (form 2)

   Example 2 of "necessary":
   Gas in the tank is necessary for my car to be driven to work.
   → If I don't have gas in the tank, I won't be able to drive to work.
   → If I am able to drive to work, then I had gas in the tank.
   Translation: $\sim G \rightarrow \sim D$ (form 1)   or $D \rightarrow G$ (form 2)

Relationship between "Necessary" and "Only." If we say something is necessary for something else, we are saying the second thing will happen *only* if the first one does. In other words, "P is necessary for Q" is the same as "Q only if P." So, if not P, then not Q (if P is not the case, then Q is not the case). This means, as the equivalent expressions in the examples showed us, that "Q only if P" can also be written "If Q then P."

6. *The Evers: Whenever, Whoever, Whatever, Wherever, Never, and special constructions of However.* Any proposition with the "—ever" construction should be treated as a universal claim. They can be rewritten as conditional claims. This is symbolized $P \rightarrow Q$.

Forms of the "evers"   P → Q
Whenever P is Q.
→ If P then Q

Note: This also applies to whatever, whoever, wherever constructions. It applies to "however" constructions in the form of "whatever way," rather than functioning as a conjunction. It does not apply to "never" (see "Negations," below).

Example 1 of the "evers":
Whenever you go on your vacation, it rains.
→ If you go on your vacation, then it rains.

Example 2 of the "evers":
Whoever is hiding behind the tree, is making grunting sounds.
→ If someone is hiding behind the tree, then that person is making grunting sounds.

Example 3 of the "evers":
However you tie the bow, it looks silly.
→ If you tie the bow, then it looks silly.

7. *Negations:* "P is never Q," "It is not true that P," "Not only P is Q," "Not just P is Q," "It is false that P." This is the same as putting the negative in front of the claim being negated.

Form of a double negative
It is not true that P is not the case.
→ P is the case. (Or just P.)

Form of "never"
P is never Q.
→ No P is Q.
→ If P then not Q.

Example of a "never":
Men can never experience pregnancy.
→ If it's a man, then he cannot experience pregnancy.
→ No man can experience pregnancy.

Form of "not all"
Not all P is Q.
→ Some P is not Q.

Example of "Not all":
Not all snakes are poisonous.
→ Some snakes are not poisonous.

Form of "not none"
It is not the case that no P is Q.
→ Some P is Q.

Basically this is a double negative. If there's not none, there are some. If it's not true that no cat bites its owner, then there is some cat that bites its owner.

Examples of a "Not none" and "Not no one":
It is false that no sauces are fattening.
→ Some sauces are fattening.

It's not true that no one can sing the national anthem.
→ Some people can sing the national anthem.

Form of "not only"
Not only P is Q.
→ Some Q is not P.

Example of "Not only":
Not only turnips are vegetables.
→ Some vegetables are not turnips.

Form of "not just"
Not just P is Q".
→ Some Q is not P.

Note: Treat this form exactly the same as a "Not only" claim.

Example of "Not just":
Not just sculptors are artists.
→ Some artists are not sculptors.

Form of "Not If/then"
It's not true that if P then Q.
→ Some P is not Q.

Note: Treat this form exactly the same as a "Not all" claim.

Example of "Not if/then":
It's not true that if babies are thrown in the water they will swim.
→ Some babies are thrown in the water and they do not swim.

Overview of the Rules for Ordinary Language

Rules of Replacement for Ordinary Language

1. Only	Form 1:	*Only P is Q.*	If it's not P, then it's not Q.
	Form 2:	*Only P is Q.*	All Q is P.
2. The only	Form 1:	*The only P is Q.*	If it's not Q, then it's not P.
	Form 2:	*The only P is Q.*	All P is Q.
3. Unless	Form 1:	*P unless Q.*	If it's not Q, then P.
	Form 2:	*P unless Q.*	Either P or Q.
4. Sufficient	*P is sufficient for Q.*		If P then Q.

5. *Necessary*   Form 1:   *P is necessary for Q.*   If not P then not Q.
                  Form 2:   *P is necessary for Q.*   If Q then P.

6. *When/what/how/where/whoever*

   Form 1:   *When/what/how/where/whoever P is Q.*   If P then Q.
   Form 2:   *When/what/how/where/whoever P is Q.*   All P is Q.

7. *Negations*

   - *P is never Q.*   Form 1: No P is Q.
                                              Form 2: If P then not Q.

   - *Not all P is Q.*   Some P is not Q.
   - *Not none/not no one of P is Q.*   Some P is Q.
   - *Not only P is Q.*   Some Q is not P.
   - *Not just P is Q.*   Some Q is not P.
   - *It is not true that, if P then Q.*   Some P is not Q.

Formal Rules of Replacement

The remaining rules of replacement are not simply focused on replacing one expression in ordinary English with an equivalent one, but focus on logical structure. These rules provide the means to translate from one logical form to another equivalent form.

1. DeMorgan's Laws.   These are two special forms of negations. With the "Not both" construction, one of the choices is being denied—either the first option or the second one. With a "neither . . . nor . . ." construction, <u>both</u> options are being denied, the first choice <u>and</u> the second one. This can be expressed as follows:

DeMorgan's law 1: Not both $\sim (P \& Q) \equiv \sim P \lor \sim Q$
Not both P and Q.
→ It is not true that both P and Q is the case.
→ Either P is not the case or Q is not the case.

DeMorgan's Law 2: Neither/nor $\sim (P \lor Q) \equiv (\sim P \& \sim Q)$
Neither P nor Q
→ It is not true that either P or Q is the case.
→ P is not the case and Q is not the case.

Example 1 of "Not both":
Not both Kung Pao beef and lasagna are Chinese food.
→ Either Kung Pao beef is not Chinese food or lasagna is not Chinese food.

Example 2 of "Not both":
Jamie does not like both blue grass and jazz.
→ Jamie either does not like blue grass or she does not like jazz.

Example 1 of "Neither/nor":
Neither gnomes nor sylphs are found in the water.
→ Gnomes are not found in the water and sylphs are not found in the water.

Example 2 of "Neither/nor":
Varoush likes neither octopus nor squid.
→ Varoush does not like octopus and Varoush does not like squid.

2. *Transposition.* The rule of transposition allows us to flip the antecedent and consequent in a conditional claim—but doing so requires the terms to change to their opposites. In other words, transposing the antecedent and consequent is only acceptable if you also change the quality of each one at the same time. (In short, "flip and switch.") This rule can be expressed as follows:

Form of transposition $(P \rightarrow Q) \equiv (\sim Q \rightarrow \sim P)$
If P then Q.
→ If not Q then not P.

Example 1 of transposition:
If Lisa doesn't hurry, then she won't make it to school on time.
→ If Lisa made it to school on time, then she hurried.

Example 2 of transposition:
If Homer eats another plate of shrimp, then his stomach will burst.
→ If Homer's stomach doesn't burst, then he didn't eat another plate of shrimp.

3. *Material Implication.* Material implication allows you to go from a conditional claim (If . . . then) to a disjunction (Either/or), with one proviso. When we make the switch the first term is negated. In other words, "If there's mud, we need galoshes" can change to the disjunction, "Either there's *not* mud or we need galoshes." Do you see why the "not" had to be interjected?

Form of material implication $(P \rightarrow Q) \equiv (\sim P \vee Q)$
If P then Q.
→ Either not P or Q.

Example 1 of material implication:
If Casey does not stop screaming, then Christina will plug her ears.
→ Either Casey stopped screaming or Christina plugged her ears.

Example 2 of material implication:
Either the basement flooded or the sand bags worked.
→ If the basement did not flood, then the sand bags worked.

4. *Exportation.* This rule allows you to restructure a conditional claim with a conjunction in the antecedent. The form of exportation is this:

Form of exportation $[(A \, \& \, B) \rightarrow C] \equiv [A \rightarrow (B \rightarrow C)]$
If A and B, then C.
→ If A then, if B then C.

Note: Do you see how the second conjunct in the antecedent was shipped back to the consequent?

Example 1 of exportation:
If he spills paint and doesn't wipe it up, then there will be a mess.
→ If he spills paint, then, if he doesn't wipe it up, there will be a mess.

Example 2 of exportation:
If the flashlight's on, then, if we aim it in the cave, the bats fly out.
→ If the flashlight's on and we aim it in the cave, the bats fly out.

5. *Equivalence.* This is also known as a biconditional or "if and only if" claim. This rule allows us to set out the two component parts of a biconditional claim in two different ways.

Forms of biconditional propositions
"P if and only Q" can be written in two equivalent forms:
→ If P then Q, and, if Q then P.
→ If P then Q, and, if not P then not Q.
Translation of form 1: $(P \rightarrow Q) \,\&\, (Q \rightarrow P)$
Translation of form 2: $(P \rightarrow Q) \,\&\, (\sim P \rightarrow \sim Q)$

Example of equivalence:
Fish can swim *if and only if* they are in the water.
→ If fish are in the water then they can swim, and if fish can swim then they are in the water.
→ If fish are in the water then they can swim, and if fish are not in the water then they cannot swim.
Translation of form 1: $(F \rightarrow W) \,\&\, (W \rightarrow F)$
Translation of form 2: $(F \rightarrow W) \,\&\, (\sim F \rightarrow \sim W)$

Group Exercise

Symbolize the dialogue below using logical connectives and variables (use the first letter of the word in CAPS).

A Day in the Life of Violet and Percy

Scenario: Cats Violet and Percy are discussing names and nicknames for their kitten.

VIOLET: LULU is a good name for the kitten only if it's a girl. Otherwise we should call him UBU.
PERCY: Provided it's a BOY and we call him UBU, then I hope no one calls him LITTLE Boo.

VIOLET: If it's a BOY and, she names him UBU and nicknames him LITTLE Boo, then there's not MUCH we can do about it.

PERCY (examining the kitten): Being called LITTLE Boo is sufficient to make me WONDER about the human mind; however, neither SILLY names nor GOOFY nicknames deter me from loving our little family.

VIOLET (wiping a tear away with her paw): Not only are you the DEAREST cat I've ever met, but I am so HAPPY you are the father of our wonderful kitten. And if neither names nor nicknames matter to the heart, then we should not mind if he is called UBU and nicknamed LITTLE Boo.

PERCY (licking the top of her head): Unless you THROW me out of the third story window, I'll never LEAVE your side, my beloved Violet.

VIOLET (sniffing his nose): Having you by my SIDE is necessary for me to find FULFILLMENT in love; although only UBU sleeping at my side has made me appreciate the JOYS of being a mother!

The End.

Exercises

Part One

Directions Rewrite the following, without the underlined word or phrase using the appropriate rule.

1. <u>Only</u> blizzards stop Carol from working out at the gym.
2. <u>Unless</u> the fog rolls in, Carol is going with Sam to the movie.
3. <u>Neither</u> hurricanes <u>nor</u> floods bother Sam.
4. <u>Only if</u> there's an earthquake, will Carol be scared.
5. <u>Whenever</u> there's a tornado, Sam sleeps downstairs.
6. <u>The only</u> time Grandma screams is when she sees a dead possum.
7. <u>Not both</u> Percy and Ubu like liver.
8. Eating escargot is <u>sufficient</u> to disgust me.
9. Being tall <u>is necessary</u> for joining the basketball team.
10. <u>Neither</u> football <u>nor</u> soccer involves swimming.
11. <u>Only if</u> you shout, can I find you in the cave.
12. <u>Unless</u> there's mustard on the sandwich, the boys won't touch it.
13. <u>Whenever</u> Norm comes over, he helps the children.
14. <u>Without</u> chocolate, Mario's diet would be boring.
15. Candle light is <u>necessary</u> for a romantic evening.
16. Ubu eats crunchies, <u>provided that</u> he doesn't get liver.

17. <u>Without</u> a friend, the little boy is sad and lonely.
18. Not both bagels and croissants are French pastries.
19. <u>It is not the case that</u> all enchiladas are made with meat.
20. A letter from home is <u>sufficient</u> to make Kevin feel good.
21. Rewrite the following sentences as categorical propositions:
    a. Most surfers are both tan and muscular.
    b. Only nudity should be banned from the beach.
    c. Not all books are worth reading.
    d. Nobody is both ornery and easygoing.
    e. Whatever ate a hole in the sweater made grandpa angry.
    f. Being a swimmer is necessary to be a lifeguard.
    g. Being a belly dancer is sufficient to be exotic.
    h. The only time Michiko sings is in the shower.
22. Rewrite the following: It is not true that if you can drive a car you can tap dance.
23. Rewrite the following: Not just oatmeal sticks to your stomach.
24. Rewrite the following: Not only a howling wind creates atmosphere.
25. Rewrite the following: It is false that if you can dance, you can swim.

Part Two

Directions: Rewrite the following using the rule of replacement as indicated.

1. Using DeMorgan's law rewrite: Not both Oaxaca and Toronto are in Canada.
2. Using DeMorgan's law rewrite: Neither Taos nor Minneapolis are in Mexico.
3. Using material implication rewrite: Either snakes are taking over Guam or the news show exaggerated.
4. Using transposition rewrite: If that's jello, then it's not protoplasm.
5. Using transposition rewrite: If that's Fatso, then it's not Casper.
6. Using DeMorgan's law rewrite: Not both novels and poetry are on the shelf.
7. Using DeMorgan's law rewrite: Neither drama nor action films interest Omar.
8. Using exportation rewrite: If the book is stolen and she can't read the assignment, Anna will not be able to finish her homework.
9. Using material implication rewrite: If the tire's not flat, then we can go home.
10. Using material implication rewrite: Either the deliveryman is sick or his car is not working again.
11. Using material implication rewrite: If the pilots walk out, we can't make it to Toledo for the wedding.

12. Write out using equivalence: The workers will organize if and only if they have a leader.

13. Write out using equivalence: The doctors will strike if and only if the nurses walk out.

14. Using transposition rewrite: If Luis gets a new car, he'll sell his hot rod.

15. Using exportation rewrite: If that's not Larry and it's a burglar, then we better run out the backdoor.

16. Using material implication rewrite: If that's a burglar, then it's not Larry.

17. Using DeMorgan's law rewrite: Neither Hector nor Salazar are lonely.

18. Using DeMorgan's law rewrite: Not both Manda and Bob eat shrimp.

Part Three

1. Name the rule of replacement used below:
   a. If the dog eats George's burger, George will be upset. So, if George is not upset, then the dog did not eat George's burger.
   b. Not both Hector and George like poetry. So either Hector does not like poetry or George does not like poetry.
   c. Either the dog ate George's lunch or someone stole it. So, if the dog did not eat George's lunch, then someone stole it.
   d. Hector can make it on time if and only if the bridge is down. So, if Hector makes it on time, the bridge is down, and if Hector does not make it on time, then the bridge was not down.
   e. The dog did not eat Hector's fruit salad and he did not eat Carol's tofu. So, the dog ate neither Hector's fruit salad nor Carol's Tofu.
   f. If the dog ate Rose's ham salad sandwich, he might not have gone for George's burger. So either the dog did not eat Rose's ham salad sandwich or he might not have gone for George's burger.
   g. If Hector got lost and ran out of gas, it doesn't matter if the bridge is down. So, if Hector got lost then, if he ran out of gas, then it doesn't matter if the bridge is down.

2. Rewrite this without the "only": Only sore feet stop Carlos from his morning walk.

3. Rewrite in two ways without the "unless": Unless Ricky can handle a staple gun, she can't be a carpenter.

4. Write this without the "whenever": Whenever Ismail thinks of Malibu, he thinks of home.

5. Name the rule of replacement below:
   a. Either Max will wrestle down the carjacker or he'll dial 911. This is equivalent to: If Max does not wrestle down the carjacker, then he will dial 911.

    b. If Rochelle does not stop singing at the top of her lungs, she'll wake the neighbors. This is equivalent to: If Rochelle did not wake the neighbors, then she stopped singing at the top of her lungs.

    c. Not both Sylvester and Tweetie are birds. This means, either Sylvester is not a bird or Tweetie is not a bird.

6. Rewrite using transposition: If the painter keeps leaving lids off paint cans, his boss will be upset.

7. Rewrite without the "only if": Only if Alex learns to hold the hammer will he quit hitting his thumb.

Part Four

Directions: Rewrite the following sentences without the underlined word (and then symbolize if you can).

1. <u>Only</u> Indiana Jones and Wonder Woman know the secret code.

2. June will come to the spring dance <u>provided that</u> she gets a ride.

3. A <u>necessary condition</u> for peace accord is that both sides must stop biowarfare production.

4. Elizabeth will go see her parents <u>only if</u> she can go with them to the Garth Brooks concert.

5. It is <u>sufficient</u> for my cat to have fleas for me to bathe him today.

6. A <u>necessary condition</u> for giving Tony a bath is that he digs holes in the yard.

7. <u>Unless</u> Kimosabe leaves the skunk alone, he's going to be very sorry.

8. <u>Without</u> proper nutrition, your body will disintegrate.

9. <u>Whenever</u> Ernie stays up too late, his eyes are red and puffy.

10. <u>Only when</u> John plays racquetball, does he feel in top shape.

11. <u>Only</u> a truck driver would enjoy my cooking.

12. Seeing a tarantula is <u>sufficient</u> for a jolt to the system.

13. Reading a good novel is <u>necessary</u> to make Lucille happy.

14. <u>Neither</u> fishing <u>nor</u> hunting excite Uncle Bob.

15. <u>Only</u> if Jim finds a pencil, can he solve the crossword puzzle.

16. <u>It is not the case that</u> all chocolate is good for your teeth.

17. <u>Unless</u> Nguyen gets a radio, he can't listen to the ballgame.

18. <u>Without</u> his shoes on, Danny can't go into the restaurant.

19. Studying logic is <u>necessary</u> for Audrey to feel powerful.

20. Studying logic is <u>sufficient</u> for Ernie to be self-confident.

21. <u>Unless</u> Alice has a nap, she feels deprived.

22. <u>It is false that</u> all dentists are into torture.

23. <u>Not only</u> clams are slimy foods.

24. <u>Not any</u> squid I've eaten is tasty.

Part Five

1. Translate the following argument using logical connectives and variables:

   If George smokes and drinks too much, then he doesn't sleep well. (S, D, W)
   If he doesn't sleep well or doesn't eat well, then George feels rotten. (E, R)
   If George feels rotten, then he does not clean his room and does not do his homework. (C, H) George drinks too much.
   Therefore, George does not do his homework.

2. Translate the following argument using variables and logical connectives:

   There are ghouls in my basement, but no vampires. (G, V)
   Only if there are vampires in my basement will I get angry. (A)
   If there are ghouls in my basement, then I'm not both dialing 911 and calling an exterminator. (D, E)
   I didn't dial 911. Therefore, I will get angry, but there are no ghouls in my basement.

3. Translate this argument:

   If I watch *Alien*, I'll be scared, but if I don't watch *Alien*, I'll be bored. (W, S, B)
   If I am bored, I get listless and start chopping onions. (L, C)
   If I start chopping onions, then my eyes water and my mascara runs. (E, M)
   If I'm scared, I'll pull my hair and bite my fingernails. (P, F)
   If I bite my fingernails, my hands won't be beautiful. (H)
   Therefore, my hands won't be beautiful.

4. Translate this argument:

   There are marshmallows in the kitchen, but no chocolate. (M, C)
   Only if there are marshmallows and chocolate, can I rest easy. (E)
   If either I rest easy or I do breathing exercises, then I can both sleep peacefully and not have nightmares. (B, S, N). I don't sleep peacefully, if it's raining outside; however, if it's not raining, my dog barks. (R, D) My dog barks.
   Therefore, I will rest easy if I don't have nightmares.

5. Translate this argument:

   If Ubu is sick, either he was chasing Wellie or he ate the meatball. (S, C, A)
   Ubu was chasing Wellie only if Wellie was out of his cage. (O)
   If Wellie was out of his cage then Silvio was home. (S)
   If Silvio was home then he wasn't working. (W)
   Silvio was working, but Ubu is sick. Therefore, Ubu ate the meatball.

6. Translate this argument:

Either George ate the lemon pie or, a thief broke into the house and stole it. (A, B, S)
If George ate the lemon pie, then Keisha will be furious. (K)
If a thief broke into the house, then either we should call the police or plan a way to trap the thief. (C, P)
Keisha is not furious, but we will not plan a way to trap the thief. Therefore, we should call the police.

7. Translate this argument:

If Wellie is out of his cage, then either the cats will start chasing him or he'll perch up on top of the cabinets. (O, C, P)
If Wellie perches on top of the cabinets and is safe from the cats, then we can relax. (S, R)
The cats will start chasing Wellie only if they are not napping. (N)
Wellie is out of his cage and is safe from the cats, but the cats are napping. Therefore, we can relax.

8. Translate this argument:

If the butler told the truth, then the window was closed; and if the gardener told the truth, then the automatic sprinkler system was not operating on the evening of the murder. (B, W, G, A)
If neither the butler nor the gardener is telling the truth, then a conspiracy must exist to protect someone in the house and there would have been a little pool of water on the floor just inside the window. (C, P)
The window was not closed. There was a little pool of water on the floor just inside the window. So, if there is a conspiracy to protect someone in the house, then the gardener did not tell the truth.

Square of Opposition: Drawing Inferences

The ability to draw inferences is not only useful it is also powerful, because we go from knowing one thing to many other things. First we'll look at the square of opposition. It sets out vital relationships between the different categorical propositions. And once we know the truth-value of one proposition, we can use these relationships to derive other truth-values.

Contrary

Two propositions are contraries if they cannot both be true, but could both be false. If one is true, then the other one is necessarily false. The truth of the A or E claim forces the contrary to be false. Only universal claims can be contraries.

Examples of contraries:
If it is true that "All drummers are musicians,"
→ "No drummer is a musician" must be false.

If it is true that "No dog has wings,"
→ "All dogs have wings" must be false.

Be careful: If an A or E claim is false need not mean the corresponding E or A claim is then true. For instance, the claim "All cats are tigers" is false, but "No cats are tigers" is also false.

Subcontrary

Two propositions are subcontraries if they cannot both be false but could both be true. This is true of the two particular claims. If one is false then the other must be true.

Examples of subcontraries:
If it is false that "Some dogs are fish,"
→ "Some dogs are not fish" is true.

If it is false that "Some mice are not rodents,"
→ "Some mice are rodents" is true.

Remember: This only applies when the particular claim is *false*. It could very well be the case that they are <u>both</u> true. For instance, "Some dogs are not chihuahuas" is true and "Some dogs are chihuahuas" is also true.

Contradictory

Two propositions are contradictories if they cannot both be true *and* they cannot both be false. All the categorical propositions have contradictories. "All P is Q" is opposite in truth-value to "Some P is not Q." "No P is Q" has an opposite truth-value to "Some P is Q."

Examples of contradictories:
If it is true that "All horses are mammals,"
→ "Some horses are not mammals" must be false.

If it is true that "Some birds are hawks,"
→ "No bird is a hawk" must be false.

Subaltern

When a universal claim is true *and* the subject class is not empty of members, we can conclude that the corresponding particular claim is also true. This is, called the subaltern. The process of going from the universal claim to its corresponding particular claim is called *subalternation*.

Examples of subalterns:
If it is true that "All Persians are cats" *and* we know there exist Persians,
→ "Some Persians are cats" must be true.

If it is true that "All flying saucers are UFOs," but we don't know that flying saucers actually exist,

→ "Some flying saucers are UFOs" cannot be inferred as true.

We can summarize these four inferences in a diagram that shows their relationship as follows:

The Square of Opposition

```
All S is P          A ——————— Contraries ——————— E          No S is P

Subalterns                                                   Subalterns

                         Contradictories

Some S is P          I ——————— Subcontraries ——————— O          Some S is not P
```

Exercises

Directions: Draw the inferences and truth-values (if unknown, just say so).

1. State the subaltern and its truth-value of "No novels are tax statements."

2. State the subcontrary and its truth-value of the false proposition: "Some insects are not sowbugs."

3. State the contrary and its truth-value of the false proposition: "No hawks are birds."

4. State the subaltern and its truth-value of the true proposition: "All werewolves are monsters."

5. State the subcontrary and its truth-value of the true proposition: "Some animals are ferocious."

6. State the contrary and its truth-value of the true proposition: "All sewer rats are rodents."

7. State the contradictory and its truth-value of the false proposition: "Some lizards make nice pets."

8. State the contrary and its truth-value of the true proposition: "No well-trained animal bites its owner."

9. State the contradictory and its truth-value of the true proposition: "All trapeze artists are daring people."

10. Given "All cocaine smugglers use airplanes for transport" is false:
    a. State the contrary and its truth-value
    b. State the contradictory and its truth-value
    c. State the subaltern and its truth-value

11. State the contradictory and its truth-value of the true proposition: "No skyscraper is a small building."

12. Given the true proposition: "No cheese is a vegetable":
    a. State the contrary and its truth-value
    b. State the contradictory and its truth-value
    c. State the subaltern and its truth-value

13. Given the false proposition: "Some chocolate fudge sundaes are non-fattening":
    a. State the subcontrary and its truth-value
    b. State the contradictory and its truth-value

14. Given the true proposition: "All Martians are aliens":
    a. State the contrary and its truth-value
    b. State the subaltern and its truth-value
    c. State the contradictory and its truth-value

15. State everything you can infer from the true proposition: "No illegal alien is a U.S. citizen."

The Obverse, Converse, Contrapositive

There are three other key moves you can make in terms of drawing inferences. These are the obverse, the converse, and the contrapositive. For these we need to know one more thing—the complement of a class.

Complement

The complement of a class A is the class of those things <u>not</u> in A. So, for instance, the complement of the set of voters is the set of nonvoters. The complement of the set of noncitizens is the set of citizens. So, given any set A, the complement is the set non-A. Similarly, given any set non-B, the complement is the set B. (Think of a non-non-B as a double negative, that takes us back to set B). Examples of complements: farmworkers/non-farmworkers; snake stompers/non-snake stompers; nonworkers/workers.

Obverse

The obverse of a proposition involves two steps: First, change the quality (from positive to negative or vice versa); then change the predicate to its complement. The result is the Obverse. It has the same truth-value as the original claim. If the original proposition is true, so is the obverse. If it is false, then the obverse is false. The obverse can be taken on any proposition.

Examples of the obverse:
All slugs are repulsive creatures.
→ No slug is a nonrepulsive creature.

Some men are not noncommunicative people.
→ Some men are communicative people.

Converse

The converse of a proposition is obtained by switching the subject and the predicate, when possible. We can take a converse on an E or I claim. However, the converse of an A claim is known as *converse by limitation,* for we must step down to an I claim. We can't take the converse of an O claim.

Examples of the converse:
No scuba divers are nonswimmers.
→ No nonswimmers are scuba divers.

Some ice-skaters are hockey players.
→ Some hockey players are ice-skaters.

All bombs are weapons of destruction.
→ <u>Some</u> weapons of destruction are bombs.

Some hikers are not people fond of heights.
→ Does not exist (no converse of an O claim!).

Contrapositive

To take the contrapositive of a proposition, follow these two steps: First, replace the subject with the complement of the predicate. Second, replace the predicate with the complement of the subject. The contrapositive cannot be taken on the I claim. It can only be taken on an A, E, and O. The E claim is *contrapositive by limitation:* step down to an O claim. Don't be surprised with a strange-looking result. Once you verify the original sentence as A, O, or E, then just flip the subject and predicate, changing each one to the complement when you do the switch and, in the case of the E claim, move it down to an O claim.

Examples of contrapositives:
All trout are fish.
→ All nonfish are nontrout.

All noncitizens are nonvoters.
→ All voters are citizens.

Some citizens are not nonvoters.
→ Some voters are not noncitizens.

No FBI agent is a person in the CIA.
→ Some nonpeople in the CIA are not non-FBI agents.

Remember we have to change the E claim to an O claim.

Neither the converse nor the contrapositive changes the quality of the original proposition. Negatives stay negative and positives stay positive. Only the obverse changes the quality: Be sure with the obverse to change positive to negative claim and vice versa. Also, the converse is the only one of these three techniques that does NOT involve a complement. So be sure that you do *not* introduce it. We can summarize all this as follows:

Converse, Obverse, and Contrapositive

Converse: A, E, and I (We can't take the converse on the O claim.)
Step: Switch subject and predicate.
       Note: Converse of an A goes to an I.

Forms of the Converse:

No P is Q.	Converse is	No Q is P.
Some P is Q.	Converse is	Some Q is P.
All P is Q.	Converse is	Some Q is P.
Some P is not Q .	No converse	N/A

Obverse: A, E, I, O (all claims)
Two steps: Change quality (positive to negative and vice versa).
            Change predicate to its complement.

Forms of the Obverse:

All P is Q.	Obverse is	No P is non-Q.
No P is Q.	Obverse is	All P is non-Q.
Some P is Q.	Obverse is	Some P is not non-Q.
Some P is not Q.	Obverse is	Some P is non-Q.

Contrapositive: A, E and O (We can't take the contrapositive on I claim.)
Two steps: Replace subject with the complement of the predicate.
            Replace predicate with the complement of the subject.
            Note: Contrapositive of an E goes to an O.

Forms of the Contrapositive:

All P is Q.	Contrapositive is	All non-Q is non-P.
No P is Q.	Contrapositive is	Some non-Q is not non-P.
Some P is Q.	No contrapositive	N/A
Some P is not Q.	Contrapositive is	Some non-Q is not non-P.

Exercises

1. What is the converse of: "All dinosaurs are extinct animals"?
2. What is the obverse of: "Some aliens are androids"?
3. What is the contrapositive of: "No electricians are scatterbrained"?
4. What is the obverse of: "No sane woman would marry a murderer"?
5. What is the contradictory of: "Some wild women are body builders"?
6. What is the converse of the subcontrary of: "Some snake swallowers are not overweight"? (*Hint:* Take subcontrary first, then take converse of what you get.)
7. What is the contradictory of the obverse of: "No woman who shaves her head is boring"? (*Hint:* Take obverse first and then contradictory of what you get.)
8. What is the contrapositive of the contrary of: "All men with tattoos are adventurous"?
9. Given it is true that "All drummers are musicians," state and give the truth-value of each of the following:
   a. The contrary
   b. The subaltern
   c. The contradictory
   d. The converse
10. Draw the inferences below:
   a. What is the converse of: "No snakes are mammals"?
   b. What is the converse of: "All mathematicians are witty people"?
   c. What is the obverse of: "Some women are not citizens"?
   d. What is the obverse of the converse of: "No friend of Damon's is a burglar"?
   e. What is the contrapositive of the obverse of: "Some voters are Republicans"?
   f. Take the obverse of the contrapositive of: "No slimy creature is a non-voter."

11. Draw the inference and then give the inference's truth-value.
    a. The contrapositive of: "All rodents are nonfish. (True)
    b. The obverse of: "Some nonreptiles are not rodents." (True)
    c. The contrapositive of: "No noninsects are grasshoppers." (True)
    d. The converse of: "All nonandroids are non-voters." (False)
    e. The subcontrary of: "Some reptiles are mammals." (False)

12. Given this is true: "All robbers are thieves," draw all the inferences you can.

13. Given this is true: "No nun is a priest," draw these inferences and give the truth-value of those inferences:
    a. The obverse
    b. The contradictory
    c. The converse
    d. The contrary
    e. The subaltern
    f. The contrapositive
    g. The contradictory of the obverse

14. Given it is false that: "Some pit bulls are not dogs," draw these inferences and state their truth-values:
    a. The obverse
    b. The contradictory
    c. The converse
    d. The contrary
    e. The subaltern
    f. The contrapositive
    g. The subcontrary

CHAPTER FIFTEEN

Syllogisms

'Twas brillig, and the slithy toves
Did gyre and gimble in the wabe:
All mimsy were the borogoves,
And the mome raths outgrabe.
—LEWIS CARROLL from *Jabberwocky*

You are having dinner with your family when you realize your father is serving your brother twice as many mashed potatoes as he served your sister. You ask why. Your dad says, "Boys need to eat more than girls, that's why." Is your father's argument defensible? Well, let's see. His argument is this: "All boys need to eat more than girls. Your brother is a boy. So, your brother needs to eat more than your sister."

You probably have no trouble with the second premise, "Your brother is a boy." By definition your brother is a male and the only dispute might be whether he is young enough to warrant being called a "boy." So, you turn to the tricky premise, the first one. Is it true that "All boys need to eat more than girls"? If your sister were an Olympic athlete and your brother a receptionist, your sister would probably need more food. If, however, she is tiny and in a physically undemanding job and he is 6'7" and jogs to work, then she may need less. But it is not patently obvious that any given boy will need more food than any particular girl. We would need to know more about the individuals concerned. In that respect, the first premise is <u>contingent</u> on the specific circumstances and is neither certainly true nor certainly false. Consequently, your father's argument could not be said to be a sound one.

▨ Introduction to Syllogisms

What your dad has done is to offer a *syllogism*. This is a three-line argument with two premises and one conclusion in which there are only three terms. In the argument above the terms are: "Boys," "your brother," and "people who need more food than girls." If we were to replace the terms with variables, letting B = boys, Y = your brother, and P = people who need more food than girls, then the argument can be written as:

All B is P.

<u>(All) Y is B.</u>

Therefore, (all) Y is P.

Now we've got it so we can examine the form of the argument and study the relationship between the premises and the conclusion. As we know from Chapter 6 on induction and deduction, this is a deductive argument. We want to know: Is it valid? Is it sound? In this chapter, we will learn how to examine syllogisms in order to determine if they are valid or invalid. We will also cover techniques for assessing validity of syllogisms, so you'll be able to check them out quickly and easily.

▨ Validity and Soundness

Your father's argument is well constructed. The problem has to do with the truth of the premises, not whether or not the premises, if they were true, supported the conclusion. If it were true that all B is P and it were true that all Y is B, then it would follow that all Y is P. No problem there. The issue isn't the construction, but the truth of the claims. Let's look at the two key issues—validity and soundness.

Validity: The argument is structurally correct (so that <u>if</u> the premises were true, the conclusion could not be false). You may remember that this means the argument is valid. It does *not* mean that the premises are necessarily true. This is crucial to imprint on our brains.

Soundness: You may also remember the two criteria for sound arguments— first, the argument is valid and, second, the premises are actually true. If an argument has both these characteristics, it is called sound. Since you need to look at the particular circumstances to determine the truth of the premises, our focus in this section will be on validity.

Validity

It is generally held that only deductive arguments can be considered valid or invalid. Validity, therefore, is an issue about the relationship between the premises and the conclusion—not about whether any statements are *actually* true or not. The question here is: Do the premises, if they were assumed to be true, fully support the conclusion? This means the conclusion could not be false if the premises were true in a valid argument.

With inductive arguments, the truth of the premises wouldn't *necessarily* force the truth of the conclusion, because there are missing pieces in the evidence. In valid deductive arguments, however, the premises could not be true and the conclusion false. The conclusion comes out of the premises, by the very structure of the argument. Look at these examples of valid syllogisms:

Valid argument 1:

All reptiles are covered in feathers.

<u>Lizards are reptiles.</u>

Therefore, lizards are covered in feathers.

Valid argument 2 (from the movie **Princess Mononoke***):*

When the land was filled with gods and demons, the earth was filled with spirits.

<u>If the earth is filled with spirits, the Boar God will be a formidable force.</u>

Therefore, when the land was filled with gods and demons, the Boar God was a formidable force.

In both of these arguments the premises provided sufficient support for drawing the conclusion. If the premises were true, the conclusion would have to be true—it could not be false. As we can see in both examples, the arguments can be valid, but not necessarily sound.

We can determine the validity of a syllogism. Note that a syllogism is an argument with two premises and a conclusion, containing three terms (called the major term, the minor term, and the middle term). We'll see how to locate the three terms shortly. First, we will set out our argument.

▦ Universal versus Particular Propositions

Basically, propositions fall into one of two categories (universal or particular), as we saw in the last chapter. They could be universal, which means something is being predicated about <u>all</u> members of the subject class (i.e., that they do or do not have some characteristic). The "all" here may refer to the collective or to "each and every one" or "any" of the subject. This includes propositions in which something is being affirmed or denied about some proper noun in the subject (e.g., the name of a person, a city, a title of a song, etc.).

Universal Claims are ALL-or-NOTHING Claims

Examples of universal claims:
- All farmhands like a big breakfast.
- No farmhand likes Caesar salad for lunch.
- Any farmhand who can drive a forklift is talented.
- Not one farmhand came to the rally for the Aryan Brotherhood.
- Every farmhand in the book group prefers *Finnegan's Wake* to *Ulysses*.
- Samuel is awfully fond of bacon and eggs for a snack.
- Rocio is not impressed by Tiramisu.
- Kalamazoo is a city with a fascinating history.
- "Unchained Melody" is one of the great love songs of all time.
- The U.S. Constitution is an important document.
- One hundred percent of Raylene's savings was spent on her trip to Scotland.
- None of her savings went to her retirement fund.

On the other hand, a proposition could be *particular*. In the case of a particular proposition, some trait is being predicated about some (but not all or none) of the subject class. Some of the subject class are claimed to have or lack the characteristic in question. That is, it predicates something of at least one member of that class, but never all of it. This includes statistical propositions of the form x percent of A is B, where $x \neq 100$ and $x \neq 0$. Particular claims are about *some*, not all. Particular claims are never all-or-nothing propositions:

Basic Forms of Particular Claims

Form 1: Some A is B (particular/positive).
Form 2: Some A is not B (particular/negative).
Form 3: x percent of A is/is not B, $x \neq 100$ or 0 (statistical).

Examples of particular claims:
- Some Italian food does not use tomatoes.
- Most people in Lamu are fond of lamb.
- Many travelers to Nairobi should bring a camera.
- Lots of hikers in the Sierra get eaten alive by deer flies.
- A few Apache at the filming of the last scene did not agree with the director.
- A bunch of Chicanos protested the racist stereotypes in prime-time TV.
- Not all Turkish desserts contain honey.
- Not every archaeologist is acquainted with Chaco Canyon.
- Ninety-two percent of southern desserts are topped with ice cream.
- Forty-six percent of the students at Cal State–Fullerton saw the poltergeist enter the faculty club.

▦ Categorical Propositions

Before we proceed to look at arguments, let's review how we can best express the propositions that constitute an argument. In using a standardized approach so we have a technique for simplifying the terms of the argument, we can then evaluate the syllogism more quickly.

From the last chapter, Chapter 14, we learned how to work with different sorts of claims. In analyzing a syllogism, it's generally easiest to do so by rewriting the premises and the conclusion in the form of categorical propositions. These are as follows:

The Four Categorical Propositions

A: All P are Q.
E: No P is Q.
I: Some P is Q.
O: Some P is not Q.

Variations of the Categorical Propositions

1. *Proper Nouns as Subject:* Remember, if you use as the subject specific individuals or proper names, like Andrea, Chicago, or the Statue of Liberty, then the claim is universal. It will be either an **A** or an **E** claim, depending on whether the sentence is positive or negative. (For example, "Lisa is a wild woman" is an **A** claim, whereas "Kareem is not a short man" is an **E** claim).
2. *Statistical Claims:* If you have statistical claims x percent of A is B, (where $x \neq 100$ or 0), then that claim is treated as an **I** or **O** claim (depending upon whether it's positive or negative). So "82 percent of donuts are greasy" is an **I** claim and "19 percent of chocolate is not addictive" is an **O** claim.

These forms (A, E, I, O) are called *categorical propositions* and are useful to provide a kind of uniformity, so we can quickly organize a syllogism and see if it is valid or invalid. Refer to Chapter 14 for a review of categorical propositions.

▦ Categorical Syllogisms

A *categorical syllogism* is a syllogism in which the premises and the conclusion are <u>categorical</u> claims. The *standard form of a categorical syllogism* is what we have when we set out the syllogism in a particular order: major premise, minor premise, and then the conclusion. This gives us a uniform way to set out syllogisms so they are easy to assess, and we aren't scrambling trying to figure out what's what. We will be learning how to do this in the sections that follow, starting with the different terms of the syllogism.

The standard form of the syllogism always starts with the major premise. This is the premise that contains the predicate term found in the conclusion. The next premise is called the minor premise and it contains the subject term found in the conclusion. This means the premise nearest to the conclusion should contain the minor term (the subject of the conclusion). Both premises have a linking term (called the "middle term") that does not appear in the conclusion. Here's an example:

Most tigers are ferocious.

<u>Tony is a tiger.</u>

So, Tony is ferocious.

Before we decide if this is a good argument, let us rewrite this argument so each proposition is in *standard form*. That is, we want to express both of the premises and the conclusion in one of these four forms (abbreviated as A, E, I, O). This is another step in streamlining the process, by making things as uniform as possible. If we put the argument above in standard form, we get:

Some tigers are ferocious animals.

<u>Tony is a tiger.</u>

So, Tony is a ferocious animal.

Notice that we had to change "*Most* tigers are ferocious" to "*Some* tigers are ferocious animals." Not only did the quantifier "Some" get added, we constructed a predicate class ("ferocious animals"). You need to do this to get the sentence into categorical form. It makes a big difference in a speedy assessment of arguments.

Why Bother

This system of analyzing syllogisms is not only a time saver; it lessens the chance of error. If you were like the Tom Hanks character in *Cast Away,* you might prefer taking a *very* long time to puzzle through the problems you face. On the other hand, you may prefer the jet propulsion model of reasoning, where speed and accuracy is of the essence. It helps to know how to organize the material to quickly determine whether or not the reasoning is worth paying attention to. Plus, you may not have time to linger.

Think about it: What if your house is on fire, you've just hit an ice slick on the road, or you're on a TV show like *Weakest Link* or *Survivor* and stand to make your fortune if you can think quickly on your feet? The ability to dismantle and evaluate syllogistic arguments quickly and correctly is more valuable than you may realize.

▦ The Three Terms of the Syllogism

Once we have the premises and conclusion expressed in standard form, we can take the next step. This is to locate the three terms. The *major term* is the predicate of the conclusion. In this case, the major term is "ferocious animals." The *minor term* is the subject of the conclusion. Here it is "Tony." And the *middle term* is the term that is only found in the two premises, and here it is "tigers."

Example of the three terms:

Some easily irritated creatures are watchdogs.

All badgers are easily irritated creatures.

So, some badgers are watchdogs.

Major term   →   Predicate of conclusion, "watchdogs"
Minor term   →   Subject of the conclusion, "badgers"
Middle term   →   Term only in the premises, "easily irritated creatures"

Exercises

Directions: Name the major, minor and middle terms in the syllogisms below.

1. All plutonium is a dangerous substance.
   No dangerous substance is a thing that should be legal.
   Thus, no plutonium is a thing that should be legal.

2. Some snakes are poisonous animals.
   All poisonous animals are things to be avoided.
   So, some things to be avoided are snakes.

3. No good driver is a person who drives drunk.
   No drunk driver is a person worthy of respect.
   Therefore, all persons worthy of respect are good drivers.

4. No sound engineer likes blaring music.
   Trent is a sound engineer.
   So Trent is not someone who likes blaring music.

5. All attractive men are people who can wink.
   Bob is a person who can wink.
   So, Bob is an attractive man.

6. Some archaeologists are Celtics fans.
   No Celtics fan is an introvert.
   So, some introverts are not archaeologists.

7. All Dolphins fans are people who like Miami.
   Some people who like Miami are Trekkies.
   Therefore, some Trekkies are Dolphins fans.

8. No electrical engineer is a person who finds the Houston Rockets boring.
   All people who find the Houston Rockets boring are people who like to read Kafka.
   Therefore, no one who likes to read Kafka is an electrical engineer.

9. Some belly dancers are Rangers fans.
   Some Rangers fans are people who like to wear caps and eat hot dogs.
   Therefore, Some people who like to wear caps and eat hot dogs are belly dancers.

10. All Nobel Prize winners are unusual people.
    Jorge Luis Borges is a Nobel Prize winner.
    Therefore, Jorge Luis Borges is an unusual person.

11. Some movies are things that waste money and time.
    Casablanca is a movie.
    So, *Casablanca* is a thing that wastes money and time.

12. Some stamp collectors are not neurotic people.
    No stamp collector is a backup singer for a rock band.
    Therefore, no backup singer for a rock band is a neurotic person.

13. Some radiologists are people who love to snorkel.
    Some people who love to snorkel are drifters.
    Therefore, some drifters are radiologists.

14. All x-ray technicians are risktakers.
    Some risktakers are mysterious people.
    Therefore, some mysterious people are x-ray technicians.

15. No flat-footed weasel is a well-behaved pet.
    All guinea pigs are well-behaved pets.
    Therefore, some guinea pigs are not flat-footed weasels.

Major and Minor Premises

Order is everything in the world of syllogisms. If we are testing a syllogism, we must first set out the argument. Our first step is to locate the conclusion. If we don't know the conclusion, we won't know where the person is headed and, therefore, can't go much further.

Our next step is to examine the conclusion to determine which term is the major term and which is the minor term. The predicate is the major term and, once you know this, you also know the *major premise*. The major premise is the premise containing the major term. The subject of the conclusion is the minor term and, once you know this, you also know the *minor premise*. The minor premise is the premise containing the minor term. To express the syllogism in standard form, set it out this way:

Standard Form of a Syllogism

Major premise	→	Contains the major and middle terms
<u>*Minor premise*</u>	→	<u>Contains the minor and middle terms</u>
Conclusion	→	Contains the minor and major terms
Remember: Minor term = Subject of the conclusion.		
Major term = Predicate of the conclusion.		

Once we have the argument in standard form, we can see its structure. The first premise should have the major term and the middle term in it. The second premise should have the minor term and the middle term in it. The conclusion contains the major and minor terms. The argument must be exactly in this order to be in standard form.

Always Double Check.   The premise <u>closest</u> to the conclusion should have the minor term in it. If not, rearrange the premises. The major term should be in the first premise, and the minor term in the second premise. Remember: The major term should be in the first premise and should be the last term of the conclusion.

Once the argument is set out in this order we can proceed to the next step. Be sure to express each proposition in categorical form.

Examples of Propositions in Categorical Form:

Quantifier	Subject	Is/Are	Predicate
All	cats	are	animals.
No	cats	are	dogs.
Some	cats	are	delightful creatures.
Some	cats	are not	ill-mannered beasts.

If the sentence does not have a quantifier, then you have to decide if it is meant to be universal or particular. For instance, "Skunks should be approached carefully" and "Scoundrels are immoral" would be written, "All skunks are animals that should be approached carefully" and "All scoundrels are immoral people."

In contrast, "Muffins were eaten at breakfast" would be rewritten "Some muffins were food eaten at breakfast" and "Nights can get cold in Alaska" would be rewritten "Some nights are times that can get cold in Alaska." You have to look at the sentence and sometimes the context to determine the most appropriate (and less cumbersome) expression. Remember, a universal claim is saying more than a particular claim—its scope is wider.

Expressing Arguments In Standard Form

Let us practice working with what we know so far. Put this argument in standard form:

Cobras are snakes.

<u>A lot of snakes are disgusting.</u>

Therefore, cobras are disgusting.

First, express the propositions in categorical form, that is in the form of A, E, I, and O claims, and then write the name of the proposition (A, E, I, O) on the left, for easy reference:

A   All cobras are snakes.

I   <u>Some snakes are disgusting animals.</u>

A   Therefore, all cobras are disgusting animals.

The next step is to look at the conclusion. The predicate of the conclusion is "disgusting animals." That is your <u>major</u> term. The major premise must contain that term, so look up in the premises and locate it. The major premise then is "Some snakes are disgusting animals." This premise—the major premise—must be listed first. The remaining premise is the minor premise (and it does contain the <u>minor</u> term "cobras"). We can now put the argument in order:

Major premise: Some snakes are disgusting animals.

<u>*Minor premise:*</u>   <u>All cobras are snakes.</u>

Conclusion: All cobras are disgusting animals.

We now have the argument in standard form. Let's run through another one for practice. Given this argument, put it in standard form: "Every student enjoys a snooze. Joe enjoys a snooze. So, Joe is a student."

The conclusion is: "Joe is a student." In categorical form, that would be written, "(All) Joe is a student." Because "a student" is the major term (the predicate of the conclusion), our major premise is, "All students are people who enjoy a snooze." That leaves our second premise, the minor premise to be, "(All) Joe is a person who enjoys a snooze." Our argument can then be expressed in standard form as:

         A   All students are people who enjoy a snooze.

         A   <u>(All) Joe is a person who enjoys a snooze.</u>

So,   A   (All) Joe is a student.

Note: The "All" was added before "Joe" to remind us that these are universal claims. The "All" is optional, because it is only a reminder. If you don't need it to jog your brain, leave it off.

Exercises

Directions: Put the following arguments in standard form, with each sentence expressed as a categorical proposition. Name the major, minor, and middle terms.

1. Every woman loves a challenge. All daredevils love a challenge. As a result, all women are daredevils.

2. Many men like to discuss sports. All sports fans are people who like to discuss sports. Therefore, most men are sports fans.

3. Many children are afraid of the dark. Therefore, many children scream loudly, because most people afraid of the dark scream loudly.

4. No crocodile should be taken for granted. Every pet is an animal you can take for granted. Consequently, no crocodile is a pet.

5. Some dogs are revolting creatures, because many dogs eat with their mouths open, and, any animal that eats with its mouth wide open is revolting.

6. All moths can fly. This is true because every moth is an insect and most insects are creatures than can fly.

7. Count Dracula sucks blood. Anyone who sucks blood is a vampire. Therefore, Count Dracula is a vampire.

8. Brush Prairie is a nifty little town. All nifty little towns have ice cream parlors. Subsequently, Brush Prairie has an ice cream parlor.

9. Possums are smarter than most people think. A large number of birds are smarter than most people think. Therefore, lots of possums are birds.

10. Any earthquake is a scary thing to experience. Many tornadoes are scary things to experience. Therefore, a few earthquakes are tornadoes.

11. A vast quantity of movie stars are people who give to charity. Wimpy is not a movie star. So, Wimpy is not someone who gives to charity.

12. A few TV shows are recognized for their artistic merit. *Six Feet Under* is a TV show. Therefore, *Six Feet Under* is a TV show that has been recognized for its artistic merit.

13. A fair amount of dental work is something unpleasant to experience. No dental work is something to anticipate with glee. Therefore, some things to anticipate with glee are not something unpleasant to experience.

14. All dreams about being swallowed whole are nightmares. Many dreams about sharks are dreams about being swallowed whole. Therefore, many nightmares are dreams about sharks.

15. Any enjoyable moment is good to note in your scrapbook. Wrestling down the alligator was not an enjoyable moment. Thus wrestling down the alligator is not good to note in your scrapbook.

The Mood and Figure of a Syllogism

After you get a syllogism in standard form, you are in a position to name the mood and the figure. These are very useful for quickly evaluating an argument for validity.

Mood of the Syllogism

The *mood of a syllogism* is the list of the types of claims (A, E, I, and O) of the major premise, minor premise, and conclusion (in that order). Because there are the two premises and one conclusion, you will have three letters indicating the categorical propositions that constitute the syllogism. For example, the syllogism below is in standard form:

All wallpaper with paisleys is something that is tiring on the eyes.

Some people have wallpaper with paisleys.

Therefore, some people have wallpaper that is tiring on the eyes.

The mood of this syllogism can then be read as AII (The major premise is an A claim, the minor premise is an I claim, and the conclusion is an I claim).

Let's get an overview of the structure. To do this we'll shrink the syllogism to skeletal form, and view it like the Terminator used his x-ray type vision to quickly assess what's what. So we'll do the following substitutions:

Abbreviations for Speedy Reference

P = *Predicate* of the conclusion → *Major term*

S = *Subject* of the conclusion → *Minor term*

M = Linking term in both premises → *Middle term*

Figure of the Syllogism

The *figure* of a syllogism has to do with the placement of the middle term. Let P = major term, S = minor term, and M = middle term. To determine the figure, we need to see where the *middle term* is located. There are four possible locations of the middle term.

As you may remember, once the syllogism is in standard categorical form, the major term P should be in the first premise, the minor term S will be in the second premise, and the middle term is in both premises. The arrangement of the middle term reveals the figure.

The Figures of the Syllogism

Figure 1	Figure 2	Figure 3	Figure 4
M P	P M	M P	P M
↘	↑	↓	↗
S M	S M	M S	M S
S P	S P	S P	S P

Figure 1	Figure 2	Figure 3	Figure 4
M's step DOWN	M's on right	M's on left	M's step UP
Left diagonal			*Right diagonal*
↘	↑	↓	↗

Examples of the different figures:

Example 1:
Mood and figure EIO—(1)

    No **M** is P
    Some S is **M**
So,   Some S is not P

Example 2:
Mood and figure AOA—(2)

    All P is **M**
    Some S is not **M**
So,   Some S is not P.

Example 3:
Mood and figure AEE—(3)

    All **M** is P
    No **M** is S
So,   No S is P.

Example 4:
Mood and figure AIA—(4)

    All P is **M**
    Some **M** is S.
So,   All S is P.

Exercises

Directions: Put the following syllogisms in standard form and then state the mood and figure.

1. No nurse is afraid to touch people. John is afraid to touch people. So John is not a nurse. (*Remember:* Claims with proper nouns are universal!)

2. Some architects love Korean barbeques. Rick is a person who loves Korean barbeques. So Rick is an architect.

3. Surgeons are people with a mind for details. A number of people with a mind for details are people who love to do their taxes. Therefore, all surgeons are people who love to do their taxes.

4. No Rolls Royce mechanic is afraid to get messy. Some cooks are not afraid to get messy. Therefore, some cooks are Rolls Royce mechanics.

5. Many purchasing agents like to do paper work. No artist likes to do paper work. Therefore, no artist is a purchasing agent.

6. All photographers have a highly developed visual sense. All website analysts have a highly developed visual sense. Therefore, some website analysts are photographers.

7. Some welders have a talent for fine metalwork. All jewelers have a talent for fine metalwork. Therefore, some welders are jewelers.

8. All lawyers are analytical people. Some analytical people are fond of playing jokes on others. Therefore, some lawyers are fond of playing jokes on others.

9. Some judges are people with a sardonic sense of humor. All people who liked *Fargo* are people with a sardonic sense of humor. Therefore, some people who liked *Fargo* are judges.

10. Some people over 6 feet tall are not gymnasts. Some gymnasts do great back flips. Therefore, some people who do great back flips are not over 6 feet tall.

11. The vast majority of waitresses are courteous. Some courteous people are crazy about stamp collecting. So, many waitresses are crazy about stamp collecting.

12. Anyone who loves the blues is familiar with Jelly Roll Morton. All guitar players are people who are familiar with Jelly Roll Morton. Therefore, all guitar players love the blues.

13. Whoever likes comedy knows about the Marx Brothers. Will Smith likes comedy, so he must know about the Marx Brothers.

14. Some people who watch MTV are computer hackers. This is because many computer hackers are people who enjoy music videos. Also, everyone who enjoys music videos likes to watch MTV.

15. Most elderly folks enjoy playing Scrabble. A few elderly folks enjoy going to the race track. Therefore, a lot of people who enjoy going to the race track will enjoy playing Scrabble.

16. Children under 10 will like *The Never Ending Story*. Here's why: All children under 10 like tales about flying creatures. *The Never Ending Story* is a tale about a flying creature.

17. Just about all rabbits are furry animals. Not all furry animals are nice to pet. It follows that lots of rabbits are nice to pet.

18. Everyone who is a friend of mine has a good sense of humor. Cuba Gooding, Jr., has a good sense of humor. Consequently, Cuba Gooding, Jr., is a friend of mine.

19. Not all of my friends are sound engineers. Some of my friends are film lovers. So, most sound engineers are not film lovers.

20. A lot of vegetarians are talented. Enrique Iglesias is talented. Subsequently, Enrique Iglesias is a vegetarian.

21. A fair amount of music is rap. All rap music is a kind of poetry. This leads me to infer that, some poetry is music.

22. The epidemiologists tracked the progress of Hepatitis C in the prisons. Anyone who tracks the progress of Hepatitis C in prisons is surprised at the rate it is spreading. Therefore, all the people who are surprised at the rate Hepatitis C is spreading are epidemiologists.

▓ Checking for Validity

Before we can test the syllogism for validity, we need to know how to tell if a term is distributed. Distribution involves the question of how much. If someone asked you to distribute all of a stack leaflets, you'd know that what was wanted was that you pass them all out. Distribution of a term is similar, in the sense that a distributed term includes <u>all</u> its members.

Distribution.   When we talk distribution, we are talking about number of members of the class in question. If the term is meant to apply to <u>all</u> members of the class it defines, then it is called distributed. Otherwise it's called undistributed. To grasp this concept, it helps to see the term "distribution" in operation. We will look at the key ways to test for distribution and then run through some examples. For any given proposition there are only two terms to examine to determine distribution—the subject and the predicate. The subject is distributed in any universal claim, the predicate in any negative claim. Let's look at this in more detail.

Distribution of Terms

Checking distribution of terms involves two steps:

Step 1: Check the location of the term (Is it the *subject* or the *predicate* of the proposition?).

Step 2: According to the location, check either quality or quantity of the proposition. If the term is in the subject place, then check the quantity (universal proposition = subject is distributed). If the term is in the predicate place, check the quality (negative proposition = predicate is distributed).

Subject Distributed.   If the claim is <u>universal</u>, the subject is then distributed, because you are saying that all of the members of the subject class either have or don't have some characteristic.

Example of distributed subject:
All possums are slow-moving creatures.
→ Claim is universal.
→ "Possums" is distributed.

Example of undistributed subject:
Some possums are animals that like cat food.
→ Claim is particular (*not* universal).
→ "Possums" not distributed.

Note: The term "some possums" tells us nothing about *all* possums in terms of liking cat food. Thus the term "possums" is not distributed. For instance, "All pajamas are comfortable to wear" is talking about *all* pajamas, not just some of them. Similarly, "No bathtub is a good place to fall asleep in," is talking about *all* bathtubs and saying that they are *not* places you'd want to sleep in. So *both A and E claims have the subject distributed.*

To determine if the subject is distributed

Check the *quantity* of the proposition.
→ See if the claim is <u>universal</u>.
→ The subject is distributed in A and E claims.

Example 1:
No cats are dogs.
Test the subject "cats" for distribution:
First, check the <u>quantity</u> of the proposition. The claim is universal ("No" refers to all), which means the subject **is** distributed.

Example 2:
Some cats are not Persians.
Test the subject "cats" for distribution:
Check the <u>quantity</u> of the proposition. The proposition is particular ("Some"), which means the subject **is not** distributed.

Predicate Distributed.   If the claim is <u>negative</u>, the predicate is distributed. This is because a negative is excluding the subject class (some or all of it) from having the characteristic set out in the predicate.

Examples of distributed predicate:
No rattlesnake is a well-mannered animal.
→ Claim is negative.
→ "Well-mannered animal" is distributed.

Example of undistributed predicate:
All rattlesnakes are creatures that like the sun.
→ Claim is NOT negative (it is positive).
→ "Creatures that like the sun" is not distributed.

Note: There are creatures that like the sun (e.g., land turtles, hummingbirds, giraffes, elephants, etc.) that are not rattlesnakes.

For instance, if someone says, "No octopus can climb a tree," they are saying that the class of animals that can climb trees does *not* contain <u>any</u> octopi—they are *all* excluded from the tree-climber class. Similarly, if you heard, "Some tall people are not basketball players," you would know that the term "basketball players" does not cover all tall people—it excludes *all* those in the subject class. Therefore, the term "basketball players" is distributed. So *both E and O claims distribute the predicate.*

To determine if the predicate is distributed

Check the *quality* of the proposition.
→ See if the claim is <u>negative</u>.
→ The predicate is distributed in E and O claims.

Example 1:
All wolfhounds are dogs.
Test the predicate "dogs" for distribution:
First, check the <u>quality</u> of the proposition. The proposition is positive ("All . . . are") which means the predicate *is not* distributed.

Example 2:
Some dogs are not chihuahuas.
Test the predicate "chihuahuas" for distribution:
Check the <u>quality</u> of the proposition. The proposition is negative ("Some . . . are not"), which means the predicate *is* distributed.

Summary of Distribution

If you want to <u>test a subject</u> for distribution, look at the quantity (universal versus particular) of the proposition. If it's universal, the subject *is* distributed. If the proposition is particular, the subject *is not* distributed. If you want to <u>test a predicate</u> for distribution, look at the quality (positive versus negative) of the proposition. If it's negative, the predicate *is* distributed. If the proposition is positive, the predicate *is not* distributed. See how the terms are distributed below:

Distribution

Type of Claim	Subject Distributed?	Predicate Distributed?
A	Yes	No
E	Yes	Yes
I	No	No
O	No	Yes

So, for example, in the claim "All novels are books," the term "novels" is distributed. In the claim, "No screenplay is a novel," both "screenplay" and "novel" are distributed. In the claim, "Some math textbooks are not great literature" the term "great literature" is distributed. But in the claim, "Some poetry is an inspiration," neither term is distributed.

Rules of the Syllogism

Rule 1: The middle term must be distributed at least once.

Rule 2: If a term is distributed in the conclusion, it must also be distributed in its corresponding premise.

- *Illicit major:* When the major term is distributed in the conclusion, but is not distributed in the major premise.
- *Illicit minor:* When the minor term is distributed in the conclusion, but is not distributed in the minor premise.

Note: This rule is not saying that a valid syllogism requires the conclusion to have its terms distributed. But *if* a term is distributed in the conclusion, it is crucial that it also be distributed in its corresponding premise.

Rule 3: At least one premise must be positive. (If both premises are negative, the syllogism is invalid.)

Rule 4: If the syllogism has a negative premise, there must be a negative conclusion, and vice versa.

Rule 5: If both of the premises are universal, the conclusion must also be universal, and vice versa.

Rules of the Syllogism

You know how to put a syllogism in standard form. You know how to find the mood and the figure. The next step is to test for validity. The quickest way is the way we'll go. And that is to use the rules of the syllogism. Any syllogism that satisfies each of the rules is valid. So you can test for validity simply by running through each rule and seeing if the syllogism checks out on each one. The rules of the syllogism are set out in the box above.

Testing a Syllogism for Validity

Note: An alternative method for testing the validity of syllogisms is Venn Diagrams. Some prefer them to using the five rules. Check it out yourself. (See Appendix C.)

Let's now test some syllogisms to determine validity. We will start with one in standard form.

Example 1:

All psychologists are insightful people.

Some cab drivers are insightful people.

So, some cab drivers are psychologists.

Look at each claim and set out the mood and figure. It is AII—(2). Run through the rules of the syllogism to see if AII—(2) is valid.

The first rule (about the middle term) is violated: Look at the middle term ("insightful people"). In the first premise, it is in the predicate. To be distributed, the predicate must be negative—but this claim is positive. So the term is not distributed in the major premise. Check the minor premise: The minor premise is an I claim and nothing is distributed. That means this syllogism has an undistributed middle and, thus, it is invalid. If you check all the other rules you will see that they are fine (rule 2 doesn't apply, because nothing is distributed in the conclusion, rules 3 and 4 have to do with negatives and there are no negatives here, and rule 5 doesn't apply, because we do not have two universal premises).

Example 2:

Some dogs are Siberian huskies.

No dog is liked by geese.

So, no goose likes Siberian huskies.

First, make sure that it is in standard form and the claims are expressed as categorical propositions. Put it into categorical propositions and then we will get it in standard form. Rewriting the argument, we get:

Some dogs are Siberian huskies.

No dog is a creature liked by geese.

So, no Siberian husky is a creature liked by geese.

Now, we must get it into standard form. The predicate of the conclusion (major term) is "a creature liked by geese." The major premise contains the major term and that means the major premise is "No dog is a creature liked by geese." That leaves the other premise, "Some dogs are Siberian huskies" as the minor premise. Note that it contains the minor term, "Siberian husky." Putting the syllogism in order (major premise, minor premise, conclusion), we get:

No dog is a creature liked by geese.

Some dogs are Siberian huskies.

So, no Siberian husky is a creature liked by geese.

Now we can test the syllogism. Note that the mood and figure of this argument is EIE—(3). Let us go through the rules to see if the syllogism obeys each rule. Rule 1 is okay, because the major premise is negative and our middle term ("dog") is therefore distributed. Now check rule 2. The conclusion is an E claim and that means both the major and minor terms are distributed, so we must check each premise to see that they are distributed in their corresponding premises. The major term is okay, because the major premise is a universal negative. However, the minor term "Siberian husky" is not distributed in the minor premise, because the claim is an I claim, where nothing is distributed. This means we have an illicit minor. It also violates rule 5 (the universal conclusion requires two universal premises). Therefore the syllogism is invalid. The other rules are fine (rules 3 and 4 are not violated). The problem is rule 2 and rule 5, which are both violated. So our syllogism is invalid.

Not all syllogistic arguments are invalid, though. Many are valid. For instance, if someone argued the following, they'd be giving a valid argument.

Example 3:

All swimmers love summer.

<u>All people who love summer enjoy fireworks.</u>

So, all swimmers enjoy fireworks.

First, put the argument into categorical propositions and then standard form. Expressing the propositions in categorical form, we get:

All swimmers are people who love summer.

<u>All people who love summer are people who enjoy fireworks.</u>

So, all swimmers are people who enjoy fireworks.

Because "people who enjoy fireworks" is the major term (predicate of the conclusion), the major premise is "All people who love summer are people who enjoy fireworks." So, we need to switch the order of the premises and then the argument will be in standard form. Our argument is now:

All people who love summer are people who enjoy fireworks.

<u>All swimmers are people who love summer.</u>

So, all swimmers are people who enjoy fireworks.

Now test for validity. The mood and figure is AAA—(1). Rule 1 is satisfied, because the middle term "people who love summer" is distributed in the first premise, the major premise. Rule 2 is fine, because the conclusion does have the minor term "swimmers" distributed, but it is also distributed in its corresponding premise (the minor premise). Rules 3 and 4 don't apply, because there are no negatives. Rule 5 is satisfied, because we do have two universal premises, but also have a universal conclusion. So our argument is valid!

Remember, a valid argument isn't necessarily sound. To be sound it would have to be both valid *and* have all its premises true, which isn't clearly the case here (the premises are not obviously true). Let's try one more syllogism.

Example 4:

Everything you eat should be full of vitamin C.

<u>Liver is not full of vitamin C.</u>

So, liver is not a thing you ought to eat.

The conclusion, "Liver is not a thing you ought to eat" can be rewritten: "No liver is a thing you ought to eat." The predicate of the conclusion (the major term) is "a thing you ought to eat." This means the major premise (which contains this, the major term) is "All you ought to eat are things full of vitamin C." That leaves the second premise, the minor premise to be "Liver is not full of vitamin C," which can be rewritten: "No liver is a thing full of vitamin C." The argument in standard form is then:

All you ought to eat are things with vitamin C.

<u>No liver is a thing full of vitamin C.</u>

So, No liver is a thing you ought to eat.

This argument has mood and figure AEE—(2). Now test it, using the rules of the syllogism. The middle term is distributed, because our minor premise (with the middle term in the predicate) is negative. Rule 2 applies, but be careful. The major term, "thing you ought to eat," is distributed, so we must check the term in the major premise. The major term is the subject of the major premise, which is universal. Consequently, the major term is distributed, so rule 2 is satisfied. The other rules check out fine, because there are not two negative premises and we have a negative premise with a negative conclusion, satisfying rules 3 and 4. Rule 5 is satisfied because we have two universal premises and a universal conclusion. Thus, the argument is valid.

If an argument is given in the form of mood and figure, just write it out using P for the major term, S for the minor term, and M for the middle term and then test. For instance, AEA—(4). This can be written:

All P is M.

<u>No M is S.</u>

So, all S is P.

Running through the rules we find: Rule 1 is fine, because the minor premise is an E claim (and everything is distributed in an E claim). Rule 2 is satisfied because the term S that is distributed in the conclusion is also distributed in its corresponding premise (predicate of a negative claim is distributed). Because P (the major term) is not distributed in the conclusion, we don't have to test it. Rule 3 is our problem. We have a negative premise and, therefore, need a negative conclusion. That means the syllogism is invalid. (Rules 4 and 5 are fine, because neither rule is violated). The trouble is with rule 3. So the syllogism is invalid.

We don't have to actually know the specific major, minor, and middle terms in order to assess validity. In fact, if we know the mood and figure of the syllogism, we can use the five rules of the syllogism to test the argument. Let's see how this is done.

Testing for Validity Knowing Only the Mood and Figure

If you know only the mood and figure, you can still test for validity. Just use S, P, and M for the minor, major and middle terms (respectively) and set it up and then test it. For example, test EAE—(3). Figure 3 means the middle term is on the left, so the argument can be written as:

No M is P.
<u>All M is S.</u>
No S is P.

Remember: P, the major term, must be in the first premise; S, the minor term, in the second premise; and M, the middle term, in both premises.

Now test the argument. Rule 1 is fine, because the first premise is an E claim and distributes everything. Rule 2 must be checked because both the subject and predicate of the conclusion are distributed. P is also distributed in the major premise (predicate of a negative claim is distributed), but S is not distributed in the minor premise (because S is in the predicate, the claim needs to be negative). This means we have an illicit minor, so the syllogism is invalid. Rules 3 and 4 are both okay (don't have two negatives, negative premise and a negative conclusion satisfies rule 4), and so is rule 5 (because we have two universal premises and a universal conclusion). The argument, because of the illicit minor, is invalid.

Constructing Valid Arguments

Say you wanted a valid argument for the conclusion, "Some vampires are bloodthirsty." Because it is an I claim, we don't have to worry about rule 2 (because nothing in the conclusion is distributed, so no problem here).

All we need to do is avoid problems with the other rules. Rule 1 means we need to have the middle term distributed. But, because the conclusion is positive we do not want any negatives in the premises (or we would violate rule 4) and because we do not want any negatives at all in the premises we won't violate rule 3.

That means we need one of the premises to be a universal positive claim, distributing the middle term. This forces the middle term to be in the subject place (because if it was in the predicate, the claim would have to be negative). The other premise cannot be universal, or we'd violate rule 5. And, because it cannot be negative (or we would violate rule 4) that means it must be an I claim. Once we distribute the middle term in the A claim, it will not matter where the middle term is in the I claim. That means we have several options. Our conclusion is: "Some vampires are bloodthirsty creatures." This means "vampires" is the minor term and "bloodthirsty creatures" the major term.

So the possible valid arguments are any of these forms: AII—(1), AII—(3), IAI—(3), or IAI—(4). These three distribute the middle term and violate none of our rules of the syllogism. So we can just pick one of these and set up our valid argument. If we pick AII—(1), our argument then is:

All M are bloodthirsty creatures.

<u>Some vampires are M.</u>

So, some vampires are bloodthirsty creatures.

Now all we have to do is make up an "M" and we are done. Let M = vampire bats. This means our valid argument is:

All vampire bats are bloodthirsty creatures.

<u>Some vampires are vampire bats.</u>

So, some vampires are bloodthirsty creatures.

A Historical Note

One of the more famous logicians in history is Lewis Carroll (alias Rev. C. L. Dodgson), author of *Alice in Wonderland* and the opening quote of this chapter. He wrote dozens of fanciful exercises and invented any number of syllogisms; many that go on for pages. Most of his examples are imaginative and humorous. Some, however, are so offensive that a 1977 edition to honor his work contained a "Note to the reader" from editor and publisher asking the reader to put such examples in their "historical setting." One such offensive example is: "No Jews are honest; Some Gentiles are rich. So, some rich people are dishonest" (cf. William Warren Bartley, III, editor, *Lewis Carroll's Symbolic Logic*). Carroll had many examples that were anti-Semitic. Simply to put them in a "historical setting" suggests that this offers some excuse.

Racism has no excuse and every "historical setting" has its racist elements. The issue is what each one of us does in our historical setting, whether to succumb to the prejudice around us or look out for it and avoid it. Obviously Carroll did not avoid it—fact that needs to be recognized. One of the messages for us in this is that we must stay aware of issues related to justice and injustice. Never assume, even in what appears as straightforward and objective as syllogistic reasoning that we should let down our guard.

Exercises

Part One

1. Test these three arguments (they are in standard form) for validity. Note any rules violated, if invalid.
   a. All monsters that live in the swamp are horrific creatures. Some horrific creatures are werewolves. So, some werewolves are monsters that live in the swamp.

b. Anyone who blows bubbles is a person who likes chewing gum. All babies are people who blow bubbles. So, all babies are people who like chewing gum.

c. No football player is an astronaut. All astronauts are daring adventurers. So, no daring adventurer is a football player.

2. Put in standard form and then give mood and figure: "Many cartoonists are zany people. All zany people are unpredictable. So, some cartoonists are unpredictable."

3. Test the argument in 2 for validity and, if invalid, note any rules violated.

4. Using the rules, decide if the following arguments are valid. Note any rules violated, if invalid:
   a. AEE—(3)
   b. EIO—(2)
   c. OIO—(1)
   d. AII—(4)

5. Using the rules, decide if the following arguments are valid. Note any rules violated, if invalid:
   a. AOA—(2)
   b. IAI—(3)
   c. AEA—(4)
   d. IEO—(1)
   e. OAO—(2)

6. Put the following in standard form and note the major, minor, and middle terms, then test for validity. If invalid, name all the rules violated:
   a. Whenever Bernie sees a rainbow, tears come to her eyes. Consequently, whenever Bernie sees a rainbow, she needs tissues. This is the case because, all the time tears come to Bernie's eyes are times she needs tissues.
   b. No woman who likes dirt between her toes should garden barefoot. Every woman who gardens barefoot needs a pedicure. Therefore, most women who need a pedicure do not like dirt between their toes.
   c. Rabid animals are dangerous. Anything dangerous should be avoided. That means we should avoid rabid animals.
   d. No one who lives in Boston is a Lakers fan. So, many anthropologists are not Lakers fans, because a lot of anthropologists live in Boston.
   e. Not all welders are naughty people. Almost all logicians are naughty people. So, some logicians are not welders.

7. Put the following in standard form and note the major, minor, and middle terms, then test for validity. If invalid, name all the rules violated:
   a. Most donuts are exquisite morsels. All donuts are greasy. So, some exquisite morsels are greasy.
   b. No jeep is a vehicle capable of climbing Mount Hood. Some jeeps are vehicles capable of crossing creeks. Therefore, some vehicles capable of crossing creeks are not capable of climbing Mount Hood.

    c. A lot of tomatoes taste like cardboard. All things that taste like cardboard are bad for your health. Therefore, some tomatoes are bad for your health.

    d. Some people who make a lot of noise are not good company. All people who are good company have a decent attitude. Therefore, some people who have a decent attitude are not people who make a lot of noise.

    e. No puppy is unlovable. All puppies are furry. Therefore, no unlovable thing is furry.

8. Test for validity and name any rules broken if invalid:
    a. Every marshmallow is white. Most ghosts are white. Therefore, some ghosts are marshmallows.

    b. All ghouls are ill mannered. No ghoul is a vegetarian. So, no vegetarian is ill mannered.

    c. No gorilla is a desirable pet. All desirable pets like to be touched. Therefore, no animal that likes to be touched is a gorilla.

    d. Most chimpanzees enjoy bananas. Some chimpanzees are well-behaved animals. Thus, many well-behaved animals are creatures that enjoy bananas.

    e. Lots of people like to go to the movies. Everyone who likes to go to the movies eats popcorn. Therefore, almost everyone eats popcorn.

    f. Most concertgoers get caught in a traffic jam. Everyone who gets caught in a traffic jam is a frazzled driver. Therefore, many concertgoers are frazzled drivers.

9. Put the following argument in standard form and then test for validity:
    a. No bird is a lizard. Some lizards are not poisonous. Thus, some poisonous creatures are not birds.

    b. Some voters are not geologists. Some stand-up comedians are voters. Therefore, some stand-up comedians are geologists.

    c. All poisonous substances are toxic things. Some toxic things are things little children get into. Therefore, some things little children get into are poisonous.

    d. Some astronomers are not fond of small children. All circus clowns are people fond of small children. So, some circus clowns are not astronomers.

    e. Most sandwiches are not spicy. Anything with mustard is spicy. Therefore, some sandwiches do not contain mustard.

    f. All chocolate lovers are interesting people. Some interesting people prefer romantic evenings at home to dining out. Therefore, those who prefer romantic evenings at home to dining out are chocolate lovers.

10. Give an example of a syllogism that has an undistributed middle, but violates no other rule. Use major: weightlifters; minor: chefs; middle: caffeine addicts.

11. Give an example of syllogisms in the following mood and figure:
    a. AEE—(1)
    b. EOE—(3)
    c. AOA—(4)
    d. AII—(2)
    e. IOO—(3)

12. Test your arguments in 10 for validity. Note any rules violated.

13. Test for validity:
    a. EAE—(1)
    b. OIA—(2)
    c. AAA—(3)
    d. AIA—(1)
    e. AII—(4)
    f. IAI—(1)

14. Give a *valid* argument for the conclusion: Therefore, no bank robber is someone to trust. Show that your argument is valid.

15. Put in standard form and then test for validity using the rules:
    Any man who can lift a refrigerator is a powerhouse.
    All men who are powerhouses are sexy.
    Thus, all sexy men can lift a refrigerator.

16. An example of an argument in AIO—(3) is:
    a. Some elephants are incredibly graceful.
    All ballerinas are incredibly graceful.
    Thus, some ballerinas are elephants.
    b. All elephants are incredibly graceful.
    Some ballerinas are incredibly graceful.
    Thus, Some ballerinas are elephants.
    c. All elephants are incredibly graceful.
    Some elephants are ballerinas.
    Thus, some ballerinas are not incredibly graceful.
    d. No elephant is incredibly graceful.
    Some elephants are ballerinas.
    So, some ballerinas are not incredibly graceful.
    e. None of the above (state what it is).

17. Put the following in standard form and then state the mood and figure: "Not all scientists are dull people. Some dull people are hilarious. So, some scientists are hilarious."

18. Give an invalid argument with an illicit minor for the conclusion, "All music lovers are discriminating people." Show it is invalid. (It's okay to violate other rules of the syllogism.)

19. Give an invalid argument with an illicit major for the conclusion: "No porridge is a lightweight snack." Show it is invalid. (It's okay to violate other rules of the syllogism.)

20. Give a valid argument for the conclusion: "All mathematicians are careful thinkers." Show it is valid.

21. Give a valid argument for the conclusion: "Some hard-working students deserve a Mercedes Benz." Show it is valid.

22. Test the following syllogisms for validity. First put in standard form then test. If invalid, state rules violated.
    a. Some women fond of dancing are exotic.
       <u>Chong is fond of dancing.</u>
       So, Chong is an exotic woman.
    b. Whoever loves to boogie loves to do the hand jive.
       <u>Whoever loves to do the hand jive will love The Temptations.</u>
       Thus, whoever loves to boogie will love The Temptations.

23. Give an invalid argument that has an undistributed middle for the conclusion: "All vampires are fond of capes." (It's okay to violate other rules of the syllogism.)

24. Give an invalid argument that has an illicit major and violates rule 4 for the conclusion: " 'Some trout fishermen are not fond of Mozart."

25. Give a valid argument for the conclusion: "Some circus acrobats are not people who are afraid of heights." Show it is valid.

26. Give an example of a syllogism with mood and figure EIO–(4). Use major term: crocodile hunters; minor term: economists; middle term: trumpet players.

27. Give an example of a syllogism with mood and figure EAE–(2) with major term: ballerinas; minor term: wrestlers; middle term: skinny people.

28. Give an example of a syllogism with mood and figure AOI–(3) with major term: carrot lovers; minor term: rabbit; middle term: vegetarians.

29. Give an invalid argument with an illicit minor having the conclusion: "All music lovers are nice people." Show it is invalid. (It's okay to violate other rules of the syllogism.)

30. Give a valid argument for the conclusion: "Some music lovers are surfers." Show it is valid.

Part Two

1. Give a valid argument for the conclusion: "No weasel is capable of doing logic." Show it is valid.

2. Give an invalid argument that has an illicit major and an undistributed middle.

3. Test for validity. If invalid name the rules violated.
   a. AAI—(3)
   b. EOA—(4)
   c. AOO—(3)

    d. IAI—(2)

    e. OAE—(1)

    f. AEE—(4)

    g. EAE—(1)

    h. IEO—(2)

    i. OIE—(3)

    j. AII—(2)

4. Why can't an argument with an A conclusion have an illicit major?

5. Give an example of an argument in mood and figure EOA—(3), with major term: rodents; minor term: pests; middle term: squirrels. Test your argument to see if it's valid.

6. Why can't a syllogism with an I conclusion have an illicit minor?

7. Why can't a syllogism with an E claim in either premise have an undistributed middle?

8. For extra practice, test the following:

    a. EOO—(1)

    b. AIO—(2)

    c. IAI—(3)

    d. AEA—(3)

    e. EIO—(2)

    f. AAA—(4)

    g. AEA—(1)

    h. EAE—(4)

    i. OEI—(2)

    j. IEO—(1)

CHAPTER SIXTEEN

Patterns of Deductive Reasoning: Rules of Inference

You have this thing called a sausage-making machine . . . anything that comes out of the sausage-making machine is known as sausage. . . . One day, we throw in a few small rodents of questionable pedigree and a teddy bear and a chicken. . . . Do we prove the validity of the machine if we call the product a sausage?

—PATRICIA J. WILLIAMS, *The Alchemy of Race and Rights*

Y ou are driving to school when you hear a "thump, thump, thump" and it is much harder to steer the car. You pull over and get out. "Gad," you think "another flat tire." A man in a pickup drives up and stops to help you. "Hey, you gotta flat!" he points out. Further demonstrating his reasoning skills, he says, "If you don't have good tires, you get a flat. You have a flat, so you must not have had good tires on your car. In fact, I'd say you were taken for a sucker! What did you pay for these tires, anyway?"

Is this an example of good thinking on his part? If you said "no," pat yourself on the back and read on to learn the type of mistake he made. If you said, "yes," you need help, so keep reading.

Think of it: What can cause your tire to go flat? You could have old tread, you could have run over a nail, your tire could have been slashed, you may have run over a pothole in the road, to name a few. Having a flat does *not* necessarily mean you have bad tires, you are a cheapskate, or you got ripped off when you bought the tire. The existence of a flat tire does not, in itself, point to one potential cause. We need more information to narrow down the list; we cannot eliminate possible causes in one wave of the arm.

There is a name for this fellow's faulty reasoning. We may remember it from Chapter 4; namely, the *fallacy of affirming the consequent.* We will examine this and other faulty patterns of reasoning in this chapter. Most of our attention, though, will be on patterns of <u>valid</u> arguments. The most common valid argument forms have specific names and are included in the rules of inference (because they indicate what can be safely inferred from the premises). Knowing the correct forms will make it easier to spot them and will help us acquire mental dexterity in argument analysis. With our minds working near optimal capacity, it will be easier to use correct reasoning when constructing our own arguments.

We will go over valid argument forms and then look at the two formal fallacies. With the rules of inference, we work with arguments and not just sentences, as is the case with the rules of replacement (see Chapter 14). A familiarity with both the rules of replacement and rules of inference provides us with the means for reformulating propositions and for drawing inferences upon the basis of the evidence we have. This allows us to greatly expand our reasoning capacity. Once we learn the rules of inference, we can spot poorly reasoned arguments like that of the roadside helper. And we'll have the requisite ability to construct well-reasoned, defensible arguments. As you might guess, this is a very powerful talent to have!

Advantages of Learning the Techniques of Logic

Some people question the value of these conventional ways of doing logic, because it puts analytical tools above the experiential and emotional; and it requires a level of precision that requires us to be attentive to fine details.

Logic elevates one kind of (rational, structured, principled) approach over other ways of thinking and problem solving. The focus here is on honing certain argumentative skills and techniques—and it does so to the exclusion of such issues as observation skills, inspirational language, values and beliefs, frames of reference, stereotypes, bias, and prejudice. Nevertheless, perfecting the techniques acquired through a study of logic can be enormously useful—and satisfying.

The advantages of supplementing these tools with critical thinking skills are as follows: An analysis should include diverse perspectives to decide key issues, the best approach, and criteria for a solution. We should be attentive to the use of language and argument structure. This helps us spot balanced versus biased presentations. We should examine underlying value systems and note just versus harmful actions. We should study policies to see if they are fair versus oppressive. And we should never use logic as a tool of racism or destruction.

We should reject oppression, not logic. Logic can be used as a tool for problem solving and analysis. Having a facility with logic gives us the techniques to examine and evaluate the many kinds of arguments we confront. This does not help us develop moral fiber, but it does help us develop *mental dexterity*.

Being good at logic is only part of being good at critical thinking, but it can be both useful and empowering. With that in mind, let's go deeper into the terrain of logic. We will first go over the different valid argument forms. Next we will go over the formal fallacies, so you will see how people go astray. At the end of the chapter will be exercises with all the rules of replacement, rules of inference, and a selection of different kinds of fallacies all mixed together.

▦ Valid Argument Forms

Let us begin with valid argument forms. Remember, an argument is valid if the premises offer sufficient support for the conclusion (see Chapter 6 on deductive reasoning to refresh your memory).

This does not mean the premises have to be true! Repeat: A valid argument does *not* have to have true premises, even if that seems like a bunch of hooey. But it does mean that, if we assume they were true, then the conclusion would have to follow—it could not be false. Moreover, the propositions making up the argument could be *entirely false* and the argument still be valid. This is due to the fact that the *focus in validity is on the form* itself, not the substance of the claims. In other words, studying validity is like examining x-rays, in that the focus is the structure. If there are problems with the structure (the bones) then the argument won't be able to "stand" on its own two feet.

The various rules of inference function like patterns of good reasoning: Anything that fits the pattern, regardless of the subject matter, is a valid argument. That means we can assess the validity of a deductive argument by examining the structure of the argument. Nothing else is necessary at this stage. Later, when we move to the issue of whether or not the argument is *sound,* we will take up the question of whether the premises are actually true claims.

▦ Rules of Inference

You are changing the tire when a woman comes by, walking her dog. She offers *her* argument: "If the tire only has a nail in it, then it can be repaired. Oh, look, that is just a nail. Good—your tire can be repaired." What do you think of her reasoning?

Her argument is a valid one, because *if* we assume the two premises are true, then she is right to suggest the tire can be repaired. Her reasoning is, therefore, correct. That does not mean the argument is sound, as you know. We also need to know the premises really are true. *Remember:* a sound argument is a valid argument that has true premises. That is, soundness goes one step beyond validity—it requires truth, as well as a good, solid structure.

If you just have a nail in your tire, she is probably right to say the tire can be fixed—though this is not certain. Your tire may be destined for the recycling bin. However, the woman has proven that she can construct a valid argument. The name of her argument is called *modus ponens.* You may recall seeing modus ponens in Chapter 6, when we looked at the major types of deductive arguments.

Modus Ponens

Modus ponens is the name of any argument in the following form:

Form of Modus Ponens

If A then B.

<u>A is true.</u>

Therefore, B is true also.

This means if there is an antecedent condition (A) for a consequent (B), and the antecedent A is given; then the consequent B follows.

Modus ponens example 1:

If that's an alligator, you better get out of the swamp.

<u>That is an alligator.</u>

So, you better get out of the swamp.

Modus ponens example 2:

If that's not an earthquake, then we can relax.

<u>That's not an earthquake we felt.</u>

So, we can relax.

Note: The antecedent is negative, so you have to carry the negative with you. Whatever the antecedent is (big or small, positive or negative), you want to repeat it in the second premise.

Modus ponens example 3:

If you've got the room cleaned and finished your homework, *then* we can either go to a movie or try out the skates I found in the shed.

<u>You've got the room cleaned and your homework done.</u>

So, we can either go to a movie or try out the skates I found in the shed.

Note: In this case the antecedent was compound (a conjunction, "C and F") and, therefore, the second premise, stating the antecedent, has to repeat the entire conjunction. Note also that the consequent is compound (a disjunction, "M or T"). Nevertheless, the form of the argument is still modus ponens.

Modus Tollens

Our next valid argument form is called modus tollens. Here we introduce opposites. That is, where modus ponens just repeats the antecedent in the second premise, in modus tollens the second premise is the opposite of the consequent.

For example, a police officer stopped to see how you were doing with your flat tire. He says, "If you cannot get the car lifted, then your jack is no good. Your jack looks good, so you'll be able to get the car lifted." Do you see what the officer did in his argument? Look at the first premise and then look at the second. What shifted? The consequent from the first premise ("Your jack is no good") has been changed to its opposite and is now the second premise ("Your jack looks good"). What follows then is the negated antecedent (So, you <u>can</u> get the car lifted). This is a good argument. It is called modus tollens.

So with modus tollens, we start with a conditional claim ("If . . . then . . ."). The second premise asserts that the opposite of the consequent is the case. Then we can conclude that the opposite of the antecedent must be the case. The form of modus tollens is as follows:

Form of Modus Tollens

If A then B.

<u>B is not the case.</u>

Therefore, A is not the case either.

Modus tollens example 1:

If you run over a nail, you'll get a flat tire.

<u>You don't have a flat tire.</u>

So, you didn't run over a nail.

Modus tollens example 2:

Only happy people sleep soundly. (≡ If you sleep well, then you are happy.)

<u>Rick isn't happy.</u>

So, Rick doesn't sleep soundly.

Note: Rewrite the "only" claim as a conditional. The second line is the negation of the consequent from line 1. It thus follows that the conclusion is the negation of the antecedent from line 1. You go to the opposite of the consequent in line 2 and the opposite of the antecedent in the conclusion.

• Think *opposite,* not positive or negative.

Modus tollens example 3:

If either toxic waste or nuclear fuel is stored here, there is a risk to public health.

<u>There's no risk to public health.</u>

Therefore, neither toxic waste nor nuclear fuel is stored here.

Note: The conclusion is a negation of a disjunction. We know from De Morgan's laws (which we studied in Chapter 14) that we could replace this with "Toxic waste is not stored here <u>and</u> nuclear fuel is not stored here." Be careful to change the "or" to an "and" when you run the negative across.

Hypothetical Syllogism

Suppose you are at home (your tire fixed!) and the phone rings. It is your mother, who has been calling all morning. She is relieved you are okay and says, "If you have another flat tire, then call me. If you call me, then I won't worry. So, if you have another flat tire, I won't worry." Your mother may be a worrywort, but her reasoning is valid. The name of her argument is called the hypothetical syllogism. As you can see, it is composed entirely of conditional (hypothetical) claims.

Form of the Hypothetical Syllogism

If A then B.

<u>If B then C.</u>

Therefore, if A then C.

It is crucial that the linking term B connecting A and C together be the consequent of the first premise and the antecedent of the second one. Otherwise there's a break in the chain and the argument will be invalid.

Hypothetical syllogism example 1:

If it hails then I can't drive home.

<u>If I can't drive home then I'll stay in a hotel.</u>

Thus, if it hails then I'll stay in a hotel.

Note: Do you see the *connecting link* ("I can't drive home")? If you don't have this connector, you don't have a hypothetical syllogism. This is the link in the chain that holds the argument together.

Hypothetical syllogism example 2:

If that's another cockroach in the living room, then either I'm calling an exterminator or I'll set out poison.

<u>If I call an exterminator or set out poison, then we can solve the problem.</u>

Therefore, if that's another cockroach crawling in the living room, then we can solve the problem.

Note: You can see that this example of a hypothetical syllogism involves a compound term (the consequent in the first premise = the antecedent in the second premise). The superstructure, however, is still in the form of a hypothetical syllogism and, thus, it's still as valid as if it had been less complex.

Exercises

Part One

1. Using modus tollens, finish the argument that starts with: "If he can clone the mouse embryo, Dr. White will file for a patent."

2. Using hypothetical syllogism, finish the argument that starts with: "If Dr. White clones the mouse, he'll clone a small mammal."

3. Using modus ponens, finish the argument that starts with: "If there's pink fluid under the car, it may be wise to check the transmission."

4. Using hypothetical syllogism, finish the argument that starts with: "If she gets another x-ray, she'll glow in the dark."

5. Using modus tollens, finish each of the following arguments that start with:
   a. If Jason uses an earpiece with his cell phone, he'll be a better driver.
   b. If Anthea hears screaming from the attic, she'll think there's a poltergeist.
   c. If there are poltergeists in the house and they're causing trouble, Bruce will hold a séance.
   d. If Ryan hears about the séance, he will study his book on egyptology.
   e. If there's no egyptologist available, Bruce will call an exorcist.
   f. If the line to the exorcist is busy, Bruce will call both an exterminator.
   g. If the exterminator is out of town, Bruce will call Jason.

6. Using modus ponens, finish each of the following arguments that start with:
   a. If the mouse embryo is cloned, then the lab experiment worked.
   b. If the lab experiments work, then people will want to clone their pets.
   c. If people cannot clone their pets, they may want to try cloning either their children or themselves.
   d. If people clone themselves and are happy with the results, they will re-think their views of death.
   e. If people clone their pets, there could be mutants on the loose.
   f. If mutants are on the loose, there may be a slight increase in crime.
   g. If there's an increase in crime and it results in more convictions, we'll need more prisons.

7. Using hypothetical syllogism, finish the following arguments that start with:
   a. If Silvio gets a speeding ticket, he'll go to traffic school.
   b. If Darin hears the joke about pig liver transplants, he'll hoot.
   c. If Dr. Snow can clone a possum, pharmaceutical companies will be impressed.
   d. If Ryan figures out hieroglyphics, he can read the writing on the wall of the pyramid.
   e. If Anthea gets rid of the poltergeists, she'll sell the story to *Entertainment Extra Extra!*

f. If the pink ooze in the New York sewer system is not transmission fluid, the police have a serious problem.

Part Two

Directions: Name the argument forms in the following statements. Each statement involves one of the following forms: modus ponens, modus tollens, or hypothetical syllogism.

1. If it keeps snowing, the skiing will be great. The skiing was not great, so it didn't keep snowing.

2. If the sun stays out, the snow will melt and the slopes will be muddy. If the snow melts and the slopes are muddy, then we can't ski. Therefore, if the sun stays out, then we can't ski.

3. If we can't go skiing, we might as well go hiking. We can't go skiing. Thus, we'll go hiking.

4. If we play Stevie Nicks albums all night, then we won't finish our homework. We finished our homework. Therefore, we did not play Stevie Nicks albums all night.

5. If you are not consistent, then you can't train a puppy. I see your puppy is trained, so you must have been consistent.

6. If neither the police nor the fire truck arrives, we may wish we picked somewhere else to live. Neither the police nor the fire truck arrived. So we may wish we picked somewhere else to live.

7. If the police helicopter lands in the yard, Virginia's vegetable garden will be flattened. If her vegetable garden is flattened, she will sue the city. So if the police helicopter lands in the yard, Virginia will sue the city.

8. If the part-time job works out and you finally get some money coming in, then we can plan a weekend away to the desert. The part-time job worked out and you finally got money coming in, so we can plan a weekend away to the desert.

9. If Sandie keeps lying in the sun, she'll get burned. Sandie did not get burned. We can conclude that Sandie did not keep lying in the sun.

10. If Steve gets everyone in the car by 3 a.m., they should be able to get to Winslow, Arizona, by evening. If they get to Winslow, Arizona, by evening, they can make it to Tulsa by Thursday afternoon. So, if Steve gets everyone in the car by 3 a.m., they can make it to Tulsa by Thursday afternoon.

Disjunctive Syllogism

There is nothing like a disjunctive syllogism. You start with a disjunction (an "either/or" claim) and then the second premise is a denial of one of the disjuncts. This forces the conclusion to be the remaining disjunct.

For example, your brother finds something weird on his plate. He picks it up and turns it over and over. He finally says, "Either this is someone's false eyelashes or they got some of the cowhide in the hamburger. This is not false eyelashes, so there's cowhide in the hamburger." Your brother shows his potential as a logician and you feel downright smug in telling him that his valid argument is called the disjunctive syllogism. Here is the form:

Form of the Disjunctive Syllogism

Either A or B.

A is not the case (or B is not the case).

Therefore, B is the case (or A is the case).

See how this works? The first premise is a choice between two options. The second premise eliminates one of the options. That leaves us with the conclusion that the remaining option must then be the case. Let's look at some examples.

Disjunctive syllogism example 1:

Either a wolf is howling or the wind is in the trees.

There's no wind tonight.

Therefore, it must be a wolf howling.

Note: Do you see how it operates? You start with an either/or choice. In the next line one choice (disjunct) is eliminated. This leaves the other one.

Disjunctive syllogism example 2:

Either there has been a peace accord between Britain and Northern Ireland and the proposal will be taken seriously, or we are in for more years of conflict.

We are not in for more years of conflict.

So, there has been a peace accord between Britain and Northern Ireland and the proposal will be taken seriously.

Note: In the first premise there is a compound first disjunct. The superstructure is still a disjunctive syllogism, however, so we proceed in the same way as if with the simpler cases.

Conjunction

Conjunction is very straightforward: Two claims that are each true are true in combination. The rule of conjunction asserts that if we have two claims that we know to be true, then they are both true together. The form of conjunction is this:

Form of Conjunction

A is true.

B is also true.

Therefore, both A and B are true.

Conjunction example 1:

That is the Vietnam War Memorial.

A huge crowd of people are gathered around it.

Therefore, that is the Vietnam War Memorial and a huge crowd of people are gathered around it.

Conjunction example 2:

A good book deserves two readings.

Molloy is a good book.

Therefore, a good book deserves two readings and *Molloy* is a good book.

So, the rule of conjunction allows us to merge together two true propositions, resulting in a third (the compounded claim) proposition that is also true.

Simplification

Another valid form of argument starts with two things given together in conjunction. If both are together true, then it must follow that each one is individually true. This is called simplification.

For example, if someone said that both the Democrats and the Republicans have a plan for an improved health care system, then it would follow that the Democrats have a plan for an improved health care system. It also follows that the Republicans have a plan. We can deduce either of the conjuncts when we know they are both true together. This then is simplification: From a conjunction, you can simplify by concluding that each individual conjunct is also true.

Form of Simplification

A and B are true together.

Therefore, A is true as well (or B is also true).

In other words, knowing that the collective, A and B, is true, it follows that each conjunct individually is true as well. Let's look at some examples:

Simplification example 1:

The reviewer liked both *A Beautiful Mind* and *Training Day.*

Therefore, the reviewer liked *A Beautiful Mind.*

Simplification example 2:

A woman with a shaved head is both daring and shocking.

Therefore, a woman with a shaved head is shocking.

Logical Addition

Our next rule of inference has a name that seems counterintuitive. It is called logical addition.

The name "logical addition" is a bit misleading, because the "adding" here is by use of an "or" not an "and." Logical addition allows you to expand when you are given one thing that is true. Here's the form that logical addition takes:

Form of Logical Addition

A is true.

Therefore, either A or B is true.

In this valid argument form, you can infer from anything that is true to a disjunction consisting of the true claim and any other proposition. Let's see some examples.

Logical addition example 1:

The basement flooded after the rain.

Therefore, either the basement flooded after the rain or I had a nightmare last night.

Note: Remember that the conclusion of logical addition is a disjunction ("or") and *not* a conjunction.

Logical addition example 2:

Seaweed has a lot of minerals in it and is good for your health.

Therefore, either seaweed has a lot of minerals in it and is good for your health, or that nutrition book I read gave the wrong information.

Note: Did you see how this example has a compounded first premise? We can still apply the rule of logical addition.

Exercises

Part One

Directions: Complete the arguments using the rule indicated.

1. Using logical addition: "Skydiving is never boring."
2. Using simplification: "Both Batman and Robin wear snug-fitting clothing."

3. Using the disjunctive syllogism: "Either I heard a seal bark or that's the neighbor's shepherd pup."

4. Using hypothetical syllogism: "If you go barefoot, people will stare at you."

5. Using conjunction: "Wellie enjoys spaghetti any time of the day. Wellie refuses to eat peas."

6. Using modus tollens: "If Tony smells a rat, the game is up."

7. Using logical addition: "Canned fruit tastes slimy."

8. Using simplification: "A good pie is warm and has ice cream on top."

9. Using logical addition: "A good book is usually better than a movie."

10. Using conjunction: "The fire destroyed 24 homes. Many people and animals were displaced."

11. Using modus ponens: "If you walk to work, you should wear comfortable shoes."

12. Using simplification: "April does not like small rodents and she doesn't care much for large rodents either."

Part Two

Directions: Name the following rules used in the arguments below.

1. If you are an art lover, then you will enjoy pottery. If you enjoy pottery, then you'll love the Zuni pots at the Southwest Museum. Therefore, if you are an art lover, then you'll love the Zuni pots at the Southwest Museum.

2. If you are a daredevil, you may enjoy race car driving. Jackie Chan is a daredevil. Therefore, he may enjoy race car driving.

3. Ed did not take the chihuahuas out for a walk. Jack did not play flamenco music. Therefore, Ed did not take the chihauhuas out for a walk and Jack did not play flamenco music.

4. If we want to see a classic film, we will watch *Wings of Desire*. Bruno wanted to see a classic film, so he'll watch *Wings of Desire*.

5. Carla didn't think *Paulie* was as good as *Babe*. Therefore, either my memory is shot or Carla didn't think *Paulie* was as good as *Babe*.

6. If Paul shows *My Cousin Vinny* at the party, Sam will laugh himself silly. Sam did not laugh himself silly. So, Paul did not show *My Cousin Vinny* at the party.

7. Either Frank will see *The Money Pit* or he'll read Plato. Frank didn't read Plato. Therefore, he saw *The Money Pit*.

8. If Rocio does not go to see *Bandits*, then she will work on her poetry. Rocio did not work on her poetry. Therefore, she went to see *Bandits*.

9. Will went to see *Blade II*, and he sat in front of a girl who kicked the back of his seat. Therefore Will sat in front of a girl who kicked the back of his seat.

10. If I eat too much popcorn, I feel sick. I ate too much popcorn. So I felt sick.

11. Either we'll see *Don't Look Now* or we'll see *McCabe and Mrs. Miller*. We didn't see *Don't Look Now*, so we saw *McCabe and Mrs. Miller*.

12. *The Vanishing* was an awfully creepy movie. Therefore, either *The Vanishing* was an awfully creepy movie or I'm just squeamish.

13. If you don't like to be scared, don't see *Night of the Living Dead*. If you don't see *Night of the Living Dead*, you might as well forget about watching *Dawn of the Dead*. Therefore, if you don't like to be scared, you might as well forget about watching *Dawn of the Dead*.

14. Provided that he enjoys a good drama, he might like *Room With a View*. He didn't like *Room With a View*, so he doesn't enjoy a good drama.

15. Ryan loved *Princess Mononoke*. He watched it three times in two days. Therefore, Ryan loved *Princess Mononoke* and watched it three times in two days.

Constructive Dilemma

In ancient Greece, they used to talk about being stuck on the horns of a *dilemma*. This means being faced with two choices where each choice has serious or problematic consequences; yet you have to pick. So you choose one, and then have to deal with the set of consequences that follow.

For example, what if your best friend said, "I'm in love"? You ask him what he is going to do and he says: "If I tell my parents, they'll want me to get married, but if I don't tell them, then our relationship will really suffer." Either he's going to tell his folks, or he's not. So either of the two consequences will then follow.

Form of Constructive Dilemma

If A then B, and if C then D.

Either A or C.

Therefore, either B or D.

If you look closely at the constructive dilemma, you will see it is like a compound modus ponens, which we can see by stretching it out:

	If A then B	and	if C then D.
	A	or	**C.**
Therefore,	**B**	or	**D.**

The second premise is a disjunction of the two antecedents from the first premise, and the conclusion is a disjunction of the two consequents. Let's look at some examples.

Constructive dilemma example 1:

If the computer crashes again, Irasema will have to reinstall the software; but if the computer quits crashing, Irasema will be able to finish her assignment for bioethics.

Either the computer crashed again or it quit crashing.

So, either Irasema will have to reinstall the software or she'll be able to finish her assignment for bioethics.

Constructive dilemma example 2:

If the band goes by bus, the concert may have to be delayed, but if the band takes the plane, the profits will be small.

Either the band will go by bus or they'll take a plane.

So either the concert may be delayed or the profits will be small.

Destructive Dilemma

There is another dilemma besides the constructive dilemma. It is called the destructive dilemma. Whereas the constructive dilemma is like a compound modus ponens, this next one is like a compound modus tollens.

Here's an example: "If you study math, it'll help you with the sciences but if you study literature, you'll be strong in the humanities. Either you are not going to be helped in the sciences or you won't be strong in the humanities. Therefore, either you didn't study math or you didn't study literature."

Form of the Destructive Dilemma

If A then B, and if C then D.

Either B is not the case or D is not the case.

Therefore, either A is not the case or C is not the case.

Destructive dilemma example 1:

If the lotus flowers are in bloom, the crowds will come to Silver Lake, but if the flowers haven't yet opened, it'll be easy to find parking.

Either the crowds haven't come to Silver Lake or it won't be easy to find parking.

So, either the lotus flowers are not in bloom or the flowers have opened.

Destructive dilemma example 2:

If Lisa takes accounting, she'll get promoted, but if she doesn't take accounting, she can spend more time with Charlie.

Either Lisa did not get promoted or she can't spend more time with Charlie.

So, either Lisa did not take accounting or she did take accounting.

Absorption

The rule of absorption fits its name quite nicely (quite the opposite of logical addition!). We start with a conditional claim, such as "If it rains, the roads will be muddy." We can then infer, "If it rains, then it rains and the roads will be muddy." The antecedent gets absorbed (think *repeated*) into the consequent when you replace the consequent with the conjunction of the antecedent and the consequent.

Form of the Rule of Absorption

If A then B.

Therefore, if A, then both A and B.

Do you see how this goes? We start with a conditional claim. We can then conclude that the antecedent condition can be "absorbed" (repeated) into the consequent. It may look like mere repetition, but it can be particularly handy for certain situations. Think of it sort of like a Phillip's head screwdriver: you don't need it very often, but when you do nothing else works nearly as well. Let's look at some examples.

Absorption example 1:

If the Lakers go to the play-offs, they will play the Kings.

Therefore, if the Lakers go to the play-offs, then the Lakers go to the play-offs and they will play the Kings.

Note: The entire antecedent had to move back to the consequent. Whatever the antecedent is—simple or compound—the whole thing has to get absorbed into (placed in conjunction with) the consequent.

Absorption example 2:

If we can make it to see either the Vancouver Canucks or the Seattle Sonics, then we can forget about staying home.

Thus, if we can make it either to see the Vancouver Canucks or the Seattle Sonics, then we can forget about staying home.

Exercises

Directions: Drawing from the constructive dilemma, the destructive dilemma, and absorption, name the rule of inference in the following.

1. If the rain doesn't stop, the roads will be flooded, but if the rain stops, we can drive to Moose Jaw. Either the rain didn't stop or it did. Therefore either the roads will be flooded or we can drive to Moose Jaw.

2. If Lisa drives the Jeep, Charlie will have to take the bus. Subsequently, if Lisa drives the jeep, then she'll drive the jeep and Charlie will have to take the bus.

3. Either the billboard got blown away during the tornado, or someone removed it overnight. If the billboard got blown away during the tornado, then we'll have a nice view of the lake, but if someone removed it overnight, then they must be planning construction on the new lot. Therefore, either we'll have a nice view of the lake or they must be planning construction on the new lot.

4. If the lightning hits the trees, there could be a fire. If the lightening misses the trees, then it could strike one of the cows. Either there was no fire or none of the cows got hit, therefore either the lightning did not hit the trees or the lightning struck the trees.

5. If the cow gets hit by lightning, it could be hurt. Therefore, if the cow gets hit by lightning, it got hit by lightning and could be hurt.

6. If the lightning hits the jeep, it could melt the steering wheel; but if it misses the jeep, Lisa won't have to worry about getting a new car. Either the steering wheel was not melted or Lisa did have to worry about getting a new car. Therefore, either the lightning did not hit the jeep or it did.

7. Either the weather report is wrong or the storm is going to strike. If the weather report is wrong, then Carol and Sam can make it to the Star Trek conference. If the storm strikes, they'll have to stay home. Therefore, either Carol and Sam made it to the Star Trek conference or they'll have to stay home.

Validity versus Soundness Reminder

All the rules of inference are valid argument forms. That means any argument in any of these forms will be <u>valid</u>. So if we assume the premises are true, the conclusion would be forced to be true as well. The conclusion can't be false whenever a valid argument has true premises.

Be aware though, in a valid argument the evidence fully supports the conclusion. So, if we assume the premises to be true in any of these rules of inference, then the conclusion will follow as true. *But it doesn't mean the evidence is necessarily true.* That's another issue altogether. To be *sound* the argument must be valid, but it must also have true premises.

We want also to have our antennae out for the formal fallacies, so we don't accidentally mistake a fallacy for either modus ponens or modus tollens, both valid argument forms. Let's then review the two formal fallacies, so we clarify how they differ from the valid forms of argumentation.

▨ Formal Fallacies

As you may recall from Chapter 4, fallacies are always invalid arguments, whether or not they have true premises. They are incorrect forms of reasoning, no matter how persuasive they may be. The reality is, people can be persuaded by bad reasoning; but that doesn't change the fact that the reasoning is still bad.

There are two formal fallacies. They are called formal fallacies because the error has to do with a misuse of form, or structure. The entire argument is structured incorrectly: even if the premises were true, the conclusion would not follow as true. These two fallacies are, basically, mutations of modus ponens and modus tollens. But where both modus ponens and modus tollens are valid forms of argument, the two formal fallacies are both invalid and unsound.

Our job is to examine the form of the argument. If we see that the structure fits these two types below, then we know the argument is invalid—that a fallacy has been committed. The two major formal fallacies are fallacy of denying the antecedent and fallacy of affirming the consequent.

Valid Argument Forms versus Formal Fallacies

We know that two famous valid argument forms are *modus ponens* and *modus tollens,* as set out below:

Modus ponens—*a* valid *argument form* (not *a fallacy):*

If A then B.

A is true.

So, B is true.

Example of modus ponens:

If the tornado crosses the stream, the farm will be hit.

The tornado crossed the stream.

Therefore, the farm will be hit.

Note: If the two premises are true, the conclusion is certainly true as well. This makes the argument valid.

Modus tollens—*a* valid *argument form* (not *a fallacy):*

If A then B.

B is not the case.

So, A is not case.

Example of modus tollens:

If the storm hits, the wedding reception will move indoors.

The wedding reception did not move indoors.

Therefore, the storm did not hit.

Note: If the two premises are true, the conclusion has to be true as well—it couldn't be false. This makes the argument valid.

If we see that an argument fits either of the valid argument patterns above, we can relax. However, that may not happen. Instead, we may be staring at a fallacy. Our job is to examine the form of the argument to make that determination.

Fallacy of Denying the Antecedent

The fallacy of denying the antecedent asserts a causal relationship between the antecedent condition (A) and the consequent (B). The fallacy occurs when the person claims that, because the antecedent doesn't happen, the consequent can't happen either. However, there may be many things that cause the consequent to happen.

The conclusion does not automatically follow if the premises are true—unless it is given that there is a one-to-one ("if and only if") connection between the antecedent cause A, and the effect B. Unless it is explicitly stated, we cannot assume it and, thus, must assume that there are other possible causal factors that could bring about the effect. The fact that one possible cause does not occur does not preclude some other factor causing the effect.

For example, "If the bank robber is hiding in the college mailroom, then we had better call the FBI." This fallacy occurs when it is argued, "The bank robber is not hiding in the college mailroom; therefore, we don't need to call the FBI." The reason this is fallacious is that, even if there is not a bank robber in the college mailroom, we may still need to contact the FBI. We might, for instance, realize that, instead of the bank robber, there are three agents from the old KGB camped out in the woodshed, plotting the overthrow of the Uzbekistan government. Or perhaps an escapee from the nearest prison is lurking in the back yard. Or it may be that we've found evidence of an e-mail scam targeting people on welfare. Simply because there's no bank robber in the college mailroom doesn't mean the consequent ("We had better call the FBI") is not the case.

Form of the Fallacy of Denying the Antecedent

If A then B.

A is not the case.

Therefore, B is not the case.

Note: A and B could be either positive or negative claims, and could be compound propositions as well.

Fallacy of denying the antecedent example 1:

If the band is too loud, Laura will get a headache.

The band is not too loud.

So, Laura did not get a headache.

Note: Laura could get a headache from other things, such as the pollen in the air or not drinking her morning mug of espresso.

Fallacy of denying the antecedent example 2:

If another snail crawls under the door, I'm pouring salt around the house.

<u>Another snail did not crawl under the door.</u>

So I didn't pour salt around the house.

Note: I might pour salt simply as a preventative measure, or to cut down on the number of slugs and mealy bugs crawling up to the door.

More examples of the fallacy of denying the antecedent:

If Carmen dyes her hair blonde, she will look sensational. Carmen didn't dye her hair blonde, so she won't look sensational.

→ *Dyeing your hair isn't the only path to looking good.*

If Wimpy jogs around the block, then he'll get in shape. Wimpy didn't jog around the block, so he didn't get in shape.

→ *There are many ways to work out; jogging is but one of them.*

If George either chases that skunk or lays a trap, he may be very sorry. George did not chase the skunk and did not lay a trap, so he was not sorry.

→ *George could be sorry for other reasons, such as losing his wallet.*

Fallacy of Affirming the Consequent

This fallacy occurs when it is argued that "If A then B. B is true (the consequent happens) and, therefore, A is true (the antecedent happens also)." As with the fallacy of denying the antecedent, having a causal connection does not make it a one-to-one ("if and only if") connection. That must be specified. If it is not stated (If A then B <u>and</u> If B then A), then the fact that B is true does not mean that A has to be true as well. There could be a number of causal factors independently causing an event.

For example, suppose someone said to you, "If the coyotes get in the back yard, the primroses will be crushed. The primroses were crushed. Therefore, there must have been coyotes in the back yard." What's wrong with this reasoning? Well, coyotes aren't the only things that can crush primroses. For example, there could have been dogs running through, or the maintenance men stomping on the primroses when they were fixing the fence in the back, and so forth.

Form of the Fallacy of Affirming the Consequent

If A then B.

<u>B is the case.</u>

Therefore, A is the case as well.

Note: A and B could be either positive or negative claims and either or both could be compound propositions.

Fallacy of affirming the consequent example 1:

If the road is muddy or full of weeds, it will be hard to go hiking.

<u>It was hard to go hiking.</u>

Therefore the road was muddy or full of weeds.

Note: There are many factors that make it difficult to hike; muddy roads are just a few.

Fallacy of affirming the consequent example 2:

If the driver in the blue Cadillac sneaks into the carpool lane, she will get a ticket.

<u>The driver in the blue Cadillac got a ticket.</u>

So she must have sneaked into the carpool lane.

Note: She could have gotten a ticket for speeding, for drunk driving, or something else besides sneaking into the carpool lane.

More examples of fallacy of affirming the consequent:

If you don't have oxygen, you will die. George died. Therefore, he didn't have enough oxygen.

→ *George could have died for another reason, such as sausage poisoning.*

If Angie gets stuck in the mud, she'll be late to the party. Angie was late to the party, so she must have gotten stuck in the mud.

→ *Angie could be late because she got lost or stopped at the bank.*

Exercises

Directions: Name the formal fallacy or valid argument (either modus ponens or modus tollens) below:

1. If Ray doesn't study logic, he'll go to the gym. Ray didn't study logic, so he must be at the gym.

2. If Max gets another Billie Holiday record, we will get a new speaker system. We got a new speaker, so Max must have gotten another Billie Holliday record.

3. If Ray becomes an aerobics instructor, he won't have time to study logic. Ray didn't have time for logic, so he must have become an aerobics instructor.

4. If Pinky feels better, he can go home. Pinky did not go home, so he must not feel better.

5. If Shannon doesn't make it to the showing of *Powwow Highway,* then she'll try to come to the next movie night on campus. Shannon made it to the showing of *Powwow Highway,* so she won't try to be at the next movie night on campus.

6. If Amelia decides to go to see *Training Day*, then she will miss the 5 p.m. showing of *Tortilla Soup*. Amelia did not miss the 5 p.m. showing of *Tortilla Soup*. Therefore, she didn't decide to see *Training Day*.

7. If the virus comes in as an attachment and you open it, all hell will break loose. I'm glad to hear you did not open the attachment with the Melissa virus in it. Therefore, no worry about hell breaking loose on your computer!

8. If the slithy toves break into Hogwarts, there'll be trouble. The slithy toves broke into Hogwarts; therefore, there'll be trouble.

9. If you burn the potatoes, the frittata won't be very tasty. Alice did not burn the potatoes, so she must have made a tasty frittata.

10. If the virus infects your e-mail system, you might as well erase your hard disk and start over. A virus infected Ann's e-mail program. As a result, she might as well erase her hard disk and start over.

11. If a cook lacks the right ingredients, he won't be able to make a good soufflé. Claude wasn't able to make a good soufflé, so he must not have had the right ingredients.

12. If Max keeps practicing his Chinese drums, he will drive Maria crazy. Max did not keep practicing his Chinese drums. So he did not drive Maria crazy.

Overview

At this point, we've covered a lot of territory in terms of the valid argument forms and the two formal fallacies. Because so many of these major forms are used in everyday discourse, as well as developed arguments that we come across, knowing the forms is extremely useful. The list below is a summary of the area we've covered.

Rules of Inference—Valid Argument Forms

Modus ponens:	If A then B. A. Therefore B.
Modus tollens:	If A then B. Not B. Therefore not A.
Hypothetical syllogism:	If A then B. If B then C. Therefore, if A then C.
Disjunctive syllogism:	Either A or B. Not A. Therefore, B.
Constructive dilemma:	If A then B, and, if C then D. Either A or C. Therefore, either B or D.
Destructive dilemma:	If A then B, and, if C then D. Either not B or not D. Therefore, either not A or not C.
Simplification:	A and B. Therefore, A. (or Therefore, B.)
Logical addition:	A. Therefore, either A or B.

Conjunction:	A. B. Therefore, A and B.
Absorption:	If A then B. Therefore, If A, then (both A and B).

Rules of Replacement

De Morgan's Laws:	Not both:	Not (A and B) ≡ Not A or not B.
	Neither/nor:	Neither A nor B ≡ Not A and not B.
Material implication:	"If A then B" ≡ "Either not A or B."	
Transposition:	"If A then B" ≡ "If not B then not A."	
Exportation:	"If (A and B) then C" ≡ "If A then, (if B then C)."	
Equivalence:	"A if and only if B" ≡ "If A then B, and if B then A." (*or:* If A then B, and if not A then not B.)	

Formal Fallacies

Fallacy of affirming the consequent:	If A then B. B. Therefore, A.
Fallacy of denying the antecedent:	If A then B. Not A. Therefore, not B.

Exercises

Part One

Directions: Using the rule indicated complete the argument or give an equivalent sentence.

1. Destructive dilemma: If truth is stranger than fiction, then they'll want to hear the truth, whereas if art imitates life, then they will have stories to tell.
2. Material implication: Either she told the truth or she deceived her friend.
3. Modus tollens: If he doesn't get an Austin Mini, then he'll buy a Z-3.
4. Addition: A marathon runner leaped over the car.
5. Exportation: If the slugs get on the lilies and eat the leaves, Ray will not be happy.
6. Absorption: If Ray is happy, then his lilies must be okay.
7. Hypothetical syllogism: If Carla serves chili, Jim will bring chips and salsa.
8. Material implication: If the band needs a sound engineer, they will call Trent.
9. Transposition: If Ed's fever does not break, he will go to the doctor.
10. Using De Morgan's laws:
    a. Neither opera nor jazz comforts a bluegrass lover.
    b. David is not guilty of both eating the tamales and gobbling up the flan.

11. Conjunction: Pulling weeds is good for stress. Nothing beats getting rid of dead wood.

12. Constructive dilemma: If they have a long talk, things will improve; but if they refuse to speak, we better put on some soul music.

13. Simplification: Omar enjoys discussing politics and is a serious soccer fan.

14. Disjunctive syllogism: Michelle is either going to watch *The West Wing* or she'll study for the chemistry exam.

15. Modus ponens: If the rumors spread, there will be trouble.

16. Constructive dilemma: If the Angels lose again, Jerry will throw a fit, but if they win, then Jerry will have to make good on his bet.

17. Hypothetical syllogism: If the Knicks win, then Anna will gloat.

18. Disjunctive syllogism: Either Madeleine is from Eagle Rock or she's from Fresno.

19. Absorption: If that's a Harvard woman, then ask her about the Peabody Museum.

20. Modus tollens: If the pizza doesn't arrive on time, Fred will eat the fudge brownies.

21. Conjunction: He's been to Machias, Maine. He knows about Helen's Pies.

22. Modus ponens: If she drops out of school and goes into web design, Gina's life will change.

Part Two

Directions: Name the rule of inference used in the following. If more than one rule is used, name both.

1. Only robins eat worms. That's not a robin. So it doesn't eat worms.

2. If something is a worm-eater it is carnivorous. John is not a carnivore. So John is not a worm-eater.

3. John does not eat squid. John enjoys his steak rare. Thus, John does not eat squid and he enjoys his steak rare.

4. Either John gets his steak rare or he'll get a hamburger. John did not get a hamburger, so he got his steak rare.

5. All steak-eaters revolt Veronica. All those who revolt Veronica won't get invited to her party. So all steak-eaters won't get invited to Veronica's party.

6. Rocio likes to eat at Farfalla. If Rocio does not like meatballs on her spaghetti, then she won't like to eat at Farfalla. Thus, Rocio likes meatballs on top of her spaghetti.

7. April does not like small rodents and she doesn't care much for large rodents either. Therefore, April does not care much for large rodents.

8. Skateboarders enjoy leaping into the air and surfers like to stand on waves. Therefore, skateboarders enjoy leaping into the air.

9. Bungie jumping is not good for those who are prone to squeamishness. Therefore either bungie jumping is not good for those who are prone to squeamishness or the sky is made of blue wallpaper paste.

10. Small alligators can be unpleasant and so can small badgers. Therefore, small alligators can be unpleasant.

11. If that's Anita and not Alice, then Gary can't be far behind. It is Anita and not Alice, so Gary can't be far behind.

12. If Leon can fix the transmission by himself, Harry will start on the radiator. Leon could fix the transmission by himself. So Harry can start on the radiator.

Part Three

Directions: Name the rule of inference or rule of replacement or formal fallacy below. *Be careful:* Not all the sentences are in standard form so translate them first and then check for the rules.

1. Unless you come with me, I won't go to see Dr. Gutierrez. I didn't go to see Dr. Gutierrez. Therefore, you didn't come with me.

2. I will talk with that Elvis impersonator if he stops teasing me. The Elvis impersonator stopped teasing me; therefore I talked with him.

3. If the operation is a success, Frank won't have to put up with a plug in his neck. The operation was not a success, so Frank will have to put up with a plug in his neck.

4. If the doctor operates and leaves in a sponge, then there'll be a lawsuit. This is equivalent to: "If the doctor operates then, if she leaves in a sponge, there'll be a law suit."

5. If that's a badger, it may be wise to stay inside the car. It was wise to stay inside the car; so, it must be a badger out there.

6. If the farmer sees another two-headed dog, then he can sell his story to a tabloid. This means if the farmer did not sell his story to a tabloid, then he did not see another two-headed dog.

7. Tod says a UFO beamed a barbequed chicken down to him. Therefore, either Tod says a UFO beamed a barbequed chicken down to him or I had another nightmare.

8. If the Elvis impersonator sings "Jailhouse Rock" one more time, the news media will not come; but if the Elvis impersonator marries the Marilyn impersonator, the news media will be there. Either news media is there or not there. As a result, either the Elvis impersonator did not sing "Jailhouse Rock" another time or the Elvis impersonator did not marry the Marilyn impersonator.

9. Una will go with Tim to the dance contest, if she doesn't have to wear her leopard tights. Una had to wear leopard tights. So she did not go with Tim to the dance contest.

10. A mudslide is a sufficient condition to mess up the freeway. If the freeway is messed up, traffic will be a tad slow. So if there's a mudslide, traffic will be a tad slow.

11. Either there's a banana slug in the kitchen or Grandpa spilled some of the linguini. Grandpa did not spill any linguini. So there's a banana slug in the kitchen.

12. Whenever Jim hears Otis Redding music, he sings at the top of his lungs. Whenever Jim sings at the top of his lungs, Nancy puts a pillow over her head. Therefore, whenever Jim hears Otis Redding music, Nancy puts a pillow over her head.

13. If Jack is squeamish, he might find riding the roller coaster a bit disturbing. Jack is not squeamish, so he shouldn't be disturbed riding the roller coaster.

14. Neither Brad Pitt nor Tom Cruise eat at my local diner. So, Brad Pitt does not eat at my local diner and Tom Cruise doesn't eat at my local diner.

15. Either Pavarotti is going to sing or he will go hang gliding over the Grand Canyon. Pavarotti did not go hang gliding over the Grand Canyon, so he's going to sing.

16. Reading Tolstoy is sufficient to get a sense of Russian literature. The Simpsons have no sense of Russian literature. So, the Simpsons have not read Tolstoy.

17. Marguerite will knit another afghan if she can get the right color of yarn. Marguerite knitted another afghan. So she got the right color of yarn.

18. Assuming John takes karate lessons, he'll want to watch Bruce Lee films. This means, either John doesn't take karate lessons, or he'll want to watch Bruce Lee films.

19. If that's not karate John's doing, then it must be tai chi. This means if it's not tai chi, then John is doing karate.

20. Having a good sense of rhythm is necessary to do rap music. Marvin Gaye had a good sense of rhythm, so he could have done rap music.

21. If the insecticidal soap doesn't work, Anita will go after the aphids by hand. Therefore, if the insecticidal soap doesn't work, then the insecticidal soap didn't work and Anita will go after the aphids by hand.

22. If the eggs come with grits, then we won't need potatoes. This means, if we need potatoes, then the eggs did not come with grits.

23. Unless we allow wolves back into Yellowstone, there will be an imbalance in the population of elk and buffalo. If there is an imbalance in the

population of elk and buffalo, the herd will suffer. Therefore, unless we allow wolves back into Yellowstone, the elk and buffalo herds will suffer.

24. John: "For economic issues, I rely on logic. For political issues, I rely on logic or on gut instinct. For moral issues, I never rely on logic."

    What follows?
    a. If John relies on logic, he may be responding to a moral issue.
    b. If John relies on logic, he is not responding to an economic issue.
    c. If John does not rely on logic, he is responding to a political issue.
    d. If John does not rely on logic, he must be responding to an economic issue.
    e. If John does not rely on logic, he might be responding to a political issue.

Part Four

Directions: More practice with the rules. Name the rule of inference or replacement below. If it's a fallacy, name it.

1. If Casper turns green, then he bears some resemblance to the *Ghostbusters'* slime. This means, either Casper did not turn green or he bears some resemblance to the *Ghostbusters'* slime.

2. Neither ghosts nor slime will stop logicians. Therefore, ghosts don't stop logicians and slime doesn't stop logicians.

3. There's a disgusting pile of slime. There's a cyborg transmutating in the living room. Therefore, there's a disgusting pile of slime and there's a cyborg transmutating in the living room.

4. If Casper turns into slime, then the traditionalists will be upset. That means if the traditionalists are not upset then Casper did not turn into slime.

5. There's an android drooling over that pit of slime and there's T1000 changing his arm into a sword. Therefore, there's an android drooling over that pit of slime.

6. If Frankenstein could get better-fitting shoes, he'd find walking easier. Frankenstein didn't find walking easier, so he must not have gotten better-fitting shoes.

7. Either that's the Wolfman or it's Ryan in his gorilla costume. That's not Ryan in his gorilla costume, so it must be the Wolfman.

8. Whenever the moon is full, there are strange noises in the forest near the old mill. Whenever there are strange noises in the forest near the old mill, the coyotes start to howl. Therefore, whenever the moon is full, the coyotes start to howl.

9. If that werewolf leers at me another moment, then I'll dial 911, and if that werewolf does not leer at me another moment, then I can sit down and read my new novel. Either the werewolf leered at me another moment or he

didn't. Consequently, either I dialed 911 or I sat down and read my new novel.

10. Either that's the house that dripped blood or our vacation cottage is haunted. That is not the house that dripped blood, so our vacation cottage is haunted.

11. If that's not Spiderman, then I'm confused about his ability to walk on walls. That is Spiderman. So I'm not confused about his ability to walk on walls.

12. There's T1000 pulling himself together over there on the floor and there's the security guard trying out his new laser gun. So, there's T1000 pulling himself together over there on the floor.

13. Waving a garlic clove is sufficient to deter a ghoul from getting within 3 feet of a human. The ghoul came up to the UPS deliveryman, so he must not have waved the garlic clove.

14. If that's not a werewolf, then he might work as a bouncer. Therefore, if he doesn't work as a bouncer, then he's a werewolf.

15. Unless that's Dr. Lecter, your threats will mean nothing. He's not Dr. Lecter, so your threats meant nothing.

16. There goes one of those pod people from that invasion last week in West Hollywood. Therefore, either that's one of the pod people from the invasion last week in West Hollywood or it's that troubled young man who works at Astro's Coffee Shop.

17. Either that's the Blob or it's slime left over from a Halloween party. Therefore, if it's not slime left over from a Halloween party, then it's the Blob.

18. Either that's an insurance salesperson or it's the Save the Oak Tree volunteer. It's not an insurance salesperson. So, it's the Save the Oak Tree volunteer.

19. If the new stereo arrives, Lulu won't leave her house. Lulu left her house; therefore, the new stereo didn't arrive.

20. If that man on the roof is not installing cable television, Ed is phoning the police. If Ed phones the police, Jack will be alarmed. Therefore, if that man on the roof is not installing cable television, Jack will be alarmed.

21. Provided that that's not the electrician, it must be an insurance salesperson. This means, if it's not an insurance salesperson, then it's an electrician.

22. Either there's a family of mice hiding in the bag of dog food or something weird is going on. Something weird is not going on. Therefore, there's a family of mice hiding in the bag of dog food.

23. If the kitten doesn't come out from under the car, we'll have to crawl after him. We crawled after the kitten, therefore, he didn't come out from under the car.

24. If that's a zombie, I'm learning self-defense, but if it's a strange person, I'll not worry. Either it's a zombie or a strange person. So, either I'm learning self-defense or I'll not worry.

25. If she doesn't cook the meat, it will taste strange. This means, if the meat doesn't taste strange, then she must have cooked it.

26. If you get a cape with fake fur lining, then you can use it as a couch cover when you aren't wearing it. Anna got a cape with fake fur lining, so she can use it as a couch cover when she isn't wearing it.

27. That's not any person I know. Therefore, either that's not any person I know or someone is playing tricks on me.

28. Someone said they saw Elvis's ghost lurking outside the Ambassador Hotel. Someone else said he was signing autographs. It follows that someone said they saw Elvis's ghost lurking outside the Ambassador Hotel and someone else said he was signing autographs.

29. Not both Harry and Leon thought the problem was with the fuel pump. Therefore, either Harry did not think the problem was with the fuel pump or Leon did not think the problem was with the fuel pump..

30. Jenny is exhausted from studying logic all night long. Ray's hard disk just crashed. Therefore, Jenny is exhausted from studying logic all night long and Ray's hard disk just crashed.

Part Five

Directions: Below are both valid arguments and fallacies. Name them using the rules of replacement, rules of inference, and fallacies.

1. I saw Mount Shasta driving from Dunsmuir to Sacramento.

2. Either you love French impressionism or you are a cultural moron.

3. Irasema was on her way to take the logic final and she found a $20 bill lying on the street. She got an A on the final. Therefore, finding $20 was her good luck and the cause of Irasema getting an A on the final.

4. Mr. Chan won $25,000 in the lottery and plans to get a new car. Therefore, Mr. Chan plans to get a new car.

5. If they patrol the border to keep out illegal refugees, there may be a shortage of farm labor. There's a shortage of farm labor. Consequently, they must be patrolling the border to keep out illegal refugees.

6. Don't let Ray read that book by Karl Marx. If he reads it, he may become sympathetic to communism. Next thing you know, he'll be organizing workers against big business and trying to set up communes all over the city!

7. My grandma said never to lie. That means I should tell my minister that the weight he's lost since Christmas makes him look like a skeleton!

8. Denise trains sled dogs for the Iditarod. Aaron teaches people how to do white-water rafting. So, Denise trains sled dogs for the Iditarod and Aaron teaches people how to do white-water rafting.

9. Your house is huge! Therefore, you must have a huge kitchen too.

10. If his new car breaks down, Mr. Chan will take a taxi. If the taxi runs out of gas, Mr. Chan will walk to the subway station and get the first train to downtown. Therefore, if his new car breaks down, Mr. Chan will walk to the subway station and get the first train to downtown.

11. If Mandy persists in her fantasy and invests her savings in making bumper stickers that glow in the dark, then she might just make it to the big time. Mandy made it to the big time. Therefore, she must have persisted in her fantasy and invested her savings in making bumper stickers that glow in the dark.

12. Most beauticians think hair dye is not carcinogenic, so it must be okay to dye your hair year after year.

13. If you eat out too much, you forget to cook. If you forget to cook, then you aren't self-sufficient. So, if you eat out too much, then you aren't self-sufficient.

14. Either you are rich or you're a fool. Charlie's no fool, so he must be rich.

15. Lightnin' Pete Perez couldn't possibly have committed the murder. Did you know he drove the Four Square Church school bus and sent money to his elderly relatives in Birmingham, Alabama?

16. Neither Ed nor Jack prefer jazz to flamenco. Therefore, Ed does not prefer jazz to flamenco and Jack does not prefer jazz to flamenco.

17. Getting brain surgery is sufficient to tire a person. Mr. Chan is tired. So, he must have had brain surgery.

18. BOSS: Hey Gloria, what are you doing digging in my desk drawer? GLORIA: Oh, Mr. Munoz, did I ever tell you how much the secretaries respect you? They think you are so much fun to work with and we love when you do imitations of Elvis. I bet your family just adores you!

19. If the journalist digs in the trash, she will find incriminating evidence about the mayor's brother. The journalist dug in the trash, so she found incriminating evidence about the mayor's brother.

20. Spencer makes rich cheesecake, so he must spend a lot of money on the ingredients.

21. Either that's Keanu Reeves on the phone or someone is playing a trick on her. That's not Keanu Reeves on the phone, so someone's playing a trick on her.

22. If you are a cynic and only see problems, then life won't be easy for you. This is the same as, "If you are a cynic then, if you only see problems, then life won't be easy for you."

23. Most people eat breakfast. Why don't you?

24. Laura is not both a cynic and a pessimist. That means either Laura's not a cynic or she's not a pessimist.

25. If you want to go bicycling, it is necessary to wear a helmet and sturdy shoes. John does not want to go bicycling, so he does not need to wear a helmet and he does not need to wear sturdy shoes.

26. If you don't like to gather pods and stones, you won't like camping. The boys liked camping, so they must like to gather pods and stones.

27. If that's a dumpling floating on Heidi's chocolate malt, then she should send it back, but if it's a very strange marshmallow, it might be quite tasty. Either that's a dumpling floating on Heidi's chocolate malt or it's a very strange marshmallow. Therefore, either Heidi should send it back or it might be quite tasty.

28. Dr. Green, you should carry more of the load in the philosophy department. If you don't I will tell your son, Evan, that there's no Easter Bunny and it's you, not Santa, who gave him that tricycle last year.

29. If Sam keeps honking his horn, Carol will have to speak to him. Sam did not keep honking his horn, so Carol did not have to speak to him.

30. Harrison Ford likes carpentry. Why don't you?

Glossary

Analysis. The process of gathering evidence, weighing premises, sorting out warranted from unwarranted assumptions, structuring arguments, evaluating the strength of an inductive argument, and assessing the validity and soundness of deductive arguments. The central task of analysis is the evaluation of an argument in order to determine its strength.

Analytical Tools. Weigh evidence, construct or dismantle arguments, analyze the various aspects of reasoning, acquire a facility for both inductive and deductive reasoning, and determine the strength of the reasoning holding the argument together.

Antecedent. An antecedent is the condition that is claimed to lead to a certain effect (known as the "consequent"). The antecedent lies between the "if" and the "then" in a conditional claim.

Argument. An argument has two parts: the conclusion and the premises (evidence). This means arguments consist of a set of propositions, at least one of which (called a premise) is offered as evidence for accepting another proposition (called the conclusion). An argument consists of *only one* conclusion and *at least one* premise.

Argument Based on Analogy. This is an argument of the form: A and B both share a set of similarities p, q, r, etc.—and A also has characteristic k. It follows that B has characteristic k as well. In other words, on the basis of a comparison that sets out a list of commonalities, it is inferred that a trait that is true of one of the terms of comparison must also be true of the other.

Assessment Tools. Assess a situation in light of any relevant policies and priorities; examine assumptions and underlying values and beliefs, and assess moral and legal reasoning.

Asymmetry. When a set of criteria applied to one group results in distinctly different results when applied to a parallel (seemingly similar) group, the resulting discrepancy would be called asymmetrical. In other words two asymmetrical things simply do not match up. Asymmetrical descriptions, thus, are what occurs when a set of descriptions of one (targeted group) are clearly dissimilar from those of the control group. For example, newspaper descriptions of one ethnic group or gender are often dissimilar from descriptions of the dominant ethnic group or gender.

Categorical Proposition. This is a proposition expressed as follows: "All/No/Some of A is/is not B." This form can also be expressed as: Quantifier + subject + is/are/are not + predicate.

Categorical Syllogisms.   These are syllogisms (two premises, one conclusion, three terms— major/minor/middle) with each proposition written in categorical form.

Cause-and-Effect Reasoning.   This is a kind of inductive argument in which it is argued that a particular event or effect occurs on the basis of specific antecedent conditions said to be the causal factor or factors.

Circumstantial Evidence.   Circumstantial evidence does not singularly or collectively definitively support a particular conclusion, but alternative explanations seem much less likely. This occurs when we have no hard evidence one way or the other, but the evidence points to the one conclusion. Circumstantial evidence works together in support of a particular conclusion that, in the absence of any reasonable alternative, seems highly likely. The key word here is "likely": no amount of circumstantial evidence can provide certainty. What gives circumstantial evidence its weight is the lack of an alternative explanation for the pieces in the puzzle.

Cogency.   "Cogent" is synonymous with "clear and convincing." A cogent argument is convincing because of the quality and persuasive force of the evidence supporting the conclusion. A cogent argument is well reasoned and clearly structured so we can follow the argument, seeing how the evidence lays the foundation for the conclusion.

Complement.   The complement of a set A is non-A (the set of all elements that are not contained in the set A).

Compound Proposition.   A compound proposition is a proposition that contains at least one logical connective (i.e., "not," "and," "or," "if . . . then," and "if and only if").

Conclusion.   A conclusion is the proposition said to follow from at least one piece of evidence. Arguments consist of premises (evidence) and one conclusion.

Conclusion-indicator.   A conclusion-indicator is a word or phrase that precedes a conclusion. If you can replace the term with "therefore" without changing the argument, the term is a conclusion-indicator. (For example: "thus," "hence," "consequently," "it follows that," and so on).

Conditional Claim.   A conditional claim is a proposition that can be expressed in the form of "If . . . then . . ." It is sometimes referred to as a hypothetical claim, because the antecedent condition (following the "if") may not be true. Rather, the antecedent could be false (but *if* it were true, then the consequent would follow).

Conjunction.   A conjunction is any proposition that can be written in the form "A and B." Note: conjunctions could have terms that are equivalent to "and," such as "plus," "also," "moreover," and "but." The rule of conjunction asserts that if A is true and if B is also true, then the claim "A and B" is then true.

Connotation.   Connotation is an issue of semantics and has to do with what words signify. The *connotation* is what the word suggests, implies, or conjures up in our minds, whereas the *denotation* of a word is the literal meaning.

Consequent.   A consequent is what is said to follow if some antecedent condition is assumed true. In an "if . . . then" claim, the consequent follows the "then."

Constructive Dilemma.   A valid deductive argument of the form: If A then B, and if C then D. Either A or C. Therefore, either B or D.

Contingent Claim.   A proposition is called contingent if it is either true or false, depending upon its component variables. In other words, contingent claims are neither tautologies (always true) nor contradictions (always false).

Contradiction.   A contradiction is a proposition that is always false, or false by definition (for example, any proposition of the form A and not A, such as "The sky is blue but it is not blue").

Contrapositive.   The contrapositive is the resulting proposition after the subject is replaced by the complement of the predicate and the predicate is replaced by the complement of the subject. The contrapositive cannot be taken on an I claim "Some A is B." The contrapositive of the E claim "No A is B" is the O claim "Some non-B is not non-A." For example, the contrapositive of "All painters are artists" is "All nonartists are nonpainters."

Converse.   The converse is the resulting proposition after the subject and predicate are interchanged. The converse cannot be taken on an O claim. No change in the quality is required, except in the case of the A claim ("All A is B," which requires the converse to be changed to the I claim "Some B is A"). For example, the converse of "No cowhands are lonely people" is "No lonely people are cowhands."

Corroborating Evidence.   Corroborating evidence is a form of reinforcement, in the sense that the corroborating evidence strengthens the case by mutually supporting one another. When evidence poses no clear conflicts or contradictions if we assume it is actually true then we have *corroborating* evidence. With corroborating evidence it is gets harder to attack a case, because the foundation gains more strength.

Critical Thinking Tools.   These are the means by which we accomplish the various tasks of critical thinking. There are four basic kinds of tools. (1) surveillance tools; (2) analytical tools; (3) assessment tools; and (4) synthesis tools.

Deductive Argument.   A deductive argument is an argument in which the premises are claimed to be sufficient for the drawing of the conclusion. This assumes that there are no missing pieces; that the evidence is purported to be sufficient for the conclusion to follow. In that sense, a deductive argument is a closed set. Examples of *valid* deductive arguments include those in the form of modus ponens, modus tollens, disjunctive syllogism, and the hypothetical syllogism.

Definition.   There are two parts to any definition: first, the word or phrase to define or clarify. This is called the *definiendum*. Then you have the explanation—words meaning the same as the word or phrase in question. This is called the *definiens*. *Synonyms* are words that are similar in meaning (e.g., warm and toasty), whereas *antonyms* are words that are opposite in meaning (e.g., hot and cold).

Denotation.   Denotation is an issue of semantics. The *denotation* of a word is the literal meaning, whereas the *connotation* is what the word suggests, implies, or conjures up in our minds.

Description.   Descriptions, like a set of facts, are statements about what is or is not the case. Generally, each item in a description is either true or false, which could be verified by an examination.

Disjunction.   A disjunction is a proposition in the form of "Either A or B." For example, "Either pudding is a vegetable or it is a creamy dessert" and "George likes pudding or so he said."

Disjunctive Syllogism.   A valid deductive argument of the form: Either A or B. Not A (or not B). Therefore, B (or therefore, A).

Distribution.   A term is distributed if all of its members are said to have a certain predicated characteristic. To determine distribution of a specific term: If it is in the subject place and the proposition is universal, then the term is distributed. If it is in the predicate place and the proposition is negative, then the term is distributed. Determining distribution of a term rests on two things: (1) the location of the term (subject/predicate) in the proposition and (2) the proposition's quality (in the case of the subject) or quantity (in the case of the predicate).

Euphemism.   When people want to avoid the repercussions of using a particular term, they may turn to a euphemism. A euphemism acts as a substitute for the targeted word, in order to achieve a particular end. The goal may be to defuse a situation that is controversial or it could be to slant it with a set of political or other values more favorable to the speaker.

Fact.   Something is called a fact if it is known to be true or could be confirmed by empirical or other means. Facts are actually the case, known by observation or reliable testimony, rather than inferred or surmised. Statements of fact include all that we can say is "true."

Factual Judgments.   Factual judgments are generally inferences drawn from earlier observations. Because the judgment is one step removed from the fact, this means that the inference drawn on the basis of the fact cannot be assumed to be true—it must be scrutinized so we are not misled.

Fallacies of Relevance.   In these fallacies the premises simply fail to support the conclusion; they are beside the point. Every fallacy contains a fundamental flaw in reasoning. The names of the fallacies relate to the form the flawed reasoning takes.

Fallacies of Presumption.   In these fallacies the argument depends upon an unwarranted assumption causing the fallacy. Every fallacy contains a fundamental flaw in reasoning. The names of the fallacies relate to the form the flawed reasoning takes.

Fallacies of Ambiguity (also known as linguistic fallacies).   These fallacies center on the use of language in terms of emphasis, interpretation, sentence structure, or the relationship between the parts and the whole. This ambiguity results in an incorrect conclusion being drawn, causing the fallacy. Every fallacy contains a fundamental flaw in reasoning. The names of the fallacies relate to the form the flawed reasoning takes.

Fallacy.   A fallacy is a deceptive or misleading argument that may persuade us, but is nevertheless unsound. There are many different forms a fallacy may take, but they all share a common trait—namely, they are poorly reasoned arguments, however persuasive they may seem on the surface. Every fallacy contains a fundamental flaw in reasoning. The flaws can take any number of forms and may involve structural or linguistic errors, mistaken assumptions, or premises that are irrelevant to the conclusion stated.

Figure.   The figure of a syllogism is determined by the location of the middle term. There are four possible figures. Knowing the figure is crucial for assessing the validity of a syllogism.

Formal Fallacies.   These fallacies occur because of a structural error. As a result, the very form of the reasoning is incorrect. The truth of the premises will never guarantee the truth of the conclusion because of a structural error. The different names of the formal fallacies refer to the pattern of that flawed reasoning.

Frame of Reference.   Each of us has a particular vantage point from which events are seen and understood. This is what is known as our *frame of reference*. This framework is shaped by our prior knowledge, assumptions, values, language or notation, among others. Assumptions and values may also influence our perceptions.

Hedging.   Hedging has the effect of undercutting the claim or raising doubts about it. Hedging can take two forms: (1) It can indicate a shift from one position to a much weaker one or (2) it can undercut a claim or suggest a negative connotation of a phrase or claim being made.

Hypothetical Syllogism.   A valid deductive argument of the form: If A then B. If B then C. Therefore, if A then C.

Idea.   Ideas take the form of solutions, intentions, plans of action, even theories. The ancient roots of the word go back to a general or ideal form, pattern, or standard by which things are measured. More commonly now, we use it to refer to insights, purposes, or recommendations.

Independent Evidence. When one piece of evidence is sufficient in and of itself, we would say that that piece *independently,* or singularly, establishes the conclusion.

Inductive. An argument is *inductive* if the conclusion can only be said to follow with probability or likelihood even if the premises are assumed to be true. The conclusion of an inductive argument never follows with certainty. Examples include predictions, cause-and-effect arguments, statistical reasoning, and arguments from analogy.

Inference. An inference is a conclusion drawn on the basis of some evidence or observations. An inference is an answer to the question, "What's it about? What story does this tell?"

Interdependent evidence. When a conclusion could not be established by any one of the premises but the premises together support the conclusion, we say the evidence is interdependent. In other words, it works as a *unit,* not singularly, to establish the conclusion.

Invalid. An argument is called *invalid* if the assumed truth of the premises does not guarantee that the conclusion is also true. In other words, if the premises could be true while the conclusion was false, the argument would be invalid. Invalid arguments are always unsound.

Linguistic Fallacy. A linguistic fallacy is also known as a fallacy of ambiguity (the lack of clarity leads to a mistaken conclusion because of the use of language). The three key linguistic fallacies are: equivocation (where there's a shift of meaning in a word or phrase leading to an incorrect conclusion), accent (where the emphasis of a word or phrase leads us to an incorrect conclusion), and amphiboly (where the sentence structure or use of grammar creates an ambiguity, leading to an incorrect conclusion).

Loaded Language. This occurs when language is value-laden in such a way that it creates either a positive or negative bias. The use of loaded terms tends to unfairly prejudge the case. Loaded language is to be distinguished from colorful, or figurative, language. With the latter, striking images (from ugly to funny to beautiful) are evoked because of the vivid use of language, but it does not function as a means of persuasion for a particular conclusion.

Modus Ponens. A valid deductive argument of the form: If A then B. A. Therefore B.

Modus Tollens. A valid deductive argument of the form: If A then B. Not B. Therefore not A.

Necessary. A condition P is called necessary for Q if Q could not occur without P. This means, if Q is the case, then P is also the case. This is commonly expressed as: "P is necessary for Q" is the same as "If not P then not Q," or the equivalent proposition, "If Q then P."

Obverse. The obverse is the proposition that results after two steps: (1) change the quality of the proposition to its opposite and then (2) replace the predicate by its complement. The obverse of any categorical proposition can be taken. For example, the obverse of "No snakes are lizards" is "All snakes are nonlizards" and the obverse of "Some cows are Jerseys" is "Some cows are not non-Jerseys."

Opinion. Opinions are statements of belief. Some opinions rely upon facts or are in response to them, but are insufficiently supported and, so, opinions are disputable. Opinions are generally based on perception and are relative to the speaker's own experience or state of mind. However, in a legal context, they may be expressed as a formal statement, a ruling, or considered advice. Court opinions, for example, function as an explanation for a decision that becomes law.

Particular claim.   This is a proposition that could be expressed in the form: "Some A are (or are not) B." This includes statistical claims of the form "X% of A is/is not B," where X is neither 100% nor zero. A particular claim is to be contrasted with a universal claim, which is an all-or-nothing claim.

Post Hoc Reasoning.   In this case an inference is drawn that something causes another thing to happen just because it happened at an earlier time. This is fallacious: The fact that something precedes something else does not necessarily mean there is a causal relationship.

Premise.   A premise is a proposition offered or assumed as evidence in support of a particular conclusion. Unstated assumptions may function as premises, so it is important for all premises to be articulated when analyzing an argument.

Premise-indicator.   A premise-indicator is a word or phrase that precedes a premise. If a word can be replaced with "because," it is a premise-indicator (for example, "given that," "in light of the fact that," "whereas," and so on).

Proposition.   A proposition is an assertion that is either true or false. Declarations and rhetorical questions may operate as propositions, in order to clarify what's being asserted.

Quality.   The quality of a proposition is either *positive* or *negative*. The quality of a proposition answers, "Are you asserting something *is* or *is not* the case?" You are either affirming that it is the case (the quality is positive) or denying it (the quality is negative).

Quantity.   The quantity of a proposition answers the question, "How much?" In other words, the quantity refers to how much of the subject class is said to have something predicated of it. The possible answer is "universal" or "particular" (i.e., all or some of it).

Rule of Inference.   A rule of inference is a valid deductive argument form allowing us to draw an inference on the basis of particular premises. By means of a rule of inference, we can draw a valid inference on the basis of the structure of the argument. Examples include modus ponens, modus tollens, disjunctive syllogism, hypothetical syllogism, constructive dilemma, simplification, and conjunction.

Rule of Replacement.   A rule of replacement allows us to restate a proposition into an equivalent form. Examples include De Morgan's laws, material implication, transposition, and exportation.

Semantics.   Semantics has to do with the meaning of words, what they signify (in contrast to syntax, which focuses on the use of grammar, sentence structure, and punctuation—structural issues).

Simple Proposition.   A simple proposition does not contain any logical connectives ("and," "or," "not," "if . . . then," and "if and only if"). For example, "Pudding is a tasty dessert" is a simple proposition; whereas "Pudding is not good for your diet" is a compound proposition.

Sound.   An argument is called *sound* if it is a valid argument with true premises. Ony deductive arguments can be sound (inductive arguments can't be sound because they could never be valid).

Speculation.   Speculation is a form of guesswork. We normally use the term "speculation" to apply to hypotheses that have little, if any, evidence to back them up. There may be a kernel of evidence, but not enough to draw a solid conclusion.

Standard Form of a Proposition.   A proposition is in standard form if it is expressed as: "A is/is not B." In other words a proposition in standard form is ordered as follows: Subject class + is/are/are not + predicate class.

Statistical Reasoning.   When an inference is drawn about a target population on the basis of what is said to be true of a sample group, it is called statistical reasoning. Key factors in statistical reasoning are the size of the sample, the diversity of the sample, and the date the study is done.

Subaltern.   A subaltern is a particular proposition that can be inferred from the truth of the universal proposition, where we know the subject class is not empty. For example, the subaltern of "all tigers are cats" is "some tigers are cats."

Subalternation.   Subalternation is the process of inferring from the universal claim to its corresponding particular claim.

Sufficient.   Sufficiency establishes minimal conditions for the truth of a proposition. This is expressed as follows: "P is sufficient for Q" is equivalent to "If P then Q" or "If not Q then not P." All three expressions are equivalent.

Surveillance Tools.   Perceive problems, recognize unsupported opinions versus facts and supported claims, spot prejudicial or biased modes of thinking, recognize the different uses of language, watch for what is not said, omitted, downplayed or discarded.

Syntax.   Syntax has to do with sentence structure, grammar, and punctuation (in contrast to semantics, which focuses on the meaning, or significance, of words).

Synthesis Tools.   Articulate goals and decisions using a defensible set of criteria; resolve personal conflicts and professional dilemmas; recognize the role of ideas and creativity in problem solving; evaluate decisions, plans, and policies; summarize arguments and synthesize information; and examine our own thinking processes and decision-making strategies.

Tautology.   A tautology is a proposition that is always true, or true by definition (for example,

"either that's a bowl of pudding or it's not a bowl of pudding").

Transition Word.   Transition words act to amplify, emphasize, introduce, illustrate, or contrast. Examples are "moreover," "to restate," "primarily," "in simpler terms," "notably," "in fact," "alternatively," "on the other hand," and so on. Transition words are neither premise-indicators nor conclusion-indicators.

Universal Claim.   This is a claim that can be expressed in the form "All A is B" or "No A is B." In contrast, particular claims assert or deny a predicated characteristic of only some (neither all nor none) of the subject class.

Valid.   An argument is called *valid* if the premises certainly support the conclusion. This means that, if we assume the premises were true, the conclusion would be forced to be true as well. The conclusion cannot be false and the premises true in a valid argument. A valid argument is not necessarily sound: soundness requires that the argument be valid *and* the premises are actually true. Validity does not apply to inductive arguments—only to deductive ones.

Value Claims.   Value claims express some kind of moral, social, or aesthetic judgment and, thus, are not normally considered either true or false. They may be used as evidence, but should be handled carefully. Value claims are usually expressed in sentences that assert a judgment of taste or moral judgments or recommendations about what one ought or ought not do.

Variable.   A variable is a letter (A, B, C, or p, q, r) used to stand for propositions. For example, "If pudding is on the menu, then George will order it" could be rewritten using variables P = "pudding is on the menu," and G = "George will order it." The proposition then would be written: If P then G.

Index